# THE MAKING OF
# VICTORIAN SALFORD

Sacred Trinity Church and the Flat Iron Market. (*Manchester Old and New*)

# The Making of
# Victorian Salford

*R. L. Greenall*

Carnegie Publishing

*In memory of my parents,*
*William Greenall (1907–85) and*
*Mary Rosslyn Greenall (1908–88)*

First published in 2000 by Carnegie Publishing Ltd
Carnegie House, Chatsworth Road,
Lancaster LA1 4SL
www.carnegiepub.co.uk

*British Library Cataloguing-in-Publication data*
A catalogue record for this book is available from the British Library

ISBN 1-85936-077-7

Typeset and originated by Carnegie Publishing Ltd
Printed and bound by Biddles Ltd, Guildford

# Contents

Acknowledgements      vi

Preface      vii

INTRODUCTION: Place and People      1

1 Going Through the Mill: Charles Aberdeen and the Factory System      13

2 Borough Making: The Life and Times of Joseph Brotherton      28

3 Voice of the People: The Radical Life of Reginald Richardson      61

4 Protestant Watchman: Canon Hugh Stowell and the Church in Salford      84

5 Manchester Man: Sir Elkanah Armitage in Business, Religion and Politics      108

6 Beer and Bible: Charles Cawley, William Charley and the Revival of Conservatism      134

7 Poverty and Pollution: Thomas Davies, the Cotton Famine and the Sanitary Question in Salford      150

8 Gladstonian Liberal: The Political Career of Benjamin Armitage      173

9 Gas and Corruption: James Mandley, Samuel Hunter and the Salford Council      193

10 Catholics: Father Saffenreuter and the Pendleton Irish      212

11 Socialists: George Evans and the Early Labour Movement      227

12 Women: the Pankhursts, Feminism and the Struggle for the Vote      270

13 Lancashire Fusilier: Sir Lees Knowles and 'The Territorial Family'      303

Notes      333

APPENDICES

Population of Salford, 1773–1911      361

The Church of England in Salford in Canon Stowell's time      362

Public Health in Salford – a Chronology      364

Vital Statistics of the Borough of Salford 1844-1912      365

Index      369

# Acknowledgements

In the research for this book debts have been incurred going back over many years. I wish to thank the British Academy and the Research Board of Leicester University for modest but timely grants at important stages of this work. I am further indebted to my University for periods of study leave, without which this project would never have been completed. Thanks are also due to archivists at the Flintshire, Ipswich and East Suffolk and Lancashire Record Offices, Manchester Archives, the Public Record Office and Rugby School, and to librarians at the Birmingham Reference Library, the British Library, Chetham's Library, Manchester, the Library of the London School of Economics and Political Science, Goldsmith's Library, University of London, the Manchester Central Library and the City of Westminster Library. I owe most, perhaps, to the staff at the Salford Art Gallery and Museum and the Local History Library at Peel Park, where the late Alan Smith was a great help in facilitating access to source material and where Tony Frankland always answered my requests for information with promptness and courtesy. Thanks are also expressed to the late J. E. C. Armitage, Tom Bergin, formerly editor of the *Salford City Reporter,* Major J. McQ. Hallam of the Lancashire Fusiliers Museum, Bury, John Seddon for photographic work, and Eveyln Vigeon, formerly of the Social History Museum at Ordsall Hall. Discussions with my colleague Robert Colls, helped me to clarify ideas on Victorian Salford and the form of this book, and Professor Brian Simon has been exceptionally generous in his support of this project, as has the Co-operative Wholesale Society. I also have to express gratitude to clerical staff of the Department of Adult Education, particularly Kathryn Baddiley, for typing and retyping inumerable drafts of this work. My final and biggest thanks are due to my wife for putting up with my obsession with Salford for so long.

## Illustrations Acknowledgements

Acknowledgement is made to the following for permission to reproduce pictures from their collections: the late J. E. C. Armitage, Esq., Flintshire Record Office, Manchester Public Libraries, the Museum of London, Northamptonshire Record Office, the Public Record Office, and Salford City Council Arts and Leisure Department for pictures in the Art Gallery and Museum and the Local History Collection at the Central Library in Peel Park.

# *Preface*

Amongst the growing number of histories of Victorian towns to be found on the library shelves relatively few are about those created by the Industrial Revolution. No doubt there are good reasons. Someone once remarked that a love for one of the old industrial towns of England – a Hunslet or a Salford – seems a hard, unfathomable passion. Given this, maybe only native sons or daughters would want to write their histories. Certainly this is the case with the present writer. Salford is where, like my parents and grandparents before me, I was born and grew up, and, in my case, left to go to university. Although I have not lived there since, no other place has ever interested me as much. Memories of one's youth are powerful and abiding: I began this book to answer questions which first arose then. Although no doubt they had their reasons, my teachers scarcely used the local environment. The Industrial Revolution stopped with the Duke of Bridge-water's canal and eighteenth-century textile inventions. Yet education goes on outside as well as inside school. Folk-memories and snippets of historical information from family, friends and neighbours stimulated interest. And in *my* Salford of the 1940s and 1950s the physical environment was still essentially Victorian, posing questions few seemed able or disposed to answer. The past seemed hugely present yet strangely absent, despite the clues which lay all around. Who was the Hugh Stowell, who had an Anglican church built as a memorial to his memory? Why did Joseph Brotherton's friends put up a statue to him in Peel Park? Whose idea was it that the Lancashire Fusilier on the Boer War monument in front of Salford Royal Hospital should be so triumphalist?

Libraries offered only limited information. Few books even refer to the place. In my youth the City Art Gallery was filled with portraits and marble busts of figures from the Victorian past, but who they were and what their life stories revealed was not explained. It seemed to be assumed that visitors would simply know. Answers to my questions would have to be sought elsewhere. Salford came into clearer focus at the London School of Economics, where such phenomena as the rise of modern industry, the growth of great towns, Capital, Labour and class were studied as assiduously as they had been avoided as school. They came into even clearer focus in my present work, teaching in university adult education in Leicester. The opportunity to undertake research led me back to Victorian Salford.

In an age of academic specialisation, the aims of this book are incautiously wide. It attempts a social history of a large provincial worktown, embracing its main economic, religious, political and cultural issues. If first and foremost this is local history, one hopes it is not too parochial. Its justification is that what took place in Salford (and similar towns) is of some importance in modern history. Here it was that industrialisation, and what accompanied it, first came upon the scene. The locating of source material was not always easy. Almost nothing of the business records of the borough's once-great firms has survived. Administrative records are better preserved, and much manuscript and printed material is to be found in archives and libraries, but its nature is random and miscellaneous. The most comprehensive source has proved to be the local newspapers and what follows is largely based on them. Vast and laborious to work through, they form a rich and fascinating source. Newspapers are, however, essentially the *public* record of people, events and actions. What they do not reveal so fully are details of the private lives and opinions of the men and women who form the subject of this book. Had more of their private papers been preserved their stories might have been more rounded. In defence of what is here it has to be said that public men (and women) are self-selected performers on the historical stage and stand to be judged by their public careers and their utterances.

Leicester, 2000

# *Place and People*

In 1905 T. R. Marr referred to Manchester as 'the great double-barrelled city',[1] drawing attention to the fact that, where strangers saw one great town of almost a million people, there were in fact two. Salford is divided from Manchester, as Southwark is from London or Gateshead from Newcastle, by a river, though the Irwell is surely no Thames or Tyne. Topographically, Salford is west Manchester, the town across the river, and as part of a greater whole Salford has always lacked a commercial or physical centre of its own. When Salfordians 'go to town' they mean Manchester, and always did.

Yet whatever the economic or geographical realities, emotionally and administratively Salford has never liked to consider itself a mere appendage of Manchester. In its modern form its administrative separation from Manchester was confirmed early in the reign of Queen Victoria. Yet even before the creation of a new municipal borough in 1844, it had become clear that nineteenth-century Manchester was going to be double-barrelled. The duality persists. In the local government reorganisation of 1974 Salford survived in name and fact, absorbing places to its west – the boroughs of Eccles, Swinton and Pendlebury and the districts of Irlam and Worsley, which all became part of the contemporary city of Salford.

So there is a paradox: on the ground Salford is, and perhaps ever will be, part of Manchester, yet for certain purposes sees itself as different and separate. There is nothing unusual in this. Individually and collectively people have a range of real and imaginary localities to which they give loyalty according to use, need or situation – continent, nation, region, county, town, district, street, religion, school, football team and so on. In the nineteenth century, in matters of local government, Salford's civic leaders and ratepayers successfully asserted their independence, claiming that what Manchester could do Salford could do as well, and if Salford could not do it better it could do it cheaper. Salford certainly did things differently, and whenever possible separately.

One of the results of this tradition is that historical (though not geographical and sociological) studies of Manchester almost invariably exclude Salford. Whilst the intention here is to redress this imbalance, the fact that Salford has always been part of a bigger entity will not be ignored. To focus on Salford is not some local obsession: the place is simply too big to ignore. As it was transformed by the rise of modern industry Salford became a very large town indeed. When this process began the township of Salford had, (in 1773), a mere 4,765 people. By 1801 its population had grown to 13,611. Fifty years later it had more than quadrupled to over 60,000, to which should be added 21,000 in the townships of Pendleton and

1

Broughton, about to be brought into an enlarged municipal borough in 1853. By the time of the Great War the three townships had a population of over a quarter of a million, making Salford the seventeenth largest town in the country.[2] Taken together with Manchester it was part of the biggest urban concentration in Great Britain outside London, Glasgow and Birmingham. Moreover, beyond Manchester and Salford was a ring of industrial towns which looked to the great double-barrelled city as their economic centre and regional capital. Victorian Salford lay at the hub of one of the world's first industrial concentrations. In the nineteenth century Manchester's connections were truly global. Lancashire's raw cotton was increasingly drawn from the plantations of the southern states of the USA, and the main markets for its finished goods were in the Far East.

No place was more a product of the Industrial Revolution than Salford. It was created by the rise of cotton manufacturing, by coal and iron, by the first important canals and railways, by enterprise, inventiveness, hard work and self-sacrifice on a monumental scale. It was also the product of bleak materialism, grasping greed, and appalling insensitivity to the consequences of rapid industrialisation and largely unregulated urban growth. If the unacceptable face of capitalism was to be seen anywhere, it was in Salford. Into the double-barrelled city poured rivers of migrants, mostly from Lancashire and counties adjoining, and Ireland, with significant minorities of Scots, Germans, Italians, Greeks, and Jews from Germany and (later) Eastern Europe. Where people came from and what their religion was were always important: in large measure they determined where people stood in an urban hierarchy dominated by North country English Protestants.

For the purposes of parliamentary representation and local government Victorian Salford was created by the union of the townships of Salford, Broughton and Pendleton. They were not brought together easily, nor was their subsequent association comfortable. If there were strong particularist feelings in Salford vis-à-vis the city of Manchester, similar feelings existed amongst the ratepayers of Broughton and Pendleton towards the township of Salford. This was partly because the speed of economic change and urban growth always outstripped people's local and mental horizons, and partly because until the late nineteenth century the social and economic profiles of Pendleton and Broughton differed from that of Salford: local politics, be it remembered, were then the exclusive province of rate-payers.

From the 1780s Salford was recognisably and self-consciously becoming urban. Pendleton and Broughton remained rural or suburban very much longer. In the eighteenth century those two out-townships had no centres of settlement, consisting of scattered farms, crofts and cottages, with a few houses of well-to-do gentlemen of more recent construction. Part of the ancient parish of Eccles, Pendleton had no church until 1773, and Broughton, within reachable distance of the old collegiate church of Manchester, had no place of worship of its own until 1836. When industrial momentum began to build up in the late eighteenth century it did so first in Salford, where, in its network of new streets, houses, cotton mills, dye and bleach works, iron-foundries, shops, slaughter houses, places of worship and public houses were promiscuously intermixed. Densely-packed Salford developed on the right bank of the enormous loop of the river Irwell. By the 1860s most of the land within this low-lying district was built up. In Pendleton, despite some very early

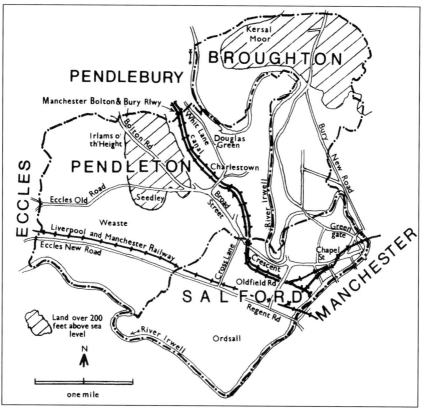

Salford, borough and townships, *c*. 1848.

cotton factories, the process advanced more slowly and unevenly. On the east (Salford) side, from about the point where Broad Street divided into the roads to Eccles and Bolton, pockets of industry and housing developed from about 1780. West of that point lay the territory of the opulent middle classes, an area where large houses, often in their own substantial grounds, dominated the landscape, with some 'ribbon development' of villas along the main roads. Even here, in semi-rural Seedley and Weaste, there appeared the occasional early dyeworks or cotton mill. Despite urban incursions, the whole area preserved its exclusive surburbanity into the present century. In Broughton the pattern was not dissimilar. Except for some industrial activity by the river near Broughton Bridge the township developed first as one of Manchester's bourgeois suburbs, Higher Broughton having a similar air to West Pendleton. However, in the last third of the century the inexorable outward spread of bricks and mortar, first into Lower Broughton, then Higher Broughton, overlapped earlier suburban developments.

The rapidity and complexity of Salford's nineteenth-century industrial growth almost defies description, thought in outline the story is clear enough. The engine of growth was cotton, and for half a century and more Salford's economy resembled that of other Lancashire textile towns. The 1851 census shows over a fifth of adult

Table 1: *The Workforce in Salford, 1851 and 1911*

### MALES, 1851

| | | |
|---|---|---|
| Total males in Salford (all ages) | 31,250 | |
| Men 20 years and over † | 22,558 | (100)* |
| Textiles | 3,801 | (17) |
| Transport and warehousing | 1,808 | (8) |
| Building trades | 1,705 | (7.5) |
| Textile finishing | 1,562 | (7) |
| Iron and engineering | 1,408 | (7) |
| Clothing trades | 1,158 | (5) |
| Agricultural labourers | 902 | (4) |
| Labourers (unspecified) | 874 | (4) |
| Coal mining | 257 | (1) |
| Domestic servants | 266 | (1) |
| Brewing | 203 | (1) |
| Chemicals | 100 | (0.4) |

### FEMALES, 1851

| | | |
|---|---|---|
| Total females in Salford | 32,600 | |
| Women of 20 years and over † | 25,997 | |
| Housewives and widows | 13,760 | |
| Employed outside the home | 12,237 | (100) |
| Textiles | 3,895 | (32) |
| Domestic service and washerwomen | 3,577 | (29) |
| Clothing trades | 1,323 | (11) |

*Source*: 1851 Census, Occupations of the People.

* Figures in brackets are percentages of the labour force aged 20 and over.

† These figures seriously distort the true extent of the Salford workforce by omitting males and females at work aged 19 and less. They also exclude the townships of Pendleton and Broughton.

## MALES, 1911

| | | |
|---|---|---|
| Total males in Salford (all ages) | 111,673 | |
| At work (10 years and upwards) | 74,286 | (100)* |
| At work (10–19 years) | 12,391 | (17) |
| Transport | 15,067 | (20) |
| Metals and engineering | 12,916 | (17) |
| Building and construction | 5,574 | (7.4) |
| Textile finishing | 4,020 | (5.4) |
| Commercial clerks | 3,756 | (5) |
| Chemicals | 2,791 | (3.7) |
| Clothing and footware | 2,399 | (3.2) |
| General labourers | 1,954 | (2.6) |
| Textiles | 1,936 | (2.6) |
| Miners | 1,163 | (1.5) |
| Domestic service | 879 | (1.1) |

* Note: Figures in brackets are percentages of the occupied male workforce in Salford in 1911.

## FEMALES, 1911

| | | |
|---|---|---|
| Total females in Salford (all ages) | 119,684 | |
| Married women and widows | 51,132 | |
| Women working outside the home (10 years and upwards) | 36,275 | (100) |
| Married women and widows engaged in occupations outside the home | 9,005 | |
| Girls and young women (10–19 years) at work | 11,124 | (31) |
| Textiles | 8,603 | (24) |
| Clothing and footware | 8,102 | (22) |
| Domestic service | 6,510 | (18) |
| Chemicals | 1,805 | (5) |

Source: 1911 Census, Occupations of the People

* Figures in brackets are percentages of the female population occupied outside the home.

25 per cent of women engaged in textile work were married or widowed

39 per cent (3,385) of the female textile labour force in Salford in 1911 were aged 10 to 19 years.

The figure for women under chemicals includes 209 india rubber and waterproof workers.

males, and a third of the adult women employed outside the home were at work in textile factories. It also reveals that almost as many women were employed as domestic servants as factory hands. However, what the printed census does not provide is information on the numbers of girls and young women *under the age of 20* then at work. Extrapolating from figures in a later census (1911), a further 40% would need to be added to the figure for female workers in the mills in 1851, and another 20% to those in domestic service. The high proportion of women in domestic service points up Manchester's class structure. There existed a multi-layered, servant- employing class which, notwithstanding the continuing exodus of the rich and well-to-do to Cheshire, Southport and elsewhere in the second half of the century, had a major presence down to the Great War. The demand of this class for goods and services is also reflected in the fact that a further 18% of working women in 1851 were milliners and seamstresses. Although the point has been made before, it is still worth noting that whilst the ethos of industrial Manchester was intensely masculine, the labour in its basic industry was predominantly female.

Already, by 1851, a substantial minority of Salford's male work force was occupied in iron-making, engineering, and transport, areas of Manchester's local economy which were to grow rapidly thereafter. By 1901 more than twice as many men in Salford worked in engineering than in textiles. Even more found employment on the railways, in other forms of transport, and in dock work and warehousing, especially after the opening of the Manchester Docks, which were in fact mainly located in Salford.

By about the time of the Cotton Famine of the 1860s textiles seem to have reached their peak in Salford. Yet whilst few major firms making or finishing cotton cloth were established after that time, old Salford firms continued to flourish and expand, and new sectors developed, so that textiles continued to provide the main occupation for working women and girls. Moreover, many of the significant developments in transport and engineering after 1870 were associated with the continuing expansion of textiles, nationally and internationally. In 1914 Cotton was still indisputedly king in Manchester. What had happened was that his court and kingdom had become bigger and vastly more complex.

Just how complex can be judged from an analysis of firms engaged in two of Salford's main industries at the end of Queen Victoria's reign.[3] First, textiles, which by 1901 can be separated out into four main sections – the old businesses of cloth manufacture and textile finishing, the newer development of clothing, and what might be called an industrial textile division, which made products ranging from ropes and railway-wagon sheets to industrial belting. At the start of the twentieth century textile manufacturing in Salford and Pendleton was carried on by some fifty three firms. In addition to the fourteen cotton spinners and manufacturers, amongst whom were such old established, large-scale employers as Richard Haworth & Co. Ltd, Langworthy Bros., Wright Turner & Son and Sir Elkanah Armitage & Sons Ltd, once all household names in Salford, there were smaller specialist firms involved in cotton doubling, and the manufacture of smallwares, checks, regattas and stripes. There were also nine cotton waste dealers, one silk spinner and one flax spinner. Textile finishing (which employed far more men than women) had always been an important speciality of Salford's cotton industry since its earliest days. By 1901 there were some 37 firms, the great majority either bleachers or dyers and finishers.

From about 1870 the manufacture of clothing for wholesale arose alongside the older cotton industry. The pioneer firm was that of Isidore Frankenburg, who came from London about 1868. His firm began what became the local speciality of water and airproof fabrics and garments for the mass market. By 1901 his garments were selling as far away as America and New Zealand, and the firm had diversified into insulated cables and wires for electric lighting, which were made at its Greengate Rubber and Cable works. By the time of the Great War Frankenburgs were employing 1200 workers.[4] Another leading firm was that of J. Mandleburg and Co. Ltd which began in Pendleton in 1885: within five years it had a work-force of over a thousand.[5] A substantial part of the clothing business was in Jewish hands, five of the eight firms in the borough being located in Lower Broughton, where considerable numbers of Jews from Eastern Europe settled in the two decades before 1900. The fourth area of textiles was that occupied by about 13 firms making rope and twine, cart and railway waggon sheets, tentings and tarpaulins, hosepiping and industrial belting.

This diversity in textiles was as nothing compared to the range of specialisation in the 117 or so firms involved in iron founding and engineering. These included (in alphabetical order) artesian wellborers, boiler makers, brass founders, brewing plant manufacturers, calendar bowl makers, coppersmiths, fire engine makers, gas-engine makers, hydraulic hoist makers, iron fencing and palisading manufacturers, iron roof and iron-staircase makers, machine makers, machinists, mechanical stoker makers, millwrights, motor manufacturers, motor-car manufacturers (2), rivet and nail makers, screw, bolt, nut and rivet makers, steel manufacturers, weighing machine and scale-beam makers, wire manufacturers and wire workers. King Cotton's great double-barrelled city was also the home of Vulcan.

Ironfounding and engineering in Salford were as old as the factory system itself. In his account of the Manchester district in 1794 Aikin noted, in addition to the five in Manchester, a considerable iron foundry in Salford. This was the business of Bateman & Sherratt, the latter described as 'a very ingenious and able engineer, who has improved upon and brought the steam engine to perfection. Most of those that are used and set up in and about Manchester are of their make and fitting up'.[6] Throughout the nineteenth century Salford's iron and engineering firms took advantage of opportunities presented by such developments as the railways, the mid-Victorian boom in dockyards and ports, the need for artesian-well and pumping equipment for waterworks in the era of Public Health, and the need for plant for the production of gas and electricity. The latter became the late nineteenth-century specialism of Salford's most famous engineering firm, Mather & Platt.

Yet, if for the successful industrial capitalist, his foremen and skilled workers the Industrial Revolution was rewarding, for many, and probably a majority, the creation of an industrialised urbanised form of society was a protean and painful experience. As the home of the factory system, Manchester was the scene of its earliest and most advanced manifestation. Industrial capitalism was an imposition of machine-based work and the culture of time-discipline on to a labour force which, in the late eighteenth and early nineteenth centuries, had to be recruited and schooled in its ways. The social transformation was distorted and rendered more painful by two decades of war, and after 1815 there followed a prolonged period of boom and slump, in which bursts of economic growth, which attracted migrants into the industrial districts, alternated with recessions which produced bouts of mass unemployment. This cyclical sequence was not interrupted until the Mid-Victorian years, and it resumed again in the 1870s.

The creation of new wealth on a prodigious scale for some was accompanied by a great extension of poverty for many – despite optimistic assumptions that industrialization would, one day, abolish poverty. In the three decades following the battle of Waterloo class conflict threatened on a number of occasions. Indeed, one might characterise the history of Regency and Early Victorian Manchester as a series of confrontations: Capital *versus* Labour; competition *versus* co-operation; individualism *versus* community; family-time *versus* factory-time. These confrontations (and there were others) cannot be ignored. But industrial life was not all alienation and conflict, and industrial society did not consist only of the rich and poor. Between them were many layers. There were those in the ranks of the skilled artisans and the 'shopocracy' who, with due observation of the tenets of thrift, seriousness and sobriety (and good luck) found life good in Victorian Salford. Defending themselves at work and from the dangers of social insecurity went beyond mere private virtue. It lay in association, which almost always provided conviviality and fostered community spirit as well. Places like Salford were honeycombed with their organisations – trade unions, co-operatives, friendly societies, building societies and temperance societies. Salford was birthplace to the Ancient Order of Oddfellows (Manchester Unity) a friendly society which spread out through Great Britain out into the English-speaking world in the course of the century. It was also where the Independent Order of Rechabites (Salford Unity) originated for temperance men who wanted a friendly society in which conviviality was enjoyed away from the public house.[7] When men began their modern love affair with sport, the places to fall most completely under its spell were the industrial towns, and none more so than sports-mad Manchester. In their various ways, and at different times, all those developments contributed towards the emergence of a viable class society, in which, for many, urban life could be satisfying and even exciting.

How satisfying or exciting depended very largely where you were in the social scale. The rise of the industrial capitalist system was based above all on the availability of cheap labour. And if cheap labour was not available by voluntary migration (as on the whole it usually was) then those in positions of economic and political power did not hesitate to import it. At bottom, this was the basis of the hostility to the poor Irish in nineteenth-century Lancashire. The prospect of work drew people into Manchester. Despite the existence of a rich mythology of 'rags to riches' stories, the chances of working people moving up the social scale by their own efforts were strictly limited. Industrialisation created a sharply defined class society in which the characteristic lot of the lower ranks of the working class was a life in and out of poverty.

Looked at from the point of view of the urban chronicler, what is marked is the scale of migration and rate of reproduction of the people of the borough, the dynamism of its industrial and urban growth, and its largely unregulated nature. What these produced at first was an urban patchwork in which the poor lived in dense pockets of courts, cellars and back-to-back houses, as close as possible to where they worked. For half a century and more, these developments were shaped by market forces rather than the bye-laws of local government. The river that encircled the township of Salford soon became one of the hardest-worked waterways in the world, and to its pollution was added that of the atmosphere by the smoke from hundreds of factory chimneys and thousands of dwelling houses. The dark red local brick and blue Welsh slate of new buildings were soon overlaid with a patina of matt black. By the 1840s Salford was already one of the most polluted places in Britain, ready for the first inquiries of the Public Health movement. The poverty, misery and ill health of the common people of industrial Britain were the grim obverse of capitalist optimism. There were few more extreme examples of their incidence than Salford, and no better place to study what the reformers came up against when they tried to improve the situation.

If modern Manchester and Salford were created in an economic and social sense by the forces of industrial growth, administratively and politically they were created by the workings of parliamentary reform. In their support for political change Manchester's liberal businessmen and religious Dissenters not only saw a chance to loosen the political grip of England's *ancien régime*, they also perceived a way to ensure their own political and social emancipation as a class. In the 1830s parliamentary reform was quickly followed by municipal reform, which enabled them to assume a role in local government and politics which matched their economic prominence. The very shape of the new Salford was the direct outcome of all this. In 1832 the three townships were united by the Boundary Commissioners to make one of the Reform Act's new parliamentary boroughs. Six years later they were brought together into a new poor law union, and in 1853 Salford (a municipal borough since 1844) was enlarged by the addition of Pendleton and Broughton.

From its gestation this new Salford was to have a very lively political history, much of which stemmed from the class-based nature of the political process. In addition to the national and local struggle between Old and New Money, the Reform campaign saw the entry into the political arena of popular Radicalism as a mass movement. Disappointment at their exclusion from the political process by the terms of the Reform Act, embittered by the sufferings of the poor, and enraged by the punitive new Poor Law, the working class turned to Chartism, which had no more active centre than Manchester. Chartist democracy was defeated in 1848, and although popular Radicals agitated for an extension of the franchise, in Manchester, as elsewhere, politics veered away from the consideration of further reform until 1866. Whatever else they were, party politics in Victorian Salford were not the politics of democracy. Even with the passing of the Third Reform Act in 1884, the electoral system became no more than proto-democratic. In 1914 only half of Salford's adult males and, (despite the best efforts of Suffragists and Suffragettes) none of its women had the parliamentary vote.

Class was a major factor in Victorian Salford, yet its history and politics cannot be explained exclusively in economic terms. One inescapable influence was religion.

Liberal and Radical leaders were often from religious Dissenting backgrounds, adding an historic animus towards the Church of England to their economic and political antipathies to the Establishment. For their part, Lancashire Tories, reborn as Conservatives after the mauling of 1832, found in 'the Church in danger' a surprisingly effective rallying cry. Faced with Ritualists within their own, ranks, and Dissenters, Catholics and 'Infidels' outside, churchmen saw themselves beset by on all fronts. No one can understand Victorian Salford without paying due attention to what ensued. Even today, when one Salfordian meets another, a question posed sooner or later is 'Which school did you go to?', the sub-text being, of course, 'What is (or was) your religion (and social origin)?' As on the economic front, politics and religion can be reduced down to a series of big confrontations – Dissent *versus* the Church, Whig *versus* Tory, Liberal *versus* Conservative, Protestant *versus* Catholic. To which, in the later Victorian years, can be added Secularism *versus* Religion and Socialism *versus* the older political parties. If all this has a fulcrum, it is *liberalism*, a word rich in meanings, to which each generation adds more. Around the time of the first Reform Act, 'liberal' as an adjective had two: the eighteenth-century usage, meaning 'generous, free, open-handed' and a contemporary one of not being bound by orthodox or established tenets in politics and religion, of being independent, and friendly to greater freedom in economics, government and administration. Needless to say, early Victorian liberals were frequently not conspicuously generous, free or open-handed. In due course, some of the liberals of 1832 emerged as 'the Manchester School', adherents of Cobden and Bright and the Anti-Corn Law League. For a decade or so the overused old cliché that 'what Manchester thinks today London thinks tomorrow' might just have had a ring of truth about it. However, Salford's political history is not only the rise and rise of Liberalism. Far from it: following Cobden and Bright proved a painful political experience after 1846. Salford is a good place to observe the phenomenon of urban Conservatism, whose appearance surprised Disraeli almost as much as the Liberals. And later on, in the Eighties and Nineties, Manchester and Salford became one of those places which proved fertile ground for Socialism and Feminism, political movements which wished a plague on both their houses.

Urban life was and is kaleidoscopic: to seek to rediscover, and do justice to the multifarious issues which make up the history of any town is to court difficulties as weighty as they are obvious. Research becomes formidable in scope, explanation takes on a Byzantine complexity, the result can be unreadable. There is a limit to the number of themes an historian can engage with. The prudent specialise. There is also the risk that within such a broad approach, people, as individuals, can vanish. Who doubts that individual leadership is not always important? It certainly was in nineteenth-century towns: their very ideology was that of assertive individualism. In what were face-to-face communities, people (always providing they were free to do so) spoke their mind. For this writer the way through all this has been the biographical approach. The story of nineteenth-century Salford is told by focusing on the public lives of certain figures, whose careers illuminate themes and events in the history of this Lancashire worktown.

Seen like this, this was a bourgeois century. With a capitalist base and a civic platform Salford provided an environment for a new middle class to lead public lives. In this urban theatre, workers, women, and minorities such as Catholics were sidelined. Their role was to be the audience, hissing and cheering. Many of the tensions of the time arose from their attempts to escape from this disenfranchisement, and play their part on the civic stage. This account begins with the life experience of a London parish apprentice drawn into the factory movement of the 1830s, and it ends with the Salford battalions of the Lancashire Fusiliers in the Great War. From the factory-floor life of Charles Aberdeen the scene moves to the life and times of Joseph Brotherton, a cotton manufacturer who gave up business for politics and became Salford's first Member of Parliament. For almost four decades there was little in the public life of the borough he did not influence. From Brotherton, pillar of the Anti-Corn Law League, we move on to Richardson the Chartist, and from early Victorian democrats to Protestants, through the life of the most influential of local Churchmen, Canon Hugh Stowell. Just as Protestant as Stowell, but nonetheless an inveterate political opponent of his, was Sir Elkanah Armitage, founder of one of Pendleton's great textile firms, a middle-class Radical who saw himself as Brotherton's political heir. To follow Armitage's career is to follow liberalism into the wilderness after the Repeal of the Corn Laws. If Armitage thought of himself as Brotherton's heir, Charles Edward Cawley was, in many ways, Stowell's. To the dismay of Liberals, 'Beer and Bible' Conservatism, that rancorous offspring of Lancashire Protestantism, displayed a powerful appeal in Cawley's time. The career of Cawley's contemporary, Alderman Thomas Davies, takes us away from politics to the Cotton Famine, and the struggle to put Public Health on to the local government agenda. From poverty and pollution the theme of the local fortunes of the Liberal party is renewed once more in the career of Sir Elkanah's son, Benjamin Armitage, who succeeded where his father failed, becoming a Member of Parliament, only to be swept away by the Irish Home Rule Crisis. In the prolonged struggle between the irascible Alderman Mandley and self-seeking Samuel Hunter, engineer of Salford's enormous municipal gas concern, we not only consider the clash of two well-developed egos and issues of probity and propriety in public service, but the inner peculiarities of Salford system of local government. From gas and corruption the focus shifts to Salford's Catholic population in the 'Second Spring'. We look at Lancashire Catholicism's inner tensions as well as its achievements, through the relationship of German-born Father Saffenreuter and his parishioners. In reconstructing the life and times of the proletarian orator George Evans we turn from Catholicism to the 'ethical Socialism' of the Eighties and Nineties, the first stage in the emergence of modern Labour. The penultimate study is of Feminism, through the career of Pendleton-born Emmeline Pankhurst and her family. Their Feminism had its origins both in Manchester's Liberalism and ethical Socialism, though the Pankhursts and their allies were to take the struggle for Votes for Women into areas of militance neither of these movements could condone. Nevertheless, there is something very Manchester (and very bourgeois) about Mrs Pankhurst. If most of the above themes are about conflict, division and protest, the book ends with patriotism and coming-together. In the career of Sir Lees Knowles, Benjamin Armitage's Unionist opponent of 1886, we look at the way local feelings and associations were harnessed for national patriotic purposes *via* the army reforms which linked old regiments to counties. Through Knowles's work promoting the Lancashire Fusiliers as 'a territorial family', it can be seen how it was the that vast armies raised in the first two years of the Great War were volunteers. It had never happened before, and it may be doubted it will ever happen again. Victorian Salford ends on the beaches of Gallipoli and in the trenches of the Somme.

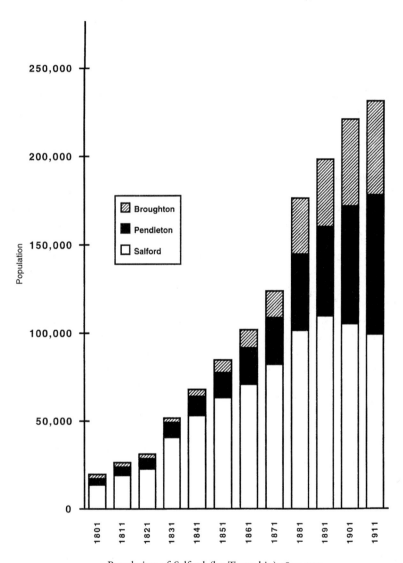

Population of Salford (by Township) 1801–1911

CHAPTER I

# Going Through the Mill: Charles Aberdeen and the Factory System

For most of his life Charles Aberdeen was an obscure factory worker. Then, not long before his death, he twice became involved in a major controversy and came briefly into the public eye. In July 1832 he appeared before Sadler's Parliamentary Committee on the Employment of Women and Children in Textile Factories. Travelling to Westminster, Aberdeen must have felt his life coming full circle, because it was from that very city he had been bound parish apprentice to a northern factory-master thirty five years before. The second occasion was the following year, when he appeared before the Royal Commission on Factories, instituted by Parliament with the intention of 'setting the record straight' on 'the one sided' evidence given to Sadler. Much of what we know of Aberdeen comes from what he said to these tribunals, and in all this his character comes across clearly. Aberdeen had strong feelings about his experiences, and expressed them bluntly. He told the Royal Commission he would have liked to have had the chance to write the history of his own life, declaring 'he would have shown up the factory system then'. He was not destined to have that opportunity: a few weeks after appearing before the Royal Commission he was dead.

The following pages attempt to repair this omission and recount the story of Aberdeen's life and times. He never lived to see Queen Victoria ascend the throne, but his story reminds us that Victorian Salford was created by the rise of the cotton industry, and that it was a proletarian city. However, the tenor of life was profoundly anti-democratic. The poor were kept in their place and their voice was rarely allowed to be heard. More by accident than design Aberdeen's was. Although unlettered, he was an intelligent man, fully conscious of what he was – a member of that first generation bred from childhood to the service of the machine and the factory.

Charles Aberdeen was never certain of his precise age. He told Sadler he thought he had been born in 1780 and apprenticed at the age of eleven or twelve.[1] In fact he was born on the 19th and baptised on the 29th December 1781; he was apprenticed in March 1797, at the age of fifteen. The son of Alexander and Jane Aberdeen of the parish of St James in the City of Westminster, the parish records contain references to his father entering and 'eloping' from the workhouse on several occasions, finally to be re-admitted in June 1796, where he died soon after. They also mention a George and a Diana Aberdeen, probably Charles' grandfather and sister.[2]

Six months after the death of Charles Aberdeen's father, the Governors and Directors of the Poor in the parish of St James were approached by the London agent of the firm of Messrs Douglas & Co. of Pendleton, Manchester, and Holywell, Flintshire, with a proposal to take on pauper children as indentured apprentices in the cotton spinning trade. The firm had recruited children from the parish before, and supplied the parish officers with their subsequent histories. In the minds of London poor law authorities there existed strong doubts about the condition of pauper apprentices in the cotton mills, but there was also a desire and duty to have their pauper children apprenticed to a trade. The St James' authorities took steps to check the employer's claims about the conditions under which the children were to live, work and be taught, and, having satisfied themselves on these matters, in March 1797 sent twenty-two children to Holywell. One of them was Charles Aberdeen.[3] At fifteen he was a little old: factory masters generally liked them younger.

Aberdeen spent the next seven or eight years in Holywell. In that early industrial colony the parish apprentice was turned into a factory hand. Normally children started as 'little piecers', and at the age of fifteen or sixteen progressed to the carding room. At about nineteen some were put to 'jobbing', assisting the spinners, or to work as card cleaners, repairing and maintaining the machines. Some rose to be spinners, and a few to be overlookers, the men who made the system work.[4] Possibly because he started late, or because he did not take to spinning, Aberdeen became a card grinder. He later recalled that the hours of work were from 6am to 7pm, six days a week. No time was allowed for breakfast, which had to be eaten whilst working, and out of the hour allowed for dinner up to half was frequently taken cleaning the machinery, stopped for the break.

In his years in North Wales Aberdeen had only two short spells away, when the mills stopped because of the wars against Napoleon. He later recollected that he had set out for London without a penny in his pocket, and while there worked as a pot-boy in public houses. Each time, however, he returned to work for Douglas. About 1804 (the information is not precise) he finally left Holywell, returned to London for a visit, but after a few months came to Pendleton, where he married Sarah Greystock, a parish apprentice from Mile End in London, and recommenced work for his old employer.[5]

The cotton mills at Douglas Green, Pendleton were amongst the first in Lancashire. In 1783 there were only two others in Manchester (Arkwright's and Thackray's) and only two more in the country (both belonging to Peel and Yates).[6] In 1777 the lease of Pendleton Old Hall, which had been in use as a bleaching croft, was advertised, and then, or soon after, William Douglas (1746–1810) constructed a six storeyed water-powered spinning mill close by, taking up residence in the Hall. Douglas later expanded his premises by constructing a second mill driven by a steam engine, purchased from Boulton and Watt in 1792. In a letter to that firm he explained that his first mill was 'going Night and Day' with 'between 3 and 4,000 Spindles'.[7] In 1782, in the great cotton boom after the Peace of Paris, Douglas went into partnership with the widow of John Smalley, one of Arkwright's original partners, at Holywell, where the waterfalls offered a more reliable source of water power than the Irwell. Smalley had founded the Holywell Cotton Twist Company in 1777. In the years thereafter the company was called variously the Holywell Cotton Twist Company, Douglas, Smalley and Co., and Douglas & Co. By 1795 its plant was the second largest insured cotton concern in the country, inferior in size only to the gigantic Peel enterprise. In that year Douglas had seven mills at Holywell and Pendleton, with a workforce of 1,225, of whom Aberdeen was one.[8]

As with other pioneer factory masters, at each expansion of his business Douglas was faced with a shortage of labour, particularly child labour. Children were in demand both for their nimbleness around the machinery, in piecing together broken yarn, and for the fact that a new workforce trained from infancy in the rhythms of the machine and the clock was needed for factory labour: spinners and weavers used to the old methods of work usually proved unsatisfactory. Douglas did what other factory masters did: he made agreements with parish overseers in the south to take pauper children as apprentices. And as well as Westminster and London children, he took others from Essex parishes.

Although its population was growing, Charles Aberdeen's Pendleton was still largely rural. Cooke's map of 1815 records a landscape of crofts (old enclosed fields), halls and scattered farmsteads. Pointers to the future were two mills, the one at Douglas Green, and Taylor, Weston & Co's factory to the south of Broad Street. This had started in 1797, and around it grew the nucleus of the future Ellor Street district.[9] Between the two mill locations developed the first streets of Charlestown, one of the earliest working-class districts of Victorian Salford. In this township of over 1,700 acres there was no settlement nucleus, though a centre was forming at Pendleton Pole, a triangular green on which there stood an eighteenth century maypole, just below the point where Broad Street, the road out of Manchester, forked, one branch turning off to Eccles and ultimately to Liverpool, the other to Bolton. This triangular green became more firmly the centre of Pendleton in 1831, when the Duchy of Lancaster gave it for the site for the new church of St Thomas ('Pendleton church') and its churchyard.

Despite its rurality, the Pendleton of this time was not exclusively given over to agriculture. Along the road out from Manchester, suburban building was taking

Paddington datestone, Broad Street, Pendleton.

place on plots often named after London districts. In Salford township there was Islington, close to the Pendleton township boundary there was New Windsor, and on Broad Street there was a row of houses called Paddington. Away from the main road, on a number of the farms and crofts, the old textile finishing trade of the district had its workplaces. On Cooke's map there is an 'Indigo field' off Whit Lane and a 'Bleach Croft' and a 'Dyeing Field' at Weaste. Whit Lane took its name from the old whitsters, or bleachers. When Pendleton Old Hall was advertised to let in 1777, sundry bleaching materials, were offered for sale.[10]The site, it was said, would be very suitable for a calico printer, but William Douglas set up there as the first Pendleton cotton spinner. Many of these crofts became the locations of future dye-works and calico printing establishments. Notable in its time was that of Russel, Bellringer & Co., down Whit Lane, not far from Douglas Green. There was a dye works at Wallness, and two later important industrial premises in Seedley originated at this time. The factory of Ermen and Engels of 1837 was sited at or near a place called Fosterwood in Weaste, where a whitster named Gee put up a bleaching croft for sale in 1763. What became the later Seedley Print Works was a dye-works in 1798, and a small calico printers in 1806.[11] The new factory system, then, superimposed itself on an older rural textile industry, which it both stimulated and transformed. And what was true of Pendleton was even truer of Salford township, closer to Manchester, but still rural. In 1794 there were some seventy cloth finishers at work there, the great majority in small workshops. Over half were bleachers, whitsters and dyers, the others being mainly cloth dressers and fustian cutters.

The firm Aberdeen worked for was important. Despite the Holywell connection, William Douglas, seems to have lived at Pendleton Old Hall and died there, a rich man, in 1810. His son John had other ideas. In 1817 he purchased the Gyrn Hall estate in Flintshire, and built Gyrn Castle, which remained in the family until 1853. Under him the firm diversified into banking. For a time it prospered, but the Smalleys withdrew in 1828, and ten years later the banking house collapsed. By then the textile business was also on its last legs, going into liquidation in 1841. The premises at Douglas Green in which Aberdeen worked became the Irwell Bleach Works, and the original mill was destroyed by fire in 1850.[12]

By then the Douglases were long gone, leaving only their name in Pendleton. Capital is always mobile and so are capitalists: as well as their Flintshire connections, at one time or another the Douglases had partners in Newmarket, Cambridgeshire, and branches of the family settled in Grantham, Lincs., Hughenden, Bucks., and Barnstaple, Devon.[13] Once the Douglases moved out of cotton no doubt they put Douglas Green out of their minds, but the people they left behind did not forget *them*. One of the strongest folk memories of Victorian Salford was the evil reputation of Pendleton's first industrial colony. A 'Douglas-greener' meant someone deformed by rickets, the mill being popularly referred to as the 'cripple factory'. Douglas, who died worth £60,000, was remembered as a driving, tyrannical employer. The author of a letter in the *Salford Weekly News* in 1863 noted the joylessness of the place, likening it to a penal colony. It was similarly described by J. G. de T. Mandley, in a lecture in 1892, and more recently by the novelist, Walter Greenwood.[14] Closer to the period, there is the evidence of John Doherty,

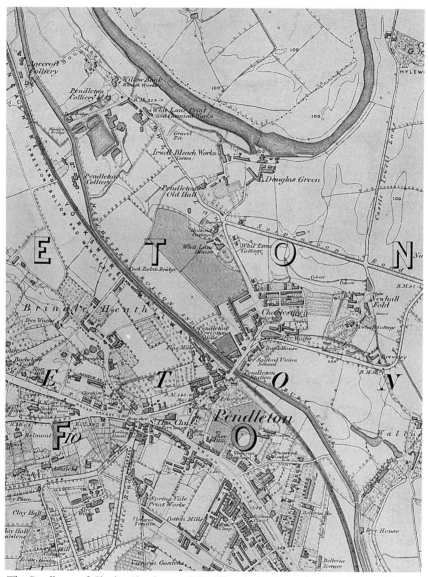

The Pendleton of Charles Aberdeen and Sir Elkanah Armitage: the first edition of the six inch Ordnance Survey map, 1848.

the trade union leader of the 1830s. To Doherty, Douglas was a 'cormorant capitalist', the worthy head of his list of 'graspalls'. Equally, if not more damning, because it came from a more contemporary witness, is that of Dr. Aikin in 1795, who referred to the condition of factory children from London and Westminster workhouses in Eccles parish, (undoubtedly Douglas's, Pendleton then being part of that parish) 'too long confined to work in close rooms, often during the whole night ... little regard is paid to their cleanliness, and frequent changes from a warm and dense to a cold and thin atmosphere are predisposing causes to sickness and disability', a point Aberdeen later made to the Sadler Committee. Aikin concluded, 'the public have a right to see that its members are not wantonly injured, or carelessly lost'.[15] Within a few years the pauper apprentice system was ended, though child labour was not.

On this question of child labour in the Industrial Revolution recent historians have fallen over backwards to be fair to the early factory masters. Yet whilst late eighteenth century entrepreneurs were not the first to exploit the labour of children of the poor, they certainly systematised it, and society soon made its unease felt at the pauper apprentice system, the last years of which Aberdeen experienced. As to the long hours and night work all good political economists would recommend using plant efficiently: time is indeed money, but the matter had always had an awkward human dimension. The nineteenth century saw the awakening of a spirit of opposition to the exploitation of children, though its application long remained patchy and partial, but the definition of the 'normal' working day became the key issue in the struggle between workers and masters in the Industrial Revolution. The 1802 Act was the first of a series regulating hours and conditions which were to be spread over much of the rest of the century. Aberdeen lived to see the 1825 Act, and played a bit-part in the events which led to the statute of 1833.

The precise dates are uncertain, but Aberdeen worked for Douglas in Pendleton for about seven years and it was there that some of the seven children born to him and his wife, none of whom survived infancy, came into this world.[16] The only one for whom any record has been traced is Dinah, perhaps named after his sister in London, whom the Parish Register of St Thomas's records as being buried on 26 March 1811, aged 9 days. Otherwise there is little information as to what kind of a life he led outside working hours at Douglas Green. Yet he seems to have had a better education than most of his fellow workers, and what he later said on the subject of bad language and morality rather implies that he was a man who stood apart from his contemporaries.

About 1814 or 1815 he gave up his long association with the Douglas firm, and moved to Salford. After working briefly for several firms, the only one of which he named being Ellis, Hughes & Co. in Factory Lane, Oldfield Road, he commenced work for the firm of Philips & Lee, perhaps the most notable of the early cotton concerns in the township. It commenced in 1791 as Atherton, Ward & Philips, became Philips & Lee, and then later Lambert Hoole & Jackson.[17] Aberdeen worked as a card grinder in that very model of a modern cotton factory until his row with the management in April 1832, which led to his involvement with Sadler's Committee. In his time the pace of the Industrial Revolution in Salford township accelerated. Despite the prolonged post-war slump, between 1811 and 1831 Salford's population more than doubled. The Twenties saw tremendous industrial expansion in the wake of the end of the recession: the number of local textile factories doubled, and there was a significant development of engineering. In percentage terms, this decade saw the most rapid population growth of the whole nineteenth century.

Aberdeen lived at Rowell Buildings, Whitecross Bank, Chapel Street, between the new industrial district growing up in Oldfield Road, and the old nucleus of the township, just across the river from the centre of Manchester. As he walked

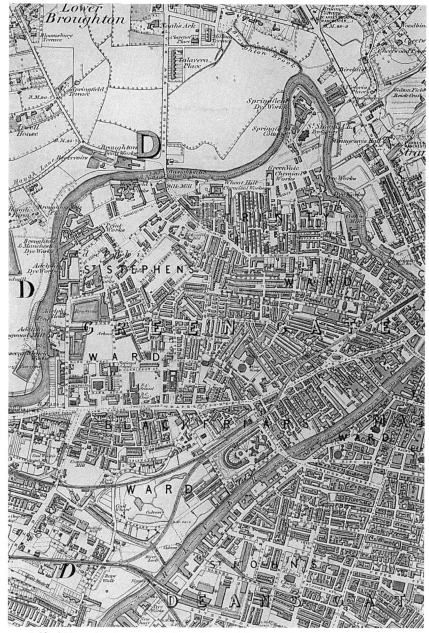

Salford Township in 1848: the first edition of the six inch Ordnance Survey map.

to work each day down Chapel Street he must have been very conscious of the rapid growth of the place, and no doubt witnessed the building of the Salford and Pendleton Dispensary (later Salford Royal Hospital), St Philip's Church, and the new town-hall in Bexley Square, as well as the more mundane appearance of new streets, houses, shops and pubs. He must have also had his share of unemployment as well, because the boom received a set-back in the commercial crisis of 1826, and was brought to an end by the severe depression of 1830–32. Those were momentous times: Aberdeen saw the passing of the Great Reform Act, followed by the election of December 1832, in which the new borough of Salford returned an MP to Westminster for the first time.

On 30 April 1832 Charles Aberdeen was taken aside by the manager at Lambert, Hoole & Jackson and told to collect his money. 'When people cannot agree,' said Mr Lambert, 'they are best asunder'.[18] Thus ended Aberdeen's time in the cotton industry, which had begun at Holywell thirty five years before. He was victimised because he refused to sign a petition opposing the Bill before Parliament to reduce the hours of child labour. According to the account he gave to Sadler's Committee in July, up to 2 March Aberdeen had been 'neutral' on the matter of the Ten Hours Bill, but when, over the following few days, heavy pressure was put on him by his employers to sign he stubbornly refused. When again pressed, Aberdeen still refused to sign, and involved himself in the public discussion of the Bill in the neighbourhood, taking the chair at a meeting at the *Duke of Lancaster* public house, expressing his views of the factory system in public.[19]

The movement to reduce child labour in the factories was by then long established in Manchester, going back to 1814, when the first short-time committee had been formed. The matter had been taken up on several occasions by parliament and no less than three acts were on the statute book, all of which had been either ineffectual, or evaded by the factory masters. In late 1830 the old factory movement, however, entered a new phase. Hitherto confined to Lancashire, that autumn it spread into Yorkshire after the publication of Richard Oastler's famous letters to the *Leeds Mercury* on 'White Slavery' in the factories of Bradford. Short-time committees had been formed, and intense anger had been generated when Hobhouse had been persuaded by the Yorkshire factory masters to exclude woollen factories from his 1831 Bill, which, when it became law, proved just as ineffective as its predecessors. The Yorkshire factory reformers then took the cause out of the hands of Hobhouse and made Michael Sadler their Parliamentary spokesman. They began to mount pressure on candidates for the forthcoming elections. In Manchester the short-time committee demanded that the electors should return only members pledged to 'ten hours, with eight on Saturday, and a time-book'. The tactic first employed by John Doherty, the trade unionist and veteran factory reformer in Manchester, was to publicise examples of oppression under which factory workers had suffered, or were suffering, and it was in this campaign he attacked Douglas as one of the 'Midnight Robbers of the Repose of the Poor'.[20] After some delay, Doherty came out in support of Sadler's Bill.

Against these attacks the employers defended themselves. They drew up petitions and pressured their workpeople to sign them, dismissing those who wouldn't, which was how and why Aberdeen was sacked. Doherty condemned such injustices. Holland Hoole, one of the partners in the firm Aberdeen worked for, retaliated by writing a pamphlet addressed to Lord Althorp, defending conditions in cotton factories.[21] Its title page carried the motto *'Laissez Nous Faire'*. Pointing out that there were many trades where conditions were worse than in the factories, Hoole blamed the attack on the cotton masters on 'agitators'.

Clearly, in March and April 1832, the obscure Charles Aberdeen found himself at the epicentre of a great political battle. If it is really correct that up to 2 March he had indeed been 'neutral' on factory reform (as he told Sadler), he now allied himself to the efforts of the local working-class factory reformers to influence Parliament to pass Sadler's Ten Hours Bill. On 7 July he appeared at Westminster before Sadler's committee as a witness, drawing on a lifetime's experience of the factory system. He was given an extensive interview, answering nearly two hundred questions: his evidence takes up nine printed pages in the published Blue Book. In addition to outlining his personal history and the circumstances of his dismissal from the mill, the bulk of his testimony was on his views of working conditions in textile factories and their effects on young people. He was first asked about the atmosphere inside mills. Aberdeen declared that in the early days the carding rooms were very dusty, but were less so now with the development of the machinery. However, he insisted that the atmosphere of the factory was still unwholesome with the friction of machinery, the smell of oil, lavatories and gas lighting. Aberdeen was clear on the effects of long exposure to mill conditions; by its 'paleness and wanness' 'a factory child may be known easily from another child that does not work in a factory' and went on:[22]

> I have seen men and women that have worked in a factory all their lives, like myself, and that get married; and I have seen the race become diminutive and small; I have myself had seven children, not one of which survived six weeks; my wife is an emaciated person, like myself, a little woman, and she worked during her childhood, younger than myself, in a factory.

Aberdeen had a way with the English language and clearly relished answering Sadler's questions. However, he did allow himself the occasional apparent exaggeration. He declared he had seen men 'more lusty than himself' 'die daily for want of breath, because they were not allowed to let the fresh air in and let the foul air out',[23] a statement later to be severely challenged. He gave his impressions of changes in the length of the working day compared to when he was an apprentice ('much the same, I think'), and working night shifts, which he declared was compulsory, less healthy than day work, unpopular, and not significantly better paid. Asked whether developments in machinery had made factory work easier, he answered it had not: on the contrary, improved and faster machinery drove operatives harder. On the hours of work, Aberdeen said he had repeatedly heard factory workers say that they were excessive, but that he had never seen any attempt inside a mill to get employers to reduce them. However, he did not think the employers would take any notice if representations were made. He alluded to the threats and bullying of his employers over the petition they got up against the Ten Hours Bill, and had bitter words about overlookers, the NCOs of the factory system. Aberdeen denied being insulting to his employers at the meeting at the *Duke of Lancaster*, and indeed in his evidence was careful not to say anything personally against any of them. On the contrary, he emphasised 'the master that I was last discharged from, had observed the Act of parliament more so than any master that I ever knew'.[24] Throughout he emphasised his quarrels were with the *system*. Finally, he was asked about the educational standards and morals of the factory children he had known. Whilst he admitted that there was positive encouragement to attend Sunday School, he did not believe that those that did derived much educational benefit. In any case most did not attend Sunday School, nor did they attend night school, for obvious reasons. Not many could read or write. In Aberdeen's opinion the 'morals' of the children in the mills were in a bad state. The reasons for this, he said, lay in the long hours worked and the 'extreme debaucheries that are practised' in factories. It is not entirely clear what he meant by the latter, though he referred with some distaste to swearing and indecent language. He declared 'if their parents, and the Sunday Schools combined, were to use all their power to teach them morality or moral precepts, the superabundant hours and extreme debaucheries that are practised in factories would entirely choke it'.[25]

Aberdeen's answers to Sadler, which were not required to be given on oath, were general rather than specific. There is, for instance, nothing in what he says that adds substance to the notion that Douglas's was any worse than any other factory. This, of course, did not prevent his former employers taking deep umbrage at what he had said. They soon got a chance to counter-attack: Aberdeen was to be picked up on certain points he had made, and weightily contradicted.

Aberdeen remains an enigma. We know very little about him. He appears a typical factory worker, yet his evidence to Sadler and the Royal Commission seem to indicate that he was better educated than many of his fellow workers. His answers were trenchant, fluent and expressed in coded language. Asked 'upon the whole, what do you think is the state of morality amongst the children in mills and factories, as compared with other classes of society?' he replied 'I cannot observe morality amongst any class of people, except they are intelligent, and their minds are well-informed'.[26] Nothing in what has been discovered about him suggests that Aberdeen was active in reform politics, trade unionism or the factory movement before 1832, but a shaft of light was thrown on his beliefs and ideas when he appeared before the Royal Commission. When asked to take the oath he refused, declaring instead, 'Truth is what I swear by, and whenever I meet her I embrace her'. 'Do you believe in a God?' he was then asked, 'Can you tell me what God is?' To which Aberdeen replied 'God is incomprehensible. I am a moral character. When I was in London I lived in Mr Carlile's shop, Fleet Street. I acted in the capacity of a servant to Mr Carlile and the Rev. Robert Taylor'.[27] The reply delighted the questioner: Aberdeen was admitting to being an Infidel, a free thinker. What could be more disgusting? Conventional outrage, no less, required Aberdeen's testimony to be disregarded as being, by definition, suspect.

Yet Aberdeen called himself 'a moral character' and declared that truth was what he lived by. His connection with Richard Carlile, the radical journalist and printer presents Aberdeen in a different light.[28] The Reverend Robert Taylor, once a minister of the Church of England, became converted to deism after reading Gibbon and Paine and was forced to leave the church in 1821.[29] Taylor and Carlile became acquainted, and Carlile took Taylor to London to present his views to the public. The question is, when did Aberdeen come under their influence, go to London and live at Carlile's Fleet Street shop? In 1829 Taylor went to help Carlile run an adult school at 62 Fleet Street. In the summer of that year the two Radical free-thinkers went on an 'Infidel Mission', which took them to the Midlands and North.[30] They attempted, with little success, to erect a popular free-thought movement based upon 'Infidel rent', the penny contributions of working men. Was Aberdeen one of the working men converted by the 'Infidel mission', and did this, on one of his visits to his native London, take him to work as a servant at Carlile's shop in Fleet Street? It seems certain he was, and it did. When Thomas Leeming, superintendent of the carding-room at Lambert, Hoole & Jackson appeared before the Royal Commission in 1833, in reply to Tufnell's question about how Charles Aberdeen came to be dismissed, he said 'I don't know exactly, but I believe it was probably owing to his principles; he was always bringing Carlile's pamphlets and others into the mill'. He also added, revealingly, 'He was always a very regular attendant, or I should have discharged him years before on that account.'[31]

When published early in 1833 the evidence of the factory reformers to Sadler's Committee caused a sensation. The manufacturers were enraged, protesting that only one side of the case had been presented, arguing that much of the evidence referred to factory conditions of an earlier era. When Parliament reassembled, the supporters of the millowners managed to get a motion carried for further investi-gation by a Royal Commission. It was now the turn of the factory reformers to be infuriated. Believing their case had been fully made by Sadler, they feared the Royal Commission would delay the Bill, and that the mill owners would be able to deceive the commissioners about factory conditions when they came to visit the manufacturing districts. The Reformers decided to boycott the Royal Commission, and to organise demonstrations against the commissioners when they appeared locally.

Hardly any witnesses who testified before Sadler agreed to do so before the Royal Commission. One who did was Aberdeen. Why is not clear: he was certainly not compelled to do so; what seems likely is that he knew that his factory days were over and he appeared as an act of defiance. If it was bravado it was perhaps foolish. His old employers were personally incensed by what he had said, and found contemporaries of his willing to refute his testimony, and the assistant commissioner, Tufnell, was certainly on their side. From the start, he went out of his way to denigrate Aberdeen. Edward Carleton Tufnell (1806–86) was one of those able, well-connected young men with an invincible sense of their own rightness, who found careers in the new agencies of the centralising Victorian state. Aberdeen came up against Tufnell on the latter's first important assignment as an Assistant Factory Commissioner. No one could call Tufnell unbiased. A political economist and a polemicist against trade unions[32] he leant strongly towards the manufacturers. His line of questioning and subsequent report lay him open to the charge of using exactly the same sort of smears of which he accused Sadler's committee.

His cross-examination of Aberdeen was not a long one. After inviting him to take the oath, which Aberdeen declined, and asking about Aberdeen's industrial experience and why he had been dismissed, Tufnell concentrated on two things

Aberdeen had said in his evidence to Sadler. The first was Aberdeen's statement of having seen men more lusty than himself die early for want of breath, because they were prevented from letting fresh air into the card-room. Aberdeen observed in reply that Mr Douglas had taken this personally, though he did not allege that of Douglas's firm particularly, but more of Lambert, Hoole & Jackson and the factory system in general. Pressed on the matter of men dying 'daily for want of breath' he replied 'I have seen men gasping in the card-room and carried out for want of breath.[33] Asked who refused to open the windows, Aberdeen said the principal carders refused because they thought cool air 'injured the surface of the fleece'. This was denied by later witnesses. The other point Tufnell pressed him on was about people being compelled to work night shifts. Asked to give instances of persons being discharged for refusing, Aberdeen said he did not recollect that part of his evidence. When asked if he remembered any person who was sacked for this he could not name any names. He said he had never been connected with throstle spinning, the only department at Douglas's that worked the night shift. By keeping the interview short and concentrating on these two matters Tufnell made Aberdeen's evidence to Sadler seem imprecise, and related to a firm he had not worked for 17 years. In concluding, he offered Aberdeen the last word. Asked if there was any further evidence he wished to give, Aberdeen defiantly declared 'If I was in solitary confinement I could write a history of my life, and I would show up the factory system then. It is a consolation to my mind, that I never put a bad example before children, either in word or action'.[34]

A series of hand-picked witnesses from the firms of Douglas and Lambert, Hoole & Jackson were then called, and in answer to Tufnell's questions proceeded to deny what Aberdeen had alleged. The card-rooms were always well ventilated; no-one forced windows to remain closed; the heat was not oppressive; no, they had never seen anyone die from want of breath; no-one was forced or had been forced to work nights; they and their wives had enjoyed health no different from other working people; children were not beaten in the mill nowadays; working people were not thought to be in favour of shorter hours and less child labour.

Despite Tufnell's leading of the witnesses, some fascinating bits of information slipped out. Asked if throstle spinning deformed children, Robert Roberts said that it did *thirty years before*, and put it down to the fact that children then worked sixteen hours a day, 'but at present the hours' (66 a week) 'are so short, there is no fear of deformity'. Tufnell hastily tried to repair the damage. 'Are you certain that you remember more instances of deformity thirty years ago than now?', he asked. 'Yes', said the obtuse Roberts, 'in Manchester there was much more then, when it was the custom to use apprentices. There are some score of men who were deformed at that time. I cannot remember more than one or two instances of persons deformed by working in our mill for the last twenty years'.[35] Tufnell decided that was enough, and changed the subject. Thomas Jones from Cockermouth, who, like Aberdeen, had worked as a child at Holywell and migrated to Salford, gave evidence on the healthiness of work in the card-room. However, he did admit that working there affected him a little 'in the asthmatical way'. Asked about children being beaten in the mill, he said they were not. However, he did recollect he was beaten himself 'many a time at Holywell, forty years ago'.[36]

Summing up matters in his report, Tufnell criticised Sadler's Factory Committee on the grounds that of the eighty nine people who gave evidence only three came from Manchester. The first was a dresser of yarn, another was an activist in the local Ten Hours campaign, and the third (Aberdeen) was an atheist. 'Considerable parts of this man's evidence ... refers to charges made thirty and forty years old; but every specific association which he or his two companions made against the cotton mills I ascertained, from witnesses of the utmost respectability, to be absolutely false.' [37] It was a weighty put-down, and some historians have taken it as authoritative.

In the following weeks of the summer of 1833 events moved briskly to a conclusion. On 17 June Lord Ashley (the future Lord Shaftesbury) who had taken over from Sadler as the factory reformers' parliamentary spokesman, introduced the second reading of the Ten Hours Bill. On 25 June the Royal Commission issued its report. Whilst largely accepting the evidence of the factory reformers on the evils of long hours on children, it rejected the allegations of the worst cruelties the reformers had made. It condemned Ashley's Bill as ineffective to protect children, and the Ten Hours movement as a front for reducing the hours worked by adults. And it condemned the movement for not co-operating with the Commission's enquiries.[38]

Ashley's Bill was heavily defeated in the Commons on 18 July. Three weeks later Lord Althorp introduced a government measure based on the recommendations of the Royal Commission. This provided for an eight hour limitation for children under thirteen, who could be worked in relays. It was to be enforced by factory inspectors, and provision was made for the daily education of factory children. It introduced the further restriction of a twelve hour day for young persons under 18. The bill rapidly passed through all its parliamentary stages and was law by the end of August.[39]

The 1833 Act was a landmark in industrial legislation. For the first time it applied to all textile factories, and not merely cotton mills, and it contained the potential for effective enforcement. It provided protection for the youngest children, and established the principle that labour and education should be combined. But it was unpopular with both sides in the struggle over the factory acts. Employers resented the introduction of inspectors, and, to punish the operatives, prepared to shed the labour of children from the workforce. On the other side, factory reformers were convinced that both the Act and the inspectors were the tools of the employers, and were soon vigorously protesting against the effects of the relay system, and the cost of the medical certificates now needed by children under the Act. Althorp's Act was a serious set-back to the Ten Hours people. However, the movement was to revive and renew the struggle for the ten hour day, which lasted almost another two decades.

It is not certain whether Aberdeen was aware of Althorp's Act, because he died just about the time it became law: the register of the Collegiate Church in Manchester records his burial on 31 August 1833. Right to the end, neither he nor his wife were sure of his correct age. In the register he is given the age of 55: in reality he was 51. His widow, Sarah, like him 'an emaciated person', was to outlive him by almost another twenty years. The last trace of her is in 1852, still living in Rowell Street, Whitecross Bank, Chapel Street, Salford.

Aberdeen died a defeated man. He started as a parish apprentice and, after a life in the mill, died poor and childless. Yet the historical argument which Tufnell and the Royal Commission thought they had settled with the denigration of Aberdeen and others who gave evidence to Sadler as liars at worst, or outdated at best, has refused to go away. The truth of the testimonies given for and against the factory system and factory masters is still debated by historians for the simple reason that they are concerned with a central issue in modern history, the nature of industrial capitalism, especially early industrial capitalism. The first historians of this period were supporters of the newly emergent Labour party in the early part of this century: in their writings on the factory system as it affected working people, Hutchings and Harrison, the Hammonds and their successors generally accept the evidence of Sadler. But in the inter-war years their findings were challenged by economic historians such as Sir John Clapham and W. H. Hutt, economic liberals in the main, for their reliance on 'literary', 'subjective', evidence and for having an anti-capitalist bias. These writers, notably Hutt, rejected Sadler and disinterred many of the arguments produced in the Royal Commission.[40] They would perhaps have been wiser to follow Althorp, who did not reject Sadler wholesale. Hutt is notably wrong on poor Aberdeen, making much of the fact that Aberdeen would not repeat his evidence to Tufnell on oath: 'If we take into account the religious feeling of the day, the importance of this must be clear.'[41] Hutt implies Aberdeen knew his evidence was shaky, and because he knew this, would not swear on the Bible. But what *was* 'the religious feeling of the day'? Hutt fails to see that Aberdeen *had* a strong quasi-religious morality, and it was precisely this which required him *not* to take the oath.

As in all academic debates, at a certain stage it is useful to go back to the primary evidence, and the life of Charles Aberdeen (1781–1833), and what he thought about it, *is* primary evidence (though one might wish it fuller). Aberdeen has to be listened to, because he lived through the period and reflected on it within his own lifetime. Despite Tufnell, there can be little doubt that much of what Aberdeen said is historically indisputable. If the parish apprentice system was only a passing phase, the textile industry was to be based on the labour of children, young people and women for a long time to come. If the worst excesses were soon over, (or only lasted a few decades) they were within the experience of plenty of people still alive in 1833, and were remembered long afterwards. The idea propounded by Tufnell, and taken up by 'Optimist' historians, that somehow the worst features of the new industrial system had been ended by 1833 is nonsense. The factory system was something new in history. The poor needed the work it created, but the demands of this new system were always enforced with harsh discipline. If by 1833 the grosser forms of physical brutality towards children was a thing of the past, as was argued in the Royal Commission, it was well remembered in the evidence given both to Sadler and to Tufnell.

Despite the welter of testimony produced to challenge the idea that the early textile factories were very unhealthy places to work, there were industrial diseases the effects of which Aberdeen described, but which the doctors of the time could not identify, (and later generations could, but would not).[42] With its factories, and other sources of air pollution, nineteenth-century Salford became the bronchitis capital of the world. As early as 1833, the physique and health of 'the race', as Aberdeen put it, had been affected, though it was to take seventy years or so before social inquirers and doctors spelt it out. In point of fact the Royal Commission agreed that much of Sadler had been correct once, but was now out of date. Yet had conditions really changed all that much by 1833? Mill machinery was improved, but was working with it all that different? When mill architecture advanced, did old mills cease to be used? If child beating had largely stopped, was the driving of young people a thing of the past? Were hours of work significantly less by 1833?

'Bringing capital to the people', as Holland Hoole put it, factory employers were increasingly conscious of being a new class, seeing themselves as benefactors, 'creating wealth', providing employment. They resented Sadler, and 'Optimist' historians have continued to resent Sadler on their behalf. In all that he said to the committee, Aberdeen did not personally attack any of his employers. The evil reputation of Douglas Green received no gloss from him. But he did attack the factory system, and rightly discerned that the division of labour, new technology and the production line were a real revolution. They were transforming the Salford townships into part of the first industrial metropolis: by the time of Aberdeen's death the process was gathering momentum.

The cotton mills of Douglas & Co., Holywell, Flintshire, in 1792, to which Charles Aberdeen was sent as a Westminster parish apprentice. (Flintshire Record Office)

CHAPTER 2

# *Borough Making:*
# *The Life and Times*
# *of Joseph Brotherton*

Charles Aberdeen and Joseph Brotherton almost certainly knew of one another. Living in the same district, they may have passed in the street. In that they were both involved in the factory movement, their political activities overlapped, and both knew where the other stood on the matter. However, a social gulf separated them. All his life Aberdeen was a poor operative; Brotherton a factory master who retired comparatively young. Aberdeen died prematurely; Brotherton lived on into his seventies in robust good health. The one died obscure and forgotten, the other had a statue erected to his memory. Brotherton was Victorian Salford's first major public figure: Salford made him, and he played no small part in making Salford. A first generation cotton spinner, Brotherton was an active agent in the industrial transformation of the district. He entered politics at the time of Peterloo, and he and his friends played their part in ensuring that Salford became one of the new parliamentary boroughs created by the Reform Act. For an unbroken period of twenty four years Brotherton sat as the Member for Salford at Westminster. He and his friends were influential in the creation of Salford's local institutions, and they saw to it that the causes close to their hearts were placed on the political agenda of their time. Despite his resolutely modest personal style, Brotherton was always their leading man. If anyone were to be awarded the title of the borough's founding father, it would surely be he.[1]

In common with many contemporaries Brotherton was a migrant from the countryside. Born in Whittington in Derbyshire in 1783, he was about six when his father, John Brotherton, a schoolmaster turned exciseman, brought his family to Manchester. Not long after he set up a small cotton mill. Ten years later, with Joseph Harvey, also from Whittington, and another Derbyshire partner, John Brotherton opened a new mill in Salford in the industrial district growing up around the terminus of the newly completed Manchester, Bolton and Bury canal.[2] Here Joseph worked from boyhood, becoming his father's partner when he came of age, and head of the business when John Brotherton died in 1810. At that time he went into partnership with his brother William and his cousin, William Harvey, whose sister he had married, the firm becoming Brothertons, Harvey & Co.

Joseph Brotherton c. 1832.
(Local History Collection,
Peel Park)

Brotherton remained a cotton spinner until 1819 when, at the age of 36, he retired from business to concentrate on other things. That year William Brotherton died, and Joseph Brotherton's only son, James, being a minor, the firm's management passed to Harvey, who went into partnership with Charles Tysoe.[3] By Manchester standards the business was not large, consisting of two small mills – the Victoria and the Albert – off Oldfield Road, which gave employment to a hundred or so workers.[4] One of the longest-lived of Salford's earliest textile firms, the business lasted three generations. In 1871 a fire did £10,000 worth of damage. Four years later the business went bankrupt, an event which obliged Alderman John Tysoe (Charles Tysoe's son) to resign his seat on the borough council.[5]

The first influence on Joseph Brotherton's development as a man and a politician, then, was cotton spinning. He spent his formative years as a Manchester manufacturer, and was always a representative of that class of men. He knew the cotton trade intimately and accepted industrialisation both as an irreversible fact and an indicator of progress. His closest friends and associates were all men of business, who were later to form the backbone of the Anti-Corn Law League in Manchester. Closest of all were William Harvey and Charles Tysoe. Their friendship was bound by ties of kinship, business, religion and politics.

After he had become a public figure two stories circulated about Brotherton's time as a factory master. One was that he had become rich by profiting from the labour of the poor. The other was that he was a factory child who had risen from obscurity by his own efforts. Neither in fact was true. The first was levelled against him by opponents who tried to prove that his frequently-declared sympathy for the poor was no more than humbug. The most notable occasion was in 1842 when W. B. Ferrand attacked him in the House of Commons in this vein, bringing the riposte from Brotherton that 'his riches consisted not so much in the largeness of his means, as in the fewness of his wants'.[6] His friends liked this so much that they had it inscribed on the plinth of his statue. Though not without some of the tendency of Dissenters to brandish humility as a weapon, Brotherton was essentially telling the truth. He never was a rich man, certainly not by Manchester standards, though he was never poor either. By the time he retired he had amassed 'a competency' which lasted him the rest of his life. If it was smaller than that of many a contemporary, it was because he adopted a lifestyle that was simple and abstemious. After his death his personal estate was valued under £1,500,[7] hardly a fortune. On the other matter Brotherton was more ambivalent. Although he had indeed worked in the mill from boyhood, he was never in any sense a factory child. He was, after all, the owner's son and became his father's partner soon enough. Yet in his political speeches he gave the impression that he knew from first hand what it was like to be a factory child. In a way that was true, and if in another it was less than the full story, he told it for a decent enough purpose: to add weight to the case for statutory regulation of the hours of child labour. The consistency of his support for factory reform is one of the most remarkable things about him. Interestingly, this never caused any serious rift with his friends. They respected his dissent: it seems to have been well understood that if on this issue Brotherton was his own man, on virtually all others he was solidly with them.

It is clear in retrospect, and indeed was clear at the time, that the provincial manufacturers of the late eighteenth and early nineteenth centuries formed a distinct new addition to the growing ranks of the middle classes. Before their emancipation in the era of Reform, social acceptance did not come easy. In Manchester there was an older élite entrenched in local positions of power and esteem. Absorption came most readily to those who, in addition to the essential prerequisite of making money, were also conventional in religion and politics. Those who were not had a harder time: they were outsiders, and made to feel it. Brotherton's career is in many ways illustrative of the way they fought their way into social and political acceptance, nationally as well as locally. One of the first Manchester Dissenters to do so, in time he became something of a trusted senior figure, with what seemed to younger men an enviably secure power-base.

Important though his manufacturing background is, it goes only some way towards explaining what made Brotherton a Radical Reformer. To reach a closer understanding it is necessary to examine his political ideas, his religious standpoint and the political experiences of his early life. Some indications of the intellectual origins of his political position can be found in the books in his library, lists of which have survived.[8] On his shelves in 1811 were some of the foundation texts of early nineteenth-century radicalism, including Paine's *Rights of Man*. In Brotherton's opposition to monopolies, to war as an instrument of state policy, and to the way taxation and the National Debt were inter-related it is not hard to detect the influence of Thomas Paine. His contempt for political corruption was thoroughly Paineite. Here lay the origins of his support for the widening of the franchise and the reform of parliament. There was not much on politics or economics in Brotherton's library then, except Adam Ferguson's *Tables and Tracts*. He had some works on practical mechanics, perhaps to be expected in a cotton spinner, and one or two volumes of a philosophical nature, including Locke's *Essay Concerning Human Understanding*. Works of poetry and imaginative literature were few, though he did have Pope's *Essay on Man* and Thomson's *Seasons*. What seems significant is the young cotton spinner's interest in diet, health and religion, topics which for Brotherton were intimately related. Above all, what his library reveals is the influence of Immanuel Swedenborg, thirteen of the fifty-eight volumes listed being writings of that author in translation.

He belonged, as did his partners Harvey and Tysoe, to a small body of Dissenters, little known outside Manchester, who defined themselves as Bible Christians. Their founder was the Rev. William Cowherd, who in 1793 had resigned as curate to the Rev. John Clowes of St John's, Manchester, and founded the New Church in Peter Street. He based his beliefs on the teachings of the Swedish scientist and mystic, Immanuel Swedenborg, to which he had first been introduced by Clowes, who for twenty years had found in their emphasis that religion was a matter more of works than faith a practical guide to the leading of a Christian life.

Clowes himself was in no hurry to move from the Old to the New Jerusalem, and stayed within the Church of England. Cowherd was a true schismatic, prepared to go where his ideas and restless spirit took him. Some years later he seceded from the New Church, building the chapel of Christ Church in King Street, Salford. Cowherd was a good preacher, a biblical scholar, a scientist and an educator. For a further nine years his theology stayed within the New Jerusalemite orbit, then, in 1809, he again rent his congregation asunder. Following a conference of ministers and laymen from New Church groups in Lancashire and Yorkshire, it was decided to throw off 'certain restraints and tendencies to hierarchy' they discerned in Swedenborgianism, break away and declare themselves to be members of 'Christ's Universal Church on Earth'. All 'who wished to join them in shunning the common evils and errors of the world' could do so.[9] Brotherton was one of the minority who accepted their pastor's new terms. Those who did not, left, and opened a New Jerusalemite Temple nearby in Bolton Street. In the years following, Bible Christian churches opened in a number of places, Cowherd ordaining the ministers. After he died in 1816, he was succeeded briefly by the Rev. James Scholefield, and Scholefield ordained Brotherton.[10] It was partly to devote himself to this ministry that Brotherton gave up cotton spinning in 1819.

There is little doubt that Brotherton owed much in his political outlook to his religion, though the Bible Christians differed from older Dissenters in having no tradition of persecution by Church or State to sustain them. Nor were they spirit-filled revivalists like the Methodists. What Bible Christianity inculcated seems to have been a simplicity in matters of doctrine, plain-living based on a disciplining of the appetites, and a belief in progress through reform and education. They had great faith in the 'march of intellect', and were prepared to take a stand against violence, the Peace Society being one of their offshoots. For Brotherton, Bible Christianity seems to have been his moral counterweight to political economy.

In matters of faith the self-defined creed of the Bible Christians aimed to be as undogmatic as possible, and stripped Christianity to essentials. Although some observers asserted that they were Unitarians in all but name, belief in the Trinity remained central to their creed. They laid emphasis on public worship, on participating in the sacraments, on family and private prayer, and on the need to meditate frequently on the word of God. They also believed that 'it is good, in order to keep under the body and bring it into subjection to the mind, to abstain from the use of animal food and intoxicating liquor',[11] a notion that to contemporaries seemed eccentric, though there are few creeds which do not impose some dietary restrictions. At any rate, Brotherton found no difficulty endorsing them enthusiastically. He was the author of what is reputedly the first tract on Teetotalism, and his wife, Martha, published the first vegetarian cookery book, which went through several editions.[12] What appealed to the Brothertons about renouncing meat and alcohol was a combination of humane and scriptural arguments against killing animals, a theory that personal character as well as physical and mental health improved that way, and, not least, the radical nature of the discipline of self denial.[13]

The Bible Christians were a small sect, but not defensive or inward-looking. One article of their creed exhorted them 'to do anything in their power to render themselves as useful to mankind as possible'. Like the Swedenborgians, with whom they remained on close terms, they were active educationists. Cowherd ran a Salford Grammar School and Academy of Sciences, and both the New Church and the Bible Christians founded elementary schools acknowledged as superior to the National Schools in Manchester and Salford.[14] It was perhaps the force of their concern for children that was one reason for Brotherton's identification with the movement for factory reform.

The Bible Christians were exceptionally open to the influence of the many new religious and social ideas then being promoted in Manchester and Salford and it is scarcely surprising then that some members of the congregation became very interested in the First Salford Co-operative Society, established in 1829, and which flourished briefly in the next few years. Aiming at social regeneration, this Owenite body promoted an evening school in which Owen's 'Religion of the New Moral World' was expounded. How interested Brotherton and his friends were in these ideas, and what the sticking point between them and the socialists was, is made clear in Robert Owen's account of discussions he had with Brotherton in 1836:[15]

> During the week I had two meetings with Mr Brotherton, the member for Salford, in which I endeavoured to enable him to comprehend some parts of our system. He admits the principles to be true, but, like many others, he is afraid that human nature is not good enough to carry them into execution. It is desirable that this error should be removed from his mind, for he appears to be a good-hearted honest man, disinterested, and a friend to the working classes with whom he is deservedly popular. He has been carefully taught from his infancy that man is bad by nature, and to believe implicitly in the Christian Scriptures; and thus he has been compelled, by his education, to receive a mass of incongruities which will require some time to remove. It is

greatly to be desired that he could be made a full convert, because many of the congregation of which he is now chief pastor, are friendly to our views, and if he was brought over, a large part of his audience would soon openly declare in favour of the Social system.

Brotherton was never a convert, but his dialogue with the Owenites later provide his opponents with arguments that were inflated into accusations that he was a a 'Socialist' and an 'enemy to religion'. Nevertheless, Bible Christians remained interested in social regeneration. A number of Bible Christians in Brotherton's time were more Radical than he was, none more so than the Rev. James Scholefield, minister of Every Street Chapel, Ancoats, a Chartist later elected to the Manchester City Council. For Brotherton, democracy, like Owenite socialism, was a Jordan he looked over, but never crossed. For religious and economic reasons he was, and remained, an individualist; for essentially class reasons he was never a democrat. Brotherton was, and remained, what Cobden described as 'a rational Radical of the middle class'.[16]

Nevertheless, Brotherton was subsequently remembered as one who wore the white hat of Radicalism when it was dangerous to do so in Manchester. He first entered local politics in 1811, a time when High Church Tories were in power. The insight Brotherton gained into the corruption and lack of accountability of the institutions of Old England as a result of his experiences in parish and township government was another influence which made him a Radical Reformer. In the early years of the nineteenth century local government in Salford and Manchester was singularly complicated. Although in the medieval period they had become 'free' or 'seigneurial' boroughs, in the intervening centuries they had never advanced to civic status. Lacking charters and corporations they were governed by a combination of local bodies more suited perhaps to villages than big towns. In Salford, as in Manchester, there were four interlocking but separate jurisdictions: the Vestry, Salford then being part of the ancient parish of Manchester; the Court Leet of the hundred of Salford, essentially a feudal survival; a body of Police (or Improvement) Commissioners, a more modern element set up by Local Act of Parliament; and fourthly the jurisdiction exercised by the Justices of the Peace.[17]

As in other towns without corporations, the basic element was the Vestry, the parish meeting which all ratepayers were eligible to attend. At the Easter and Michaelmas vestry meetings held in the Collegiate church in Manchester Salford's township officers were nominated, and the work and accounts of the past year's officers and their servants scrutinised. This parochial form of government provided a minimum of rough and ready administration. In practice its most important function was the administration of poor-relief and the town charities, and the upkeep of roads not under the jurisdiction of turnpike trusts. It was as township overseer of the poor that Brotherton first took part in local government in 1811.

Complicating the pattern of government in the township was the Salford hundred court leet. Its full title was 'the Court Leet, View of Frankpledge, and the Court of Record of our Sovereign Lord the King for his Hundred or Wapentake of Salford'. The King's Steward, the Earl of Sefton, through his deputy (a barrister) held this court twice a year in Salford. Its jurisdiction was not, however, confined to Salford township. It had two main functions, which complemented those of the vestry. A jury, chosen from the ratepayers of the district, was sworn, whose job it was to appoint a borough-reeve and two constables, a deputy (paid) constable for the township of Salford, and constables and deputy-constables for certain of the other townships within the hundred. Its second function was to enable such 'nuisances' in these townships as smoke and noxious smells from factories, obstructions of the highway, foul ditches, the sale of unwholesome food and use of false weights or measures to be 'presented' and 'amerced' (fined) before the deputy steward. Whilst the Court was nominally one for the whole hundred, in practice its jurisdiction applied to only those townships which had no court leet of their own. It did not, therefore, have anything to do with Manchester, which had its own, but it nominated constables for such townships as Pendleton, Ardwick, Crumpsall, Chorlton Row, Heaton Norris, Crompton, Hulme, and Cheetham. The main business of the court related to the borough of Salford. In addition to a borough-reeve and two constables, it appointed a dog-muzzler, an ale-taster, 'bye-law men' and inspectors of flesh and fish. Although archaic, the hundred court seems to have been the only active police and sanitary authority the township enjoyed in the early nineteenth century, although in practice it was closely interwoven with the vestry.

A third and more modern element in the township government of Salford was the body known locally as the Police Commissioners. The local Act of Parliament which brought it into existence granted the elected Commissioners powers to improve the cleansing, lighting, watching and upkeep of the streets beyond those possessed by the vestry and court leet. The first of these Acts had been obtained in 1765, and in that, and the next one of 1776, Manchester and Salford were treated as one town, only one body of Commissioners being provided for. In 1792, when another Act was obtained, once more only one body of commissioners was provided for. But this Act was an important landmark because what followed ensured that the ancient tendency to separate development in Manchester and Salford was perpetuated into the modern era. At their first meeting the Commissioners appointed under the Act promptly divided and formed two distinct bodies, one of Commissioners resident in Manchester, the other of those resident in Salford. Henceforth, these two bodies confined their activities to their respective townships. This separation was quite extra-legal, and remained so until Manchester obtained a new Act in 1828, the preamble of which acknowledged the *de facto* separation of the two towns. In the same year as he became overseer of the poor, Brotherton became involved with the Salford Police Commissioners as an assessor.

The fourth element in the local government of Salford was a 'county' influence in the persons of local Justices of the Peace. Apart from their principal role in the hearing of cases at the Petty Sessions, their responsibility extended to the maintenance of bridges and culverts, and the upkeep of the New Bailey Prison in Salford. In addition they formed a 'court of appeal' in disputes arising from the levying of the rates, or the administration of poor relief, and one of their functions was to formally ratify the appointment of overseers of the poor nominated by the vestry.

This, then, was the system which Brotherton came to know from 1811. His intimate knowledge of its shortcomings, and the political battles with the local

Tories entrenched in it moulded him as a politician. Brotherton first made a name for himself as a parish reformer, and local government always remained one of his main preoccupations. His first battle was the campaign to expose the mismanagement of the considerable income of the Salford charities. Despite all efforts, it was not until 1841 that the accounts of the Salford charities were ever published in full, and it took the Booth Charities Act of 1846 to regularise the administration of the two principal charities. And that was by no means the end of controversy over this matter.

Another issue in which Brotherton involved himself during these years was the collection and honest disbursement of the poor rates, and getting the accounts opened to scrutiny. In 1819 the Sturges Bourne Act gave legality to the device of a Select Vestry, a committee to oversee the overseers. Salford adopted the Act in 1821, and a Select Vestry, on which Brotherton served, came into being. However, in 1824, finding this control irksome, the overseers turned the tables on the parish reformers. Choosing a time when ratepayers had lapsed into apathy, they neglected to summon the meeting at which the Select should have been chosen, and it therefore lapsed.[18]

The ousting of the Select Vestry was followed by an initiative of some importance in the history of Salford. In 1825 a committee of Tory burgesses acting independently of vestry, court leet and police commissioners resurrected a claim to ancient rights to hold a market in Salford. Despite the fact that the committee failed to find the original charter of 1230, it did secure from the Duchy of Lancaster (Salford being a royal manor) permission to erect a partly-covered market on what was then the edge of the township. When it was finished this included offices and a town hall, and was to remain Salford's Town Hall until 1974.[19]

By the later 1820s it was apparent there was need for the reform and modernisation of the machinery of local government. In towns like Salford it was becoming clear that the powers of the existing authorities were insufficient to tackle the problems of uncontrolled urban growth. However, a national solution was not something which could be sought at that time. For Parliament, local government was a local matter and it was to be some time before this was to change. There was a Parliamentary Select Committee on Select and Other Vestries in 1830 (to which Brotherton gave evidence), but it was to become clear that the way forward lay not *via* the reform of the vestries, but through local Improvement Acts. Salford was forced to seek a new one in 1828 when Manchester obtained its new act which rendered that of 1792, under which Salford's Police Commissioners operated, out of date.

At the Michaelmas vestry in 1829 the draft of a new local Act, proposed by the police commissioners, was discussed and it was decided to apply to Parliament for legislation on it. Early the next year, a deputation consisting of Joseph Brotherton and Robert Pilling travelled to London to see the Bill through the initial stages of the parliamentary process. There was little delay, the Act receiving royal assent on 19 March.[20] Popularly known as the Salford Police Act, it was designed 'for the better Cleansing, Lighting, Watching, Regulating and Improving the town of Salford'. With this Act the modern history of the borough may be said to commence. In the next fourteen years the centre of local political influence shifted away from

'Chaste Grecian Colonnade': Salford Town Hall. (Baines' *History of Lancashire*)

the vestry and court leet to the Police Commissioners. Under them Salford got its first introduction to continuous and moderately effective government.

By the time the new Police Act came into force Brotherton had been a full-time minister of religion and local politician for more than a decade. Brotherton assumed the ministerial duties at King Street in 1819. Although he never seems to have been known formally as the Rev. Joseph Brotherton, he exercised them for the rest of his life. After his election to Parliament he was assisted by the Rev. Joseph Thompson and the Rev. J. B. Strettles. Despite frequent absences Brotherton never remained anything but intimately connected to the chapel and its people.[21] It remained central to his life, his closest friends were there, and he used his political position to promote its causes.

However, Brotherton left cotton spinning as much for political as religious reasons, and it was no accident that he did so in 1819. By then he had become one of the circle of Manchester Reformers which formed around John Edward Taylor.[22] After remaining covert since the heyday of the 'Church and King' mob and the trial of Thomas Walker in 1793–94, Reform began to stir again in Manchester in 1812. A crucial factor, which middle-class reformers such as Taylor and Brotherton were not slow to appreciate, was the shift in popular opinion. Under the effects of the long war against the French, the cause of 'Church and King' lost its appeal to the Manchester artisans. In 1808 there were weavers' riots, and four years later the calling of a 'loyal meeting' in Manchester to welcome Castlereagh and Sidmouth to high office provoked a counter-demonstration which culminated in the burning of the Royal Exchange.[23] The anonymous author of the placard *Now or Never* was held responsible by Tory High Churchmen, who attributed it to Taylor. This led to a famous libel trial from which Taylor emerged triumphant. By then, this merchant son of a Somerset Unitarian Minister had found his true vocation. For some time he had been contributing articles to Cowdroy's *Manchester Gazette*, the only local liberal newspaper. For Taylor (as for Brotherton) the 'Peterloo Massacre' of August 1819 was a decisive event. He and Archibald Prentice, later the historian of the Anti-Corn-Law League, sent eye-witness accounts to the London papers the same evening, which were corroborated by *The Times* correspondent. For Taylor this led to his editorship of a new paper, the *Manchester Guardian*, which commenced in 1821, financed by his friends.[24] The spectacle of what Toryism was capable of propelled Brotherton full-time into politics. He became caught up in the victims' support campaign and in the resistance to the attempts of the government and its local supporters to cover up what had been done.[25] At first, the way forward was not easy. The 'old regime' showed no inclination to disintegrate. The Tory government stayed firmly in control, and in Manchester the old élite resisted Dissenters and Reformers with great bitterness. When it finally came, the victory of Reform came suddenly. The collapse of Old Toryism, which had seemed so durable after Peterloo, was spectacular. It was the result of a tremendous groundswell of popular demand for Reform which built up towards the end of 1830. This received impetus from the revolutions in France and Belgium, the worsening economic situation, and the accession of a new king who, it was felt, could not legitimately obstruct the course of Parliamentary Reform for long. In those heady days Brotherton's Radical friends addressed meetings organised by shopkeepers, artisans and operative democrats, the backbone of the Political Unions which sprang up to press for reform.[26]

When the first Reform Bill was being drafted Brotherton and his friends reacted strongly to the fact that there was no provision to give Salford a seat in Parliament. In January 1831 a town meeting was called to petition for representation. Led by the Unitarian J. B. Smith, then the most vehement middle-class Radical in Manchester or Salford, Brotherton's friends forcibly put the case for enfranchisement.[27] A deputation, which included Smith and Brotherton, was despatched to deliver the petition to Lord Althorp, and the Whig government in due course accepted these arguments, awarding Salford one seat in the Bill, in addition to Manchester's two. This was a momentous step in Salford's history, for in upholding Salford's claim to separate parliamentary representation the Whigs created two boroughs in what (to outsiders) appeared to be one great town. The Whigs had their reasons for enfranchising Salford: they were intent on separating county and borough constituencies, and it was a way of giving 'liberal Manchester' three seats rather than two. The decision was also historically important in that when the boundary commissioners defined the new constituency of Salford, anticipating future population growth, they included in it the adjoining townships of Pendleton and Broughton, together with a detached portion of Pendlebury. What the Whigs did in 1831 was to define the Victorian borough and the 20th century City of Salford.

In 1831, Salford Reformers, confident that the Reform Act was imminent, announced Brotherton's acceptance of their invitation to stand for Parliament.[28] In the event it was a year too early: the second Reform Bill passed the Commons, but the Lords threw it out in early October. The result was the agitation which brought

Brotherton's election
agent. John Benjamin
Smith, MP for Stirling
Boroughs, 1851. (*Illustrated
London News*)

this country closer to revolution than perhaps at any other time in modern history.
All over the country middle-class reformers joined with the radical political unions
to agitate, bishops were publicly insulted, Nottingham Castle was burned, and in
November, the most serious rioting since 1780 took place in Bristol. In Manchester,
meetings of the democratic Manchester and Salford Political Union at which
'Declarations of Rights' were read out created an atmosphere given an insurrectionary
edge by the thousands of starving handloom weavers in the town. In December
there was mob violence, and troops were brought into the New Bailey Prison, with
others in temporary barracks.[29] Yet even at this stage, class divisions remained
paramount. The real pressure was mounted by the political unions, at whose meetings
such middle-class Radicals as the Potter brothers and Alexander Prentice were happy
enough to make speeches. But in February 1832, as the third Reform Bill was being
introduced in Parliament, the leading 'revolutionary' Manchester agitators, Ashmore,
Broadhurst, Curran and Gilchrist, were arrested, tried, and effectively removed from
the scene with stiff sentences for unlawful assembly.[30] Although this did not damp
down popular agitation, it marks the point where the middle-class Reformers were
able to see their way to more decisive action. At the height of the Reform crisis in
May they formed the Manchester Political Association and the Salford Reform
Committee to press for the Bill to pass unmutilated.[31] In late May it did, receiving
the Royal assent on 6 June. On hearing the news, multitudes took to the streets,
the bells of the Collegiate church were tolled incessantly, and the discharge of pistols

and muskets went on throughout the night and the greater part of the next day.32

A year after he had first stepped forward, Brotherton renewed his bid as candidate for election to Parliament. He stood as a local man, formerly in business but now of independent means, with a twenty year record as a local reformer. In economic matters he was for free trade and against monopolies. As a good Radical he stood for a general reduction in taxation, public expenditure, the armed forces, and sinecures. He was for the ending of West Indian slavery, the abolition of tithe, the reform of the legal system, and an introduction of a national system of education. 'I am for the move-along system,' Brotherton declared (in 1838) 'I know of no finality in political or social improvement'.33 He was, he said, in favour of the ballot, shorter Parliaments and the extension of the suffrage. His election committee was made up of radical Dissenters like himself, consisting in the main of Bible Christians, Swedenborgians and Unitarians. Prominent among the latter were Thomas Potter, the Manchester merchant, and J. B. Smith, who was very active in the campaign. Significant support for Brotherton also came from active 'non-electors', who saw in him a 'Friend of the People' who could be trusted not to be duped by either Tories or Whigs. As the long election campaign drew to a close the Salford and Pendleton Political Unions circulated a broadside threatening 'the most rigid system of exclusive dealing' against shopkeepers who 'voted against the people' by voting against Brotherton.34

His opponent, William Garnett, was also a local man. A Manchester merchant for thirty years and President of the Chamber of Commerce, Garnett was extremely wealthy, a strong churchman, and President of the Salford Royal Dispensary, founded a few years before. Garnett's manifesto bore a marked resemblance to Brotherton's. He too (it declared) was a believer in reform, an anti-monopolist, a free-trader, and an enemy of public expenditure and sinecures. He too wanted to settle the issue of tithe, and he too (under certain conditions) was in favour of ending West Indian Slavery. His committee was headed by Robert Gardner, a rich manufacturer, and included men prominent in Manchester business circles. But what united them was not so much loyalty to the political system now overthrown, as devotion to the Church of England, seen as about to come under threat from Dissenters, Radicals and the Catholic Irish. They were in the main drawn from the Evangelical party, and the militance of their temper (not to mention the money in their pockets) was to be influential in shaping the sort of Conservatism to emerge in Victorian Salford.35

The prolonged election campaign of 1832 grew increasingly rancorous as the polling days (21 and 22 December), drew near. The Reformers' attack on Garnett concentrated on the recent nature of his conversion to Reform and Free Trade, and his previous inactivity in these causes. For their part, Garnett's supporters stigmatised Brotherton as socially unfit for Parliament, a charge which Brotherton countered by saying that if not as rich as Garnett, he was just as independent. The Tories also sank to considerable depths of scurrility in attacking him for his religious unorthodoxy and alleged political extremism. On the eve of the election a handbill appeared advertising a mock sale sale of the 'Pythagorean Chapel' of the Bible Christians which was so libellous (in suggesting he had swindled Mrs

Cowherd) that Brotherton threatened legal action if it was not withdrawn.[36] Brotherton was accused of being an Owenite, a republican, an admirer of Cobbett and an advocate of universal suffrage and annual Parliaments.[37] In point of fact he was none of these things.

As expected, the first ever election in Salford proved a robust affair and set the scene for a decade of violence at the hustings. Fearing the police would be biased towards Garnett, on the first day of the voting (20 December) a great crowd of 'non-electors', preceded by the band of the Political Union, swept into the township waving the white flags of Radical Reform and the green and gold of Brotherton's colours. They paraded the town, intimidating the opposition, smashing the windows of public houses displaying the red of the Garnett supporters. At 3pm, in the interest of civil order, polling was suspended. Next day it was agreed bands and flags would not be allowed when it resumed, an agreement Brotherton's supporters ignored. However, there was no violence and eventually Garnett conceded: Brotherton was returned with the comfortable majority of 194.[38] It was the first of a remarkable run of election successes.

Middle-class Reformers were euphoric. Old Toryism had been pulled down. With considerable adroitness, and a generous measure of luck, bourgeois reformers had used the popular Political Unions to batter on the doors of the constitution, but when it came to admission only they and the 'shopocracy' found they had the right credentials. The dividing line between those who were enfranchised and those who were not – the possession of a £10. household qualification – was drawn with near-mathematical precision to exclude the working class and all but a few artisans, news of which the friends of Brotherton received with equanimity. They had the vote; their class had completed its move into the political nation; the Salfords of England were now represented in Parliament.

At Westminster, once election euphoria had worn off, Brotherton cannot have felt anything but strong sense of isolation. In a House of Commons dominated by the landed, legal and military élites, an ex-cotton spinner with an unorthodox religion was distinctly an odd man out. There was only a small group of Radicals for Brotherton to align with, and they were soon at odds with the Whig Government. Brotherton, however, earned the respect of the House, though he never cut more than a minor figure. He did not intervene in debate very often, and never took more than fifteen or twenty minutes of the House's time. But when he spoke he did so with admirable good sense. Brotherton was liked and became something of a favourite with both sides of the House. Contemporaries referred to his genial manner, 'unaffected courtesy' and good humour. His personal appearance too was an asset: inclined to be stout, his ruddy countenance and jet black hair reminded people of nothing so much as a respectable country squire who had given up field sports.[39] What Brotherton became best known for was his nightly motion that the house should adjourn its business at half past midnight. 'Mr Brotherton's "early closing" motion never failed to amuse the Commons'.[40] In its sturdy provincial refusal to be afraid of appearing absurd, it was somehow typical of the man.

Brotherton represented Salford in Parliament for an unbroken twenty four years. Although the Tories did not contest the elections of 1847 and 1852, his supremacy

Brotherton's Tory rival:
William Garnett. (Salford
Art Gallery and Museum)

was hard won. The 1830s saw some very bitter contests, and in 1837 he got home by the narrowest of margins. In this period the reaction of local Tories to the fact that the power they had so long enjoyed was slipping away was one of impotent fury. Acutely conscious of wealth and status, they found it almost unbearable that a man of no great means or social standing, and a Dissenter into the bargain, had defeated them. Symptomatic of their fury and frustration were their attempts to humiliate Brotherton and besmirch his good name, attempts they made again and again in the next few years. Confined to a relatively few voters, politics in Salford were extraordinarily personal and vindictive: Brotherton survived by cultivating a thick skin.

Brotherton had little difficulty winning the election of 1835. Garnett trying his luck at Carlisle, he was opposed by an old-style Tory in the person of John Dugdale, a calico printer. As previously, polling took place in an atmosphere of near riot. On the first day the Tories paraded what they saw as a symbol of Old England – a scarred and bemused old bull, the survivor of many a day's baiting at village wakes round Manchester. On the second, real violence erupted when they attempted to roast a sheep in mockery of Brotherton's vegetarianism. For this they were treated to a thorough drubbing by a body of Manchester Irishmen, who marched into Salford with their green flags and band. When the votes were finally counted Brotherton was returned with a majority of 225, his most comfortable victory ever.[41] There followed the customary insults. But soon threatening portents appeared to indicate that in future the party of Reform would face sterner opposition. 'We have a Reform Association in Salford and the Tories have formed one for watching the Registration – so we shall have a struggle next time', Smith warned Brotherton.[42] In fact, the Tories founded two, a middle-class Constitutional Society and an Operative Conservative Association. These organisations announced that their aim was to prevent England falling into the 'hands of Popish intolerance on the one hand, or a democratic ascendancy on the other'.[43]

In 'Popish intolerance' (the modern version of 'No Popery') Tories discerned a way forward from defeat. The opportunity presented itself with the rise of the Irish national movement. After his success in forcing the Tories to grant Catholic emancipation in 1829, Daniel O'Connell began to press for an end to the Established Church in Ireland, Whig dependence on Irish votes at Westminster giving him leverage. All over England, even in parts where Ireland seemed remote and Catholics thin on the ground, 'Popish intolerance' and the bogey of O'Connell were used by Conservatives to arouse their supporters. In Lancashire factory towns, where Irish immigrants had been used to force down wages, or so it was alleged, anti-Catholic and anti-Irish sentiments were easily inflamed, and were to enjoy a long existence. 'Popish intolerance' also had the effect of bringing the Church of England more directly into politics. Churchmen feared that if the Irish Church could be disestablished, their opponents might apply the same treatment to the Church in England. And indeed extreme Dissenters – 'Liberationists' – were already dreaming of such. It so happened that the most vigorous Church element on both these fronts was the Evangelical Party, and in the person of the Rev. Hugh Stowell, a Salford clergyman, it had its most formidable local leader. Although the immediate danger receded in 1835 (the Irish Church Bill being thrown out by the House of Lords), it became Stowell's mission to ensure that anti-Catholicism did not fade away. Banging his anti-Popery drum, Stowell was to play a significant part in Salford's history.[44]

In the next two years the political balance began to tip away from the Whigs and Radicals and at the election of 1837 Brotherton came the closest he ever did to defeat. He lost support not only because of Protestantism and his opponents' improved organisation, but because of the severe disillusionment with the Whigs felt by many Radical voters and non-electors since the Reform Act. They were disillusioned over inaction on factory reform and the starving hand-loom weavers, the suppression of trade unionism and in particular by the harsh punishment meted out to the Tolpuddle Martyrs. The issue most threatening to Brotherton, however, was the passing of the Poor Law Amendment Act of 1834. In 1837 the Poor Law Board in London began to introduce the workhouse system into Lancashire. In January an Assistant Poor Law Commissioner, Alfred Power, met with Salford's parish officers to discuss the formation of a Poor Law Union for the district, which he soon decided would be co-extensive with the Parliamentary borough.[45] Power's proposals pleased hardly anybody. Imposed by central government and designed for the rural south, the workhouse system seemed inappropriate to the needs of industrial districts. Locally, Broughton and Pendleton objected to being linked to Salford, and Salford township ratepayers disliked what Power proposed. His arrival was followed by angry meetings, and a Tory Radical alliance emerged to plan a campaign of resistance and non-co-operation. As the election campaign began in June it did so against a background of hardening resistance to the New Poor Law.

Brothertonians were in the difficult position of having to react to a piece of legislation which some of them disliked, passed by a government which, in general, they supported. They hotly denied the accusation that they had instructed Brotherton to vote for the Bill, and in fact Brotherton had voted against the third reading in 1834.[46] Once the bill had become law, faced with demands for local non-co-operation with the authorities in Somerset House, they were put on the spot. This was the situation when polling began in July 1837. There ensued the closest and most exciting electoral contest in Salford's political history. Brotherton's opponent once again was William Garnett, the main plank of whose platform was the injustice of the New Poor Law.[47] Determined not to lose control of the street a third time, the Tories distributed drink in large quantities. A combination of 'Garnett's Elixir', anti-Popery and hatred of the workhouse almost brought Brotherton down. Had the election come a year later, he would certainly have lost, and might never have got back into Parliament.

Election day revealed just how far Brotherton had lost support. A torrent of 'Popish Intolerance' handbills brought an invasion of Ancoats Irishmen on his behalf, as in 1835. They assembled in front of the Market Hall, and laid about them with their sticks. Later, another fight in Oldfield Road resulted in three premises being burned down. Fighting resumed that evening, and ended with an Irish retreat after a terrible beating at the hands of an army of bricklayers and colliers, united under the orange flag of Protestantism.[48] Any satisfaction Garnett's supporters derived from their street victory dissipated into fury when the election result became known. Brotherton had won by two votes (890 to 888), and the fact that he had voted for himself when it became clear that a close result was likely, led to the jibe of 'self-elected Member for Salford'.[49] The Tories petitioned to overturn the result. When the petition went before the Commons Committee the case hinged on the allegation that the Borough-reeve of Salford had acted incorrectly as returning officer. The committee decided he had not, and Brotherton was confirmed as the Member for Salford.[50] He had survived the greatest political crisis of his life.

After the 1837 election the bitter political struggle in Salford over the implementation of the Poor Law Amendment Act moved to its climax. Scheduled to come into operation in March 1838, it was in fact delayed until later that year. Organising the opposition was the South Lancashire Anti-Poor Law Association, whose secretary was R. J. Richardson, a Salford carpenter. At Easter 1838 the Tory Radicals at last succeeded in ousting the Brothertonians from the Select Vestry, and elected one of their own.[51] The Select Vestry pursued a policy of non-co-operation and obstruction towards those creating the new Poor Law Union. However, the Select soon found itself in a technical and legal morass. Tory Radicals were in a battle that they could not win. As one of them put it, 'the government were not going to be intimidated by the Salford Select Vestry'.[52] In June 1838 Power took steps to by-pass them. Deciding the time had come to implement the new system, he announced that the first Board of Guardians for the Salford Union would be elected in July. The 'out-townships' agreed that the election would be uncontested in their districts. In Salford no less than five lists of candidates were published – two Reform, two Tory and one Tory Radical. After Power remonstrated, the Whig/Radicals proposed a list of five Reformers and five Tories to avoid a contest. Characteristically, the Tories overplayed their hand by demanding a ratio of seven to three, and a say in the choice of the three Reformers. The Reformers refused and withdrew.[53] So the first Salford Guardians were all Conservatives, friends of William Garnett. After so many setbacks they were satisfied to have excluded the Brothertonians from an important new local body, and ditched their working-class radical allies.

In late 1838, as the economic situation worsened, two great Radical movements developed for which Manchester was to become a notable centre over the next decade; Chartism and the Anti-Corn Law League. Essentially rival campaigns, their followers divided along the lines of class. Offering different explanations of the current economic and political crisis, they proposed different ways forward. The Chartists insisted that action to improve economic conditions must be preceded by the creation of a democratic political system; the workers, 'cheated by the Whigs since 1832', were prepared to wait no longer. The middle-class Anti-Corn Law League argued that a change in national economic policy in the direction of Free Trade was more important than immediate changes in the political system.

When the Free Traders began to organise in late 1838, Brotherton's friends were in it from the outset. The first provisional Committee of the Manchester Anti-Corn Law Association included the names of Thomas Potter (Manchester's first Mayor), William Harvey (Brotherton's brother-in-law and ex-partner), Charles Tysoe (Harvey's partner), Elkanah Armitage and William Lockett (later Salford's first Mayor).[54] Several were long standing Repealers, none more so than Brotherton's election agent, J. B. Smith, whose single-mindedness earned him the names 'Corn Law Smith' and 'Mad Smith'.[55] He was the League's first treasurer and one of the triumvirate who gave it leadership, the others being George Wilson, the chairman, and Richard Cobden.

A liberal trade policy had long been one of the cornerstones of Brotherton's economic beliefs. He advocated the Repeal of the Corn Laws long before the climate began to change in its favour. It had appeared in his first election manifesto, and thereafter he never neglected a chance to promote the idea. For him, as for many a provincial businessman, the eight-year campaign which began in 1838 became the central heroic experience of his life. It not only resulted in the famous political victory whereby national economic policy went over to Free Trade but it also marked another stage in the acceptance of the new provincial manufacturing class into national life.

As one of only a handful of Free Traders in the House of Commons in these years, Brotherton did his duty on every occasion when the question was debated. By the Spring of 1841 the Whig government was on its last legs, and it was obvious a General Election was coming. Declaring that it was struggling principally for justice and humanity, the League concentrated on the benefits the 'Big Loaf' would bring the poor, once Repeal was carried. It also persuaded the reluctant Whigs to make trade policy an election issue, though Russell and the other leaders were at that stage more in favour of replacing the sliding-scale with a moderate fixed duty rather than total Repeal. For Brotherton the 1841 election was to be his fourth and last contested election, and his Tory opponent once more was William Garnett. The campaign took place against a background of appalling unemployment and distress: it was feared Manchester was on the verge of rioting. Whilst the electors were invited to listen to arguments for and against the sliding scale, the Chartists were urging the non-electors to mount pressure for the carrying of the Charter. Brotherton was an all-out Repealer, whilst Garnett argued for modification of the sliding scale. Garnett also campaigned for education to be based on religious principles, and opposition to the centralised Poor Law. This time the local electors were more on Brotherton's side than Garnett's.

The Salford election campaign of 1841 was, as usual, highly charged and scurrilous. Brotherton was assailed, not only by the Conservatives, but by Chartists, Tory Radicals and anti-Popery fanatics, and the old attacks on his character and good name were given one last airing. The attack failed: the electors came out for Brotherton on the Corn Laws, the principal issue in the election. His argument that protection led to 'dear bread for the people in hard times' proved telling. When the votes were counted he had a comfortable majority of 117. At an election in which League candidates generally did badly, and the country returned a Conservative ministry, Brotherton's victory was memorable. After this defeat, Garnett indicated that he had had enough, and retired to Quernmoor, an estate near Lancaster. With his going, Toryism in Salford collapsed. After being seriously pressed for six years Brotherton now found himself in sole possession of the field.

Brotherton remained as active in the cause of free trade after 1841 as he had been before. In Parliament he spoke to the issue whenever it came up.[56] However, from that time, the advocacy of the cause in Parliament passed more and more into the hands of Cobden and (from 1843) of Bright. Brotherton stepped into the background. Characteristically, he bore no resentment that the lead had passed to younger and more brilliant men. When Parliament was not sitting Brotherton busied himself speaking at meetings of the Salford Operative Anti-Corn Law Association, and others arranged by the League.

In the following years Brotherton was invariably present at the events the League organised as the campaign rose to its peak. He spoke at the great meeting in Manchester on the 14 November 1843 which raised £120,000 in an hour and a half.[57] By now big money was coming over to the League, and the Whig grandees announcing their conversion to free trade. In 1845 the Irish potato crop failed and the League increased its pressure on Peel, already moving towards Free Trade. All over the country there were demands to 'Open the Ports'. In the political crisis which ensued, Peel could not carry the Commons and resigned. Russell failed to form a Whig ministry, and Peel came back. The League decided on one last great push. On 13 December it started a fund of £250,000 – double its previous target. At a great meeting in Manchester on 23 December 60,000 people subscribed, which created an immense stir nationally. Brotherton was one of the speakers. He also took part in the great debate in Parliament the following February on Peel's proposals for repeal in the Queen's Speech.[58] Though totally outshone by Cobden and Bright, the League's historian recorded 'Mr Brotherton made a sensible speech which told well in the House'. In May, Peel's proposals passed the House of Commons: the Corn Laws were to go in three years.

Repeal was full of ironies. It was passed by a Conservative prime minister who had resisted his own supporters' demands for Protectionism as well as the League's demands for its abolition. In the last analysis Peel was swayed less by the League than by the Irish Famine. Repeal split his party and ruined his career. When he died, not long after, following an accident, the League turned him into a liberal hero. There are Peel statues all over the North of England: the first was in Salford's new municipal park. Inevitably, the honour of unveiling it fell to Joseph Brotherton MP.[59]

Brotherton's career was crowned by the almost simultaneous triumph of another cause he had served long and faithfully: the passing of the Ten Hours Act in 1847. It is Brotherton's unusual achievement not only to have served the cause of the factory masters loyally but the cause of the factory workers as well. His connection with the movement went back to 1816. The first piece of factory legislation was Sir Robert Peel's Act of 1802, which applied solely to pauper apprentices. The next phase started up in 1814 with the aim of relieving the long hours worked by non-pauper children. The first reform group was started in Manchester by Nathaniel Gould. Brotherton became associated with it soon after and stayed with the cause for the next three decades. He was the first factory master to join, and was unusual in that those who did were usually Tories. His commitment to this cause never wavered and he won the reputation as a 'friend of the people' which, even at the height of the fierce political controversy over the New Poor Law, he never really lost.

In a matter which could always be rendered complicated by technicalities, his views were straightforward. He believed the factory women and children worked

The great Free Trade banquet, Free Trade Hall, 1843. 3,400 were said to be present.
(*Illustrated London News*)

hours that were far too long for their general good, and campaigned for a working day fixed by statute. Although generally an advocate of political economy, he always held that in this matter Parliament had a positive duty to intervene.[60] As long as employers found ways to evade their legal responsibilities, Brotherton remained convinced that the campaign for factory reform should be maintained and the law amended. He realised early that what the factory masters resented and feared most was precisely what was needed – effective inspection. It was always going to be a long struggle. In the early years Brotherton made himself into the well-informed expert to whom Parliament would listen. It was in this role he appeared before a committee of the House of Lords in 1819 in support of Sir Robert Peel's bill, which sought to forbid the employment of children under nine, and to limit the hours of those between the ages of nine and sixteen. The campaign was successful, and the Bill became law that year.[61] However, it did not work as intended, and in 1825 Brotherton was campaigning strongly for Hobhouse's Bill to reduce the working week to sixty six hours. For his efforts in helping to get the 1825 bill through he received many tributes. One from the cotton spinners of Chorlton Row recorded that he had 'attended the masters' meeting and almost singly combated a host of foes to the measure ... He was an enemy of every kind of tyranny and oppression'.[62]

Within a very short time evasions of the law again led to the movement's revival. In late 1828 Brotherton began to work with the Manchester-based 'Society for the Protection of Children employed in Cotton Factories', organised by John Doherty and Thomas Foster of the Grand General Union of Spinners. In December 1832 Brotherton became even more useful to the factory reformers. Henceforward he could advocate their cause where it mattered most, inside the very seat of British political power and influence. When Fielden and Lord Ashley introduced their Ten Hours Bill in March 1833, Brotherton gave his active support. In the next fourteen years he continued to do so, though he largely confined his efforts to Parliament.

In March 1836 the clause in the 1833 Act came into operation by which mill owners were prohibited from employing children under 13 for more than 9 hours a day, or 48 a week. The manufacturers did not like this at all. Many tried all they could to get round it.[63] A Ten Hours Bill office was opened in Manchester with a permanent secretary and a committee. By the end of 1836 the factory masters by and large were obeying the Act because there was a way round it: working the under–13s in eight hour relays to keep the rest of the workforce on long hours.[64] Ashley duly presented a Ten Hours Bill early in 1837; its failure led to another lull, factory reform being pushed aside by the Anti-Poor Law movement, the start of Chartism and the launch of the Anti-Corn Law agitation. In the late summer of 1841, however, the campaign began to move again. When Lord Ashley came to Manchester to meet the local committee and to inspect some factories Brotherton accompanied him.[65] This campaign led to the 1844 Act, which reduced the working day for children to six and a half hours, brought in compulsory half-time school attendance, and had regulations against dangerous machinery. However, it was made a twelve hour Act, with a nine hour day on Saturdays, and, as a sop to the manufacturers, actually lowered the minimum age for child workers to eight.

After this, the prolonged campaign for the Ten Hours Bill moved into its final phase. In October 1845 the Manchester Short Time Committee arranged for a great meeting at which there was a deputation from every mill to welcome Lord Ashley. Brotherton was again by his side. Local Anglican clergy now came out in support, and a few manufacturers unilaterally reduced hours.[66] As the operatives had predicted, output and profits did not fall, a blow to the employers' argument that it was in the last two hours work of the day that their profits were made.

In May 1846 the Ten Hours Bill was narrowly defeated. It had been bitterly opposed by Cobden, Bright and the League at *their* moment of triumph. But so narrow was the majority that it was clear Parliament would pass it the following year. The Conservatives, defeated over protection, saw to its triumph. In the Spring the Bill finally went through. In Driver's words, 'it is particularly gratifying that it should have been two manufacturers – Fielden and Brotherton – who finally piloted the bill through the House . . . their motives were surely beyond the suspicion of political colouring'. There was much praise for Brotherton; the *Scotsman* called him 'a staunch and incorruptible friend of the people', and in May 1848 he was presented with a commemorative medal by the delegates of the Factory Workers of Lancashire and Yorkshire for his part in the passing of the Act.[67]

Brotherton was always an assiduous member of the House of Commons, and eventually found a niche as chairman of the Private Bill Committee, a useful if unglamorous position, the main requirement for which was regular attendance. In this role Brotherton provided a service fellow MPs appreciated. Apart from Free Trade and Factory Reform, the most notable parliamentary causes he associated himself with in the 1840s were the movements for the opening of museums and libraries. Brotherton became involved in drafting a bill which finally appeared as the Museums Act in 1845, working closely with a fellow Radical, William Ewart.[68] This led Brotherton to the idea of a permissive bill for public libraries. There is evidence that Brotherton had been planning a Free Libraries scheme for some time. He always had been a 'March of Intellect' man, welcoming the forming of educational institutions for the people. He had other motives as well. Speaking in support of libraries and reading rooms he told the annual meeting of the Salford Literary and Mechanics' Institution in 1845 he did so because 'ignorance and crime were closely allied, and as a means of removing that ignorance and raising the standards of morality of the people'. Brotherton worked closely with Ewart and Edward Edwards on the Libraries Bill, and they proved an effective team.

Brotherton was very keen for Salford to set an example by opening a free library, and found an ally in E. R. Langworthy, the Mayor. A public meeting in July 1849 set up a 'Salford Borough Museum and Library Association', and Langworthy gave an initial donation of £250, followed by £100 each from Brotherton and seven others. Many lesser sums were also contributed. A committee was formed to raise funds, buy books and receive gifts and specimens from donors. Under the 1845 Act the Corporation's part was limited to purchasing and equipping a building, and appointing and paying the staff. The Corporation already possessed a suitable building, Lark Hill, William Garnett's old home, which it had acquired with the land for Peel Park five years earlier. In November 1850, shortly after Brotherton and Ewart had successfully steered the Free Libraries Act through Parliament,

The richest man in Victorian Salford. Philip Westcott's 'very spirited and gentlemanly portrait' of E. R. Langworthy, 1852. (Salford Art Gallery and Museum)

the Salford Borough Royal Museum and Library was formally opened. Salford's Museum and Free Library was one of the first in the land, situated in one of the earliest municipal parks. In the mid-Victorian era both were used and visited by vast numbers of people, especially at holiday times.[69]

In these years Brotherton advocated a range of causes outside Parliament some of which, if they reflected his particular brand of Radicalism, were destined to play a prominent part in Victorian political and social discourse. Brotherton was always a social regenerator, and this shows in his lifelong advocacy of Temperance and Teetotalism. As already noted, he was the author of the first published tract on abstinence from intoxicating liquor, published in 1821, which records Brotherton's horror at the scale and extent of contemporary drunkenness. 'The drinking of intoxicating liquors,' he wrote, 'is at the root of almost every evil in Society.' The Temperance movement started in America and from there was introduced into Ireland, Scotland and then England. The Salford Temperance Society was an early one, founded on 7 January 1830, Brotherton being one of a committee which included the Rev. J. A. Coombs, an Independent Minister, William Higgins, a Conservative factory master, and the Rev. Hugh Stowell, who, on most other matters opposed Brotherton.[70] Brotherton's life encompassed the first phase in the history of the movement. The Manchester and Salford Temperance Association was founded in 1835, and by 1851 was claiming that some 60 Societies existed in the Manchester district.[71] By 1853 Temperance was poised to enter politics. The United Kingdom Alliance for the total Suppression of the Liquor Trade, a pressure group which aimed at legislation to allow a local licencing option, was formed, which was to have a long existence. In its early years it was Manchester-led, and some of Brotherton's closest friends were involved. In 1854 the committee started a fund to promote the idea of the 'Maine Liquor Law' in Britain.[72] Old Anti-Corn Law campaigners tended to believe money and organisation could achieve anything. Not surprisingly, the drink trade organised in its own defence, and the Mid-Victorian battle between the pint pot and the tea pot commenced.

Brotherton was a leading spirit in two other organisations which reflected his particular blend of idealism – the Vegetarian Society and the Peace Society. The former, which started in 1847, articulated the vegetarian case through its journal, the *Vegetarian Messenger*. Its first president was James Simpson, a Bible Christian, who was succeeded by William Harvey.[73] By 1852 the Society claimed a membership of 800, and that year it held its annual meeting in Salford Town Hall in a room decorated with portraits of famous vegetarians – Plato, Plutarch, Pythagoras, Swedenborg and Benjamin Franklin.[74] In its early years Brotherton was also President of the Manchester and Salford Peace Society. His wife was also active on both these bodies, and accompanied Brotherton, Simpson, and Harvey to the 'Peace Congress' in Paris in 1849.[75]

Until the very last phase of his political life, Brotherton was a member of the 'Manchester School' and served in the campaigns it lost as well as those it won. An example of the former was the twenty year agitation for improving elementary education, which began in 1837. He was closely identified with Cobden, the Brights and the Potters, Mark Philips and Absalom Watkin in the Manchester Society for Promoting National Education and its successor bodies, the Lancashire Public Schools Association, the National Public Schools Association, and the Manchester and Salford Committee on Education.[76] The issue here was to find a formula that would improve the elementary schools, make them non-sectarian, and fund them out of the rates. Their efforts foundered on the opposition of the Church of England to non-denominational education, led by Stowell and the Evangelical party.

In the two decades following the Reform Act there important developments in Salford's local institutions too. Brotherton's historic election victory in 1832 was followed by efforts on the part of his friends to tilt the balance of power in local government their way. In this they were largely successful. In 1838 the Radicals ousted the Tory overseers of the poor and a Select Vestry, a body much favoured by parish reformers, was re-established, the first since 1826. It was almost wholly Whig Radical, Brotherton having a seat on it himself.[77] Soon after, they turned their attention to the Court Leet, where the principal township officers were nominated. Hitherto, invariably these had been Tories, but in 1835 a group of Brotherton's allies persuaded the Earl of Sefton, a supporter of the Reform Bill, to instruct his deputy steward to cease packing the jury with his political opponents.[78] From then on the township officers were usually Reformers. At this time, too, Brotherton's friends began to take the lead on the committees of the Police Commissioners.

In the early 1840s, with Brotherton's active support at Westminster, the Radical Reformers commenced a campaign to obtain a municipal charter and a new local Act for Salford. The town's local government had undoubtedly improved under the 1830 Police Act. The gas works had been purchased by the commissioners and Salford had started supplying Pendleton as well as its own consumers, using some of the profits to finance township improvements. The new Town Hall in Bexley Square had been acquired, and a new cattle market opened. After the 1832 cholera visitation the Scavenging and Improvement Committees had made efforts to improve street cleaning and carried through some street improvement, and the two oldest bridges into Manchester had been rebuilt. Salford streets were better lit than ever before, and some steps had been taken towards creating one force from the hitherto separate day police and night watch.[79] Yet, much remained to be done: as the population multiplied the problems of town government were increasing apace. From 1835 a small but cohesive body of Brotherton's friends on the Police Commission emerged as the leading force in Salford's local affairs. They were led by William Lockett, Brotherton's election committee chairman in 1837 and 1841. A retired silk mercer, Lockett now devoted his active life to politics and emerged as something of a local party boss. Energetic and able, he possessed in full measure that self-righteous domineering style which was to make Anti-Corn Law Leaguers so cordially hated by opponents.

Progress in urban government hinged very much on Westminster. If reform was to come, it needed a lead from government, but few politicians at that time had much interest in urban problems. Yet despite being largely a political move to get rid of old Tory corporations, the Municipal Corporations Act of 1835 *did* offer a way forward for local government reformers. It contained provision for

Salford's first Mayor: Philip Westcott's portrait of William Lockett, 1855. (Salford Art Gallery and Museum)

towns without borough councils to petition the Privy Council for charters and so begin to reform their local government. In early 1843, with Brotherton's strong support, a plan for a municipal charter was put forward. It proposed a Greater Salford taking in Pendleton, Broughton and the detached part of Pendlebury, making the borough co-extensive with the parliamentary constituency and the Poor Law Union. The plan had demographic logic as well as administrative tidiness on its side, for it recognised the likely pattern of future growth in this industrial district. This did not prevent bitter hostility developing. Opposition came principally from a group of Pendleton ratepayers, and opponents of the Radicals in Salford. Pendleton opponents expressed fears that in a greater Salford their township interests would be over-ridden, Pendleton's councillors would be outnumbered and outvoted, their rates would increase, and the cost of the turnpike roads would fall on the ratepayers. Lockett, who was extremely active on this issue, countered most of these arguments, but he could produce no compelling reasons why Pendleton would be better off incorporated with Salford. Within Salford, opposition came, as expected, from Conservatives, Tory Radicals and Chartists representing the smaller ratepayers.

The matter came to a climax in the spring of 1844. A government Commissioner arrived in the district to ascertain the wishes of the ratepayers, to decide whether or not to include the out-townships, and to divide the borough into wards. It soon became clear that Pendleton would be excluded and, because of that, so would Broughton, despite the fact that a majority of the ratepayers *there* had signified their assent. Salford's charter of incorporation was granted on 16 April 1844. Henceforth, the inhabitants, through the Mayor, Aldermen, and Councillors, were to be recognised as one body corporate. The new municipal borough was to consist of Salford township together with a tiny portion of Broughton which lay south of the river, and was to be divided into four wards. The first municipal election was fixed for 12 July, with Lockett named as returning officer.[80]

Despite the exclusion of Pendleton and Broughton, the charter was an achievement for the middle-class Radicals. They had acquired it without any expense, and the transfer of power and authority from the Commissioners to the new municipal council was not to be accompanied by the confusion Manchester experienced. However, Salford's first local government election was an embittered and highly-charged affair because not only was it the culmination of the party struggle over incorporation, but because of another issue which was, if anything, a greater source of local discord. In January 1844 Lockett introduced the draft of a new Street Bill at a special meeting of the Commissioners. Its principal objectives were to rectify the shortcomings of the 1830 Act. This Bill was concerned with street widening rather than public health; life and death in the back streets would be largely unaffected. Nonetheless, it was important. The local authorities were to be given the right to purchase hundreds of small properties and to increase the mortgage debts of the borough. New powers were also to be granted on a wide range of matters including street offences, nuisances and licensing. Two, in particular, were of some importance in the development of local administration. The Bill provided for the transfer of all the powers of the Commissioners to the Corporation, and for a new system for the selection of borough-reeve and constables. In fact, from

1844, when Salford got its first Mayor, the position of the borough-reeve and constables ceased to have any significance, though they continued to be nominated for some years. It was, however, important to have effected the transition from borough-reeve and Commissioners to Mayor and Council smoothly, so that rival jurisdictions did not survive to confuse local government, as happened elsewhere.

The appearance of the improvement proposals provoked far more hostility than those for incorporation. The fear that it would lead to increases in the rates thoroughly alarmed the small ratepayers. The arguments of Lockett and the Improvers that township assets and the gas profits were enough to underwrite and service the debts were met with disbelief, and in the spring and early summer of 1844 a fine Salfordian row developed. The bitter rivalry was carried into the committee rooms of Parliament itself, where William Wanklyn, the Tory borough-reeve and the constables, together with their legal advisers, tried to have the Bill rejected. They failed. The Radicals produced enough evidence in favour of the Bill to convince Parliament and it became law on 6 June. Each step had been closely followed by Brotherton, who was strongly in favour of both incorporation and the new Improvement Bill.[81]

Preceded by a furious pamphlet war, Salford's first municipal election took place the following month. After a heavy poll the result was a great victory for the Brothertonians: seventeen of the twenty-four councillors elected were Reformers, six were Tory, one was a Tory Radical. After the election they shared out the spoils. Lockett became Salford's first Mayor, serving a second term the following year. Harvey was made an aldermen, together with Charles Tysoe, and Edward Ryley Langworthy. The latter, who had hitherto stood rather aloof from the political in-fighting was a significant addition. A millionaire Unitarian cotton merchant and manufacturer, head of Langworthy Bros. of Greengate, he was Mayor in 1849–50, and MP for a few months after Brotherton's death. Langworthy was generous to causes he approved of. His bequest £20,000 to Manchester Grammar School was so munificent that he is remembered as its 'second founder'. He also left £10,000 to Owen's College. The Salford institution which benefitted most was the Museum and Free Library: over the years he gave it nearly £20,000. Other notables were attracted on to the Council at that time, the most outstanding of whom, perhaps, was Thomas Agnew. Born in Liverpool, the son of a Scotsman, he be came the partner of an Italian dealer in clocks, barometers and opticians' wares in Manchester, but eventually concentrated on print-publishing and picture-selling. Ideally placed to supply the emergent new provincial middle class, he founded one of the great art firms of modern England. His son, Sir William Agnew, became one of the most sought-after art experts in the Victorian era. Thomas was a Swedenborgian and a Radical, and his son inherited both his father's religion and his politics. As a Salford Police Commissioner Thomas had been a close ally of Lockett, whose daughter he married, and played a leading part in the early years of the Salford council. He was soon an alderman, became chairman of the Nuisance Committee, and was Salford's Mayor at the time of the royal visit in 1851.

The nine years between the establishing of the municipal borough and its extension in 1853 form a distinct era in Salford's history. Never again was the council to be quite so dominated by the liberal business élite of the district as it was then. They made it the finest club in Salford, a cachet it never lost in Victoria's reign, and took the step of employing well-paid borough officials. If their first qualification had to be that they were Reformers, the precaution was also taken of appointing men of some ability. Charles Gibson, formerly law clerk to the commissioners was made town clerk at a good salary, and the able David Chadwick became borough treasurer, at the age of 23. A Swedenborgian in religion he served the borough until 1860, when he left to become superintendent of the Globe Insurance Co. and later a partner in a firm of accountants. For a time he had a seat on the Salford Council, which he gave up in 1868 when elected Member of Parliament for his native Macclesfield.[82]

There were other developments too. For the first time Salford appointed a chief constable: the history of the borough police really begins in 1844. As the scope of the council widened, its committees grew from the seven inherited from the commissioners, to twelve by 1853. In this period the framework of authority seemingly worked well, though the transition from old to new was not without its difficulties. In establishing the new borough council as go-ahead and progressive, perhaps the most notable development was the opening of Peel Park and the Free Library and Museum, objects with which, as we have seen, Brotherton was closely identified. In these years there were also some important developments in street improvement and public health. After the passing of the 1844 Improvement Act there was some widening and straightening of the thoroughfares of old Salford, chiefly to facilitate the better passage of traffic into Manchester. By 1849 £40,000 had been spent on this, by which time most of the objects of the Act had been accomplished. Attempts to extend this work were thwarted because of lack of powers, and so by 1850 a further local Act was in contemplation. At the same time interest in public health began to develop. Information on such matters as slums, sanitation and overcrowding, had, of course, been available long before 1845, but it was not until the publication of Playfair's *Report on the Condition of Large Towns in Lancashire* in the second volume of the reports of the Health of Towns Commission in that year, that the issue had much immediacy. Minds were concentrated on sanitation by the threat of cholera, the passing of the Public Health Act of 1848, and the publication of reports on Broughton and Pendleton by the General Board of Health in London.[83]

As all these reports and descriptions make clear, the problems of sixty years of largely uncontrolled urban growth were now acute. Salford had acquired features which were to distinguish it for the rest of the century. Certain parts of its working-class districts were desperately crowded. Playfair observed that the value of land in the town had led to intensive use, and the poorer districts were mazes of narrow streets, blind alleys and courts. He directed attention to other overcrowded dwellings of the poor, the worst being the inhabited cellars, but found even worse conditions in the common lodging houses. The extreme filthiness of the environment in which this mass of people lived had two further causes: lack of a sewerage system, and lack of effective scavenging. In the pages of the Health of Towns Commission Report Playfair and Dr Roberton catalogued, in often horrifying detail, what happened as a result. They also provided a wealth of information on the other aspects of the sanitary state of Salford, including the range of nuisances, smoke from the factories, putrid emanations from the sewers and gas works, pig-sties in crowded districts, and slaughter-houses in courts. Two other sanitary problems also stood out: the over-crowded burial grounds, and the inadequacy of the water supply. Playfair made it clear that one key to sanitary improvement was a plentiful supply of water at pressure.[84]

The result of all these sanitary shortcomings were high mortality rates. With a death rate of 30.9 per 1000 in 1845, Salford township was considerably over the national average of 21.6 Pendleton was somewhat less unhealthy, though its mortality rate of 24.5 per 1000 was still high. By contrast, middle-class Broughton, with a death rate of 16.3 per 1000, was as salubrious as almost any suburban or rural district in the country. The average age at death in Salford was 21 years 8 months, the lowest in the whole of Lancashire, except Liverpool. Of those who died over the age of twenty, the average was 49 years 6 months. A major feature of the death rate was the gross wastage of infant life.[85] Yet, despite high mortality rates, the population increased fast because of the high rate of migration into the manufacturing districts, and because, if the death rate was high, the birth rate was even higher.

In the later 1840s the promotion of the concept of public health had a long way to go. Major changes in attitudes were needed, but did not come rapidly. Some first steps in these directions were taken in these years. The centre of activity was the Nuisance Committee, which from 1845 to 1850 came under the chairmanship of Thomas Agnew. Together with the work of the Paving and Soughing and Scavenging Committees, for the first time efforts were made to pave, sewer and cleanse the streets of old Salford in a systematic way. The most impressive achievement was that the cholera visitation of 1844 had little impact. When the Medical Superintendent Inspector of the Board of Health visited the following year, he declared 'Salford was second to no town he had visited in the Sanitary Department'.[86]

A further step was the securing of a new local Act in July 1850. It was badly needed. Street improvement could not go ahead until the Council had greater powers. There was pressing need for Salford to come under the 1848 Public Health Act. And there was urgent need to secure an adequate supply of water. This was the immediate reason for the new Act, and Salford was also forced into action by what Manchester was doing. In this case, the Manchester Council under Acts in 1847 and 1848 bought out the Manchester and Salford Waterworks Company and instituted a large scheme based on supplying the town from reservoirs in Longdendale in Derbyshire. Under its 1850 Act, Salford corporation was to purchase the plant of the old company in Salford, and be supplied with water by Manchester at prices laid down in the Act. The improving of the water supply was a significant step forward on the sanitary front. The 1850 Act also re-defined the way gas profits could be used for improvement, and gave new powers over paving, sewering and street improvement. The equivalent of a local Act under the General Board of Health, it granted most of the powers against nuisances the lack of which had hampered the authorities since 1844. These extended powers were important, though it must be observed that the Act, like most pieces of legislation, looked back towards what had been needed before, rather than forward to more positive concepts of public health.[87]

Sidney Webb's impression of this period in Salford's local government, of a 'somewhat energetic council going on vigorously with paving, putting down smoke and nuisances and developing its gas and water and parks and library and gallery',[88] seems in general not seriously wide of the mark. However, there were shortcomings, the details of which are more instructive of the realities of local government than Webb's generalities. The story of the early years of the Salford police is a case in point.[89] By coming under the Municipal Corporations Act the borough was committed to police reform. Its initial reaction was to try to carry on in much the same way as before. 'Reform' consisted of increasing the numbers of policemen, putting them in uniform, and making Diggles, the old superintendent of the day police, chief constable. In the next four years the force was beset by problems. Within a year Diggles and the night superintendent had been dismissed for financial irregularities. Eight years later Salford was being served by no less than its fourth chief constable. Diggles' successor Sheppard had apparently been honest and efficient enough, and had seen the borough safely through the 1848 Chartist crisis. But he resigned after discovering that members of the Watch Committee had engaged a subordinate to spy on him. Neal, his successor, seems to have been as competent as Sheppard. However, he promoted a campaign against the retailers of beer and 'evils attendant upon Sunday evening municipal entertainments, as carried on by certain publicans of the Borough'. If this was a kind of zeal that perhaps appealed to well-to-do Bible Christians and Swedenborgians on the bench of aldermen, it earned him nothing but trouble with the Watch Committee. In August 1852 his employment was terminated. The reasons given were vague, to say the least. Failing to extract more precise ones, Neal issued a pamphlet to vindicate himself after his appeal for reinstatement had been turned down. He claimed that he was unfortunate enough to get on the wrong side of the dominant figure on the Watch Committee, Councillor Gendall: 'it was this same Mr Peter Gendall who persecuted my predecessor, Mr Sheppard, an able and efficient officer, who after two years of continued annoyance, retired from your service in thorough and unmitigated disgust'.[90]

Gendall is a Salfordian figure whose career deserves notice. It started on the Police Commissioners in 1836 and only came to an end with his death in 1881. By trade a joiner and builder, he was an authentic representative of the small businessman in politics. Whether Gendall was a Liberal or a Conservative is unclear – at different times he seems to have been one and then the other. In early life he opposed the Poor Law, the 1844 Improvement Act and Incorporation, wore the colours of a Tory Radical and associated with the Chartists. Probably always more a Tory than a Liberal, his true party was the Salford Ratepayers Retrenchment Association, founded in 1845 to elect men on to the Board of Guardians and the Council to watch the interests of the small tax payer. The Association was formed originally to resist the domination of Lockett and his circle and put a brake on expensive improvement schemes. As early as 1849 it was noted that the Salford Association was more influential than the one in Manchester, and had in fact become the most effective organisation for fighting council elections.[91] By the mid 1850s it was said it was in a position to decide on who would, and who would not, get on the council each November. Gendall's elevation to the aldermanic bench in succession to Langworthy in 1857 was an indication of his position in that Association, and he remained a Salford alderman for almost a quarter of a century. In his early years he sat on nine of the ten Council committees, and was chairman of the Watch Committee. That was the body which impinged most on the interests of the publican, the beer seller, and the small shopkeeper. In these years Gendall was powerful enough to get rid of any over-active policeman insensitive to the way they did things in Salford.

Neal's request for reinstatement was not granted. It was under James Taylor, the former superintendent, who succeeded him in 1852, that relationships with the Watch Committee were put on an agreed basis. However, the extension of the borough and the introduction of the Police Act of 1856 revealed serious shortcomings in the Salford force. Because of the Watch Committee's zeal for economy, the three townships were considered seriously underpoliced. Numbers had to be hastily increased in preparation for the first visit of HM Inspector of Police.

At the time of Neal's dismissal in 1852, matters in Salford local politics had reverted back to a reconsideration of the problem shelved in 1844: the relationship of Pendleton and Broughton to Salford. It had become clear that the need for sanitary reform in the two townships could be put off no longer. The choice which faced them was either to have local Boards of Health under the 1848 Act, or amalgamate with Salford. In the twenty years up to 1851 the population in the two townships had more than doubled: there were now over 14,000 people living in Pendleton, and over 7,000 in Broughton. Yet they remained largely without modern local government, being serviced from outside with regard to policing, lighting and gas. In the face of growing concern with sanitary matters some ratepayers felt this situation could not go on. In 1850–51, in response to petitions from the townships, the General Board of Health in London produced reports on their sanitary state. The effect was to give support to those who argued that Pendleton and Broughton could no longer continue to act independently of Salford in matters of sanitary improvements.

It was Brotherton who took the initiative in bringing the townships together to apply for an Amalgamation Act.[92] In the mid-winter of 1851–2 he met the local authorities in Pendleton and Broughton. Referring to the recent sanitary reports, he put proposals for union to them. Aware of the extreme touchiness of feelings in Broughton, Brotherton proposed an intricate federal arrangement. To demonstrate that Salford was not out to steamroller the others, what he proposed was that Salford should have four wards, eight aldermen and twenty-four councillors, and Pendleton and Broughton each to have two wards with four aldermen and twelve councillors, so that Salford's representatives could not outnumber those of the other two. There would be borough committees and a borough rate for such matters as police, but for such purely 'local' matters as lighting, paving and sewering there would be township committees levying township rates. A share of the gas profits would go to Pendleton and Broughton, and Salford would supply them with water.

The Salford Extension and Improvement Act was the crowning achievement of Brotherton's career, the culmination of a forty year association with the reform of local government. Under the new arrangements the borough was enlarged to become co-terminous with the Poor Law Union and the Parliamentary constituency. However, extension created almost as many problems as it solved. Broughton remained unassimilated into the borough: given the class dimension, maybe this was inevitable. The intricate 'borough' and 'district' arrangements made improved local government difficult. Borough finances took on a Byzantine complexity, inter-district jealousies over finance, gas and water were virtually in-built, and it may be doubted whether the sanitary improvement of the borough, the main reason for incorporation, was well served by these arrangements. A local wit designated Salford 'A Trinity without Unity'.[93] In a town growing ever more industrialised and populous, this complex administrative framework was to be a brake on effective local action. Changing it proved very difficult. These arrangements continued largely unmodified until 1891.

The Extension and Improvement Act was Brotherton's last major service to Salford. Although then seventy, he never retired. When he died, early in 1857, he was still the Member for Salford. In retrospect, his death almost seems another example of his well-developed sense of political timing. For a veteran Radical Reformer there could have been no more appropriate time to bow out: within months the friends of Cobden and Bright took a terrible beating at the general election. What Dissenters called the 'Stoning of the Prophets' marked the final demise of the League. Its survivors were to wander in the political wilderness for some years before they found their Moses in William Ewart Gladstone.

It was not so much a Conservative revival that defeated them, as a sea-change in liberal opinion. The immediate cause of the alienation of many of their erstwhile supporters was the 'unpatriotic' opposition of Cobden and Bright to Palmerston's foreign policy. But splits in the party of Reform in Manchester went back a long way. Once the Corn Laws had been repealed there was no great issue on which to concentrate its collective mind. For many reformers, 1846 was the culmination of all that had been achieved since the Reform Act. They, the new provincial middle class, had elbowed their way into the political nation and had seen their ideology absorbed by it. Reform had done its work. The royal visit in 1851 and the great Art Treasures Exhibition of 1857 signalled to the world that the transition of Manchester from Coketown to provincial metropolis was complete: they found it deeply satisfying that it had done so under their leadership. *They* had arrived, and found their world nicely in balance. Increasingly they came to dislike the attempts by Radicals to press for further change. The rift between Whiggish moderates and advanced Radicals in Manchester went back to a dispute which arose in 1846 over who should succeed Mark Philips as reform candidate at the next election. Cobden was asked, but declined, and the Radicals pressed for John Bright. Viewing Bright as a vulgar demagogue, moderates loathed the idea, and their hostility was voiced in the columns of the *Manchester Guardian*. The Radicals won this one: Bright was duly adopted, and returned with Milner Gibson in 1847. But a rift had opened up in the ranks of liberal Manchester.

Support for the policies of Lord Palmerston crystallised the new alignment. In the early Fifties Manchester was turning against the Manchester School. Would Brotherton have got in 1857 if he had lived? It seems unlikely he would have stood. He had been very tired in 1852 and reluctantly agreed to carry on to see the Salford

Matthew Noble's statue of Joseph
Brotherton. (Photo: the author)

Extension and Improvement Act through parliament.[94] If he *had* stood, it is just conceivable he would have been returned against the general swing, as in 1841: he had a considerable personal following in Salford, and the Conservatives had been disorganised for a long time. There is also another reason to suppose he might have made it yet again. In his last years Brotherton moved discernably to the right. He played no part in the attempts of the middle-class Radicals to agree a programme with the Chartists, and he resigned from the presidency of the Manchester and Salford Peace Society over their criticism of the way he voted in the House of Commons on the enrolling of the Militia. Defending his action, Brotherton made it clear he did so for two reasons: one technical and one patriotic. He voted for one of two resolutions on the Militia as the lesser of two evils, and because there was a fear that the nation might be invaded.[95] Brotherton was old enough to remember the war against Napoleon, and had joined the local Volunteer company back in 1804. In distancing himself from extreme anti-war Radicals Brotherton was moving with popular opinion. Palmerston's visit to Manchester and Salford in November 1856 turned into a triumphal progress, the prelude to the 'Stoning of the Prophets'. In his speech of welcome Brotherton recalled that when Palmerston's conduct as foreign minister was attacked over Don Pacifico he had given him his support, and had continued to do so after Palmerston became Prime Minister in the Crimean War.[96]

After Brotherton's sudden death on the Pendleton omnibus on 7 January 1857, little of this was recalled. It was the broad sweep of his long life which filled the obituaries. Brotherton's career went back to the beginnings of modern Manchester, and his life seemed a classic example of the boy from the country finding success in the big city. With his background in cotton spinning and his heterodox religious beliefs, he was an authentic representative of the new liberalism of industrial Lancashire. If he lacked personal charisma, contemporaries respected him for his integrity. A subscription was got up to commemorate him, a thousand guineas of which were spent on Matthew Noble's statue for Peel Park, unveiled in August 1858.[97] In raising this monument his friends and fellow townsmen were commemorating more than just plain Joseph Brotherton. They were celebrating the rise of the borough with whose fortunes he had been so intimately connected, the arrival of their class, and the memory of the Anti-Corn Law League. Currently their cause was at a low ebb. After Langworthy's brief sojourn as Brotherton's successor at Westminster, a Palmerstonian defeated a League candidate at the general election of 1857. In parliamentary terms this was the end of Radical Salford. Brotherton's death exhibited nice timing in one other sense. Salford's new municipal cemetery was in the process of completion, and his was its very first internment. The subscription raised enough to pay for an imposing funerary monument. The rest and residue went to endow prizes of books at the newly-founded Salford Working Men's College.[98]

The arms of the Borough of Salford. Brotherton was much involved with their design and is credited with suggesting the motto 'Integrity and Industry'. (Author's collection)

CHAPTER 3

# Voice of the People: The Radical Life of Reginald Richardson

The agitation for the extension of the franchise to working men, and the prolonged resistance to it on the part of those who held the reins of power, is one of the great themes of nineteenth-century history. At certain junctures in the Early Victorian years, the possibility of welding together a democratic movement capable of mounting pressure on the political system presented itself. At these times local men emerged to assume the mantle of Tribune of the People. One such was Reginald John Richardson, a Salford Radical, who, in the first phase of the great Chartist agitation, was a local leader, organiser and journalist, and also played a part in the movement nationally.

Richardson's biography has to be constructed from scattered references in newspapers and other sources, and fragments of personal history in his writings.[1] Scarcely anything is known of his early life. He was born in Salford in 1808, and evidently had a good basic schooling. He received his political education from the writers of the unstamped press, and his debt to Cobbett and Wade is evident. After their deaths, Richardson seems to have taken it upon himself to spread and perpetuate their ideas. A self-made intellectual, with a library of his own, like Samuel Bamford he interested himself in Lancashire dialect and local history as well as politics.

After school, Richardson was apprenticed as a carpenter and joiner. A strong trade unionist and a keen Friendly Society man all his life, he showed a marked preference for self-employment, and had an active dislike of big employers, whom he viewed as tyrannical almost by definition. His class consciousness was sharpened by the sufferings of the working people around him, being ground down under the twin pressures of the factory system and unemployment.

His political apprenticeship was served in the great Reform agitation. For him, as for other Radicals, the lesson was that it was mass pressure and the threat of insurrection rather than the parliamentary process which toppled Old Corruption. The subsequent refusal of the Whigs to enfranchise the working class, and the abandonment of their erstwhile allies by middle-class Reformers once they had secured their objectives in 1832, also made big impression on him. Richardson's abiding hatred of the ruling élite was hardened by their subsequent policies: the suppression of the trades unions, the New Poor Law, and the passing of the Municipal Corporations Act. By 1838 Richardson had come to believe that the Whigs were capable of anything.

Richardson started as a trades union activist and was politicised by the resistance campaigns against the Whig governments, finding work for his talents as an organiser, speaker and writer. About 1836, he seems to have given up carpentry to become a bookseller and stationer in Chapel Street, though for a time he was both. Her husband frequently being away on political business, Elizabeth Richardson looked after the shop as well as bringing up their family. As his fame grew, politics took him away from home for longer periods and eventually to gaol. Although we know very little about Elizabeth Waite, who married Richardson in 1833, she seems to have been a supporter of her husband's activities and a woman of some strength. Their first son was born in 1834, and he soon had three brothers.

Richardson's political life falls into distinct phases: the years as a union activist and Anti-Poor Law campaigner, his involvement in the early Chartist movement, and the last twenty years spent in the Radical wilderness. In the aftermath of the passing of the Reform Act we find him at the meeting in the Dyers Trade Union room in Manchester, at which it was resolved to form a Political Union for Manchester and Salford to meet weekly to debate the issues of the day, and watch events locally.[2] At their meetings Richardson first established himself as a platform man, and was involved in Manchester's part in the national protest movement against the transportation of the Tolpuddle Martyrs in 1834.[3] He also began to make a name as a drafter of resolutions and printer of handbills. Associated with Doherty's great cotton spinners union and the Owenite Consolidated Union in 1834, he was active in the protest campaign against the transportation of the Glasgow spinners four years later.[4]

Richardson never lost touch with the trade union movement, but was drawn into wider politics by the passionate resistance campaign to the New Poor Law gathering momentum in Lancashire and Yorkshire at this time. Salford became a notable centre of this agitation: with local Radicals such as Joseph Hodgetts and William Willis, another bookseller, Richardson soon found himself in alliance with local Owenites and Tory Radicals to organise resistance to the workhouse system. The New Poor Law was received by the poor, and those sympathetic to them, with deep hostility. It was seen as inappropriate to local conditions, an attack on the ancient rights of the poor to parish relief, and an assault on local government by a centralising state. It was also seen as a major ideological development. No one expressed this more cogently than George Mandley, a Salford Owenite, who, in May 1834,[5] declared it was

> evidently founded on the suggestions of political economists filled with the prejudices of a particular school, ignorant of the habits and feeling of the poor, and whose almost exclusive attention to the rise and fall of markets led them to treat human beings and their concerns as mere commodities, subject to the same laws and influences as any article of commerce.

What gave the northern reaction to the workhouse system its emotional intensity was a sense that it was heaping punishment on the tens of thousands of handloom weavers who had already suffered twenty years of falling wages and severe bouts of unemployment. The new Act not only enraged Radicals. Some Tory paternalists and certain Methodist ministers abominated it for its harsh philosophy, and others feared that the Boards of Guardians would transfer local government into the hands of the rich.

The northern opponents of the Bill attacked it as it passed through Parliament, sought to have it repealed when it became law, and resisted its implementation on the ground, union by union. Their campaign lasted several years, reaching a climax in 1838–9. In Salford it was part of the wider political battle which, as we have seen, was fought with singular rancour. Tories used it as a stick to beat Whigs and Reformers, and it posed real problems for Brotherton and his supporters. The latter took the view that once it was law it was pointless to resist its implementation. To Richardson and *his* allies this was anathema. They fought to capture control of the Salford Select Vestry, petitioned Parliament and the Poor Law Commissioners, and, when the time came, tried to obstruct the formation of the Salford Union.

They first tried to capture the Salford Select from the Whigs and Brothertonians in 1835. They failed that year, and the next, but with the appearance of Alfred Power, the Assistant Poor Law Commissioner in Lancashire, in December 1836 to discuss the formation of the new unions, resistance stiffened.[6] Power's arrival provoked a great outcry in 1837 which Richardson figured very prominently. However, it was not until a year later that the movement began to attract mass support, which was lucky for Brotherton, who narrowly managed to retain his seat at the 1837 election. Attempts by Richardson to organise a Tory Radical victory at the Easter vestry again failed that year, as did a petition to the Poor Law Commissioners. The Salford Select Vestry, however, refused to meet Power and furnish him with the information necessary to bring the new Registration Act into operation.[7] Power's reaction to all this was that he would carry on as best he could, with or without local co-operation, and create a Salford Union.

The next stage began in the mid-winter of 1837–8. A great meeting in Manchester in February 1838 of delegates from various places in Lancashire, Yorkshire, Cheshire, Derbyshire and Staffordshire was held to get up a petition for the repeal of the new law. The following month Richardson became secretary of the newly-formed South Lancashire Anti Poor-Law Association and soon organised a petition to Parliament, reputedly signed by 85,000 people. Brotherton's refusal to present this to the House of Commons led to allegations that he had snubbed the delegation, and his enemies put around the story that the reason was that Brotherton entertained hopes of an Irish Poor Law Commissionership. Such was the bitterness against the proposed new Salford Poor Law Union that, at Easter 1838, the old Select Vestry was finally defeated and a Tory Radical one replaced it. Richardson, Hodgetts and Willis were elected, and theirs were the most vehement voices arguing for resistance and non-co-operation.[8]

For several months the Salford Select fought a rearguard action against Power. In June, Power formally announced the structure of the new Union and its Board, and in July, nomination lists of guardians were drawn up. As we have already seen, to avoid the controversies of a contested election a party political compromise was attempted. When it failed, the Whigs and Brothertonians withdrew, and so it was that the first Salford Board was a Tory one.[9] On the first of January 1839 it formally took over the relief of the poor.

The new poor law regime in Salford got off to a conspicuously bad start. The Conservative board of guardians won a Pyrrhic victory. After all they had said about the iniquities of the system, they now had to work it. The Board was seriously divided along township lines, Pendleton and Broughton hating the idea of having to maintain Salford's poor, and no sooner was it formed than it ran into one of the severest depressions of the century. The guardians were soon being accused of being extravagant with ratepayers' money. At the 1840 election they were ousted by Whigs and Reformers.[10] In the first decade of its existence the Salford Board mismanaged its affairs badly, and in 1848 nearly collapsed into financial chaos. It was not until 1852 that the new workhouse in Eccles New Road was built, and it was only from that time that the union began to operate relatively free from trouble.

The problems the New Poor Law brought to the ratepayers were as nothing to the pain it gave to working people. The threat of the workhouse over the lives of the poor was both physical and psychological. In a way it was terribly effective: people went to the extremes of privation to avoid seeking relief, and when they did so were almost broken. In the good old British manner it was brutal to encourage the others. Nonetheless, for fifty years respectable Victorians believed, as if it were the eleventh commandment, that the threat of the workhouse was necessary to counter idleness and improvidence.

If, by the end of 1838, the battle in Salford had been lost, for Richardson the war was not over. As secretary of the South Lancashire Association he was actively involved in a campaign to keep up the pressure on parliament to repeal the Act, and encourage local resistance.[11] The Association's meetings attracted great crowds, and significantly raised the level of anger against the government and the economic system. If ultimately it failed to prevent the setting up of the new system, it did delay the process in places where local anger was strongest, or thought to be volatile by the authorities. In the later stages of the Association's existence, as the law had its way, the Tory Radical alliance began to fall apart. The Radicals began to move towards Chartism, leaving the Rev. J. R. Stephens to carry the Anti-Poor Law movement into its last phase, in which his allegations were couched in very inflammatory language.[12] By later 1838 the situation in Lancashire and Yorkshire was, in Carlyle's famous phrase, 'discontent grown fierce and mad'.

In early 1839, Richardson was already deeply involved in Chartism. His activities over the past six years had transformed him from a trade union activist into a full-time political agitator. They had developed his organising abilities and public speaking, and he was about to launch into journalism. They had raised his prestige in the ranks of the popular Radicals, and his name was now widely known in South Lancashire. Most important of all they had put him on to platforms alongside the first leaders of northern Chartism.

Chartism was the first great national working-class political movement. It welled up from below as a result of the turbulent conditions of the times, and was united on the six points of the People's Charter in 1837–8. Below the veneer of an agreed national platform it was always sectional and fragmented, a movement of localities in search of an organisation. In origin and temper, London Chartism was different from that of Birmingham; and Lancashire and Yorkshire Chartism was different again. Even within the manufacturing districts the movement was strongly localised: country Chartists were always fiercer and more uncompromising than those within Manchester and Salford. Given this sectionalism and regionality, the fact that Chartist leaders were able to create a sense of being part of a national movement was an achievement in itself.

The 'physical force' character of early Northern Chartism arose directly out of the Anti-Poor Law Movement and the bitter privation suffered in the depression of 1838–42. In this, the worst sufferers were the tens of thousands of hand-loom weavers. Chartism was essentially their cause. Although the movement ebbed and flowed, it managed to sustain itself for a full decade as a movement capable of disturbing, and even menacing the existing political order. For Radical leaders the essential problem was to find ways of creating a movement out of unfocused discontent. As with any new political development, the first stages were as much a matter of faith and illusion as of organisation. Chief amongst the conjurors-up of northern Chartism was Feargus O'Connor, a Protestant Irish barrister, briefly MP for Oldham in 1835. Addressing Radical meetings in Lancashire and Yorkshire he sensed the possibility of a movement forming.

Hunt and Cobbett recently dead, O'Connor saw himself as the inheritor of their mantle. In the *Northern Star* newspaper O'Connor discovered a way to unify the scattered pockets of local Radicalism. Starting in 1837 as a factory movement and Anti-Poor Law weekly for the West Riding, the following year the *Star* began to focus more on the People's Charter, and to print reports of local activities from correspondents up and down the country.[13] In addition to selling the *Star* and other Radical journals in his shop, Richardson soon became a contributor to its columns. It is principally through this source that his Chartist career can be followed. As well as being a local platform man and organiser, he played a supporting role nationally. In 1838 and 1839 he shared the same platforms as O'Connor, Stephens, Jackson and O'Brien and spoke at virtually all the major meetings in London, Birmingham and Manchester. Using talents developed in the Anti-Poor Law movement, in September 1838 he helped to organise one of the biggest demonstrations ever seen in this country, and from his pen poured a stream of reports, letters, handbills and pamphlets. All this began with a letter in the *Star* in March 1838 urging the people to put pressure on the government through a 'run for gold', by withdrawing money from the savings banks.[14] Richardson's arguments were borrowed from William Cobbett, who saw in what he called THE THING, the fiscal and banking system, the main agency of state oppression of wage earners and the poor. This was, and remained, the basis of, Richardson's critique, which was directed more against the State rather than industrial capitalism.

The following month Richardson was at the Carpenters' Hall in Manchester when a Political Union was founded on the Birmingham model. A committee was constituted to agitate for annual parliaments, universal suffrage and ballot votes, and Richardson was appointed its secretary *pro tem*. On 6 September he represented Lancashire at the Newhall Hill meeting in Birmingham, usually taken as the start of

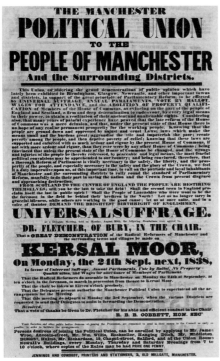

Richardson's work: poster of the great Kersal Moor Chartist demonstration of September 1838. (Public Record Office)

Chartism as a national movement.[15] The following month Richardson attended and spoke at the rally in Palace Yard, Westminster, held to make Parliament aware of the new movement, and rouse London Radicalism. Richardson's speech was full of the rhetoric of 'physical force'.[16]

The Palace Yard meeting was a failure. It did not bring out the London Radicals and it was ignored by Parliament. In his speech Richardson drew attention to the next step in the campaign – the great demonstration of the people of South Lancashire on Kersal Moor the following Monday, which he had been organising.[17] Richardson said he expected 300,000 to be present. On Monday 25 September 1838, with their bands and banners, vast processions from the Manchester, Oldham and Ashton districts converged on the Moor (on the north west edge of Broughton township). Just how many were there became the subject of some dispute.

The Chartists claimed half a million, the *Manchester Guardian* (using the estimates of the military, who watched the meeting carefully) put it at 30,000.[18] Whatever the true figure, it was very large, and the meeting was an impressive demonstration of the support Chartism enjoyed at that juncture. Kersal Moor was the first of many rallies across the industrial north. The specific objective of these was the nomination of delegates to the forthcoming People's Convention in London. Richardson was one of eight men nominated to represent South Lancashire.

Kersal Moor aroused South Lancashire. That Autumn, as the depression worsened, activity intensified. In the country round Manchester, despite a government ban, torchlight processions were held, weapons displayed and the language of physical force freely used. Such developments put Richardson and other platform men under severe stress: the situation demanded they use the language of force, but they were only too well aware that, if things came to confrontation, ultimately, real physical force lay with the army. They were also worried that it was a well-tried government tactic in these situations to stand-off, infiltrate *agents provocateurs*, and let agitators convict themselves out of their own mouths. On 15 December, Richardson issued a handbill addressed to the men of Worsley, Leigh and the neighbourhood, warning them of the recent Royal proclamation against torchlight processions: 'the Whigs have sent their spies to entrap you'. However, when the Rev. J. R. Stephens, fieriest of the Chartist orators, was arrested, Richardson again employed the language of physical force at the protest meeting in Manchester: 'there was no hope for the people of England but in hanging a sabre or some other offensive weapon over his [*sic* ] mantlepiece'.[19]

Through that winter and into the spring of 1839 tension was racked up. 'We are by no means in a comfortable state here at present,' wrote Lord Derby to the Home Secretary, 'the language both in this town and the neighbourhood is very much what it was immediately preceding the days of Peterloo; of a forceable seizure and appropriation of Property etc. and most notoriously and openly the working men are arming themselves with Pikes, Pistols etc'. However, it was clearly seen by the Manchester authorities that the threat of physical force came more from *outside* Manchester than from within.[20] Nonetheless, the authorities in Manchester prepared themselves. A committee was formed, and masses of special constables were sworn in, local Chelsea pensioners were were called up and reinforcements of regulars were posted to the army barracks in Manchester and Salford.

Around Christmas 1838 a local Chartist organisation had emerged in Salford. By the following April the Salford Radical Association had rooms in St. Stephen's Street, and its leading organisers, Jabez Barrowclough, William Willis (the secretary) and Anyon Duxbury (treasurer) were all friends of Richardson from the Anti-Poor Law campaign.[21] Heavily committed elsewhere, Richardson played little part in the Association, though he remained close to its leaders, and was admired by its members.

Richardson was now entering the most exciting period of his life. Between February and the end of May 1839 he attended the Convention as delegate for South Lancashire. Whilst he was away, his wife Elizabeth looked after the shop. 'Thronged on Saturdays,' she informed him in a letter opened by the Home Office, they were selling 300 copies of the *Northern Star* a week.[22] In the early summer, together with the other platform men, Richardson went on tour to speak at rallies across the country, to 'test the mood of the people'. At this time he produced his first series of political pamphlets, articles and letters to the press. His *South Lancashire Political Union Almanac and Englishman's Manual* was issued in March, the *Star* printed a letter attacking the 'centralising system' of the Whigs, and he produced a pamphlet on *The Right of Englishmen to have Arms at this Time.*[23]

For the individual delegate, especially the family men of modest means, life at the Convention, was a mixture of exhilaration and anxieties. Richardson's show clearly. Within days of the opening of the Convention the *Star*[24] printed his declaration 'To the Men of Manchester and South Lancashire': He reminded them that 'You have placed us in a position of danger … but with the mighty phalanx of Kersal Moor at our backs, urging us forward, and inspiring our souls with ardent zeal: our course will be forward our motto 'No Surrender', our grand *ultimatum* will be liberty.' Behind the rhetoric, Richardson's nervousness is unmistakable.

Debates in the Convention were dominated by the question of proceeding by 'moral' or by 'physical' force. Gammage notes 'the majority were more disposed to the advocacy of physical force than otherwise'. However, it is clear that by now Richardson was through his physical force period. March saw the seceding of batches of moderates from the Convention. Eventually a package of proposals was agreed – the organisation of mass-signings of the Charter; the collection of 'the

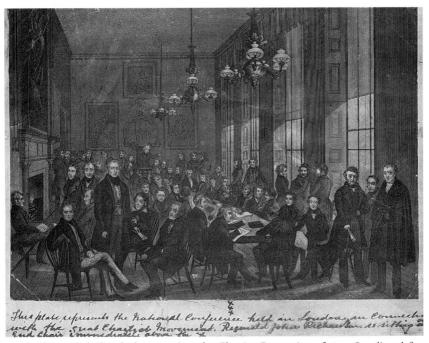

Richardson (marked with the crosses) at the Chartist Convention of 1839. Standing, left, is Feargus O'Connor. (Manchester Public Libraries)

Rent', a national Chartist subscription, a 'Run for Gold' on the banks, 'exclusive dealing' to pressurise shopkeeper voters, a boycott of excisable articles to deny the government revenue, and a decision to go out into the country over Whitsuntide and hold monster meetings 'to test the people's resolution'. When these measures were attacked by Harney, the ultra-physical force man, Richardson rounded on him.[25] The National Petition, with its quarter of a million signatures was presented to Parliament on 13 May. Shortly after, the Convention transferred itself to Birmingham, and then adjourned until 1 July. Delegates left to prepare for the 'monster meetings'. Some never returned: Richardson was one.

In Manchester and Salford all attention once more was on Kersal Moor. The rally of 25 May 1839 was attended by another vast concourse. The prospect of the rally caused the authorities the gravest anxieties. The magistrates were very nervous, and General Napier, the military commander, when he heard a rumour that the Chartists had acquired five brass cannon and were planning desperate things, laid on an artillery exhibition for some Chartists with whom he was acquainted. He also let them know what his cavalry would do if Chartists ever started to act like a military force. In the event, the people arrived on the Moor on the 25th, listened peacably enough to the orations and dispersed under the watchful eye of the authorities, who were extremely careful to avoid any provocation.[26]

One notable absentee was Richardson and, shortly after, at the end of May, he resigned from the Convention. He had fallen out with his Manchester and South Lancashire supporters, who nominated Christopher Dean, a stone-mason, to replace him. The reasons did not become public until two years later. Meanwhile, though, Richardson had no intention of withdrawing from the wider Chartist movement. He accepted an invitation to visit Scotland, and his speech to a vast crowd in Glasgow delighted them with its humour and sarcasm.[27] At the time Richardson was making enemies in Manchester, he was making friends in Scotland.

In the summer of 1839 the events of the first Chartist agitation moved to a climax. On 1 July the Convention reconvened in Birmingham and delegates reported on the feelings of the rank and file, subjectively tested in the great meetings. For better or worse it was decided that if the Petition was rejected by Parliament on 12 July, a general strike, or 'National Holiday', would be called in August. The Petition *was* rejected. The press poured scorn on it and on the whole notion of universal suffrage. Plans for the Holiday began to be formulated. In a letter printed on 21 July, Richardson, said the decision was ill-timed; it had little support in the country; even in Manchester it could not be effective with so many operatives on short-time.[28] His attitude found little support amongst local Chartists. Since the Kersal Moor demonstration there had been a lot of activity. A policy of exclusive dealing towards local shopkeepers had been attempted, and, because this was essentially a women's cause, a Female Radical Association had been set up in Salford. A series of open air meetings in the township urged the adoption of the National Holiday, and the language used was inflammatory. James Campbell, an emerging new local leader, declared that they would do no work during the Holiday 'unless to make coffins for tyrants'.[29]

As 12 August, the day of the Holiday approached, the civil authorities prepared themselves to meet the Chartist challenge. As tension started to rise in the Manchester area in early August the authorities moved. Police, backed by hundreds of special constables and the army, seized arms at Stockport and arrested nineteen local leaders: a subsequent riot was dispersed. Public meetings were banned by the Manchester magistrates. On 12 August the police and military cleared the crowds in the streets as they tried to get local factories to turn out. The only Chartist success in Salford was at Nathan Gough's mill in James Street. At the end of that day the Mayor of Manchester informed the Home Secretary that, in his opinion, the arrests, and the failure of the Holiday, had caused a complete cessation of Chartist activity in the town.[30]

For reasons which became clear later, Richardson was out of Manchester that August, but he was duly arrested as part of the general round-up of platform men which followed the defeat of the Holiday. He was released on bail put up by Peter Gendall, Anyon Duxbury and James Garratt Frost, JP.[31] In the half year between bail and his trial Richardson was very active. In late 1839 political excitement was highest in the Bolton area, with incendiarism and illicit meetings addressed by physical force men. By contrast, in Manchester and Salford the main forms of activity were the defence and support of the families of political detainees, and aiding the national campaign in support of those arrested after the Newport Rising in South Wales. In Salford, the Radical Association published a 'Declaration of Opinion' supporting Universal Suffrage and professing undying hatred of the New Poor Law. It also took the decision to open a co-operative store, 'on the principles of that at Newcastle'.[32]

In January 1840 the nationwide campaign to have the death sentences on the Newport leaders, Frost, Williams and Jones lifted succeeded. Richardson spoke as delegate from Salford at a great Manchester meeting, and the following month was in London for a meeting of the committee now agitating for a free pardon. This failed, and the Newport men were duly transported, but the agitation kept Chartism alive in early 1840. In those months Richardson started the *Regenerator*, a short-lived newspaper, produced a pamphlet, *The Rights of Englishmen*, an anti Poor Law tract, and brought out his *Political Almanac for 1840*, a compendium of facts on the working of the British state culled from government publications. He also had a series of eight letters on banking and currency printed in the *Star*. A ninth appeared in the issue of 25 April. Headed 'Secure in the Embrace of the Whigs', it was addressed from Lancaster Castle, where Richardson was starting a gaol sentence.[33]

Richardson was tried at Liverpool Assizes. Arising out of what he had said in a speech in April 1839, he was charged with 'conspiracy and combination to create discontent in the minds of Her Majesty's subjects, incitement to tumult and insurrection and to use force to procure resistance to the Laws of the land, and to disturb the peace and security of the land'. He was convicted largely on the testimony of one journalist, and sentenced to nine months in prison, afterwards to enter into his own reognizancies for good behaviour for three years in £100, and to find two sureties in £50 each.[34] In all, the Spring Assizes of 1840 saw the despatch of some ninety three Chartist leaders and activists, including Feargus O'Connor. The first Chartist challenge had been made, met and repulsed. But if the government hoped the movement was now snuffed out, they were to be disappointed.

Despite financial worries and natural anxieties over his wife and four small sons, once inside Richardson acquitted himself well. He took the view that he was a political prisoner and refused to wear prison dress and do prison tasks. This was permitted, provided he maintained himself, which added to his financial worries. Barrowclough appealed on his behalf in the *Star*, and money was subscribed in Manchester and further afield. In a letter of thanks to the Burnley National Charter Association Richardson affirmed that prison was not changing him – he was still an inveterate enemy of the New Poor Law and 'greedy grasping cotton masters'. But Richardson had enemies as well as friends. In another letter to the *Star* Barrowclough vigorously denied a story printed in the *Manchester Guardian* that Richardson's poor rates had been paid by a Tory agent, reminding Chartists that it was the evidence of a *Guardian* reporter that convicted Richardson.[35]

If the authorities thought that prison would silence him they were wrong. It took something to shut Richardson up. He addressed a series of 'Letters from Prison' to the *Star*. When the government Report on the condition of the handloom weavers was issued, he penned another series, the first of which was addressed to 'the Radical Reformers of Colne', which the *Star* printed. The paper also reviewed his *Political Almanack and Annual Black Book for 1841*, containing 'many stern facts calculated to generate deep reflection in a tax-payer's mind'. The same issue noted that the Leicester Chartists had nominated the still-incarcerated Richardson to the executive council of the new National Charter Association, a position he never took up. Richardson had also received support from Scotland, and announced in the *Star* that he was coming out of prison on 23 December and would visit that country.[36]

Whilst Richardson was in prison, Chartism revived with the formation of the National Charter Association in July 1840. This was an attempt to form a party with branches and card-carrying members. Older Chartist bodies began to dissolve themselves, and join the Association. The focal point of all this was Manchester, where the provisional executive Council was formed. Although the revival started whilst O'Connor was in prison, from the time of their release he and his followers came to dominate the Association. In Salford the Radical Association dissolved itself, and by September five new Chartist classes, meeting on Sunday afternoons, had come into existence. By late October they had their own room in Great George Street and formally joined the National Charter Association. In James Campbell, their secretary, they had a figure destined to play a leading part in this phase of the movement.[37]

Plans were made to give the prisoners a great welcome on their release, and

Feargus O'Connor
(*Illustrated London News*)

when Richardson and seven others arrived at Eccles on Christmas Day 1840 they were met for breakfast by a deputation and then conveyed to Stephenson Square, Manchester. With bands and banners they processed through the streets of Manchester and Salford. At the meeting at the Hall of Science, Campfield, which ended the day, Richardson, 'chief of the liberated "patriots"', was the lion of the hour. He made a fine speech villifying the Whigs. He assured them that prison had left him unchanged.[38] On that Christmas Day, Reginald John Richardson was at the peak of his popularity. It did not last very long.

The next few months he spent writing, and fighting one last anti-Poor Law battle. He contributed articles to the *Star*, and in the summer of 1841 three more tracts for Radicals were published. In February Richardson attended a Chartist Delegate meeting in Manchester as the representative for Burnley, where his writings on the weavers had earned him many admirers.[39] About this time he became involved in the first election for Guardians of the Manchester Poor Law Union. The Radicals put up their own candidates, of whom Richardson was one. He got a mere 21 votes. The final Anti-Poor Law episode came in March. A Salford meeting to protest against the renewal of the Poor Law Commission for a further ten years, attended by Chartists, Operative Conservatives and some leading Tories heard speeches from Richardson and others.[40] Despite petitions from many such meetings, Parliament duly renewed the Commission. Further resistance was pointless.

June 1841 found Richardson in Scotland. For the next fifteen months he resided in Dundee. What took him there was an invitation from the Scottish Radicals, the prospect of paid journalism and a pressing need to get away from Manchester. Information on his Scottish year is contained in 'Richardson's Works', a book of cuttings preserved in the Manchester Archives. It contains articles from the Radical *Dundee Chronicle*, of which he became editor, and from the *British Statesman* and the *Illuminator*. Ostensibly Richardson's reason for going north was to take part in the Perth election of 1841. Richardson went to the hustings to swell the number of Chartist candidates in the general election, to report the proceedings, and to try to ensure the defeat of Fox Maule, the Whig candidate, a former Home Office civil servant. Richardson was in good form at Perth. Mauling Maule was excellent sport.[41]

Fox Maule won Perth comfortably enough. As expected, Richardson did not go to the poll. Nonetheless he had put up a good show. The *Perth Chronicle* saw in him a representative of 'who the man would be whom "the people" Fox Maule speaks about, would support, if the appeal actually were made to them'.[42] Which was the reason Richardson and other Chartists went to the hustings. The Anti-Corn Law League were doing the same thing. J. B. Smith, Brotherton's old election agent, contested Dundee the following day as a Free Trader, losing to a Whig. Richardson made an impression and stayed on. As Chartism revived, there was room for Radical writers. His Dundee pieces range over economic issues, current questions such as Free Trade, the Poor Law, the rural police question, and examples of extravagant public expenditure, mostly based on information published in the civil list and other sources. Whilst there, he brought out his *Exposure of the Banking and Funding System*, printed in Dundee and published in London, Manchester, Salford, Glasgow and Dublin.

The 1841 General Election brought the return of the Conservatives under Peel. Richardson argued that a new chapter in Chartism had begun.[43] The 'physical force' era which had started with the Chartist Convention in early 1839 was over. These were not arguments calculated to endear him to Manchester, where O'Connor was God. Still less was his next step. A month later Richardson was urging 'rational Chartists' to support Joseph Sturge's 'New Move', an attempt to unite moral force Chartists with middle-class Radicals around a new 'moderate' programme.[44] Richardson's metamorphosis from physical force orator to respectable Radical was now complete.

At the time of his move to Scotland he became involved in a painful split with his erstwhile friends and supporters fought out in public in the columns of the *Star*. Perhaps foolishly, Richardson started it. In a letter printed on 17 July 1841 he complained of his financial plight, notably debts incurred over the great Kersal Moor demonstration of September 1838. Such had been his inability to meet the demands of his creditors he had, he said, been obliged to flee to Ireland in 1839 to avoid arrest for debt. There (he claimed) he had stayed for several weeks in hiding. Whilst in prison the following year he had been served notice from printers to whom he owed money, and had asked the Manchester Committee for help. Richardson said that he had told them that when he came out of prison he wanted no triumphal reception, unless there was an agreement to help, and had received a promise to that effect. However, since then, apart from some money from Oldham, he had received very little, been obliged to go into hiding and ultimately to flee to Scotland. He again appealed for help.

The next issue of the *Star* printed a letter on behalf of the Manchester 'Tib Street (National Charter) Association' which said their committee were looking into it. A further letter from them appeared in the issue of 31 July, which claimed that a thousand reports of the Kersal Moor meeting had been printed and sold, implying that Richardson must have received the money and further claiming that Richardson had been paid £5 a week as a Convention delegate. The committee demanded to see Richardson's books. There followed a bitter retort from Richardson. He denied receiving £5 a week while at the Convention, alleging that all he had had from February to July was travelling expenses. This provoked an even more acrimonious reply, printed on 4 September. It denied his version of what he had been paid, accused him of being a self-confessed Tory Radical and a calumniator of O'Connor and O'Brien, and of informing against another Chartist at Liverpool.

Just over a month later, on 9 October, the *Star* printed a pitiful letter from Richardson, forwarded by his friend T. R. Smart of Leicester. It revealed that while he was in Dundee the bailiffs in Salford had seized and sold his furniture and his wife and children had been turned into the street in the middle of the night. Richardson himself had been arrested and held as a debtor until his legal costs could be paid. Some money had been realised by all this, but £60 was still owing, and he had turned to Smart for help. 'Nine months ago' reflected Richardson, 'I entered Manchester in triumph, now I leave in disgrace'. One final, appalling letter appeared in the *Star* of 20 November. Written by 'An Old Chartist' it is headed 'Mr Reginald John Richardson. Is he a Traitor?' It alleges that back in the summer of 1838 Richardson cancelled a lecture tour in Dublin, and instead stayed in Liverpool to give evidence against Christopher Dean, the Manchester Chartist. It alleges Richardson stayed in Liverpool on expenses of six guineas a day, and that the police who arrested Dean paid Richardson a sovereign to point out the house Dean was in.

Richardson made no reply. However, in an editorial in the *Dundee Chronicle* of 9 December 1841 there is this note:

> TH. Mr Richardson does not intend to take any notice of what appeared in the *Star* but treat it with contempt; at the same time he is willing and anxious to satisfy Mr Dean himself as to the falsehood of the charges against him; such is the proper course. If Mr Dean be aggrieved let him write to Mr Richardson upon the subject; if not why should other people interfere and abuse the liberty of the press by unwarrantable slanders?

Where lies the truth in all this? What it highlights is the fact that in poor men's politics in the nineteenth century much bitterness and envy turned on the question of money. In times of great privation money was collected from the rank and file and suspicions that their leaders were on the make over expenses easily arose. But there was more to it than money. The rift between Richardson and the Manchester committee went back to May 1839, when they forced him to resign as their delegate and replaced him by Dean. Richardson alluded to this in a speech at Perth:[45]

> He could tell Mr Maule why he was superceded by Dean; it was because he was not physical force enough for the Manchester people – because he would not go far enough and fast enough for them.

As we have seen, being disowned by the South Lancashire delegates in the summer of '39 did not lead Richardson to withdraw from Chartism, though it does explain his absence from the second Kersal Moor demonstration. Still much in demand as a speaker on Chartist platforms, his Glasgow speech led to the Perth and Dundee invitations after he came out of prison. Moreover, the way he refused to be silenced during his time in Lancaster Castle brought him fresh admirers. If he had quarrelled with the Manchester leadership, to the rank and file he was still a hero, and treated accordingly on his release. Richardson's problem was that, as he was moving away from O'Connor's brand of Chartism, Manchester was going over to it. Meanwhile, the bailiffs closed in.

One mystery in all this is where was Richardson at the time of 'the Holiday' of the late summer of '39? His version is that he was in hiding in Dublin, but did he stay in Liverpool and betray Dean, for whom he could have felt little affection? Evidence as to his whereabouts is lacking, not surprising if he was indeed in hiding. There is little reason to suspect he was not. He was facing arrest for seditious libel as well as debt. The Home Office Papers give no support to the charge that he was an informer, or ever took money, and the idea that he did seems quite out of character. With all his faults, Richardson was an old Radical with supreme contempt for the ruling élite and its new policemen: in all his life he never changed on this. He was duly arrested and tried and sentenced. Had he been an informer, he would surely have escaped this. It is thus highly unlikely that what the Tib

Street Chartists alleged against Richardson is true. To them his chief offence was that he had turned against physical force and O'Connor. That was enough. They threw everything they could at him.

When the Chartist movement revived in late 1841 there were several schools of thought on how best to proceed. Still working in Dundee, Richardson threw in his lot with those who argued for an alliance with followers of the Birmingham Quaker, Joseph Sturge. Sturge, having abandoned the Anti-Corn Law League for its 'lack of principle' put forward his 'New Move'. In an editorial in the *Dundee Chronicle* of 23 December, Richardson indicated his approval of this development, even though it did not embrace all the points of the People's Charter. In April the following year Richardson attended the Sturgeite conference in Birmingham, which attracted those Chartists who, for various reasons, were at loggerheads with O'Connor and his friends. Richardson played a not insignificant part in the proceedings (in which, despite the intentions of Sturge, the six points of the Charter were carried).[46] Efforts were made to meet middle-class objections to swallowing the Charter whole, and, after the conference, the Complete Suffrage petition was drawn up and presented to Parliament. But by then the short-lived coming together of Chartists and middle-class Radicals had dissolved away.

In May 1842 the second Chartist petition, with over three million signatures was presented to Parliament. It was heavily defeated after a debate which heard weighty speeches arguing for political rights being soundly based on property. In the late summer tension was racked up once more by the worsening economic situation in the manufacturing districts. In a re-run of the events of 1839, that August the movement peaked a second time with the 'Plug Plot' riots and an attempted general strike. Another large-scale round-up of Chartist and union activists followed, with the handing down of severe prison sentences.

Though Richardson now had no part in it, a flourishing Chartist culture had developed in Salford.[47] In the summer of 1842, when the Charter Association's influence reached a peak, there were plans to build a Chartist Hall. To keep members out of the pubs, the Association ran an 'amusement class' on Saturday evenings, organised a Chartist Sunday School and set up a youth section. At their meetings they sang the Chartist 'National Anthem' ('God Save our Patriot Frost/Let not his cause be lost/God save John Frost'), made efforts to popularise the wearing of white hats again, and ran a co-operative store. How large the membership was is hard to determine. In June 1841 a figure of 200 is mentioned: a year later, the Association claimed it had doubled its paying members.[48] Its political activities included forming a committee, half electors and half non-electors, to consider contesting the 1841 election (after much argument it was decided to support Brotherton); supporting and welcoming home O'Connor and the Manchester Chartists released from prison in September; organising signatures to the National Petition; and debating with the Free Traders. At this time its leading figure was James Campbell, an Irishman, general secretary of the National Charter Association and it is clear there was a strong Irish element among the Salford Chartists. However, the Manchester Irish O'Connellites had no love for O'Connor, and their leader Kelly disputed with Campbell in the columns of the *Star*.[49] Eventually the

O'Connellites threw in their lot with the Anti-Corn Law League, who used them to break up Chartist meetings in Manchester.

The rejection of the National petition in May 1842 took place against a grim economic backdrop. In July a local paper commented 'the picture which the manufacturing districts now present is absolutely frightful. Haggard and half-clothed men and women are stalking through the streets begging for bread'.[50] That August, despair led to a series of strikes and attempts to bring those mills still working to a standstill. The Manchester Chartists tried to use this attempt at a general strike to further the cause of the People's Charter. The events in Salford connected with these moves occurred between the 9th and 23rd August.[51] On the first of these days a large crowd from Manchester marched along Greengate ordering the workers in the mills and workshops to turn out, breaking windows where they met any opposition. The Manchester and Salford authorities swore in seven divisions of special constables, and, to back the specials, the 72nd Highlanders were drafted in from Liverpool. They were soon in action. On Friday 12 August, an alarming situation arose at the Adelphi Calico Print works of Wilson & Co. On the Wednesday the gates had been forced and the men turned out, but had gone back to work. On Friday a crowd of some 3,000 besieging the works were fired on by a watchman with a blunderbuss, who injured five people. An attack had just started when the Highlanders arrived and dispersed the crowd. Some rioters were apprehended.

The strikes had been widespread, and the authorities were expecting trouble the following week. Inside Manchester, a series of meetings were held by trade delegates in the Carpenters' Hall, the Chartist Headquarters, but it was the prospect of 'physical force' men coming in from Ashton, Stockport and Bury that really alarmed the magistrates. A volunteer mounted patrol kept an eye on things in the central districts, and a circle of outposts was set up, controlled from Manchester Town Hall. In the event, this well-organised defence system was not tested. The strike was solid, but the workers were never sure what to do next and were debating. Salford township itself was quiet, except for one incident, but there was some

August 1842. 'Plug Plotters' attack Wilson's Print Works, Adelphi, Salford, Friday 12 August. (*Illustrated London News*)

trouble at the Victoria Mill on Eccles New Road, at the Seedley Print works, and fifty seven colliers were arrested after a meeting at Kersal Moor. On 20 August the *Manchester Times* noted the paradox that 'while at a distance Manchester is thought to be in a state of siege, the whole town may be traversed without a single act of violence being witnessed'. The 'irrationality' of the situation puzzled middle-class observers. The strike was solid, but the workers made no demands on the employers, and the trade delegates' meeting at Manchester produced no plans: the cotton masters offered no concessions. In the third week of August the strike began to collapse. The chairman of the trade delegates was arrested, the meeting dissolved, and by the 23 August the men began to go back to work.

The events of August 1842 once more exposed the weaknesses of physical force strategy. When offered a chance of insurrection, both Chartist and trades union leaders hesitated and the moment was lost. They hesitated with very good reason: revolutions only happen when authority crumbles. In the manufacturing districts in August 1842, whatever the reality of their true organisational strengths, neither the Home Office nor the middle-class forces of local government gave any outward sign of irresolution. Chartism and labour failed to make their challenge, and, though it was to last another six years and more, the first great working-class movement was never the same again. Nonetheless, government had been frightened, and exacted retribution. But it had survived another of the challenges to its authority in the nineteenth century.

Away from Salford for most of 1842, Richardson played no part in these events. However, analysing things as he saw them in his newspaper articles, he was deeply influenced. On 11 July we find him writing from Salford in O'Brien's *British Statesman*. O'Brien commented 'We are happy to find Mr Richardson once more in the field, and feel great pleasure in informing our readers that Mr Richardson is henceforward to be a regular weekly contributor'.[52] Unfortunately for both of them, the journal proved short-lived. Richardson was still writing for the *Dundee Chronicle* until September. In July and August some of his pieces were addressed from London, but his last contributions were from Salford. Another indication that Richardson had returned home is the survival of subscriber's tickets for 1842 and 1843 to the Salford Lyceum, a workers' educational institute.[53]

In September 1842 Richardson lost his employment in Dundee because of his attacks on O'Connor, and returned home. That month he wrote several 'Letters to Sir Robert Peel' in the *British Statesman*. In the issue of 20 September he was caustic about the round-up of Leach and others in Manchester. The trial of the Chartists and Plug Plotters at Liverpool and Chester brought a 'Letter' in the *British Statesman* of 12 October. The last of the cuttings in 'Richardson's Works' is another letter to Peel, 'Commerce, Corn and Industry', dated 'Salford 10 November 1842'. Again the text is from Cobbett, and the burden of the argument that a total change in the 'paper system' (of money) was wanted.

If Richardson hoped to carve out a permanent career as a journalist, he was to be disappointed. He produced more pamphlets and booklets, but from the end of 1842 evidence of his literary efforts is fragmentary.[54] Richardson's reaction to, and participation in the later stages of Chartism are not very clear. He played no direct part in the movement in Manchester or Salford after 1842, and, with the curtailing of his connection with the Dundee paper and the failure of O'Brien's *British Statesman,* he had no outlets for his journalism. He seems to have paid off his debts, and the shops in Chapel Street, and later New Bridge Street, were the mainstay of the family's finances until about 1850. The truth is, we know all too little about Richardson in those twelve years.

Back home in Salford Richardson was soon involved in local politics. In 1842 he became a Salford Police Commissioner for Blackfriars district and was to figure prominently as spokesman for the grouping who opposed Brotherton's proposals for a new Improvement Act and the incorporation of the Borough. What Richardson and his allies objected to was the concentration of local power in a Council whose members were restricted to those with a high property qualification. Their support for old institutions was not because they were old, but because in the vestry, court leet and township meeting small ratepayers at least had a voice. He and his friends also feared that more local government would mean greater taxation and that compulsory purchase for street improvement would hit the small property owners and rate payers. Richardson and his allies were trying to fight the trend of the times. Parliament was inclined to grant the urban middle-class access to power in the town halls.

The battle over incorporation and the new Improvement Act took place in the first half of 1844. Richardson fought the bill and its promoters as hard as he could, likening Lockett and his friends to 'a greedy grasping junto, like those in Spain. Some twenty of them kept all the power in their own hands'.[55] However, once the parliamentary stage of the Bill was reached, it was the Tory Police Commissioners who carried on the most effective opposition. The Chartists and small ratepayers were weak because they were essentially outside the system. The successful passage of the Municipal Charter and the new Act left them even further outside. The first municipal election saw the friends of Brotherton firmly established in the Town Hall. However, one development in the campaign did point to the future. The Ratepayers Association that had come into existence indicated a way to influence the Council that was soon to make its presence felt in Salford politics.

The following year Richardson was again in the public eye over his involvement in a fierce dispute within the ranks of the Odd Fellows Friendly Society. By the 1840s, the Independent Order of Odd Fellows (Manchester Unity) had grown into the largest national 'affiliated order', offering death and sickness benefits to workers, artisans and shopkeepers and their families. The Unity was Manchester-based, with head offices in Aytoun Street, and had 30,000 members in the Manchester, Salford and Eccles districts alone. Richardson was a zealous Odd Fellow, a Past Grand Master of 'Morning Star' Lodge. At the centre of the dispute which arose in July 1845 was an issue dear to Richardson's heart: self-government *versus* centralisation. By the 1840s membership of the Unity had increased to an extent its founders never anticipated. Attempts of William Ratcliffe, the Corresponding Secretary, and the rest of the Aytoun Street people to bring its rules up to date at the Annual Moveable Conference of 1844 caused a serious revolt. Essentially, what Ratcliffe was arguing was that the system of representation at the AMC (where important decisions were made) needed to be reformed and that every Lodge should supply the Board of Directors with a Financial Statement of its affairs, with a view to ascertaining (for the first time) the true position of the Unity's finances.

Many lodges and districts refused to make any returns. Their point was that the society as a whole was flourishing, and they saw no reason why it should not continue to do so. The main opposition lay in Manchester. Many lodges and Districts were suspended for their refusal to obey the Resolutions of the AMC. Out of the 15,840 members suspended, 8,316 came from Manchester, 2,905 from Salford and 733 from Eccles.[56] Richardson was one of those, and threw himself into the protest movement. He declared that self-government was 'the inalienable right' of every lodge. Attacking 'the Star Chamber of Aytoun Street', Richardson composed a 'Declaration of Independence' for the Salford district, and the Manchester Odd Fellows followed suit. The battle of words was fought in the columns of the *Northern Star*, and the paper eventually came out against the 'Aytoun Street Junta' over its suspensions in the Manchester, Salford and Eccles District, which the *Star* condemned as dictatorial and high-handed.[57]

The upshot of this affair was that the disaffected members and branches in Manchester and Salford split from the Manchester Unity, and organised themselves into a separate society – the National Independent Order of Odd Fellows. Long after the split, they remained more numerous in the Manchester area than the Manchester Unity, though nationally, and in the rest of Lancashire, the Manchester Unity was far bigger. By 1849 Richardson was a prominent member of the 'Sir Oswald Mosley' Lodge. What had happened to 'Morning Star' is not clear: it disappears from sight after 1845.

1847–48 saw the culmination of the major political campaigns of that troubled decade. In the serious economic depression of those years, the Chartist movement came to its third and final climax. Conditions amongst the Manchester poor once more were truly appalling. Events first came to a head in early April, and then again in the summer. But civil order was resolutely maintained by Mayor Armitage, the police and the regular army.[58] Richardson's role in all this was confined to that of commentator. In 1847 he produced his *Blue Book of the Commons*, a rather dull parody of official publications. Prefaced from 'Salford 1st November 1847', it was published by Abel Heywood, the ex-Owenite Manchester publisher, a figure with whom Richardson increasingly allied himself.

The following year, he brought out another version under the title *The Annual Black Book and Political Almanack for 1848*. For Richardson, for Chartists, the interest on the National Debt was 'Taxes on bread, sugar, tea, coffee, tobacco etc. paid by the people, from whose labour all wealth is derived'. Amongst his 'seditious facts' and Radical analysis, Richardson found space to have some fun at the expense of those who enjoyed government sinecures and pensions, and extracted from official sources the ugly fact that the number of strokes of the Cat-o'-nine-tails in floggings in the army in 1845–46 totalled no less than 38,394.[59]

In the events of 1848 Richardson played no part. By now committed to co-operation with those middle-class Radicals who were not convinced that all that could be accomplished had been accomplished with the Repeal of the Corn Laws, in 1848 he produced a pamphlet entitled *A New Movement*, jointly with John Bright. But the New Movement came to nothing. Both Chartists and middle-class

Radicals had fragmented. In the late Forties and early Fifties many attempts were made to form associations to devise an agreed programme, but all failed to come up with one. In February 1850, Richardson was on the platform with Abel Heywood and J. R. Cooper at a meeting in Manchester organised by O'Brien's National Reform League,[60] but this, too, led nowhere. As trade improved and Palmerston shifted the nation's attention to foreign policy, politics underwent a sea-change. Chartism was effectively buried, its supporters cast in the guise of physical-force fanatics.

Possibly because he now had more time, Richardson's interests turned to education and intellectual matters. In early 1850, he was at a meeting at the Music Hall, Brook Street (until recently the Carpenter's Hall), to promote the idea of a People's College for Manchester. Two years later, he was arguing that now that the new Manchester Public Library had been opened (in the former Hall of Science, Campfield), a Museum of local antiquities should be started in the building. At this time he was studying Lancashire dialect, and some writings of his survive which indicate he was planning a work on the etymology of Lancashire place-names and a glossary of dialect words.[61]

In these years, Richardson did not lose contact with the local trade union movement. When, in 1849 an apprentice at Worrall's Dye Works was victimised for taking part in a strike, sent to prison for a month, and threatened with flogging for breaking his indentures, Richardson plunged in. The Dyers Union and Sick and Burial Society challenged the decision, and started a campaign to get the boy out of prison. Richardson was on the platform at a public meeting to promote the campaign. The union won.[62] Ten years later Richardson was at the Jubilee Dinner of the Lancashire, Yorkshire and Cheshire branches of the Friendly Society of Iron Moulders, one of the oldest craft unions (founded at Bolton in 1809). A likely reason for his presence was that his son, Alfred, was a member. The only one of Richardson's sons to become anything of a public figure, Alfred later quit the iron trade and set up in business as an oil merchant. Involved in Salford politics, he was briefly on the Council from 1894–7. A sportsman, a churchman (St Bartholomew's) and a Conservative, Alfred was an Odd Fellow and Friendly Societies advocate like his father, and for more than 40 years also kept up his membership of the Iron Moulders' Society. Besides Alfred, the Richardsons had three other sons by 1840, and at least one other later: this was Henry, born 1844, who lived only seven months.[63]

About 1852, Richardson became involved in the Manchester Association for the Preservation of Ancient Public Footpaths, a revival of a body that had been active for about ten years from 1826. It had always been supported by Radicals, many of whom – such as the Potter brothers, Archibald Prentice and William Harvey – had by now become very prominent citizens. The Association was revived in 1844, when cases involving the closing, or threatened destruction of ancient rights of way in places such as Cheadle, Bowden, and Altrincham were brought to their notice.[64] Together with Richardson, its leading figures included Alderman Sir John Potter, Edward Harford, the Manchester coroner, and Samuel Pope, the Temperance man. Treasurer of the revived Association was Sir Elkanah Armitage, recently knighted. Richardson became the Association's leg-man, their on-the-spot investigator and writer of letters to the press, bringing these matters regularly to the attention of the public.

A number of Salford cases no doubt sharpened this commitment. Footpaths were in danger on Kersal Moor as a result of its enclosure by Col. Clowes and Miss Atherton, on the Walness estate of Mr Fitzgerald, and on the route from Cross Lane to Mode Wheel. There was a complaint against Mr Egerton about an Ordsall Lane footpath, and concern about what the railway companies were proposing about cutting across Weaste Lane.[65] Not all the cases the Association contested were successful, but one that was was Kersal Moor. It is easy to see how close to Richardson's heart this was, and he was certainly very active. Sir John Potter agreed the destruction of footpaths upon enclosure was monstrous, and Richardson argued that not only should they seek to restore footpaths, but see if they could 'establish a common right which the inhabitants believed to exist'. He was keen to take Col. Clowes to court, but the Association decided on negotiation instead. In the event, the landowner proved acquiescent on access, and to the idea of 40 acres being let as a park.[66]

For two years Richardson's activities took him considerable distances from Manchester and it is clear that investigating footpath cases was something he enjoyed. However, in April 1855, at an Association meeting the secretary pointed out that 'Mr Richardson had been unable to report upon the alleged diversion of a footpath ... near Hall i' th' Wood (Bolton) in consequence of his having been appointed to the officer of inspector to the Newton Board of Health'.[67]

Some time about 1850, Richardson gave up his bookselling and stationer's business in Salford, moved to Byrom Street, Manchester and set up as a surveyor. In 1854 he was appointed clerk of works to the recently formed Newton Heath Local Board. However, he remained involved in the footpaths association. Fighting for the preservation of ancient rights of way was a form of resistance to the inexorable industrialisation of his native township.[68]Writing to the *Salford Weekly News* towards the end of his life he reminded readers that, if Salford was now an industrially-polluted town, it had not been so for very long.[69]

> How many thousands yet living remember the beautiful walk from Oldfield Lane and down the Adelphi, across Bank Mill Yard, and along the southern side of the river, with its fine green bank shelving down to the pure stream, overshadowed by tall poplars ... Along the river bank to Springfield Lane; every inch of this has been absorbed – to use a mild term – by the rapacity of those who have built works along the river side.

One of the tasks involved in Richardson's post with the Newton Heath Local Board was to act as inspector of nuisances. In this he found another way of rendering himself useful to the working people of Manchester. Ever since he had come back from Dundee Richardson had attended meetings of the old parish and manorial bodies, the only bodies accessible to him as a small ratepayer. After the establishment of the municipalities of Manchester and Salford he found, or tried to find, ways of continuing to use their now nearly defunct powers. In 1855, after being sworn one of the jury of the Salford Hundred Court Leet, Richardson stated that as servant of the Newton Heath Board he had succeeded in putting down

View of the River Irwell from the Crescent. The poplars mentioned by Richardson are seen on the left. From Bradshaw's *Manchester Journal, c.* 1841 (Local History Collection, Peel Park)

the 'slink trade' – the slaughtering of diseased cattle, and the dressing of dead and unsound beasts for sale as human food within that township.[70] For some time, tons of unsound meat had been supplied to Manchester, Liverpool and other towns in the area. However, all that had happened was that the offenders escaped his jurisdiction by moving to such unregulated townships as Gorton, Droylsden and Clayton. Two years later Richardson was still drawing attention to fish and flesh unfit for human consumption being brought into Manchester and Salford and sold at cooks' shops and other places.[71]

At the Easter Vestry of the Parish of Manchester in 1858 Richardson raised another matter, when he used the occasion to urge the inhabitants of the outlying townships to look carefully at the administration of their local charities, and had hard words to say about the trustees of the extensive Booth charities in Salford. He pointed out that, some years before, £1800 had been spent to obtain an act to regulate this charity and its leases on land left to it in Manchester, 'the property of the Salford poor'. Despite this 'reform' Richardson, like Brotherton before him, was very critical of the lowness of the rental and the length of leases granted by the trustees.[72]

Despite these worthy activities, these were years of political frustration for Richardson. Not a lot happened to encourage popular Radicals. In 1858 another move to try to unite Radical Reformers got under way, and he wrote to George Wilson, former chairman of the Anti-Corn Law League, offering his services.[73] Nothing came of it. Save for one occasion, his name does not appear in reports of the flurry of Reform's 'New Movement' in Manchester in 1858–59. He was, however, sufficiently encouraged to bring out a new issue of his *Black Book*.

Nationally and locally it was a bad time for Reformers. Since their defeat of 1857, middle-class Manchester Radicals were in disarray and Palmerston was riding high, supported by most of the Manchester Whigs and liberals. The New Movement of 1858 was an attempt to reorganise. The Chartists were just as divided. Ernest Jones was urging them to co-operate with the lower middle-class Radicals, and exploring the possibility of working with the rump of the League. This involved some watering down of the six points of the charter. Some Chartists would not wear this: Jones's Political Reform League was opposed by O'Brien, and a National Political Union was set up in 1858 whose programme was 'the Charter, and nothing but the Charter'.[74]

The most significant step came when Abel Heywood, Richardson's old ally, formed the Manchester Manhood Suffrage Association, which tried to unite Jonesite Chartists with John Bright's followers. Disraeli countered Bright's Reform Bill with a government one in February, and the defeat of this led to the General Election of 1859. Without an electoral organisation, Abel Heywood contested Manchester, and Richardson spoke at one of his meetings. Heywood was not elected, but he pushed a Palmerstonian into fourth place, to the the surprise of middle-class Radicals, and consternation of 'liberal Conservatives'.[75] Nationally, Palmerston got back into power. For the time being, the prospects of Reform were finished.

Against the background of these events Richardson published *The Extraordinary Black Book*, which once more reproduced a mass of information collected from government publications about the costs to the taxpayer of the armed forces, the church, the law, the civil list and the diplomatic services. It was the last of his political almanacs. In thirty years Richardson's diagnosis of the ills of the political situation had not changed, nor had his cure. Richardson published only one more work, a Popular Abstract of the Refreshment Houses and Wine Licensing Act, in 1860, the outcome, apparently, of his appointment as secretary of the South Lancashire Beersellers Association, which had been organised in the face of threatened changes in the law.

Richardson died in January 1861. He was 53. His death excited little notice, though he was given decent enough obituaries in the *Salford Weekly News* and the *Manchester Weekly Times*.[76] It was his recent activities which received most attention. He was remembered as a zealous reformer who had scarcely missed a parish vestry meeting in Manchester for the past twenty years, and one who took 'a great interest in everything connected with the political economy of Manchester, and perhaps no other inhabitant was better acquainted with the antiquities of Manchester and the surrounding neighbourhood'. His efforts to improve the administration of local charities and his support for the Footpaths Association were recalled, but little was said of his Chartist days, except that he had been a moral rather than a physical force man. In 1861, Radicals were not given much credit for their Chartist days. By then there was an agreed collective amnesia on the subject: Chartism was written out of history, and if remembered at all, recalled as a sort of desperate irrationality.

# CHAPTER 4

## *Protestant Watchman:*
## *Canon Hugh Stowell*
## *and the Church in Salford*

If a man's standing as a public figure was measured by the scale and nature of his funeral, as it often was in the nineteenth century, it would be hard to underestimate the Rev. Hugh Stowell's in Victorian Salford. 'Never in the history of this country, nor in the history of the Church of England had a private clergyman such a funeral.' The procession which followed his coffin on that day in October 1865 was a mile long. It took an hour to cover the distance from his home in Pendleton to his church in Salford, where he was interred with all due solemnity. The Bishop of Manchester and 160 of the clergy were accompanied by hundreds of laymen, representatives of other churches and public bodies. Shops were shuttered, private houses drew their blinds, and the streets were lined with silent onlookers.[1] The sense of a lost leader was palpable.

Salford erected no statue to Stowell, but his friends found a very effective way of perpetuating his name. Within a short time of his death a new district church, consecrated the 'Stowell Memorial', was opened. To commemorate a clergyman of the Established Church in this way was perhaps not unique in the nineteenth century, but it was highly unusual. Stowell Memorial's lofty steeple, set at the corner of Eccles New Road and Trafford Road, was a fine piece of townscaping, one of Victorian Salford's more conspicuous landmarks.

No student of the Victorian period can fail to miss the importance of the Church of England in Lancashire. In few towns was it more active than in Salford. Yet there was nothing inevitable about this. Institutionally and temperamentally, the early nineteenth-century Church was ill-equipped to face the challenge of the rise of great towns and its early efforts were not all that impressive. However, in the third decade of the century it was galvanised into life by the energy of its own people and threats from outside. In this Stowell played an important role. Whilst he had his counterparts in other places, McNeile in Liverpool, Miller in Birmingham, he was the most vigorous and best-known clergyman in the Manchester of his day, and achieved a wider fame as one of the spokesmen of a particular party within the Church. Coming to Salford with few connections, he quickly made a name for himself. Despite offers from elsewhere, he never left, dying in harness forty years later.

In a city of migrants few were more conspicuous than those from the Celtic West. Stowell, who from his vocabulary and style might be mistaken for a Protestant Irishman, was in fact a Manxman.[2] Born in 1799, he was the son of the Rev. Hugh Stowell, rector of Ballaugh. Stowell revered his father, and in later life loved to recall the plain life and staunch Protestantism of the people of his Manx boyhood. Delicate as a child, after receiving his early education at home, he was placed under the care of the Rev. John Cawood, incumbent of Bewdley in Worcestershire. From Bewdley Stowell progressed to Oxford. His academic achievements were no more than ordinary, though he distinguished himself as a debater. He was up just before the Tractarian movement began, and no high church influences seem to have affected him at St Edmund Hall. When he graduated in 1822 he held the religious opinions of a convinced Evangelical under a gentlemanly Oxford veneer, a combination Salford was to find irresistible. The Bishop of Gloucester and Bristol ordained him the following year and he went to Shepscombe in the Cotswolds to serve his first curacy. But scenes of rural idiocy were not for Stowell. He soon moved to a curacy in Huddersfield, and in 1825 became curate of St Stephen's, Salford.

There Stowell found himself in sole charge of a private chapel-of-ease, erected at his own expense by a clergyman of means.[3] St Stephen's was an expedient to

'Extemporaneous Firebrand'. The young Hugh Stowell, c. 1835 (Local History Collection, Peel Park)

The proprietary church of St Stephen, St Stephen's Street, Salford, 1794, drawn by L. S. Lowry, 1957. Now demolished. (Salford Art Gallery and Museum)

minister to the well-to-do and middling sort in a growing town short of church places, and its curate could never forget he was part of a private enterprise venture. To keep his pew-renting congregation, the curate had to preach well. Happily, this was Stowell's forte, and he was soon thrilling his hearers. It was not long before they made it clear that this man must be kept in Salford at all costs. But there was a problem: virtually all livings in the vicinity were in the gift of the Warden and Fellows of the Collegiate Church in Manchester, or patrons similarly minded. With them, local connections counted. There seemed little chance of an outsider, particularly one with Stowell's Low Church principles, being presented to one of their livings.[4] To prevent Stowell accepting an offer he could not refuse, as well as for their own good reasons, a group within his congregation secured the Trustees Church Building Acts of 1827 and 1831, which empowered trustees to erect district churches endowed from pew-rents having at least a third of the sittings free.[5] Building upon the older expedient of the private chapel-of-ease this proved a more than useful strategem, not just to keep Stowell in Salford, but for the Church generally.

The first Trustees' Church in England was Christ Church, Acton Square, Salford. Built for Stowell at a cost of £6,000, it was consecrated in 1831. In Stowell's time another £9000 was spent endowing it with schools and enlarging the fabric.[6] Every penny was raised by his supporters: it said that if Stowell wanted funds for any purpose he had but to ask. The work of Thomas Wright, a local architect, Christ Church consisted of a circular preaching auditorium, dominated by a great pulpit set high before the communion table. In 1845 an octagonal tower, relieved by eight circular columns topped with Corinthian capitals was added. Two years later it was given extensive galleries, which increased the seating to 1,900, about half of which was free.[7]

Christ Church, Salford was an important prototype. In Trustees' churches the Evangelical party of the Church of England devised a way of increasing the number of places of worship less expensive than those paid for by government grant (a local example of which was St Philip's, Salford, erected in 1825), and a flexible way round the difficulties of patronage or dividing ancient parishes. In doing so they made it easier for the Church to compete with the Dissenters and Methodists, whose provision had expanded more rapidly than the Church's before 1830. In this way the Evangelicals became the spearhead of Anglicanism in Salford, and elsewhere in

Lancashire. As well as gathering in their 'natural' supporters in the middle-class, their avowed aim was to reclaim support within the working class with a church whose spirit was energetic, combative and, above all, Protestant. The Evangelicals were also prepared to take on Dissenters in the name of England's 'matchless constitution' and Tractarians and papists in the name of the Reformation. Stowell played a leading part in projecting this kind of Anglicanism. He was soon the district's leading Evangelical, and his fame spread far beyond the confines of Lancashire. He accepted many invitations to preach and speak in other parts of the country, and became a star performer in Exeter Hall, the favoured venue of the Evangelicals in London.

Stowell had three essential talents. The first was his preaching. He had 'that rare gift of commanding rather than soliciting the rapt attention of vast crowds'. Endowed with a 'stately ease of bearing', he had a deep, melodious voice and an imposing solemnity. Moreover, he preached without notes, as the spirit moved him. Initially the Bishop of Chester had some hesitations about licensing an 'extemporaneous firebrand', but a personal interview with Stowell banished his lordship's doubts.[8] 'His sermons', recalled Marsden, his one-time curate, 'began with a rush of words: everyone waited to see what would become of it. But in a few minutes his course became simple and direct'.[9] Victorians revered their orators and preachers, men 'touched by the divine afflatus'. But they were not uncritical.

The church they built for Stowell: Christ Church, Acton Square, 1831, drawn by L. S. Lowry in 1956, shortly before demolition. (Salford Art Gallery and Museum)

Evans, in his essay on Stowell, identifies weaknesses as well as strengths. Stowell's preaching 'owed far more to fervency and eloquence of sentiment than to any striking amount of deep cogitation. He seems to express himself in greater abundance from the heart than from the brain'. Yet Stowell was no ranter. He possessed a suavity of manner which rough old Lancashire adored: his pulpit demeanour struck observers as manly and open. But that was in the pulpit: 'Mr Stowell on the platform is a different speaker altogether', Evans informs us, 'We have heard and seen his speeches on sundry occasions, but, forsooth, never encountered one in which he did not fly off at a tangent from the main point under discussion'.[10]

Stowell's second attribute was that of diligent pastor. He was immensely hard-working and had great organisational talents. In his thirty four years at Christ Church he gathered in a large and devoted congregation. 'No one', Marsden remembers, 'who have worshipped within its walls will soon forget the stirring service. The full burst of almost of 2,000 voices in sacred song, the deep and subdued but universal peal of response in the responsive parts of the liturgy ... the heart-warming utterances which flowed from the pulpit. The number of communicants at Christ Church was never less than 400 and sometimes rose to 600'.[11] Making due allowance for the *ex parte* nature of Marsden's recollections, the picture is impressive.

Stowell put great energy into parochial duties. With the aid of two curates, five services were held in the parish every Sunday: three in Christ Church, two elsewhere. Stowell preached morning and evening every Sunday, and hated to miss it. Once a month he catechised his church on Sunday afternoon. On a Wednesday evening there was a service followed by an expository lecture on the Bible. Frequent weekday evening cottage and schoolroom lectures were given, and on the Saturday evening previous to the monthly celebration of holy communion there was a preparatory service in the church. His staff of volunteer district visitors (36 of them in 1852) sought out the poor in their own homes. The Evangelicals introduced the Church in Lancashire to the Gospel of Work.

Christ Church ran day and Sunday schools on an extensive scale. Stowell also introduced the first Ragged School into the borough, and organised a refuge for 'fallen women'. There was a Church library, clothing clubs and a Mutual Improvement Society. Once a month Stowell met his voluntary workers and teachers, and his curates every Saturday evening for prayer and 'reading the word'.[12] In Christ Church he provided an environment in which his earnest followers could totally immerse themselves. Many men and women, prominent and active in Salford before and after Stowell's death, were given their church and political schooling there.

Despite all this, Stowell was possessed of an energy that could not be contained within the bounds of his own parish. He was the leading light, and not infrequently instigator, of a network of church associations in Manchester and Salford, not all of which were solely for the middle class. He was the first, and for many years the *only* Anglican clergyman to support the Temperance Movement: most took another thirty years to come round to his view on this. Stowell had a vision of a reconstructed working-class: it would be respectable, respectful, sober, Protestant and Conservative. And in time, a part of the Lancashire working class came to be rather like this. Although Stowell perhaps did not live to see its emergence, he did more than most to make it possible.

In his relationship to his congregation Stowell seems, in some respects, more like a great Dissenting preacher than a conventional Anglican parson. He never owed his position to a patron, and it is pretty certain he never intended to. In his eyes Salford, the new urban England, was where the great challenge to the modern Church lay. Not that he ever suffered in any pecuniary sense for this unfashionable belief. Based on pew-rents, plus the income from the investment by the Christ Church trustees of a thousand pounds in consols, Stowell's stipend rose as his congregation grew. By 1850 it was around £800 a year, a handsome salary in his day. Moreover, from time to time, his large and rich congregation pressed gifts on him: £1,500 in 1846; a silver salver and banker's pass-book, in which the sum of £5,000 had been placed to his credit, fifteen years later.[13]

Stowell's relationship with his congregation was a marriage of true minds. Had he been forced to seek preferment elsewhere at the termination of his curacy at St Stephens, Stowell, no doubt, would have made a worthy enough clerical career. What he almost certainly would not have found was the appreciation verging on adulation he received in Salford. In the ranks of these ardent Protestant churchmen a Joshua found his army. The appearance of Stowell in the pulpit of St Stephen's Chapel made it plain to his hearers just what it was *they* were seeking: a re-affirmation of English church Protestantism, a creed based four square on the Bible as the literal word of God, expounded by powerful preaching. Just as importantly, they wanted active lay-involvement, a partnership with their clergy. As events in the next few years unfolded, they sought leaders to rally around, vigorous in church defence, who would also organise a general counter-attack on the enemies of the Establishment. With some truth, they felt that the official leadership – the Bishop of Chester and the Warden and Fellows of the Collegiate Church, Manchester – was both supine and unwilling to utilise lay talent and energy. In Stowell they found someone who was. With *him* they could move forward. With *them* Stowell could operate, when he chose, outside the constraints of conventional parochial arrangements (not that he was ever, deep-down, anything other than a conventional son of the Establishment).

Stowell and his friends, moreover, wanted a Church that was active on a broad social front. Although middle-class, with some extremely rich people amongst them, the Evangelical party wanted churches and schools opened in the working-class districts to ensure that at the very least the people came under Protestant and Conservative influences: Dissenters, Wesleyans, Catholics and Infidels had to be challenged in the streets. Once they found their leader, and their way forward, these people were prepared to put their money at the service of their convictions. This combination of will-power and financial strength characterised the Anglican offensive in Lancashire over the next half century and more.

More remains to be discovered about the rank and file of Stowell's followers, but it is clear who his close friends were: business and professional men, Tories in politics, devoted to the Church, Protestant by conviction. Stowell's right hand man was Robert Gardner, treasurer of the Christ Church trustees. A merchant and manufacturer on a large scale and a Free Trader, Gardner, like many Lancashire

Tories, was something of a paternalist. In 1844 he became the darling of the factory reformers when he unilaterally reduced the hours of work in his Preston factory.[14] On the many platforms Stowell occupied over the next thirty years Gardner was invariably at his side. Himself a generous giver, Gardner became treasurer of innumerable Evangelical organisations. Another supporter was Stephen Heelis. Garnett's agent in the famous Salford election of 1837, Heelis was later an alderman and Mayor of the borough.[15] Another friend, also a solicitor, was William Whitelegg Goulden, who as a young man studied for ordination and had a long career as an ardent Evangelical churchman in Manchester and Salford. When Stowell died in 1865, Goulden devoted himself virtually full-time to Church matters and Conservative politics. A trustee of several other churches, and a manager of five schools, Goulden was, for a number of years, Vice-Chairman of the Salford School Board which was always controlled by the Church of England.[16] Other wealthy and active men close to Stowell were E. R. Le Mare and Joseph Rice. In the many campaigns he fought over three decades, they gave Stowell their closest backing, and after his death, carried his Protestant banner.

When Stowell came to Salford, political events were threatening the Church's old supremacies in a serious way. The repeal of the Test and Corporation Act in 1828 freed the Dissenters from political disabilities which had lain on them since the 17th century. The following year the Catholic Emancipation Bill became law. The further triumph of Reform and the election of 1832 saw the apparent collapse of England's *ancien régime*. To churchmen, the Dissenting middle classes seemed to be carrying all before them. They got men such as Brotherton into Parliament, where straightaway they lent their support to the Government's reform of the Irish Church establishment,[17] and even worse things seemed likely. Locally, Dissenters attacked the Church on the church rate issue. By 1835 the Manchester United Dissenters Committee had ended compulsory church rate locally.[18] Elated by this victory, their zealots began to press for the ending of the Establishment of the Church of England itself. The Society for the Promotion of the Disestablishment of the Church of England, ('the Liberation Society') was relatively strong in the Manchester district, with powerful advocates in local Dissenting chapels.

To Stowell and his friends, Church resistance to this series of disasters seemed unnervingly weak. Local leadership was ineffective, and the feebleness of the Brunswick Clubs over Catholic Emancipation suggested that the old 'Church-and-King' tradition was as good as dead. Into this vacuum stepped the Evangelical Party, and began to organise an Anglican reaction to the advance of religious and political liberalism. If old traditions were dead, new ones had to be invented. To this end they set up a network of clerical and lay organisations to take on Dissenters and Catholics. Stowell was their prize controversialist and acknowledged leader. In the next three decades he involved himself in innumerable organisations and campaigns: his energy for such work seemed inexhaustible.

He first established his credentials as a militant apologist for the Church of England. To rally the faithful it seemed important to restate the reformed, Protestant virtues of Anglicanism. Sermons he gave were printed and widely distributed as penny leaflets. Yet for Stowell there was always more to Church Defence than apologetics. The pressing need was to tackle abuses and build new churches and schools. On abuses, Stowell, as a dutiful son of the Church, was somewhat muted. But he had an aversion to clerical malingerers: 'He quarrelled with no man's income', recalls Marsden, 'but he did quarrel with the man who would receive the income and not do the duty attached to that income'.[19] In the Evangelicals' battle of 1846–50 with the Dean and Chapter (as the Warden and Canons of Manchester had then become) over Canon Parkinson's presidency of St Bees College and the Manchester Rectory Division Bill,[20] Stowell said very little in public, but the fact that the leaders of the Manchester Church Reform Association were all his closest friends indicates where his feelings lay on these matters.

Stowell was, however, a severe critic of the Church's building programme. He believed that the great sums expended by the government in the 1820s on the building of vast unendowed churches were largely wasted. Not surprisingly he advocated the way forward pointed by the Trustees Church Building Acts. In 1835 a meeting was held in Manchester to form a society for the building of new churches in the diocese of Chester. The Bishop, the Warden of the Collegiate Church and other leading clerical and lay figures were present. In his speech Stowell outlined how Christ Church had been built, urged them to harness the wealth of the laity and launched the fund with a promise of £500 out of his own pocket. By the following February this body (now the Society for Building and Endowing Churches and Chapels in the Parishes of Manchester and Eccles) had raised £4,000, of which Gardner had donated £1,000.[21]

In the serious depression in the latter years of the decade progress was slow, but in 1841 another appeal was launched, the Society now being called the 'Association for the Building and Endowing Ten Churches in the Boroughs of Manchester and

The Commissioners' Church of St Philip, 1825. (Baines' *History of Lancashire*)

Salford'. Stowell was one of its four secretaries, Gardner its treasurer. The target was to raise £40,000 to build and endow seven churches in Manchester and three in Salford. Each was to accommodate about a thousand, and at least half the seats were to be free. The right of presentation to each new church was to be visited in five trustees.[22] Within a short time the three planned for Salford were in being: St Bartholomew and St Matthias were opened on the same day in 1842, and St Simon followed in 1847.[23] The former two were provided by the Ten Churches Fund: St Simon's was the first church built by the Incorporated Society under a new church building Act of 1845.

The three new churches were all located in expanding districts in Salford township. Their first rectors were men who had built up their congregations in temporary accommodation and, rather like Catholic priests, (though with somewhat richer supporters to call upon) had been expected to raise at least some of the money themselves. Needless to say, these men, were all Evangelical partisans. Some of these new district church clergymen were Irishmen, graduates of Trinity College, Dublin.[24] Like Stowell, what they brought into mid-Victorian Lancashire was a Protestantism driven by an Irish rather than an English sense of urgency. The churches they served were large, not to say cavernous. It may be doubted whether the Evangelical party, which was always sanguine about its prospects, ever expected to expect to fill them with working-class church people. What they were about, however, is clear enough: they were planting active and highly visible Protestant institutions in the streets of this rapidly growing town.

The Ten Churches Association did not in fact build ten churches: that was an ambition too costly for even its subscribers. But the Association did concentrate church people's minds on the matter of Church Extension. Its successor was the Manchester Diocesan Church Building Society (founded September 1851) which saw its task not so much to build churches as to grant-aid to those willing to do so. Instead of raising capital sums, it existed to assist and encourage the well-to-do to subscribe to local projects.[25]

The period between the founding of the Diocesan Society and Stowell's death in 1865 was the Golden Age of church building in Salford. No less than seven were built, or near-completed, in these years, and no corner of the borough, however sparsely populated, was neglected by this burst of voluntarism.[26] Indeed, so much building was there, it is hard to resist the conclusion that it was, in part at least, a case of cash looking for somewhere to spend itself. The most generous individual subscriber was Herbert Birley, Manchester's leading lay Anglican at this time. He gave generously to St Paul's, Paddington, St George's Charlestown, and he built St Anne's, Bridleheath entirely out of his own pocket.[27] Others who made big contributions were the Heywood brothers, Robert Gladstone, William Langton and Edward Tootal, who personally gave £10,000 to St Luke's, Weaste,[28] Land-owners also played their part by donating sites: Lord Egerton for St Bartholomew's, Miss Atherton and Colonel Clowes for St Paul's, Kersal, Sir Robert Gore-Booth for St Luke's, Weaste, and J. P. Fitzgerald for St George's, Pendleton.

After gathering-in congregations and building new churches the next step was the creation of church schools. In Stowell's time the education question became a major issue, and he played no small part in determining the way schools and schooling were to be provided in Manchester and Salford. The education of the urban masses first became controversial in the mid-1830s. Provision in Salford at that time was largely in the form of Sunday schools (the Dissenters and Wesleyans providing the majority of the places) and some seventeen 'Public Day Schools', together with a range of 'Superior Private Schools' for the better-off, and 'Common Schools' and Dame Schools for the children of ordinary folk.[29] Beyond those who attended some sort of school, there was a mass of poor 'street children', who did not go to any school at all.

By the mid-1830s it was clear that this undirected mixture of private enterprise and religious voluntarism was inadequate to the needs of growing towns. However, private enterprise and religious voluntarism was the English way, and education was a local matter. All the government had done in response to the growing evidence of the system's inadequacy was to provide a modest sum each year from 1833 towards the building costs of new schools. Important as this step was in marking the start of state involvement, it did not amount to much. But government was aware that schooling was contentious. The Church of England's position was that if there was to be 'national education', it would have to be under the Church's aegis, and Stowell and the Evangelical Party were in business to defend this at all cost. Nonconformists, Catholics and 'Unsectarians' for their part would never agree to Church control, and provided their own schools as best they could. However, lacking the resources of the Church, they relied heavily on Sunday Schools to instruct their children.

In 1837 a Manchester Society for Promoting National Education was started by liberals and Dissenters, prominent amongst whom were Brotherton and Cobden, to press for non-sectarian schools paid for out of local taxes. With Stowell in the van, the Church party vehemently opposed the scheme.[30] Education became an issue again as a result of certain clauses in Sir James Graham's Factory Bill of 1843–44, which this time seemed to Dissenters too favourable towards the Church of England. At a meeting in Salford Town Hall in April 1843 prominent non-conformist ministers objected to the levying of a local rate which Dissenters would have to pay, but which might be used to maintain church schools.[31] This was a line they were to maintain until the early years of the next century. Stowell on the other hand, in a letter to Peel, whilst agreeing that educational provision needed improvement, agreed that 'to alienate it from the Church would be to drive a fatal wedge between her and the State'.[32] Peel did not agree. When the Bill became law the following year, grants from central government were to be made to all denominations on equal terms, but schools were not to be paid for out of the rates.

'National education' and local schemes for funding schools from the rates came up on other occasions in Stowell's life-time (notably in 1849, and 1854–55), but the Act of 1844 set down the basis of denominational rivalry aided with grants from the government, and overseen by Her Majesty's Inspectors of Schools, for the next generation. The Evangelical party girded its loins to work the system, and Stowell, as one of the clerical secretaries of the Manchester Church Education Society, founded in 1854, figured prominently.[33] Stowell played his part in ensuring that the Church of England established and maintained a lead as provider of schools in nineteenth-century Salford. By 1861 it had more schools than those of all other providers combined: that year 64% of all 'attendances' were in Church Schools. Even as late as 1903, at the close of the School Board era, there were twice as many children in Church Schools as in Nonconformist and Catholic voluntary schools combined.[34] The consequences of this were of some significance. If going to Church Schools failed to turn more than a minority of the working-class into adult communicants, it was more successful in giving them a general sense of being Protestant. To Stowell and the Evangelicals this may have been a second-best achievement, but it was one for which they were prepared to settle.

Mid-Victorian voluntaryist education had many shortcomings. The most serious was the failure of the schools to gather in the children of the poor. School attendance was not compulsory, nor was it free; the payment of 'school pence' was an insoluble problem for them. In an attempt to do something on this, the Evangelicals started a scheme in connection with the Manchester City Mission which in 1849 began to help with the payment of school pence for poor children. This attracted subscribers, and in 1855 E. R. Le Mare, one of Stowell's congregation, took it over and extended it. In 1864 this scheme was emulated by the Manchester and Salford Education Society, and the next year Le Mare's society joined forces with it. In fact its most valuable work was not paying school fees but in exposing the sheer extent of poverty suffered by the children of Manchester and Salford. Ironically, what the Society demonstrated was that there was a mass of poor children who could not be got into school by voluntary efforts alone. By this time even government was beginning to get the message: School Boards were just round the corner.

What the Society documented was known much earlier. When an appeal for schools for the destitute had been made in 1851 Stowell had been one of the first to respond. The setting up of the Salford Borough Ragged and Industrial School in Greengate was in great measure due to his efforts, or so it was claimed.[35] By 1870 Salford had eight Ragged Schools. As with many such missions the Ragged Schools were part fishing-expeditions for individual souls, and part efforts at crime prevention, but there was probably always as much love as calculation in their promotion.

As a logical extension of his role as Anglican expansionist, Stowell was an untiring supporter of the growing network of Church associations in the Manchester district. Evangelicals were organisation-men *par excellence*. There seemed no limit to the efforts they were prepared to expend to encourage old associations and found new ones. Amongst old Evangelical bodies were the British and Foreign Bible Society's Manchester Auxiliary and the Religious Tract Association, the latter devoted to winning hearts and minds from 'infidelity' and 'immorality'. Over thirty years Stowell was said to have raised £16,000 for missionary work through sermons preached at Christ Church.[36] He was also a strong supporter of the Society for Promoting Christianity among the Jews. This operated through the distribution of New Testaments and missions usually conducted by converted Jews. Ever sanguine, Stowell proclaimed that the conversion of the Jews was as desirable to Protestants as the conversion of the Irish, and was always ready to speak at the Society's annual meetings and preach sermons to raise funds.[37] Not surprisingly, Manchester Jewry bitterly resented these efforts to convert them.

As well as supporting older Church associations, Stowell was active in, and often the founder of, some of the newer associations of the time, particularly those which were anti-Catholic or anti-Ritualist. He was one of the first secretaries of the Manchester and Salford Auxiliary of the Church Pastoral Aid Society. Stowell declared that the Society felt bound to ensure that the men and women it supported 'were honest protestants of the Church of England, neither diverging to Latitudinarianism on the one hand, or on the other to Romanism'.[38]

Towards those who 'diverged to Romanism', Stowell displayed a robust and unremitting hostility. 'He had no sympathy,' Marsden informs us, 'with that party in the Church which avow their disapprobation of the work of our Reformers, and some of whose leaders have told us they become less and less the children of the Reformation'. When Newman became a Catholic convert Stowell bade him an unfond farewell, declaring 'I believe the whole Tractarian movement, from first to last was Romeward – a pitiful, Jesuitical, dark conspiracy to un-protestantize England, and re-unite us with Rome'.[39] Although Stowell always preferred to concentrate on the Catholic Church as England's main foe, he spent considerable effort on a two volume theological refutation of Anglo-Catholicism, published under the title *Tractarianism Tested by Holy Scripture and the Church of England*, in 1845.

Although Anglo-Catholics were to play their part in the history of the Church in Victorian Salford, they did not do so in Stowell's time. This was largely because the Evangelical party seized the leadership of the Church in the period when the townships were first expanding. They dictated its tone and physical form, and in this Stowell took a leading role, as we have seen. When the Rt. Rev. Dr. James Prince Lee, the first bishop of the newly-created diocese of Manchester, arrived in 1848 he found the church in the district in relatively good shape. Thanks to the Evangelicals, it had been resolving its problems vigorously. The new bishop's position was one of hard-edged orthodoxy, and he found the religious standpoint of Stowell and his friends congenial. Within three years he had made Stowell his chaplain, and rural dean. For his part, Stowell appreciated the new bishop's vigour as an administrator, and his zeal as an opponent of Ritualism. He and his friends gave Lee their support in his long alienation from the dean and chapter of the cathedral, which commenced in 1850 over the Manchester Parish Division Act. For some years Manchester was diverted by the sight of its first bishop shunning his own cathedral.[40]

In the religious drama of his time Stowell cast himself in the role of Watchman on the walls of Zion. Many enemies beset his spiritual fortress, and the danger lay not merely in their numbers, but in the direction whence they came. Some (Dissenters, Catholics) were clearly external; others (Tractarians, liberal churchmen) were enemies within; and the Church's oldest friend, the State, appeared increasingly unreliable. Moreover, social England was changing around them, nowhere more visibly than in Lancashire.

Stowell was not incapable of seeing the Church's enemies rationally, as separate problems to be combatted separately. But the essence of his message and style was that they were all part of one great conspiracy:[41]

> The adversaries have laid their heads together, and taken counsel craftily, for the expulsion of Protestant truth from this Protestant land. Oh, what a motley

group do they form. The Infidel and the Papist, the Chartist and the Liberal, have united their forces, and are advancing in one compact battalion, and shame, shame upon them, among their ranks are some that profess to fight under the broad banner of the Church of England.

Among them was one arch-enemy, formidable in itself, but busily manipulating all the others in its grand design, 'the subversion of the Church of England'. Stowell was not merely anti-Catholic, he was paranoid about popery. It is not just his anti-popery which needs understanding, it is the popularity such ideas commanded in his time. Whatever else he was, Stowell was never a lonely prophet preaching in the wilderness.

He preached a message which had all the requisites of successful propaganda: it was simple, it appeared to bear on reality and was repeated endlessly. Catholicism is rising up and threatening to take over Protestant England. Because the Rome of the nineteenth century is essentially no different from the Rome of the sixteenth, Protestants have to fight the battle of the Reformation all over again:[42]

> Rome's principles are unchanged, her Bulls and Decretals are unrepealed, and she has the same spirit now that lighted the fires at Smithfield ... Would you wish to be like Italy – to be like the serfs of that country ... Would you wish to have your houses infested by spies, and your families invaded by priests? Would you wish your daughters and wives to be dragged to the confessional?

Beset by a ring of enemies, Protestant churchmen must build up their defences, and then go on the attack.

It is easy to find his picture of Rome as the moving-spirit behind working-class Infidelity or middle-class Dissent laughable, but to frightened Conservative contemporaries, Catholic Emancipation was a shock: the more they dwelt on it, the more bitter a betrayal it seemed. Emancipation heralded the 'Second Spring', the Catholic revival after centuries of an outcast, half-secret existence. In few places was the revival more apparent than Stowell's Manchester. As the population grew and native Catholic numbers were swelled by waves of Irish migrants, it became one of the principal centres of the Faith in England. Schools and Chapels were opened, priests were recruited and founded mission districts, the bases of later Catholic parishes. In 1848, St John's, Chapel Street, was consecrated, not a mile from Christ Church. Built on a grand scale, with the tallest steeple in Lancashire, it was conceived from the start as pro-cathedral of a future Catholic diocese.[43]

As Stowell perceived it, the reappearance of Catholicism was a reversal of history, a challenge not only to the supremacy of the Church of England, but to the Reformation itself. His first task was to restate the Church of England's essential Protestantism for contemporaries. His polemical sermons on the subject were widely disseminated as penny tracts, and through them his fame spread. He went through lists of theological points and practices in which Catholicism was compared unfavourably with the Church of England.[44] An important part of Stowell's argument was that Catholicism is essentially foreign, and that England's freedoms were the result of the Reformation. Because absolution can only be had through a priest, Catholicism imbues its people with 'a spirit of bondage and disquietude of mind'.[45] The Church of Rome had a shameful history of persecution, and if modern Rome lacked the opportunity to persecute, it did not lack the disposition. Popery was responsible for the backwardness of many a country, not least Ireland, and the sooner the Irish could be converted to Protestantism, the sooner that unfortunate land could begin to rid itself of its backwardness. It was an assumption widely shared. Stowell's dislike of Catholicism also focused on the 'unnatural' celibacy of its clergy, and on their alleged power through the confessional. The refounding of religious houses (especially nunneries) attracted his special hostility. Yet if Stowell's anti-popery verged on a prurience and a crudity which deeply offended Catholic sensibilities, there is no reason to suppose that his arguments were out of step with what the non-Catholic public felt. There was a latent pool of anti-Catholicism to be tapped in Early and Mid-Victorian England, and Stowell knew how to tap it.[46]

St John's, Chapel Street, the Cathedral of the Catholic Diocese of Salford. (*Manchester Old and New*)

With the benefit of hindsight, all this seems exaggerated and over-wrought. The Church avoided Stowell's funeral pyre. Catholic expansion and 'encroachment' always had its limits. Yet there remains the question of why Stowell's scenario had such appeal. Anti-popery was deeply embedded in British history, and had demonstrated its potential for re-use on many occasions in the past. Stowell can be seen as the last (or almost the last) in an old tradition. Against this, it can be argued that the Victorian version was something new. Certainly before Stowell (and McNeile in Liverpool and Miller in Birmingham) got to work there seemed little serious overt anti-Catholicism about. Other reasons for its revival should perhaps be sought. One was baffled Conservative anger over Reform, conjuring-up visions of catastrophe and social collapse. In addition, there were anxieties over what kind of society was being created in the new industrial districts. Stowellite Church Protestantism was perhaps a way of assuring industrial Manchester that it was part of old England. It did this by offering the non-Dissenting middle-class a place in a reconstructed Conservatism and a remodelled Church. Moreover, it offered them a way of relating to the urban masses. When de Tocqueville visited Manchester in 1835 he observed that, though it kept a very strong hold on the upper classes, Protestantism seemed to be losing its power over the lower classes.[47] Perhaps what the Church of England has always feared is that, deep down, it is insecure in the affections of the people. But Stowellite Protestantism not only offered the industrial middle classes a way of relating to the already dangerously alienated poor, it offered to the new urban working-class (or at any rate a part of it) a form of self-definition. It offered Protestantism as a principal component of contemporary Englishness.

What Stowell brought to all this was a Celtic vehemence. Imbued with an hereditary animus against Irish Catholicism, it was the Irish dimension of the 'Second Spring' which gave Stowell's anti-popery its resonance. Stowell, and Tories generally, knew full-well that Catholic Emancipation had been pushed through for essentially Irish reasons, and that when the Whigs came to power the Irish Protestant Ascendancy was endangered. The Irish Church in the 1830s was the springboard from which Stowell launched his thirty-year career as Protestant Watchman. From the start, Stowell and the Manchester Evangelical party were involved in resisting Whig reforms of the Irish Church establishment. They urged resistance against the government scheme for National schools in Ireland, arguing that the absence of Bible teaching would deliver Irish children 'into the hands of the priesthood'.[48] They were soon promoting the relief of the 'distressed Irish clergy,' suffering through the withholding of the tithe. Early in 1834 a deputation led by the Rev. Dr. Mortimer O'Sullivan came to England to whip-up support. They met the friendliest of welcomes in Manchester. A relief fund was established at a great meeting of the South Lancashire Conservative Association on 'the coming crisis', well-attended by clergy, landowners and the party rank-and-file. Stowell was appointed its secretary.[49]

The Irish Church turned out to be a rich source of Anti-Catholic ideas and associations to propogate them. If not all these bodies were new, most were new to Manchester. A local Auxiliary of the Irish Society of London (an old Evangelical body) was promptly formed, its avowed objective 'to enable the Irish peasant who cannot read or speak English to peruse the Scriptures in his native tongue':[50] Gardner became first treasurer, and Stowell was always ready to place his talents at the service of this cause. Another association close to his heart was the Manchester and Salford branch of the British Reformation Society, which also originated amongst the Irish clergy. Two years later the branch appointed its first Protestant missionary in Manchester, and for over twenty years the Society maintained this work, largely amongst the poor Irish. Over the years its annual meetings gave a platform to such lions as Stowell and McNeile and various itinerant anti-Catholic agitators. They rarely lacked a contemporary issue to focus in on. In 1844 there was Tractarianism and Stowell treated his listeners to a rousing attack on Newman. In 1850 misrule of the Papal States provided the text and the meeting was addressed by Dr Achilli, recently released from a papal dungeon.[51]

The Protestant and Reformation Society was essentially a middle-class body, but Stowell and his friends did not neglect to try to recruit working people. As early as 1835, in Stowell's own district, they formed the Salford Operative Protestant Association. In the main, its work was the distribution of tracts, the circulation of petitions and the promotion of anti-Catholic lectures. However, an important device in building up a Protestant network was the practice of visiting supporters in their own homes. Over many years Stowell never faltered in his commitment to this body. A similar Association was formed in Manchester, the Protestant Tradesmen's and Operatives' Association. Neither had very large memberships, but they made much noise and were always given good coverage in the local press. Their importance lay in the fact that they put about the idea that Protestantism was a national issue, and incorporated anti-popery into contemporary popular culture.

Compared to what came later, their tone, if not their message, was relatively tame. In Stowell's time they were always firmly under clerical leadership. Orangemen attended their meetings, but the Operative Protestant Associations were kept separate from the Orange lodges. For this reason, and perhaps because hard-core Orangemen were usually Scots or Irish with little or no love for the Church of England (or the Church of Ireland), Stowell was never hand-in-glove with Orange violence. He stood outside of all that, although he undoubtedly contributed to the climate in which it flourished.

At street level anti-popery could be pretty rough. Dr Achilli was the first, or one of the first, in a line of continental anti-Catholic agitators, often ex-priests or ex-religious, who claimed to have suffered (and often had) at the hands of the Catholic Church. They were brought to England to whip up feeling against Catholicism, often treating packed meetings, through interpreters, to lurid accounts of papal dungeons or life in nunneries. Achilli was followed by Signor Gavazzi, an Italian ex-priest, the Rev. Count Wlodarski, DD., and the 'Baron' and 'Baroness' de Camin, apparently Poles, the latter an escapee from a nunnery. This pair were real trouble makers. Their meetings not infrequently led to serious mayhem, local Irishmen not always being prepared to let the claims and insults of these agitators pass unchallenged. They in turn were often set upon by Orangemen and the 1850s saw a series of violent incidents, riots and near-riots in Lancashire and elsewhere.[52]

Although this street theatre was never Stowell's particular milieu, he never relaxed or relented his anti-popery: he preached the message undiluted for more than thirty years. He was always sure of an audience because this period continually threw up national and local issues to which he could react. One which gave him considerable mileage was the parliamentary grant to Maynooth College. On each occasion renewal came up, the Protestant lobby created a song and dance against the principle of (Protestant) taxpayers' money being used to fund a seminary for the training of Irish priests. Maynooth first arose in 1839 and Stowell attracted notice at a 'Great Protestant Meeting of Lancashire and Cheshire' held in Manchester. Appearing in a supporting role to O'Sullivan and McNeile, Stowell treated the vast audience of three to four thousand people to his own combination of patriotism, Protestantism and paranoia. In 1845 it was a Conservative government which was the recipient of his onslaught ('Et tu Brute') for their additional grant of £21,000 to the College. And ten years later another mighty Protestant effort was made to end the grant.[53] Parliament ignored it. By now, anti-popery was more important locally than nationally.

The great Manchester Maynooth meeting of 1839 advanced Stowell's career as an anti-Catholic controversialist. The following year the Hearne libel case made him famous. A well-known Irish priest in Manchester, Father Hearne, brought an action for libel against Stowell, who had publicly accused him of refusing the sacrament to a poor Catholic until he had done penance by crawling on his hands and knees for four hours a day. At the Liverpool Assizes the case caused a sensation. The plaintiff was able to demonstrate that the penitent was a simpleton, was duly exonerated and awarded forty shillings damages. However, largely thanks to the efforts of W.W. Goulden, a rule to arrest the judgement was obtained on the ground that the statement as made upon the record did not amount to a libel. The case went to the Court of Queen's Bench, where a verdict was found in Stowell's favour.[54] His friends were jubilant. If the case vindicated Father Hearne, it also demonstrated that Stowell had temporal resources which were beyond what Catholics could match. In this respect it illustrated a general truth of the time.

The anti-Maynooth agitation of 1845 coincided with the great Irish Famine and Stowell and the Evangelicals thought they saw a great opportunity to advance the cause of the conversion of the Irish. Stowell was prominently involved in forming the Manchester branch of the Church Mission to the Roman Catholics of Ireland, and gave it his usual energetic support. If in hindsight the project seems sanguine, at the time the Catholic Church took it seriously enough to found a Catholic Defence Association.[55]

Especially galling to Stowell was what was happening on his own doorstep. The Catholic leadership in Manchester was forced to organise and expand its institutions as a result of the enormous influx of poor Irish after the Potato Famine of 1830, which, if not so well known and catastrophic as that of 1845, was still a considerable tragedy leading to large scale emigration. Local Protestants, with Stowell at their head, did all they could to oppose the opening and operation of these Catholic schools, convents and chapels. Nonetheless, the formation of a Catholic infrastructure was slowly accomplished. In 1843 an Association for the founding of Salford Catholic Day and Sunday Schools was formed, and the opening of St John's Catholic Schools, the first in Salford, was an important moment in the Second Spring. The next year, St John's Chapel was opened for worship, and its consecration on 8 August 1848 by Dr Wiseman, attended by the flower of the Catholic gentry, was probably unmatched for colour and pageantry by any other occasion in Victorian

Salford.[56] Two years later, St John's became the cathedral of the new diocese of Salford, which extended over industrial East Lancashire, and saw the installation of the Rev. Dr. Turner as first Bishop of Salford. Five years later, in September 1855, Wiseman, now Cardinal, returned for the consecration of the choir and chancel, and preached from the text 'One Body and One Spirit'. The same evening Stowell preached a counter-sermon from the same text, challenging Catholic assumptions of universality. Christ Church was crowded to excess, and hundreds were unable to obtain admittance.[57] No event in these twenty years of local Catholic advance was allowed to pass unchallenged by Stowell's Evangelicals.

Yet if Evangelicals generally failed to prevent the spread of papal influence in Palmerston's England, they put anti-popery on the social agenda; it became part of the spirit of the age. It entered the literature of the time through the writings of Thomas Hughes and Charles Kingsley, and it percolated through the layers of social class right down to the non-Catholic poor. It drove a wedge between the English and Irish working class: Protestantism gave the poor something to look down on. Poor they might be; Catholic, like the 'low Irish', they were not.

Offensive Protestantism, too, had a formative effect on Catholicism. If the carrying through of the Second Spring in the face of their own acute poverty and Protestant bullying was to become a source of pride to Catholics, the latter in large measure imprisoned Catholicism inside a psychological ghetto, giving it a mentality quite different to that of any other religious denomination. Other influences, social and economic, helped to foster that particular blend of defensiveness and ultramontanist optimism which characterised Lancashire Catholicism,[58] but 'No popery' did most to keep Catholics and Catholicism on the defensive, and out of the mainstream of civic life for the rest of the century. Catholics never had the public acceptance or recognition that their numbers in the population perhaps entitled them.

There was always more to the religious drive of the Evangelicals than building churches and schools and opposing the enemies of Zion. They devoted much energy to a series of quasi-religious causes which perhaps impinged more on the lives of the poor who existed outside the sphere of organised religion than some of their more direct religious efforts. For causes such as Sunday Observance, Temperance and Ragged Schools, Stowell was an energetic and lifelong campaigner. It is not that his brand of authoritarian godliness and good works was all that different from that of other Evangelical leaders in other places, but Manchester and Salford puritanism had local characteristics, some of which might justly be attributed to Stowell. Such was the strength of his views and of his power as the acknowledged leader of the Evangelicals, he imparted a character to Church Protestantism which made it more intolerant and bigoted than that of the Dissenters, the true descendents of old puritanism.

On his visit to Manchester in 1835 de Tocqueville observed that on a Sunday 'the workers stay in bed ... or pass it in the pub'. He found this unsurprising: 'What room for a life of the spirit can a man have who works for about 12 hours a day every day except Saturday? What a need he must have for rest or lively distraction on Sundays.'[59] French sociology was not for Stowell. He saw nothing but sinfulness and social danger in the People's Sunday. In 1834 the Evangelicals founded the Manchester and Salford Auxiliary Society for Promoting the Due Observance of the Sabbath Day. Stowell was made one of its clerical secretaries, and its committee included the names of Le Mare and Gardner.[60] Over the next thirty years, as it gathered support, the impact of the Society and the other bodies involved in Sabbatarianism became increasingly effective. In few towns were they more strident than Salford. Stowell was in the van in a campaign in 1849 against a proposed extension of cheap railway excursion tickets on Sundays. A notable local victory was the ending of letter deliveries on Sunday. In 1858 they petitioned the officer commanding Salford Barracks to march his men to church on Sunday mornings without a military band because of the nuisance arising from large crowds of persons being collected on the footpaths' to enjoy the spectacle. General Smith acquiesced.[61]

By then, Sabbatarianism was fully incorporated into the middle-class Protestant ethos. In a letter in 1861 from Germany, a country which in so many respects he admired, the young Salford engineer, William Mather, (a follower of Swedenborg) complained:[62]

> My Sundays do not please me at all that I spend here in Germany. There is something so loose about the habits here; so different from my Sunday school work at home. There one felt as if something, though only a trifle, had been done 'to earn a night's repose', but here it is all passing the time away.

In this respect, Dissenters such as Mather did not differ from churchmen like Stowell. In order that they might earn a night's repose they put a massive effort into trying to prevent working people passing the time away on their day off work.

In 1860 a little phalanx of Conservatives sought to persuade the borough council to further the aims of Sabbath Observance, and succeeded in getting through a resolution enabling hackney-cab proprietors to withdraw their cabmen on Sunday. Salford was the first municipality to do this, or so they claimed. As with many such initiatives, unforeseen effects followed. It appeared that one regular use of Sunday cabs was to convey the well-to-do to their place of worship: the cabmen's day-off inconvenienced the godly. After due consultation between councillors and cab-proprietors, a rather brilliant compromise was arrived at. Henceforth a half cab-service would be permitted. Let it be the ungodly who were inconvenienced.[63]

Compromise was also the result the following year, when Councillors Pellett, Bowman and Husband, rising Conservative stars and Stowellites all, sought to induce the 230 or so sweetshops and provision dealers in Salford who opened on Sunday, to close. Previous initiatives to persuade them to do so voluntarily had failed, so the matter was referred to the General Watch Committee to enforce the law against Sunday Trading. Liberals opposing the motion declared that as good Protestants they too were in favour of Sunday Observance, but opposed rigid enforcement for fear of making the law into a mode of personal oppression (with fines of five shillings for the sale of a bottle of milk, etc). In any case where would things stop? Would the Sunday baking of bread, or the manufacture of gas be banned? Would the railways have to stop running trains? The Watch Committee decided to go for friendly persuasion. A printed address was circulated.[64]

Such pussyfooting enraged Stowell's zealots. A new Sabbath Association for

Salford was formed. The borough was divided into districts, and two members went round each to remonstrate with those who opened on Sundays. When this failed, the Association brought prosecutions under legislation of Charles II. Ignoring the defence plea that the Act was obsolete, the Salford Stipendiary magistrate fined five shopkeepers five shillings each, and asserted he would fine them that every time they appeared.[65]

The Association's initiative provoked fierce reaction, particularly when it was revealed that Henry Mead, one of Stowell's home missionaries (a notable anti-Catholic and anti-Ritualist bulldog) had played the part of *agent-provocateur*. The Bishop of Manchester himself regretted 'that in the righteous effort to enforce the law as regards the Sabbath, the convictions had been attained through the exertions of persons who tempted the miserable creatures to commit the sin for which they were brought to justice.' A fine Salfordian row developed. Attacks were made on Meade and the Association. Evangelical preachers (with Chalmer of St Matthias to the fore) leapt to their defence. A shopkeepers' association was formed to defend those prosecuted. In the end the Sabbath Observance Association backed off, contenting itself with an exhortation in the newspapers:[66]

> Working people, don't shop on the Sabbath. Young men who smoke, why purchase tobacco on the Sabbath? Sunday trading is unfair, unjust, and illegal, and ought to be put down.

Obstinately, the Association retreated only to advance on another front. Meetings were called to petition Parliament for an act to close the public houses on Sundays. This was a clever move: it married Sabbatarianism to Temperance, which brought in the Dissenters. This was an important development in Victorian social life. It was also an important conjunction in Stowell's. He had advocated Temperance when scarcely any other man of the cloth had done so. As with so many causes, he had been in at the start. Stowell joined with Brotherton and his liberal friends in their attempt to get legislation against the proliferation of beerhouses. Characteristically, Stowell proved himself more puritanical than they. He never really believed that if parks, mechanics' institutes and 'rational amusements' were promoted they would turn people away from drink. As he observed on one occasion, 'Where we have one mechanics' institute, church or chapel, we have some thirty beerhouses, ale-houses or dram shops.'[67]

Co-operation between Sabbatarians and Temperance advocates started in 1854 when, with legislation against the Sunday opening of licensed premises being considered in Parliament, the Manchester and Salford Temperance Society convened a meeting on the Sunday Liquor traffic, which, in Stowell's words, changed 'the day of God into the day of Satan'[68] In the 1850s the joint Temperance and Sabbatarian lobby had had some success cutting the hours beershops were permitted to open on Sunday, and in the method of licensing them. The United Kingdom Alliance was formed to persuade Parliament to suppress the liquor trade along the lines of the Maine Liquor Law in America, the so-called 'Permissive Bill'. This, as we have seen, was the brainchild of Harvey, Brotherton and other local men and was entirely a Nonconformist initiative. When Stowell threw in his lot with them it was something of a coup.[69] The fact that Conservatives (and the Church) traditionally acted in defence of the liquor trade, made no difference at all to Stowell. On such matters he followed the dictates of his conscience.

In politics he always had. He was a Conservative, but the fact that he always saw party politics solely in terms of Evangelical morality meant that his interventions were almost always eccentric. Stowell played little or no part in the elections of 1832 or 1835, though his friends did.[70] In 1837 Stowell was active 'in defence of the Protestant Church', though that was not the main issue. It was rather more so in 1841, and Stowell published *A Letter to the Protestant Electors of Great Britain on their Duty in the Present Crisis*, in which he appealed for the return of MPs who would support the 'Reformed Faith' against papist encroachments. He saw Jesuits everywhere: 'those masters of mischief are skulking up and down the country plotting crime and sowing sedition'.[71]

Whilst Brotherton was alive there were no further party contests in Salford, but the Chartist/Irish crises of 1848 brought typical interventions from Stowell. In a pamphlet he warned the workers against Irish leaders ('Irish Papists? – Jesuits perhaps'), and those 'who like the toil of the tongue better than the toil of the hand'.[72] Workers' interests were identical to those of their employers, and he called for 'meek and manly submission in these troublesome times', urging the working class to put its collective trust in God. If order could be preserved a little longer, Stowell held out the prospect of abundant trade just around the corner. To give him his due, Stowell did follow this pamphlet with another, *A Plea for the Working Man: Do not lower his Wages. Addressed to the Employers.* These were but two in a series of homilitical addresses Stowell delivered to the working class over the years.

After the 1841 election, organised Conservatism in Salford collapsed. As MP for the borough, Brotherton had a freehold for life. Yet, if there were no more contests in Salford there was always Manchester. There, in the next decade, the targets for all right-thinking conservatives and churchmen were Bright and Milner Gibson, the avowed enemies of Palmerston and all he stood for. The prospect of an alliance of Conservatives, Whigs and former Anti-Corn Law League supporters disillusioned with the Radical leadership was very inviting for Stowell's Evangelicals. The 1852 election presented them with a chance to oust Bright and Milner Gibson who were thoroughly castigated by Stowell over the way they had voted on the Ecclesiastical Titles Bill and Maynooth, and the issue of the inspection of nunneries was dragged in.[73] Despite the growing divisions within Manchester liberalism, Bright and Milner Gibson were returned safely enough. At this election Stowell was active in other places as well. July found him in Oxford, where he had been invited to lend his weight to the political opponents of Gladstone.[74]

The tide turned against Bright and Milner Gibson over the Crimean War, an issue which revealed what peculiarities could result when Stowell insisted on viewing contemporary events from the standpoint of an anti-popery monomaniac. Going to war with the Czar to protect the Turkish Empire was perfectly acceptable to him, as it was to a majority of the patriotic electorate. The problem was that it all originated with the protection of Catholic rights against the encroachments of the Orthodox in the Holy Places in Palestine, and involved in an alliance with France, the Pope's protector. Stowell confused his contemporaries by insisting that

The Protestant Watchman
in his prime: Hugh
Stowell, about 1857.
(Author's collection)

the war was caused 'by the aggrandising and aggressive character of the Church
of Rome led by the artful conspiracy of the Jesuits'.[75]

After the Crimea, Stowell had far less to say on politics. One reason was that
he was getting old, and played the role of an elder Church statesman, speaking
on many platforms and preaching in many pulpits, including that of Westminster
Abbey, before the Queen herself. Another was that the political tide was running
favourably for Protestants and Conservatives. Brotherton died in January 1857 and
was replaced for a few months by E. R. Langworthy. At the general election that
year the Liberal candidate was defeated by the Palmerstonian Massey. Stowell and
the Evangelical Party gave him their support and helped to ensure the humiliation
of Brotherton's old allies. Stowell's closest friends, however, were involved in a
much bigger affair – the 'Stoning of the Prophets' in Manchester, which saw the
defeat of Bright and Milner Gibson.

So Stowell lived long enough to see the political defeat of the local Dissenting
Radical élite. After the Second Reform Act, which Stowell did not live to see, Salford
became one of those large parliamentary boroughs where Liberals were always going
to have a hard time defeating Conservatism. For this, some of the credit must go
to Stowell and the brand of Protestant churchmanship he spent his life promoting.

Hugh Stowell died the 5th October 1865 at his house, Barr Hill, along the Bolton Road, in rural Pendleton. Had he lived a little longer he would have completed forty years in Salford. Delicate as a child, Stowell had suffered few illnesses thereafter, and his 'robust manliness', an important part of his pulpit and platform appeal, enabled him to lead a full and active life. However, in his early sixties he had a heavy fall, from which he never fully recovered.

Regrettably little is known of him as a private man. Marsden tells us 'he kept no journal; he wrote few letters except those of affection to his family, or of business to his friends'.[76] He married Anne Ashworth, daughter of Richard Johnson Daventry Ashworth, barrister, of Strawberry Hill, Pendleton in 1828, and they had a family of six daughters and three sons, two of whom, Hugh and Thomas, followed their father in the clerical calling.

Stowell died in the same year as Lord Palmerston, Abraham Lincoln and Richard Cobden, and his admirers did not hesitate to include him in their company. Although in one sense absurdly exaggerated, such a judgement is indicative of his local standing in a place which took its own importance very seriously. Stowell died full of honours: he had been Bishop's chaplain, he was honorary canon of Chester, he had served as rural dean and he had preached before his monarch. A marble bust of him had been commissioned from the sculptor Papworth, and a full length portrait in oils by Mercier, a local artist, was hung in the Town Hall.[77]

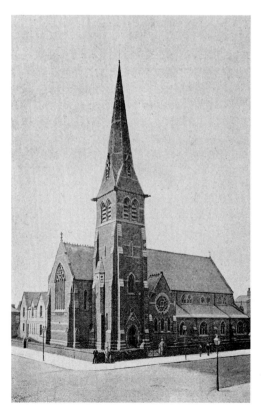

Stowell Memorial Church, 1867.
(*Manchester Faces and Places*)

Stowell was given a funeral of almost civic splendour, and his funeral sermon was preached by Hugh McNeile, Dean of Ripon, the only Evangelical in the North of England who cast a longer shadow than he.[78]

Within weeks his friends convened a meeting to decide upon a memorial. It was agreed to open a new church and endow scholarships at Oxford, for which purpose £8,000 had already been subscribed. In October 1867 the foundation stone of the Stowell Memorial Church was laid and it was consecrated eighteen months later, the Rev. William Doyle, a graduate of Trinity College, Dublin, being first rector. It was a trustees' church, and the five founder trustees were all men who had been close to Hugh Stowell.[79]

His death left Protestants with a sense of a great man gone, a leader lost. No one filled, or could fill the space he left. His second son, Thomas Alfred, was invited to do so, succeeding him at Christ Church, and was minister of his father's parish for a quarter of a century. He had a good career which, in many ways, followed that of his father. He was an able preacher, and his flock were devoted to him. In 1886 he announced that they had raised no less than £57,000 for church and charitable purposes in his twenty years there.[80] Active on the Diocesan Board of Education and in the Temperance movement, Stowell played his Protestant role as president of the Operative Reformation Society. He was made rural dean in 1876 and, three years later, honorary canon of Manchester. When he left, in 1890, to spend his latter years as rector of Chorley, there had been a Stowell at Christ Church for almost six decades.[81]

L. S. Lowry's painting of St. Simon's Church, 1928. (Salford Art Gallery and Museum)

# CHAPTER 5

# Manchester Man: Sir Elkanah Armitage in Business, Religion and Politics

When Joseph Brotherton collapsed and died on the Pendleton omnibus in 1857 he was in the company of two close friends, Sir John Potter and Sir Elkanah Armitage. So close were they that Brotherton bequeathed each of them 'a handsome gold ring' in his will. At the time, all three were important figures in Manchester and Salford. Armitage, then 62, was at the height of his powers. A prominent Pendleton factory master, a former Mayor of Manchester knighted for his handling of the Chartist troubles of 1848, he had good reason to see himself as Brotherton's natural successor as MP for Salford. A few years at Westminster would round off a career which seemed to contain all the ingredients of the archetypal provincial success story.

Alas for Sir Elkanah, things were not to work out that way. In 1857 politics were moving into a new phase, and the shifts which brought Palmerston to the fore could turn old allies into opponents. The friendship of Sir John Potter and Armitage is a case in point. Potter was a leading figure in the opposition which formed against the old Anti Corn-Law League leadership in Manchester, of which Sir Elkanah was a member. By the time the Palmerstonian period had ended and Liberal prospects were improving, Armitage was an old man. Politics aside, the long life of Sir Elkanah Armitage was illustrative of his time, place and class. He was one of Victorian Manchester's great capitalists. The firm he started, Sir Elkanah Armitage & Sons, lasted until 1959, and he was the founder of a dynasty whose members played their parts in the history of Victorian and Edwardian Salford. He himself lived to a great age. When at last he died in 1876 he was remembered as one of the last links with the era before Manchester and Salford received their municipal corporations.[1]

Born in 1794, he was the third of the six surviving sons of Elkanah Armitage of Failsworth, a small farmer and linen weaver. Though a man of modest means, 'Old Elkanah' was a pillar of Dob Lane Chapel, Failsworth and respected in the district for his upright character, charitableness and piety. Even in 1794 few parents gave their sons such ringing Old Testament names as Elijah, Ziba and Elkanah without wishing to make statements, and the first clue to the Armitages is that

Mayor of Manchester: Sir Elkanah Armitage. (Salford Art Gallery and Museum)

they were old Dissenters. They took a pride in their descent from Godfrey Armitage of Lydgate, near Huddersfield, the friend and supporter of Oliver Heywood, one of the Yorkshire ministers ejected under the Act of 1662. With other Presbyterians, Unitarians, Quakers, Independents and Baptists, for over a century the Armitages had suffered for their Dissent. One branch of the family emigrated to America 1719, and as recently as 1793 a 'Church and King' mob had rabbled Dob Lane.[2] In common with certain other old Dissenters, the Armitages felt they had come down in the world, a trend Sir Elkanah was to reverse rather spectacularly. Above all, Sir Elkanah was a *political* Dissenter, an opponent of Church, Toryism and the landed élite.

Their religious attitudes and chapel connections did much to prepare the Armitages for the business opportunities which Manchester offered in the early years of the nineteenth century. Although Elkanah's school days finished when he was eight, family connections secured him entry into the cotton trade. He joined his brothers Elijah and Ziba in the firm of George Nadin & Nephews. There, as a warehouseman, he learned the business. He started at the bottom, but his employers always liked the strict attention he paid to his work, and he got on. As puritans, Dissenters took life, and especially business, seriously. Armitage was fond of recalling that he only ever had one master (though in fact he worked for him for twenty years). When Elkahah left Nadins' he was their manager, which upset them. What upset them even worse was that he was already in business on his own account and was soon in competition with them.

In Manchester the sons of 'Old Elkanah' came under many influences, not the least of which was the rich pattern of religious diversity on offer. In 1829 a Government return revealed that there were over twenty denominations and 15,000 Protestant Dissenters in the town.[3] In Manchester the three boys came under the influence of the Rev. William Roby, minister of Cannon Street and later Grosvenor Street Independent Chapels. So involved were they with religious matters that, when the Rev. William Hill, a representative of the London Missionary Society came to Manchester to recruit for the South Seas mission, Elijah responded to the call. Elijah stayed in Tahiti for about fifteen years.[4] Somewhat reluctantly, Elkanah accepted Nadins' offer to take Elijah's place as manager.

His reluctance was based on the fact that he was about to set up on his own. Elkanah had married young. His bride was Mary Bowers, whom he had first met at Roby's Sunday School: they went to the altar in 1816 when he was 21, and their marriage lasted twenty years, ending with Mary's death in 1836. She bore him eight children, all of whom survived. The first, a son named Elkanah after his father and grandfather, was born in 1817. The young couple were ambitious. They started in business with a draper's shop in Chapel Street, Salford, which Mary managed. Sir Elkanah later remarked that in these years his wife 'earned him 12*s.* a week'.[5] On the premises he kept a small warping-mill, which he worked constantly during his evenings and spare time. In 1822, soon after becoming Nadins' manager, Armitage and his wife decided to strike out on their own.

Armitage set up as a manufacturer, taking a James Thompson as a partner. This arrangement did not last long, and Armitage never had another outside his family circle. He took in work from the handloom weavers of Irlams o' th' Height, for which he paid ready cash, which he then sold in Manchester, and built up capital out of his profits. In 1829, starting with a workforce of 24, he opened a weaving shed at Swinton. Now in business as a nankeen, bed-tick and smallwares manufacturer, he had an office in Manchester and the shop in Salford. In the next few years he did so well that when his brother Elijah returned from the South Seas in 1837 (with his family of ten), Nadin (it is said) offered him a loan to start up in opposition to Elkanah, which Elijah refused, though in fact he and his sons went into the cotton business.[6]

# The Family of Sir Elkanah Armitage

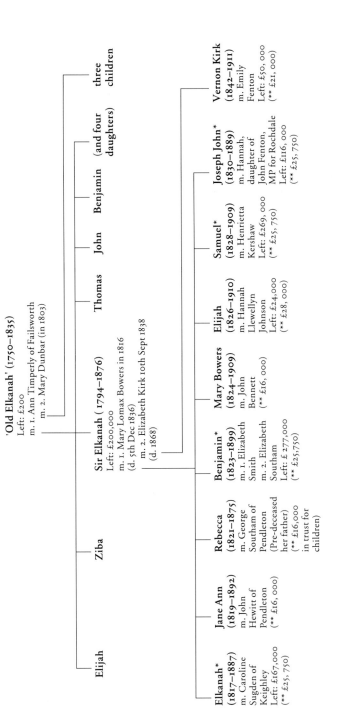

'Old Elkanah' (1750–1835)
Left: £200
m. 1. Ann Timperly of Failsworth
m. 2. Mary Dunbar (in 1803)

Elijah    Ziba    Sir Elkanah (1794–1876)    Thomas    John    Benjamin    (and four    three
                  Left: £200,000                                             daughters)   children
                  m. 1. Mary Lomax Bowers in 1816
                  (d. 5th Dec 1836)
                  m. 2. Elizabeth Kirk 10th Sept 1838
                  (d. 1868)

Elkanah*        Jane Ann       Rebecca          Benjamin*        Mary Bowers      Elijah           Samuel*          Joseph John*     Vernon Kirk
(1817–1887)     (1819–1892)    (1821–1875)      (1823–1899)      (1824–1909)      (1826–1910)      (1828–1909)      (1830–1889)      (1842–1911)
m. Caroline     m. John        m. George        m. 1. Elizabeth  m. John          m. Hannah        m. Henrietta     m. Hannah,       m. Emily
Sugden of       Hewitt of      Southam of       Smith            Bennett          Llewellyn        Kershaw          daughter of      Fenton
Keighley        Pendleton      Pendleton        m. 2. Elizabeth  (** £16, 000)    Johnson          Left: £269, 000  John Fenton,     Left: £50, 000
Left: £167,000  (** £16, 000)  (Pre-deceased    Southam                           Left: £24,000    (** £25,750)     MP for Rochdale  (** £21, 000)
(** £25, 750)                  her father)      Left: £ 277,000                   (** £28, 000)                     Left: £116, 000
                               (** £16,000      (** £25,750)                                                        (** £25,750)
                               in trust for
                               children)

* Partners in the firm
** Sum bequested in will of Sir Elkanah

Three things gave Armitage the lead in his particular branch of the textile trade: his business ability; his success in dyeing and weaving colours in such a manner as to avoid running; and, most important of all, being the first to apply the power loom to the production of his particular lines of fancy cotton prints. Eventually he looked round for a site to build a new factory and found one in Pendleton. There he built Pendleton New Mills, employing about two hundred people making fancy ginghams, checks, sailcloth and yarns. And there he prospered. Armitage was no tycoon: methodical and cautious, he was spoken of as one 'whose ventures never failed because he never ventured ... few Lancashire manufacturers in those days suffered so little from bad debts, and few ever had a more steady increase of profits'.[7]

Armitage was undoubtedly wise to be cautious: in the first decade of its existence his business at Pendleton New Mills had to survive three bouts of depression in the economy, each of which brought crops of bankruptcies. Between slumps, however, there were brisk booms from which Armitage evidently benefited, because he enlarged Pendleton New Mills in 1848 at a reputed cost of £60,000, and his workforce grew to around 600. By now the firm was said to be the most noted in Lancashire for coloured goods.[8] Armitages' prospered even more in the boom years of the mid-Victorian era, and always made it a point to instal the latest machinery. Pendleton New Mills was one of the showplaces of contemporary Manchester. In 1854 the King of Portugal and the Duke of Oporto were conducted round, and were amazed to see great weaving rooms with 600 power looms in them. Two years later, Lord Palmerston was received, and Queen Victoria paid a visit when she came to Manchester for the Great Art Treasures Exhibition. Another royal visitor, in the person of the French Empress Eugénie, was given a conducted tour in 1860. By then Armitages' had a workforce of around 1,700, the majority women, girls and young lads. There was more growth in the 1860s. By the time Sir Elkanah retired in 1873, he was the employer of around 2,500 people, including those in the firm's great warehouse in Mosley Street, Manchester.[9]

The opening of Pendleton New Mills was an important step in the development of industrial Pendleton. After the colonizing of Douglas Green, Charlestown and Croft Street, the growth of Pendleton had been fairly slow. The next developments came in the 1820s with the development of coal mining and the opening of the flax mills. The latter belonged to James Kay & Sons, an Ulster firm who brought with them their fellow countrymen to work as doffers, piecers, spinners and weavers in the mill, the first in Mill Street, by the canal. Kays' survived until the 1870s, passing to another Irish firm. The premises were eventually taken over by Mandelberg's.

In the 1820s John Purcell Fitzgerald, the owner of much of that part of Pendleton township, made efforts to develop the coal under his land, and that of other proprietors. He commenced operations in 1824 from a shaft sunk just south of the Manchester, Bolton and Bury canal, leased from the Duchy of Lancaster. In 1832 his engineer Robert Stephenson drilled through the thirty yard-thick red sandstone and found coal. Unfortunately for Fitzgerald, the main feature of the colliery's early history was a continuous struggle against water, which first flooded the workings in 1834. This was overcome, and for a time Fitzgerald expanded the business. But in the end, in December 1848, his efforts bankrupted him. The leasehold was sold to Andrew Knowles & Sons, who thereafter ran Pendleton Pit, purchasing

Pendleton New Mills, Broughton Road, Pendleton. (Photo: the author)

the site and mining rights in 1897.[10] The firm built streets of cottages down Whit Lane near the colliery, and a mining element was introduced into a population which had hitherto been largely textile in character. Close by, there were also pits at Agecroft.

At the time Armitage started Pendleton New Mills, another textile firm was opened in another part of the township. This was Ermen & Engels at Weaste. Founded by Peter Albert Ermen, a Dutchman who had emigrated to Manchester after completing his studies at Nassau in Germany, it started in 1837: no doubt because of the accession of the Queen that year, it was called 'Victoria Mill'. When he first came to Manchester, Peter Ermen had worked for a firm of shipping agents, but in the early 1830s he set up a small mill in Blackfriars, Salford. He then took two of his brothers and Friedrich Engels, senior, into partnership. They then built their new mill at Weaste. It was to learn the business that the younger Friedrich Engels came to Manchester, with consequences the whole world knows about, and remained connected with the firm until 1874. After he left, his uncles went into partnership with H. J. Roby. Three years later, they gave up the mill at Weaste, which passed to Archibald Winterbottom & Co., manufacturers of bookbinding cloth.[11]

From about 1840, then, the industrialization and urbanization of Pendleton township quickened. Elkanah Armitage saw its population grow from 11,000 (in 1841) to 26,500 (in 1871) and, triggered by the boom of the early 1870s, Pendleton's growth became phenomenal in the last three decades of the century. In Armitage's time there was a diversification of industries, with the opening of Thom's Soap Works (in the 1840s), Spence's Chemical Works and Barningham's Iron Foundry, Strawberry Road.

In 1843, not long after Pendleton New Mills opened, Armitage moved from Adelphi Terrace, Salford, to Rose Villa on the corner of Broad Street and Broughton Road. A few years later he moved to The Priory in Ford Lane, closer to the mill. In 1853, he moved again, this time to Hope Hall, two miles or so to the west, along Eccles Old Road. The extensive gardens of the Priory and other houses nearby, shown on contemporary maps, were laid out for building, and the Armitages themselves erected houses for their workers in Broughton Road, Hope Street, Smith Street, Lissadel Street and Hall Street.

The Armitages were a prolific race. Elkanah had eight children, and there existed an extensive cousinage. All his children married, and in his old age he loved to play the family patriarch, surrounded by his children, their spouses and his fifty or so grandchildren. The first objective of his life was to create a business which would provide for this posterity, and he do so with some considerable success. When the time came, each of his sons were given a chance to join the firm, which became Elkanah Armitage & Son in 1842, when Elkanah junior was given an interest, and Elkanah Armitage & Sons two years later when Benjamin was made a partner. In their turn Samuel and Joseph John became members. The only son of his first marriage who did not stay with the business (for reasons, it seems, of ill-health) was Elijah; Vernon Kirk, the child of his second marriage, did not join either. The positions Armitage's sons took in the firm were later somewhat folksily described by a local writer: 'Young Elkanah was learning weaving and "bossing" ... Sam was learning spinning, Elijah jobbing, and then went to farming: Ben and Joe were selling, and Vernon Kirk toiled not neither did he spin, for he went for a lawyer'.[12]

The coloured goods business provided handsomely for all of them, non-members of the firm as well as members, female as well as male. After his death, Sir Elkanah's personal fortune was assessed at £200,000 for probate purposes. He bequeathed £16,000 to each of his surviving daughters, Jane Hewitt and Mary Bennett, and the same in trust for the children of Rebecca Southam, his other daughter, who pre-deceased him, and doubtless each had received a suitable dowry when they married. To Elijah, of High House, Kendal, he made a bequest of £28,000, and to Vernon Kirk, £21,000: the rest and residue was divided equally between his other sons.[13] Each of these had, of course, benefited from their part in the business for many years. All died considerably richer than Elijah or Vernon, the 'non members', and two of them, Benjamin and Samuel, died worth more than Sir Elkanah himself. The Armitages were, (at least for as long as Sir Elkanah lived), a close-knit family. After his move to Hope Hall, an old mansion with some land attached, his sons settled close by with their families: Elkanah at the Rookery, Benjamin first at Bank House, and later at Chomlea, Samuel at Seedley House and then at Chaseley, and Joseph John at Chaseley Field, which he built in 1868.

Doubtless Sir Elkanah bought Hope Hall for reasons of status, as well as the fact that it afforded the opportunity to his children to settle with their families close by. His possession of it was probably the reason why he alone of Salford's prominent capitalists, some of whom were considerably richer, got an entry in A. B. Thom's *The Upper Ten Thousand for 1876. A Biographical Handbook of all the Titled and Official Classes of the Kingdom* (1876), though another reason might have been that in 1866 he had served the office of High Sheriff of the County. The cultural influence of England's titled and official classes was certainly a factor in Armitage's considerations as he grew rich and became one of Manchester's leading citizens. Yet Sir Elkanah's economic and political philosophy was always Cobdenite; behind it there was the provincial businessman's hostility to hereditary power based on land. Moreover, as a Dissenter, Armitage had little affection for the religion of England's ruling élite. His children, or at any rate those of his first marriage, were brought up as Congregationalists. They were educated at home, and, though Benjamin was sent to a Moravian school in Yorkshire, none went to public school. The family generally stayed Dissenters, worshipping with Sir Elkanah at Hope Street, Chapel, Pendleton and then Eccles Congregational Chapel, towards the building of which they contributed handsomely.

However, not all died Dissenters. In his late years, Elkanah, the eldest son, attended St James, Hope, though he never ceased to make contributions to the Congregational body, or so it was said.[14] The truth was, that as they became rich, married into other families, moved in other circles, different influences began to impinge on the Armitages. In this they were not untypical of their class and time. The effect on the Armitages of rising in the world can best be seen in the case of Vernon Kirk Armitage. Born in 1842, he was twelve years younger than Joseph John, the youngest of Elkanah's first family. Vernon's mother was Eliza Kirk, daughter of Henry Kirk of Chapel-en-le-Frith, Derbyshire, whom Armitage married in 1838, just over a year after he was widowed. The Kirks had some landed and military connections,[15] and Vernon, the only child of the three Eliza Armitage bore to survive childhood, was given a very different education to that of his step-brothers. Educated at Harrow and Trinity College, Cambridge, and, as a young man a cricketer good enough to play for the Gentlemen of England, it is perhaps not surprising that Vernon Armitage did not join the firm. In the 1860s the Gentlemen of England did not manufacture anything, let alone coloured goods. For a time he practised as a barrister, but gave it up to live off his income. And yet, he was, and remained, very much a son of Sir Elkanah. His main interest was politics. Several times he tried to get into Parliament, and was unlucky not to do so. Instead, he had to be content with a place on the Salford Council and later one on the Lancashire County Council, of which he became an Alderman. For some years he lived at Swinton Park, near to the rest of his family, though in later life he succumbed to the attractions of Birkdale.[16]

What made Elkanah run? Money was always the key, and Armitage and his sons made plenty. Yet for them, and for him in particular, wealth was not an end in itself. As soon as he could, Armitage began to involve himself in other things, leaving the running of the business to his sons and managers. From the time he was about forty Armitage began to play a part in public affairs. For him, as for many another of his type and generation, public recognition was a necessary accompaniment of business success: *fame was the spur.*

Armitage's public career began in 1833. He was one of the group of Dissenters associated with Joseph Brotherton. In that year he became a Salford Police

Commissioner, and served his time as Chairman of the Town Hall and Markets and Watch Committees. The parliamentary election of 1835 saw him very active in the South Lancashire Reform Association, and he closely supported Brotherton in all his election battles. Two years later he was nominated borough-reeve, and it fell to him to lay the stone to mark the opening of Victoria Bridge, which replaced the ancient one linking Salford to Manchester.

However, in 1838 Armitage moved into the bigger arena of Manchester politics. Closer, perhaps, to the mainly Unitarian group around Thomas Potter and John Edward Taylor than to the Bible Christians and Swedenborgians around Brotherton, he became an active participant in the movement to incorporate Manchester. Ever ready to back his convictions with his money, Armitage stood as one of the financial guarantors of the campaign to secure a borough charter from the Privy Council. He became a protagonist in the remarkably rancorous struggle which ensued. In this Armitage and his friends emerged triumphant over old Tory ruling élite, and the fruits of victory were soon theirs. In December 1838 he was elected to Manchester's first municipal council. 1838 was something of an *annus mirabilis* in his life. As well as getting on to the council he joined the first provisional committee of the Anti Corn Law Association, and was therefore in at the very start of the movement which was to play a formative part in his life and opinions. He also began to build Pendleton New Mills. It was in the large room there, empty as yet of machinery, that Brotherton celebrated his victory over Garnett with his speech 'I am for the move-along system ...'.[17] That year Elkanah also married Eliza Kirk.

Armitage was a member of Manchester Corporation for over a quarter of a century. In his time he served on virtually all of its committees, and for long periods was Chairman of the Watch and the Waterworks Committees. Though never much of a speaker, Armitage was well suited to the work of local administration. A close attender to detail, he was above all resolute in seeing matters to their conclusion, no matter how long it took. His rise to the top was remarkably rapid. By 1841 he was an alderman and one of the borough's first magistrates, and was Mayor from 1846 to 1848. All this was as much to do with circumstance as talent. Defeated over the charter of incorporation, the Tories boycotted the first council election, and for the next few years dissipated their energies contesting the legality of the charter and what the new borough council was doing. The Whigs and liberals were handed a monopoly in municipal matters, and Armitage was one whose career benefited.[18]

By the time Armitage became Mayor, controversy had been largely resolved. But only just. These local battles had been fierce and bitter. The borough-reeve and constables, the churchwardens and the Manchester Police Commissioners had done all they could to obstruct the new council. They had denied it use of the Town Hall, obstructed it over finance and the transfer of judicial business from the hundred to the borough, and had opposed it over the police. So confused was the situation, that in the end the government stepped in and appointed a special Chief Commissioner of Police, Sir Charles Shaw, to hold the ring. When Shaw arrived he found Manchester had no less than three law enforcement bodies. By the time Shaw's term expired in October 1842, this period of disputed jurisdictions was largely over. The validity of the 1838 Charter had been tested in court and upheld, and 'adjustments' were being made with the Anti-incorporators. In victory, Armitage and his friends were not generous to their opponents.[19]

All this had taken place against a background of deep depression, two Chartist crises (which Sir Charles Shaw had had to police) and the agitation for the Repeal of the Corn Laws. Like Brotherton, Armitage was in that great cause from first to last. He was platform man, one of the League's proposers and seconders, and a committee member whose time and income was always at the disposal of the promoters of Free Trade. In November 1842 he was 'a hundred pound man' when the League raised a fighting fund of £50,000. Three years later he pledged £500 towards another.[20] Free trade was the cause of Manchester's businessmen, but it was especially dear to Dissenters, uniting, as it were, God and Mammon. Not only did it coincide with their economic interests, it also gave them the psychological satisfaction of having a political issue they could invest with overtones of morality. If the battle for Free Trade was a vehicle for the political emancipation of their men, it also offered opportunities for their women. Mrs Armitage and a Miss Armitage were much involved in the great League Bazaar of February 1842, and many a bourgeois marriage was contracted from family friendships made in the cause of Free Trade. One particular friendship the Armitages made at this time was with the Brights. The oratorial gifts of the Rochdale Quaker made him a hero with the extreme Free Traders and leading Dissenters, though it upset the more staid elements in liberal Manchester. Armitage and his friends were delighted when Bright was elected MP for Manchester in 1846, on the retirement of Mark Philips. The Armitages were friends with the Brights over three generations. They shared the pleasure of John Bright's triumphs and fame, and they also had to suffer the pains of his rejection. But, in 1846, all that was in the future.

The repeal of the Corn Laws was achieved just weeks before Armitage was elected Mayor of Manchester in late 1846. By then the corporation was pushing ahead with improvement schemes, and in his time in office Armitage was involved in a number of these. Several main streets were widened and new ones constructed; Blackfriars Bridge was freed of tolls; a Markets Improvement Bill was secured, (the manorial rights having been purchased the year previously from Sir Oswald Mosley), and in 1846 work commenced on the new borough goal in Hyde Road. Mayor Armitage also became involved in the negotiation and bargaining that preceded the construction of the Woodhead reservoirs, regarded in their time as one of the finest achievements of English local government. Armitage's role in this was important: for seventeen years he was Chairman of the Waterworks Committee, and the problems of presiding over the project, not finally completed until the 1880s, made him frequently express the regret that he was not a man of science as well as a man of business. In those years his application and resolution served Manchester's civic interests well.[21] They also served him well over the matter for which his mayoralty was remembered, and for which a grateful government gave him a knighthood: the political crisis of 1848.

The editorial in the *Northern Star* of 18 March 1848 was headed 'THE COMING STRUGGLE. THE BEGINNING OF THE END', and ended 'France has a republic. England must have the Charter!' Amongst members of the National Charter Association and the National Land Company there was a strong feeling that it was now or never. The Irish saw it as a chance to press home their demand for the Repeal of the Union. All could see what insurrection had achieved in Paris. The English situation was, however, much more problematical. Once again, the Chartist, and indeed the Irish leaders, were faced with the dilemma of wanting their objectives gained peacefully, via Parliament, and the need to use the rhetoric of violence both to bring their own people on to the streets and to pressurise the government. As the situation developed, the questions for Mayor Armitage were, did the Irish and the Chartists mean it? If they did, how to meet it? For his part, Armitage had no intention of presiding over another Peterloo.

Since early 1846 the fortunes of Manchester Chartism had been on the upturn. The Chartist Land Plan was flourishing: by early 1848 there were 4,000 members in Manchester.[22] The most important factor was the appalling level of unemployment, which had been growing for more than a year. In no place was it worse that in South East Lancashire. As early as February 1847 half the mills in Manchester were said to be on short time, and by then some had been stopped eleven weeks.[23] The army of the unemployed included thousands of hand-loom weavers. By 1848 these were very desperate men. Most were outside Manchester and Salford, though there were pockets inside the city whose plight shocked people. A deputation to the Mayor, with a request for him to convene a public meeting to assess the unemployment problem, was met with a straight refusal.[24] For Armitage, unemployment was a result of market forces, and there was nothing local authorities or public meetings could (or even should) do.

The crisis which faced the authorities in March 1848 was triply serious, in that it had an Irish as well as a Chartist dimension to compound the economic unrest. It had always been an ambition of Feargus O'Connor's to unite the English and Irish workers behind Chartism. Until that very month it had proved impossible. As early as 1833 O'Connell had opposed O'Connor's politics, and most Irishmen followed O'Connell.[25] They joined his Precursor Society, well established in Irish centres by 1838. The Manchester Irish also supported O'Connell's next campaign – the Repeal of the Union. Their network of Repeal branches was a rival organisation to Chartism and to the Anti Corn Law League. Irish priests were at one with O'Connell in their dislike of trade unionism and Chartism. In Manchester, Father Hearne played an important part: 'virtually every Chartist attempt at fraternization with the local Repealers was frustrated by the vigilance of this Irish-born priest.'[26] Like O'Connell, Hearne favoured the League's programme of cheap food and free trade to Chartism's 'one man, one vote'. And he also shared the views of the Dissenting League leaders on such issues as Temperance. As already noted, relations between Chartists and Irish Repealers deteriorated into physical confrontation in 1841 – 42. In retaliation for the use of Chartist physical force to disrupt Free Trade meetings, the League made an agreement with the Repealers and used Manchester Irishmen to turn the tables on the Chartists.

Despite many efforts, in the next few years Chartism signally failed to win over the Irish. Neither the Famine nor the secession of the Young Ireland group from the Repeal Association (in July 1846) made any difference: Young Irelanders showed no desire to co-operate with Chartists. After O'Connell's death (in May 1847) most Irish stayed loyal to his Repeal Association. When the Irish Confederation, a rival nationalist organisation, was founded, Chartist hopes were raised. Led by Young Irelanders, it attracted a sizeable minority away from the O'Connellite body to press for a vigorous but peaceful agitation for Repeal. By the end of 1847 there was a network of Confederate Clubs in Manchester and Salford. However, these Irish organisations remained opposed to Chartism, and, on the grounds that they seemed to have no interest in parliamentary democracy, Chartism was opposed to them.

Yet, only a few weeks later, O'Connor's dream of an entente had come about, for two reasons. The first was the decision, under the influence of the radical ideas of James Fintan Lalor on the Confederate Council, to press for Ulster tenant right to be extended to the rest of Ireland. This opening up to new ideas led to contacts with the Chartists, and there was a visit to Dublin by some Manchester leaders, and a joint rally was planned for Manchester on St Patrick's Day, 17 March 1848. The second reason was the effect of the French Revolution, which had a big impact on Irishmen of all shades: physical force could no longer be ruled out. In Manchester a joint committee of Confederates, 'Conciliation Hall Repealers' and Chartists was established 'to watch passing events and to act as might be required'.[27]

There followed six months of tension and pressure on the civil authorities, especially on Armitage, as Mayor of Manchester, and William Jenkinson, Salford's first Tory Mayor. As in all the Chartist crises there was an out-of-town dimension: would the Chartists and Irish from the Bolton, Oldham and Ashton districts converge on Manchester and join up with their allies in the great city? In these six months, there were in fact three periods of crisis. The first, and perhaps most serious was in March and April. It was triggered by the events in Paris and the sufferings of the unemployed. Some of the largest open air-meetings ever to take place in Manchester were held. Armitage received deputations of handloom weavers at the town hall to put the case for relief of the unemployed, to petition for the release of Frost, Williams and Jones, and to press the case for justice for Ireland. Huge joint Chartist-Irish meetings were addressed by O'Connor and Daniel Donovan, the Manchester leader, to protest over the arrest of Smith, O'Brien, Meagher and Mitchel.[28] On 4 April, the Chartist National Convention assembled in London and the familiar debate about tactics commenced once more. Situated between the discontents of the people and a government which showed no sign of yielding, it was decided to convey the third Chartist petition to Parliament on 10 April, accompanied by a vast procession, which was to assemble on Kennington Common. As with the other petitions this was rejected by Parliament, and with its presentation the Chartist movement peaked for the last time. After ten years, it had finally run its course. Democracy seemed no nearer.

For the crisis of March/April 1848 to have become a revolution the authorities would have needed to have been ill-prepared and irresolute. Anxious they certainly were, but never anything other than well-prepared and resolute. In Manchester most of the credit for the way they handled the crisis lies with Armitage. His leadership was firm, well-prepared and confident. To the Chartists and Irishmen he was defensive, unprovocative, conciliatory. At the start, to back-up the police and the regular army, there in force, great numbers of special constables were sworn for six months. The two boroughs were divided into well-patrolled 'police districts'. When tensions rose, the bridges and toll bars were guarded, and the alarm was to be raised by the ringing of church bells. Armitage also recruited a 'town hall guard', chiefly clerks and porters from the warehouses, some of whom were mounted. Their role was to keep the centre constantly in touch with the periphery. Armitage made his name by his constant presence at the Town Hall, being at his desk at 5.00 a.m. each morning, and never going home for several nights in succession at the height of this April crisis.[29]

There was a second peak in early June. A demonstration of Irish Repealers and Chartists, planned for 31 May to protest against the sentence of 14 years' transportation handed down to Mitchel, was banned by Armitage. An attempt to put on a massive show of strength in Manchester was made by calling on the men from the out-townships to converge on the city and link up with the local Chartists and Irish. Backed by solders, the police and specials dampened the crisis by making it impossible for open-air meetings to be held in Manchester. It was only in such places as Failsworth that crowds could gather, and they could not get into the town because the toll bars were heavily guarded. The great fear was that the men from Oldham would march on Manchester, and the old Radical, W. H. Chadwick, tried to raise them, but failed. Rank-and-file anger was then turned on their leaders, and the second crisis of 1848 was over.[30] In the days following, there was a round-up of leading Chartists, many being sent to prison.

The final peak came in August. Late in July, the Irish Confederate Clubs in Manchester and Salford held a demonstration at which 3,000 well-drilled and disciplined men formed up in ranks, in a quasi-military show of strength. This caused great unease and Mayor Armitage put the police, the fire brigade and the specials on alert. Early in August, Smith O'Brien was arrested, and by the third week of the month Manchester was in a state of excitement, with talk once more of Irish, Chartists and colliers planning to march on the city. Inside Manchester and Salford, the Chartists and Confederates congregated in their clubs, closely watched by the police. The plan (if there was one) failed once again because the out-districts failed to arrive. Once more, the crisis was followed by another round-up of Chartist and Irish leaders. By early October all talk of physical force was over. The Mayor was informed that Chartists were currently turning their creativity towards co-operative provision shops.[31]

The events of the past six months marked the end of an era whose beginnings went back to the situation after the end of the Napoleonic Wars, or even to 1812. Political Radicalism in its old form had reached the end of its particular road. The significance of Mayor Armitage's contribution to the defeat of the Manchester Chartists and Irish did not pass unrecognised. At the end of October, a grateful government informed him that Her Majesty wished to bestow a knighthood upon him. If fame was the spur, by 1849 fame was what he had achieved.

One of Armitage's last duties as Mayor was to open the new borough goal in Hyde Road: it seems appropriate, symbolic even. An era of turbulence had come to an end: the authorities were firmly in the saddle. When Queen Victoria visited in 1851 the contrast with 1848 could not have been more marked. 'The order and good behaviour of the people, who were not behind any barriers', wrote the Queen, 'were the most complete we have seen in our many progresses through capitals and cities ... Everyone says that in no other town could one depend so entirely upon the quiet and orderly behaviour of the people as in Mancheter'.[32]

Sir Elkanah Armitage was a prominent Manchester figure for another two decades, but for him, as for his friends, the great days were the 1840s. There was no cause the Reformer party fought in which he was not involved. He was prominent in the movement to secure a half day holiday on Saturdays for the Manchester warehouses, which achieved success in 1843. As a strong Dissenter, he supported the Liberation Society, gave generously to the building of Congregational Chapels, and supported his co-religionists when they crossed swords with the Church on the education issue. When the Manchester Society for the Repeal of Taxes on Knowledge was set up in 1852 he was invited to be its first president.[33] He supported the Reform party in the battles with the foeffees of Manchester Grammar School, and when the Court of Chancery came down on the Reformers' side, Armitage played his part in laying the foundation of that School's nineteenth-century success. He was one of the first trustees in 1849, and was chairman until shortly before his death. When he died, his part in the rebuilding of the School in 1870–71 was recalled.[34]

The early years of Armitage's public career seemed one long catalogue of triumphs for his brand of liberalism: Parliamentary Reform, Municipal Reform, the defeat of Chartism, the Repeal of the Corn Laws. The latter gave its supporters immense pleasure: they felt they had won a great ideological battle. So they had: but it was not as important as they thought. The real rulers of England took Free Trade on board in much the same way as they had accepted political economy in the 1820s: they simply *absorbed* it, and carried on. A new political situation soon emerged in which Armitage and his friends found themselves marginalised rather brutally. But before that, he was to have one more triumph. Although it was merely a dispute between him and his workers, the Pendleton Weavers lock-out was also a significant confrontation in local industrial history. Its outcome further strengthened Armitage's image as the knight with the grim visage.

On the morning of 19 September 1850 a trade union deputation went to see Armitage to try to negotiate a pay rise for the weavers at Pendleton New Mills. They were told to their faces that in twenty years in business he had never negotiated with any trade union, and did not intend to start now. When the workpeople came back after breakfast the doors stayed closed and the bell silent: Armitage had locked them out.[35] In all they were idle for 35 weeks. Down to the 53 week carpenters' and joiners' strike of 1877 it was the longest single dispute in Victorian Manchester, a classic example of the way the struggle between Capital and Labour was fought at that time.

The depression of 1847–8 was followed by a boom which carried on for most of the Fifties. In times of depression trade unions often collapsed, only to re-form when things revived. The Power Loom Weavers of Great Britain was just such a union. In 1850 its stronghold was in the mills of Armitages' competitors at Stand and Radcliffe. When the union discovered that the firm was paying wages lower than in their district, its organiser, Matthew Shaw, stepped in. He argued that low wage firms like Armitages' were bad for good wage firms, like Farrars of Radcliffe, and urged his Pendleton members to press for equal wages. From the very start,

Sir Elkanah's object was to break the union, and he applied himself to this with his customary resolution.

To his great annoyance, the dispute became a public issue when it was reported in Abel Heywood's *Manchester Spectator*, which, from the start, took the workers' side. It reported Armitage was paying eight to ten shillings a week compared to the twelve shillings average of the 'high wage' employers. To refute this, Armitage bought space on the front page of the *Manchester Guardian*.[36] In over two columns of print he listed every single one of his employees by name with their earnings over the previous three weeks. The *Guardian*, the mouthpiece of the manufacturers, was consistently pro-Armitage and alleged that the *Spectator* was the union's dupe.

Industrial disputes are rarely resolved in the columns of newspapers. This developed into a contest between an employer who was determined to lock-out his workers, the majority of whom were female, until they submitted, and a union which felt it was financially strong enough to support its members until the employer gave way. In an attempt to break the union, other employers in the vicinity, became involved in disputes with *their* workers. Very soon the union was having to support almost a thousand workers and their children in Pendleton and Swinton. Help came from union members in Stand and Radcliffe, and from the Central Committee of Factory Operatives, representing Oldham, Ashton, Royton, Droylsden and Gorton. Some employers gave in and agreed to pay the union rate. Armitage was made of sterner stuff. He kept production going and recruited blackleg labour. He turned down all efforts at mediation.

In Pendleton, Armitage's efforts to recruit blackleg labour was regarded as going too far. The Rev. Thomas Lee, minister of New Windsor Independent Chapel stepped in. At a public meeting he did not mince his words. He declared Sir Elkanah was the sort of man 'who, to gain his purpose, is capable of starving the very operatives who have made him what he is'.[37] To appeal to public opinion, Lee began a weekly *Trades Union Magazine and Precursor of a Peoples Newspaper*, which started on the 23 November 1850 in the ninth week of the dispute, and came out regularly until the following May. Lee's main intention was to report what was happening in Pendleton, but, as an avowed Christian Socialist, used the dispute to advocate the cause of Co-operation.[38]

One offshoot of the dispute was the Whit Lane Weaving Company, run on co-operative lines. Co-operative production, or 'Associative Labour', was much in the news at the time, and several ventures were launched, including the Salford Universal Family Society, which had a store and a shop which produced shirting. The Pendleton weavers co-operative leased a small mill and set about raising two thousand pounds. By March 1851, much to Armitage's annoyance, they were in production. For a while the project was 'quite the co-operative lion of Manchester and its neighbourhood'.[39] For a year or so it employed fifty people weaving nankeens, florentines, ticks, regattas and stripes. It created widespread interest. Hotfoot to Pendleton came leading Christian Socialists. At New Year 1851 Lee shared a platform with Professor F. D. Maurice of Kings College, London, and Thomas Hughes the barrister, author of *Tom Brown's Schooldays*, to air co-operation, Christian Socialism and to publicise the new Pendleton Mechanics' Institute.[40]

These developments did something to fortify the morale of the men and women out of work. However, after facing a bleak Christmas, some were giving in, and the union admitted that Sir Elkanah was to keep production going. Outside the mill, blackleg workers had to run a gauntlet of hooting crowds, which assembled each day. In January, Armitage brought prosecutions for intimidation with, however, very little success.[41] From the 17th week, the union's expenditure was greater than its income, though it was prepared to fight on. A second attempt at mediation was made, but failed to move Armitage from his opposition to standard rates of pay. In the *Trades Union Magazine* of 25 January 1851, Lee, in an open letter to Joseph Brotherton, publically accused Armitage of trying to starve his workers back. Armitage replied in the columns of the *Guardian* and the *Spectator*.[42]

On 3 May Lee's magazine reported 'Sir E. Armitage thinks he has conquered his opponents', and the *Manchester Spectator* reported the end of the dispute on 17 May. With strike pay gone, many weavers had returned to their looms. Armitage had won a great victory, and one with far-reaching consequences. The great Pendleton lock-out was never so much about pay as union recognition. Though the union at Stand and Ratcliffe soon revived, there was no women's union in Pendleton for half a century. Addressing a meeting in 1909 in connection with the recently formed Manchester, Salford and Pendleton district of the Textile Weavers' Amalgamation, its president declared, 'Manchester was the black spot in the weaving industry as regards wages, and the women workers were paid anything from ten to twenty five per cent less than the standard list in the trade in the Lancashire towns ... In Manchester the women lacked organisation.'[43] Armitage's victory was thus a major one, long remembered. Down to the Great War, the firm never had another strike.

Of the other protagonists, the Rev. T. G. Lee remained at New Windsor

The former Pendleton Mechanics' Institute, Gardner Street, Pendleton. (Photo: the author)

Congregational Chapel until he retired in 1877. He retained his Christian Socialism, campaigned against the Crimean War, preached Temperance, and from time to time did battle with his congregation. He was the first clergyman of any denomination in Salford who took the side of the working class in a dispute.[44] Abel Heywood's *Spectator* did not survive very long, but Heywood became a successful publisher and book seller, a prominent Liberal and a future Mayor of Manchester.[45] The Whit Lane Co-operative Weaving Company ceased production in 1852, and its affairs ended in confusion. The organisation to survive longest was Pendleton Mechanics' Institute. In 1857 it moved into purpose-built premises in Gardner Street, and survived as an adult education institution until 1874, when its buildings became a branch of the borough library.[46]

After his triumph in Pendleton in May 1851, Armitage was liberal Manchester's foremost hard man. If military rank had been bestowed in the class war, Armitage would surely have been a Major-General. No-one underestimated his importance, least of all the Government: in 1853 Sir Elkanah was made a Deputy-Lieutenant for the County Palatine of Lancaster. All the signs were that further social distinctions lay in wait.

In the early 1850s Sir Elkanah and his friends in Newall's Buildings could have been forgiven for feeling bullish. Their economic and political objectives had been achieved: their Conservative enemies were split, and soon to be beaten out of sight. In the election of 1847, Bright, Milner Gibson and Brotherton were all returned unopposed. In 1848 the League leaders presided over the policing of Chartism's last hurrah. However, political victories recede rapidly into history. It took time to become apparent, but from 1848 Sir Elkanah and his friends began to flounder. They were clear as to which path of Reform *they* wanted to follow: what they could not do was to reconstitute a movement similar to that for Free Trade.

In May 1848, in response to an initiative from the (short-lived) Chartist Universal Suffrage Association they launched their so-called 'New Movement'. But the programme of the New Movement aroused little interest when League branches were circulated.[47] It slowly became clear that, in the middle-class electorate at large, there was no support for new initiatives on Reform. The Chartist initiative also collapsed: after 1848 the non-electors, too, were disillusioned.

Discerning perhaps that the logic of events pointed to an alliance between middle- and working-class Radicals, meetings were convened in Manchester in the summer of 1848 by the People's League, another short-lived body, consisting of the sort of men who, for some time, had argued that the only way further Reform could be achieved was by an alliance across class. But this initiative also sputtered out.[48] Much had to be suffered by Radicals of all complexions before a party emerged which could gather them all in. Early the following year another initiative, which originated with the Liverpool Financial Reform Association, was launched with a banquet to mark the final abolition of the Corn Laws, but it came to little. There were also fresh moves to create a platform in Manchester on which Financial Reformers, the People's League and such advocates of cross-class co-operation as Abel Heywood could unite.

There were, however, factors working against the development of a grouping on these lines. To the bulk of Manchester Whig and liberal opinion the continued existence of the League increasingly seemed a wilful provocation. In particular, they disliked Bright for attacking the politicians at Westminster. Jeremiah Garnett's *Manchester Guardian* voiced this opposition to Bright, portraying him and his friends (including Sir Elkanah) as 'extremists', out of touch with 'moderate' opinion.[49]

In 1851 Stowell and his followers took their chance to drive a wedge into the Protestant Dissenters, attacking Bright for his opposition to the Ecclesiastical Titles Bill. Politically more dangerous to Bright and his friends was, however, their opposition to Palmerston's aggressive foreign policy, and the *Guardian* began a long campaign of bitter criticism over this.[50] They were to find that being branded unpatriotic was much more damaging than being accused of being unprotestant.

An opportunity for the Financial and Reform Association to bounce back from all this came in February 1852 with the fall of the Whig government. Seizing upon a fear that Lord Derby was contemplating the re-introduction of tariffs, they laid on a bit of old style League politicking. Free Trade meetings were called, to which former activists responded eagerly. A fighting fund to defend Free Trade raised £35,000 within days, and Sir Elkanah contributed his mite, in this instance £500.[51] However, the threat of Protectionism was short-lived: Lord Derby's government lasted only a few months before a general election was called.

Sir Elkanah was heavily involved: closely in touch with Brotherton in Salford, he was also chairman of John Cheetham's committee in South Lancashire. In the event both were returned unopposed. The real battle was in Manchester, where an alliance of Conservatives, Whigs and moderate liberals emerged to try to unseat Bright and Milner Gibson. Sir Elkanah was the treasurer of the latter pair's election committee. Opposing them was the so-called 'Manchester Independent Electors Committee', formed to support candidates of 'Liberal but moderate political views'. Largely a Conservative organisation, it was led by Stowell's Evangelical friends. The champions they brought to the hustings were the Hon. Captain Denman, RN, and James Loch, the Earl of Ellesmere's agent. Though not local men, both had powerful connections. To the chagrin of this coalition, their attack was insufficient to unseat Bright and Milner Gibson, whose supporters were brought out by the cry 'Free Trade in danger'.[52]

Sir Elkanah and his friends celebrated with an enormous Free Trade and Reform banquet on 2nd November. Nearly three thousand people, including 42 MPs, sat down to dinner in the Free Trade Hall. From the chair George Wilson referred proudly to the League's ability to revive itself when Free Trade was threatened, and to the huge sum (£70,000) they had raised. Described as 'the last blow on the head of the last nail in the coffin of Protectionism', this banquet was seen as a demonstration of the League's strength and determination.[53] So it was. But it was the last. Within five years the ambition to make it the focus of a new Radical party of Reform was scotched by a terrible defeat.

What alienated the moderates from the friends of John Bright was their refusal to keep quiet on Reform and their opposition to the Crimean War, which began in March 1854. For over a year the Radicals had watched the Near Eastern crisis develop, and denounced the aggressive anti-Russian posture of the Foreign Minister and the government. Most of the battles in the Crimea which aroused the patriotic gore of the nation – the Alma, Balaclava, Inkerman and the start of the siege of Sebastapol – took place before the end of 1854. Bright's famous letter to Absolom Watkin, in which he argued that Britain had no right to intervene in the Russo-Turkish War, and that action should have stopped with the recommendations of the Vienna Note (which Russia accepted), was printed in the *Manchester Guardian* of 8 November, just after the bloody battle of the Alma, and at a time when local energy and interest was involved in the raising of a Patriotic Fund. At a protest meeting prominent Manchester Free Traders disassociated themselves from Bright's letter: a list of their names appeared on the *Guardian's* front page. Bright was burned in effigy at New Cross, with a placard round his neck inscribed 'The Friend of Nicholas'.[54]

His friends, including Sir Elkanah, rallied round at his annual meeting with his constituents in January 1855. All the local middle-class Radicals (except Brotherton) were there, and leading Dissenting ministers lent support by their presence. In a great speech Bright attacked the government and the war. Sir Elkanah was one of a deputation which, in March, took a memorial containing 11,000 signatures to the Prime Minister requesting the government to suspend hostilities during the diplomatic meetings at Vienna. Palmerston cheerfully told them that he was unconvinced by their arguments.[55]

The long drawn-out siege of Sebastapol (which did not fall until September) gave the Peace Party the chance to attack the conduct of the war, the competence of the army, the raising of Palmerston to the premiership and the arrogant and intoxicated state of the nation. This provoked a furious counter-attack in the press, and when Cobden's pamphlet *What Next – and Next?* appeared, a movement to 'de-select' Bright and Milner Gibson started in Manchester. Palmerston led the country to victory in the first war since 1815 seriously to inflame British patriotism, and his visit to Manchester in November 1856 (which included a visit to Pendleton New Mills and Peel Park Library and Museum) was little short of a Roman triumph.[56] The *Guardian* rejoiced in it as a severe blow to Bright and Cobden. Just how severe was soon to become apparent.

When Brotherton died in January 1857, Armitage was at the height of his involvement in public affairs. As a temporary arrangement it was agreed by all parties in Salford that E. R. Langworthy should have the unopposed nomination as a tribute to his status and generosity to Salford. Sir Elkanah served as chairman of the committee. What made Langworthy so acceptable as the new Member for Salford was that he would be a presentable specimen of the Northern businessman in Parliament, and that he had no intention of staying long. A general election was not far away. Langworthy was in Parliament only a matter of weeks, and liked it no better than most businessmen. The election was caused by the sensational defeat of Lord Palmerston in the House of Commons in early March 1857, largely the work of Cobden (Bright had suffered a serious nervous breakdown and had been absent for the session). In his attack on the government's policy towards China and Persia (which led to its defeat by 16 votes), Cobden was supported by Gladstone. Westminster had not witnessed scenes like it since the Repeal of the Corn Laws.[57]

In Manchester, their supporters began preparations to re-elect Bright and Milner Gibson, Sir Elkanah being committee treasurer. It was clear the 1857 election was going to be difficult to win: there was no 'Free Trade in Danger' flag to wave and businessmen were strongly pro-Palmerston over China and Persia. More widely, middle-class opinion was clearly against the Cobdenite 'peace at any price' philosophy, bourgeois Manchester having convinced itself that there were more honourable things in life than the promotion of trade and the pursuit of profit. A very strong committee, which combined liberals and Conservatives, was formed to return two prominent local figures, Sir John Potter, son of Manchester's first Mayor, himself an ex-Mayor, and James Aspinall Turner, a Unitarian cotton manufacturer, chairman of the Manchester Commercial Association. With Bright still convalescing in Rome, their supporters were confident they would oust the League from the representation of Manchester.[58]

The situation in Salford was somewhat less clear, not least because it had been fifteen years since there had been a contested election. Party organisation (such as it was) had long since disintegrated, and some confusion was evident in a public meeting called to discuss the representation of the borough, Langworthy having stood down. Pro- and anti-Palmerston feelings were expressed, as was a call for a man with local connections 'to represent the interests of moderate persons on both sides'. Cobden's name was proposed. Cobden seriously considered standing, and came to Salford to discuss matters, well aware that Sir Elkanah's hat was in the ring. In the end Cobden elected to take his chance in Huddersfield, and commended Sir Elkanah to liberal voters. At an election meeting a few days later, Armitage indicated that he was aware of the difficulties facing him when he declared himself a free-trader, and an 'independent pledged to neither Cobden nor Lord Palmerston' at that time.[59] He fooled no one.

As for the Palmerstonians, Oliver Heywood, suggested as an Anti-League candidate, declined to stand, preferring the role of *eminence grise*, supplying his own replacement in the person of W. N. Massey, a professional politician with no local connections. Until the dissolution MP for Newport, Isle of Wight, and Under Secretary of State at the Home Office, Massey knew what he was about in coming to Salford. On his first appearance he said all the right things. As an old free trader, he flattered Cobden. He stoutly defended Palmerston's foreign policy and the Crimean War. On Reform, he pronounced himself cautiously against, unless it was 'reasonable and moderate'. A member of the Church of England, Massey made the sort of anti-Tractarian remarks that commended him to Evangelicals. In proposing Massey to his election meeting, Thomas Baines Potter (Sir John's brother), reflected on how they in Manchester and Salford had too long suffered under 'the tyrannies of the League', and how his late father had been the only man in Manchester who could handle them. It was apparent that Massey was going to enjoy broadly-based support.[60]

At the election of March 1857 the Prophets were well and truly Stoned. Massey defeated Sir Elkanah in Salford, Turner and Potter ousted Bright and Milner Gibson in Manchester and Cobden lost at Huddersfield. The election was one great Palmerstonian victory, and the League virtually disappeared from parliament. The Peelites were damaged and scattered, though Gladstone was emerging as an

Armitage's vanquisher: W. N. Massey, Palmerstonian MP for Salford, 1857–65. (*Illustrated London News*)

important figure. The Whigs, under Lord John Russell, survived scarcely strong enough to impede the actions of the government.

Massey had scored a remarkable victory in Salford. A total stranger, arriving only a few days before the election, he got in with the substantial majority of 616, receiving 1,880 votes to Sir Elkanah's 1,264.[61] Yet his victory had little to do with him personally and Armitage's defeat was not in any important way due to *his* defects. What Armitage stood for was out of tune with the middle-class electorate which shared Palmerston's scepticism over Reform and endorsed the aggressive patriotism of his foreign policy. The judgements of history (though they always depend on who is making them) are often less severe than the judgements of contemporaries: in the long term the ideas of the Manchester School Radicals ('Peace, Retrenchment and Reform') were taken on board by the Liberal Party. But in 1857 the *Manchester Guardian* castigated Cobden and his followers for not sharing the sentiments of the British people 'on the question of national greatness, duty and policy towards the outer world, which are embodied in the traditions of England, and deeply rooted in the attachments of the people'.[62]

The defeat of 1857 was the probably the greatest blow Armitage ever suffered: it ended his ambition of a seat in Parliament. He bequeathed this ambition to his son, Benjamin, by general agreement 'a chip off the old block'. Benjamin's career, which eventually culminated in a seat in Parliament for Salford, started with the

Crimean War and the Stoning of the Prophets, the men who were, and long remained, culture heroes of the Armitage family.

However, Sir Elkanah's active life was by no means over. Like his old friend Brotherton, he was a politician to his fingertips. As a Manchester Liberal chieftain, he stayed close to events to the end of his life nineteen years later, lending his name and subscribing his money to Liberal and Dissenting causes. Sir Elkanah lived to see Lord Palmerston buried, Disraeli's Reform Bill, which brought a significant instalment of democracy (and gave Salford a second seat in Parliament), pass into law, and Gladstone's first and greatest reforming Ministry. For the most part, for old League men like him, these were years of painful adjustment and frequent setbacks, the only consolation being that, as they grew older, many of them gew even richer and more successful.

After the election the Salford Radicals reorganised. In May 1857 a Salford Ballot and Reform Association was formed. Benjamin Armitage was a leading figure and soon served his turn as president. Recognising 1858 would be a year of Reform agitation, Liberal associations were springing up everywhere. When the Manchester New Reform Association began early in the New Year, Sir Elkanah was on the platform at the meeting to launch it.[63] At the same time, important moves were taking place within working-class Radicalism. Ernest Jones was arguing at Chartist meetings that the way forward was to co-operate with middle-class Radicals, and was generally successful in defeating hard-liners who argued against trusting any middle-class compromise.[64] For them the six points of the Charter were not for

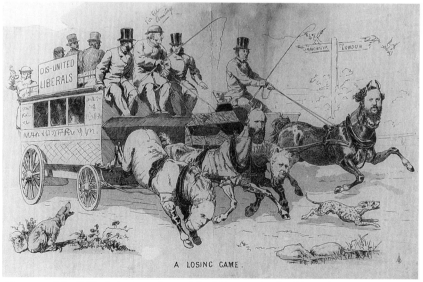

Cartoon of the Salford election of 1857. The 'Dis-united Liberals', with Jeremiah Garnett of the *Manchester Guardian* kicking over the traces, are being overtaken by Massey, hauled into the lead by Sir John Potter. (Original in the possession of the late J. E. C. Armitage, Esq.)

modification.[65] When the Manchester New Reform Association was formed it received a deputation of 'respectful working men', who came with an offer to co-operate, which was accepted. R. J. Richardson's request for a place in this development, as we have seen, was not. However, there were, and long remained, difficulties in agreeing terms on which to base an acceptable Reform programme. The most obvious was that, whilst Radicals of both classes could agree on the ballot, more equal constituencies and shorter parliaments, middle-class Radicals wanted to limit the franchise to male householders, whilst popular democrats wanted a universal male franchise.

Unwilling to move further towards democracy than manhood suffrage, 1858 brought a slight improvement in the League's other problem, its relationship to moderate liberal Manchester. Following the early death of Sir John Potter, MP, a meeting of electors considered the matter of his successor. The name of Thomas Bazley, president of the Manchester Chamber of Commerce, was proposed. The League, in the person of George Wilson, opposed Bazley, and hoped Manchester would call on Cobden, as yet still out of the House of Commons. Bazley was supported by Edmund Potter, who said he had spoken with Cobden, and had informed him that no candidate favoured by the League would stand the slightest chance in Manchester. Cobden told Potter that nothing would induce him to stand. Attempts were made to get Wilson to withdraw his amendment. He refused, and lost. The original motion was put, and Bazley's name was agreed on. The League then gave in. Wilson made a graceful speech of support for Bazley, and Sir Elkanah agreed to act as treasurer. Bazley was duly elected unopposed.[66]

The *Guardian* reviewed the business coolly. It recollected that Bazley had been Bright's proposer in 1857, and reminded Bazley not to forget 'he was the representative of the whole liberal party of Manchester, and that his presence there is regarded as the symbol of peace and harmony among us'. The paper expressed itself suspicious of Bazley's 'extreme friends', and said there are those who regard him as 'a dove sent out from the ark to see if the flood that destroyed their friends last year is yet assuaged'.[67]

The Manchester Reform Association, buoyed up by the way things were moving, ended their year with a soirée for Bright and Milner Gibson at the Free Trade Hall. It was just like old times. The people who voted for them in 1857 were invited, and over 3,500 attended. Sir Elkanah and all the leading figures were there, together with class-bridgers such as Henry Vincent and W. P. Roberts, the Chartist lawyer. Bright, now fully recovered, was stumping the country for Reform and in his speech gave the subject a thorough airing: Milner Gibson concentrated on 'aristocratic mis-rule.' Out of this meeting came the Lancashire Reformers Union, whose aim was to agitate for Bright's Reform Bill to extend the franchise. Armitage became hon. treasurer.[68] At this time, the Manchester Manhood Suffrage Association came into being at a meeting under the chairmanship of Abel Heywood, with Dr Watts and Edward Hooson as the two leading speakers.

The 1859 election gave greater encouragement to Reformers in Manchester than in Salford. Middle-class Manchester was surprised when the Manhood Suffrage Association nominated Abel Heywood. Hooson was one of the men behind this move, and the Chartists came out in support, recalling with approval Heywood's promotion of cheap literature in the days of the *Poor Man's Guardian.* Manchester shopkeepers were pleased at the chance to vote for someone of their class for once. Heywood's committee appealed to Sir Elkanah's friends for support, and sent a deputation to the Council of the Lancashire Reform Union: it was a testing search of that body's commitment to Reform. A lawyer-like response was forthcoming. Whilst *individually* supporting the candidature of Alderman Heywood, the Council said it was not *constitutionally* in order for them to endorse any candidate. At the last minute the Manchester Conservatives brought back the Hon. Capt. Denman to partner J. A. Turner in opposition to Bazley and Heywood. Bazley and Turner were duly returned, but the popular hero was Heywood, who beat Denman into fourth place. The middle-class Reformers were surprised and impressed that Heywood got 5,448 votes without any organisation or money behind him, and, in public at any rate, were generous in their praise for Heywood.

The *Manchester Guardian* moderates took some consolation from the result in Salford, though not much. Sir Elkanah wisely declined to stand, but played his part on the committee supporting the Bolton manufacturer and Free Trader, Henry Ashworth. The election was a boisterous re-run of 1857: questions of Reform and manhood suffrage were pushed into the background behind the issue of 'League tyranny'. It was also very personal. Massey's supporters saw him as the man who had defeated the League. Ashworth's supporters saw Massey a phoney liberal elected by the votes of Salford Conservatives.[69] Ashworth was a poor candidate, tedious even when proclaiming his support for Bright's version of Reform. Massey, on the other hand, was a seasoned campaigner. He concentrated on the one idea that united all his supporters – 'League dictation'. Massey claimed he was proud to be 'no nominee of any club or millowner', and the *Guardian* (whose editor was on Massey's Committee) compared the League Rump to the Jacobin Club in the French Revolution. There was a high turn-out (84 per cent of those registered) and a close finish, Massey winning by 132 out of a total of 3,706 votes cast.[70]

For Sir Elkanah Armitage and the Salford Ballot and Reform Association the return of Massey was a disaster, and within weeks a new penny newspaper, the *Salford Weekly News*, was on the streets.[71] It was Salford's first successful paper, and although it claimed its appearance was a result of the repeal of the newspaper duties, it was financed by Salford liberals, and Armitage was involved in its launch. It never hid its politics. In its early years it was anti-Whig, pro-Reform, pro-Temperance, against government spending and Dissenting in religious tone. In local matters it was vehemently pro-Salford *vis-à-vis* Manchester. Most of all, it loathed Massey and never neglected a chance of attacking him.

It was to have plenty of opportunities. Massey remained the Member for Salford until February 1865, when he resigned to join the Indian government as Finance Minister. His spell as Salford's representative coincided almost exactly with the duration of Palmerston's second ministry, and to Salford Reformers Massey typified everything they hated about Palmerstonian 'conservative liberalism'. Massey rarely visited the constituency and obstructed Reform whenever it came up. His career advanced steadily. In 1859 he left the Home Department to become Chairman of Committees in the House, and earned the hatred of Salford Reformers for his influential speech against Lord John Russell's Reform Bill in March 1860, which led to the failure of that measure.

Nevertheless, the years of Massey's incumbency were not all bad for Sir Elkanah and his friends. Out of events and movements of this time the alliance of interests which was to coalesce into the future Liberal party began to form. But it was Benjamin Armitage rather than Sir Elkanah who was the active participant. When Massey at last resigned (in February 1865), a committee was formed to elect John Cheetham, another of the League's grey men. The Armitages all turned out to serve: Sir Elkanah, Benjamin and his brothers, Elkanah, Samuel and Joseph John. Cheetham was elected unopposed, and was returned again at the general election that July.[72] Palmerston was now dead, Palmerstonism was dead, and Conservatism was as yet showing few signs of life.

In Sir Elkanah's last years there were more surprises in store for liberals. When Disraeli's Reform Bill came, it proved far more Radical than anything they had ever proposed. In the first election after the Reform Act, Gladstone won a great victory, and Sir Elkanah lived to see Gladstone's first great ministry pass many of the reforms he, as a great political Dissenter, had campaigned for for so long. However, to the intense chagrin of the Armitages and other Liberals, at the 1868 election Salford returned two Conservatives. It was as great a defeat as 1857.

In his last years Sir Elkanah could look back on a long life, full of achievement. The patriarch of a large family, he had become the grand old man of Manchester Liberalism. In the Cotton Famine the hard-faced master of the Pendleton lock-out emerged as something of a paternalist. When the Unionist blockade of the Confederate States cut off supplies of cotton, the mills of Lancashire ground to a halt, and unprecedented efforts were made to relieve the thousands of jobless operatives in Britain's greatest industry. Sir Elkanah served as a member of the Central Relief Committee, and in November 1862 the *Times* correspondent, visiting Manchester, reported that[73]

> Sir Elkanah Armitage, of Manchester, has fed and clothed the whole of his workpeople, some 1,200 in number, ever since the mills have been closed, and intends to do so as long as the necessity may last. He has been heard to say 'I will share my property with my distressed workpeople as long as I have a shilling left; this is my special mission and as I do not ask the public to give one penny to anyone who has been in my employ, but take the whole burden on myself, so it will account for no large sum against my name in the subscription list.'

In point of fact, when the list appeared a few weeks later, the sum contributed by Sir Elkanah Armitage & Sons was twice that of any other single contribution.[73]

After the enforced shut-down, the firm did well in the boom which followed. Just as the firm had expanded after the 1848 depression, it did so again after the Cotton Famine. To add to their productive capacity the Armitages purchased Nassau Mills, Patricroft, in 1867. From the time he took the last of his sons into partnership, Sir Elkanah had been content to leave the running of the firm to them (though he did not finally retire until 1873). He continued active on

Manchester Council until 1866, at which time he was elected High Sheriff of the County. Sir Elkanah remained chairman of the Manchester Grammar School trustees, and served as a governor of the Manchester Infirmary.

Sir Elkanah Armitage died on 26 November 1876, in his eighty second year. His life, informed by the triple influences of Dissent, political economy and bourgeois party politics of the Radical kind, had passed through many phases. There was the boy whose childhood ended at eight; the diligent warehouseman; the young entrepreneur striking out in business with his wife; the 'patient plodding manufacturer'; the Independent ever ready to promote the cause of Dissent; the politician who was an alderman of Manchester almost as soon as he entered the town hall; the Free Trader; the class warrior; the downcast politician sharing to the full the setbacks which befell the party of his friends; and finally there was the patriarch, the Grand Old Man of Manchester Liberalism.

Armitage lived through one of history's greatest and most rapid periods of change. He and his type knew who they were, and what they were. They personify the rise of the nineteenth-century northern capitalist. They nurtured a certain style, and seized the chance to direct the development of the new industrial towns and mould their institutions. By the time of his death, Sir Elkanah was almost the last of the Manchester men whose political lives went back to Napoleonic days, Peterloo, the Great Reform Act and the Anti-Corn Law League, and he passed the mantle of Liberal chieftain to his second son Benjamin. For him, as for his father, fame was the spur, and he was to enjoy the one triumph denied Sir Elkanah. Yet, Benjamin, in his turn, was to suffer another Stoning of the Prophets.

Crowds flocking to the Manchester Art Treasures Exhibition in 1857.
(*Illustrated London News*)

CHAPTER 6

# Beer and Bible:
# Charles Cawley, William Charley and
# the Revival of Conservatism

When Canon Stowell died in 1865 the political effects of his life's work had not become fully apparent. True, in his time, the Evangelical party had done much to revive and determine the character of the Church in Manchester, and, on the political front, he and his friends had started to roll back the advance of Liberalism. At the time of his death, all the predictions were than the future lay with the Liberals. But their politicians at Westminster, floundering in the bog of 'fancy franchises', were outmanoevred by Disraeli. Exercising the prerogative of Conservative leaders to astonish their party from time to time, in his Reform Act of 1867 Disraeli gave an unexpected measure of democracy to working men in parliamentary boroughs. In the election which followed, Lancashire surprised those who expected the industrial districts to vote Liberal. And Salford surprised them more than most places, by returning not one, but two Conservatives. On a visit a few years later, Disraeli told delighted Salford Conservatives 'It seems a strong place; I had the pleasure of giving it two members – I wish I had given it four.'[1]

One of those returned in that famous victory was Salford's Mayor-elect, Charles Edward Cawley. In one celebration speech, Cawley acknowledged Conservatism's debt to Stowell: 'that great and good man, though dead, yet speaketh. I attribute the result ... very largely to the healthy church feeling which he created in the borough.'[2] If, for about a quarter of a century after the first Reform Act Salford had been a 'Radical' seat and then a Palmerstonian fief, after the second Reform Act, more often than not, it returned Conservatives. In the first era of proto-democratic elections they were the party to beat. A consideration of Cawley's life and politics, offers some explanations why.[3]

Cawley's Conservatism perhaps owed something to his origins and to his chosen profession. Born in 1812, he was the son of Samuel Cawley of Gooden House, Middleton, near Manchester, agent to Robert Gregg Hopwood, Esq. of Hopwood Hall. His background and character were thus formed, in part at least, by the relationship between agent and landowner which was, and is inherently conservative. After attending Middleton Grammar school, the young Cawley was engaged to Thomas Longridge Gooch, engineer to the Lancashire & Yorkshire Railway

Company. He showed aptitude in his chosen career, and when only twenty three was given charge of building a part of the Manchester-Leeds line. One local monument to his railway engineering is the Clifton viaduct.

In 1846 Cawley was elected a member of the Institute of Civil Engineers and, soon after, set up on his own in business in Manchester. In 1843 he had married Harriet Motley, daughter of George Motley of Nottingham, by whom he had a son and a daughter. The young couple settled in Broughton. In his professional life Cawley moved on from railway construction to public works, his firm building, amongst other projects, waterworks at Heywood, Burnley, Windermere and Buxton. He became a respected figure in the world of civil engineering, called in to act as umpire on several occasions in disputes involving technical matters.

Portrait of Charles Edward Cawley, Conservative MP for Salford, 1868–77. (Salford Art Gallery and Museum)

However, his rural upbringing and profession had much less to do with Cawley's brand of Conservatism than religion. Cawley was a hard Evangelical in the Stowellite mould. His first entry into public affairs was when, in his late thirties, he attracted notice as one of the leaders of the Manchester Church Reform Association, founded in March 1847 in reaction to the failure, as Evangelicals saw it, of the dean and canons of Manchester to give a vigorous enough lead in church matters. In particular, what provoked such people as Richard Birley, Robert Gardner, Charles Cawley and other followers of Hugh Stowell into organising was the action of Canon Parkinson in accepting the presidency of St. Bee's College, in addition to his other preferments and duties. Cawley then went on to play a leading part in the subsequent campaign to secure the Manchester Rectory Division Act of 1850, and was a strong supporter of Bishop Lee in his acrimonious dispute with the dean and chapter of Manchester Cathedral. By then, Cawley was churchwarden of Manchester Parish, and churchwarden and Sunday school superintendent of St. Anne's, whose vicar, the Rev. James Bardsley, a leading Evangelical, was a close friend. Cawley was one of the promoters of the building of St. Paul's, Kersal, founded, it was said, to provide a living for the Rev. W. H. McGrath, another Evangelical son of thunder. Cawley became his churchwarden too.

In the 1850s Cawley busied himself in a number of Evangelical causes. He was one of the hon. secretaries of the Manchester and Salford Protestant Alliance, which evolved from the Protestant Defence Committee of 1851, set up to campaign against the Maynooth Grant, 'Papal Aggression' and the opening of nunneries.[4] These campaigns tapped a deep well of Protestant feeling: 'We recognise,' confessed a somewhat surprised *Manchester Guardian,* 'it is an undeniable fact that the hostility to the Roman Catholic faith is a passport to greater popularity than it could have commanded some years ago.'[5] It was a passport Cawley was to flourish throughout his life.

About the time he first became active in Evangelical causes Cawley's career in local government also commenced. In 1848 he was one of those who urged that Broughton should adopt the Public Health Act. Five years later, when that township became part of the borough, he was one of the first councillors to be elected. On the council he made a name for himself in his attempts to reform and improve the working of that body. When they took their places in the council chamber, Cawley and the new Broughton and Pendleton Councillors found themselves part of a body with well-established customs and practices. By 1853 the tradition was of strong committees which had enjoyed a high degree of autonomy and had their own ways of proceeding. The full council exercised little over sight or control over these committees, whose chairmen wielded considerable power.

Not long after Cawley took his seat on the council a question arose about the way in which the full council was informed about what committees were doing. In January 1858 a critical account of a council meeting appeared in the *Manchester Guardian.*[6]

> The proceedings of the committees were then gone through, in the incon-venient and unsatisfactory manner usual in the Salford Council Chamber. Instead of the results, at least, of the proceedings of each committee being read, as a matter of course, nothing is ever read from any minute book unless the chairman or some member of the particular committee requests that a specified portion of the minutes should be read. There is no established rule (or none is insisted upon) when discussions upon the minutes shall be taken; and hence, yesterday, the subject of increasing salaries was partially discussed upon some of the minutes, and the discussion was resumed upon the motion of confirming the minutes of all the committees in a batch.

These criticisms were discussed at the following month's council meeting, and the Mayor (William Harvey) made suggestions as to how chairmen of committees could keep the full council better informed about their business. Cawley, for his part, emphasised that the matter was important, and uttered the prophetic words that, if the present mode of informing (or not informing) the council was not improved, 'irregularities' would inevitably appear, which, in the course of time would bring municipal government into disrepute in Salford.[7]

At a later meeting, Cawley moved a motion that the present system was 'irregular and inexpedient' and that it was important that the non-routine committee questions should be brought before the council, and that the General Purposes Committee be instructed to consider the best mode of seeing that improvements were made was adopted. That committee duly recommended that a synopsis of 'all nonroutine committee business' should be made available to the full council. When this was agreed to, the Town Clerk (with what seems appalling candour) was moved to comment that the Water and Watch Committees were quite out of the control of the Council.[8] In real terms it seems that little improvement was effected. The ultimate outcome was the scandal over the gas works contracts of the 1880s. But as early as 1866, Salford was humiliated by the defalcation of a Borough Treasurer with council monies, an indication of how inefficiently the council oversaw Salford's municipal business, despite the criticisms of a decade earlier. Once more, Cawley was the chief critic. At this time, too, there was considerable disquiet over allegations of indiscipline and inefficiency in the police, and the council's failure to do enough on Public Health.[9]

Cawley sat on the Council for eighteen years. He was active on a number of committees, notably those to do with Broughton township, the Museum and Library, and was Chairman of the Gas Committee for the ten years from 1861. He was made an alderman in 1859, and served two terms. When he was elected to Parliament in November 1868 he was Mayor-elect, and had to decline the chief magistrate's office in order to fulfil his duties at Westminster.

As befitted a civil engineer, Cawley showed some interest in improving sanitation and public health. In 1855 he was chairman of a sub-committee of the Manchester and Salford Sanitary Association looking into the state of Manchester's 'River Sewers', in particular the appalling state of the Medlock as it emptied into the Bridgewater Canal.[10] Over the next decade, the question of public health loomed larger and larger in local government, but, just at the time the Salford Council could no longer avoid taking action, Cawley departed for Westminster.

Cawley finally resigned from the Council in 1871. Of late, he had not attended many meetings because of the difficulty of combining business commitments and duties as Member for Salford with local government service. He had been a vigorous, ascerbic local government politician, and if his attempts to improve the way the Salford Council carried on its business had not been crowned with much success, he had served the borough diligently. Yet, if Cawley was an improver, he was never prepared to go beyond a certain degree of criticism. For him, the prestige of his position as councillor and alderman was a useful way of building a local power-base: it made him into one of best-known Conservatives in Salford. Nor did his brand of Protestantism in any way harm his standing with the largely Protestant middle-class electorate, or, indeed, the new working-class voters.

Cawley's party political career commenced about the time he entered municipal politics. Its pattern demonstrates how a new Conservatism re-emerged out of defeat over the Corn Laws and Brotherton's long supremacy. It did so via 'conservative liberalism' and Protestant militance. Cawley's first real political battle was the Manchester election of 1852. As one of the leading figures in the Manchester And Salford Protestant Alliance Cawley was drawn in, and first attracted attention, as a member of Loch and Denman's committee.[11] Although Bright and Milner-Gibson were safely re-elected, Cawley and his friends had discovered the way for Conservatism to climb back on to the hustings. For the next dozen years they sang hosannas to Lord Derby and clung to the coat-tails of Lord Palmerston. Events moved their way over the Peace Party's opposition to Palmerston's foreign policy. Cawley played his full part in the Stoning of the Prophets. He was a relentless opponent of Sir Elkanah Armitage and a leading figure on W. N. Massey's committee in the 1857 election, and the one which followed two years later. In a speech to supporters at Salford Town Hall after the latter victory Cawley gave his views on where modern conservatism now was.[12]

> If opposition to all change and progress, the old Tory doctrine, was now called Conservatism, Mr Massey was certainly not a Conservative; but if Conservatism meant the preservation of all that was valuable in our institutions, with the introduction of such improvements as the increased knowledge of the people and the altered circumstances of the country might require, then Mr Massey was both Liberal and Conservative, as so also was he himself.

In the years of the Palmerstonian supremacy, Cawley and the Salford 'conservative liberal' Committee stayed firmly behind their hero.

The Palmerstonian coalition provided a refuge in which the shorn lamb of Salford Conservatism was protected from the chill wind of party confrontation. Yet this sheltered accommodation did not foster a vigorous and free-standing Conservatism. This became apparent in 1865, when, first, Massey resigned to go to India, and, even more so, when Lord Palmerston died. To replace Massey, Cawley and his allies tried to persuade Oliver Heywood to stand. Had he done so, there is little doubt that he would have been elected. However, he declined, and they could find no-one else suitable. The Liberal John Cheetham was returned unopposed, and again at the general election a few months later.[13] In the Manchester by-election in November 1867, Jacob Bright easily beat both a Whig and a Conservative. Suddenly, Liberalism was on the ascendant and Conservatism seemed bankrupt. After the death of Lord Palmerston, moderate Liberals in Manchester and Salford seemed to be moving left again. However, in the next three years the political situation was re-cast. Not the least of the surprises of this time was the appearance of a vigorous popular Conservatism, the first result of which was the election of Cawley and another Conservative for Salford in 1868.

Palmerston died on 15 October 1865, and the government which succeeded his was a Whig Liberal one. In March 1866, a cautious Whig Reform Bill was introduced. Anodyne though it was, it was defeated by the efforts of Liberal defectors. Russell was succeeded by Lord Derby, who formed his third administration, whose leading figure was Disraeli. His Reform Bill was more democratic than any Bright or any other Radical, Liberal, or Whig had contemplated. Disraeli's famous 'Leap in the Dark' extended the borough suffrage to all (male) householders paying the poor rate, and to all lodgers of one year's residence, paying an annual rent of £20. Boroughs with a population of less than 10,000 lost the right to return two members to Parliament; Manchester, Birmingham, Liverpool and Leeds were each given a third seat, and Salford, together with Merthyr, received a second.

When the Salford Overseers of the Poor's new list was published, the electorate had increased by two hundred and fifty per cent. 'The great bulk of the working-class here will, we take it, be found Liberal to the core,' wrote the *Salford Weekly News*, 'To assume otherwise would be the greatest insult to their understandings.'[14] Unfortunately for that prediction, at the next election (November 1868), while the country as a whole elected Gladstone's first Liberal government to power, Salford returned two Conservatives.

As the statistics of the contest (Table 3) indicate, the election was extraordinarily close. Salford's electorate was not then (or later) as Conservative as its parliamentary election results would seem to suggest. In fact the two parties were almost evenly balanced. This is not to say that the emergence of popular Conservatism in Salford was not a remarkable phenomenon: manifestly it was. How was it that a Conservative party was able to spring up, apparently fully-armed from what seemed a situation increasingly favourable to Liberal recovery, and to attract enough first-time working-class voters to win in 1868, and again in 1874?

In the first place, Conservatism was able to call upon a folk memory of Tory/working-class co-operation in the past. Before the First Reform Act, Salford had been Tory-dominated, and the capture of the seat at the first Salford election had been a great shock. Popular enthusiasm for Whig 'Reform' had been short-lived: as we have seen, there had been an upsurge of Tory Radicalism over the New Poor Law, and, with Chartist support, the Tories almost unseated Brotherton in 1837 and 1841. There was also the memory of Conservative and working-class co-operation over the Factory issue. But, at the party political level, Conservatism had withered away until propagated anew in the Palmerston years. In 1867–8 Conservatives began to envisage a new Tory Radical scenario.

Table 3. *Voting by Districts in the Salford Election, 1868*

| Polling District | Voters on Register | Votes polled for | | Majority | |
|---|---|---|---|---|---|
| | | Liberals | Conservatives | Liberals | Conservatives |
| Lower Broughton | 976 | 890 | 790 | 100 | |
| Higher Broughton | 582 | 411 | 567 | | 156 |
| Seedley | 1,592 | 1,366 | 1,266 | 100 | |
| St Thomas's | 1,529 | 1,351 | 1,341 | 10 | |
| Pendlebury | 120 | 132 | 76 | 56 | |
| Blackfriars | 397 | 263 | 398 | | 135 |
| Crescent | 1,769 | 1,210 | 1,722 | | 512 |
| St Stephen's | 603 | 468 | 525 | | 57 |
| Greengate | 1,148 | 922 | 945 | | 23 |
| Islington | 661 | 560 | 533 | 27 | |
| Oldfield Road | 2,182 | 1,840 | 1,719 | 121 | |
| St Philip's | 1,925 | 1,630 | 1,535 | 95 | |
| Trinity | 1,375 | 1,116 | 1,076 | 40 | |
| | | | Conservative Majority: | | 344 |

A second reason is that Conservatives in Salford, and elsewhere in Lancashire, were better organised than their opponents. They seem to have had a more instinctive feel for the new situation, and were faster off the mark. The Salford Constitutional Association was founded in February 1867, immediately after the Queen's Speech announcing Reform, and by April had branches in Crescent, St Stephen's and Trinity wards. Its founder and leading spirit was Daniel Hall, a foreman in an engineering works, who declared at its inaugural meeting that he believed that 'the principles of the association were such as were entertained by very many of the working-class of Salford.'[15]

Hall was one of those working-class conservatives whose political career bridged the years between the Operative Conservatism of the 1830s and the new Conservatism of the 1860s. Born at Hickleton, near Doncaster, in 1818, he migrated to Salford with his elder brother, John, whilst still a boy. After a time in a silk mill near Broughton Bridge, he went to work at the King Street Ironworks of Higgins & Sons. The Higgins family were strong Conservatives. Hall rose to be a foreman, and later their general manager. In 1835 he became actively involved with the Salford Operative Conservative Association and was later a supporter of Massey. 1866 found him in at the formation of the Salford Constitutional Association, and he became its first chairman. He got on to the council in 1868, and, with one three year break, sat continuously until 1898, the last sixteen as an alderman. Like his brother John, he was an ardent churchman and a prominent Odd Fellow.[16]

Middle-class Conservatives, on the other hand, seemed slower to come forward. At the second annual meeting of the Salford Association, the chairman confessed that 'one of their principal difficulties had been to induce gentlemen of position and influence to join them.' By October 1868 the Association had started its own weekly newspaper, the *Salford Chronicle* to oppose the *Salford Weekly News* and act as 'exponent of that large and daily increasing Constitutional feeling which has so unexpectedly discovered itself in Salford.'[17]

By contrast, the Liberals were slow to organise and were divided along class lines. No 'United Liberal Party' emerged in 1867 or 1868. When Reform came to life again at the start of 1866, middle-class Liberals organised a branch of the National Reform Union. In the autumn, branches of the working-class Reform League had been formed, but Salford's Liberal leaders failed to see the need to reach an understanding with the League and Liberal trade unionists. They apparently believed that once the Reform Bill became law the political battle was as good as won. Insensitivity towards working-class political feelings is well illustrated in the way the Liberal candidates were nominated in July 1867. At a meeting of Liberal electors, the veteran Anti-Corn Law Leaguers who stage-managed it tried to persuade Sir Elkanah Armitage to stand. When he declined, an offer was made to his son Benjamin, who also declined. So they invited John Cheetham and Henry Rawson, the latter a son of the old treasurer of the Anti-Corn Law League.[18] It never occurred to them to consider nominating someone acceptable to new voters. They were therefore surprised when a meeting of trade unionists, Reform League, Temperance and friendly society men resolved 'That as the non-electors to be enfranchised in the coming Reform Bill they have the right to nominate at least one of the two candidates for the borough', and called upon Cheetham's committee to withdraw Rawson's name. Working-class resentment at the 'twenty-two faceless men' on the Liberal committee was met with conciliatory words, delay caused by Rawson's illness, and an eventual bland assertion that Rawson represented all classes: 'broadly their interests ... were identical'.[19]

Cheetham and Rawson were not such effective candidates as the Conservatives. Both were rather colourless and their impeccable League pedigrees cut no ice with working-class voters. The Conservatives were an altogether more formidable duo. As a running partner Cawley had William Thomas Charley, a 35 year-old barrister from Ulster, whose name betrayed Lancashire (Chorley) origins. A good platform

man, Charley knew how to butter-up the electorate. He also had more 'bottom' than was at
first perceived. When it came to Protestant militance the Ulsterman was more extreme than the
Salfordian. During his election campaign Charley
played the role of 'Protestant dog tear 'em' to the
limit. When he first appeared in Salford, however,
he was best known as a promoter of organised
Conservatism. The previous year he had stepped
on to the stage of Lancashire politics as a 'forger
of unity' between the working men and the
Anglican clergy in Liverpool. Charley had also
played his part forming Conservative Associations in London, and was later president of the
Metropolitan Alliance. He also had impeccable
patriotic credentials, as a major in the Middlesex
Rifle Volunteers. Last, but not least, he also had a
ready-made campaign song in George Leyburne's
'Champagne Charlie', then sweeping the music
halls.

William Thomas Charley,
as Common Sergeant of
London, Conservative MP for
Salford 1868–80. (*Illustrated
London News*)

A perennial explanation for the ability of English Conservatism to revive itself
is deference to the country's 'natural rulers'. Although always difficult to gauge,
deference was certainly a factor. In the autumn of 1868 declarations of reverence
for the landed classes were *de rigueur* on Tory Platforms, and Lord Derby's
contribution of £10,000 to the Relief fund in the Cotton Famine did not pass
unremembered. A landed magnate, the tangible benefits from whom were more
locally apparent, was Lord Egerton of Tatton. The owner of most of Ordsall, he
had already made his influence felt through the provision of churches and schools.
Other Salford landowners who were prominent, or willing to allow their names
to be used in the Conservative election campaign, included Sir Robert Gore-Booth,
who owned land in Salford and Pendleton, C. P. Fitzgerald, the owner of an estate
and coal mines in Pendleton, and S. W. Clowes, the biggest landowner in
Broughton.

However, it was the Conservative claim to be the 'true friends of the people
'which struck more of a chord than deference. Pieces of legislation such as the
Coal Mines Act, the abolition of Truck and the Factory Acts were paraded as
evidence. Lord Derby's voting record on issues from Catholic Emancipation to the
Second Reform Bill was compared favourably to that of John Bright, the current
hero of the popular Liberals.[20] By and large, the Salford factory masters were the
backbone of the Liberal party, though there were important exceptions, such as
Richard Haworth, the most successful of the new entrepreneurs of the 1850s, already
well on his way to becoming 'the largest ratepayer in Salford'.[21] Ironfounders and
engineers were mostly Liberal, Brewers were Conservative virtually to a man.
However, there can also be little doubt that a significant number of workers voted
against their Liberal employers. After the Ballot Act was passed in 1872 there were
even more.

Accompanying these attitudes was another, based on the argument that the workers stood to gain more from Conservative than Liberal governments in such legislation as a new Master and Servant Bill. The most outspoken advocates of this view were two men in positions of influence, W. H. Wood and S. C. Nicholson, secretary and treasurer respectively of the Manchester and Salford Trades Council. Wood, in particular, was passionately anti-Liberal. He hated Free Trade and was a fierce denouncer of the French Treaty of 1860. It may be that Wood did not speak for the majority of Manchester and Salford unionists, but his arguments raised interest in Protectionism. 'Reciprocal Free Trade', or 'Reciprocity 'was much discussed at this time, the *Salford Chronicle* giving it great support. Although 'Reciprocity' faded in the boom after 1870, it was to re-appear thereafter. Wood is an interesting figure of this period: his name appears in all sorts of areas where working-class Conservatism was being revived – trades unionism, journalism (he was actively involved with the *Salford Chronicle*), and, it goes without saying, he was a hard-line Protestant.[22]

The main issue of the 1868 election in Salford, however, was not economics, or deference, or the quality of the candidates: it was religion. The Conservatives were swept into parliament by a gale of near-hysterical Protestantism, aroused by Gladstone's proposal to disestablish the Irish Church. The campaign against this policy began in the spring of 1868. The *Salford Weekly News* scented danger: 'Nobody who has not the sublime audacity of Mr Disraeli dare now raise the old anti-social 'No Popery' cry; but there are a great many left who have a lingering instinctive dread of Roman Catholicism gaining ground.' It added, 'It is not easy work combating a feeling of this kind.' [23] Indeed it was not, thanks to almost forty years of Evangelical effort in Salford. As Engels noted, in this election the parsons showed unsuspected power and influence.[24] In at least one Salford church the national anthem was sung the Sunday before polling day. The clergy's cry of 'No surrender, no robbery, no spoilation' was amplified into the more resonant 'No Popery'. Cawley and his Evangelical friends hammered home the message that the attack on the established Church in Ireland was the first step towards the abolition of the Protestant Constitution and monarchy. They implied that the disestablishment of the Irish Church would, in no time at all, lead to Catholic supremacy in England. At street level, they said the election was about 'whether you will have the Pope or the Queen', or, more basically still, 'Will you vote with the low Irish?' [25] Cawley and his friends employed the paranoid style perfected by Stowell. Henry Mead, for many years a Protestant missionary in Salford, assured his listeners that 'The Conspiracy of 1868' was in the same category as those of Guy Fawkes or James II, and that 'Infidels, Quakers, Independents, Fenians, Baptists, Reformers and ratteners all combined in one unholy League to overthrow the Protestant institutions of our land, and to bring us under the heel of priestly despotism.' [26]

The question is, why were the voters of Salford so receptive to such overblown arguments? By 1868 there was a strong anti-Irish tradition in many Lancashire towns. After the election, one observer declared that Lancashire was as Liberal as Yorkshire except on one issue: the Irish in Lancashire, he declared, are the 'poor whites', and 'nowhere is the illiberal notice "No Irish need apply" more fully carried out in the social and political relations of life … Lancashire has contracted towards the Irish much of the feeling which actuates the Orange Protestants in Ireland.'[27]

The life-long efforts of Stowell and the Evangelical party were of obvious importance in explaining the outburst of anti-Catholicism of 1868 and the Conservative victory in Salford. It did not pass unnoticed that the election of 1868 was won and lost in the Crescent. Here Stowell's church stood, and here his army of curates and lay helpers laboured. Hope Street was Henry Mead's stamping ground.[28] Yet, in 1865, the year Stowell died, Protestant watchmen must have felt that things had gone cold on the Catholic and Ritualist fronts. But scarcely had Stowell passed away, than a series of events came along which did much to pave the way for the 'Conservative reaction' of '68. In the first place, a Tractarian curate was appointed to St. Stephen's. Finding his church unheeded amongst the working people who surrounded it, the Rev. George Huntington tried to change matters by abolishing pew-renting, reorganized the schools, employed district visitors and introduced an element of Ritualism into the services. The Salford Operative Protestant Association whipped-up feelings to such an extent that, after two years, Huntington was forced to resign. They then went on to form the Church of England Laymen's Defence Association, which aimed to create a nation-wide movement in opposition to 'priestly incumbents' and the ritualistic English Church Union. Cawley was a vice-chairman, and amongst its members were the men who were to be the leaders of the 'new Conservatism' in Salford.

But it was Fenianism which really racked-up anti-Catholic and anti-Irish feeling. Prior to the 'Manchester Outrage' of 1867, in which a policeman was murdered, there had been rumours that Fenians were active amongst the Manchester and

The Fenian attack on the Manchester police van, which led to the escape of the prisoners and the death of Sergeant Brett, 1867. (*Illustrated Times*)

Salford Irish. The rescue of the Fenian prisoners from the police which caused Sergeant Brett's death, and the subsequent trial and public execution of the 'Manchester Martyrs' just one year before the 1868 election brought anti-Irish feelings out into the open.[29] After the hanging of Allen, Larkin and O' Brien Protestant militants had no intention of letting anti-Irishness fade. In the itinerant rabble-rouser, Murphy, they found a suitable instrument. Murphy stumped the industrial districts with his anti-Catholic performances in the weeks before the election

The first election in Salford under a proto-democratic franchise was a rough and close-run thing. So close, that the Liberals petitioned Parliament, alleging that the scale of 'treating', hiring of 'roughs', picketing of voters and the use of pubs and beer-houses as committee-rooms constituted a case for unseating Cawley and Charley. In his summing up (in March 1869), the Petition Court Judge, Baron Martin, found that the case was not strong enough, though he was moved to say that he was not sure that, hearing the same things on another occasion, he would not put the other verdict.[30] Judges are always saying things like that. It was no consolation to the Liberals, who were doubly furious. After the election they turned to improving party organization.

Early in 1869 the Salford (District) Liberal Association came into being, and, in those Pendleton and Salford wards where they had worked efficiently, the election committees turned themselves into branches of the Association. Yet the party proved slow to learn its lessons. The Salford Liberal leadership was manifestly uneasy in the new political situation. But even if the Liberals had been able to spring back from defeat, they could not have stopped the onward march of Conservatism. In places like Salford the political consequences of the early legislation of Gladstone's government gave Conservatives the opportunity to widen the gap with the Liberals.

The passing of the Bill which disestablished the Irish Church in 1869 was the cue to Conservatives in Lancashire to intensify the anti-Popery campaign. In these months Lancashire lost its head. Aristocrats and respectable local figures shared platforms with Orangemen and rabble-rousers, whose verbal excesses make strange reading. One favourite description of Gladstone was 'Judas Iscariot', (who, it was claimed, was 'more of a gentleman than the present Premier of England').[31] In all this, Charley and Cawley were well to the fore. The first result of this campaign (and the deteriorating situation in Ireland) was the revival of the Orange movement in Salford, largely defunct since the late 1840s. By the end of 1870, there were eight lodges in the township, and one in Pendleton,[32] though Orangeism never grew much after that. In April 1869 Charley told an Orange demonstration in Exeter Hall in London that, although not an Orangeman himself, 'in point of principle' he was entirely at one with them.[33] That June, Cawley was in Rochdale to lay the cornerstone of an Orange Protestant Hall. By the end of that year the most rabid phase of anti-Popery was over, a process initiated by a robust attack on Murphyism by the Bishop of Manchester in a speech at Accrington.[34] In July 1869 the Irish Church Reform Bill became law and the fight against it collapsed, though anti-Popery was to reverberate through local politics for some time yet. But by the start of 1870 a new political controversy was arising out of Gladstone's programme – the Education Act.

Before the Bill there had been much talk about the introduction of unsectarian and 'godless' education, and the Church of England and the Catholics had organised early for the coming struggle. Yet when Forster's Bill was published it could scarcely have been friendlier to the Voluntarists. It was Liberals who were thrown into disarray. Middle-class opinion in Salford was generally voluntarist, and working-class spokesmen and Dissenters who argued for 'non-sectarian' Board School education found themselves out on a limb. The Liberal Association, therefore, on this issue had to stand by and witness the rivalry of friends. Although it made efforts to put up an agreed list of candidates for the School Board election, it failed. The result was that the 1871 Salford School Board comprised nine Voluntarists (seven church-men and two Catholics) against three Nonconformists and three Wesleyans.[35] In the 33 years of its existence the combination of churchmen and Catholics never lost control of the Board, and ran the system so as not to harm church and parochial schools. All that Liberals and Dissenters could do was reflect on the irony of the situation whereby the Church party, which had fought recent politics on the anti-Popery ticket, was now involved in an alliance with the Catholics. Of course, there was more to the educational history of the Salford School Board era than that. The Board had much to do in a borough which grew very rapidly after 1870.[36] But by 1900 there were still considerably more children in voluntary than in Board schools.[37]

The area where the 'Conservative reaction' in Salford was most clearly seen was in local government politics. Straight party-political contests began as early as April 1868. Their superior organisation meant that the Conservatives were better able to take advantage of the partial democratization of local government which followed on the heels of parliamentary reform, and which doubled the burgess roll in Salford. The Conservative take-over of the borough council was swift, and in the case of the Salford to township wards, spectacular. By 1870, eighteen of the twenty-four Salford district councillors were Conservatives, and, after the municipal election of 1871, the party had a clear majority on the council, a dominance they were never to lose down to the Great War.

If middle-class Liberals were generally behind the administrative reforms of Gladstone's first ministry, there were elements in the programme which pleased working-people a lot less. These made it that much more difficult for the Liberals to win the next election in Salford. Gladstone's government eventually fell in January 1874. In the businessman Henry Lee, a partner in the firm of Tootal Broadhurst Lee, and the barrister Joseph Kay, brother of that eminent Victorian, Sir James Kay-Shuttleworth, the Liberals had stronger candidates than six years before. Local party workers made strenuous efforts, canvassing, organising meetings and covering the walls of Salford with brilliant red-lettered placards. The election was another close one, the Conservatives getting back with a majority of 454.[38] This time Salford was in step with the rest of the country: a Conservative government under Disraeli was returned to power.

Gladstone professed himself in no doubt as to the reason for his defeat: 'We have been borne down in a torrent of gin and beer.' It is said his Licensing Act of 1872 created a nation-wide alliance of the Drink trade and Conservatism, and made public houses into Conservative club rooms.[39] In Salford that was nothing new. Local Liberals were more inclined to lay the blame on two other causes:

Disraeli receiving addresses from Lancashire Conservative groups in the Great Hall,
Pomona Gardens, Manchester, 1872. It was in his speech that Disraeli joked that he
wished he had given Salford Borough four MPs instead of two. (*Illustrated London News*)

the estrangement of erstwhile supporters (especially Catholics) over the way the
Education Act worked, and trade union dissatisfaction with the government's
industrial legislation. The Education Act focused the Catholic Church's attitude
to local party politics more directly than ever before. Catholics voted Conservative
in the municipal election in 1872 on this issue, to the great annoyance of the
Liberals. But when the church became entwined in a bitter dispute with the Board
of Guardians over the education of Catholic children in the workhouse, Conservatives fought a successful campaign to defeat Catholic candidates in the poor law
elections that year. This led to the forming of a Catholic Political Association.

Bishop Vaughan expressed the view that in 'all matters of morality and religion' (i.e. education) Catholic voters should bind themselves to neither party: in what he defined as 'matters of reason' they were free to make up their own minds.[40] In a close contest the votes of the Salford Catholics were crucial to the Liberals. The Catholic Association could not advise Catholics to vote for Cawley and Charley, but because of the equivocal attitude of the Liberals towards paying fees of poor parents whose children went to denominational schools, advised Catholic voters to abstain. On the morning of the election, Kay had an interview with Bishop Vaughan and told him that he was opposed to denominational education, but was *not* opposed to *religious* education and would not support taking the capitation allowance from denominational schools. The Bishop pronounced himself satisfied, but in the way of last minute concordats, it was too late to stop most Catholic voters abstaining.[41]

A second explanation for the Liberal's narrow defeat in 1874 was trade union disatisfaction with Gladstone's industrial legislation. Whilst the unions approved the Trade Union Act of 1871 (which finally clarified their legal existence), they were not at all enamoured of the Criminal Law Amendment Act of the same year, which surrounded picketing with legal restrictions. But what really annoyed organized Labour was the attitude of free-market Liberal politicians to the proposed Nine Hour Day. Just after the election one friend of the trade union movement noted that 'From what I have heard I am inclined to think that no single fact had more to do with the defeat of the Liberal party in Lancashire ... than Mr Fawcett's speech on the Nine Hours Bill.'[42]

Early in 1875 Gladstone resigned as Liberal party leader and, with his pamphlet on Papal Infallibility, took a holiday from politics to go on an anti-Popery diversion of his own. Conservatives exulted in Liberalism's disarray. Scenting interesting possibilities, Charley declared 'The collapse of Liberalism entails great responsibility on us, the Conservative party. The people's health, the people's dwellings – the social condition of the people – these are subjects which I hope and believe will engage our attention for many sessions to come.'[43] The relative failure of Gladstone's first ministry in these areas gave the Conservatives a chance to forge a shining new version of Tory Democracy.

Cawley lived long enough to play his part in the passing of the Public Health and the Artisans Dwellings Acts of 1875, legislation which stands central in the tradition of Tory concern with social questions. They were issues which concerned Cawley's business as a civil engineer, and his interests as a local councillor. Certainly from this time, the efforts of local government to improve Public Health became more energetic than ever before, an important development for Salford, where the cumulative environmental problems arising from almost a century of industrial development were about as severe as anywhere in the country.

Cawley also lived long enough to see the onset of Disraelian Imperialism. He supported his leader's purchase of the Suez Canal shares and his Royal Titles Bill, which created Queen Victoria 'Empress of India'. Cawley also saw the start of the Near East crisis. But, dying on 2nd April 1877, he did not live to take part in the furore over the Russo-Turkish War and the Turkish atrocities, which divided political Manchester in much the same way as the Crimea had done twenty years before. Nor did he live to see the wars with the Afghans and the Zulus. Had he done so, it can hardly be doubted that he would have sung all the Jingo songs. Dying when he did, Cawley was also spared the revival of Liberal fortunes which all this did so much to stimulate.

Cawley's political life encapsulates the rise of Victorian popular Conservatism. Rooted in an energetic, if bigoted, church Protestantism, he was a characteristic product of the Lancashire version of that political creed. Manchester Evangelicals like Cawley did not dream of Barset: they were animated by a sense of what the church should be up and doing in an age of great cities. In anti-Catholicism and a remodelled Conservative ideology, they found ways of expressing their hostility to the disturbing challenges of a new, more pluralistic, industrial society. There was more to their Conservatism than anti-Catholicism, but in their time their conjuring-up of the Reformation and anti-Popery struck a popular chord. On these matters Cawley's opinions were unchanging over more than a quarter-century. Very successful in business and politics, Cawley's life was not without tragedy: his only son died when he was an undergraduate at Cambridge. Although active in the debates on the Disestablishment of the Irish Church in 1868–9, Cawley never made much of a name for himself in Parliament, restricting himself to church and sanitary topics. His abilities as a civil engineer were utilised by Select Committees of the House, and with two other eminent engineers he was responsible for a report to Parliament on the state of the water supply to the Metropolis. But his years at Westminster were unremarkable.

Cawley's sudden death in 1877 at the age of 65, apparently from typhoid, occasioned a by-election, in which the Conservative, Oliver Ormrod Walker, principal of one of the largest textile firms in Bury and a Colonel in the Rifle Volunteers, defeated Joseph Kay, Q.C.[44] This election was fought on a number of issues. But the one which mainly excited the electorate was the first intimations of Irish Home Rule, a thorn in the side of the Liberal party from that time on. Again, it was a desperately close contest: out of 17,148 votes cast, Walker got home by a mere 270. Liberals attributed their defeat once more to anti-Irishness and the alliance of parsons and publicans. 'When the two influences are combined, as they have been in the recent election contest, they are irrisistible, especially in a town like Salford where religious bigotry is as rampant as it was in the days of the Puritans, and drunkenness is a great and crying evil.'[45] It was alleged that at least two hundred licensed premises displayed 'Vote for Col. Walker and Religious Education' posters in their windows.[46]

The Salford result was a blow to the Liberals nationally. Gladstone had hoped that popular indignation against Disraeli's pro-Turkish Near Eastern policy would show itself. Instead, Irish Home Rule provoked a backlash. But 1877 was the last Conservative success for some time. In its wake the Salford Liberals really did reform their organization, and ousted Charley and Walker in 1880.

By then national events were swinging their way, and they enjoyed themselves attacking 'the Admirable CRICHTON of Belfast, Lancashire and London.' 'Mr Charley,' declared the *Salford Weekly News,* 'is a child of Nature. He would have been the delight of Jean Jacques Rousseau, or the father of Maria Edgeworth. His vanity has little guile in it; his flagrant political shallowness is wholly free from the taint of hypocrisy; he plays all the characters in his comical repertoire with the impulsive, egotistical familiarity of Toole, or of Bottom the weaver.' [47] The loss of his seat in Salford effectively ended the political career of 'Champagne' Charley, by now Common Sergeant of London, and the recipient of a knighthood. In the parliamentary seats he contested after quitting Salford Sir Thomas's particular blend of blarney and bigotry never served him as well as it had in Lancashire after the Second Reform Act. Charley died in 1904, his later years no doubt consoled by the material rewards accruing to a successful Judge in late Victorian England. But, after 1880, Salford knew him not.

A posed yet evocative photograph of about 1900 of women weavers believed to be employees of Wright Turner & Sons, Pendleton. Some are clearly sisters. (Local History Collection, Peel Park)

CHAPTER 7

# Poverty and Pollution:
# Thomas Davies, the Cotton Famine
# and the Sanitary Question in Salford

In 1871, shortly after the close of his term of office as Mayor of Salford, the admirers of Alderman Thomas Davies presented him with a purse containing a thousand guineas. They also had him portrayed in oils and sculpted in marble, and for the benefit of posterity lodged these likenesses in the Art Gallery and Museum in Peel Park.[1] Such expressions of esteem marked a decade of exertions in the service of the borough – three years as Mayor, three years as hon. secretary of the local Cotton Famine Relief Committee and three years as chairman of Salford's first Health Committee.

Both personally, and in his devotion to public service, there can be little doubt that Thomas Davies deserved these tributes. He seems an admirable if somewhat puritanical man, the very model of Wesleyan uprightness.[2] Yet, it might also be observed that such tributes were as much a product of relief as admiration, in that someone (at last) had taken the lead in the battle against the more appalling consequences of Victorian capitalism. The Cotton Famine was the nemesis of an industry which scoured the world to buy in the cheapest markets, and in the end became dangerously over-reliant on one. The accumulated sanitary problems of Salford resulted from the greatest industrial expansion so far seen in the modern world. Virtually unregulated, it had been pushed forward with a fine disregard for what it was doing to the environment or the lives of the people. As de Tocqueville noted of Manchester thirty years before, 'Everything in the exterior appearance of the city attests to the individual powers of man; nothing the directing power of society. At every turn human liberty shows its capricious creative force. There is no trace of the slow continuous action of government.'[3] It fell to Davies to lead the council towards that sort of 'continuous action' needed to make Salford a healthier place in which to live and work.

Davies was a Salfordian first and last; born in Bury Street in 1811, the son of a baker, he died seventy five years later in Leaf Square, Pendleton. Carrying on business as a shopkeeper and flour merchant he prospered, so much so that when he became a member of the council for the second time in 1859 he had been able to retire. Now Thomas Davies, Gentleman, he was free to devote himself to matters close

to his interests. One of these had
always been Methodism. Davies
was one of Mid-Victorian Salford's most influential Wesleyan
laymen. In boyhood he had been
connected with Gravel Lane
Chapel, where his father was
treasurer. When Irwell Street
Chapel was built in 1826, the
Davieses moved there, and
Thomas began a life-long connection, eventually becoming
Sunday School superintendent,
trustee and treasurer. In the
eighteenth and nineteenth centuries Manchester was the scene
of great Methodist effort. By
1802 the Manchester circuit
had 28 preaching places served
by three travelling and 22 local
preachers.[4] Seventy years later
there were 11 Wesleyan chapels

Portrait of Alderman Thomas Davies by Measham,
1871. (Salford Art Gallery and Museum)

in Salford alone, as well as another 11 belonging to other Methodists.[5] Add these
to the pattern of Church, old Dissent, Roman Catholics, Swedenborgians and Bible
Christians already noted, and something of the religious heterogeneity of Victorian
Salford may be appreciated. If, in the main, these churches and chapels lay intermixed
with the houses and other buildings, in certain places their proximity to one another
could make for memorable townscapes. One such, which survived until swept away
in recent 'urban renewal', was the few hundred yards of Broad Street, Pendleton,
between St Thomas's Church and Frederick Road. On the north side of this
throughfare below St Thomas's were located four large chapels, the first and biggest
of which was Brunswick, founded in 1814 as the great double-barrelled city's fifth
Wesleyan chapel, rebuilt in Gothic splendour with new Sunday schools in 1880. A
few yards further on towards Manchester lay Pendleton Congregational Chapel,
which originated as an offshoot of New Windsor in 1826, and was re-located on
Broad Street in 1847. It, too, was Gothic, its front being modelled on the east end
of Whitby Abbey. Next, on the corner of George Street was a large Primitive
Methodist Chapel, erected in 1874. And the last chapel on that side of Broad Street,
by Milton Place, was that of the Welsh Calvinistic Methodists, also built in 1874.
On the other side, facing this remarkable soot-blackened row of conventicles, stood
one whose origins were older than any of them, Bethesda Chapel of the Methodist
New Connexion, which went back to 1806.[6]

Davies, however, focused his religious energies on Salford township. Ignoring the
drift of the more affluent of his co-religionists to Broughton and Pendleton, where
they founded new chapels, he stayed loyal to Irwell Street. When the chapel came
to celebrate its jubilee, Davies, as one who had helped to make it, was the obvious

'Memorable Townscape': Broad Street, Pendleton, with its 'soot-blackened conventicles'.
On the left is Bethesda Chapel, Methodist New Connexion. On the right, the Welsh
Calvinistic Methodist Chapel. In the distance can be seen the spire of Brunswick
Wesleyan and, on the skyline, the tower of St Thomas' Church. (*Manchester Old and New*)

choice to write its history, which he did in his *Memorials of Irwell Street Wesleyan
Chapel* (1876). Two years later the chapel honoured *him* with a testimonial presentation to mark his fiftieth year of membership. His commitment to Wesleyanism
immersed Davis in education, and this in turn led him to face up to 'the condition
of the people' question. At the start of the nineteenth century Protestant Evangeli-
calism opened Sunday schools in places like Salford, where the streets teemed with
children. Formed by the 'Committee of the Sunday Schools for Children of all
Denominations,' Salford's first Sunday School remained undenominational for
almost two decades. Eventually, however, sectarianism took over. With Methodists
and Dissenters taking the lead, new chapels such as Irwell Street and Brunswick
had their own Sunday schools from the start. The objects were the conversion of
scholars so that they became 'members of society' and of 'select religious classes'.
But instruction was given free to children of all denominations (or none), and these
schools operated on a large scale. In 1831 the four Salford Wesleyan Sunday Schools
had 2469 scholars between them. A good part of their effort was devoted to secular
teaching, which was one reason why they so well-attended.[7]

One local development associated with this activity were the 'Whit Walks', street
processions of the Sunday Schools during the great annual holiday, which began
in 1801. These developed into one of the great annual Manchester events, one
which survives to the present day. Methodists and the Protestant Dissenters led
the way, Anglicans and Catholics lagging behind, though, in the end, pride and
prestige brought them in.

Whilst immersing themselves in their Sunday Schools, not to mention the other associations for their fellow church or chapel members, Christians as committed as Davis could never ignore the masses of people who, for a variety of reasons, lay outside the influence of organised religion. The Wesleyan circuits formed 'Home Missions'. One of the bodies Davies was much involved with was the Irwell Street Juvenile Missionary Society, founded in December 1864 to concentrate on trying to bring the young of the district within the scope of religious influences.[8] Another initiative devoted to this end was the Ragged Schools movement, launched in the 1850s to try to provide education for some of the thousands of 'street arabs' of Manchester and Salford. This new movement was actively promoted by the Manchester and Salford Ragged School Union. By 1866, twenty three schools were affiliated, of which seven were in Salford. One such was Spaw Street, founded in 1862. The district just south of Chapel Street was one of the poorest and most neglected in Salford. Spaw Street Ragged School's first home was under a railway arch. The place dripped water, and the atmosphere was polluted by the stench from nearby piggeries. Eventually, better premises were found in Worsley Street. Perhaps because it was located so close to his chapel, Davies became a strong supporter, and a frequent chairman at its annual meetings.[9]

At one of these in 1864 he estimated that there were perhaps 50,000 children in Manchester and Salford whose parents were 'wholly destitute of the means of affording them education'. In Salford alone he supposed there were 12,000. Despite his powerful belief in the voluntary principle, he had come to the view that elementary schooling, financed by a farthing rate, should be provided for all, though he recognised that this was, as yet, politically impossible.[10]

The faith of middle-class Liberals such as Davies in the efficacy of education to change society also found an outlet in their support for the Salford Working Men's College, which came into existence in the same year as the first Ragged School. The call for colleges for working men in Manchester was first made in a letter to the *Manchester Guardian* in 1856.[11] In fact three were founded, including one in Salford. At its inaugural soiree in June 1858 it was claimed that the latter was one 'which had originated with the working classes themselves', a provisional committee of working men having been formed when the project was launched, and the constitution of the College was always reasonably democratic. Nonetheless the College could not have been launched but for financial support from Salford's Liberal élite, particularly E. R. Langworthy, Sir Elkanah Armitage, William Harvey and David Chadwick, who was the College's principal advocate, serving as its treasurer until eventually succeeded by Davies.

Alongside these activities, Davies had become involved in local government. Unlike many prominent Wesleyans, his political instincts were never Conservative. Yet, though a firm Liberal, he was never a narrow party man, nor much to the fore in the excitement of parliamentary elections. For him, local government was, and always remained, the focus of his energies. Davies was first elected to the Council for Blackfriars Ward in 1847, and served nine years. However, in 1856 he declined to stand again. Davies was not absent from the Town Hall for long. In 1859 he was again elected for Blackfriars and soon became Chairman of the Water Committee. He was made an alderman in 1861, and remained a member of the corporation until his death twenty four years later. Contemporaries chiefly remembered him for his efforts in the field of public health. But before his involvement on that front, Lancashire was hit by the Cotton Famine. In the early 1860s local unemployment relief was to have the first claim on his attention.

In 1861 four-fifths of the raw cotton used in Lancashire came from one source, the southern states of the USA.[12] The alarming political instability of America in the 1850s did not pass unnoticed in Lancashire. In 1857 a Cotton Supply Association was formed with the intention of investing in schemes to develop alternative sources of supply. But the Association had scarcely progressed beyond formation before being overtaken by the start of the American Civil War in the spring of 1861.[13]

The first effects of the Famine began to manifest themselves in Salford in September, when it was announced that hours in local mills were about to be reduced by one third. By Christmas just over half the textile workers in Salford were on some sort of short time, and by the end of that first winter the sheer scale of the problem was becoming all too clear. In April 1862 the local paper noted 'The Great Cotton Famine has spread mischief through the working population of Salford as elsewhere: though, perhaps, not to the extent as has been seen in Blackburn, Stockport, and other towns exclusively devoted to the cotton industry.[14] The Famine was more serious in Salford township than in Pendleton. However, some mills never stopped, most notably those of Richard Haworth, who used fine cotton from Egypt and the Levant.

By mid-1862 efforts were being made to make-up the shortfall of American cotton with 'Surat' (as Indian cotton was called). It was called other things as well. The textile workers loathed it. Their unconquerable aversion arose, from the fact that Indian cotton was inferior in quality and often dirty, making it difficult to earn anything like the piece-rates they could with American. However, it was soon Hobson's choice: Surat or nothing. It was often nothing; increased imports of Surat

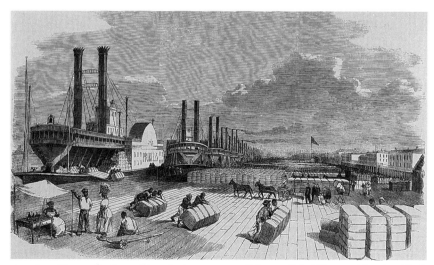

American Cotton for Lancashire: the levee at new Orleans, 1858. (*Illustrated London News*)

simply did not meet the shortfall from America. In the second half of 1862 the situation worsened. That winter as the sufferings of the mill-workers and their families increased, pressure mounted for better forms of relief than those resorted to so far.

In the absence of any social security system other than that afforded through personal or organised thrift, the only recourses of the destitute were to local charity, soup kitchens and the Poor Law. Soup kitchens first appeared in the St Stephen's district at New Year 1862. Using money collected locally, soup was distributed at taverns, some mills and chapels, and by individual shop keepers. But soup kitchens were always a temporary winter expedient, and by May 1862 many were closing because of lack of funds.[15] Other, less *ad hoc*, initiatives had to be sought. The principal burden of relieving the poor fell on the Poor Law authorities, and in the Cotton Famine the Boards of Guardians spent more on relief, and helped more people, than all other agencies put together. By July 1862 it was reported that the Manchester, Salford, Chorlton and Prestwich Boards were giving support to an estimated 25,000 persons weekly.[16]

Table 4. *The State of Employment in the Borough of Salford on 17 January 1862*

| Factories | Total | Usually Employed | On full-time | | Short-time | | Stopped | |
|---|---|---|---|---|---|---|---|---|
| Cotton | 29 | (9,405) | 11 | (1,470) | 15 | (1,523) | 3 | (2,812) |
| Flax | 5 | (1,783) | 5 | (1,783) | 0 | (0) | 0 | (0) |
| Small wares | 6 | (289) | 3 | (65) | 3 | (151) | 0 | (73) |
| Silk | 3 | (1,230) | 3 | (555) | 0 | (0) | 0 | (675) |
| Total Textiles | 43 | (12,707) | 22 | (3,873) | 18 | (5,274) | 3 | (3,560) |
| Other Businesses | | | | | | | | |
| Dye, printworks | 20 | (2,234) | 2 | (175) | 18 | (1,951) | 0 | (108) |
| Bleachworks | 14 | (617) | 3 | (145) | 10 | (375) | 1 | (97) |
| Oilcloth | 2 | (220) | 1 | (160) | 1 | (60) | 0 | (0) |
| Machinists | 47 | (4,040) | 39 | (2,438) | 8 | (665) | 0 | (937) |
| Brewers | 11 | (166) | 10 | (156) | 1 | (6) | 0 | (4) |
| Sawmills, joiners | 15 | (579) | 12 | (476) | 3 | (75) | 0 | (28) |
| Industrial chemists | 9 | (125) | 7 | (109) | 2 | (12) | 0 | (4) |
| Miscellaneous | 57 | (1,851) | 35 | (1,417) | 22 | (347) | 0 | (87) |
| Totals | 218 | (22,539) | 131 | (8,949) | 83 | (8,715) | 4 | (4,825) |

Source: *Salford Weekly News*, 18 January 1862.

The Famine presented the New Poor Law, and the social philosophy which underpinned it, with many difficulties. In this situation how could the 'workhouse test' be applied in all its rigour and purity? How could the aim of keeping down poor rates be reconciled with the need to relieve people *en masse*? How could the principle of no relief to the able-bodied without a 'labour test' be applied to thousands of young women? How could the 'respectable' working class, who had never in their lives applied to the Guardians for relief, be persuaded that now, in this new situation, relief was their *legal right*. What really shocked public opinion was the revelation of the utter destitution of the hitherto 'respectable' working class. In November 1862 James Dickson, one of the relieving officers of the Salford Board of Guardians, reported 'I have been an officer since March 1844, in all the branches of the Poor Law, but I never witnessed scenes such as now'.[17] Dickson described visiting houses that had no fire, no bedding, no furniture, and no clothes other than those the people stood up in. He described an almost physical 'shrinking in their frames at the idea of going into the [work]house' when he suggested it to them. The Board reacted by giving relieving officers the power to give bedding at once where it was urgently needed, but it was fast becoming clear that other methods of relief needed to be found.

From the end of the first winter (1861–62) poor law policy in Salford was in any case being modified in direct response to the growing anger of the unemployed. At protest meetings resolutions were passed against the level of relief, and labour tests were viewed 'as that kind of labour which common felons are required to perform' and demonstrations against them were organised. Unemployed operatives in Salford also protested against the use of relief tickets instead of cash, and the 'miserly conduct' of the Guardians in general.[18]

With the coming of the Famine's second winter the need for new initiatives became pressing. 'We are all beginning to see the hopelessness of making the Poor Law responsible for the unemployed,' confessed the *Salford Weekly News*, adding optimistically, 'but there is much voluntary liberality which has yet to be evoked.'[19] In fact new initiatives in the form of Famine Relief Committees, funded by national as well as local subscription, were already beginning, and it was as honorary secretary of Salford's Famine Relief Committee that Alderman Davies was first to make his mark.

'Reduced to their last stick of furniture'. A Salford family in the Cotton Famine, 1862.
(*Illustrated London News*)

Table 5. *Short time and unemployment in the winter of 1862–63*

| Date | Usually Employed | On Full Time | On Short Time | Out of Work |
|------|------------------|--------------|---------------|-------------|
| 1862 | | | | |
| 23 Aug | 19,218 | 10,029 | 5,020 | 4,159 |
| 6 Sept | 20,984 | 9,613 | 6,731 | 4,640 |
| 20 Sept | 21,181 | 9,056 | 6,805 | 5,320 |
| 4 Oct | 21,227 | 8,920 | 6,791 | 5,516 |
| 18 Oct | 21,328 | 8,882 | 6,665 | 5,781 |
| 1 Nov | 21,331 | 8,599 | 6,802 | 5,930 |
| 15 Nov | 21,347 | 8,566 | 6,519 | 6,262 |
| 29 Nov | 21,389 | 7,880 | 6,944 | 6,565 |
| 13 Dec | 21,456 | 8,349 | 6,568 | 6,539 |
| 27 Dec | 20,576 | 9,560 | 5,891 | 6,125 |
| 1863 | | | | |
| 10 Jan | 21,536 | 9,946 | 5,388 | 6,202 |
| 24 Jan | 21,536 | 10,257 | 5,673 | 5,606 |
| 14 Feb | 21,614 | 9,674 | 5,836 | 6,104 |

Source: *Salford Weekly News.* Between August 1062 and February 1863 the paper published detailed figures in the form listed each week. The dates in the left-hand column are those of the issues of the newspaper.

A preliminary meeting to form a Central Relief Committee in Manchester was held in May 1862. The argument for a new initiative was put by Alderman Pochin, who disclosed that while the Guardians helped some, and the District Provident Society others, 'there was nothing doing to lend a helping hand to the better class of those sufferers who were unwilling to become paupers, and amongst whom it was desirable to maintain this healthy feeling'. A Central Committee was duly formed to receive donations.[20] Despite what was said about raising money locally and not relying on aristocratic largesse it was material aid from such figures as Lord Derby (who gave £20,000), and from the Mansion House and Bridgewater House Funds, tapping a nationwide outburst of sympathy for the suffering operatives of Lancashire, which enabled the system based on a Central and local Relief Committees to function through the Famine.

The Salford Committee began in the second week of August 1862 (six months after the effects of the Famine began to be serious). Soon help was being mobilized on a larger scale. In the week ending 26 December 1862, 17,793 people (5,238 cases) additional to those relieved by the Guardians were assisted, at a cost of about £1,000.[21] One of the first things the Committee did was to open 'sewing schools' for the vast army of unemployed females for whom the Poor Law was seen as inappropriate. In return for relief payment the women and girls were to sew, 'make useful articles' and be given lessons. By February 1863 some 1,100 were attending the eleven Salford schools. They were required to attend from 6.00 a.m. to 4.00 p.m., 'in order', it was bluntly admitted, 'that the work … would not be easier than in the mills and so that the girls would not lose their habit of early rising.'[22]

What is observable, is the effect that such mass deprivation had on the hitherto inflexible Poor Law. As a result of concern over the plight of the respectable poor

The Cotton Famine: a Society of Friends' Soup Kitchen, Manchester, 1862. (*Illustrated London News*)

(and the protests of the unemployed), within weeks of the sewing schools being formed, the workhouse test for men was replaced by a so-called 'educational test'.[23] By November 1862 the Guardians had set up 'outdoor schools', or attendance centres for men in Chapel street, Ellor street and Great George street, and others followed. To qualify for relief, men had to attend on Mondays from half past one to half past four and Saturdays from nine until half past twelve, and the remainder of the week from nine to four thirty (with time off for midday dinner).[24] This timetable represented the Guardians' attempts to enforce a form of 'workhouse test', whilst giving time for men to look for work. In an effort to keep Salford's children at school, relief was conditional on parents agreeing to send their children to school, fees being paid by the Committee.[25]

In the overall Relief effort, never far from the minds of ratepayers was a fantasy that, as a result of their prolonged lay-off the factory operatives might develop a taste for the leisured existence, and, when it was all over, decide not to return to factory life. 'Labour', pontificated the *Salford Weekly News*, 'is the true glory of the mass of our population, and we must ever keep them in love with a fair day's work for a fair day's wages'.[26] That December the paper carried an advertisement which said that 'if any persons in receipt of relief have been offered work with reasonable wages and have refused it' employers should contact the Board of Guardians. It printed it every week for over a year. In fact, the textile workers wanted nothing more than to go back to work. Whatever illusions tax payers entertained about life on relief, it bore little comparison to life on regular wages.

Mass unemployment reached a peak at Christmas 1862, and by then the Salford Committee was facing a funding crisis. It was calculated that if more resources were not forthcoming they would not be able to carry on beyond the last week in January. Relationships with the Central Relief Committee in Manchester rapidly worsened, Salford (as always) feeling that it was at a serious disadvantage being linked in with Manchester for the receipt of outside funding.[27] Their task was not, in any case, easy. They had to organise systematic relief for thousands of people on a weekly basis. They had to maintain working relationships with the Board of Guardians, the Central Relief Committee and the District Provident Society. On the one hand they were urged to be more liberal than the Guardians (whose relief payments, the *Salford Weekly News* frankly admitted, was 'quite insufficient for the maintainance of the family or the paying of rent'), whilst on the other hand they had to keep their payments within the amount 'the head of a family might earn by half a week's work' because, as the paper put it, 'half work may be next year's prelude to a return to the old five and a half days work out of seven'.[28]

In fact, in February and March 1863, the Salford Committee came under pressure from the Central Committee to *reduce* its relief rates, said to be marginally higher than in other areas. Davies and his colleagues were forced to comply. Since December very little subscription money had come in and they were increasingly dependent on the Central Committee, through whom help from the outside was channelled. Average relief was brought down to 2s. 2d per adult per week. This enforced belt-tightening angered the unemployed, and led to disturbances in Preston, Ashton, Dukinfield and Stalybridge, and outbursts of quite serious rioting. In Salford things were quieter, though Canon Stowell received an anonymous threatening letter, having moved the resolution to comply with the Central Committee's instructions. The Committee did so reluctantly.[29]

One solution advocated in 1863 was emigration. Would-be emigrants were wooed with press advertisements from such organisations as the Lancashire and Queensland Co-operative Emigration Society Ltd.[30] However, emigration proved no panacea. It was not cheap and was generally opposed by Boards of Guardians. In general, those who emigrated paid their own passages. Another reason was the hostility of factory masters, who had a vested interest in keeping their workforces intact during the Famine, sometimes spending, as in the case of Sir Elkanah Armitage & Sons considerable sums in unemployment assistance. Not many followed their lead: most employers accepted what had happened as nothing more than the unfortunate consequences of American politics, and, as such, not their responsibility.

In 1863, as the power of the Manchester Central Committee grew, that of the local committee waned. To shift the financial burden the Central Committee urged upon local bodies the adoption of work schemes under the recently passed Public Works Act. In Salford a scheme to dredge mud from the river at Peel Park was started in March 1863, employing a few men eight hours a day, three days a week, for 3d an hour, and the Poor Law Union employed paupers on the Broad Street sewer, then under construction. Finding suitable projects to come under the Public Works scheme was a problem in itself. Eventually (in September) the council received loans of £52,000 for paving and sewering in Salford and Broughton, the completion of a manure depot at Ordsall, and for extensions to Salford Cattle Market.[31] Notwithstanding the need for such schemes, not least on the sanitary front, public works were rarely more than a sideline. Compared to the thousands seeking relief scarcely more than a few hundred found employment on public works.

The winter of 1862–63 was the worst. The following spring and summer employment prospects improved, largely through the increased use of Surat. However, there was a limit to which Indian production could be expanded. By July 10,674 Salford operatives (just under half the estimated total) were on full time, 5,164 were working between two and four days a week, whilst 6,071 were still entirely out of work.[32] The situation worsened again in the winter 1863–4. In January 'many mills which have, at least, been partially working, are now dropping off one by one into gloomy silence, causing the list of the unemployed operatives to swell into formidable dimensions.'[33] It was to be almost another year, in the spring of 1865, that unmistakable signs of recovery began to manifest themselves. It was to be another five before the Lancashire cotton industry recovered to its 1861 position. As late as 1869 the USA was supplying a mere 31 per cent of the cotton Lancashire was using, compared to the 85 of pre-Famine days.[34]

By the end of August 1864 the Salford Relief Committee was optimistic enough to believe that the end of its work was in sight. It was being over-sanguine. As winter approached, pauperism began to increase once more. Alderman Davies told the *Weekly News* there was work to be done because 'cotton operatives would apply to the Guardians only from extreme necessity … they would struggle with their hard fate manfully, and with patient endurance … the new applicants to the Guardians were not factory workers, but mainly those who had been engaged in outdoor work.'[35] And, in the event, the Salford Relief Committee's work was not completed until May 1865. In just under three years it spent about £43,000, £9,000 of which had been locally subscribed, most of the rest being drawn from the Mansion House and Bridgewater House Funds. It distributed around £15,000 in food relief, spent £8,000 on clothing, and distributed more than a thousand tons of free coal over the three winters of the Famine. The committee paid out some £9,000 in cash to the unemployed, and over £7,000 to girls and women in the sewing schools: another £500 were spent on school fees. There was pride (not unmixed with relief ) that no-one in Salford had died of starvation, and the committee claimed (quite wrongly) that public health was no worse than usual.[36] Order had been preserved, and there was general satisfaction at the level of co-operation shown on the committee.

Table 6. *Relief in Salford in the Cotton Famine*

| Year | By the Guardians of the Poor | | By local Relief Committee | Total |
| | In-Relief | Outdoor Relief | | |
| | £ | £ | £ | £ |
|------|-----------|----------------|------------|-------|
| 1861 | 3,718 | 5,339 | – | 9,057 |
| 1862 | 3,944 | 6,995 | – | 10,939 |
| 1863 | 4,728 | 24,419 | 25,296 | 54,443 |
| 1864 | 4,338 | 19,226 | 17,162 | 40,766 |
| 1865 | 3,889 | 13,076 | 681 | 17,646 |

*Source:* G.F.Watts, *Lancashire and the Cotton Famine,* 1866.

The committee also took pride in the scale (and complexity) of the work it had undertaken for nearly three years. It added up to a great voluntaryist effort, which called forth organising skills and leadership of no mean order. From the expressions of admiration (and gratitude) which Thomas Davies received from his friends and fellow members it is clear that his role as hon. secretary had been a key one. He had given leadership when it was badly needed, and never stinted with his time or effort. Presenting him with a testimonial in October 1864, Alderman Wright Turner referred to the early funding crisis. At Davies' prompting they sought (and received) assistance direct from the Mansion House Committee. More clearly than the other members, Davies foresaw the scale and likely duration of their task. In standing up for Salford *vis-à-vis* the Central committee in Manchester he also earned the gratitude of the borough's élite. In reply, Davies reflected what had been the main concern of the middle class all along: 'it had been the high endeavour of the Committee in helping the distressed operatives not to degrade themselves in any way, or wound their self respect, or add to the normal pauperism of the borough'.[37]

It has to be observed that the Relief Committee also relieved several other middle-class anxieties. The Poor Law had not been overwhelmed. If the rates had gone up, the Government Rate Relief Scheme ensured they had not go up too much, and to aid Lancashire the nation's generosity had been tapped. To support 'the respectable poor', a parallel system to the Poor Law had been created. The workhouse system survived. Thirty years later Poor Law Reformers were to find the public adhering to the principles of 1834 as strongly as ever.

Those who had been unemployed played no part in this post-Famine self-congratulation. Before receiving help they had been required to exhaust all, or very nearly all, of their resources. For most this meant reducing their homes to the last stick of furniture. Application for relief was received with all the suspicion the system demanded, and their 'case' was investigated just as intently by the District Provident Society on behalf of the Relief Committee as by Relieving Officers on behalf of the Guardians. Relief pay was very low, the bare minimum needed 'to sustain life', as was openly admitted. The figure almost universally arrived at for the sustaining of life was about two shillings per week per head, with occasional help with bedding, clothing and coal. In the Famine a sizeable part of the working class existed on a maximum of that for two, and sometimes three years. If no-one starved, those mill-working families who lived well before the American Civil War learned what 'clemming' (going hungry) really meant. If relief was not given without scrutiny, it was not given unconditionally either. Inside the workhouse there were the usual labour tests: outside there was attendance at men's 'outdoor schools' and women's sewing schools. Small wonder that when the mills reopened in 1865, local shopkeepers put out flags and there was rejoicing in the streets.[38]

The unemployment and stagnation of the Sixties was followed by the phenomenal boom of the early Seventies. With America concentrating on recovery and Germany and France at war, Britain played out the last phase of its period as 'Workshop of the World' virtually unchallenged by competitors. In Salford the effect of this was a decade of growth. Between the censuses of 1871 and 1881 the popula-tion of the borough increased by upwards of 51,000 to a total of 176,000. The greatest relative increases were in Pendleton and Broughton (up by 59 per cent and 120 per cent respectively), but the population of Salford township also grew by more than a fifth.

To some extent this great boom overlaid the memory of the Famine – more easily, perhaps, for some than for others. For the working class, the Famine had been traumatic and their sufferings were remembered vividly. For some members of the middle-class the way the respectable operatives bore their privation with what seemed Christian forbearance, was profoundly moving, and helped to create the myth of an almost saintly working class. In fact, working people were not nearly as passive in the face of a minimalist and grudging scale of relief as this myth had it. One indication is the anger which occasionally erupted. Another is that when they were given the vote in 1867, Lancashire operatives were as willing to vote for the party of those 'aristocrats' and 'outsiders' who came to their aid in 1862 as the party of their mainly Liberal employers.

In Thomas Davies's first period on the council the sanitary state of Salford was a grumbling ulcer, a problem the corporation was painfully aware of, but reluctant to investigate. Yet, almost yearly, some event or inquiry raised the sanitary issue anew and periodically the sensibilities of the reading public were sickened by accounts of slums or some example of gross industrial pollution. It is not that the council or its members were indifferent, or had no achievements to their credit in these years. As already noted, their efforts resulted in the opening Peel Park and establishing a Nuisance Committee, a good deal of paving and street improvement, and the laying on of a good supply of water. Compared to the sheer scale and dynamism of the problem, in retrospect they appear scarcely more than first tentative steps.

One difficulty was that every revelation about the sanitary condition of Salford, and every action taken, served only to reveal greater dimensions to the problem. In the 1860s it came to be perceived that sanitary improvement needed more than street paving, nuisance removal or even a reasonable water supply. It grew to embrace the condition of Salford's older housing, the almost incredible population densities in the oldest part of the township, the state of drainage in what was a low-lying district almost encircled by the great bend of the Irwell, the appalling state of the river itself, the problem of night-soil removal, the close proximity of slaughter houses and piggeries to human dwellings and the worst air pollution in the world. Before 1860 sanitarians were not unaware of Salford's high death rate. But, because no regular statistics were gathered, no picture of *trends* in public health was available. The Council itself was daunted by the awareness that not only did it have a backlog of problems but also by the fact that, despite recent setbacks, industrial Salford continued to grow inexorably.

Whenever action was initiated in these years, it nearly always ran up against the problem of limited legal powers. By the late 1850s Salford had a series of local Acts, each widening the powers, or rectifying the shortcomings of previous ones. Above all, councillors and aldermen were working within an individualist ideology, which even the most ardent sanitary reformers endorsed. In particular, the rights of property were most tenderly protected. Capitalism created Salford's slums, and was protected from those who wanted to make it accept the consequences of its own workings. In 1854 and 1856 when the Nuisance Committee, prodded by Pendleton villa owners on the matter of increasing air pollution, prosecuted Messrs. Barningham's Iron Works and Spence & Dixon's Chemical Works, they experienced a backlash from workers, businessmen and the local press, the severity of which took them by surprise.[39] Fines for air pollution were derisory, and, though businessmen promised to adopt 'patent smoke consuming boilers', the problem simply worsened as new factories and foundries opened. Above all, there was a powerful feeling that business was too important to be interfered with.

Beginning as Chairman of the Water Committee, Thomas Davies was to become the man most remembered for cajoling the Council into action on the sanitary front. The motives of Davies and those like him who took up this cause are summed up in the words of William Mather in a lecture in which he roundly stated 'The state of social life in England below the upper working class is a disgrace to civilization, a mockery of the religious fervour of which we boast, and it is the badge by which, among other nations, our own is distinguished, or rather, notorious.'[40]

For Davies the Cotton Famine was profoundly educational, bringing him into even closer contact with the grim realities of the lives of the poor. However, his interest in sanitary matters pre-dated the Famine. In the Fifties he and other middle-class reformers were influenced by the Manchester and Salford Sanitary Association. This propagandist body promoted meetings, held lectures and published pamphlets on the 'laws of health' and the prevention of disease. It aimed to influence local authorities as well as public opinion, and took it upon itself to bring sanitary nuisances to their attention.

By 1860 a certain amount had been achieved in Salford. Under the Nuisance Act there had been some cleansing of the filthiest corners of the courts off Greengate and Chapel Street, and action had been taken against common lodging houses. Following a report by David Chadwick in 1854 on the provision of public baths and wash houses in Liverpool and London, the Manchester and Salford Baths and Laundries Company opened its first premises in Collier Street, Greengate two years later. The Collier Street complex of two swimming baths, private baths and a laundry was the first of five such planned for Manchester and Salford.[41]

Undoubtedly, the most significant development of these years was the Sanitary and Nuisance Committee's decision in 1860 to gather statistical information on a regular basis. Over the next nine years the reports compiled by John Pickering, Salford's Sanitary Inspector, for the first time brought some precision to discussions about the extent of Salford's problems. On the appearance of his first report, Salford congratulated itself on what was claimed to be the most detailed statistics for any town in England, almost as if the mere act of their publication did something to solve the problem.[42] A certain amount of satisfaction was also taken that Pickering seemed to show that Salford was by no means the unhealthiest in a select list of large towns. It was in the breakdown of these statistics that the real impact of Pickering's work lay. The death rate of the borough was arrived at by averaging that of Salford township with those of Pendleton and Broughton, the latter then a pleasant middle-class suburb.[43] However, over seventy *per cent* of the borough's population was concentrated in Salford township, and more than half of those in Greengate Registration District, the tightly-packed older part. It was there that the borough's sanitary problems were worst. Pickering's method of drawing attention to this each year was to list streets with an abnormally high mortality rate, an effective descriptive device.

From 1860 Pickering's annual reports kept the sanitary question before the ratepayers, and what he was saying was periodically reinforced by information from other sources. The most significant fact revealed by Pickering's reports was the steady worsening in Salford's mortality rates:

Table 4. *Mortality in Salford by Districts, 1861–68*
*(per 1000 of the population)*

|      | Borough | | Registration Districts | | |
|      |         | Greengate | Regent Rd | Pendleton | Broughton |
|------|---------|-----------|-----------|-----------|-----------|
| 1861 | 24.6 | 26.1 | 27.8 | 21.8 | 13.8 |
| 1862 | 25.3 | 27.8 | 29.4 | 19.6 | 14.7 |
| 1863 | 26.0 | 29.1 | 28.3 | 22.5 | 15.0 |
| 1864 | 26.5 | 31.0 | 28.7 | 21.7 | 14.6 |
| 1865 | 29.1 | 32.8 | 32.3 | 25.2 | 14.8 |
| 1866 | 28.8 | 33.9 | 32.2 | 23.0 | 13.6 |
| 1867 | 28.2 | 31.9 | 31.9 | 22.8 | 15.7 |
| 1868 | 30.5 | 33.0 | 34.3 | 28.7 | 14.9 |

Source: *Annual Report of the Medical Officer of Health for Salford* (1902), pp. 62–5.

In view of the Cotton Famine this was perhaps not unexpected, but Davies and his fellow reformers were alarmed that the 1868 figure was the worst Pickering recorded (though the mortality rate had touched 32.7 in 1846, 30.6 in 1849 and 30.4 in 1858).[44] Other factors were that, despite the recession, the town's population continued to grow in this decade and there had been outbreaks of epidemics. Furthermore, if the sanitary efforts of the Council were successful in minimising the effect of such events as the cholera in 1866,[45] they were proving hopelessly inadequate in big environmental matters, such as the state of the river, slum houses and middens and cesspools.

As well as gathering statistics on Salford's general mortality rates, Pickering also assembled those for infant mortality, marriages and births, and also attempted to analyse some of the causes of premature death. During the Cotton Famine, the incidence of marriage in Salford fell, but began to pick up again in the second half of the decade, reaching a peak in the boom years of the early Seventies. Throughout the Sixties the birthrate remained high. It was invariably higher than the death-rate, in which deaths of infants played a very significant part.[46] In any one of the years examined by Pickering, deaths of those under five accounted for just under half of all deaths in Salford, and half of these were of infants in their first year of life. Thereafter, Public Health measures slowly succeeded in levelling off and then reducing the general mortality rate, as in other great towns. However, they failed to effect any improvement in infant-mortality rates, which, until about the turn of the century, remained appallingly high.[47]

In 1864 Pickering produced a 'Table of Deaths from Certain Diseases, in each

Division of the Borough, during Five years', in which, despite the medically imprecise terms of the day, he demonstrated that Salford's excessively high mortality rates were environmentally caused. For adults the greatest causes of death were bronchitis, 'phthisis' (tuberculosis) and pneumonia. The greatest killers of children were 'convulsions' and 'diahorrea', and in those five years there had been epidemics of 'Hooping cough', measles and scarlatina.[48]

In his reports Pickering also gathered together and published information on population densities, which illustrate very graphically the accumulated problems of the many decades of unregulated urban growth. In 1861 in Greengate district the density was 142.8 persons per acre, against 31.7 in Regent Road, 9.0 in Pendleton and 7.0 in Broughton. By 1870, Greengate's density had fallen to 139.4, whilst Regent Road's had increased to 42.7, Pendleton's to 10.8 and Broughton's to 10.2. In fact, Regent Road District's population overtook that of Greengate in 1864, and for the rest of the century its density grew, whilst Greengate's fell. Yet, however much the expanding districts of the borough grew in the last third of the century, they never saw anything like the degree of overcrowding found in Greengate in the first eight decades or so years of old Salford's expansion.[49]

Despite a background of the Cotton Famine and the deep anxieties it engendered amongst taxpayers, Pickering's reports brought a certain amount of action on the part of the Council. In 1862 a new Salford Improvement Act was obtained. Primarily a consolidating and amending statute, it superseded and updated all previous local acts since 1830. Largely concerned with gas and water, sanitary improvement was not its primary purpose. However, the Act did contain some sanitary provisions. It granted the corporation powers to purchase the market rights of Salford and regulate fairs, cattle markets and slaughter houses. The Council's powers over sewers, house drainage and house building were also extended.

In the early Sixties the state of the river and the drainage of Salford township began to cause concern. Always liable to flood, it was estimated that, because of the dumping of rubbish, the Irwell was silting up at a rate of an inch or more a year. 'Our river communication with the sea,' declared the *Salford Weekly News*, 'is a vile common sewer – an overflowing mud channel', the stench from which was abominable in summer. Three years later, an engineer's survey noted, 'The River Irwell has been appropriately termed "the Grand Trunk Sewer" receiving as it does, the entire drainage of the borough from 46 separate contributories.'[50]

In 1863 the Salford Drainage Committee had a report prepared on construction of a much-needed main sewer to intercept and carry away the surface water of the borough. This scheme was shelved, partly for reasons of cost, and partly because of the lack of the necessary legal powers. However, events continued to keep the question alive. In July 1864 the setting up of a Parliamentary Committee of Inquiry into the Sewage of Towns was announced, followed shortly after by a Royal Commission on River Pollution, whose representatives duly visited the borough.[51]

Two years later, the river made its presence felt yet again: that November Salford had its worst floods since 1837. Four hundred acres disappeared under water, 3,500 dwellings and 40 mills were affected, three lives were lost and the cost to business alone was estimated at upwards of £100,000.[52] 1866 is a key year in the history of sanitation generally, and Salford's in particular. In addition to the floods, its livestock markets were closed by the Cattle Plague, and the cholera paid one last visit. In other ways, 1866 was not a good year for local government in Salford. There came the revelation of low standards and inefficiencies in the police force, and the defalcation of William Noar, the borough treasurer, caused something of a shock. It was at this point that Thomas Davies, freed from service on the Famine Relief Committee, began to assume the role of leading sanitary advocate on the Council.

In point of strict accuracy, he had started the year before. In April 1865 there had been a typhus outbreak in Back William Street.[53] That summer the Privy Council warned local authorities to take action against the approaching cholera. At a council meeting Davies severely criticised the Sanitary Committee; producing statistical reports was not enough, more inspection was called for. In reply, Councillor Nuttall, the chairman, made the damaging confession that nowadays only he and the deputy-chairman attended meetings. Davies moved that the committee be reformed, and that members with cottage property interests should not sit on it. He also proposed employing medical officers from the Poor Law Union, because, under the Nuisance Removal Acts, no proceedings could be instituted unless information was laid by a medical officer. Davies' resolution was carried, and he was elected chairman in Nuttall's place.[54]

His next five years of activity mark a turning point in the history of public health in Salford. He, more than any other individual, forced its 'economiser' Council to face up to its responsibilities, first over 'nuisances', then on a broader sanitary front. The first task was to act against cholera. The borough was placarded with notices advising people on suitable measures – whitewashing dwellings, removing accumulations of filth and rubbish, ventilating and draining, and being personally clean. Cottage owners were threatened with the Nuisance Removal Act, and the Scavenging Department dusted down the most insanitary corners of old Salford with deodorising powder.[55]

In general, these precautions proved successful. Salford largely escaped the cholera, and there was a certain amount of satisfaction that, in Pickering's table of death rates in 21 large towns in England that year, Salford was 13th. Nonetheless, there was no hiding from the fact that 1866 was a very bad year. If only 21 people were identified as dying of the cholera, the death rate in Salford township was the highest yet recorded.[56]

The Sanitary Act which followed the cholera visitation legislated against over-crowding in private lodging houses, and Davies and his committee lost no time in getting to work. They found some 900 houses in Salford sub-let, and the bye-laws they drew up for lodging-houses provoked considerable opposition from small property owners. The committee had also started to enforce the Regulation of Buildings Act. Salford's 'spec-builders' proved worthy opponents. Davies reported that *after* new buildings had been approved by the committee, builders and owners often proceeded to alter them to defeat the purposes of the law.[57]

In 1867 the council secured another multi-purpose Improvement Act. It gave powers to construct a new street in Pendleton, extend the Gas concern, and to take steps to resolve the long standing triangular dispute over water between

Pendleton district and the councils of Manchester and Salford. It also contained a few sanitary clauses. It conferred on the Council powers to decide the width of new streets, to stop-up streets when necessary and to order the cleansing of ponds, ditches and sewers. It also contained clauses relating to the removal of filth, the closing of piggeries, and offensive trades. Most significantly, it sanctioned the appointment of a Medical Officer of Health.[58]

Davies took up the latter question in a speech to the Council in 1868. He declared that in the past two and a half years as Committee Chairman he had done all he could, but the time had now come to have a qualified medical practitioner. Initially, he said, he had been in favour of up-grading a sanitary inspector, but having gone into the question Davies was convinced that it was essential for Salford to have one of its own, and cited the fact that only a medical officer could enforce certain of the clauses of the Sanitary Act. Opposition came from Ratepayers' Association councillors. Their suggestion that Pickering, or another sanitary inspector, be promoted and placed in charge was rejected, and a motion that a Medical Officer be advertised for and appointed was carried.[59] In due course Dr John Edward Syson was appointed Salford's first Medical Officer of Health.

When Pickering fell ill in 1868 Davies saw through the last of the annual reports prepared by the sanitary inspector. It escaped no-one's notice that the recorded death rates were the worst since statistics began nine years before.[60] Davies was automatic choice as first Chairman of the new Health Committee, serving six years, and in November 1868 was elected Mayor. He was then prevailed upon to serve a second and then a third consecutive term. Clearly, Salford needed Thomas Davies.

In the next few years Davies worked closely with the new Medical Officer. Together, they tried to create a more positive attitude to sanitary reform in the borough. They were helped by new legislation, particularly the Public Health Act of 1872. Nonetheless, it was uphill work. The main achievement of Davies' mayoralty was the Salford Improvement Act of 1870, the primary object of which was to make the Blackfriars street extension, the most important piece of town improvement for years. The Act also raised the council's borrowing powers, further extended its controls over builders and building plans, divided Salford townships four wards into eight, allowed for profits from water as well as gas to be used in aid of the rates, and extended the power to disburse the income from the borough's other charities to the distributors of the Booth Charities.[61]

The following year saw yet another Improvement Act, the main provision of which was to empower the council to construct a sewage-treatment works at Mode Wheel. It also gave the corporation powers to act against the dumping of solid matter in the river, and further amended the building regulations.[62] The year after, Salford appointed its first Borough Surveyor and Engineer to try to secure some uniformity of action in the matter of drainage schemes, in place of each township making its own arrangements. In 1873 a Building Committee was set up, taking over powers then vested in an overworked Health Committee. This was also the year Salford appointed its first Borough Analyst.[63] Two years later, under the Salford Tramways and Improvement Act of 1875, powers were given to the Council to demolish slums. First to go was the notorious Birtles Square, Greengate.

These years saw an attack on the more outlandish old-world nuisances in Salford. The worst of the piggeries were swept away, and the council followed Pickering's suggestion on central abattoirs, opening six new ones next to the cattle market in Cross Lane in 1870. Butchers in Salford continued to slaughter, but from now on under rather more control than hitherto.[64] In his brief tenure of office (he moved in 1873) Dr Syson drew attention to Salford's high infant mortality, arguing that this was in some measure preventable, although he was under no illusion as to the difficulties in achieving this. However, he tried. Using 'Sisters connected with the Church of England', he started a day-nursery in Greengate. Although it operated in a very modest way, it served to focus some attention on the problems of child care, 'baby farming' and the waste of infant life.[65]

The most daunting feature of the years Davies and Syson were at the helm was the fact that the more that was done, the more needed to be done. Massive issues now had to be faced, the technical solutions to which were either not at that time clear, or were conceived of (for financial or ideological reasons) as near-impossible. One such was river pollution. In 1868–89 the Royal Commission visited the borough, and both Davies and Syson appeared before it to answer questions on the state of the Irwell, and outline ways they thought it affected the health of the district.[66] The basic facts were simple: the difficulty was what to do about them.

In his evidence Davies reported on the abortive 1863–4 scheme for an intercepting sewer. Using powers in the 1871 Improvement Act, the corporation were now able to achieve this: an intercepting sewer for Salford was constructed, the work being finished in 1879. Four years later the sewage works at Mode Wheel was completed. This was no mean achievement. Whilst this reduced river pollution and improved drainage, it did not end flooding – which occurred again in 1877, 1890 and 1901. Nor did it lead to speedy emulation by other authorities. In 1874 a deputation from the Salford Council waited upon the Home Secretary to propose a River Conservancy Board for the whole length of the Irwell. They were told that they must confer with the other authorities and come back if they reached agreement.[67] This proved impossible.

The visit of the Royal Commission ushered in a long debate on the midden question. From its outset the water-closet and water-borne sewage system (the modern solution of how to dispose of human excrement in cities) had its advocates. The problem was that Manchester and Salford were then almost entirely midden cities, and the cost of a water borne system seemed impossibly high. Nonetheless, the nightsoil question was the central one in the battle to reduce the urban death rate, as the title of Dr Syson's 1870 pamphlet – *The Great Sanitary Question of the Day – How to Dispose of our Refuse*, makes plain.

In his first annual report in 1873, Syson's successor, Dr Tatham, described the four methods of excrement and rubbish disposal then in operation in the borough. In addition to the almost universal 'Lancashire midden cesspit 'there was the 'modified midden' – a privy and ashpit with a much shallower cesspit, roofed over to prevent (in theory) the admixture of rain water. After commenting on the disadvantage of both reconstructed and unreconstructed middens, Tatham turned to the two others – water closets and the 'tub cinder-sifter closet', a tub under the privy with an absorbent layer. The former were confined to the houses of the better-off and, in Tatham's considered opinion, 'For general adoption amongst the poorer classes they are bad in principle and practice.' He found it hard to see where the necessary water would come from, and the 'bulk of the scientific evidence' (he said) 'was in favour of keeping all excremental matter out of sewers', using sewers for surface water and household slops. Tatham was personally inclined to the fourth method – 'the tub cinder-sifter closet'.[68] Unlike his predecessor, Tatham was also a believer that the waste product, once removed, could be converted into manure.

Fowler, Salford's Borough Surveyor and Engineer disagreed. He was the advocate of a patent water-closet of his own design, to use rainwater and household slops to flush the lavatory. There followed several years of experiments with different systems to find the most satisfactory. These ended in the Depression of 1879. Finding it was more expensive to empty the 11,000 receptacles under the 'tub-system' than to empty the 32,000 ashpits, the Council backed away from further experiment.[69] In the 1880s and 1890s Salford's 'mixed economy' approach to nightsoil-removal changed little. By the latter decade the supremacy of the water-closet system and pumped sewage, allied to the activated sludge process, emerged as the most effective methods of removal and treatment, and from 1894 all new homes erected in the borough were on the water-closet system. Under the Local Act of 1899 the Corporation took absolute power to require owners to adopt the water-carriage system in 1902. From then on both ashpit and pail systems went into decline. But that was long after Davies's time.

In the years he and Syson were Salford's sanitary leaders the Cotton Famine was superseded by a new phase in economic history. The early Seventies saw one of the greatest booms of the whole century, which lasted, despite a setback in 1873, until the last year of the decade. As already noted, Salford's economy, population and built-up area all began to expand prodigiously. This burst of growth had important implications for public health, which show in the statistics gathered by Dr Tatham. In the five years 1876–80, marriage and birth rates reached their highest recorded figures. The crude death rates also peaked in 1866–70 and in 1871–75.[70] Clearly, another era – one in which the emphasis had to shift from Sanitation to Public Health – was beginning. Davies, however, had shot his bolt. He indicated in November 1870 that he had no wish to serve a third term as mayor. No suitable alternative suggested himself. Cawley was perhaps the natural choice, but he was too involved in Parliamentary matters. Davies was importuned to carry on, and it was proposed that the next mayor be paid an allowance of 300 guineas towards the unavoidable expenses of the position. In the ensuing debate the Council managed to transform this into an insult. The vote in favour was extremely narrow, as always where expenditure of ratepayers' money was concerned. Davies in the end agreed to serve a third term, but declined an honorarium so tardily proffered.[71] Happily, a year later they got it right. When he finally relinquished the mayoralty, a purse of a thousand guineas was subscribed in recognition of his decade of service to the borough, which he accepted in the spirit in which it was offered. And, as we have seen, Davies also received the accolade of a civic portrait and a marble bust.

Although he severed his direct connection with Public Health three years later when he retired from the Health Committee, it was not possible for him, or anyone else on the council, to ignore the matter. As mortality rates reached a peak in the middle of the decade, 'the Sanitary and Social state of Salford' was taken up in the local press. Columns were filled describing the conditions which gave rise to Dr Tatham's and the Registrar General's statistics. In April 1875 the scandal of a gigantic tip near Phoebe street, in the rapidly growing Regent Road district, was revealed in the *Salford Weekly News*. The General Health Committee was horrified by this revelation, and of the general inefficiency of the scavenging of Salford's ashpits and tubs. What was also clearly outdated was the system of each of the three townships having scavenging departments, between which there was little, if any, co-operation. But when it was proposed that the Salford Scavenging Department's functions be taken over by the General Health Committee, the district committees united in opposition to the proposal, which was abandoned.[72]

Early in 1877 the same newspaper drew attention to the fact that, in the quarter just ended, the death rate in Salford was higher than in any of the twenty great towns compared in national statistics. 'We have the highest death-rate of children under one year of all the large towns, Oldham only coming anywhere near us'.[73] Davies sprang to the defence of the Council, and was supported by the journal the *Sanitary Record*, which pointed out that Salford was one of the first towns to appoint a medical officer 'entirely devoted to health work'; that it had been the second to appoint a Health Committee with power to apply all public and local acts (save those on scavenging); that it was a pioneer in getting sanitary powers inserted into its local acts; that it had been energetic in paving and the making of new streets; that every new house had to be certified as fit by the Medical Officer and surveyor, that plans must be submitted, and that each must have a separate yard and privy.' The Local Acts of Salford', it declared, 'have been copied up and down the kingdom'. It did, however, come back to the central issue:

> Salford is essentially a 'midden town', and its old parts must be excrement sodden. By this time all middens ought to have been abolished. The energy that has directed the paving and draining has not been at work with the acres of middens which reek in the midst of the people, and on the face of it the weak spot would appear to lie here. No matter what system of closet is adopted, frequent removal is the great secret, of course, coupled with removable receptacles.

The *Sanitary Record* concluded, 'We are not inclined to think that the Health Committee has been idle, whatever the apparent result as measured by the death rates of the last few months.'[74]

In August of that year a new General Improvement Committee was set up in an attempt to improve the sanitary state of the older parts of the borough, and to get away from the piecemeal approach inherent in the existing arrangements. It was the idea of the Conservative Mayor, Francis Walmsley, who was a doctor.[75] Davis was a strong supporter of this move and took his place on the committee. Having become a convert to the idea that the sooner the separate districts of the borough were amalgamated the better, he strongly urged that it should be a *borough* committee, which it duly became.

Davies was always a stout defender of the Council's record. In a speech in 1880 he pointed out that in the past decade it had built the great Intercepting Sewer, ended 'jerry building', opened three new parks, (Broughton Recreation Ground, Seedley Park and Albert Park), three branch libraries and its first public baths in Blackfriars street, possessed a museum and art gallery which attracted half a million visitors a year, and made the point that Salford's death rate was falling, as indeed it was. He might also have added that, in response to a strong plea from William Mather for children's playgrounds, one had been recently opened in Greengate, on land formerly occupied by slum property demolished by the corporation.[76]

Perhaps he did not do so because this might have drawn attention to Salford's conspicuous failure to do much about housing. In the past dozen years or so, there had been a certain amount of slum demolition but not much in the way of replacement. Under the Labouring Classes Dwelling Houses Act of 1866, by which money was available from the Public Works Loan Board to buy up slum cottages, demolish them and erect 'model' dwellings, a tentative first move had been made in that direction. Davies had been a supporter of the Salford Improved Industrial Dwellings Co. Ltd Land (between Boond street and Caygill Street, Greengate), was acquired, and two blocks of dwellings erected However, when building commenced in 1869, only about a third of the shares had been taken up, which is probably why no other Improved Industrial Dwellings followed. Even more glaring was the failure of the Council to take action under the Artisans' Dwellings Act.[77] The provision of housing was regarded as a matter best left to market forces, and not really the concern of local government at all.

Davies's life was remarkable in its consistency: local politics and Methodism remained his abiding passions to the end. He was still on the Council at the time of his death in 1885 at the age of seventy-four, a respected aldermanic figure. On the sanitary front, in his old age he could draw some satisfaction from his years of effort: from its peak in the early Seventies, Salford's death rate was now on the decline. In a review of Salford's record on public health over the past decade, published shortly after Davies's death, Dr Tatham noted that the fall in death rates was chiefly the result of improvements in the prevention of infectious diseases, largely through compulsory notification and the opening of an isolation hospital. He could also point to several other achievements. The adulteration of food had been reduced since the appointment of a Public Analyst and the Adulteration of Food Act, and dairies, cowsheds, milkshops and retail bakeries had now come under his aegis. As well as being a legitimate source of municipal pride, the new public baths and parks had been beneficial to the health of Salford's people, especially the young.[78]

Despite their public claims, Davies and Tatham were not naive enough to believe that the battle for a healthier Salford was really being won by 1886. The mortality statistics for the borough continued to conceal startling differences between its poorest and richest districts. And if Salford's mortality rate was falling, its position in the table of great towns remained very much the same. In 1871 (on this criterion) it was the third unhealthiest town in the country, after Newcastle-on-Tyne and Sunderland.[79] In the period 1892–1900 it was still third. The same was true of infant mortality: in 1900 only Preston and Blackburn had higher rates than Salford.[80] Nor could it be seriously suggested that much progress had been made on air and river pollution, or in the clearance of slums. In the late Victorian period most other large towns were improving faster than Salford.

Second hand boots for sale at the Flat Iron Market, in the poorest part of Salford, about 1894. One of a fine series of photographs by S. L. Coulthurst. In order to take unposed pictures Coulthurst would go about the streets with his camera concealed in an old clothes cart. Is the bearded man staring at the camera suspicious? Note the shawled women on the left, by the railings in front of Sacred Trinity Church.
(Local History Collection, Peel Park)

CHAPTER 8

# Gladstonian Liberal:
# The Political Career
# of Benjamin Armitage

In December 1898 the corporation of Salford bestowed the honorary freedom of the borough for the first time upon two men, B. W. Levy and Benjamin Armitage.[1] As well as honouring them as individuals, the city fathers were also giving civic recognition to what they represented. In Levy's case this was Manchester and Salford Jewry, whose leaders were coming to play an increasingly prominent part in public life and whose overall numbers had increased markedly as a result of recent emigrations from Eastern Europe. In addition to paying tribute to Armitage as a leading employer, former Member of Parliament and public benefactor, the corporation were also tacitly acknowledging the part Liberal Dissent had played in the life of the district for three generations.

Born in 1823, the second of the six sons of Elkanah (later Sir Elkanah) Armitage, Benjamin was, by common recognition, the one most like his father. From early life he was groomed as Sir Elkanah's political heir, willed to succeed where his father had failed. Given a thorough Nonconformist schooling by the Moravians in Yorkshire and the Rev. Mr Giles at Barton Hall, Worsley, what might be termed Benjamin Armitage's 'higher education' was completed in the 'Manchester School' of Cobden and Bright.[2] When the family business started up at Pendleton New Mills he was about fifteen, and he and his brothers played their parts in the successful development of the firm for which they received their due reward. At twenty-one Benjamin was given a partnership. The following year he married. His bride was Elizabeth, daughter of John Smith of Turkey Mill, Bingley, in Yorkshire, one of that network of Anti-Corn Law Leaguers whose alliance was strengthened by inter-marriage. In the ten years of their marriage Elizabeth bore Benjamin Armitage five sons and a daughter, and her early death was a great loss. A year later, in 1856, he married Elizabeth Southam, by whom he had another daughter. Evident subscribers to the notion of keeping things in the family, Southams and Armitages intermarried on more than one occasion. In 1842 Benjamin's sister, Rebecca, had married Dr. George Southam, a Salford physician who rose to be President of the British Medical Association. *Their* son, George Armitage Southam (1843–98), joined the business at sixteen, and was groomed to be managing director

173

'A chip off the old block':
Benjamin Armitage, MP for
West Salford, 1880–86.
(*Manchester Faces and Places*)

in succession to his uncles in the third generation of Sir Elkanah Armitage & Sons'
existence as a family firm. It was Southam's sister (*i.e.* his niece) that Benjamin
took as his second wife. Southam in his turn married Benjamin's daughter, Mary
Elizabeth, in 1893: for both of them it was a late and brief marriage, and there
were to be no children.[3]

Although Sir Elkanah remained head of the firm until his last years, he had,
from the 1840s, been content to leave the day-to-day management to his sons. In
business Benjamin specialised on the sales side, becoming a familiar figure on the
floor of the Manchester Exchange, and a leading light in the Chamber of Commerce.
'In business', recollected one admirer, 'he was inflexible. Having once asked a price,
neither Greek, nor Jew, nor Gentile, shipping or home-trade house could get him
to deviate from it. He was a chip off the old block – a Colossus of industry'.[4]

If Sir Elkanah relished his role as family patriarch and great man of business it
is clear that he was not as dictatorial as such men sometimes are: he respected,
and was prepared to listen to his sons. Under their influence, the knight with the
grim visage became a paternalist. There were, of course, more than mere filial
influences in this. For a time at least, the Cotton Famine created greater feeling
of mutuality between employers and workers than had existed before, and there
were good political reasons for the lessening of class antagonisms as well. The most
visible product of the new Armitage paternalism was the opening of the Pendleton
Club in 1862. At the start of the Famine, this hall for their workers was opened

# The Family of Benjamin Armitage of Chomlea

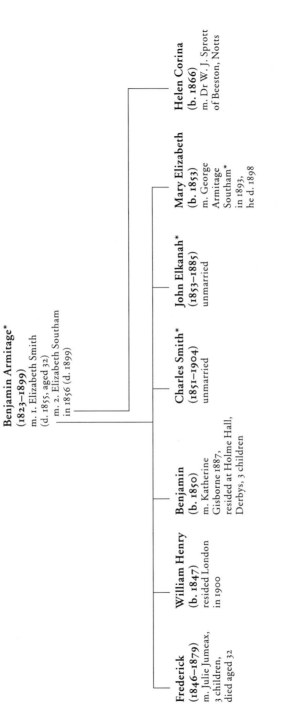

**Benjamin Armitage***
**(1823–1899)**
m. 1. Elizabeth Smith
(d. 1855, aged 32)
m. 2. Elizabeth Southam
in 1856 (d. 1899)

**Frederick**
**(1846–1879)**
m. Julie Jumeax,
3 children,
died aged 32

**William Henry**
**(b. 1847)**
resided London
in 1900

**Benjamin**
**(b. 1850)**
m. Katherine
Gisborne 1887,
resided at Holme Hall,
Derbys, 3 children

**Charles Smith***
**(1851–1904)**
unmarried

**John Elkanah***
**(1853–1885)**
unmarried

**Mary Elizabeth**
**(b. 1853)**
m. George
Armitage
Southam*
in 1893,
he d. 1898

**Helen Corina**
**(b. 1866)**
m. Dr W. J. Sprott
of Beeston, Notts

* Member of the firm

in Ford Lane, Pendleton and its first use was as a relief centre. Later it became an early working men's club and community centre. During the day it served as a work's canteen and in the evenings as a club. For a small weekly subscription members had the use of reading and recreation rooms, which could be hired by local groups and societies. At the official opening, Sir Elkanah explained that the whole thing was Benjamin's idea, paid for by him out of his own pocket. In 1882 it celebrated its twentieth birthday, and within its walls many Pendleton associations got their start. One such was the Pendleton Lads' Club (formed 1889).[5]

Armitage paternalism: datestone of their school for 'half-timers', Broughton Road, Pendleton. (Photo: P. A. Greenall)

At that time the most usual form of industrial paternalism was the annual works treat. At Pendleton New Mills these were large-scale happenings, spread over six evenings, on each of which around 250 operatives and their families were entertained by the firm at the Pendleton Club. Another (perhaps) was the provision of houses. As the streets around the mill were built up, Benjamin and his brothers put some of their money into cottages (with 'back doors and other conveniences'), the majority of which were rented by their own employees. Following the 1870 Education Act they also provided a British (Nonconformist) School for their 'half-timers', and a few years after, in keeping with the new spirit of sanitary reform and healthy recreation, opened one of the first children's playgrounds in the town, close by the mill in Borough Street. Armitage money also went into the two Pendleton Congregational Chapels and their Sunday schools.[6]

Not all of this was necessarily the pure milk of human kindness. There were obvious 'public relations' benefits in paternalism. Other large employers, such as William Mather, were providing similarly for their workers and cemented closer relationships with their workforce than the Armitages. There never seems, for instance, to have been a works' band at Pendleton New Mills, as there was at the Salford Ironworks. As well as promoting 'good feelings', behind the new paternalism lay a certain amount of political calculation. From the time he first became politically active, Benjamin Armitage had always argued that one way forward for their kind of Dissenting politics was by trying to convince working-class Radical leaders that they could only prosper if they all united behind the banner of Reform.

Benjamin Armitage's political apprenticeship began with the 'Stoning of the Prophets' and his father's defeat in the Salford Election of 1857. It was to last twenty years. His first success in public life came in November 1859, when he was elected to the borough council for St. Thomas's Ward. However, local government held little attraction. Armitage was always a party politician, a staff officer in the Manchester Brigade of the Liberal Army. When the Salford Ballot and Reform Association was formed in the aftermath of Massey's second victory in 1859, Benjamin Armitage became its chairman and then president. 1860 saw him one of the Manchester delegation to Paris to witness the signing of the Anglo-French Trade Treaty, which its sponsors hoped would initiate an international movement towards the liberalising of trade. These years were very busy for the young politician. He was involved in local efforts to persuade the government to give the borough a second seat in Parliament, and was a leading light on the Manchester Garibaldi Reception Committee in 1864.[7] That year organised Radicalism began to revive with the formation of the National Reform Union. Armitage became a vice president of the Manchester Branch and busied himself with the formation of one in Pendleton, the power base of his future political ambitions.

With Palmerston gone, Reform in 1865 seemed unstoppable. The Armitages ardently supported John Bright and his Reform programme.[8] Unable to bring themselves to swallow manhood suffrage, these Radicals spent much time and ingenuity doing 'fancy franchise' sums, calculating how many new electors would be added to the roll if occupiers at such and such a rateable value were enfranchised. As Reform became inevitable, their excitement mounted. In Salford the campaign for a second seat was resumed. Claiming to be the largest of the single-member Parliamentary boroughs, it was pointed out that there were no less than eighteen others (piddling places like Calne, Wilts.) each sending an MP to Westminster, whose combined electorate was smaller than Salford's.[9] By the following June this issue was resolved. It became clear that Salford was indeed going to have a second seat. At last things seemed to be going their way. However, as we have seen, in his Reform Act Disraeli not only dished the Whigs, he dished Radical Lancashire as well. The Conservative revival in 1868 consigned Salford Liberals to another dozen years in the political wilderness. Perhaps the Armitages saw this coming, because both Sir Elkanah and Benjamin declined offers to stand, though the latter served as Cheetham's election committee chairman.[10]

After the local defeat, Liberals tried to put on a brave face. Things could have been worse. At least the country had a Liberal Government, and Gladstone was to carry many of the reforms for which they had agitated for so long. Moreover, within its gift the government had rewards for the party faithful. Armitage received his in the form of elevation to the County Bench in April 1869, as did Wright Turner and William Agnew.[11] But this was scant consolation, and could not compensate for the pain of Salford being represented in Parliament by Cawley and Charley and seeing the control of the council fall to the Conservatives.

In the aftermath of defeat it was important to get Liberal momentum going again. Led by Benjamin Armitage, William Agnew, William Mather and Robert Leake the party set about becoming better organised. In the next year or so ward election committees transformed themselves into permanent associations, and a Central Association was formed, with Benjamin Armitage as its first president.[12] But they fudged it: party democracy was not something the League's Young Guard took to too readily. They were the products of a tradition in which participatory politics meant big public meetings with agendas and speakers decided on beforehand by an unelected leadership. The function of followers was to turn up, subscribe and do as they were told. Armitage and friends were slow to learn what the new situation required.

For a variety of reasons, many beyond its control, Liberalism was heading for another defeat. In retrospect, Gladstone's first ministry was one of the great reforming governments of the nineteenth century. Unfortunately for Liberalism, at the local level Gladstonian Reform frequently left Liberal activists dissatisfied, whilst at the same time providing ammunition to the Conservatives. Gladstone's Irish policies in particular inflamed Conservatism, whilst such measures as the Disestablishment of the Irish Church and the Education Act upset the Dissenters, the former because it did not lead on to any further advance of 'religious liberty' (*i.e.* Disestablishment in England or Wales), the latter because it turned out so tender of the interests of denominational schools.

But if Salford's Liberal Dissenters were unhappy over government legislation, they were also having difficulty winning over the new voters. Their programme, as defined in late 1869 – the Ballot, a new Education Act, solving the Irish Land Question, 'Free Trade in Land 'in England, curbing the Drink Interest, cutting public expenditure, the promotion of 'religious liberty' – reflected the concerns of middle-class Dissenters and businessmen rather than those of Radical working men. In defence of the government, its supporters could point to a series of measures of direct interest to working people, Public Health, Regulation of the Mines, the Ballot, the Adulteration of Food and Liquor Licensing. However, weighing heavily against these was the anger of trade unionists over the Criminal Law Amendment Act (which made picketing difficult) and the hostility of Parliamentary Liberals toward the Nine Hours Question. Grasping their importance to the working-class, when it came to power in 1874, Disraeli's government passed a Trade Union Act and an important Factory Act, which instituted the half day on Saturday. At the election of 1874, Salford went with the national swing, and, borne along on that famous torrent of gin and beer, Cawley and Charley were returned once more for Salford. Local Liberalism reached its lowest point in 1877 when Oliver Ormerod Walker succeeded the deceased Cawley.

But, if the past nine years had been dog days for the party faithful, they had not been unkind to the Armitages. The firm survived the Cotton Famine in good shape, and when trade began to revive was able to expand with the purchase of Nassau Mills in Patricroft. The death of the founder in 1876 necessitated some reorganisation. A 'Family Limited Company', was formed with a capital of £300,000 in £100 shares. The subscribers were Benjamin and his brothers Elkanah, Samuel and Joseph John ('governing directors'), together with Benjamin's sons Charles and Elkanah John, Benjamin's son-in-law, George Armitage Southam, and James Lings of Didsbury, the only person brought in from outside.[13] Now one of the most prominent men in Manchester, Benjamin was a leading member of the Manchester Reform Club, President of the Chamber of Commerce and a Manchester Grammar School trustee.

Some confusion and amusement arose from the fact that Armitage had a namesake in his cousin Benjamin, the second of his uncle Elijah's sons. Born in Tahiti, where his father had gone as Protestant missionary, on returning to England *this* Benjamin Armitage went into business with his brother Jeremiah and took over the mill in Whit Lane, Pendleton, which had once housed the Whit Lane Weaving Company of 1851. Later, after Jeremiah emigrated to Australia, Benjamin and a new partner built Albert Mill in Orchard Street, close to Pendleton New Mills. This remained his until he retired to Southport. Benjamin Armitage of Sorrel Bank (or 'Black Ben', as he was sometimes called) prospered, was elected to the council, became a JP and was, like all the Armitages, an active Liberal. To distinguish the two men, his older and more famous cousin was usually referred to as Benjamin Armitage of Chomlea, or 'White Ben'. Both were art connoisseurs, and the collection of nineteenth century masters of Benjamin Armitage of Sorrel Bank was said to be one of the finest in Lancashire. It was from him that one of the best-known of all Victorian pictures – Ford Madox Brown's 'Work' – was acquired by the Manchester City Art Gallery.[14]

On the political front things had started to look up for Benjamin Armitage of Chomlea after 1877. The way forward was pointed by John Bright. After the fall of Gladstone's first administration he called on local Liberal associations all over the country to reform themselves on the model of the Birmingham caucus. This involved the creation of a genuinely representative organisation from ward level up, the opening of Liberal clubs, the employment of paid agents and a systematic attempt to get Liberals elected to local councils and boards. The essential matter was to strengthen links between party grandees and the grass-roots. The man who more than any other persuaded Salford Liberals to organise along these lines was Harold Rylett, a journalist, who demonstrated what could be done by organising the Regent Ward Party.[15] Rylett's example was copied in other wards, and in 1877 a new party organisation for the borough was announced, consisting of a General Council with representatives from each of Salford's twelve wards, and an Executive formed from the officers of the association, together with elected representatives from each ward, and a new full time secretary (J. Wigley).[16]

The leaders of Salford Liberalism, Armitage, Mather, Leake and Agnew recognised the necessity for new men and new organisation, because without them they were not going to win elections. If many of these new men – such as J. G. de T. Mandley, R. D. Rusden, or Richard Pankhurst – were more Radical than they were, there were also advantages. The new organisation men gave the old leaders space, and left them freer to look around for constituencies to cultivate. For their part, the new organisation men in the main recognised the importance of these hereditary chieftains. Liberalism, no less than Conservatism, had its deference systems. The party selected its candidates for the next election in November 1878. The men they chose were Benjamin Armitage and Arthur Arnold, regarded as a well-balanced pair, a matter of no little importance in two-member constituency elections. The one a Dissenter, a local manufacturer and hereditary Liberal leader: the other, a journalist and speaker on political and economic matters, a Churchman from the south of England, who first came to Lancashire during the Cotton Famine as a assistant commissioner under the Public Works Act of 1863. Arnold had left 'with the thanks of the Poor Law Board and a large number of local authorities', and strengthened his Lancashire connections with his *History of the Cotton Famine*, published in 1864.[17] By 1878 Liberal activists were optimistic about their chances in the election, which was to be fought on two main issues – Imperialism and the state of the economy.

What revived Liberal politics was another Near Eastern Crisis. This had started with risings in Bosnia and Herzegovina and later Bulgaria, all suppressed by the Ottoman government. A war between Serbia and the Turks ensued, and the victory of the latter led to a Russian invasion. The prospect of war with Russia always stimulated Conservatives, whilst an alliance with the Turks (which threatened a repetition of the Crimean War) had an equally powerful effect on Liberals, nowhere more so than in Manchester. In January 1878, when the Russians advanced on Constantinople and the government ordered the fleet to the Straits, war seemed very close. These were the days of 'Jingoism'. There were pro and anti-war demonstrations in Manchester in February, but in the end war was averted, a treaty signed between Russia and Turkey, and a conference of the great powers convened. If the Congress of Berlin was a Conservative triumph, from that point Imperialism began to tilt politics towards the Liberals. In anti-Imperialism they found an issue which re-united their party, so that, at the time of their nomination, Armitage and Arnold found things moving their way. There was an uproarious town's meeting in Manchester in November over the war with the Afghans at which the Liberals bested the Conservatives,[18] and the following year the Zulu War and the government's South Africa policy gave the Liberals further ammunition for their attacks on Beaconsfield's declining administration.

Even more serious for the government was the economic recession. In late 1878

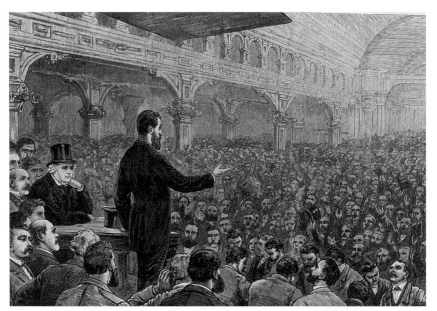

Great Liberal demonstration, Pomona Gardens Palace, Manchester 1879. The speaker is Lord Hartington. Seated, in top hat, is John Bright. (*Illustrated London News*)

Manchester was hit by the worst bout of unemployment since the Cotton Famine. The Depression was the main reason the Conservatives lost the election of 1880. Demands for Protection revitalised the Liberals. Free Trade *versus* 'Reciprocity' was one of the main election issues and one on which Arnold and Armitage could out-argue Charley and Walker any time.

In 1880 they won at a canter: Armitage topped the poll with 11,116 votes, Arnold received 11,110, Charley 8,400 and Walker 8,302. Manchester returned two Liberals to one Conservative, whilst in South East Lancashire William Agnew and Robert Leake ousted the Conservatives. In a letter to the *Pendleton Reporter* Benjamin Armitage of Sorrel Bank cockily suggested changing the name of Eccles Old Road to

William (later Sir William) Agnew, the great art dealer and Liberal politician. (*Manchester Faces and Places*)

'Parliament Road' to mark the fact that no less than six Members of Parliament now lived there.[19] It was a great moment for Liberals, and for his cousin Benjamin. Now fifty seven, he had succeeded where Sir Elkanah had failed. He celebrated by building 'Chomlea' in Claremont Road, a house grand enough for an MP to entertain his friends and maybe even Gladstone. He also donated a white marble statue to the newly opened art gallery in Peel Park, erected under the bequest of E. R. Langworthy. Entitled 'The Genius of Lancashire', a sturdy classical female bends a sword under one knee. It is housed in the Victorian Gallery with other marbles donated under the Armitage Bequest and some fine pictures by contemporary artists presented by William Agnew, G. W. Agnew and Oliver Heywood, all of whom had cause to rejoice in the genius of Lancashire.

All the good fortune that was going in 1880 went the Liberals' way. The campaign presented no issue which Beer and Bible Conservatism could exploit. Moreover, Conservative 'Jingoism' backfired by providing an issue on which Gladstone could base his spectacular re-entry into the political limelight in Midlothian. The Liberals also got the full support of the local Irish, better organised than ever before. This was the result of growing self-confidence of the Parliamentary Irish Party, whose leaders urged Irishmen in England to organise. From 1877 Irish parliamentarians such as Biggar, O'Connor Power, Mitchell Henry and Charles Stuart Parnell made regular visits to Manchester and Salford. Full Irish endorsement in this election was given following a speech by Arnold, an ardent Land Reformer, at Salford Town Hall in October 1879.[20] The Irish now looked to the Liberal Party to further their desire for Home Rule, emerging as the main object of the Irish Nationalists. This Liberal-Irish alliance, predictably, brought an Orange reaction. But, for the moment, it fell on deaf ears: Conservatives were too dismayed to respond.

Virtually everything Gladstone and his second ministry touched went wrong. When Bradlaugh – freethinker, republican, birth-controller, and hero of the popular Radicals – tried to affirm instead of taking the member's oath, the government mishandled the situation. The Opposition (aided by some Liberals) were able to turn it into a constitutional wrangle which embarrassed the Government for five years. In foreign affairs, after withdrawing from Afghanistan and making concessions to the Boers (though not the Zulus) in South Africa, the government of 'Peace, Retrenchment and Reform' turned out to be remarkably warlike. Anti-Imperialist opinion was disturbed when the government, acting in what seemed more in the interests of the Suez Canal Company than peace, invaded and virtually annexed Egypt. In its last years, trouble over Afghanistan almost led Gladstone's government to go to war with Russia.

Though these matters agitated some Radicals in Salford, by and large they had little impact on the position of Armitage and Arnold, both ardent Gladstonians. The issue which did was Ireland. Amongst the Irish, support for Armitage and Arnold quickly turned to hostility. Agricultural depression brought Irish agrarian society to crisis, and when Davitt founded the Land League, violence, intimidation and then murder followed. When the Conservative Peace Preservation Act expired in 1880, the government found it could not maintain law and order without further special legislation. A stern Coercion Act was passed, which Armitage voted for. This turned him into the *bête noire* of the Salford Irish. Arnold voted against the Bill, but that did not save him from becoming just as unpopular as Armitage. Indeed, in the long run, this harmed Arnold more, because opinion in all sections of the general population, except amongst Radicals, became more and more anti-Irish. What was disliked was the way in which the Land League subverted law and order, the way Irish Nationalist MPs disrupted Parliament and the revival of Fenian violence. When a bomb exploded in a meat store adjoining the armoury of the Regent Road infantry barracks in January 1881, serious anti-Irish feelings were aroused again in Salford. No military personnel were injured, but 5,000 rifles belonging to the Volunteers were destroyed, and a seven year old boy was killed.[21]

The government tried to balance Coercion with Reform with the 1881 Land Act. It pleased neither landlords nor tenants and the situation worsened. Intimidation and murder increased and, in October, Parnell, now the Irish leader in Parliament, was gaoled for inciting the Irish to intimidate tenants who took advantage of the new Act. Irish disillusionment with Liberalism deepened. A branch of the Land League of Great Britain (the 'John Dillon') was formed in Salford, and at the inaugural meeting its leading figure, George Murray, reflected that though they had worked hard for the Liberals at the last election 'he felt sure that there was not an Irishman who would disgrace himself by voting for Mr Armitage again for he supported Mr "Coercion" Forster'. Another speaker denounced Arnold as a 'place seeker', and both Salford MPs as 'hypocrites'. A Land League branch (the 'Thomas Brennan') was formed at the Irish National Hall in Cavendish Street, Regent Road, and another in Pendleton on the eve of the 1885 election specifically to try to unseat Armitage.[22]

In May the following year (1882) the government made the so-called 'Kilmainham Treaty' with the imprisoned Parnell, Dillon, O'Kelly and Davitt, that in return for a promise to cease 'boycotting' and to co-operate with the government, they would be released. The Lord Lieutenant, and the Chief Secretary for Ireland, resigned in protest. The following week their successors, Lord Frederick Cavendish and Thomas Burke, were brutally murdered in broad daylight in Phoenix Park, Dublin. There was tremendous public revulsion against the Irish. Dr Vaughan, the Bishop of Salford, instructed Catholics that 'secret societies were the mothers and nurses of treason and of murder, the instruments made use of for carrying out revolutions of the most bloody kind; they were the overthrow of all social and civil order which had God for its author'.[23] Irish workmen were threatened and insulted on the shop floor.

For a time the election of 1880 stimulated interest in Parliamentary politics, and the Borough of Salford Parliamentary Debating Society, which started in 1881, offered a platform for its members to debate current issues and act out being Liberal, Conservative, Independent or Home Rule 'MPs'. Though it flourished briefly, it was always something of a charade, and for those interested in real politics there were plenty of other associations to join, and live issues to debate.[24] For those radically inclined, there was, in 1880, the Manchester and Salford Radical Reform Union, which was replaced the following year by the Democratic League, with active branches in Pendleton and Salford, whose members debated the merits of Home Rule, Land Reform, Free Trade and the Bradlaugh case. The latter was the reason why a branch of the National Secular Society was founded in Pendleton in 1882 which had debates on secularism and the 'truth of Christianty', heard lectures on other great world faiths, and was graced that year by visits from Bradlaugh and Mrs Besant, his co-worker in the secularist cause. In 1884 a new Salford Radical Association was formed to spread ideas on how Reform could be further advanced.[25]

The debating of such advanced political and religious ideas aroused the fierce opposition of Evangelicals, Orangemen and such working-class Conservative leaders as James Houston, 'Hon Member for Belfast' in the Parliamentary Debating Society, and a Member of the Protestant Reformation Society. They set up a short-lived anti-Bradlaugh Salford Representative Political Committee in 1882, which was soon replaced by a better organised Salford Working Men's Constitutional Union, which was particularly strong in Broughton.[26] Most of these associations had brief lives, but their importance should not be missed. They provided ways for working men to imbibe and debate the ideas of the time, and the same names tend to re-appear as their leading spirits – men like William Horrocks, R. D. Rusden, Thomas Knowles, A. F. Winks and George Mason amongst the Radicals, and R. J. McCartney and E. Edeson amongst the Conservatives.

Within the two main party organisations there was a good deal of activity in these years. Despite their parliamentary victory the year before, losses in the 1881 municipal election stung the Borough Liberal Party, under the presidency of William Mather, to improve party organisation and be more active in Council elections. The Conservatives, by contrast, were slow to recover from their severe defeat in 1880. Lord Beaconsfield's death in 1881 marked the end of a glorious Conservative era, and seemed to put a damper on Tory spirits. The Church was in no immediate danger, and, even after the Phoenix Park murders, 'No Popery' lacked the resonance it once had. The awareness that Irish leaders, from Parnell to local Land Leaguers, were urging Irish voters to vote Conservative next time were also incentives not to beat this drum. Others were inclined to blame Conservative lethargy on the lack of an effective Conservative newspaper, and very unkind things were said of the *Salford Chronicle*. There was a good deal of friction between the leadership and maverick local Tory activists, such as Councillor J. E. Middlehurst, for 20 years the leading Tory in Islington Ward.[27] In many ways the problems of the Conservative Party mirrored those of the Liberals before they got their act together in the late '70s. Old leaders, and with them old-style party politics, were passing away. When W. W. Goulden died in late 1878 the *Chronicle* gave him a black-edged obituary which began 'Know ye not that there is a prince and a great man fallen this day?', and the death in 1883 of Richard Haworth, a major local cotton manufacturer and Conservative was a shock. Trying to find new ways of appealing to working-class voters was the reason they founded the Salford Working Men's Constitutional Union in late 1882.[28]

Despite its sea of troubles, Gladstone's government produced some reforms, the chief of which was a Bill in 1884 to extend the franchise to (male) voters in the counties on pretty much the same terms as borough householders received it in

Lost Conservative leader: Richard Haworth (1820–83), cotton manufacturer, reputedly the largest ratepayer in Salford. (Author's collection)

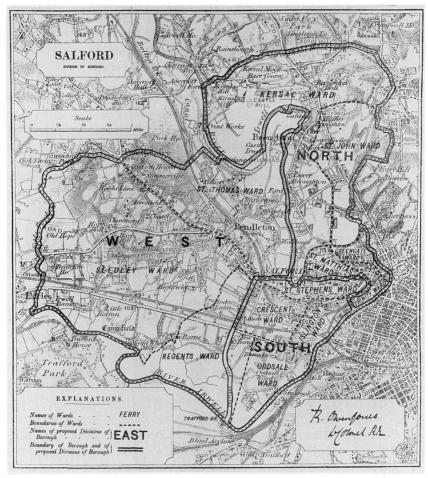

The Boundary Commission's map of Salford's new single-member Parliamentary
constituencies, created by the Redistribution Act of 1885

1867. It was to add another two million voters to the register. When the Bill was
at first rejected by the House of Lords in the summer a crisis threatened, and it
was this that brought the Salford Radical Association into existence. In the end
Gladstone negotiated the passage of the Third Reform Act at the price of acceding
to Conservative demands for an accompanying redistribution of seats. The following
year this Redistribution Act passed on to the statute book. Shortly after, Gladstone
resigned and Lord Salisbury formed a government, which lasted seven months.

These reforms marked the beginning of a new era in politics. The historic
division of parliamentary counties and boroughs came to an end, to be replaced
by single-member constituencies. Salford was no longer the two-member borough
it had been since 1868, but was divided into three single-member constituencies,
an arrangement which was to last for a century. In their wisdom, the Boundary
Commissioners defined Salford's three new divisions thus:

Table 9. *The new Salford Parliamentary Constituencies in 1885*

| Constituency | Wards | Population (1881) | Voters on the Register (1885) |
|---|---|---|---|
| West Salford ('Pendleton') | St Thomas's | 18,444 | |
| | Seedley | 24,673 | |
| | Regent (part of) | 11,280 | |
| | | 54,397 | 8,197 |
| North Salford ('Broughton') | St John's | 14,038 | |
| | Kersal | 17,819 | |
| | Trinity | 6,521 | |
| | St Matthias's | 10,899 | |
| | Greengate | 7,075 | |
| | | 56,352 | 7,728 |
| South Salford ('Ordsall') | Islington | 9,523 | |
| | Ordsall | 25,300 | |
| | Crescent | 12,126 | |
| | St Stephen's | 9,497 | |
| | Regent (part of) | 9,038 | |
| | | 65,484 | 8,717 |

*Source*: *Salford Reporter* 17 Jan and 28 Nov 1885.

As candidates, the Liberals nominated Benjamin Armitage for West Salford, Arnold for North Salford and William Mather for South Salford. Arnold had the difficult task of opposing Edward Hardcastle, the leading figure in the Salford Conservative Party, who had been MP for South East Lancashire from 1874 to 1880. Mather's opponent was Thomas Gibson Bowles, proprietor of *Vanity Fair*, who had previously contested Darlington and Banbury. Bowles had impressive, if hidden, Manchester connections in that he was the illegitimate son of Thomas Milner Gibson, Bright's old running mate, though no-one was ungentlemanly enough to refer to this in public. After some considerable delay, the Conservative nominated to challenge Armitage was Sir William Worsley, Bart., of Hovingham Hall, Yorkshire, President of the North Riding Conservative Association, who had previously contested Whitby and Malton.[29]

Armitage fought a vigorous campaign in November 1885. His manifesto addressed every element in the Liberal alliance. Dissenters were assured that he favoured the separation of Church and State. On political reform, he was in favour of changing the constitution of the House of Lords and was in favour of women ('duly qualified') having the same parliamentary franchise as men. On economic matters he was strong for free trade and urged electors not to be taken in by the arguments of 'fair traders'. To his Temperance allies he declared he wanted to see the effective control of 'licensing by the people' at the local level. The Pendleton Irish were informed that he wanted to see the 'redress of Irish grievances', but to working men and trade unionists he had little to say, except that he supported Thomas Burt's demand that there should be legislation for the prevention of accidents in mines.[30] Armitage was a seasoned election campaigner, and fought this one as hard as he could. Gladstone and the Liberals were returned to power, but they did badly in Lancashire, where they won only 17 out of 55 seats. They were defeated in every one of Liverpool's nine constituencies and won only one out of the six Manchester seats. Vernon Armitage lost narrowly at Eccles. However, Agnew got in at Stretford and Leake at Ratcliffe-cum-Farnworth. In contrast to Manchester, Salford was a scene of some considerable Liberal rejoicing, with the return of Benjamin Armitage by 274 votes, and Mather taking the allegedly unwinnable South Salford by 55. Arnold also did well, losing by a mere 176.[31]

At the election Gladstone had a majority of 86 over the Conservatives. By coincidence, this was exactly the number of Nationalists elected in Catholic Ireland. Just before Christmas, news of Gladstone's conversion to Home Rule leaked out. From the time that it became public it was clear that Home Rule was a political decision which could blow the Liberal alliance apart. After the fall of Lord Salisbury's government early in 1886, Gladstone formed a Ministry of those Liberals who were willing to pass a Home Rule Bill. The first sign of trouble soon appeared. When Lord Salisbury's government fell, 18 Liberals voted with the Conservatives. A powerful Whig faction cut itself off from Gladstone.

On 8th April 1886 Gladstone outlined his scheme for Home Rule. In practice, this would have meant little more than putting local government into the hands of a Dublin Parliament, but it provoked fierce opposition. Home Rule Bill was seen as having implications which went far beyond what it actually proposed. When Hardcastle protested vehemently at the 'surrender by 33 millions of the

William (later Sir William) Mather, of the firm of Mather & Platt, captain of industry and Liberal politician. (*Manchester Faces and Places*)

people of the United Kingdom to the disloyal minority of 3 millions' he was not just articulating the prejudices of the old Tory school. Nor was he when he argued that Home Rule was giving in to assassins, or that it was fraught with danger for the Empire at a time when the German Empire was consolidating its unity.[32] In the second week in May, a packed Liberal meeting in Broughton heard strong anti-Home Rule arguments. It was pointed out that since the Redistribution Act the Irish had had fair representation at Westminster, there was much sympathy for the Loyalists in Ulster, and bitter hostility towards Parnell for his recent conduct. As John Bright put it in a letter to Benjamin Armitage dated 6 May,[33]

> To hand over a million and a half of Protestant and loyal people of the north of Ireland to the tender mercies of the ruffians and rebels who sat opposite to us in the last Parliament is more than I can consent to.
>
> The 'Party Associations' are ready to accept anything apparently. I am not ready, and am silent amid the strife of tongues – perhaps it is a sin to be silent. I sometimes fear it is – but I am too old for the warfare of former times and I hesitate to become the assailant of Mr Gladstone tho' I condemn his policy – which I think is insulting to the Party and may be injurious to the country.

In the event, Bright did speak out: when the election came he and Chamberlain secured Birmingham for the 'Unionists'. In Salford a small but influential band of old Liberal stalwarts defected from the party immediately: John Mather, Richard Hankinson, who had been very active in the 1880 election campaign, George Milner, the Temperance leader, and Henry Davis Pochin, a former Liberal mayor, came back to Salford from Bodnant in North Wales to attack Home Rule in the strongest terms. Salford Conservatives beat their Loyalist drums more incessantly than at any time since 1868–9 and their meetings witnessed much in the way of 'disorderly proceedings'. With the unity of the United Kingdom and the integrity of the Empire seen to be in danger, their peculiar venom focused on Gladstone. With him, said Alderman Dickens, 'it was a question of "open your mouths, shut your eyes and see [sic] what one man of principle will do for you."'[34]

In June the first Home Rule Bill was debated in the House of Commons. More than 90 Liberal MPs ( roughly equal numbers of Whigs and Radicals) went into the 'No' lobby, and, amidst scenes of the wildest excitement, the Home Rule Bill was defeated early on the morning of the 8 June. Parliament was dissolved there was a General Election, and 'Gladstonians' were swept away by the close alliance of Conservatives and Liberal Unionists. All things considered, in this atmosphere the Liberals did remarkably well in all three Salford seats. In South Salford Mather was faced with a new opponent, H. H. Howorth, who found Conservatives and Unionists in bouyant mood. One of their election squibs read[35]

> South Salford Stakes. The Straight Tip. Put your money on Howorth. He rides a good horse; it is called Union, by Patriotism out of Danger, goes straight and needs no blinkers. Mather rides a poor tit called Separation, half-brother to Fenian by Premier out of Vanity.

Mather found 'Stand fast by the Union' and 'No Parnellite dictation' hard to counter, but went down by only 126 votes. In North Salford, Arnold actually did better than in the November election, reducing Hardcastle's majority from 176 to 162. The biggest blow to the Liberals was Armitage's defeat in Pendleton, by 116 votes. Various reasons were advanced: good Conservative organisation and a good candidate in Lees Knowles, whose family name was a household word in Pendleton, Swinton and Pendlebury. In fact, Knowles polled fewer votes than Sir William Worsley the year before. The Liberals lost because important figures defected and Liberal voters abstained. The best known defectors were Henry Lightbown, until then a leader of the Pendleton party, and other leading employers and former Liberal activists such as James Johnson, T. C. Horsfall, Alderman Harwood, Armitage's cousins 'Black Ben' and Robert Armitage, his own half-brother Vernon and his son-in-law, George Armitage Southam. Home Rule was an issue which split families.[36] Bright summed up the atmosphere in another letter to Benjamin Armitage, just after the election[37]

> It shows what a shock was given to the public mind when Salford rejects you and our friend Mather, whose services to the Borough have been so great. We have had a great example not of the wisdom but of the folly of statesmanship and the effects and the mischief seem likely to be lasting.

As indeed they were. For virtually twenty years, with the exception of a brief spell in 1892–5, the Liberals were out of office. If the swing against Liberalism in Salford in 1886 was tiny, in the next three elections the party managed only one victory – in North Salford in 1892. Whether he knew it or not, Benjamin Armitage's parliamentary career was finished.

For the next four years Irish matters dominated politics. Salford Liberals and Irish had perforce to pick themselves up from defeat and reorganise. In July 1886 the Pendleton Irish formed a branch of the Irish National League, and the following year another was formed in Greengate.[38] The passing of Balfour's Coercion Act in April 1887 led them to redouble their efforts. Faced with the spread of Socialist ideas and the rise of trades unionism amongst a working class badly affected by two hard winters, the Liberal party looked to the matter of keeping working-class Liberals loyal. In October 1886 a Salford Working Men's Radical Association was formed under the presidency of Alderman W. H. Bailey: it soon changed its name to the Salford Reform Association.[39] In the main, Salford Liberals had stayed remarkably loyal to Gladstone and Home Rule. But the policy of the Land League widened the split with Liberal Unionists. As Vernon Armitage made clear in a speech to the Pendleton Liberal Club, 'In his opinion Mr Dillon was advocating a course which was absolutely illegal and which, if he was successful, would strike at the root of all law and order, not only in Ireland but elsewhere.' The Gladstonians refused to condemn the Land League, and in the next few years the Liberals and Irish co-operated closely. When Balfour's draconian Prevention of Crimes Act was passed they united to oppose the government's policy. Liberal Unionists, on the other hand, strongly supported Coercion, and this led them to organise on a more permanent basis. In July 1887, an Eccles Constituency Association was formed, and a Salford Association followed in March 1888. Two of its leading figures were Benjamin Armitage of Sorrel Bank and George Armitage Southam.[40]

After his bitter defeat, Armitage was inactive in politics for some time. Though he remained a Home Ruler and loyal to Gladstone, the secession of people close to him was profoundly upsetting. So were the activities of the Irish MPs and the Land League. Armitage looked upon Dillon's activities in much the same way as his half-brother (though Vernon was eventually drawn back into the Liberal fold). There were perhaps other reasons as well. He was now in his sixties and suffered a number of personal blows: his youngest son, John Elkanah, died of tuberculosis at the age of 31, and his brothers and partners, Elkanah and Joseph John, died in 1887 and 1889 respectively, necessitating new arrangements in the business. In June 1890 Sir Elkanah Armitage & Sons became a public company, the directors being Armitage and his brother Samuel, his son-in-law George Armitage Southam, G. H. Gaddum and J. Leigh. The firm was apparently in good shape: potential investors were informed that over the past five years profits 'represented upwards of ten per cent upon the present issue of share capital'.[41]

In the immediate aftermath of the loss of his seat in Parliament, Armitage became involved in a characteristic Salford battle. Fought over the evergreen issue of Sabbath Observance, it cast him in the congenial role of sturdy individualist against Evangelical bigotry, and won him many friends and admirers. Since Hugh Stowell's time, the matter of the opening of the Free Libraries and Museums on Sundays had been raised on several occasions but always rejected by the Conservative majority on the council. In 1888 Benjamin Armitage took up the cause. In this he co-operated closely with W. E. A. Axon, a Liberal educational reformer. When the Libraries Committee, upon which Armitage sat as an honorary member, voted in favour of recommending Sunday opening on the Manchester pattern, on the eve of the question being debated in the council he published a penny pamphlet. Armitage outlined arguments in answer to those of the Sabbatarians (led by Rev. Thomas Alfred Stowell) who claimed that Sunday work would inflict hardship on library and museum employees.[42]

By a vote of 30 to 20 the council refused to allow Sunday opening 'until the sense of the burgesses had been taken'. To test that, Armitage suggested ballot papers be posted to all ratepayers, and when he agreed to be responsible for the cost, his proposal was accepted. The poll of the ratepayers gave Armitage his victory. In all, 6607 votes were cast, and, by a majority of 283, the supporters of Sunday opening carried the day. Conservatives took some comfort that only one in five bothered to vote. When Alderman Bowes moved in the council that the museums and libraries be now open on Sundays, the matter was adjourned.[43] But, soon after, the council reversed its policy. It was a victory that had been long in coming. Sabbatarianism was forced to give way by a rich Liberal individualist using his own money to embarrass a Conservative council. It was a gesture in the Armitage tradition.

Armitage's campaign cheered up Salford Liberals. By the end of the decade the party was recovering from the defeat in the Home Rule election, and was given a boost in 1891 when the *Salford Reporter* abandoned political neutrality and announced that it was 'now ranged on the side of the Liberal Party'.[44] Early in

1888 the South and North Salford Liberal Party Associations selected new parliamentary candidates. Mather declining to stand (he was shortly to become MP for Gorton), he was replaced by Alexander Forrest, a Scots engineer with good local connections. However, the Socialists put up a candidate against him. The Liberal candidate for North Salford was W. H. Holland, a cotton spinner, employer of a thousand people at Miles Platting. As to the candidature for West Salford, there was no question who had first refusal, and Benjamin Armitage of Chomlea signalled that he was prepared to do battle one last time for Gladstone and Home Rule.

Fighting on a platform of Home Rule and 'the Newcastle Programme' (a package of Liberal reforms), Gladstone was returned to power, though again dependent on the votes of Irish Nationalists for his majority in the House of Commons. So close to being a triumph, in the event the election of July 1892 was once again a great disappointment for Salford Liberals. Holland got in for North Salford with a majority of 287. Forrest lost by 37 in a three-cornered contest in South Salford: the 552 votes cast for the Socialist cost the Liberals the seat. In West Salford the contest was also close run: at the end of the day Armitage had lost a second time to Lees Knowles, by a mere 40 votes. Liberals were left to reflect that, with a little luck and the tiniest of swings towards them, they could have taken all three seats.

Liberalism, however, was alive and well in 1892 and responding to social and political change, as the list of new Salford magistrates after Gladstone's victory reveals. As well as rewarding businessmen such as Councillor Stephens, the West Salford party leader, Herbert Lee, President of the South Salford Association, and James G. de T. Mandley, a fierce opponent of corruption on the council, six Temperance men, Irishmen, Jews and trade unionists were also elevated to the bench. Councillor H. B. Harrison, a Wesleyan who had sat on every Salford School Board since the Elementary Schools Act, and F. H. Smith, a Churchman who had started the Pendlebury Blue Ribbon Army twenty years before, were the Temperance men. Dr. Richard O'Gorman, a Broad street physician and president of the West Salford branch of the Irish National League became Salford's first Irish Catholic JP, and Thomas Dreydel, a Manchester merchant and treasurer of the North Salford Liberal Association, became Salford's first Jewish JP. The three trade unionists – George Sunley, general secretary of the National Amalgamated Society of Operative House Painters and Decorators, George T. Jackson, General Secretary of the Northern Counties Amalgamated Association of Tramway and Hackney Carriage Employees and R. Isherwood, Treasurer of the Lancashire and Cheshire Miners' Union, became Salford's first working-class JPs.[45]

Once again, another Liberal victory turned to ashes. In 1893 Gladstone introduced a second Home Rule Bill, the principal difference from his first being the provision that the 80 Irish representatives should sit at Westminster. It passed through the Commons but was rejected by the Lords on 8 September. Although, in retrospect, almost certainly right in his Irish policy, Gladstone's Liberal rationality could not overcome nation-wide Unionist feelings. Having lost his final battle, the Grand Old Man resigned in March 1894. He left the party shattered and, after a year under the premiership of Lord Rosebery, the Liberals resigned and lost the 1895 General Election. They were out of power for another decade. Paradoxically, after the failure of the second Home Rule Bill, for the first time for many years Ireland faded from political prominence. Morley, the Liberal Irish Secretary, had ruled with a sure touch and for another decade Conservative policy of 'Killing Home Rule by Kindness' with Land Purchase Acts worked. However, Home Rule remained on the agenda of both Irish Nationalist and Liberal parties.

Armitage finally withdrew from politics on the eve of the 1895 election, and his half-brother, Vernon, long since back in the Liberal fold, was nominated. He lost by 100 votes, and the Conservatives took all three Salford seats. If Benjamin Armitage's life (and it was a very political life) ended in disappointment, it had been a remarkable one nonetheless. One of the great Manchester businessmen of his day, he left a personal estate valued at over a quarter of a million pounds. He sat in Parliament for six years and, though he made little impact there, he was accepted as a worthy representative of that rare species in the national legislature, the Northern businessman. In Manchester he was a giant: prominent on the floor of 'Change, president of the Chamber of Commerce, governor of the Grammar School, trustee of the Infirmary and much involved in the Manchester and Salford Sick Poor and Private Nursing Institution, he was a member of the bourgeois élite, and it was fitting that Salford honoured him with the freedom of the county borough a year before his death.

Inevitably, there were sadnesses at the end. His wife, Elizabeth, died shortly before his death, as did George Armitage Southam, in his fifties. None of Benjamin's sons were then involved in the firm and Southam was being groomed as chairman in the next generation. The firm, however, went on and prospered, notably in the boom which preceded the Great War. And subsequently there was rarely a time when the firm did not have an Armitage in it. As capitalist and politician, Benjamin Armitage had been a worthy successor to his father. Between them, the two had been intimately involved in virtually all the main issues in the public life of Victorian Manchester and Salford.

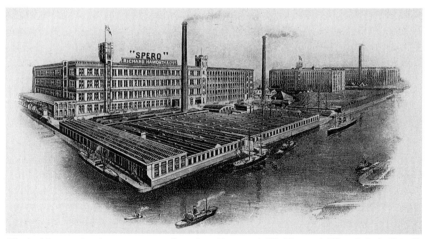

Vertical integration in cotton manufacturing. Egerton Mill, Tatton Mill and Ordsall Mill of the firm of Richard Haworth & Co. Ltd. (founded 1852), with their weaving sheds. By 1889 these premises were equipped with 139,000 spindles and 3,200 looms. 'Spero' was the firm's trade name. (Author's collection)

# CHAPTER 9

# Gas and Corruption:
# James Mandley, Samuel Hunter
# and the Salford Council

When, at a borough council meeting in August 1878, the recently elected Councillor James Mandley rose to propose a motion on the subject of municipal gas contracts his action provoked an unusual and disturbing response. Members of the gas committee interrupted his speech and, in an apparently concerted action, rose and quit the chamber. Lacking a quorum, the meeting was counted out.[1] This insulting behaviour was their way of putting an upstart in his place. In voicing criticism of a committee of which he was not a member, Mandley had offended against one of the canons of the council. Mandley declined to be sat upon. He served notice that the matter would be raised again on the next available occasion. This scene marked the start of a running battle which lasted more than a decade. Despite the fact that he was subsequently proved correct on virtually every allegation he made about the Salford gas concern, for much of this period Mandley achieved little. Eventually, matters reached a point when even he despaired of opening up the workings of the gas committee to scrutiny. Then, in a turn of events, his enemies delivered themselves up to him. What he had long been saying in public was vindicated in a court of law. Not only were the singular workings of the gas concern exposed, long established customs and malpractices of the borough's municipal system were opened to public scrutiny.[2]

Mandley was not the first to voice criticism of the gas concern. A few years previously some councillors, newly elected in the great Conservative victory of 1868, had been insensitive enough to ask questions about the management of the gas works. Supported by the rest of the council and the local press the gas committee closed ranks and succeeded in silencing them.[3] However, it seemed that the critics' efforts had not been entirely fruitless. In 1875 the gas committee was quietly reconstituted under the new chairmanship of Councillor Sharp, a prominent businessman and a rising star of the corporation, and a new engineer appointed. What Mandley was to demonstrate was that, despite outward appearances, this reformation had not changed much.

The gas works was the brightest jewel in Salford's municipal crown, and had been for a very long time. One of the oldest managed by any local authority, it

'An almost Carlylean hatred of every description of cant and sham': Councillor J. G. De T. Mandley (1835–1903). (*Manchester Faces and Places*)

dated back to 1831 when the Salford township police commissioners purchased the works from the original proprietor. The importance of gas to a rapidly growing industrial district was obvious, and the acquisition of a massive and potentially profitable concern seemed evidence of Salford's business-like way of conducting its local affairs. In the four decades of its existence the Salford Gas concern had grown with the town. By the late 1870s there were three gas works supplying over 30,000 consumers; some £400,000 had been invested in the plant, which consumed 73,000 tons of coal and cannel a year.[4] Successive local acts specified how the profits were to be applied to both the servicing of the debts of the business and easing the burden on the ratepayers. This vast concern was managed by the gas engineer who was responsible to the gas committee, one of the most prestigious of the council. The new engineer appointed in 1875, Samuel Hunter, was not only highly esteemed by all who knew him, but personally was more impressive than any of his predecessors. Yet, despite the confidence he exuded, a grumbling sense of unease about the efficiency of the gas works persisted and it fell to Mandley to voice it. If he entertained any illusions about the difficulty of getting at the truth, his treatment in August 1878 must have disabused him of them. Mandley, however, was not the sort to let go easily.

The son of George Frederick Mandley, who had played some part in the earlier history of the borough in his own right as Owenite socialist, Anti-Poor Law reformer and businessman, James George de Thiballier Mandley (de Thiballier was his French grandfather's name) was born in 1835.[5] At the age of thirteen he had started work in his father's business of commission agent to the cotton trade. In his twenties he was sent to Mexico to assist the firm's partner there, and travelled widely in the Americas. In 1861 he was given a partnership and the following decade visited India, starting up a connection which subsequently formed the main part of the firm's business. It was also his task to produce a trade circular started by his father which gave the monthly prices of raw cotton, yarn and cloth, and for some time he wrote and edited this himself. A cultured man, Mandley had a wide range of interests. A member of the Manchester Literary Club, he published works on the position of women in non-Christian societies, French colonisation in Africa, and, some years later, on the Manchester Ship Canal project. A local historian who gave lectures on Salford's history, he later produced a two volume edition of the records of the old Salford Portmote and Court Leet, published by the Chetham Society. Mandley, however, was no bookworm. By temperament he was well qualified for the role of sweeper of the Augean Stables. A contemporary noted his 'almost Carlylean hatred of every description of cant and sham'.[6] On the Salford council he was to find much to feed this hatred. He first stood for election in 1876, unsuccessfully. A year later he got in as a Liberal in the normally Conservative ward of St John's, Broughton.

A month after his initial rebuff, the upstart Mandley, as promised, again raised the matter of gas contracts, drawing attention to the gas works' lack of profitability since 1870, compared to Manchester's. He demanded information about its workings. This time the gas committee offered a prepared explanation of certain 'difficulties' it had encountered.[7] The chairman, Alderman Sharp, admitted that for some time they had been aware that there had been inefficiencies, and Alderman Sinclair, in a bantering Mancunian manner, launched into an apparently frank explanation of how 'some years previously' 'an unfortunate error of judgement' had been made. Acting on the advice of the gas manager of the time they had gone in for 'gambling in futures'

> A few years ago when the price of material had reached a price that was never known in the country before, and when it was stated by coal proprietors and iron and other manufacturers that there would never be a reduction in the price ... everyone – cotton spinners and others – went in to protect themselves against a further possible rise and the Gas Committee were advised to enter into a very large contract for materials at the very highest prices ... When the price of materials fell they could not charge the ratepayers the heavy prices they had been charging them for gas and consequently the concern sustained a very great loss.

All that was unfortunate, but was a thing of the past. Now that they had the services of the experienced Samuel Hunter, such mistakes were unlikely to be repeated. Under his able direction the works were being expanded, and already showing very satisfactory profits. Mandley's criticisms, it was suggested, were out of date.

In all this there was much that was new, and, in view of later developments, what was said about awarding contracts more revealing than appreciated at the time. But they had not supplied the information Mandley had requested, so he produced his own calculations of gas profits and losses for the years 1870–78. There were more of the latter than of the former. Meanwhile, his seconder, Councillor Walker, touched on other matters. For years, he declared, 'there had been a nervousness, a timidity, a shirking of any exposé in connection with the gas department' on the part of the council. They had had officials 'who had been their masters, and who had dictated what had been done'. Walker suggested that the gas committee were still not in control of the financial management of the concern. Although subsequent events were to bear out what Mandley and Walker were alleging, in the event, the council was quite happy to accept the gas committee's word that mistakes, understandable enough to men with experience of these matters, had been made, and that a Hunterian reformation was now under way at the works. Mandley and Walker's allegations were regarded as wild and unsubstantiated, and their motion rejected.[8]

Mandley reacted with the publication of his pamphlet, *Salford Gas Management*, in October 1878. In clear language he set out the reasons why he had started his campaign, what had happened so far, and what needed to be done in the future. His interest had first been aroused by the widespread dissatisfaction he had found among ratepayers about the high cost and poor quality of Salford gas. Examining the performance of the concern since 1870, Mandley showed that in reality the losses were worse than the committee had admitted, and for a reason that any man of acumen could spot right away. In their figures, they had not allowed sufficient for depreciation. For sixteen years not a penny had been set aside for depreciation of the plant in Regent Road, on which £92,000 had been spent by June 1875. Dryly, he observed 'the Works and Plant of No 3 Station must have been looked upon by the Gas Committee as though they were port wine, the older they were the more valuable they became'.[9]

He took particular exception to Alderman Sinclair's taunt that he and Walker were busybodies. 'Is the Gas Committee a private concern looking after its own interests only, that every member of the council, not being a member of that committee, who shall seek to acquaint himself with its operations, is to be set down as a "busybody"'? 'Was the council master of its committees, or the committees masters of the council'? Mandley was to find out that in Salford the latter was indeed the case. On the committee's policy of 'let sleeping dogs lie', Mandley commented 'I fully believe that at the present our Gas Committee is composed of honourable, and in the main shrewd and intelligent men, and I believe that we are equally fortunate as regards our Gas Manager. My action relates to the past on account of its bearings on the future'. What was really on his mind were the enormous contracts placed by the committee, and the way they awarded them. Referring in general terms to malpractices that were rumoured to exist, he suggested that what was imperative was that in future contracts should be for no longer than twelve-months, and that such materials as coal, cannel and iron pipes, ordered in large quantities, should be purchased direct, not through middlemen, and that the council should adopt standing orders to that effect. He further suggested that councillors at large should have far more information than was available to them at present. In a pamphlet that was almost wholly factual and businesslike in tone, Mandley ended by allowing himself one flash of his 'Carlylean anger'. He declared the poor of Salford had been betrayed by the mismanagement of the gas concern. Profits which should have been used by the Health Committee to demolish slums had been incompetently squandered.[10]

Although selling 2,000 copies, *Salford Gas Management* was ignored by the council. Mandley found himself in a classic dilemma. His criticisms were rejected by the very body without whose action the system could not be changed. Denied access to essential information, Mandley's allegations could be brushed off as intemperate and inaccurate. Thus frustrated, Mandley's contempt for his fellow councillors and the ruling aldermanic clique grew. Highly individualistic, very undiplomatic and easily provoked to anger, increasingly he declined to hide his contempt. Not able to work well with other councillors, Mandley preferred to appeal direct to the ratepayers, but with council and press opposed to him, Mandley was to find he was in a weak position. At this stage of mid-Victorian municipal history, with a narrow ratepayer franchise, arrogant oligarchies able to control ward elections had little to fear from public opinion – at least, not in Salford. Just how little, was made clear early the following year. At a council meeting in January 1879 there was an angry scene when Mandley accused the town clerk of denying him access to information on current gas contracts. When Mandley was impudent enough to declare that he would leave the meeting believing there were men present guilty of fraud, once again the members of the council rose as a body and walked out.[11]

Certain that past iniquities were still flourishing at the gas works, Mandley's attentions were, perhaps for the first time, focusing on Hunter, the gas engineer. However, his first attempts to bring matters into the open rebounded upon his own head. Rather more than a year later, in September 1880, a motion of his touching on bribery over gas contracts was defeated, following acrimonious exchanges. At this meeting of the council, new (long-term) contracts for coal and cannel, to the value of £150,000, were considered. Severely criticised by Mandley, it was agreed that the matter should be put into the hands of the general purposes committee for investigation. Two weeks later the committee reported back, finding nothing at all untoward. Mandley, much discomforted, came under fire in the press. 'After a full investigation Mr Hunter has triumphed over his enemies in the Salford Town Council. When Councillor Mandley submitted his motion to the judgement of the council at its last meeting it was generally understood to be aimed at the Gas Engineer and the Gas Committee.' Now that the matter has been investigated, declared the *Reporter*, 'the specific charges preferred by Councillor Mandley have been proved to be as false as the innuendoes he employed were base and discreditable'. Noting that Mandley was up for re-election in November, the editor suggested that his obsession with gas and his 'wild performances' in the council might not commend themselves to the good burgesses of St John's Ward.[12] He was to be proved wrong. Mandley was returned unopposed. When he secured a seat on the new gas committee he made it clear that nothing had changed. 'In going on to the gas committee. I know I have a great work before me,' he declared.[13]

In the meantime, Hunter was riding high. The following March (1881), he brought a court action against Ellis Lever, one of the largest coal contractors of the district. It alleged Lever had libelled him in a letter to the chairman of the gas committee which stated that there had been corruption in the matter of a cannel contract, which had gone to a rival firm. Lever was forced to retract, settle out of court, and pay Hunter's costs.[14]

For the better part of a year, though the matter simmered away outside the council, there were no overt developments. Then, in January 1882, a letter appeared in the columns of the *Salford Weekly News* which offered £100 for an independent audit of the accounts and transactions of the Salford gas committee. It was signed VIGILANCE, and if its writer was not Mandley, it was someone close.[15] It was timed to agitate ratepayer sensibilities, already ruffled by increases in local spending. Recently, feelings had been made plain at angry meetings of ratepayers over a proposed new Improvement Bill for Salford, and the proposal had been abandoned. At another angry meeting in March, a motion of censure was passed on the gas committee after allegations that there had been twenty years of mismanagement (which had cost the ratepayers a sum in the region of £180,000), that the concern would not stand comparison with Manchester's, and that what was needed was an independent investigation. When Hunter attempted to address the meeting, he was shouted down.

Inside the council things were very different. A proposal for an inquiry was turned down flatly by the gas committee and the council concurred. Alderman Makinson assured members that the committee carefully scrutinised every item, and voiced an opinion that VIGILANCE was a disappointed contractor. When Mandley made circumstantial allegations about irregularities over contracts, virtually the whole council voted against his motion of censure. The *Reporter* took the same line. It declared that recent meetings of ratepayers were unrepresentative, and branded VIGILANCE as nothing more than a pettifogging libeller. Hunter got his vote of confidence at the next meeting of the council, and Mandley, increasingly undiplomatic, accused a fellow member of being a liar and refused to withdraw. The members of the finest club in Salford declared themselves scandalised at his utter lack of gentlemanly manners. Unabashed, Mandley attacked Hunter, drawing attention to the extravagance of his life-style, inferring that Hunter was growing rich on the pickings of his position.[16]

And, undeniably, Samuel Hunter lived well. Indeed, he never sought to hide the fact. He had a house worth £8,000, two carriages, and a hunting box in Cheshire. Visitors to his house were regaled with cold turkey and champagne, and much appreciated these were. It was not unknown (it later transpired) for him to arrive at gas committee meetings dressed in hunting pink, and for business to be despatched briskly, to allow him to be away to the meet. He travelled abroad. He shot grouse on the moors. In 1882 it was rumoured that he had recently paid £12,000 for the *Ashton Reporter*, and it was later revealed he had invested heavily in a grey-cloth company which traded with Australia, made other newspaper investments and had £6–7,000 in gas shares.[17] A respected member at Brunswick Wesleyan church (where he occasionally preached), Hunter was not unmindful of the poor. Early in 1881, at his own expense, he issued a thousand coke tickets to be distributed in that inclement season.[18]

Not least amongst the benefits Hunter enjoyed were the confidence and esteem of the gas committee. Indeed they supported him in a way that later seemed to have transcended mere loyalty to a paid official. True, they had selected him and exceedingly pleased with their choice they were. But, not to put too fine a point on it, Hunter bedazzled them.[19] Few things delighted a certain kind of nineteenth century businessman than the sight of another joining their ranks. They took it as a compliment. A special fondness was reserved for those who could claim to have risen from a humble background and Hunter's was humble enough. He began his working life as a Lincoln errand boy who eventually was appointed to a post in the Huddersfield Gas Works. Thereafter he progressed, first to Louth, thence to Rochdale. In 1875 he was appointed to revitalise the Salford concern at the very decent, but scarcely princely, salary of £500 a year. In retrospect, it was apparent that the attraction was not merely the salary but the way the concern was run. It operated on a large scale. Huge contracts were there to be awarded. And, rather unusually, both the technical and financial management was concentrated in the hands of the Engineer. Even more tempting, perhaps was the knowledge that the gas committee delegated the running of the business very extensively indeed.[20]

From the start Hunter set out to impress, and certainly succeeded. A scheme of extensions was launched, and was soon delivering up 'record' profits, for which, after only two years, a grateful committee raised his salary.[21] When Mandley pointed out that it was suspicious that someone on £810 a year lived like a '£5000 a year man' the council declared itself outraged. Then, and later, a host of explanations, were advanced: Hunter was an astute investor, he dealt in horses as a sideline, he was in receipt of consultancy fees, Mrs Hunter had money. No matter that most of these were the purest of fictions, Hunter exuded confidence, consumed conspicuously, and was defended vigorously by his admirers on the council – Aldermen Sharp, Makinson, Hubbard and Robinson. To them Hunter was indispensable, Mandley unspeakable.

The vote of confidence of April 1882 virtually silenced the critics for nearly five years. Hunter, to all external appearances, advanced from strength to strength. He persuaded the Council to build splendid new municipal gas offices in Bloom Street, and when the Institute of Gas Engineers held their annual meeting m Manchester in 1885 their president expressed profound admiration for Salford's Engineer, declaring the borough's gas plants were looked upon as model works. Hunter's business ventures prospered. In 1886 the borough of Ashton-under-Lyne made him a Justice of the Peace.[22] Occasionally, as in August 1885, Mandley raised his voice, alleging on that occasion that a tender had been awarded to a firm that had entertained Hunter. The committee replied that Hunter had done nothing without their approval. Yet, as time passed, some strains did begin to show. The gas manager produced annual statistics of the gas business for circulation within the council, and the time came when even the Salford council found them too much to swallow. In late 1886 some sharply critical observations were voiced by Councillors Snape and Keevney, hitherto Hunter supporters, after Hunter produced figures purporting to show that Salford was making greater potential profits for the relief of the rates than was Manchester. Keevney was moved to point out that Manchester gas was superior in quality, cheaper to the consumer, and produced profits that met the costs of street lighting, something Salford had not yet even so much as contemplated. When Hunter's figures were defended, Keevney suggested it was high time there was a full inquiry. As always, this suggestion found little support, and in the debate a weary and discouraged Mandley was moved to declare that, though he continued to believe that there was something very odd about the working of the gas concern and the style in which Hunter lived, 'he had fought a big fight, but had dropped it'.[23]

Given that, in the end, Mandley was to be proved right in almost all he had alleged, why was it that after eight years he had achieved so little, and had virtually given up? Contemporaries would certainly have pointed to his defects. There was a choleric side to him which led him to be provoked into personalising arguments and alienating people. Yet it must be said the treatment he received from fellow members of the council goes far to exonerate him. The Salford system meant that anyone could be denied the essential information to substantiate criticisms of its workings. In practice, if not in theory, the gas committee *was* autonomous; it *did* delegate to the point of negligence and the rest of the councillors and aldermen suspended their disbelief and acquiesced. In Salford the desire not to rock the boat transcended any feelings of unease about maladministration and corruption. Ironically, for Mandley (and for Hunter), just at the point when it seemed that the gas committee had silenced its critics, the great Salford gas scandal blew up in all their faces.

Early in 1887 another action for libel was brought against Ellis Lever, the coal contractor, then much in the public eye as a leading promoter of the great Manchester Exhibition of Arts and Industry to mark the Queen's Jubilee. Somewhat to the surprise of the rest of the council, members of which had not been informed beforehand, the action was brought not by Hunter, but by the gas committee. At the police court hearing the matter took an interesting twist. Imputations against the members of the gas committee being withdrawn to the court's satisfaction,

Ellis Lever, the great coal contractor, friend and then enemy of Samuel Hunter. (*Manchester Faces and Places*)

Lever was committed for trial solely on charges of having libelled Hunter.[24] When, at his subsequent trial at the Assizes, a verdict of 'not guilty' was returned, these allegations were in effect upheld. Thus, though Lever was the defendant, it was Hunter who was put on trial. A flood of information about the workings of the Salford gas concern, the borough municipal system, and the gas manager's life-style was released at these hearings. It substantiated what Mandley had been alleging for nearly ten years.

The gas committee and the council came out very badly. Under cross examination, the Mayor, Alderman James Farmer, was made to look a confounded fool. At one point counsel asked him 'Is there anything about the Corporation you do know?' Alderman Sharp, chairman of the gas committee for the past twelve years, fared as badly. Counsel was able to show that Hunter had run rings round him and the committee for years, from time to time tossing them such titbits of information as he judged they should have, refusing access to the books to anyone asking awkward questions. Under cross-examination, Hunter never lost his confident air, supplying explanations as to how, on his salary, he could live as he did. The trial hinged on Lever's accusations about why his coal had been replaced by that of another contractor, Wrigley. Hunter argued that this had been done because of a 'bad debt', but Lever alleged that the real reason was that Wrigley had paid Hunter a 'sweetener'. A figure of ten shillings per ton was mentioned. Between 1877 and 1886 Salford gas works had consumed over 800,000 tons of coking coal, of which Wrigley had supplied about half.[25] Explanations as to why Hunter was now reputedly worth £100,000 after ten years on a salary of £810 per annum began to suggest themselves.

Not surprisingly, the case aroused more than mere local interest. Every town had a gas works, and it was implied that what went on in Salford was hardly unique. One early casualty was Hawkins of the Wigan gas works, a close friend of Hunter's, who gave evidence on his behalf. Shortly after, his employers dismissed him. At the first Council meeting after the trial Mandley demanded that Hunter should not be allowed to resign quietly, but fired and prosecuted, and did not neglect to round on those who had denigrated him over the years. He made two demands; the resignation of the gas committee, and the setting up of a full enquiry. The gas committee chairman, Alderman Sharp was too shell-shocked to offer a defence. It fell to Alderman Makinson to defend their record. He argued that Hunter had increased profitability, had reduced the cost to the consumer, and that charges against him had always been circumstantial. All this rang hollow. Nonetheless it took a fortnight for the gas committee to resign and they went full of self-righteousness, Makinson even laying claim to the gratitude of the public for having brought Hunter to court.[26]

The Gas Investigation Committee reported at the end of the summer and produced a devastating, if limited, exposé. Capital expenditure since 1877 had created enormous debt charges, and had failed in its aim, output having fallen short of its targets by full fifty per cent. Running costs were found to be excessive, and it was stated that 'undue latitude' had been allowed the late gas engineer, and 'greater confidence, which was undeniably misplaced, reposed in him than was desirable'. Hunter had frequently been away from the office for days on end. Visits to the works by the committee had been rare and supervision perfunctory. Much irregularity could have been prevented by more frequent inspection, thought the committee. It professed itself 'astonished' to find that as late as 1886 tenders for three years' supply of coal and cannel (valued in the region of £140,000) had been accepted without any examination or analysis of the material to be supplied. Moreover, no real check was ever made of material actually delivered to the works. Clearly, as the Lever trial had strongly suggested, the gas concern had been, and probably still was being swindled by contractors over deliveries. There was, moreover, laxity in the collection of consumer accounts; a higher proportion of bad debts were found in Salford than in other places.[27]

In the debate on the report Mandley was very critical, not so much over what they had looked into, but what they had not. In particular, in the welter of statistics produced, he professed himself anxious that the scale of Hunter's fraud and embezzlement might get lost. Almost inevitably his personal criticisms of certain committee members led to a row. In the midst of this the matter of their resignation from the council was lost.[28] None did resign, or at least not immediately. In the end the report was tamely referred to the (new) gas committee for implementation, and in October, after 36 meetings, the Investigation Committee was dissolved. More angry scenes followed Mandley's and Rycroft's allegations that there was a cover-up. They also accused the town clerk of dragging his feet over the prosecution of Hunter.[29]

In fact, it was not until March 1888 that Hunter was committed for trial for perjury and for issuing a forged authority for payment of monies. He pleaded guilty, professing at the same time a willingness to make restitution (in cash) to the council. It did not impress the Judge, who gave him five years with hard labour.[30] But, in the sense that it went down well in council circles, this was a shrewd attitude to take. How shrewd soon became clear. The council now went in for a damage-limitation exercise. If Mandley and other reformers hoped for a sweeping of the stables they were to be frustrated. Moreover, reaction to Hunter's sentence revealed considerable ambivalence in certain quarters on the whole matter.

Samuel Hunter at his trial, 1888.
(*Reporter*)

Detectable in an editorial in the *Salford Reporter* is a distinct note of relief. 'Those who were anticipating disclosures of an important nature inculpating people whose names have been freely mentioned since Mr Hunter's arrest have been doomed to disappointment. We believe Mr Hunter was too shrewd and wily a man to trust any member of the Salford Town Council with the secret spring from which his wealth came'.[31] A distinctly anti-Mandley tone is apparent. As guardian of the good name of the borough, the *Reporter* had never liked his accusation that there was something rotten in the state of Salford. The Lever trial forced it to change its tune. The paper's priority now was now to limit the ramifications of the scandal. This was prompted by other reasons than the mere preservation of Salford's good name.

Suggestions were once again being mooted that there were advantages in the uniting of Salford and Manchester for the purposes of local government. First given serious consideration in 1883, Salford had rejected it. It arose once more in 1888 in the context of the new County Councils Bill before Parliament and the construction of the Manchester ship canal. There was considerable alarm in Salford when a Manchester and Salford Society was formed, led by such prominent citizens as William Mather and George Chester Haworth to promote the creation of a new administrative county out of the great double-barrelled city. Such a proposal was anathema to the *Reporter*. In the end, the proposal was turned down, a Salford committee having concluded that it offered no financial advantages to the ratepayers. However, the mere suggestion caused Salford's élite to close ranks over the gas affair.[32]

There were other factors. That year another scandal broke when it was found that the Town Clerk, Graves, had defalcated with a large sum. The fact that he had taken more from the clients of his law practice than from the ratepayers was little consolation. Once again the glaring inadequacies of Salford's highly compart-mentalised municipal system, with its fondness for delegation and secrecy, were exposed.[33] A third factor was that, when the County Councils Bill was being debated in Parliament, the possibility of Salford becoming one of the new county boroughs was raised, and serious consideration started to be given to ending the local arrangements of the 1853 Act, and bringing the three townships into a more unitary system. In the light of this, the *Reporter* and all patriotic Salfordians were very anxious to limit the extent of further self-inflicted wounds.

However, the Hunter saga had still some way to run. In November 1888, pressed by Mandley, the council set up a committee to consider legal action against Hunter. In August the following year there was much surprise when it was announced that an out-of-court agreement had been reached with his solicitors. In return for dropping litigation and all claims against Hunter or his abettors, the council had agreed to accept a once-and-for-all payment of £10,000 from its former gas engineer. In support, it was argued that, in the light of the difficulties unravelling all the implications of the affair (Hunter having covered his tracks so well) this was a satisfactory conclusion to the business. As usual, Mandley differed. As usual, events were soon to prove him right. In his view, the deal was wrong anyway, the council backing out of civil proceedings just at the point when they were within reach of information of the utmost importance – the Court of Appeal having just confirmed an order giving the corporation the right to inspect the books of a certain firm of suppliers. Hunter, he went on, now knew the game was truly up, which was why he was offering £10,000 to compound. Mandley also pointed out that nearly half that sum had been swallowed up in legal costs already, and that more could also have been said about both the legality and morality of such an agreement. Once again, Mandley found himself in a minority. When it was put to the vote only four councillors voted with him.[34]

Not the least surprising development at this juncture (although perhaps not so surprising with the virtue of hindsight) was the getting-up of a petition to the Home Secretary for the early release of Hunter from prison signed by the town clerk and an overwhelming majority of the council. The *Salford Reporter*, too, had nothing but sympathy for Hunter, supported the financial deal, and accused those who disapproved it of 'a lack of courtesy and want of faithfulness towards their colleagues'. On Hunter, the editor declared[35]

> The facts revealed are so decisively in his favour that we cannot any longer withhold saying that anything short of his immediate release would be a public scandal and a grievous wrong to Hunter. It is now admitted that there never was any proof, and two and a half years of investigation ... has failed to produce proof that the random assertions about the enormous amount of bribes and commissions had any foundations in fact.

At a special meeting of the council the settlement with Hunter was approved. However, it aroused a chorus of very unfavourable comment outside, notably in the Manchester press. Incensed, the mayor was moved to make a statement. The general purposes committee had not met in secret behind closed doors to devise a settlement, his worship declared; it *always* met behind closed doors. To alter it would mean rewriting standing orders. He added that he, with others, believed Hunter's sentence was severe 'considering that his offence was not a criminal one to all intents and purposes'. It was Mandley's turn to be embarrassed when Alderman Keevney read out a letter of his to the *Manchester Examiner* alleging that Keevney and Ashton supported Hunter because all three were members at Brunswick Weslyan Church. Mandley had to confess that he had indeed sent the letter, intending it 'for information not publication.' His motion regretting that the petition for Hunter's release had been signed by 42 members of the council was resoundingly defeated. Another motion of Mandley's, petitioning for a Royal Commission on Salford's local government, was defeated 32 to 4. He was to persist with this as a way of preventing the agreement with Hunter being finalised and was to find support from amongst leading citizens and local Socialists pressing for a 'clean' and more accountable system of local government in the borough.[36]

As had become almost pre-ordained, it was a matter of mere months before Mandley's opposition to the Hunter agreement was vindicated. Again, it rose out of litigation involving Ellis Lever. An action brought by the council against Lever to recover certain monies alleged to have been paid to Hunter was heard at Leeds Assizes a few months later (in March 1890). Details were revealed in court which added new dimensions to the scandal. In the first place Lever's reputation was tarnished. Since the libel case three years before, he had been playing 'the great purist'. Evidence produced in court stripped him of that particular mantle. It emerged that Lever had offered a bribe of a shilling a ton to Hunter to grant him three contracts for 56,000 tons of coal. After paying Hunter an advance, Lever had in the end been denied the contract. It was in revenge for this that he had written to the corporation in June 1885, first exposing Hunter, posing as a discoverer of wrong doings. However, as we have seen, Hunter's threatened action for libel was settled out of court, part of the deal being Lever agreeing to pay Hunter more of the money 'owed'. They quarrelled again in 1886, and Lever sent a telegram to the Mayor of Salford alleging bribery, corruption and fraud. The gas committee forced Hunter to sue for libel, which case he lost, and was eventually sent to prison. Only when the council investigated the matter further did the long-term nature of the relationship between the two men become apparent. What was also revealed was that Hunter originally offered £20,000 (not £10,000) to the council 'to get him out of his difficulties'. Hunter gave evidence, and one of the more risible pieces of information revealed was that the good Wesleyan had spent one of Lever's bribes on a visit to the Holy Land. Lever was ordered by the judge to repay the corporation £2,300 – a shilling a ton on the coal purchased under the contracts in question.[37]

This trial was yet another severe discomfiture for the corporation. Public criticism sharpened, and in the Manchester press Salford was branded 'the rotten borough', the severest attacks appearing in the *Manchester City News*. Against this background, Mandley pressed for a Royal Commission, and for a time it seemed his demand was irresistible. But he was up against fudgers of proven ability: the matter of whether such an inquiry should be confined to Salford, or whether it should cast its net wider was raised. With Salford's honour at stake, Alderman Makinson pressed for the latter, and the council came down in favour of a 'roving commission'. By now, the whole thing was thoroughly tangled up in the Manchester amalgamation issue. In the council and in the *Reporter* bitter attacks were made on Mandley for aiding and abetting those 'treasonable' Salfordians who favoured amalgamation. In the end, it was the Home Secretary himself who scotched the idea of a Royal Commission, narrow or broad. Until every legal remedy had been exhausted, he told a delegation from Salford, Parliament could not act.[38]

On 7 May 1890 the council debated the matter of fixing the common seal of the borough to the 'release' agreed with Hunter, by which he was to pay them £10,000. Mandley, Rycroft and other opponents managed to get the matter adjourned, and at a public meeting it was agreed to make one last attempt to prevent the council giving this agreement the legal status of a contract. Application was made to the Court of Chancery, but the Court declined to grant an interim injunction. On 4 June the council, by a majority of 16, decided to seal the Hunter release whereby the ratepayers were to receive £10,000 in discharge of all claims against him. The *Salford Reporter* applauded the decision, and once more urged the council to press for Hunter's early release.[39]

The matter was now as good as over, though Mandley persisted in arguing that the release was wrong. He received little support inside the council, but was yet again vindicated in court. At a hearing in the Divisional Court of the Queen's Bench in July 1890 Lever petitioned for a new trial. He was refused, and in delivering judgement, Mr Justice Vaughan Williams referred to the contract between Hunter and the corporation as 'illegal, *ultra vires*, and of no effect'. For good measure he also considered it immoral. When the case went to appeal, the Master of the Rolls said he considered the agreement infamous; it amounted to a 'bribe of the corporation to Hunter to give evidence which he was bound to give'.[40]

The infamous release of 1890 was evidence, if further evidence be needed, that right to the end Hunter outfoxed the gas committee, the corporation and its legal advisers. They apparently believed that, in return for Hunter depositing securities for £10,000, they were to proceed against the persons who had bribed him, and that by so much as they recovered, the £10,000 would be diminished, in order that (in effect) Hunter might not pay the money twice. The whole tenor of the argument was that £10,000 was to be the amount taken as the sum Hunter had received in bribes, and that this was the sum to go back into the coffers of the corporation. But when the council attempted to proceed against certain contractors they found that, in making the release with Hunter, they had disqualified themselves from doing so. The opinion of learned Counsel was[41]

> If the deal of June 4 1890 releases Hunter from liability from the joint fraud of himself and the contractors it acts as a release to the contractors. We are of the opinion that it does release Hunter from liability for such frauds. The very general words at the end of the said deed must be considered as qualified by the recitals; nevertheless we think there is sufficient in the recitals to cover frauds committed jointly with the contractors, and that in so releasing Hunter the contractors are also released.
>
> We think the corporation have now no right of action against any contractor who contributed to the sum of £10,000 mentioned in the release, and that under all circumstances they would not be reasonably justified in instituting proceedings against them.

In this manner, with the council and its legal advisers to the end exuding the incompetence of the desperate, the matter died. The council's relief was palpable. The contractors escaped further exposure. And, with his payment of £10,000 as a sort of tax on profits made, Hunter was probably not inconsolable, although it may be doubted if he ever found Her Majesty's Prison, Portland, much to his taste.[42]

The Hunter affair raises profound questions about local government in Victorian Salford. Why would the corporation not listen to Mandley? How was it that, when unease became widespread, investigation was resisted so long and so resolutely? How could the council afford to ignore the ratepayers? And why were its members so anxious to sweep matters under the carpet when Hunter was finally exposed, and even press for leniency for him? Answers to some of these questions have been touched on, but others have to be sought at a deeper level than mere inquiry into the peculiar workings of the gas committee. They lie in the history and structure of the borough's local institutions, and in the psychology and motivation of the men who got themselves elected to the council in the middle and late Victorian years.

By the time the Hunter scandal broke, extreme committee autonomy was part of a scheme of things which went back to Brotherton's 'Limited Liability partnership' of 1853, and even beyond, to the era of the Police Commissioners. If Salford's famous 'trinity without unity,' with its complex 'borough' and 'township' committees, had been designed in recognition that township loyalties were, if anything, stronger than borough ones, the Hunter affair revealed some of its shortcomings, at least to its critics. What proves harder to fathom is the egotistical arrogance on the part of elected councillors and aldermen, which covered up for so long the gross inefficiency and lack of answerability on the part of the gas committee. Salford's local constitution was not unique. In these years, townships were federated for borough purposes in other places. Until amalgamation in 1874, the six Manchester townships were organised in a not dissimilar manner. What Salford lacked in comparison to its neighbour was (amongst other things) an effective executive. Salford never had anyone remotely comparable in power or influence to Sir Joseph Heron, Manchester's town clerk from 1838 to 1889. Salford's first town clerks, Gibson and Chadwick, had been able enough, though scarcely of Heron's stature. But after Chadwick resigned in 1860, there seems to have been a fall in the quality of the men, as well as a weakening in the role of the office. The reasons would appear to lie both in the part played by Ratepayers Associations (with their fondness for internal appointments), and in the temper and at attitudes of the sort of men who came to the fore in local politics in the 1860s and 1870s.

If it were to be asked why men sought election to local institutions in the nineteenth century it would be wrong to deny that some did not do so out of a disinterested sense of public duty. No doubt Salford had its share of such men. However, by no means all were motivated by such a spirit. There were not too many Thomas Davieses. Many, possibly most, sought election first and foremost to gratify legitimate bourgeois ambition. There was no clearer way known to Victorian businessmen to underline their success in life than to be elected to the town council or, if they were smaller fry, to the board of guardians. For many, the object of getting on the council was getting on the council. Once elected, new members did not, as a rule, feel impelled to take on the role of gadfly. Older members, thinking of promotion, or out of self-satisfaction, were just as unlikely to criticise the corporation's structure or practices. Indeed, many grew enamoured of its traditions. Most were only too happy to belong to a club that would have them as members. Moreover, party feelings, always sharp in Salford, in most instances prevailed over all other considerations. It is true that in the 1850s and 1860s Ratepayers Associations had been stronger than party organisations for the purpose of local elections, but these really only brought a different kind of local politician to the fore, and by 1868, Ratepayers Associations had faded in importance. From then on, council elections became a sector of the local party political battle.

On these traditionally autonomous council committees, chairmanships and deputy chairmanships were largely an aldermanic preserve. Safe for long periods from direct ratepayer influence, Salford aldermen could ignore public opinion. Moreover, elevation to the bench of alderman was invariably a question of party. Promotion on grounds of seniority did not come until 1899, and, after the early years of the council, there was no co-option from outside, as in some other places.

From the early Seventies the council came to be dominated by a phalanx of Conservative aldermen; and the Hunter scandal served to unleash a wave of vituperation against this 'aldermanic gang'. If some of this can be put down to Liberal resentment of 'vulgar Tory' hegemony, there was much in the charge that what had earned Salford the epithet of 'the rotten borough' was aldermanic arrogance, incompetence and slackness. Moreover, the businessmen who dominated the council in this period failed to apply to the public's business the acumen they displayed on their own account. Another feature noted at the time was that Salford men of the first rank frequently stayed out of local elections altogether, or preferred to stand in Manchester where their offices were located.

The Hunter affair brought changes. In 1887, for the first time, the books of the corporation were opened to professional auditors. It transpired that hitherto outside auditors had only ever been allowed to look at the cash books, and the gas accounts had *never* been looked at all.[43] The Salford Corporation Act of 1891 removed some of the structural inadequacies of the council when it united the three townships, abolished the township committees and reduced Salford's twenty-four committees to sixteen.[44]

Yet these consequences of the gas scandal were oddly unsatisfactory and incomplete. Another damaging *cause célèbre* was required to further the progress of reform – the 'Financial Muddle' of 1894–5. This time what was revealed was not so much corruption as incompetence. The Muddle brought to an end the domination of the old aldermanic bench, which had soldiered on through the Gas Scandal, unrepentant and oblivious to criticism. The Muddle arose over a budget deficit of some £76,000, the origins of which lay in the methods used to fund large new sewering and slum clearance schemes. This burst of activity arose out of the increasing mass of contemporary legislation enlarging the responsibilities of local government. In trying to finance these large capital projects out of current income an alarming deficit built up. Only late in the day did the finance committee consider applying to the Local Government Board for loans.[45] The deficit exposed alarming financial incompetence. The committee, the borough treasurer and the borough engineer all came in for heavy criticism. 'Men who could not distinguish between capital and revenue charges were not men who should be sent to the council', declared one incensed ratepayer.[46] At first, councillors attempted to lay the blame on officials. But the Local Government Board, the ratepayers and Socialist campaigners for 'clean government' made sure that this line of defence was swept aside. Hall, the borough treasurer, was honest, but he was old. After serving the council for over 20 years he had been made town clerk after Graves's defalcation six years before. It was recognised that the job had simply been beyond him.[47] Inside the council, Mandley led the attack on the finance committee and the inept system of financial control then in operation. Once again Mandley employed his own special combination of incisiveness and tactlessness, which this time provoked a fellow councillor into a physical assault upon him. Mandley took out a summons, and it required the personal intercession of the Mayor to smooth things over.[48]

The great Financial Muddle took three years to straighten out. Procedures were tightened, old staff (including the borough treasurer) retired, and new appointed. Economies were introduced, the rates were increased, even the Technical Education

Fund was raided. The council election of 1895 saw an influx of new men, so that within three years half the council had served four years or less. It was also the year that Aldermen Keevney and Makinson died and Alderman Sharp finally retired. 1895 also saw Mandley elevated to the aldermanic bench. For a time, however, the old party system of promotion continued: out of eight new aldermen created, six were Conservative Party men.[49] It was not until four years later that Salford began to promote on grounds of seniority only.

As a result of the Gas Scandal and the Financial Muddle, Salford's municipal system began to change. Some judgement on how far and how effectively can be made from notes on a visit in 1899 made by Sidney Webb, the Fabian Socialist historian of English local government.[50] Webb's unpublished notes record interviews with the mayor, the deputy mayor, the chairman of the gas committee and 'an old committee clerk.' Webb found the mayor, Alderman Rudman, 'a flashy publican', and Alderman Robinson, the deputy mayor, 'an aged property owner', a 'Conservative of a vulgar type', smoking in the mayor's parlour, with many bottles of drink on the table (at 11am.). Alderman Phillips, chairman of the gas committee since the Hunter scandal, was marginally more to Webb's liking: 'a Manchester businessman, somewhat Jewish, of easy familiar manners – [who] represented the honest element in the corporation but a common unimaginative man, simply regarding the corporation as a business enterprise to be done honestly, economically and efficiently, though without fads'. Webb noted that the council had always been political, and that the Conservatives were dominant, the division then being 'something like 37 to 27'. There was no Socialist or ILP man, the nearest being Jackson, a Tramways Union secretary, made a JP by the Liberal Government. The Social Democratic Federation vote at one time had been 'noisy and strong', but had declined. 'In spite of a huge Catholic population in the borough', no Roman Catholic sat on the council. The mayor and deputy mayor went out of their way to express to him their intense objection to amalgamation with Manchester. Salford, they protested, was a quite different entity from Manchester, divided from it by the river and absolutely requiring different sewerage and gas systems. They disagreed when Webb suggested that London north and south of the Thames was analogous. They were indignant that Salford was rarely given the recognition it deserved as a major town, larger, for instance, than Leicester or Nottingham. In their opinion, Manchester wanted to annex Salford to rival Glasgow in size and spread the burden of its debts. Amalgamation would not, in their eyes, find 'half a dozen supporters' in the Salford council, and they assured him they were determined that the new electric tramways were going to work as separate systems. This issue was destined to exacerbate the rivalry between the two councils, as well as inconveniencing passengers, for years to come.

Webb's notes of his discussions with Alderman Phillips are very revealing about council practices in the immediate post-Hunter era. Little had changed. No committee *documents*, other than its minutes, could be seen by an 'outside' councillor, said Phillips, and he told Webb he should refuse to give a committee report, or even mere information to an 'outside' councillor, except by way of an answer in full council. If this was some advance on what Mandley had come up against, it was not much. The council had modernised itself in that it now produced a 'synopsis'. Formerly the minutes were read, and much slipped through that ought not to have. 'Things', said Phillips, 'were managed very loosely then'.

Alderman Phillips told Webb the old gas committee was very weak, the chairman aged, and Hunter, 'a consummate manipulator of men', had led them by the nose. For years there were rumours of his corruption, but the committee would not listen, made no inquiries, and frowned on those who asked questions. At length, when it was all found out, Phillips had put down a motion calling on the gas committee to resign, which they did *en bloc*. In all this, the alderman made no mention of Mandley.

Under the present gas committee, said Phillips, things were now very strictly looked after. Tenders had to be sent to the town clerk (when formerly they had gone to the gas engineer). The town clerk brought them, unopened, to the gas committee, where they were opened and initialled by the chairman and his deputy and handed to the gas engineer to tabulate. When the committee had made its decision, they recommended the firms and quantities to the council in a specific motion, but neither price nor any information as to other tenders was given. One may be excused for wondering if anything *had* changed since the days of Hunter and Sharp. Phillips made clear his objection to allowing prices to be published. Colliery owners, he said, objected to having the special rates they quoted to so large a buyer revealed. ('I gathered', noted Webb, 'that in the first flush of revolt against Hunter, they had once published prices, but gave it up on these representations being made'). In other words, even after all these years, secrecy was alive and well in the gas committee, though bribery and corruption had apparently been suppressed.

In 1908 the matter of the publication of contract prices caused another bitter local battle in Salford, which was to last four years. When challenged, Phillips, still chairman of the gas committee, argued that secrecy was widely used in these matters. In support, Alderman Snape claimed thousands of pounds were saved as a result of negotiations with regard to the price of coal. If prices were to be published the savings would be lost to the ratepayers.[51] The battle raged between those who wanted 'clean and open' government and those who supported secrecy and 'hush'. The old system, proposed by Phillips himself over twenty years before, was to advertise for tenders in the press. This had come to be supplemented by the practice of bargaining with intended suppliers 'to beat prices down'. In a series of articles in the *Salford Reporter* in September 1911, W. Hunt, a Socialist, criticised this system so devastatingly that it was discontinued. The dictatorial Phillips (Salford's Mayor in 1910–11) proved more than a match for the opposition. Using all the latitude allowed by standing orders and council custom and practice, he was able to turn the tables on them in classic fashion in 1912. What Phillips and the gas committee did was to go back to the Hunterian system of soliciting 'offers' from favoured firms. The council and ratepayers were now presented only with those 'offers' accepted by Alderman Phillips. It transpired that, since 1902, three coal firms had gradually increased their share of the coal and cannel, so that, between them, they regularly supplied about half of the 160,000 tons the gas works used each year. It also transpired that not only did the gas committee not advertise, they kept no records either. As the *Reporter* commented, 'In future the only method of obtaining information open to members of the council will be by personal and private application to Alderman Phillips, for the Alderman intends to maintain in public an attitude of impenetrable secrecy'.[52] As of yore, the council supported its committee against the critics. It was only when, in August 1912, the committee decided not to allow even the prices to appear in the minute books that the reformers made some progress. A vote of censure was passed. Policy was changed: from 1913 the prices of coal were to go in the minutes.[53] Apart from that gain, the secrecy and bargaining power concentrated in the hands of Alderman Phillips went on. Phillips had inherited the power once enjoyed by Hunter. The difference was that Phillips was not using his position to line his own pockets.[54]

All this took place in another era: Mandley had died in August 1903. What his attitude might have been can only be guessed at. Essentially an old individualist, he had been averse to 'New Liberalism' and, not surprisingly, did not care for Socialism. It is sad to record that one of his obituary notices mentions that, in his later life, he was contemptuous of those who campaigned for purer government, and that many of his former admirers 'had in consequence of this change, come to regard him with great aversion, and he lost the hold on the public he once had'.[55] Most old politicians get left behind by the changing times, but it is ironical to reflect that Mandley may have succumbed to the sin of aldermanic arrogance.

As for Samuel Hunter, the last Salford heard of him was that, at the time of his wife's death in 1899, he was alive and well and living comfortably at Shavington Lodge, near Crewe, in rural Cheshire.

Sidney Webb's 'flashy publican'. Alderman Samuel Rudman. Born in Somerset in 1851 he came to Salford at the age of fourteen and eventually went into partnership with his brother in the Park Hotel, Ordsall. From the start he identified himself with the Conservatives. Elected to the Council in 1882, he was the first to serve four terms as Mayor of Salford, from 1898 to 1902. A sidesman at Manchester Cathedral, he personifies 'Beer and Bible' Conservatism. (*Manchester at the Close of the Nineteenth Century: Contemporary Biographies*)

# CHAPTER 10

# Catholics: Father Saffenreuter and the Pendleton Irish

Early in 1890 Father Gustavus Saffenreuter celebrated twenty five years as a priest in the Manchester area. Born and educated in Germany, he had been ordained by the Bishop of Bruges for the English Mission in 1865. After a few years at St Wilfred's, Hulme, he was moved to Salford: for almost two decades he had been rector of the mission district of St James, Pendleton. There was much to celebrate. When he arrived, Catholics did not even have a church of their own, hearing Mass in an old school-chapel.[1] By 1890, through much saving and self denial, Saffenreuter and his flock had built a church, and two more schools. Now in his early fifties, he was approaching the peak of his career. A successful senior priest esteemed by his Bishop, he was also a member of the Salford School Board and Instructor to the Catholics in the workhouse. Nine years later Father Saffenreuter was a ruined man, forced into a humiliating resignation, the direct outcome of a vendetta against him by some of his parishioners. Despite the Bishop of Salford's firm support throughout the affair, nothing could save him from the disgrace and ignominy which followed his dismissal by the Board of Guardians upon charges of sexual misconduct.

Saffenreuter's story has a fascination all of its own, but it also illustrates many of the tensions and pressures affecting the Catholic church in Victorian Lancashire. As well as its successes, it touches on the problems the Church faced as it gathered in congregations drawn mainly from the ranks of the poor and how it had to operate in a pervasive atmosphere of anti-popery. There were also tensions within Catholic ranks, in particular between lay aspirations and a sometimes heavy-handed clerical authoritarianism and the occasional flaring up of a strong mutual antipathy between English and Irish Catholics. Above all, Father Saffenreuter's story provides an extreme example of what could happen when the hierarchy had to be made to understand that if the Lancashire Irish took their religion from Rome, they were determined to take their politics from Dublin.

Because of poverty the evolution of a nineteenth-century Catholic mission district (technically there were no parishes until 1918) was usually more a matter of decades than years. The first stage in its formation was invariably renting rooms for a Sunday School. There then followed a slow accumulating of funds to finance the next stage, usually without the help of those well-heeled supporters virtually all other denominations could call upon. Catholics achieved it on a penny-a-week from the faithful, collected door-to-door. The church in Lancashire was built on the heroic efforts of the poor, and priests gave the lead by saving out of their meagre stipends. As the saying went, 'When a priest builds a church he had better order his coffin'.[2] Stage two was entered upon with the opening of a purpose-built school, which doubled as a Sunday school and chapel. The next stage was the building of a church, at the consecration of which (or sometimes thereafter) a 'mission district' would be designated by the bishop, with its own rector. In the large towns the process would be extended with the opening of school-chapels served by curates in populous sub-districts, which in the course of time became mission districts in their own right.

The evolution of the mission of St James, Pendleton nicely illustrates the process. It began as a Sunday School in a room in a Charlestown cottage in 1828. This was the first Catholic Sunday School in the Salford district. Commencing with a dozen children, the rent was paid by the teachers of the Manchester Catholic Sunday Schools of the time and subsequently by the Catholic Board of Education, formed in the 1830s. Until St John's was opened in Salford, Pendleton remained within the mission district of St Mary's, Mulberry Street, Manchester. A further landmark was the building of the school-chapel of St James's in Ellor Street in 1850, enlarged several times in the years following. In spite of the dire poverty of a district severely affected by the Cotton Famine, resources were husbanded so that money and land for a church were there when Bishop Turner gave it the status of a mission district in 1870, Father Saffenreuter becoming its first rector.[3]

Instead of having the satisfaction of being able to go ahead as planned and build his church, the new rector found himself faced with more urgent demands on his

The school/chapel of
St Charles (Borromeo),
Whit Lane, Charlestown,
1871. (Right) its prettily-cut
datestone.
(Photo: P. A. Greenall)

funds. The 1870 Education Act forced all the religious denominations to rush into building new schools before the deadline in the Act expired, at which time undenominational Board Schools were to fulfil their role of plugging educational gaps in the poorer districts. Saffenreuter's task was not made any lighter by the rapid growth of the district in the early 1870s, which saw one of the greatest industrial booms of the whole century. People poured into Pendleton. To provide school places the rector spurred his flock into tremendous efforts. In 1871 a new infant school dedicated to St Charles Borromeo was opened in neglected Charlestown, which came into use as a school-chapel three years later.[4] It was fortunate that more than half the money for St Charles's had already been raised by the time work commenced, because Saffenreuter was then informed by the owner of the land earmarked for the new church of St James that he wanted them to start work at once, or abandon it to him for other building purposes.[5] So a bigger debt than first envisaged was shouldered, the money raised, and the church built. St James was formally opened in the presence of Cardinal Manning in 1875,[6] and St James' school was enlarged again four years later. In the following decade Saffenreuter's building programme reached a further stage with the erection of All Soul's School at Weaste, in the south west of the township. In these years he had spent upwards of £12,000, of which two-thirds had been paid off.[7] His method of repayment was to settle responsibility for a portion of the debts on each particular part of his flock, and he was a hard taskmaster, demanding much of his people. When trouble came for Father Saffenreuter, ostensibly it was over the inequity of

'A natural stateliness of manner': the Rt Rev. Herbert Vaughan, 2nd Catholic Bishop of Salford, 1872–1892. (*Manchester Faces and Places*)

this policy. But that lay in the future. In 1890 Saffenreuter's flock thanked him for his leadership and example, and he, for his part, congratulated them on their loyalty, charity and Catholic obedience.

In the four decades down to 1890 the solid progress of the Catholic cause in Pendleton was matched in the other parts of the borough. As we have seen, in Salford township a major development came in 1844 with the establishment of St John's, Chapel Street which became the cathedral of the new Catholic diocese of Salford, with Dr Turner as its first bishop.[8] To meet the spiritual needs of Catholics in the populous districts around it the school-chapels of St Peter's, Greengate, and Mount Carmel were opened in the 1860s, becoming separate missions the next decade. St Joseph's, at first a dependency of Mount Carmel, founded to serve the growing Regent Road district, and the school of St Anne's, for children in the Adelphi area, were also opened in the 1870s, as was the mission of St Thomas of Canterbury in Higher Broughton. The Catholics of Lower Broughton got their school-chapel, St Boniface's, in the late 1890s.[9]

The way Catholics saw themselves towards the end of the nineteenth century is summed up in the words of Salford's third Bishop: 'at the present day, we the Catholics of England are but a "a remnant saved according to the election of grace" (*Rom*, XI,5) weak, isolated, and scattered in the midst of others enjoying almost the monopoly of wealth and power and worldly privilege'.[10] In the optimism of the 'Second Spring' this lonely if heroic sense of being a minority religion was overlaid by a series of more positive perceptions, no less real for being romantic. In the first place was a local pride in history of Lancashire's fidelity to Catholicism, and in those martyred for it. There was optimism also in the knowledge that numbers were swelling, thanks largely to Irish immigration. Although it is said Irish exiles brought nothing with them to Protestant England but their Faith, 'It was the only heritage their fathers could leave them', the Irish loved to point out that not only were they reviving Catholic Christianity in the nineteenth century, this was the second time they had done so. Remembering Celtic missionaries to early Saxon England, Irishmen reminded one another 'We taught them how to read and spell/And saved their pagan souls from Hell'.[11] Catholics also got something of a boost from the existence of the recusant gentry, who gave them an upper class of their own to look up to who added colour to such events as the enthronement of bishops or the consecration of cathedrals. And every time some prominent convert was received into the Church this vein of snobbery was reworked by the clergy and Catholic apologists anew. In the 1870s Ultramontanism added yet another layer on to Catholic perceptions. The Ecumenical Council and the promulgation of Papal Infallibility gave the humble Catholics of Lancashire a renewed awareness of the universality of the Church. One offshoot of this was the way in which official Catholicism embraced what had hitherto been one of the more exaggerated claims of extreme Protestantism – that what the Catholic revival was really about was the reconversion of England. The papal Bull of 1896, *Apostolicae Curae*, which denied the validity of Anglican Orders, made it perfectly clear that if the churches of England and Rome were ever to be reunited, the reunion would be entirely in terms of Anglican submission. This progression from the remnant tradition to Ultramontanism can be followed at the local level, not least in terms of the personalities of the Church's Lancashire leaders.

Most of Saffenreuter's years in Pendleton coincided with the episcopate of the Rt. Rev. Herbert Vaughan, second Bishop of Salford from 1872 to 1893. In character, temper and social origin Vaughan was something of a contrast to his predecessor. William Turner was Lancashire to the core. Born at Witheringham near Preston, where his father was a solicitor, Turner had been educated in the north country seminary of Ushaw and then went on to Rome, where he rose to be Prefect of the English College. Ordained priest in 1826 all his cures were served in Lancashire – in Bury, Rochdale and Manchester, where he rose to be senior priest at St Augustine's and vicar general of the hundreds of Salford and Blackburn. When Pope Pius IX re-established the Catholic hierarchy in England it was a logical step to choose a leading local priest to become first Bishop of a diocese which took in all of industrial East Lancashire. On both sides Turner's family was old Catholic, his mother taking special pride in counting Father Arrowsmith, the Lancashire martyr, amongst her forebears. Turner clearly understood his role in the Second Spring. It was to establish and strengthen the infrastructure of the Church in one of England's most populous but poorest Catholic districts. This he did with considerable success, but his personality and style were relatively low-key. Bishop Turner was remembered as a man of retiring habits, an administrator able but discreet, a preacher persuasive but not oratorical.[12] The same could never be said of Herbert Vaughan, who was anything but low-key.

In 1869 Bishop Turner went to Rome for the Ecumenical Council, but ill-health brought him home early, and he died in July 1872. What his attitude was to the new era ushered in by the Council never became clear. There is little doubt of his successor's. Ultramontanism well-suited the bullish Catholicism of the Rt. Rev. Herbert Vaughan. Like Turner, Vaughan was descended from impeccable Catholic stock, but from quite a different social class.[13] The eldest son of Lieut. Colonel J. F. Vaughan of Courtfield, Hereford, his was an old landed family of Welsh extraction. Of the Colonel's five daughters all became nuns, and six of his eight sons became priests. Born into the Catholic division of the English officer class, Herbert Vaughan was to advance effortlessly through that process of accelerated promotion which depends upon family connections as much as suitability for the task in hand. His uncle was Catholic Bishop of Plymouth. One brother became Archbishop of Sydney, Australia. Another became a celebrated Jesuit. Yet another was for a time private secretary to Cardinal Manning, before going to South Africa as a missionary. It was, however, as Cardinal Wiseman's protégée that Herbert Vaughan was to rise so high.

After Stoneyhurst he spent three years at a Jesuit school in Belgium, then a year with the Benedictines at Downside. In 1851 he went to Rome to study for the priesthood and, despite never having been to a seminary, was ordained in Italy three years later. Vaughan's educational record was undistinguished. His 'natural tastes', says his first biographer, 'were those of an ordinary country gentleman'.[14] He loved plain dealing and plain speech. Although his mind was not speculative or subtle, there was an element of romance in his nature to which large and bold enterprises appealed. What Vaughan also possessed in abundance was 'a natural

St Peter's Catholic School,
Greengate, Salford, built
1863. Behind is St Peter's
Church built in 1872
(Photo: the author)

stateliness of manner', an unmistakeable 'habit of authority', money of his own,
and a powerful single-mindedness.[15]

He served no apprenticeship. Vaughan's first post was the vice-rectorship of St
Edmund's College, Ware. This he owed to Cardinal Wiseman, who desired to
have his own man in the oldest Catholic school/seminary in England. Vaughan's
time at Ware was not a success, and he soon moved on to a project of his own.
It was characteristically grandiose. At a time when England could not train enough
priests for itself Vaughan conceived the idea of founding a College for Foreign
Missions. In 1863 he sailed for the Caribbean and America and for two years
journeyed in the New World expounding his scheme to audiences in many cities.
It was to be his Grand Tour. When recalled to England in 1865 he brought with
him £11,000 raised for his project, with promises of more. Land was purchased at
Mill Hill, and St Joseph's College began work the next year. Five years later it
sent its first priests to the USA to work amongst coloured people. Vaughan visited
America a second time and whilst there became convinced of the power and
importance of the press. On his return he bought the Catholic journal *The Tablet*,
and for three years exercised editorial oversight. In the heady days of the Ecumenical

Council he was a strenuous advocate of the Ultramontanist case. It was as if the Church's internationalism was for him an antidote to its marginality in England, an idea which soon pervaded Catholic consciousness more generally.

When Bishop Turner died in 1872 it was thought likely that his successor would be Canon Benoit. A mission priest from Belgium, for two decades he had played an important role in the history of local Catholicism, rising to become Vicar General of the Diocese. As an active member of the Salford Famine Relief Committee he had become known and well-respected in the wider community. However, Cardinal Wiseman wished for the elevation of Father Vaughan. Benoit was persuaded to stand aside, and, in a neat job-exchange, left Salford to become Rector of St Joseph's, Mill Hill.

How would Vaughan take to the multifarious problems of running a populous industrial diocese, and how would the proletarian Catholics of East Lancashire take to their very upper-class new Bishop? The answer is that on both sides it was a case of love at first sight. Soon after arrival, Vaughan wrote 'On Wednesday I spoke to about four thousand people in the Free Trade Hall and you can form no idea of their enthusiastic shouts as they saw their new Bishop. It beat anything I had ever dreamed of'. Two months later he declared: 'This is the grandest place in England for popular energy and piety. May they never change'.[16]

In Bishop Turner's time the greater part of the efforts of clergy and laity had gone into churches and schools. Inevitably, concern with other problems had been limited. Three stood out, all inter-related – how to bring lapsed Catholics back to the faith, how to prevent 'leakage', the loss to the church of children born to Catholic parents but deprived of a Catholic upbringing by their poverty and how to increase the supply of locally trained priests and teachers. Like other denominations, Catholics used revivalist methods as a way of recalling those fallen by the wayside. In 1846 the Italian Father Luigi Gentili carried out a long-remembered mission in Manchester, and eighteen years later St John's was the setting for a fortnight-long mission by four Redemptorist Fathers, which drew vast crowds.[17] Deeply stirring though these events were, they were not the answer. Their success was limited to individuals, and they could never stem the general losses of the time. In 1866 Father C. J. Gadd, at the meeting of the Catholic Association for the Suppression of Drunkenness, reported 'a diminution of 8,000 in the number of Catholics in Manchester and Salford within the last few years, several years ago the number having been 92,000, while it was now only 84,000'. The reasons were, he said, two-fold: the large number of Catholic children without education (and his estimate was that fully half were not in Catholic schools), and the large numbers of children being brought up as Protestants in workhouses.[18] Given the numbers involved (Father Saffenreuter told the Salford School Board in 1885 there were then 28,000 Catholics in Salford), and the demands upon church finances, for the time being nothing more could have been done than was being done.

The basic strategy had to be to carry on building schools. In Vaughan's time the number of Catholic schools in Salford was doubled (from five to ten), the number of places provided increasing from 3420 to 6371.[19] In the politics of the School Board era, Catholics entered into a tacit alliance with the Church of England to restrict the impact of this new Board provision as far as possible. In Salford School Board elections seven of the fifteen seats invariably went to Church candidates, two (and occasionally three) to Catholics, the rest to Liberal Non-conformists or 'unsectarians'. Father Saffenreuter was elected a member of the Board in 1882, and served diligently for eleven years. There the policy was to try to limit the ability of the Board's own schools to compete with denominational schools. This (in the sacred name of the ratepayers) involved resisting the opening of new schools, a tight rein on expenditure and an eventual policy of refusing to implement free education when this came in in 1891. Catholics and Anglicans claimed (not very convincingly) that Board Schools were seedbeds of atheism. And Vaughan even declared 'a man who has his children educated by the rates pauperises himself'.[20]

The truth was that denominational schools faced collapse if their income from the 'school pence' ceased. It followed that the very poorest Catholic children often could not afford to go to Catholic schools, and went to Board Schools instead. Given the rapidity of Salford's population growth, denominational schools could never have been expanded fast enough, though this did not prevent them from making the greatest of efforts to do so. The Catholic Church, and none more clearly than Bishop Vaughan, saw that in the long term the only way to maintain denominational education for working-class children was to campaign for funding on the same basis as the Board Schools. In 1884 Vaughan founded the Voluntary Schools Association to argue for a twenty five per cent increase in government grant to the denominational schools and equal treatment with the Board Schools. This many Liberals would never agree to, but under the Conservative Education Act of 1902 this is substantially what Catholic and Anglican Schools got.

But denominational schools was only part of the answer. What gave the Catholic church deep anxiety was the question of the poorest children. In this matter the position of the Salford Board of Guardians and its policy towards Catholics in the workhouse was central. For half a century the church had battled to counter the strong and open anti-Catholic bias of Boards of Guardians, backed-up by the central authorities, whose general policy it was that workhouse chaplains should be clergy of the established church. In Salford, however, in recognition of the number of paupers who were Catholic, the Board in 1870 appointed a priest to minister to them and Catholic inmates were free to attend Mass. This priest was Father Saffenreuter.[21] What Catholics wanted just as much was to have their own representatives on the Board of Guardians. Because of the fewness of Catholic ratepayers this had proved difficult, through not impossible in the 1870s and 1880s. However, when the Poor Law electoral system was eventually widened, Catholics at last began to achieve better representation to the Board, though they were never in more than a tiny majority.

'Leakage', the loss of the children of the poor, was a source of particular anguish to Vaughan. Vaughan's estimate was that, in his own diocese, 10,000 children 'ran in peril of their souls' through parental neglect, the anti-Catholic bias of poor-law institutions and Protestant missionaries. Vaughan launched a 'Crusade of Rescue' with the publication of his pamphlet *The Loss of our Children* (1889). A Catholic Protection and Rescue Society was founded, and, as his pastoral letter, printed with its second annual report, shows quite clearly, its objective was as much to tighten up Catholic cohesion as to rescue the lost. In it he stressed 'In order to turn out Catholic children virtuous and well conducted citizens it is of quite capital importance that the homes, schools, lads' clubs, and similar societies intended for their training and preservation should be thoroughly and frankly under the influence and direction of their own religion'.[22]

In the generation which followed great efforts were made to carry out the Bishop's policy at school and institutional level. More problematically, the Society operated an emigration policy to resettle 'rescued' children in North America. Although the children were escorted across the Atlantic by priests it may be doubted their best interests were always served by this uprooting from their native land. Modern experiments in such organised migration suggest that much anguish and exploitation has been the lot of such children. Vaughan seems to have had little doubts as to its wisdom. He was enamoured of American Catholicism, and in any case he was not the doubting kind.

Another great cause of concern to the church, and one which also played its part in Saffenreuter's story, was the question of the inadequate supply of locally produced priests. In 1878 Vaughan estimated that of the two hundred or so priests in the diocese only about thirty were native-born.[23] What was required was the establishment of good secondary schools and seminaries. In 1862 Bishop Turner had founded a Salford Catholic Grammar School in association with the Cathedral, whose most distinguished pupil, Louis Casartelli, was to become fourth Bishop of Salford, and shortly after the arrival of Bishop Vaughan a seminary for pastoral training was established. A notable development came in 1880 when Vaughan raised £6,800 to purchase the Manchester Aquarium, on whose splendid site in Alexandra Park, Manchester, St Bede's College, was erected, a middle-class school with which the older Salford school was amalgamated in 1891. In 1885 a school was set up in Adelphi House, Salford, by the Sisters of the Faithful Companions of Jesus, to educate and train girls to become teachers in Catholic schools.[24] Important though these developments were, it would be some time before they began to make an impact. In the last twenty years of the nineteenth century priests had still to be recruited where the supply was available, which meant Ireland and the continent, most notably Belgium. It was a policy pursued long before Vaughan became Bishop, but in the 1880s the accusation arose of the Bishop's alleged preference for continental priests over Irishmen.

The origin of this lay in party politics. The idea of Home Rule for Ireland first appeared in 1874. Conservative victories in the general election of that year, and the by-election three years later which followed the death of Cawley, bitterly divided English and Irish Catholic voters in Salford. The suspicion that the English Catholics, supported by the Bishop, had voted against Gladstone enraged local Irishmen, as 'A Crusader', in a letter to a local newspaper, demonstrated[25]

> they [English Catholics] are looked upon as fitting tools and instruments of the prelatical mind ... Being English Catholics, they detest the Irish people because of their nationality, and on every occasion insult them. In this course of conduct they are supported by English priests ... The 'Catholic vote'

therefore is confined to the drummers and blowers in the bishop's band, and I sincerely hope your readers will not consider the 'Irish vote' means the same thing.

He went on

> The election has not been without its good, and one of its fruits is that a powerful Irish Association has been formed with good men and true at its head, and in a short time these English Catholics will find they might as well whistle jigs to a milestone as be able to influence a single Irish voter in Salford.

In the following decade the Catholic vote was not only split along national lines, but the volatility of Irish nationalist politics led to a fraught relationship with the Liberal party. 1886 altered all that. The aftermath of the Home Rule crisis threw Irish politics firmly in with the Liberal party. In Pendleton the local branch of the Irish National League and the Liberals began to co-operate closely, and this brought the sort of recognition and respect Irishmen had never enjoyed before. As already noted, in 1893 the first Irish Catholic magistrate in Salford was appointed to the bench in the person of Dr O'Gorman, President of the Pendleton branch of the Irish National League.[26] Elevated 'for services to the Liberal Party', Irishmen correctly interpreted this as an acknowledgement to themselves as well.

Vaughan was not the man to respond sensitively to this change in Irish attitudes. In many ways he made an impressive Bishop, but in manner and social attitudes he was very distinctly the English gentleman. In the words of his biographer, 'a seeming haughtiness and lack of sympathy lessened his attractiveness'. This was something Vaughan was aware of, and even recorded in his diary, but could not change.[27] His manner, and essentially romantic brand of Catholicism did him no harm with English Catholics, who perhaps expected, and certainly liked a habit of authority in their leaders. To the Irish, or at any rate to those politically active, it had far less appeal. They were convinced that he was biased against them, a charge his biographers try somewhat unconvincingly to refute.

Never one to mince his words Vaughan made it plain he had no sympathy with Irish nationalism, and was outspoken in his condemnation of acts of violence such as boycotting, the Phoenix Park Murders, and secret societies and brotherhoods. However, suspicions of anti-Irish bias were not only levelled at Vaughan but at the diocesan authorities more generally, notably Monsignor Gadd, the Vicar-General. In particular it was alleged that Irish priests in Salford seemed destined to be mere curates forever. If there was good Father Beswick at St Peter's, Greengate, there were continentals in most of the other mission rectories – Father Schepercels at St Joseph's, Father Schneiders at Mount Carmel, Monsignor de Clerc at the Grammar School (all Belgians), Father Carruccio (a Neopolitan) at All Souls, Weaste, and, of course, there was Father Saffenreuter, at St James's, Pendleton. This bias was in part generational: continental priests had come at a particular time to fulfil a particular mission. In the years after the Home Rule crisis it was beginning to seem to local Irishmen that this phase was being prolonged unconscionably.[28] Just as this issue came to a head Vaughan quit Salford for the arch-diocese of Westminster and a Cardinal's hat. His successor, the Rt. Rev. Dr.

Bilsborrow, Lancashire born, was personally much more like Bishop Turner than Vaughan, but in policy or attitudes it may be doubted if he differed from Vaughan in any significant way.

Father Saffreneuter's troubles began with the dismissal of his curate in Charlestown in 1893. On the surface, the dispute which led to this appeared to be about parochial finances, but as the affair widened it became clear that it was about much more. The year previously Charlestown, where there were said to be 5,000 Catholic Irish, had been designated a mission district and given its own priest. However, for the time being, Father Smith was to remain a curate, subordinate to the rector of St James's. The new priest quickly established a rapport with his congregation in one of the oldest and poorest industrial districts in the whole borough. He seemed to understand their sense of social and religious neglect. One of the first things he was involved in was a great procession on May Day 1892. It was very well attended, very colourful, and was the first open-air Catholic demonstration ever held in Charlestown. Only a few years before such an event would never have been contemplated for fear of anti-popery. Smith also busied himself in social and community matters, notably in the promotion of the St Charles's Temperance League of the Cross and the Charlestown Household Co-operative Society Ltd.[29] In doing so he committed the *faux pas* of establishing good relations with non-Catholics in his district.

It came as a great shock in Charlestown when, in September 1893, it was announced that Father Smith was being transferred to Burnley. All the curate would say was that he was going because he disagreed with the rector and the Diocesan Board of Finance over 'unjust debts' settled on Charlestown. Apparently Saffenreuter had laid £1,000 on the mission as its share of the general debt of the district. Smith protested, and the debt had been reduced by a quarter. When he protested further the Bishop transferred him. As a dutiful priest, Smith obeyed: his parishioners declined to show the same spirit of submission. Great efforts were made to get the Bishop to change his mind, and when he would not, relationships between Saffenreuter (backed by the Diocese) and Charlestown became very strained. Much comment was caused in Salford when a group of local Protestants sought an interview with the vicar-general to intercede on Father Smith's behalf. Monsignor Gadd refused to see them.[30] The quarrel was conducted in the open, both sides expressing their views with considerable frankness in the press. Feelings normally suppressed or hidden were given a full airing.[31]

> The rector of St James [*wrote the pseudonymous* VERB SAP] is an estimable man in many ways ... [but] we want a man more in sympathy with the temporal needs of the age instead of the conservatism and coldness which have done so much to injure Catholicity and spread Infidelity in France and Germany. This conservatism seems to be a characteristic of Continental priests. They do not understand us; they shrink from and are afraid of our liberalism, they have no sympathy with our aspirations, our desire for progress.

The quarrel dragged on into the winter, becoming notably bitter after Saffenre-uter's taunt that the Charlestown Defence Association reminded him of the Three

Tailors of Tooley Street (who once circulated a handbill beginning 'We the People ...'). Eventually the Bishop himself stepped in. To quell what was becoming an incipient anti-clerical revolt, Dr Bilsborrow went down in person to St Charles's. At eleven o'clock Mass on 14 January 1894 he rebuked the errant parishioners most sternly, enjoining Catholic obedience. The revolt was quelled. Saffenreuter had apparently prevailed. Soon after the Bishop made him Dean. But behind the scenes a deal was made. The Charlestown debt was reduced to £550, ironically enough the figure Father Smith had asked for. The Defence Association dissolved itself.[32]

In the next few years there were further developments in Charlestown. With continuing population growth the accommodation at St Charles became increasingly inadequate and in 1896 a new school chapel for the mission district was built in Gerald Road, some distance away, at a cost of £4000. Priestly duties were shared by Fathers Poole and Divine. Two years later they were moved on and replaced by Fathers Hyancinthe Koos and Moran, two Dominicans, who were charged with the enlarging and extending of the Charlestown mission, whose nucleus was now to be a new church and religious house. The foundation stone of St Sebastian's was laid in September 1898 and the church consecrated three years later, Father Koos becoming the first superior.[33] To serve the parishioners a new secular priest was appointed curate of Charlestown, Father N. C. McCarthy, an Irish nationalist. He was already controversial, having caused offence in Bolton by refusing to take part in celebrations to mark the jubilee of Queen Victoria.

Early in 1899 a letter, signed significantly 'English Catholic', appeared in the local paper protesting about McCarthy laying the foundation stone of the memorial to the 'Manchester Martyrs' – the Fenians executed in 1867. Shortly after, the Bishop dismissed Father McCarthy.[34] The affair provoked another public quarrel which revealed the extent of the gulf between English and Irish Catholics in Pendleton. To the former the Fenians were nothing but terrorists, to the latter they were martyrs who had died for Ireland. The Pendleton Irish were incensed at McCarthy's dismissal and their anger focused on their 'cold and conservative' German rector.

Unlike Smith, McCarthy had no intention of going quietly. His correspondence with the Bishop was leaked to the press: scathing remarks were made about the 'genteel (English) Cawtholics' running their church, and he was strongly backed by the Manchester Irish. On 12 February the Central Manchester Martyrs Memorial Committee organised a demonstration march from Ancoats to Pendleton. Starting with between 600 and 800 by the time it reached its destination it had swelled to over 5,000. A handbill called for 'a demonstration of sympathy to the good and real *Soggarth Aroon* (dear Priest), Rev. Father McCarthy, who blessed the foundation stone in Moston Cemetery on November 27th to our honoured martyrs Allen, Larkin and O'Brien ... another Irish priest sacrificed on the altar of English hate and animosity'. The scene, observed the *Reporter*, 'was an inspiring one. Green was the prevailing colour worn, men, women and children wearing some article of clothing of an emerald tint'. At the meeting which followed in the Pendleton Town Hall that evening much strong language was employed against English Catholics and German priests. McCarthy alleged that Monsignor Gadd was motivated by envy, having wanted the kudos of blessing the Martyrs Memorial for himself, and that official animosity towards him stemmed from the fact that he, an Irish priest, had carried out the task. He further declared that 'As Irish Catholics they were not going to be sat upon or Saxonised ... they were not going to be Saxonised by an English Catholic Bishop'. The real struggle centred on the person of Saffenreuter. McCarthy declared 'he was not going to run away until he had shifted Dean Saffreneuter'. A resolution was passed declaring the parishioners would withdraw financial support from their parish church and attend Mass elsewhere until the present situation was remedied by Saffreneuter's removal.[35]

On the eve of his departure for America, Father McCarthy was presented with an address and a purse of 200 sovereigns. The address alleged that

> for the past twenty eight years a long succession of virtuous and talented Irish priests have been dismissed from their posts in Pendleton, and had been compelled to leave the parish in which their own countrymen were a pre-dominating majority, without adequate or justifiable cause. This humiliating and irritating policy culminated in you, and we are confident that the protest we organised, goaded on by this injustice will prove not only a powerful vindication of the Irish clergy, but the death blow to the state of things that produced it.

On arrival in New York McCarthy was given a hero's welcome by O'Donovan Rossa and other prominent Fenians.[36] However, he found it no easier in the New World to find a parish than in the Old.

It being axiomatic that the Catholic hierarchy would back clergy against laity in almost any dispute, the way the Salford Irish struck at Saffenreuter was not through religious channels. The dean was brought down through his workhouse chaplaincy. It so happened that the McCarthy affair coincided with the democratisation of elections for Guardians of the Poor (which began in 1894). A group of Catholics were elected, a Catholic Registration Association having been formed for this purpose. Three were Irishmen, J. P. Byrne, T. Hall and W. Burns. In July 1899 Saffenreuter was suspended by the Board of Guardians as Catholic instructor at the workhouse for alleged immorality with girls. The charge was brought by Byrne, supported by Burns. The dean was strongly defended by James Thompson, an English Catholic member of the Board, and a Conservative. However, five Guardians deputed by the board to interview the children reported that the charges could be substantiated. Saffenreuter was suspended, and then dismissed by the Finance and General Purposes Committee of the Union. However, at the weekly meeting of the full Board this decision was reversed.[37]

The issue split Pendleton's Catholics. The English declared themselves outraged by the charges against the dean, which they saw as an attack on Catholicism. The executive committee of the Registration Association demanded the resignation of Byrne (its own President) and Burns who had first brought the charges. The Irish National Club in Ancoats in turn bitterly attacked the Registration Association. As far as the poor law authorities were concerned the matter was settled at a special meeting of the Finance and General Purposes Committee which heard the evidence of the girls concerned. It was told that the priest had sat the girls on his knee, kissed them, and gone further (at this point the *Reporter* draws a veil over precisely what happened). By a vote of 10 to 6 Saffenreuter was dismissed. The full Board of Guardians confirmed the decision.[38] Saffenreuter's supporters pinned their hopes on a ruling from the Local Government Board in London, but this body declared it was not a matter within its jurisdiction. The Irish had wreaked their revenge on their cold German. After almost twenty eight years in the employ of the Salford Guardians, Saffenreuter was dismissed, humiliated and ruined. There seems little doubt that Saffenreuter had done things that an adult in a position of authority, let alone a priest, should not have done, and that it had been his custom and practice over the years, if his enemies are to be believed. To them, it was typical of a man who had been too powerful for too long. Nevertheless, the whole business was damaging to Catholics, enabling the representatives of Mrs Grundy and the anti-Catholic populace at large the luxury of having their worst suspicions of the celibate priesthood confirmed. This at least must have tempered the rare pleasure the local Irish took in combining at one and the same time revenge and moral outrage.

After his dismissal, the church strongly supported Saffenreuter. In a pastoral letter read at Mass in all churches in Salford the Bishop took a strong legalistic line, declaring that the dean had been dismissed 'on the contradictory evidence of workhouse girls of immature years', without a proper hearing by a Board of Guardians, who had acted both as judge and jury. After over thirty years' dedicated service Saffenreuter was disgraced. The whole thing, the letter suggested, was a miscarriage of justice. Incensed, the Bishop declined to nominate a short list from which the Board could choose the next Catholic instructor. The Board advertised the post and, because no-one applied, for the time being, Catholic services at the workhouse were discontinued. The Board of Guardians was even more beset by Protestant-Catholic antagonism, as it had been ever since 1894.[39]

That October Saffenreuter resigned from St James. It was said that a five-man commission appointed in Rome had inquired into the case and that the Dean had resigned following its findings. This the Bishop categorically denied, insisting that Saffenreuter had gone voluntarily. Interestingly, a number of bitterly hostile anti-Saffenreuter letters appeared in the press. In the first week of the New Year, at a large and well-attended meeting in Pendleton, Saffenreuter, like McCarthy before him, was presented with an illuminated address and a purse by supporters. Tribute was paid by the Bishop to his work as rector and as a great builder of schools and churches. Dr Bilsborrow could not forbear to castigate Byrne, Burns and the testimony of the workhouse children: to the end feelings remained bitter and undisguised. Saffenreuter went on to St Anne's, Fairfield, Ashton, for four years, before retiring to Germany, where he died in 1911.[40]

There was a postscript. When the workhouse scandal surfaced Father McCarthy re-entered the fray, hoping to be re-called to Pendleton. His hopes were soon dashed. In a letter written from Cork he reacted angrily to what the Bishop had said about him in his pastoral letter. Yet, when Saffenreuter departed, he was replaced by an Irishman, Father Crilly. McCarthy was effectively barred from the Diocese of Salford. Three years later a short letter published in the local press indicated he had been brought to heel. McCarthy apologised: 'I herewith withdraw whatever I may have said or written derogatory to the sacred office of his Lordship'.[41]

The story of Saffenteuter's downfall is a minor episode in the history of Catholic Salford. If its reverberations re-awakened Protestant bigotry, and traditional 'Rome never changes' attitudes, these did not seriously hold back its institutional or social progress. Yet it remains a very revealing episode, shedding light on grass roots Catholicism at the time, and on myths which have grown up since. If there was Catholic unity on purely religious matters (which by and large there was), there was less on organisational ones, and unity could be severely strained by politics, nationalism and class. In the case of politics the ethos of the clergy and hierarchy was Conservative, yet, apart from a sprinkling of professional people, the membership was Irish and proletarian. In the case of Irish national feelings, if the English church leaders were for too long insensitive, it is clear that by the end of the century they had got the message. Perhaps the Saffenreuter case played a part. Where Irish people predominated, it came to use Irish or Lancashire Irish priests, and the line thereafter was maintained that Catholics do not quarrel. Time was on the Church's side; despite Father McCarthy, the Irish *were* destined to be Saxonised. However, the Church could react as clumsily to other contemporary questions as it did to Irish national feelings. In the 1890s, at the time the Saffenreuter affair was developing, the Church was also thundering anathemas against Socialism, free education and state-directed social reform, just as young Catholic men were coming into contact with such ideas and starting to join the emergent Labour movement.

Workhouse children. A rare photograph of about 1900. Note the regimentation and the shaven heads. With its scrubbed wooden floors and wooden ceilings the place is as stark, as unwelcoming and as clean an institution as Sir Edwin Chadwick could have wished. One supposes the pictures on the walls are a late 19th century humanising gesture.
(Local History Collection, Peel Park)

# CHAPTER II

# Socialists: George Evans and the Early Labour Movement

On the morning of 8 April 1893 the people of the Regent Road district were drawn into the street by the sound of a brass band playing the *Marseillaise*. What greeted their eyes was an unusual funeral procession. Many who followed the coffin were wearing red rosettes, others the regalia of Friendly Societies and a number held banners aloft. As the cortège wound its way to the cemetery, crowds assembled. Nineteenth-century Salford witnessed many a notable celebration of the Victorian way of death, but this was no grand bourgeois funeral. Here was something distinctively proletarian. At the same time as being a sorrowing, it also contrived to be a celebration.

They were burying George Evans, the Socialist activist and orator, a painter and decorator by trade. The *Reporter* treated him to a fine obituary, but, presumably because no suitable photograph could be found, illustrated it with a woodcut.[1] Evans has the emaciated appearance of some religious zealot, which was not at all inappropriate. Though only fifty, he was prematurely aged. The awareness that Evans had worked himself into an early grave by his unsparing efforts in the cause of Socialism gave an edge to the occasion. Converted to Socialism as to a religion, he was given an appropriate funeral. At his request the Red Flag was draped over his coffin and his body was followed to the grave by friends and representatives of the working-class associations to which he had belonged. The funeral service was read by the chaplain to the 'True as Steel' Division of the Sons of Temperance, and orations over the grave were delivered by Frederick Brocklehurst of the Labour Church and William Horrocks on behalf of the Social Democratic Federation. Afterwards, the *Marseillaise,* the Socialist anthem of the time, was sung. From the very start of its revival, Evans had been totally involved with Socialism, preaching its message in Salford and the industrial towns of South Lancashire. His last eight years witnessed the emergence of the modern Labour movement.

Evans came to Socialism late. Always a man of deep political conviction and moral seriousness, he had a long history of working-class activism behind him. Born in 1842, he was the son of a Kidderminster carpet weaver and at the age of nine he started in the factory. After his father lost his job following a wages dispute, the family led a migratory existence. They moved to Scotland, where for some time he was employed in domestic service. In his teens he worked back in Kidderminster and also seems to have spent some time in Liverpool. Later, after

'The emaciated appearance of some religious zealot of a bygone era': the woodcut of George Evans. (*Reporter*)

he married and had a family, he was obliged to leave Birkenhead because of his part in a strike. Eventually he and his wife and five children moved to Langholme in Scotland, the domain of that great British landowner, the Duke of Buccleuch and Queensberry. By then a Liberal and an ardent teetotaller, Evans was caught up in Gladstone's Midlothian campaign. He organised a penny subscription and led a deputation to present the Liberal leader with a suit of local tweed, which he later came to regret as an act of sycophancy. He had cause to regret it at the time too: the Duke's son and heir, Lord Dalkeith, was the sitting MP whom Gladstone ousted. Evans and his family were evicted and he later recollected that no-one in the village dared offer them help or accommodation. After a spell in Carlisle they moved to Manchester. It was here, at a Sunday morning open-air meeting near Trafford Bridge in 1885, that Evans first came into contact with Socialism.

Socialism had made its appearance in Salford in January that year with the formation of a branch of the Social Democratic Federation, an organisation founded in 1884 by London Socialists, notable amongst whom were H. M. Hyndman and William Morris.[2] It drew its ideas from the writings of Marx and Engels and the American Henry George, and at the meetings of the Salford branch in the clubroom of the *Crescent* Inn the principles of 'scientific Socialism' were expounded and their application to contemporary society debated. At this time, Salford was in a state of political ferment. The third Reform Act had just been passed, and Salford transformed from a two-member borough into three single-member constituencies. Meetings in the *Crescent* Inn drew speakers from a wide range of political beliefs with whom the Socialists debated contemporary issues.[3]

The first Social Democrats usually came from the ranks of Radicals disenchanted with the Liberal Party. Prompted by the worsening economy, alienated by local Liberal caucuses and challenged by the reappearance of Socialism as a viable creed, from 1884–5 they began to switch allegiance. Their conversion was often not as sudden as perhaps it seems. Many had a history of involvement in ultra-Radical and democratic politics behind them, and, though their clubs and societies had often been short-lived and small in membership, a thread going back to the brief appearance of Socialism after the Paris Commune in 1871 can be discerned. After the Commune, continental political refugees migrated to London and an International Working Men's Association was formed with the object of maintaining contact between the workers in each country and the refugees in England. A Manchester District Council was formed in 1872, which had a Salford section.

Dissension in London soon led to decline and by the end of that year the Salford branch was no longer in existence.[4] However, it revived again as the Salford Republican Club, which held its first meeting on 23 December 1872 and for about a year had a fairly active life.[5] With its demise, democratic societies were not to reappear for almost a decade. Radicals generally threw in their lot with Gladstone's Liberal Party, but things began to change with the formation of the Democratic League, which had branches in Salford and Pendleton in 1881, and the Bradlaughite National Secular Society, established the following year.[6] In these clubs the politics of the day were debated, including Henry George's Single Tax and land nation-alisation ideas, the future of the House of Lords, Irish Home Rule and support for Bradlaugh's attempt to take his seat in the House of Commons. The 'truth of Christianity', its relevance to contemporary society and the possibility of alternative ethical bases to living were also much discussed.

It is through individuals rather than institutions that the continuity of the Socialist tradition can perhaps best be seen. Although the International Working Men's Association was short-lived, a link through to the Socialist revival has been traced in the person of John Darbyshire, one of the members of the Salford Republican Club. Early in 1883 he succeeded in re-forming a branch of the IWMA and one of his recruits was Henry Musgrave Reade.[7] The son of an army officer

The organiser of the Salford Social Democrats, Henry Musgrave Reade (from his *Christ or Socialism. A Human Autobiography,* 1909)

Reade had been influenced in his youth by the Paris Commune and the French revolutionary tradition and reacted against his upbringing. He read widely among progressive thinkers of the day and his studies led him to free-thought: in 1882 he became secretary of the Salford branch of the National Secular Society. Finding secularism too arid and Bradlaugh's Radicalism too individualistic, Reade joined the revived IWMA and discovered what he was looking for.

When Hyndman and the others formed the Democratic Federation in 1882 and published their manifesto *Socialism Made Plain*, Reade was impressed. However, he declared he was not prepared to associate with an organisation which merely called itself 'democratic': Reade considered Salford republicans well in advance of such ideas. William Morris wrote to Reade to seek his co-operation in forming a united group, but until Hyndman came to Manchester and met Reade this was rejected. Hyndman was able to convince him that the newly formed organisation was based on real *socialist* principles and that a change of name was imminent. In August 1884, following the national delegate conference, it became the Social Democratic Federation. Reade was satisfied, and promptly set about forming a Salford branch, which began to meet at the *Crescent* Inn, Salford, in January 1885.[8]

Seeking like-minded companions, Reade had joined the Liberal party in Pendleton, where he met working men ripe for Socialism. Among the members was William Horrocks, a turner by trade and a member of the Salford branch of the Amalgamated Society of Engineers. In December 1884 Reade and Horrocks proposed that a working man should be put forward as a candidate for the new constituency of West Salford. Their resolution was rejected and Benjamin Armitage adopted.[9] Perhaps it was Horrocks or Reade who penned the letter which appeared in the issue of the *Reporter* of 17 January 1885 above the pseudonym A DEMOCRAT. 'I ask as a working man how long is this sort of thing going to last? How long are we working men to be deprived of *real* representation, namely, by one of our own class?' A DEMOCRAT declared that he intended to vote Tory at the coming election to teach Liberals that working men would not stand for this sort of thing any longer, and warned the Liberal Association that they would lose some of their most active workers if they did not change. These words might well have proved empty had not the economic conditions of the time reinforced the idea that it was time working-class activists bestirred themselves to create a party devoted primarily to their own interests.

By the mid 1880s it was becoming abundantly clear that the great years of the Mid-Victorian era, when Britain stood alone as 'the Workshop of the World', were over. In the last quarter of the nineteenth century capitalism was entering that uncomfortable phase which came to be called the 'Great Depression'. Despite the fact that this name is in some ways misleading, it stuck. In the sense that these years were ones of unbroken depression, it is a misnomer: interspersed with the slumps were years of industrial expansion. But it was the slumps, bringing large scale unemployment which dominated the thinking of the time, coming as they did at the end of nearly a quarter of a century of economic expansion. And other trends – deflation, falling profits, foreign competition, rising tariff barriers and growing Great Power rivalries depressed the spirit of businessmen. 'We are now driven from the proud position of being the cotton lords and kings, and controlling the cotton trade of the world,' said George Chester Haworth, head of the firm of Richard Haworth & Sons, in 1903, 'to one of three – America, the Continent and ourselves'.[10]

For working-people the slump of the winter of 1878–79 brought unemployment and mass deprivation on a scale not experienced for many years.[11] To prevent the Poor Law being overwhelmed, and to mobilise relief on the scale needed, arrangements were resorted to not seen since the Cotton Famine. Subscriptions were raised and soup kitchens and relief centres opened.[12] In the early 1880s trade briefly recovered, but by 1884 the economy was hit by what was to prove one of the severest depressions in the whole of the nineteenth century, on a par with those of the Peterloo years and the time of the first Chartist crisis. By February 1884 40,000 workers were said to be jobless in Manchester and Salford.[13] 1884 is a year of some significance. Workers began to demand that the unemployed should be given work. Anger was replacing acceptance, and new tactics began to be tried. Socialists did not create this discontent, but Evans, Reade, Horrocks and their comrades in the SDF saw their opportunity and threw themselves into the campaign, putting up candidates for local office, and playing their part in the 'New Unionism'. The sheer magnitude of their task would have daunted any but enthusiasts. Not least among their difficulties was how make an impact on old labour associations created out of working-class experience before (and sometimes long before) Socialism made an appearance.

By the mid-Eighties, Salford, was honeycombed with organisations which, through the principles of thrift and mutuality, sought to mitigate the harsh conditions of the life of working people. One of the oldest strategies in devising an alternative to competitive individualism was through Co-operation, which by this time was beginning to flourish. It had not always done so. Salford had a long history of co-operative experiments, the common fate of which was a failure to survive. Earliest of these was the First Salford Co-operative Society, a body which, for a few years from its foundation in 1829, existed to promote the Owenite Religion of the New Moral World and had attracted the attention of Joseph Brotherton.[14] One ambition of the Salford Owenites was to found land colonies, and some of its people joined a rural community at Ralahine, Co. Clare. This venture soon failed, as did this first burst of Utopian Socialist co-operation. There was, however, another Owenite co-operative initiative in 1840 which saw the promotion of a 'Universal Community Society of Rational Religionists' in Salford. Attacked by the Church of England as 'blasphemous, licentious and absurd' this too was short-lived.[15]

In the Forties Salford Chartists promoted several co-operative ventures. One in 1840 failed almost immediately. The following year Chartists were buying provisions in bulk and trying to persuade the working class to purchase shoes, clothes and newspapers direct from Chartist suppliers as 'the way to bring the shopocracy to their senses'.[16] In 1845 a cotton mill was established upon co-operative principles in Whit Lane, Pendleton. It, too, had only a short existence.[17] In 1848 a Co-operative Land and Building League was started in Manchester by local Chartists, but it too failed.[18] The collapse of Chartism in the depression of 1848 led to experiments in 'Co-operative Associative labour', their promoters being influenced by the 'National

Workshops' set up in Paris after the 1848 Revolution. In Salford 'The Universal Family Association' established a provision shop and began to put out work to one unemployed weaver. Later that year the trades unions in Manchester organised a conference on 'Associative Labour' which brought together Owenites, Chartists, trade unionists, middle-class 'Friends of the People' and Christian Socialists. Inspired by the French example, delegates discussed such ideas as replacing the wages system by 'exchanges of labour'.[19] This was the background against which the great Pendleton lock-out of 1850–51 took place, which produced the Pendleton Mechanics Institution and the Whit Lane Co-operative Weaving Co.

Neither the Universal Family Association nor the Whit Lane Weaving Co. survived. What is remarkable, is that, from every set-back, there was revival. From the late Forties, particularly in the smaller textile towns where the working-class was more homogeneous than in Manchester and Salford, co-operatives were established which survived, the Rochdale Equitable Pioneers being the archetype. From about 1858 the belief that for working-class people co-operation was the most viable alternative to the competitive system became established, and was destined to spread, not only through the working class but among educated opinion formers, appalled by the continuance of mass poverty and the structural inequalities of the capitalist system. The year 1859 saw the establishment in Manchester and Salford of retail societies which were to survive and flourish, the first of which was the Manchester and Salford Industrial Co-operative Society, which came to be known as 'the Hulme'. Within ten years the Society had around 2000 members and shops which sold bread, meat, groceries and clothes.

Two other Co-operative Societies soon had branches in Salford. The Manchester and Salford Equitable started at almost exactly the same time as the 'the Industrial'. By July 1860 it had a store at Bank Parade, Salford. By 1883 membership had grown to 12,230, served by 16 shops in Manchester and Salford. Co-operation in Pendleton began in 1860. Hardly had they moved into their first shop when the Cotton Famine started and the venture almost collapsed. When they got into 'trouble over the books', they had to call in the help of the Secretary of the Rochdale Pioneers Society. Under his steady hand the Pendleton Industrial Co-operative Society survived, though by 1870 it still only had 378 members and share capital of £1,158. However, in the boom of the next few years, membership and share capital grew rapidly, and it eventually opened seven grocery shops. It rapidly became West Salford's main society. In 1874 it was agreed that its territory stretched as far as Cross Lane, districts east of which belonging to the Equitable. To the west it agreed not to overlap into the domain of the Eccles Society. In 1881 the PICS expanded into Lower Broughton, and three years later into Higher Broughton. Eventually the PICS took over the Ordsall and Regent Road Districts and the premises rented or owned there by the Manchester and Salford Equitable Society. The early Eighties saw phenomenal growth. With the opening of its warehouse, bakery and slaughterhouse in Cheltenham street and magnificent new Central Premises in Ford Lane in 1887, the PICS established as impressive a presence as any of the factories in central Pendleton. In 1889 it sold 13,000 tons of coal, delivered almost 700,000 quarts of milk, and baked close on a million 4lb. loaves. It was advancing money on mortgage, was about to go into the tailoring business, and planning to rent a farm at Swinton. Between 1885 and 1890 membership almost doubled again.[20]

By the mid-1880s the Co-operative movement was in many ways the most impressive 'old labour' body in existence. However, if more and more working people and labour leaders were becoming co-operators, leading co-operators were clear that the movement must remain non-political. In point of fact the Co-op was almost the last working-class organisation to become politicised. It did not come into the movement until 1917. On the other hand, the Co-op Societies did not hesitate in their support of labour in the bitter trade disputes of the last decade of the century. In 1893 the PICS sent money and bread to the locked-out cotton operatives of Oldham, and gave generous financial and food aid to the Pendleton miners in the autumn and winter of that year.[21]

Victorian Liberalism's principal message to working people was the encouragement of the pursuit of thrift and sobriety. As in other industrial towns, a wide range of bodies were founded for their promotion in Salford. First there were the institutions for independent savers. The most basic were the Savings Banks established early in the nineteenth century, and millions of people across the country trusted them with their small savings. For bigger savers a characteristic nineteenth-century development was the Building Society, which offered higher returns with the added incentive of being able to invest in property. In the course of Queen Victoria's reign scores of such societies were founded in Manchester and Salford. Savers through building societies were largely middle class, though at the upper end of the working class any one inheriting some money, or in a position to save, would join one. The encouragers of thrift made much of working-class membership, and working men were constantly urged to join. If working people were not major subscribers as individuals, they certainly were collectively. John Blythe Foden, President of the National Independent Permanent Benefit Building Society, remarked at its 17th annual general meeting 'there are upwards of 40 lodges holding shares in the society, amongst which we observe Sunday School clubs, the Sons of Temperance, widow and orphan funds, funeral, sick and burial, and mutual improvement societies, besides many lodges of Druids, Oddfellows and Foresters'.[22]

The number of such clubs in Victorian Salford defy computation. At the top were undoubtedly the Friendly Societies belonging to the great 'affiliated orders'. In 1872 it was said there were 325 lodges in the Manchester district,[23] and these orders, with their large aggregate memberships and national (and sometimes international) networks, constitute the second of the 'old labour' bodies Socialists had to win over to the idea of a political organisation separate from the Liberal party. At the pinnacle of the nineteenth-century Friendly Society movement were the Odd Fellows and the Foresters, and Manchester and Salford played no small part in their history. It was in Salford, at a meeting at the *Ropemakers Arms* in Chapel Street in 1809, that the first Odd Fellows' lodge was founded.[24] The way in which these Affiliated Orders spread is a testimony to the working-class genius for association. Despite their vast and complex organisation, the basic units were the local lodges, with often quite small memberships and a jealous sense of their own autonomy. The tension between local lodge and 'central office' not infrequently caused rifts and breakaways, as we saw in the life of R. J. Richardson.[25] By about

1880 the Manchester Unity of the Independent Order of Oddfellows was the largest of the affiliated orders, though it was being overtaken by the Ancient Order of Foresters (which, at the close of 1878, had a membership in excess of half a million, and funds which amounted to over £2 1/2 million).[26] Whatever the national position of the Foresters, they were weak in Salford. Salford was Odd Fellow territory. In 1891 there were lodges belonging to no less than five different orders: the Manchester Unity, the Nottingham Ancient Imperial United Order, the United Oddfellows (Bolton Unity), the Loyal United Order, and the National Independent Order. The National Independent Order was the largest, with nine lodges in the Salford District and six in Pendleton, and a total membership of 2,743.[27]

Alongside the Odd Fellows there was a spread of lodges, branches, 'Courts' or 'Tents', of Foresters, the Royal and Ancient Order of Buffaloes, the Ancient Order of Druids, the Independent Order of Rechabites, the Sons of Temperance, and the Independent Order of Good Templars. The last three were Temperance Societies. Oldest was the Rechabites, which, as the 'Salford Unity' part of its name records, originated in the township in 1835. By the time of its jubilee half a century later, its 'Tents' and districts had spread throughout England and Wales, and had a presence in Scotland and in the Belfast district in Ireland. They had also been exported to the Australian colonies, New Zealand, Barbados and the United States.[28] The tide of thrift and temperance also flowed the other way. Buffaloes, Good Templars and the Sons of Temperance all started in America. The latter was founded in New York, the first Salford 'Division' (or branch) being established in 1850. By 1891 in the Salford Grand Division there were 12 Sub-divisions boasting a membership of 1,110.[29] 'True as Steel', the Division to which George Evans belonged, was the biggest, with a membership of over 500.

The Friendly Society movement was the self-help social security system of Victorian England. By the 1880s many of the societies had spread their benefits to female and juvenile members. As well as adding colour to the lives of their members through the rituals and conviviality of the lodges, their demonstrations, outings and church parades (with be-sashed members, banners and brass bands) added colour to the

Past Chief Ruler's certificate, Independent Order of Rechabites, Salford Unity. (Author's collection)

common scene. By about 1890, however, there were signs that people were becoming aware of their limitations as providers of social security. Addressing an Odd Fellows rally that year, the mayor of Salford observed 'we have in Salford something like 25,000 working men. My friends both right and left of me say that there are something like 5,000 members of benefit societies. That is a very small proportion.'[30] For very obvious reasons, the major orders of Friendly societies were limited to the upper echelons of the working class and salesmen, clerks in warehouses, shopkeepers and other small businessmen. Only they had the regularity of employment and levels of pay which gave them the ability to keep up their dues.

Although the great affiliated orders of Friendly Societies were the 'élite' organs of self help, as providers of basic forms of social security they were in a decided minority. There existed in Salford, as elsewhere, a range of 'penny a week' clubs providing burial, or 'sick and burial' benefits to their members. Some were based on public houses, some on churches and chapels, some were offshoots of co-operation or temperance. Like Friendly Societies, from small beginnings certain of them developed into considerable enterprises with branches in many towns. The Salford Funeral Friendly Society, founded in 1815, had 41 lodges in various places by 1871, with 15,153 members: twenty years later its subscribers had more than doubled.[31] Many of the purely local clubs were very long lived. The New Windsor and Pendleton Burial Society, founded 1811, was still going strong eighty years later with 8,000 members.[32]

The Friendly Society and the Sick and Burial Club network reflected the nature of urban self-help: associative, federal yet intensely local, independent, suspicious of state interference. It also reflected the highly stratified nature of the working and lower middle classes. Each stratum had its own clubs, providing what its members were able and willing to insure for. By definition, it was a poor man who could not pay for his own funeral. If Friendly Societies saw themselves as the basis of respectability, they were very much 'Labour bodies', and did not hesitate to act as such when necessary. At the time of the great engineering lock-out in 1895 the Royal Archer Lodge of Buffaloes in Broughton supplied two thousand loaves to local men and their families suffering as a result of the dispute.[33] Nevertheless, the Friendly Society movement, as a movement, was impossible for Socialists to politicise. Tradition decreed that differences over party and religion were left at the lodge door. If members of Friendly Societies were to play a part in the emerging Labour movement, they were to do so as individuals. In fact, most Labour activists like George Evans *were* Friendly Society members, and often convinced Temperance men as well.

In trying to create a sense of class consciousness, Socialists were only too well aware of the difficulties. The recollections of Robert Roberts of the district between Oldfield Road and Cross Lane offer the most graphic picture available of working-class life in Salford in the early years of this century. Above all, they dispel notions of working-class homogeneity. In what Engels had described sixty years before as a 'classic slum', Roberts delineates no less than five distinct inter-related and self-conscious social layers.[34] Top of his pyramid were shopkeepers and publicans. Next came the skilled workers, 'aristocrats, cut-off from the rest by the barrier of seven-year apprenticeship.' Below them came the textile workers. Below textile workers came the 'semi-skilled'. What Roberts underlines most graphically is the pecking order in working-class life. 'The engineers and textile workers patronised the labourers and had a kind of friendship with them, but the people they hated were the drillers and planers who would, if they didn't watch out, sneak into their jobs without serving the apprenticeship.' Even the workers at the lower end, the 'unskilled', had a pecking order. Anyone in regular work looked down on the casual worker, docker, seaman or street trader. Those, in turn, looked down on the almost destitute, small-time thieves or prostitutes. In The *Classic Slum* (1971), Roberts was reacting (and perhaps over-reacting) against memoirs and reminiscences which had appeared celebrating the warm-heartedness and solidarity of working-class life, now thought to be becoming a thing of the past. Whilst not ignoring warm-heartedness and decency, what he chose to emphasize was the repressive, hierarchical and competitive characteristics of everyday life in the terraced streets. The nature of the institutions founded by and for the different parts of the working class reflected its stratified nature, and, as we shall see, what was true of the clubs and friendly societies was just as true of the trade unions.

Alongside the clubs and Friendly Society lodges in Manchester and Salford in 1872 were 125 trade unions with an estimated 25,000 members.[35] Most were small and fiercely independent, usually (though not exclusively) representing craftsmen – painters, carpenters, joiners, masons, iron-moulders, bakers, confectioners, tailors, rope and twine makers, bleachers and dyers and miners. By the 1880s behind them lay three quarters of a century of struggle. Employers enjoyed the power to coerce, dismiss, combine together and 'blacklist', and rarely hesitated to use them. When workers combined they ran foul of the law, which was heavily weighted against labour combination. Industrial relations was Victorian society's most abrasive interface. By the 1860s there was a well established pattern: in times of boom, workers (often belatedly) pressed for pay rises, and in slumps (often belatedly) organised to resist pay cuts. In most cases the resultant disputes were brief and swiftly resolved, though Salford had witnessed several major confrontations, Sir Elkanah Armitage's dispute with the Pendleton weavers being the longest and most bitter down to 1877.

In the 1860s organised labour was becoming stronger. A movement was being created by well-organised craft unions which had survived in the face of defeats and other set-backs. Helping them was the burst of prosperity which began in the early Fifties. This fortuitous turn in economic affairs reinforced a spririt of optimism in the minds of influential elements in the middle-classes. Fear of revolutionary disorder faded, and, after the death of Palmerston, Parliament was soon ready to admit the upper stratum of urban workers to the franchise. One result of this was that Parliament itself came under pressure for a major recasting of trade union and labour law.[36]

The first significant step for local trades unionism was the founding of the Manchester and Salford Trades Council in 1866. The background to its formation was a series of disputes involving operative joiners, plasterers, labourers, tailors, gas works employees, Pendlebury miners, and engine drivers and firemen, most of whom had been defeated by lock-outs.[37] Another factor was outbreaks of 'rattening' which began locally with the destruction of tens of thousands of unbaked bricks in June 1864 in the Regent Road district. There were similar incidents in other places around Manchester and in the background were the Sheffield 'trade outrages'. In response to great public alarm over these attacks on property and people, a Royal Commission was appointed which visited Manchester in 1867.[38] Not least because some Commissioners were strongly of the opinion that the climate was right for the adoption of conciliation and arbitration in industrial relations, the unions were able to convince the Commission that such incidents were not characteristic of trades unionism, which, they argued, was generally respectable, law-abiding and in favour of conciliation.

The new Trades Council attracted delegates from 32 trade societies representing about 9,000 members to its first annual meeting. C. S. Nicholson became president, and W. H. Wood secretary; both were members of the Letterpress Printers' Society. The latter told the meeting they were working for the promotion of courts of arbitration, a new Master and Servant Bill, the extension of the Factory Acts to workshops, and legal protection for the funds of trade societies.[39] In its early days the Trades Council was walking a tightrope, and knew it. In claiming (as it did in 1874) that it had been successful in reducing public prejudice against trade societies, and that it had lessened bad feelings between employers and workers, it was being sanguine. With only a minority of local unions affiliated, its leaders knew perfectly well that inter-union co-operation was fragile, that arbitration was favoured by few on either side of industry, and that strikes, violence and intimidation were not about to disappear from trade disputes. However, Trades Council members were undoubtedly correct in arguing that the time was ripe for campaigning for changes in the legal position of the unions and for further parliamentary regulation of certain trades.

One reason why the Trades Council wanted to steer clear of political agitation was that party politics were an obvious source of dissension. As we have seen, it was widely assumed that working-class respectables enfranchised by the Second Reform Act would be Liberal. Lancashire demonstrated that this was not necessarily so. The leading spirits on the local Trades Council, Wood and Nicholson, were both active Conservatives. As trade unionists, however, they argued that union business and party politics were separate spheres and should be kept that way. In this, they were not untypical. As late as 1887 the Salford branch of the Steam Engine Makers Society passed a resolution of censure on the Trades Union Congress for 'introducing and voting on questions of a distinct and party nature ... calculated to cause disruption in our ranks.' [40]

The late Sixties saw significant developments on a wider front. The passing of the Master and Servant Act of 1867, which for the first time placed employers and workers on the same footing in breach of contract cases, was a landmark; 'the first positive success of the Trade Unions in the legislative field.' [41] The same year also saw a Workshops Regulation Act and the passing of the Second Reform Act. Another development of potential significance was the establishment of a national 'Parliament of Labour'. The Trades Union Congress owed its formation to an initiative of the Manchester and Salford Trades Council. In April 1868 that body issued a circular convening a Congress in Manchester in Whit week. From this meeting emerged the idea of an annual Congress. The modern TUC can be said to have been launched when the 1871 Congress in London set up a Parliamentary Committee to fight the battle of the Trade Union Acts going through Parliament.[42]

The legislation put through by Gladstone's Government in an effort to regularise the legal position of trade unions consisted of two Acts in 1871, one welcomed by the unions, and a second which alarmed and politicised them. The Trade Union Act laid down that no trade union was henceforth to be illegal merely because it was in 'restraint of trade', and registration under the Act gave a union protection for its funds. The Criminal Law Amendment Act summed up and codified previous legislation and judicial decisions by declaring as criminal a range of activities which had led to court cases over picketing during industrial action. It seemed that the law now said that to strike was lawful, but anything done in pursuance of a strike was criminal. The struggle to have the Act repealed was the dominant preoccupation of the trade union world fought at the national level by the TUC and at the local level by the Trades Council, with Wood and Nicholson to the fore. The unpopularity of the Criminal Law Amendment Act was a factor in the defeat of Gladstone in 1874.

The Conservative Government stepped in with the Conspiracy and Protection of Property Act, 1875, which laid it down that no one was liable for criminal conspiracy for any act done in contemplation or furtherance of a trade dispute, except in certain circumstances. An Employers and Workmen Act of the same year freed workers from another ground of criminal liability, by declaring breach of contract by a worker (a crime for centuries) to be no longer criminal. In August 1875 Wood was presented with a £60 gold watch by local trade unionists for his services to the cause over almost a decade.[43]

On the local industrial front the boom of the early seventies led to an increase in trades union recruitment and confidence. Claims for a share in the profits of the boom publicised many examples of underpay and overwork. An accident on the Irish Mail revealed that railwaymen worked twelve hours a day on a thirteen day work cycle before they got a day off. Disputes in the tailoring trade revealed systematic 'sweating'. In May 1873 there was a big strike of Manchester carters, and in August the Dressers, Dyers and Finishers Union demanded a rise of two shillings a week.[44] In June 1874 Manchester saw a huge rally in support for the locked-out agricultural workers in Joseph Arch's Union. There was considerable industrial unrest in 1875, the most notable local case of which was a bitter dispute at the Atlas Iron Works in Manchester. On the wider front, a big issue of the day was the lock-out of the South Wales miners, and unions in Manchester sent money to support the men out of work. A strike at Cottrills' Britannia Mills in Pendleton in April-May 1875 resulted in unionists being taken to court for breach of contract.[45] The most significant general advance of these years, however, was the Factory Act of 1875 which brought in the Saturday half day, closing the mills at 1 o'clock, a landmark in the history of working-class life and leisure.

The disputes in the boom of the early decade were as nothing to those in the slump, which became serious in late 1877. A reduction in wages in Bolton led to a great strike. In May the following year, a Salford newspaper declared 'Lancashire seems to be in a state of ferment such as has been unknown since the miserable Peterloo business'.[46] Employers cut wages by ten per cent and, what was new, agreed to act together. The biggest strike and lock out in the history of the cotton industry ensued. Although it was centred on towns outside Manchester, there were local reverberations. Locally, workers were locked out in disputes at Messrs Haworths' Mills in Ordsall, at Hall, McKerrow's Windsor Mill in Pendleton, and at the Irwell and Medlock Mills of the Dacca Twist Co, Regent Road, though nowhere did the resistance last as long as in the textile towns to the north.[47] By far the bitterest industrial battle in Manchester was in the building trades, where the strike of the carpenters and joiners lasted 53 weeks from May 1877.[48] In the end the union lost. In May 1878 the men had to return to work at the old wages and hours. Although contemporaries did not immediately appreciate it, the country was entering a new era. Capital and Labour were now beginning to organise in bigger battalions than in the past. It was into this situation that modern Socialism arrived. However, Socialists were to find that many of the working men most actively involved in co-operation, friendly societies, trade unionism and party politics were not easily persuaded of the relevance of the Socialist message.

In the twenty or so years prior to the appearance of Socialism, trade unionists and politically conscious working men in Manchester were seriously divided over party politics. When access to political participation began to open up, the most startling result, as we have already seen, was the appearance of that brand of Conservatism which propelled Cawley and Charley into Parliament. Although the influence of individuals should not be over stressed, the activities of Wood and Nicholson were clearly important. Their Conservatism was a mixture of Protestantism, Protectionism and the argument that working people had benefited more from Conservative than Liberal legislation in the past, and would probably do so in the future.[49] These ideas had some appeal, and Wood's ability to influence public opinion was much increased with the appearance of the Conservative *Salford Chronicle* in October 1868, his name appearing as its proprietor. An ardent protectionist, Wood was fond of pointing out how Free Trade had damaged British industry, especially the silk trade. He also took a special pleasure in pointing out how strongly John Bright, the middle-class Radical most admired by Liberal working men, had no love for trade unions and had always opposed factory legislation.[50]

This brand of Conservatism enjoyed a decade of success. However, by the late Seventies bridges had been built, and many trade union activists were identifying with Liberalism or Radicalism. One sign of this was the loss of Wood's position on the Trades Council. At its 11th annual general meeting in 1877, in the election for the post of secretary Wood was defeated by P. Shorrocks of the Journeymen Tailors, and Henry Harry of the same society was elected chairman for the ensuing year.[51] A few years later Harry was to be the first SDF man to stand for office in Salford.

As we have seen, when Radical politics revived after the death of Palmerston, a combination of old Chartists, trade unionists, temperance men and co-operators founded the Reform League in Manchester and Salford, and once more began to explore the possibilities of an agreed platform with middle-class liberal Reformers. At the time of the Second Reform Act Ernest Jones was the acknowledged leader of Manchester's Popular Radicals. The son of a major in the 15th Hussars who was equerry to the Duke of Cumberland, Jones stands in that tradition of popular leaders from upper-class or professional backgrounds which includes Major Cartwright, Henry Hunt and Feargus O'Connor. Converted to Chartism as a very young man, he threw himself into the movement and was its last leader in the years of its decline after 1848. He had a long connection with Manchester, being involved in assembling the 'Labour Parliament' which met there in 1854, and the Association for Manhood Suffrage formed four years later. In 1861 he came to live in Broughton, practised as a barrister, and was counsel for the defence in the Fenians' trial. In the Autumn of 1866 Jones presided over a meeting in Manchester to promote the Reform League in the north of England. A series of large scale open-air meetings were organised, the like of which had not been seen since Chartist times. From the very start, popular Radicals challenged Gladstonian Liberalism on Labour representation: 'Let cotton lords represent themselves, and let land be represented but ... let working men also have their representatives', demanded Thomas Ellis at the inaugural meeting of the National Reform League's Pendleton branch early in 1867.[52] In July a delegation from the newly formed Manchester Trades Unionist Political Association met the council of the Reform league and selected Ernest Jones as 'the most fitting man' the represent Manchester 'as its 3rd member'.[53] It was one thing to select their own candidates: it was quite another to get the Liberal party to accept them. As we have seen, Ernest Jones contested the 1868 election in Manchester as a Liberal, without the formal support of the party leadership, who were surprised (and annoyed) by the size of his vote. The success of the Conservatives presented the Liberal chieftains of Manchester and Salford with some dilemmas. Clearly, in order to prevent candidates like Jones splitting the Liberal vote in future, accommodation needed to be reached with the popular Radicals and their supporters. At the same time, the middle-class leaders had little desire to deny themselves the ultimate reward in political life, a seat at Westminster, by gratuitously offering one to an ex-Chartist, a modern Radical or a Trade Unionist.

Had Ernest Jones lived longer the situation might have proved more awkward for the Liberals, for they must surely would have had to accept him as a candidate. However, Jones died in January 1869, in his 49th year, and was given one of the great funerals of Victorian Manchester. His coffin was borne to his grave in Ardwick Cemetery by four old Chartists, and his pall-bearers included Jacob Bright MP, Thomas Baines Potter MP, Abel Heywood, Sir Elkanah Armitage, his son, Benjamin, Elijah Dixon, the veteran Chartist and others prominent in Manchester Liberalism. Behind these came about a thousand mourners, including representatives of the National Reform League branches from many parts of the country, members of the local Bar and numerous personal friends. Jones was a much loved figure, and there was a tremendous sense of loss. And, in truth, Jones was irreplaceable in local Radicalism. A memorial fund was raised, and two years later Elijah Dixon unveiled the Ernest Jones monument in Ardwick Cemetery.[54]

Despite Liberal businessmen's dislike for trade unionism, they were forced to take cognisance of it after 1868, for political reasons if nothing else. The same was true for trade union leaders about Liberalism: despite the tradition that political and union matters belonged to different spheres, they were being drawn more and more into party politics. What, of course, drew them in was the need to repeal the Criminal Law Amendment Act of 1871. The miners showed the way. At a meeting of delegates from all over the country in Manchester that year a resolution declared that 'the interests of the working classes will never be truly served until Labour is properly represented in the House of Commons. We, therefore, pledge ourselves to do our utmost to send working men to parliament, and we call upon the trades to co-operate in carrying out this object.' [55] In 1874 Alexander MacDonald and Thomas Burt, both miners, became the first working men to be elected to Parliament. From this time on, trade unionists pressed the union case to politicians.

In the late 1870s trade unionists were not thinking about a party of labour. What they were pressing for was *labour representation*. Most unionists nationally, and perhaps even in Manchester, were Liberals, and believed that labour representation would come as a result of local deals with the Liberal party. Socialists did not think this collaboration with the class enemies of the workers was either likely or desirable, and grew increasingly contemptuous of Liberal trade unionists. Through involvement in the extension of trades unionism to the 'unskilled', the organisation of the unemployed, the exposure of 'sweating' and campaigns against slum housing, they began the process whereby the old consciousness of class was, however, imperfectly from a Socialist viewpoint, transformed into *class consciousness*. George Evans only lived long enough to see its first stages.

From early 1884 to late 1888 (when trade began to improve) Socialists led a campaign to have the seriousness of unemployment recognised, and to try new methods to alleviate it. In February there was a large demonstration of the unemployed in Manchester from which deputations were sent to wait upon local councils. Official reactions were predictable. Boards of Guardians denied that the scale of the problem was anything unusual, and said that Socialists were exaggerating the scale of unemployment for their own purposes. The new tactics, however, disturbed the authorities. As the depression reached its lowest point the Socialist campaign intensified. They stepped up the lobbying of local authorities and the guardians of the poor. Another tactic was to demand work instead of relief. At the height of the crisis the sanitary department of the Salford Council did provide a little scavenging work, and some jobs were made available on the grounds of the new poor law Infirmary at Hope as alternatives to the detested workhouse labour tests. In terms of changing ideas and public policy, the Socialists' campaign had achieved little. It remained a basic free market tenet that there was work for all who strove to find it, in good times as well as in bad, and that the unemployed were those who did not strive energetically enough. Yet something had been achieved. Socialists had challenged the traditional view that unemployment was something to be borne with resignation and fortitude. Consciousness had been raised a little. Moreover, Socialists had seized the initiative from the trade unions, who, by and large, accepted the inevitablity of unemployment. Most significantly perhaps, the campaign on unemployment started the process by which informed opinion would slowly begin to rethink its attitudes to what caused poverty and unemployment, which bore fruit in the next twenty years or so in the social inquiries of Booth, Rowntree and Beveridge.

These years saw the rise of another movement in which Socialists played a prominent part – 'New Unionism'. Workers hitherto unorganised, or thought to be unorganisable, began to join unions. New Unionism exposed the appalling conditions of work and rates of pay existing in many of the industries of the district. In the wider history of New Unionism the struggle of the London gas workers played a major part, and it was in the Salford Gas Works that Socialist involvement was submitted to an early test. Trouble started there in 1888 as a result of changes introduced by Hunter's successor, Shoubridge. A strike occurred over the sacking of men who had worked there for many years. At first, public sympathy was on the side of the workers and the initial dispute was settled by a compromise, which did not last.[56] A battle commenced between the Gas Committee and the workers, supported and led by Socialists, George Evans playing an active part. In September 1889 we find him giving a characteristically fiery speech at the meeting at which a branch of the National Union of Gasworkers and General Labourers was formed: 'My blood boils to see you before me listening quietly, and then as soon as the beerhouses are open you are off to get a pint, and you forget all about it ... I do not plead for you. If it was only you that were concerned you would deserve to die and get out of your apathy and make way for better people'.[57] Even more closely involved was William Horrocks, who became district organising secretary of the union.

At first things went well. In October, as part of the national campaign by the gasworkers, the men got a pay rise and the hours of some workers were reduced. But trouble soon stirred. The union alleged that pressure was being put on men not to join the union, and predicted that when time became slack, union men would be laid off first. A 'closed shop' was demanded. The men gave two weeks' notice: the Gas Committee retaliated with one week's notice. It soon became a Manchester and Salford issue – the two Gas Committees *versus* the union. Much interest was aroused in this first trial of the New Unionism's strength. Horrocks, Evans and the other local leaders were given strong backing from such national figures as John Burns, Tom Mann and Will Thorne. The men on strike were replaced by non-union men, who worked and slept in the gas works. In pressing for a closed shop, the union had made a mistake, enabling the employers to fight on the issue of 'the freedom of labour'. Just before Christmas 1889 the strike collapsed. Union men were sacked: much recrimination followed. Socialist leadership was blamed for the defeat, and Horrocks made the scapegoat. Allegations of dishonesty were levelled against him; he was suspended by the local branch of the union and forced to vindicate himself at a public meeting in Manchester.[58]

A similar experience of optimistic intervention, followed by setback, resulted from early attempts of Socialists to stand for election to public bodies. In the Parliamentary election of 1885 a Socialist candidate was fielded in opposition to Benjamin Armitage, in the person of Henry Harry, a Jewish tailor from Lower Broughton. Although in the end he did not go to the poll, the coverage Harry received in the local press was extremely good, his manifesto being reported in some detail.[59] Arguing that the interests of employer and employed were diametrically opposed, Harry said his conviction was that the Liberal caucus was organised in direct antagonism to labour candidates. He argued that both Tory and Liberal legislation had been a failure from the point of view of the labouring classes. In

November that year the Salford Socialists had their first taste of electoral success when George Smart, a working painter, defeated Alderman Husband, a prominent churchman and former Mayor of Salford, in the school board election.[60] Each year from 1887, the Socialists put up candidates in the borough council elections. Despite increasing their vote fairly steadily, not once were they successful in these early years, and Smart lost his seat on the school board in 1888. Such reverses did nothing to deflect them from their aim of a political movement independent of any other as the way forward for the working class.

To most working people this must have seemed political cloud-cuckoo-land. Socialists were few and, despite all their efforts, failed to win over workers in any numbers. Their sectarian manner, and perhaps above all their contempt for 'old Labour' politics set them apart. Moreover, Socialism no sooner appeared then it fragmented. The Socialist League broke with the Democrats, and in Manchester a Social Union was formed independent of both the SDF and the Socialist League.[61] To most Radicals and trade union leaders the only realistic way forward seemed accommodation with the Liberals over Labour representation. Reform, they argued, had changed politics in the past, and was currently delivering an increasingly democratic system. Capitalism could be, and was being tamed by co-operation, mutuality and parliamentary legislation. The main proponent of this line was the influential Charles Bradlaugh, who engaged in acrimonious debates with Socialists on the subject of Reform *versus* 'State Socialism'. The trades union scene was, however, changing. The rise of New Unionism had to be accommodated by the TUC and local Trades Councils. Their gradual support for Socialism began to have effect on the rank and file of the older, stronger unions. It became clear that if the labour movement was to become more catholic and embrace the politics of New Unionism, for their part Socialists would have to widen their appeal. In the final years of Evans' life Socialism began to do this, and he was to play no small part in the process. A factor of significance was support received from the press, and in this, the part played by Robert Blatchford, the William Cobbett of his day, was crucial.

Like Cobbett, a soldier turned journalist, Blatchford moved to Manchester in 1887 to work for Edward Hulton's *Sunday Chronicle*, a popular sporting newspaper. He was not a Socialist when he arrived, but Manchester and its slums soon made him one. Blatchford's articles introduced Socialism to a far wider public than the SDF could have ever reached. Blatchford was no idealogue: for him Socialism was the commonsensical way to restore happiness to a miserable and impoverished world. One of his characteristic initiatives was the Cinderella Club, which provided toys and treats for poor children. Inevitably, Blatchford's political views caused a rift with the proprietor and Blatchford parted from Hulton. In December 1891 he launched the *Clarion*, the best loved and most influential Socialist newspaper ever published in this country. Together with such writers as A. M. Thompson and T. W. Harris, Blatchford popularised Socialism. The *Clarion* was an important reason why, when a broader party of the left was to emerge a year later, it was to have a greater appeal than the SDF. The 'Clarion Movement', with its discussion groups, philanthropic efforts and cycling clubs, appealed to the optimistic and convivial instincts of young northern men and women far more than the more narrowly doctrinaire Democrats or Socialist Leaguers ever could. Henry Reade, in the final period of his influence in the Socialist movement in Manchester, became secretary of the Manchester Clarion Club, organised to attract 'unattached Socialists'.[62]

Another influence was the Fabian Society, which originated in London in 1884, and began its Lancashire campaign in 1890. Henry Reade was an early recruit and so was Blatchford. A Manchester Society was founded in January 1891. Another leading figure was Dr Richard Pankhurst, the best-known middle-class Radical in Manchester. Pankhurst, a barrister, was typical of another type attracted to this broadening vision of Socialism. 'The Doctor' never quite shed his Baptist origins. Disliking their insistence that economic self-interest was the all-embracing drive in men, he had never joined the Social Democrats. Nor did he and Mrs Pankhurst much care for the opposition to women's suffrage of Hyndman and others on the SDF executive. Whatever differences there were between Fabians and Social Democrats in London, there were fewer in Manchester and Salford. Alongside Reade, Blatchford and Pankhurst, the leading lights of the Manchester Fabian Society included J. K. Hall, Alfred Settle, (SDF) T. W. Harris, A. M. Thompson, and John Trevor of the Labour Church.[63]

The latter organisation was another which helped to widen Socialism. John Trevor was born in Liverpool and brought up a Baptist in Cambridgeshire. A nervous, rather unsociable young man, he first intended to be an architect, but in the end trained for the Unitarian ministry.[64] A formative influence was Philip Wicksteed, whose assistant minister in London he became for a while. Wicksteed had a profound concern with social and economic problems, and new ideas on what modern christianity should be doing about them. In the summer of 1890 Trevor moved to Manchester. Aware of the ways established religion excluded working people, Trevor decided on another approach. His first 'Labour Church' meeting was in Chorlton Town Hall in October 1891. There Trevor spoke of the need to bring religion 'into the struggle'. The next Sunday Blatchford spoke to an overflowing congregation. Support for this new organisation spread rapidly. One influential recruit was Frederick Brocklehurst, the Cambridge-educated son of a journalist.[65] Originally intended for the Anglican ministry, Brocklehurst gravitated towards Socialism after becoming convinced of the inadequacy of modern religion in the face of the social evils of the time. Brocklehurst met Trevor and came to Manchester, where he became the Labour Church secretary.

The Labour Church commenced in Salford in November 1892, with Sunday afternoon meetings in Pendleton Town Hall. Three years later a separate Salford Church started up in the Prince of Wales Assembly Room in Liverpool Street. At its first meeting John Hempsall, an SDF man, declared, 'it is the intention of both Churches to emphasize more strongly than ever the ethical and altruistic aspects of Socialism and to insist on the essentially religious character of the Labour movement.' One early preacher was Keir Hardie, who addressed them on 'the Gospel of Jesus'.[66] Whether or not the Labour Church was essentially a religious movement, or a political one in which Christian and Socialist ethics were fused (or confused) matters little. Its effect was to recruit to Socialism serious people in search of a moral creed outside conventional religion. It attracted local SDF men such as T. M. Purves and George Evans, for whom Socialism was already a religion.

The spirit of the age which led to the emergence of the Labour Church was not without its effects on conventional religion. In 1891 the minister of the Pendleton Unitarian Free Church began monthly 'Peoples' Services', and the PSA (Pleasant Sunday Afternoon) movement was also launched at this time. Although this attempt to attract working people was spearheaded by Nonconformists, it was soon taken up by the Church of England. In a sermon to working men at St Bartholomew's Church, Canon Hicks, rector of St Philip's, admitted that the Church for too long had been the opponent of democracy. Sympathetic to trades unionism, Hicks became involved in the questions of the poverty and unemployment which surrounded him at St Philip's.[67] Hicks remained a Liberal, but it was not long before active Socialists appeared amongst the clergy. One of the most notable ILP supporters was the Rev. C. P. Wilson of St Luke's, Weaste. A follower of Henry George, Wilson allowed the Weaste Clarion Fellowship to meet in his schools and gave them talks on such subjects as 'The Land Question'. The Christian Social Union had its adherents in Manchester and Salford, as did the later Church Socialist League (founded in 1906), whose secretary was the Rev. E. B. Hooper, curate of St Philip's.[68]

No church was unaffected by the rise of Socialism, but none opposed it more vehemently than the Catholic clergy. The Church's position was defined by *Rerum Novarum,* the Pope's Encyclical of 1891, which, whilst it affirmed the right of workers to 'a family wage' and opposed economic liberalism, condemned Socialism, stressing the inviolability of private property. On the other hand, the laity could not be immune to the advance of Socialism. Ultimately the rise of Labour was to enfranchise working-class Catholics in Manchester and Salford in a way the older political parties never had. By 1908 the strain between the hierarchy and the awakening political activism of individual Catholics was out in the open. Respectable Catholics in Salford were scandalised when service in St John's Cathedral was interrupted by one Joshua Batty, who tried to address the congregation on the plight of the unemployed. A lapsed Catholic, Batty was passionately outraged by the sufferings of the unemployed. The following year he was imprisoned again for inciting the unemployed to riot.[69] Lest Batty should be seen as a martyr, sermons were preached against Socialism in local Catholic churches. 'Pope after Pope has condemned Socialism, and no Catholic can be a Socialist and remain a Catholic,' warned Father Carroll at St Joseph's. Yet, the emergence of Socialist ideas attracted young Catholics such as Joseph Toole, future Member of Parliament for Salford. When the priest at Mount Carmel warned him off, Toole went his own way.[70] Socialism also had unsettling effects on Irishmen. In 1895 the *Reporter* printed a letter which disputed the claim of the Irish National League to represent the Salford Irish in the alliance with the Liberals: 'There were more Irishmen connected with the Independent Labour Party than with the Irish National League' insisted the pseudonymous writer, provoking a furore in the correspondence columns.'[71]

By the end of the 1880s the first attempts of Socialists to win credibility where it counted, in local politics, had not gone well. As the Chartists found half a century earlier, working-class movements faced special difficulties. Not the least of these was the problem of trying to fight elections without money and an organisation. To remedy this a Salford Labour Electoral Association was formed in August 1891. Although Evans was a vice-president, it was not entirely a Socialist initiative, with non-Socialist trades unionists such as John Kelly as vice president and George

T. Jackson as treasurer. The Association's sudden appearance bewildered the Trades Council. The Electoral Association was accused, amongst other things, of being a Socialist front. The Trades Council was also surprised by the appearance of three other 'Labour' candidates in the forthcoming School Board election (of whom Evans was one). In the end, although the Trades Council endorsed these efforts, it could do little to prevent all of them coming bottom of their respective polls.[72]

Most disconcerted by these Labour stirrings was the South Salford Liberal Party, particularly when, in 1892, the Fabian Society and the Labour Electoral Association persuaded T. W. Harris of the *Clarion* to stand in the forthcoming general election. Liberals were not amused when Harris declared that Socialists should 'place themselves in one solid phalanx to fight a losing battle and lose it brilliantly'.[73] Their fear was that a Socialist would split the anti-Conservative vote and allow Sir Henry Howorth to retain his seat, which, as we have seen, was what happened.

In the long run losing brilliantly in Ordsall was less important to Socialists than an event which took place a few weeks before – the founding of the Manchester and Salford Independent Labour party. This was the outcome of a meeting in the *Clarion* office in Manchester, following a May Day rally. Present were Blatchford, Reade and William Johnson (Fabians), John Trevor, and (it is thought) Evans, Purves and Settle, all of the SDF. The ILP's objectives were the nationalization of the land and the means of production, and to organise to elect representatives to public bodies. One rule stipulated that 'no member of any organisation connection with the Liberal, Liberal Unionist or Conservative parties be eligible for membership of this party', and another that members were to pledge to abstain from voting for any candidate for election who was the nominee of any other party. Blatchford characterised the ILP as 'an organisation formed to rouse, educate and unite the vast masses of the workers and to give the strength of sympathy and cohesion to the scattered companies and isolated forlorn hopes of Social Reformers.'[74]

The Manchester and Salford ILP was a 'Keep Left' organisation, founded to 'bury the old Labour Electoral Association.' Its 'Marxism from a moral angle' certainly roused and educated many people the Social Democrats or the Socialist League could not reach, and gave Socialism a boost. On the other hand, it did not bury the Electoral Association, which survived several years longer. Within months there were ILP branches in most electoral divisions of Manchester and Salford, and in October a county federation was founded to co-ordinate programmes and speakers for Lancashire, Cheshire and the Manchester area. In January 1893 at the famous meeting in Bradford a *national* Independent Labour Party was launched. In Broughton the ILP opened Pankhurst Hall in memory of Dr Pankhurst, whose premature death in 1898 was a major loss to the movement in Manchester. Its first year programme of activities illustrates the social purpose of life in the ILP. Pankhurst Hall had facilities for billiards and chess, dances were held twice a week and there were monthly members' 'at homes.' The Hall was to have its own football, swimming and cycle clubs, and housed debates, visits by the Manchester Socialist choir and plays put on by its Amateur Dramatic Society. An adult education programme was organised, with lecturers from the Manchester University Settlement in Ancoats, and from Ruskin Hall, and there was a Socialist Sunday School for the children.[75]

The Manchester Fabian Society seems to have merged with the ILP right away, as did its North Manchester and Gorton branches. However, many Clarion Club people and the SDF remained separate, although individual members, George Evans for one, joined the ILP in much the same spirit as they had joined the Labour Church. Evans served as ILP treasurer from the start, though the SDF was always his first love.[76] Localism was important. The ILP never developed in South Salford as strongly as in Pendleton and Broughton. Ordsall was SDF territory. Interestingly, the more proletarian the district the less likely was Socialism of any kind to make headway in Salford: the poverty stricken area around the Flat Iron Market in Chapel Street was acknowledged by a slightly baffled SDF to be 'a hot-bed of Toryism'.[77]

The appearance of the ILP coincided with (and probably stimulated) a revival of the Socialist League in Manchester, whose members now turned to 'anarchist communism'. However, some activists, notably John Ritson and Leonard Hall soon left, and joined the South Salford SDF. Hall became a prominent figure in local Socialism and later joined the ILP. Within the membership of the Socialist League a significant proportion consisted of immigrant Jews, many of whom had encountered anarchist and communist ideas on the continent. For a year or so the League expounded its brand of revolutionary Socialism in the political clubs and at meetings in Stevenson Square and Ardwick Green in Manchester. The authorities showed far less tolerance to the League, whose speakers were harassed and arrested by the police, than to the SDF and ILP, whose speakers, on the whole, had less trouble. Soon, the Socialist League faded into obscurity.[78] It was to rise again in due course.

The formation of the ILP was a landmark in Labour history, and George Evans deserves to be remembered for his part in it, and for his activities in the whole Socialist revival. His anger at the sufferings of the poor, his unsparing commitment to the cause, and, above all, his personal qualities inspired his comrades. 'I wish I could say how much I am indebted to this good man', wrote John Trevor, 'It has been a help to me in all I have done simply to know him.'[79] But Evans' days were numbered. In November 1892 he became seriously ill. After a three-week convalescence in Southport, he returned to his work as a painter, only to fall ill again, and died on 2 April 1893, leaving little provision for his wife or family, which now included an adopted orphan child. It is not known whether or not he was aware that the Trades Council, now with a membership of 25,000, had recently agreed to work harmoniously with the ILP. The first manifestation of this was the joint Labour demonstration on May Day in Alexandra Park, Manchester.[80] But by then Evans was dead. Being what he had been, and events moving the way they were, it is readily apparent why his funeral was not only a sombre occasion, but, as one journal described it, a 'triumphal march' as well.

In the two decades or so between Evans' death and the outbreak of the Great War, Socialism and, more broadly, 'Labour', advanced. Yet they did so slowly, unevenly and with numerous set-backs and disappointments. The enthusiasm engendered by the appearance of the ILP only went so far. Supporters of the idea of a political party of Labour were to find there were no short cuts to local credibility and the creating of a strong organisational base.

In the first place, if the formation of the ILP widened Socialism, and if made it a little easier to work with other bodies on particular issues, it nonetheless added to Socialism's tendency to fragment. Moreover, beyond the ILP, the SDF and the Socialist League, there was always a body of 'unattached' Socialists, whose common link was the *Clarion* newspaper. Blatchford remained Socialism's finest recruiting sergeant, and 1894 saw the appearance of his *Merrie England*, which sold a million copies in this country, and was published abroad in pirated editions.[81] Yet Blatchford and many Clarion Socialists were unwilling to be drawn into organisational politics. Another element in the fragmentation of Socialism was the spirit of local independence of the ILP in Manchester and Salford. A rift opened up with the National Executive Committee which was never overcome down to 1914. At first this was personified by the strong mutual antipathy between Blatchford and Keir Hardie. Within Manchester and Salford there were pro-Blatchford and pro-Hardie factions, which lasted until Blatchford began to lose interest in the ILP, and started to promote the idea of 'one Socialist Party' in the *Clarion* in 1895.[82] In any case the appeal of the ILP should not be exaggerated. In the broader Labour movement many trade unionists stayed loyal to Liberalism, and from the time of the 1892 election, the Liberal Party not only took on the ILP and the SDF, but gave more attention to the interests of Labour in constituencies such as South Salford.

The limits of Socialist advance are shown in their failure to make much impact in local elections. Despite increasing their vote, the best that Salford Socialists could manage was to elect Joseph Nuttall to the School Board in 1892 and 1895. Not a single Socialist made it on to the Salford Council in that period. However, two trades unionists did. In 1893 George T. Jackson, the Tramways Workers Union leader, got in for Crescent Ward as a Liberal, and, as we have seen, earlier that year he had been made one of the first trades union magistrates for Salford. The second was R. W. Watters, a letterpress printer and an ex-chairman of the Trades Council, elected under the wing of the West Salford Liberal Association in 1896.[83] In municipal elections in 1894 all seven candidates were defeated. In the general election of 1895 the SDF again put up a Socialist in South Salford, W. H. Hobart, a London compositor. On election day Hobart polled 813 against Sir Henry Howorth's 3,384 votes and Forrest's 3,310.[84] Once more Socialists demonstrated that they had the power to ensure that a Liberal would be denied victory. On the other hand, after two parliamentary contests, there was no significant move of voters into the Socialist camp.

After this election, the ILP lost ground nationally. In Manchester the party managed to sustain enthusiasm for another three years, mainly because of the Boggart Hole Clough contest. When the Manchester City Council banned the use of this park for political meetings in 1896, Socialists resisted on the grounds of free speech. Speakers arrested for breaking the bye-laws took the matter to court, refused to pay fines and were sent to prison. Their case was effectively presented by Dr Pankhurst, and in this struggle his wife Emmeline first came to appreciate the potential of civil disobedience. Supported by much of the local press, the ILP campaign over Boggart Hole Clough was a success, Frederick Brocklehurst in particular making a name for himself. Eventually the City Council gave in, drafting new bye-laws allowing the use of the park for open air political meetings.[85]

One reason for the slowing of the advance of Socialism in the latter half of the decade was the sharpening of the ideological opposition: collectivism provoked a strong reaction. One local manifestation was the rise of the Young England Patriotic Association, which began in North Salford in May 1894. Founded to challenge Socialism by using similar methods – debates in the clubs and open-air meetings – and addressing itself to the same class of the population, Young England preached a simple but effectual message: Socialism is atheistic, Socialism will destroy family life, Socialism is the antithesis of individualism. For many years its chairman and leading figure was R. J. Macartney, a young man of Protestant Irish origins. From Broughton, the YEPA spread out into East Lancashire. Eventually it became part of the national Anti-Socialist Union, Macartney making his name lecturing for its North West Counties branch.[86] At the outset, it was denied that Young England was linked to any political party, but the way it shamelessly played the Orange card indicated that it was a modern manifestation of old Protestant Toryism. Just as Socialism provided an ideological education for future Labour activists, so the Young England Association provided a grounding for working-class Conservatives, prominent amongst whom were future Salford councillors John Royle and Abraham Williamson. Eventually superceded by 'Conservative Labour' organisations more directly controlled by the party, Young England's existence was ended in 1912. It had, however, fought collectivism for 18 years in the Manchester area.

Socialists had to contend with other forms of individualist and patriotic reaction in the Nineties. Founded in response to advances in trades union organisation, a resurrected National Free Labour League had an active Manchester branch, which provided strike breakers in the great Engineers' dispute in 1897. A more potent anti-Socialist force than either individualism or 'Free Labour' was the extreme patriotism provoked by Imperialism, which culminated in the Jingoism of the Boer War years. No Socialist candidate contested the 'Khaki election' of 1900. In South Salford Sir Henry Howorth's successor, J. G. Groves, a local brewer, won handsomely. The Social Democrats knew that if they had contested the seat, as they said they fully intended to do before the Boer War came along, they would have been humiliated. On the electoral front, by 1900 Socialists seem to have been back where they were a decade before.

The rise of Labour, however, was always about more than contesting elections. In the course of the Nineties Socialists were able to play leading parts in a number of movements which helped to establish their credentials locally and nationally. In 1892 the cause of the unemployed was once more taken up and placed firmly on the political agenda. Socialists played their part in the extension of trades unionism to the mass of largely hitherto unorganised workers, and in doing so forced the older trade organisations to contemplate the idea of an independent party of Labour. And by agitating for action on such local matters as sanitary reform, slum demolition and improved education they helped to extend their credibility not only with the working class but also with some of the clergy and other professional people.

Unemployment in Salford became pressing in the winter of 1892–3 and once more it was Socialists rather than the trade union movement which tried to provide the spur to local action. The public authorities proved somewhat more sensitive than a decade before. In Salford the Borough Council set up a sub-committee to register the unemployed in December 1892. The following April the Council opened a permanent 'Labour Exchange'.[87] The economy began its upturn in 1895, which vindicated political economists. But few did not expect unemployment to fail to return, which vindicated Socialists, whose stance on unemployment brought them increasing appreciation with the working class.

They were to earn even more through their part in the spread of New Unionism. As trade improved towards the end of the Eighties there had been a general trade union revival. First on the scene was the Pendleton, Pendlebury, Clifton and Kearsley Miners' Association. Founded in June 1888, it was the first successful miners' organisation in the district for twenty years. In the early Nineties New Unionism found fertile ground amongst transport workers in Salford. In 1892 the Amalgamated Society of Railway Servants had a mere 500 members in Salford, though there was a lively branch in Pendleton. Kept very much at arm's length by the management, a drive for members was launched. In that year evidence was assembled to put before the Select Committee of the House of Commons looking into working conditions on the railways, for which the Pendleton branch gave an illuminated address to Councillor Albert Fletcher for his services.[88]

In these years trades unionism extended into another sector of Manchester and Salford's transport system, the horsemen. In 1890 there were perhaps as many as 14,000 horsemen in Manchester and Salford. The road transport system was vast and fragmented but broadly they fell into two categories – lurrymen and carters working for railway companies, breweries, coal merchants and other employers, and 'car drivers' working for Tramway companies or as hackney carriage men licensed by the local authorities. Working conditions were notoriously harsh. It was not unusual for the working day to run from early in the morning to late at night, with no set time allowed for meals. For this, carters were paid weekly wages varying from 17 to 23 shillings. By 1890 three unions had established themselves, two for carters and one for the tramway workers and hackney carriage men. The first to be set up was the United Carters, led by James Plunkett. Alongside it was the Manchester and Salford Lurrymen and Carters Union, whose secretary was a Salford man, John Kelly. And in 1889 George T. Jackson organised the Manchester and Salford Tramways Employees Association.[89] Union leaders soon realised the advantages of amalgamation, and, in February 1892, Kelly, desiring to link 'corporation men, brewery men, and all description of horseman into one solid society' organised the Manchester Salford and District Lurrymen and Carters Union. Meanwhile, Jackson had widened his local tramways union into the Northern Counties Amalgamated Association of Tramway and Hackney Carriage employers by recruiting in Bolton, Preston, Burnley, Huddersfield, Leicester and Nottingham. By 1893 he had 3,500 members. Soon after, Kelly's union joined with Jackson's, forming the Amalgamated Association of Tramway, Hackney Carriage Employees and Horsemen in General. However, the United Carters remained separate from the Amalgamated Association, which, under Jackson's leadership was to grow very considerably in the next decade. By 1906 it had a hundred branches with a membership of 13,000, spreading as far north as Dundee and as far south at Portsmouth.[90]

The construction of the Manchester Ship Canal between 1887 and 1894, and the opening of the Manchester docks, the greater part of which were in the Ordsall district of Salford, greatly enlarged the number of transport workers in the local economy. The docks began business on 1st January 1894, the Queen officially opened the Port of Manchester the following May.[91] The presence of large numbers of ununionised navvies, and, later on, dockworkers, was a challenge Socialists and the New Unionism could not ignore. In late 1890 the Navvies, Bricklayers and General Labourers' Union began holding recruiting meetings. These met with

Trade Union leader, George T. Jackson of the Amalgamated Association of Tramway, Hackney-Carriage Employees and Horsemen in General. In politics a Liberal. (*Pike's Contemporary Biographies of Manchester and Salford*)

some success. The district organiser was Leonard Hall, a leading local Socialist.[92] The following year Hall helped to organise the Lancashire and Adjoining Counties Labour Amalgamation and became its general secretary.

The Manchester docks opened at a time when the boom of the early Nineties started to give way to recession. Men from other ports, notably Liverpool and Hull, came to Salford seeking work. The reaction of local men was to send deputations to the dock manager claiming these new jobs. A demand from the Union for eight hour shifts 'to spread the work' was ignored.[93] This was the background against which No. 9 branch of the National Union of Dock Labourers was formed in Salford in 1894. It did not have to wait long for its first test of strength with the management. A demand that the Union men should wear their union badge at work was refused by the company, and men wearing the badge were locked out. A rough and fierce dispute ensued, in which the employers were aided by 'Free Labour' support and the men, led by Thomas Purves, secretary of No. 9 branch, an SDF man, were strongly supported by local Socialists. The dispute ended in victory for the Ship Canal Company. No dockworker was allowed to wear the union badge at work. Nonetheless, the Union survived. A year later, when it opened its new club house in Stamford Street, Ordsall, it was estimated that about half the men in the docks were members, and Purves was still branch secretary.[94]

In 1890 attempts were started to unionise textile finishing, tailoring and the predominantly female workforce in the mackintosh and shirtmaking trades. For the Bolton-based Bleachers, Finishers and Dyers Association (founded in the late Sixties) Salford was a black spot. Pay was poor and scarcely anyone was in the union. The new approach had some successes. By 1893 membership of the Bleachers Union had gone up in Salford from 90 or so to about 600, and an increase of from four to five shillings a week had been secured. However, most of the workers in dressing, dyeing and finishing were still outside the union, both in Salford and in the wider Manchester/Bolton district. These years also saw efforts to unionise the predominantly Jewish trades of tailoring and shirtmaking. Once again, although branches of the Amalgamated Society of India Rubber Workers were started, it proved extremely difficult to improve pay and conditions in trades in which women and poor immigrant workers were so routinely sweated. Nonetheless, organisation went forward in neglected corners of the textile and clothing trades.[95]

In the changing world of engineering, new unions emerged to recruit men ineligible to join the old established Amalgamated Society of Engineers. In 1891, a branch of the National United Trade Society of Engineers was formed, and five years later, on the eve of the great engineering lock-out, the Amalgamated Society of Toolmakers, Engineers and Machinists started up in Salford. These years also saw the beginning of the Electrical Trades Union.[96] Trades unionism also began to spread to hitherto undreamed of areas: Paper Mill workers, shopworkers and life insurance agents and collectors. And, finally, in these years, tradesmen defeated in past battles picked themselves up and re-formed their unions. A General Union of Joiners and Carpenters was resurrected in 1890.[97] Men and women were being organised in trades hitherto thought unorganisable. And that was something new. Socialists had played important roles in this. Labour was on the move.

The spread of New Unionism forced old trade unionists to modify some of their preconceptions; grudgingly craftsmen began to acknowledge those beneath them. In 1890, after lengthy discussion, the Trades Council resolved to 'admit such other labour and industrial organisations, not strictly designated as of skilled artisans, as the Executive Committee may recommend for admission'.[98] Old Labour organisations were forced to take notice of the Socialist programme by the vigour and action of its supporters. In 1892 New Unions and Socialist Societies demonstrated with Trades Council Unions at the first Manchester May Day rally, at which the formation of an Independent Labour Party was announced. 'Labour Sunday' in Manchester on 5th May 1895 was celebrated by the largest ILP meeting ever held there. The five platforms included one from which speeches were made in Yiddish. The main address of the day was given by Keir Hardie, who, that evening lectured on behalf of the West Salford ILP at the Pendleton Co-operative hall, supported by Dr Pankhurst.[99]

The message of Socialism was also able to make an increasing impact in the Nineties because of the sharpening conflict between capital and labour. In the latter part of 1893, nationally the scene was dominated by the great lock-out of the miners, but there were some local disputes, the one which attracted most attention being a strike at Reddaway & Co., Pendleton. Threatened with big pay cuts, the belting and hosepipe weavers struck, the dispute lasting some three months. The hiring of blacklegs led to violence on the picket-line, followed by prosecutions in the magistrates' courts. Despite support from the General Labourers Union, the workers lost. 'None of the men who had misbehaved themselves during the strike', Mr Reddaway bluntly informed the *Reporter*, 'would ever find employment at these works again'.[100]

The most significant example of the developing confrontation was the national lock-out of the engineering workers between July 1897 and January 1898. The Amalgamated Society of Engineers was the acknowledged archetype of the skilled workers' union, and had not been involved in a strike for 50 years. The battle began in London and spread to the provinces. Its immediate cause was the demand for the Eight Hour Day. The real friction, however, was over 'de-skilling' and the increasing use of machinery. Once started, the dispute spread rapidly and soon, according to contemporary estimates, 80,000 men were affected.[101] The dispute came to be regarded in trade-union history as the first major example of the skilled and the 'unskilled' fighting together against capital. On the employers' side it led to the growth of a Federation large and powerful enough to square up to a union with some 90,000 members. The industrial scene was changing: localism and fragmentation were being replaced by big battalions.

Despite the scale of the conflict, only about half of Salford's fifty or so engineering firms were directly involved. At Mather & Platt, which employed 1600 men and boys, not a day's work was lost. Only about 420 men, a third of the total membership of the ASE branches in the borough, were directly involved. However, both unionists and employers subscribed heavily to their respective sides in the battle, and all understood its significance. The Masters Federation won. In January 1898 the union withdrew the demand for a 48 hour week, and its grip on the old pattern of rigid job demarcation loosened: resistance to new machinery, however, continued. Union membership fell, and for a time recruitment remained difficult. However, the demand for the 48 hour week remained part of its programme. The first firm in Salford to concede this was Mather & Platt, who did so unilaterally.[102]

The events of the Nineties advanced the Socialist message and began to erode the sharp distinctions between 'skilled' and the rest of the working class. A growing sense of Labour unity can be detected. The great engineering lock-out engendered a sense of solidarity, with Friendly and Co-operative Societies giving financial help and organising fund-raising activities. But these advances should not be exaggerated; old industrial attitudes and old political loyalties were not easily surrendered when challenged by Socialists, however convincingly. Moreover, as we have seen, the more Socialist ideas took hold, the clearer the representatives of Capital and the advocates of individualism became about the need to assert opposition. Most seriously of all, the heady atmosphere of the Boer War demonstrated (once again) the power of patriotism and imperialism to override local, class, and indeed almost all other loyalties.[103]

In these years Socialists were able to make an impact on society beyond the working class by raising the 'condition of England' question. In particular, they were able to force the supporters of individualism to face up to the failure of industrial capitalism to reduce the extent of poverty over the past century. In Salford the issue which concerned people most was slum housing. The matter came to the fore as a major issue following the publication of Dr Tatham's Report for 1887. The housing question provided Socialists with the opportunity to make common cause with other social reformers, and take a lead. The Salford Workingmen's Sanitary Association had its origins in a meeting on 'How to improve the homes of the people', one of a series of conferences for working men promoted by the Rev. Henry Smart, minister of Gravel Lane Methodist Church, one of several Salford clergymen actively embracing social action. After speeches from the Dean of Manchester and the Bishop of Salford on the disgraceful state of the housing of the poor, a good deal of anger was expressed at the failure of the Council to do anything constructive. The Artisans Dwelling Act was permissive, and Salford had exercised its right to do nothing. When Councillor Bradbury ridiculed the idea of providing housing on the rates, the meeting reacted by proposing the formation of an association. A 25-man Committee, which included Socialists such as W. K. Hall, George Smart and William Horrocks was elected.[104]

The Council came under immediate attack. Why did it not apply the Artisans Dwellings Act, asked John Marshall of the SDF, in a letter to the *Reporter*. It spent money on baths, libraries and museums – why not on houses? The Reporter published a series of articles. One described back-to-back housing opening on to a street twenty-nine inches wide, with a midden opposite. Another described a row of back-to-backs forming the right hand side of one Salford street and the left hand side of another. The measurement from pavement to the eaves of the houses was eight feet. Some were one-roomed, others two: 'built for a race of Lilliputians', it concluded. The author pointed out that the Council had powers under a series of local Improvement Acts and the Artisans Dwellings Acts but had chosen not to use them. The Council responded in June, setting up a committee on insanitary housing. It reported in October, listing the most insanitary pockets in the borough, and recommended the erection of new dwellings for 900 persons.[105]

By now, Socialists were raising the wider subject of 'municipal misgovernment', and discussing the idea of petitioning for a Royal Commission on Salford's local government. A proposal to establish a Municipal League in Salford, the object being to give working people a voice in municipal affairs, was made at a meeting in January 1890. The importance of getting working men elected on to the Boards of Guardians, the School Board and the Council was urged, and the problems of financial qualification, morning meetings, etc. were discussed. Its members included George Evans.[106]

Housing focused resentment against the slowness of Salford's Council to act on the matter of public health generally. One of the main critics was Dr William Fraser, who attacked the quality of much new housing in Salford. He was shortly to publish *The Salford Death Rate Scandal. A Pamphlet for the People* and contribute a series of articles in the *Reporter* on 'Sanitary Salford' contained scathing attacks on the Council's inaction.[107] Under this sort of pressure, things began to happen. A Company to erect Dwellings for the Poor was started, and, in November 1890, the Council began a scheme of slum clearance. At a meeting of the Salford Workingmen's Sanitary Association Evans and other speakers strongly urged the Council not to be satisfied with clearance, but to go on and build houses. The mayor said that the plan was to build one large model lodging house in Bloom Street, and others, if private enterprise did not step in. The meeting found this limited ambition unsatisfactory, and made its feelings plain.[108]

The Sanitary Association was very active in 1891. Their efforts received plenty of support from the clergy, Catholic and Protestant alike, the Bishop of Salford accepting the presidency of the Association. In point of fact, with the forcing of the Council into one slum clearance scheme and the erection of the model lodging house for 258 males, which opened in October 1894, it had shot its bolt. The scheme involved almost ten thousand square yards of property south of Chapel Street, and the clearing of buildings on four smaller sites in the Blackfriars Road and Greengate areas. Apart from the erection of the Bloom Street Model Lodging house, all that was built in this first era of 'Council housing' were 36 artisans cottages in Linsley and Hopwood Streets and 69 tenement dwellings in Queen Street.[109] Other dwellings erected by the Council were to be built in 1903, 1905, and 1909. The grand total of 'council housing' erected before the Great War in Salford (excluding the model Lodging House for 285 men) amounted to a mere 701 dwellings. Set against the scale of the problem this amounted to the smallest of gestures. Nonetheless, the Salford Workingmen's Sanitary Association was dissolved in December 1894, claiming it had achieved its objects by exposing insanitary dwellings and calling the attention of the Health Committee of the Corporation to their duty.[110] Socialists (Evans to the fore) had played a vigorous part in its activities.

In the wake of the Hunter Scandal, yet another crisis in Salford's local government, the Financial Muddle of 1894–7, gave Socialists a further opportunity to play a part in public affairs, which they took with both hands. On the eve of the 1894 Council elections, John Hempsall of the SDF, in his role of Elective

Auditor, made Salford's large budget deficit a major issue, receiving strong backing from the *Reporter*, which attacked the Council over its 'conspiracy of silence' and unseemly efforts to scapegoat Council officials. At public meetings and in print Hempsall proved an effective critic. His pamphlet, *The Muddle in Salford. Twelve Months Work as Borough Auditor,* was published by the SDF the following year.[111] All in all, if Socialists were not yet able to influence the Council from inside, they emerged as an external force to be reckoned with.

The passions aroused by the Boer War caused divisions and re-alignments within the ranks of Socialism. Blatchford, always the old soldier, took a strongly patriotic line.[112] Most Socialists opposed the war, Keir Hardie in particular taking a strong Pro-Boer stance. On the other hand, many rank and file trades unionists came out for Queen and Country, and Fabians generally sided with the Liberal Imperialists.

Nonetheless, despite Socialism being at a low ebb, 1900 saw developments of huge importance in Labour history. The first was the formation of the Labour Representation Committee, a coup engineered by Keir Hardie to by-pass opposition to political involvement on the part of the more conservative union leaders. Ramsay MacDonald became LRC secretary, and thereby began to make a name for himself as a Labour leader. The second was the legal judgment in favour of the Taff Vale Railway Company against its employees. This case (and that of Quinn *v.* Leatham) threw the legal rights and immunities of trades unions into confusion, and made union leaders think more seriously than ever before of political involvement. The Labour Representation Committee was to be the penultimate step in the emergence of the modern Labour party (which duly declared independence in 1906). Set up to elect Socialists and trades unionists to Parliament, the LRC committed Labour to 'the Parliamentary road to Socialism', a strategy which very soon provoked a reaction on the left. Pragmatism suggested that reforms through Parliament were the only way to Socialism in Britain: Socialists saw 'reformism' as collaboration with the enemy.

Although a Manchester and Salford Representation Committee was not established until 1903, and scarcely did anything for another two years, the regiments and intelligence units of Labour's as yet unmustered army began to re-form and recruit in the years immediately after the Boer War. One reason for this was the prolonged depression which followed the war-time boom. To the workers, especially the general labourers, the winters of 1903–4 and 1904–5 brought immense privation. Socialists once more threw themselves into the activities of local unemployed workers' associations. Early in the winter of 1903–4 Salford Council appointed a sub-committee to look into what might be done for the unemployed and their families. When its report was debated, the general response was unsympathetic. A letter writer in the local paper invited the Council to go 'any morning to the vicinity of John Street, Pendleton where they would see children running to school pale-faced, bare-legged and bare-footed, which in this exceptionally prosperous Christian borough of ours is heart-rending.' Plenty of hearts remained unrent.[113]

In some ways the winter of 1904–5 was a turning point in the history of unemployment. The findings of the great social inquiries of the time began to enter public discourse. Some began to use the concepts and language of Charles

Booth, who was quoted by the Rev. Neader Anderton in a lecture in Salford in 1905: 'our modern system of industry will not work without some unemployed margin, some reserve of labour.'[114] William Beveridge was saying the same thing: Socialists had been saying it for over twenty years. In early 1905 Arthur Smith set out a Socialist 'Manchester Scheme' for the unemployed in a lecture to the South Salford SDF. A Minister of Labour should be appointed by the government, and a 'Labour Bureau', where the unemployed could be registered should be opened in every town or district. Another Socialist tactic in 1905 was the 'Hunger March'. Arrangements were made to organise a march on London by the unemployed of Manchester and the surrounding towns.[115] These marches (of which there were a number from different industrial centres that year) made a big impression on the country, and were a factor in forcing the Conservative government to pass the Unemployed Workmen's Act.

Important as the first piece of legislation to accept that society had some responsibility towards the unemployed, the Act did little more than give local authorities powers to form 'Distress Committees'. Trades unionists assumed that, amongst the latter, places would be found for working-class representatives, and for the first time allied themselves with those involved in the unemployed workers movement. A Trades Council Committee was set up, with a sub-committee for Salford which included representatives from the SDF, the ILP and the Women's Co-operative Guild. When the membership of Salford Distress Committee was finally announced it consisted of the mayor, four aldermen and six councillors, twelve Guardians and the seven persons 'experienced in dealing with distress' on charitable bodies. A deputation from the unemployed which asked for trades union representation was snubbed: Labour's sole representative was Joseph Nuttall, by virtue of his being one of the councillors on the committee.[116]

Despite the fact that the Act carried no provision for Distress Committees to do anything more than collect statistics, the snub was felt acutely. At Salford meetings scathing references were made to the meanness, ignorance and vulgarity of certain committee members. However, as the winter of 1905–6 arrived and the scale of local unemployment remained undiminished, the new mayor, Alderman Frankenburg, went out of his way to be conciliatory. The request for public works met with a response: the River Conservancy Committee took on 250 men and the Highways and Paving Committee and the Electricity Committee took another seventy. With this, and a subscription list 'of sufficient dimensions', the mayor expressed the hope that the worst suffering could be alleviated. He was being sanguine: unemployment continued to be a nagging social problem well into 1906, and the Manchester and Salford Unemployed Association continued to hold meetings, demonstrations and devise other ways to confront the authorities.[117]

And there were other causes which gave Socialists and trades unionists scope for action and co-operation. One such was the continuing criticism of Salford's borough council record, and a Socialist successor of Hempsall in the role of Elective Auditor was able to mount a well-argued 'clean government' campaign. In his pamphlet *In Darkest Salford* (1899) William Hunt attacked the Council for its 'bitter factionalism', and Hunt also mounted vigorous support for municipal trading, pointing out in 1902 how gas profits over the past decade had been used to relieve the rates in Salford.[118] The year previously the Council has passed a resolution on the paying of 'fair wages' by Council contractors, a decision the ILP and the trades unions had been pressing for some time. In late 1904 the Socialists on the Council were successful in having a resolution adopted that a minimum wage should henceforth be paid to all Council employees, which, if modified later, was nonetheless a considerable achievement.

But no domestic issue in the dozen or so years down to the Great War caused more concern than the housing question. Interest in slum clearance and rehousing the poor revived with the rebuilding of the old infantry barracks site in Regent Road. The site was acquired by the Health Committee, who vowed to make its redevelopment 'the finest piece of corporation property in Manchester and Salford.' In fact, their efforts to do so high-lighted the problems encountered when local authorities overcame their reluctance to interfere with market forces in land and building. It was pointed out that slum clearance so far had led to an increase rather than a decrease in overcrowding in these wards, and that when the Council built new housing the poor could not afford the rents. This was certainly the case with the Barracks site, on which were erected 32 shops and upwards of 300 new houses. Even when the Health Committee agreed to reduce the rents a little, the same complaint was made.[119]

The principal Socialist contribution towards finding solutions to these and other associated problems came from people such as T. R. Marr, a Fabian active in the University Settlement in Ancoats. In an address in 1904, he outlined the findings of the recent Report of the Inter-Departmental Committee on Physical Deterioration, which had been prompted by the alarming number of men from the industrial towns who volunteered for army service in the Boer War and had been rejected as physically undersized. This Report was very influential. Hearts that had long remained unrent by the misery of the unemployed and the poor, became quite alarmed at the notion that industrial society was creating a stunted race unable to defend the Empire. In fact the 'physically undersized' men from the industrial towns were soon to come forward and 'save' the Empire. Nonetheless, the Report was correct in emphasising the considerable differences in physique between those of different social classes, and within the working class. Anthropometric measurement of samples of Salford Board School boys in 1903 confirmed this. Considerable variations were revealed between boys from Grecian Street School in Broughton and those from John Street School in Pendleton. By the age of thirteen, boys from the former school were, on average, almost four inches taller and sixteen pounds heavier than those from the latter. Salford boys measured were, on average, *seven inches* shorter than boys of the same age in Boston, USA.[120] The Inter-Departmental Report gave a filip to practical attempts to institute new social policies and to the provision of decent housing for the working class, and Marr put the case for Councils to stop nibbling at the problem and produce comprehensive plans for slum clearance and rehousing. He also made it plain that he did not think councils, as at present constituted, were prepared to deal with so vast a problem. How right he was. In the period between the Boer War and the Great War there were only three municipal housing projects in Salford: the old Barracks site which provided 317 houses, the provision of another 228 houses in Seaford Road, Pendleton, and the erection of 51 houses in Springfield Lane in Salford township. A quarter of a century of effort on the housing front had produced little if any improvement.[121] There were a few less slums and a few less back-to-back houses, but the problem was too vast, the will too weak, and the means too puny to achieve much else.

The Inter-Departmental Report, and the great social surveys of the time helped to stimulate a growing discussion on the extent and causes of poverty. A figure often quoted at that time was that there were 10,000 families in the borough, about a quarter of the total, who had to subsist on less than £1 per week. In 1904 the Rev. J. A. Storey estimated 'on Mr Rowntree's basis the number of people in Salford in down-right poverty would be 62,000, while Mr Charles Booth, the London expert, would make them 66,300. 'Now these 66,000, for I think this number would be found not to exceed, but to fall short of the mark, cannot afford to pay even a reasonable rent.' [122]

Reaction against the jingoism of the Boer War, the Taff Vale judgement, rising unemployment and the developing focus on housing and poverty brought a Socialist revival. The first move was an alliance between the ILP and other 'Progressives' in Manchester to fight the School Board election in 1900. Attracting members from all over the great double-barrelled city, the formation of a Manchester Central branch gave the ILP a boost it badly needed. By 1906, with 13 branches, the ILP in Manchester and Salford was in better shape than for the past few years. The SDF also revived, though total membership of these societies remained unimpressive. By 1906 the Manchester and Salford ILP had 810: the SDF was much smaller. Yet their influence was out of all proportion to their numbers.[123]

In 1901 no Socialist or Labour candidate in Manchester or Salford ventured to stand for municipal election. However, the following year Joseph Nuttall became the first Salford Socialist ever to be elected on to the Council. A stamp-cutter by trade, and general secretary of his union, Nuttall was to become secretary of the Manchester and Salford Labour Representation Committee as well as secretary of the Manchester and Salford ILP. Nuttall's triumph had taken the best part of two decades of Socialist effort. He was re-elected in 1905, and the following year made a JP. In 1903 he was joined on the council by John Hayes, president of the West Salford ILP, a member of the postmen's union, who got in for St Thomas's ward, Pendleton. In 1904 another Socialist was elected, J. F. Thompson for Trafford ward. The following year H. Mottershead, another ILP postman, was successful, but A. A. Purcell of the SDF, general secretary of the French Polisher's Union, was narrowly defeated though he was elected the following year. If Socialists and Labour representatives made something of a breakthrough in these years, it was very modest. By and large, Labour candidates were less successful in Salford than in such districts of Manchester as Bradford, Openshaw, Blackley and Newton Heath. Even in Manchester, success was very moderate: in 1905 only nine of the 124 members of the Council were Labour representatives.[124]

By 1904 local trades unionism had become more politically active. What was galvanizing them was the Taff Vale case. Unionists were also alarmed by the growth of unemployment, and 1904 found John Hempsall speaking on the case for Protectionism under the auspices of the Tariff Reform League. That same year, joint Jewish and Labour meetings were held to protest against the Aliens Immigration Bill. These years saw the start of a period of growth in the national membership of trades unions. At the end of 1907 total membership stood at just under 2.5 million, half a million more than at the end of 1904. As a Board of Trade Report pointed out, this was 'a greater rate of increase than in any previous three year period since statistics were compiled' (in the 1860s).[125]

The political revival after the Boer War led to plans to put up candidates for Parliament in the next general election. What these revealed was a state of some disunity. The ILP had plans in some constituencies, and the SDF in others, and the latter looked with little favour on the growing influence of the Labour Representation Committee. In August 1905 the LRC in London indicated to G. D. Kelley, secretary of the Manchester and Salford Trades Council, that they had under consideration the question of establishing a permanent organisation to deal with municipal and local elections. The Trades Council agreed to raise a fund to pay the expenses of Labour men fighting local elections. It was also decided to hold a conference of delegates of all Labour societies to consider the question of getting more representatives on to local councils – and to include not just those affiliated to the Trades Council. This was held the week following, and it was resolved that all the societies represented there should contribute a penny a week to a central fund, the stipulation being those candidates should accept the conditions imposed by the national Labour Representation Committee. This posed no difficulty for the ILP, whose members were in positions of influence on the Manchester LRC. However, the South Salford SDF declined to associate: they had decided that the class struggle, rather than deals with the trades unions, remained the only real basis for Socialism to advance.[126]

Almost immediately the Conservative government disintegrated, and a General Election was fixed for the following January. The Liberals, sensing victory, offered local deals to the LRC. Labour agreed not to contest West Salford, and moved their candidate, J. R. Clynes, to South Salford. When the Liberals offered an agreement in North East Manchester, Clynes was transferred there. In return, the LRC offered no opposition to the Liberal Hilaire Belloc in South Salford. The SDF (having now reversed its previous decision and come into the LRC) agreed and Belloc was able to oust Groves by 852 votes.[127] The scale of the Liberal victory in 1906 took everyone by surprise. In Salford all three seats went to the Liberals. In Manchester four of the six (including that of Balfour, the late Prime Minister) fell to them as well, whilst the others were won by Labour: Clynes in North East Manchester, G. D. Kelley in South Manchester, and J. Hodge won Gorton. In parliament there were now 29 members under the banner of the Labour Representation Committee, plus another 24 Liberals of working-class origins. The Labour Party, as the twentieth century was to know it, made its appearance.

The revival of Liberalism and the emergence of a Labour Party, effectively the instrument of the trades unions, precipitated a move to the left amongst Socialists. In Manchester and Salford there were splits and re-alignments accompanied by intense debate about the state of contemporary capitalism and what Socialists should be doing. The return of unemployment in the winter of 1907–8, the failure of the government to come up with anything new, and the growing spirit of confrontation in industrial relations also encouraged this, as did the success of Victor Grayson, the first avowed Socialist to be elected to Parliament, at the Colne Valley by-election of 1907.

By this time, the Left in the Manchester area was again in crisis. The ILP had ceased to grow and began to fragment. In 1908 the SDF withdrew from the Labour Representation Committee. Early in 1909 the *Reporter* noted that Victor Grayson was bent on forming a new Socialist party separate from the ILP. He had won over Blatchford, the *Clarion* and the Clarion Clubs, 'many of which have recently sprang into existence'. However, so far, the SDF stood aloof. In 1910 steps were taken to unite SDF, ILP militants and unattached Socialists. A Manchester and District Socialist Representation Committee was established, consisting of six from the ILP, six from the SDF and nine from unattached Socialist groups. The following year, the British Socialist Party was formed after a conference in Salford. In essence the BSP was the old SDF, enlarged to include ILP dissidents and other unattached Socialists. By the middle of 1912 the BSP was overshadowing the ILP as the dominant Socialist organisation in Manchester.[128]

The success of the Labour Representation led to the formation of a Conservative Labour party, which appeared in Salford in 1904. It declared its opposition to Socialism and 'any section of thought that may seek to make use of trade union branches for political ends.' How separate this body was from the Young England Patriotic Association is not clear, though it is significant that its organising secretary was R. J. Macartney. It claimed to have been started by Conservative working men, the leading three of whom were Abraham Williamson, John Royle and Frank Fearneley. The latter was an ex-marine from Preston who came to Salford after his service days, and became an active member of the congregation of St Bartholomew's. So active, indeed, that the rector made him a lay-missioner. Together with six of his friends he was in at the start of the National Conservative Labour Party in Manchester. In addition to the Manchester and Salford branches there were soon others in Stockport, Crewe, Heywood, Rochdale and Oldham.[129]

The first efforts of Conservative Labour in Salford were not very impressive. Nonetheless missionary work by the Conservative Labour Party Van, lectures and meetings spread the word, and, by the final year of Balfour's government several branches had been formed. The one in Ordsall was named 'Hampson Lodge', in honour of Councillor Fred Hampson. And an appreciative government made Abraham Williamson a JP in 1905. Williamson had been one of the Young England activists who made names for themselves in the Anti Pro-Boer Crusade in Lancashire. When the Conservative Labour Party started, he became its first treasurer.[130] Both Young England and the Conservative Labour party were shaken into greater activity by the successes of their political opponents in 1906, and remained part of the local political scene until absorbed into the Conservative Party organisation in 1912.

Conservatism was not the reason why, between 1906 and the Great War, Socialist and Labour successes in local elections were so few. In February 1907 James Dudley, a 'Socialist Labour and Trade Unionist candidate', got in for St Paul's ward in a by-election. Although that November, James Openshaw, an ILP postman, won in Seedley, Councillor Thompson was defeated in Trafford, and a Young England Patriotic Association man defeated Dr Shand in St Paul's ward. In 1909 all six candidates were defeated. Rivalry between the various Socialist and Labour bodies on the ground, poor organisation and lack of money made electoral success difficult to achieve. Although the Manchester and Salford Labour Representation Committee was placed on a permanent footing after 1906, its impact before the Great War was surprisingly weak. The only role it performed was providing candidates at parliamentary elections. As we have seen, in the pre-war years Socialism was moving left, and the gap with the bulk of the trades unionists was, if anything, widening. There was little evidence of voters defecting from the Liberals to Labour. Most importantly, there was as yet no mass-electorate. If just over half the Salford ratepayers were working-class, only about thirty per cent of working-class men were local or national voters. Even allowing for all this, Labour's performance in local government elections in Salford in the pre-War years was unimpressive. From a peak of five councillors (out of 64) in 1906, their number fell to four in 1911, and one in 1913. In Manchester the picture was a little better, with the nine (out of 124) in 1904 remaining the average until 1911–12, rising to sixteen in 1912, falling again to fifteen in 1913.[131]

The position was rather different in the parliamentary elections of 1910, with the LRC being actively involved, and the Lib-Lab pact remaining operative. In the January election in Manchester, Clynes held the seat he won in 1906, and J. E. Sutton, leader of the Labour group on Manchester Town Council, was successful in East Manchester, and Hodge got in again for Gorton. The Liberals won three seats, but took a dim view of the fact that they narrowly lost the South West to a Unionist, because an Independent Labour candidate had made it a three cornered fight. After a bitter dispute between the local ILP and the SDF, A. A. Purcell fought West Salford as an 'Independent Labour' candidate and polled 2396, the largest vote for any Socialist in Lancashire.[132] Yet this did not prevent G. W. Agnew winning comfortably for the Liberals, who once again, won all three Salford seats. No Socialist candidate contested North or South Salford.

In the second (December) election of 1910 the Socialists were unable to make any interventions in Manchester. Clynes and Sutton held their seats, as did Hodge; Liberals won in the other four. In Salford, Agnew and Byles were victorious once more in the West and North divisions, whilst a Conservative, Montague Barlow, beat a Liberal in South Salford, after Belloc had withdrawn. No Socialist challenge was offered.[133] Lack of money and inadequate organisation were reasons, but by now the Left was beginning to focus on the industrial front, where an unprecedented Labour unrest was starting to manifest itself. The years 1911, 1912 and 1913 saw the sort of massive and widespread national industrial confrontations Socialism had so often predicted, but rarely experienced. Many concerned transport workers, and Salford found itself one of the main national centres of industrial unrest.

The cause of the discontent of 1911–13, however, was not unemployment, which had fallen since 1908–9, but the inflationary increase in the price of food and coal.[134] What this triggered amongst tens of thousands of low paid workers was something new: a widespread spirit of anger, unity and militance which proved capable of shaking the government. The location of the first industrial battle of 1911 was the nation's docklands. Because of the casual and migratory nature of their work it had been traditionally hard to unionise port workers. In the past, when a union had been formed and managed to get concessions out of the Ship Canal Company, the men often fell away afterwards. The first moves to increase the strength of dockers and transport workers in Salford took place in April 1911. The chosen strategy was Federation. At a public demonstration of dockers, firemen and sailors addressed by Socialist speakers, Purcell told them they had now registered themselves under the National Federation of Transport Workers. Tom Mann called for the co-operation of railwaymen and carters, not merely by being identified with their own unions, but with the Federation, which had come into existence three months before.[135]

The great transport strike of 1911 began in June with the extension of a national strike of the Seamen's and Firemen's Union to Salford docks. The seamen demanded a pay rise, improved terms of employment, union recognition and a conciliation board. When the ship owners tried to import blackleg labour, the dockers came out on unofficial strike, an act of altruism which brought them great privation. However, the dockers saw in this a chance to improve *their* pay and conditions. The strike leaders were confident that by striking in the busy summer season, at a time of generally good industrial conditions, they would catch the employers napping. The Seamen's employers were soon willing to settle, but the seamen refused until the dockers' employers agreed to *their* terms. Soon the port of Manchester was idle and the pickets winning: no strike-breaking labour was entering the gates. Eighty four ships were tied up. The grip was further tightened when 4,000 carters and lurrymen came out in sympathy and there was strong, though unofficial, support from local railwaymen.[136]

The first week of July saw serious rioting. Police protecting food vans and supplies of newsprint were subjected to violent attacks by carters, and reinforcements

Salford Dock Strike, 1911. A show of hands being taken by Mr Tom Fox. (Local History Collection, Peel Park)

were drafted in from other towns. 'Never before has Salford and Manchester witnessed such scenes,' declared the *Reporter*. When pickets tried to prevent coal leaving Pendleton colliery, this led to the miners walking out in sympathy. Troops and metropolitan policemen were hastily drafted in and the Government sent out a senior civil servant from the Treasury to bring the sides together. Salford was subjected to a virtual military occupation, which ended the fighting. Pickets ceased to bar the movement of foodstuffs. A local coal shortage, produced by the colliers' strike, shut down the big Salford mills. The streets were thronged with idle, anxious workers. Friday witnessed the last scene in a remarkable week of mass industrial confrontation – a demonstration by the dockers' wives. About 2,000 Salford women marched into Manchester in support of the men on strike. Clad in tattered shawls and gowns, many with infants in their arms, the women were visibly exhausted by the march. 'The procession in its every aspect bore the impress of poverty' commented the *Reporter*.[137]

The first great transport battle of 1911 ended the following week. The seamen got what they wanted. The dockers also won a victory. However, the dockers would not go back to work until the carters got what they struck for. At the 'Peace Conference' at Manchester Town Hall it was soon announced that the railwaymen, carters, dockers, watermen and sailors all agreed to go back to work together. The workers were jubilant. It was a great victory, though it had not been won without great hardship. But they thought it had all been worth it: the strike had brought knowledge of the appalling conditions of thousands of dockers' and seamen's families into the public domain.

A second great transport strike followed hard on the heels of the Dock strike. The first ever national Railway Strike began locally at Central Station, Manchester, on Friday, 11th August 1911, when the men came out in sympathy with the Liverpool railwaymen, and the strike spread to other stations. As with the dockers, the railwaymen were demanding shorter working hours, a minimum living wage, overtime pay and union recognition. In Salford the army of workers in the massive goods yards of the Lancashire & Yorkshire Railway Co. came out on Monday 14th August, and were supported by railwaymen and carters. Railway workers at the Salford Docks joined the strike, stating that they wanted grievances over pay and conditions, the subject of negotiation for the past 18 months, settled. Dockers were not asked to come out in sympathy. They did not need to: the docks were effectively paralysed. The railwaymen were soon joined by the carters, whose grievances had their origin in the aftermath of the June strike. Unable to distribute their coal, the collieries of Andrew Knowles & Co. closed on the Wednesday. By Friday the strike was being observed by 18,000 workers in Manchester and Salford.[138]

Alarmed at the extent of support for the dispute, the Government (which at first was determined to support the Railway Companies) changed tack, and pursuaded the employers to accept conciliation. Askwith, the Government conciliator, arrived once more to try to sort things out, and a settlement was arrived at on Sunday 20th August. A Commission was to be set up, whose findings would be accepted by the Railway companies. However, when the Secretary of the Manchester Strike Committee put a resolution agreeing to wait for the report to a meeting of the men he ran up against the temper of the times. Amongst the workers there was a growing impatience both with unions and conciliation, and a growing preference for using the strike weapon as the one sure way to bring results. The ill-timed arrival of troops and the imposition of martial law again in Salford on the 21st also caused outrage, and the men voted to stay out, encouraged to do so by Socialist speakers. Despite this the union executive called off the strike, anxious to escape from their embarrassing situation. The eventual settlement went some way towards achieving union recognition, but did little to alleviate the basic complaints of the railwaymen – low wages, long hours and tyrannical discipline. The most important result was a rapid growth in union membership and a new confidence amongst railwaymen. Askwith also made a settlement with the carters, who got the principle of a basic minimum wage established.[139]

As well as these manifestations of national confrontations, there were local strikes. 'Disputes have broken out in various parts of the borough, the persons responsible,' noted the *Reporter*, 'being workmen of the lower grade, who have no connection with any trade union.' Firms involved included the Broughton Copper Works, Ellisons Cabinet Works, F. H. Smith's Wireworks, and Greengate Mills. As well as revealing what male labourers earned, the level of wages paid to poor women was brought before the public. The case which caused the greatest outrage was that of the women at Renshaw's Broughton Flax Mill, where the best standing wage in a week, *including bonuses*, was eleven shillings.[140] The wages at Renshaw's were thoroughly exposed in the local papers, and the (non- unionised) women's case taken up by the Women's Trades Union Council. After a strike (without any strike pay) wages were forced up a little – from eleven to twelve shillings a week.

On the face of it, the industrial strife of 1911 presented a tremendous opportunity to the Left, and the British Socialist Party was launched that September. For Leonard Hall, the object of the new party was to exploit the potential of the Labour unrest, and adherents of Syndicalist ideas like Hall, Tom Mann and A. A. Purcell sought to do so. However, the BSP was soon split on this: Hyndman and the old SDF guard retained control of the new party, and held their old view that that it was not a Socialist Party's task to interfere with the industrial responsibility of the trades unions.[141] A lively debate between Syndicalists and anti-syndicalists ensued over the next two years.

1912 was another year of national industrial strife. A national miners strike commenced on the last day of February. This action, which brought out one and a half million miners, was a well-planned official strike in pursuit of a minimum wage of seven shillings a day. Its scale led the Government to rush through a Miners Minimum Wage Bill, which became law on 29th March. However, local employers had ample notice of the strike and built up stocks accordingly, whilst the Lancashire Miners Federation had funds for the payment of no more than two weeks' strike pay. It was not long before people began to feel the pinch of poverty in the Whit Lane and Irlams o' th' Height districts of Pendleton, and in the poorer districts of Salford generally, when lack of coal temporarily shut down the mills. The Whit Lane Soup kitchen, last used in 1905, was re-opened, as were several others. After six and a half weeks the miners returned to work with great reluctance.[142]

The next incident in Salford in 1912 was the arrest and trial of Tom Mann.

The organiser of the Transport Workers Union and leader of the 1911 Liverpool transport strike, Mann was president of the Industrial Syndicalist Education League. He was charged in connection with speeches he made in Salford on the 13th and 14th March, and his 'Open Letter to Soldiers' in the columns of the *Syndicalist,* urging troops to disobey orders to fire on workers. His arrest and trial at Manchester Assizes, at which he was sentenced to six months in prison, brought widespread protests, and the *Reporter* drily noted that what the whole episode mainly achieved was to give publicity to Syndicalism. The Home Secretary evidently agreed, and reduced Mann's sentence. After 46 days in Strangeways, he was released in cheerful form. Mann told the *Reporter* he had been well-treated, had lost a stone in weight and been able to give his throat a much needed rest. Mann had not altered his views, and took the opportunity to explain Syndicalist ideas for wages and conditions to be regulated by 'direct action' independently of Parliament, and the ultimate establishment of 'workers' control.' [143]

Mann was out in time for the national dock strike of 1912, called in support for the London men battling with the Port of London Authority. In Manchester and Liverpool there was little enthusiasm. Dockers locally had no immediate grievances, and their union leaders were not really in favour of striking. More out of solidarity than conviction, the men came out on Thursday 13 June. Disappointed by the response in Liverpool and other ports, the strike fizzled out the next day, though, it was observed, 'on the very eve of its failure the strikers seemed in a stronger position than ever.' The national strike failed, and London dockers battled on for another month or so until their struggle, too, ended in failure.[144]

Locally, the bitterest local dispute of 1912 was in the furniture working trades, which lasted more than six months. On the union side a leading part was played by A. A. Purcell, who in September was taken to court and fined for using abusive language on the picket line. There were, however, agreements as well as disputes in 1912. After decades of trying by voluntary agreement to get a half holiday each week for shop assistants (who worked notoriously long hours), the Shops Act of 1912 gave local authorities the power to make an order for shops to close one afternoon a week, and also provided for statutory breaks and meal times. In June that year improvements in pay and hours of work for employees of the Lancashire & Yorkshire, and the London & North Western Railway Companies in Manchester and Salford was secured, the agreement to last until 1915. Within a year, the Amalgamated Society of Railway Servants, the General Railway Workers Union and the United Pointsmen and Signalmen's Union joined to form the National Union of Railwaymen, which brought a potential end to the sectionalism of the vast army of workers on the railways. On the political front the new union prepared itself to sponsor candidates for parliamentary election, and resolved that men so returned must act with the Labour Party. On the other hand, within the ranks of 'the largest trade union in the world', the Amalgamated Society of Engineers a bitter internal controversy raged in 1912–13.[145]

The national industrial unrest continued into 1913, which saw 1,500 strikes, more than ever before recorded. Outside the mining industry (quiet after the national strike of the year before), the number of working days lost was greater than in any year since 1892. Most of these disputes had no local ramifications. The big battles were in the metal industries of the Midlands, a transport workers strike in Dublin and strikes of building workers and busmen in London. There was, however, an eighteen week strike in Pendleton at the glass bottle works of Connolly & Steele, with violent scenes on the picket lines. And there was another strike at the docks, which was of some considerable significance in the history of trades unionism there. It originated with a demand for a pay rise by timber carriers, who were not included in the agreement made after the 1911 strike. Their demand triggered off claims by other dock workers. Although the men involved were almost all outside the unions, they were given massive support by other workers, some four thousand men coming out. The Company decided to fight: no pay rises would be granted. Despite the fact that the strike was technically unconstitutional, appreciating the strength of feelings, the union moved swiftly to take over the leadership, seeing the chance to recruit non-union men and also to improve their position *vis-à-vis* the Ship Canal Company. The strike was peaceful and well-conducted, and there was strong public sympathy for the men. It lasted two weeks and a day. Although impressive, it had never quite been total. Nonetheless, the dockworkers and their union were well pleased with the result. The Company undertook to make a full inquiry into pay and conditions compared to those in other ports, conceding the union argument that Manchester had the reputation of being the lowest paid port in the country. The Company also agreed to the suspension of the 'cap' system, whereby some 1,400 picked men had preference in employment every morning. The union got 'sole and complete recognition', and the company also undertook not to victimize anyone.[146]

A few months later, at the end of April 1914, there was a sequel, the ceremonial unfurling of the new banner of the Salford district of the Dock, Wharf, Riverside and General Workers Union. It carried portraits of Ben Tillett, and J. Wignall (organising secretary) and R. Blundell (branch secretary) the two who had led the last strike and negotiated recognition by the Company. In his speech, Wignall spoke of plans for a 'Triple Alliance' of railwaymen, transport workers and miners. The main speaker was George Lansbury, former MP for Bow, who told the men the industrial atmosphere was changing. What they wanted to do, said Lansbury, was to 'link up Labour', so that it would present one united front.[147] 'The Triple Alliance', duly came into being, the most impressive demonstration of Labour unity of the time.

Whilst the unions moved towards federation and labour alliances, the question amongst Socialists in 1913 was whether to pursue Syndicalism or political action. In March that year, A. A. Purcell and W. Pickles debated the question at a public meeting at the Co-operative Hall, Pendleton.[148] Purcell put the case for 'direct action' as being more likely than the parliamentary route to being changes in the direction of Socialism. The threat of a general strike, declared Purcell, would be sufficient to secure the acquiescence of Parliament to what the workers wanted. Pickles argued that Syndicalism would fail because the capitalist power of resistance was greater than that of the workers. Capitalists used the political system to give themselves the advantage: it was now up to the workers, through their vast numerical superiority and the power of the vote, to follow suit. The way forward was to elect their representatives into positions of power and influence in Parliament, on Municipal Councils and on other public bodies. Purcell replied that capitalists feared the industrial power of the workers more than their political power. It had taken twenty-five years for them to get two men on the Salford Council. At the present rate it would take 'hundreds of years' to gain a majority. He wanted to get down to business immediately. So far as political action was concerned, the bulk of the labouring classes still did not have the vote. The Trade union movement had done far more for the working classes than Parliamentary action had ever done.

Purcell was undoubtedly right about the paucity of success on the political front. After thirty years of Socialism, by late 1913 representation in Salford was down to one Councillor. The mould of late Victorian party politics seemed some considerable way from being broken. The revival of the fortunes of the Liberal Party was one factor in the failure of Labour to make greater advances. But there were others. The Socialist movement was as fragmented as ever. Within the BSP, the Syndicalists lost the argument. In September 1913 the Party announced its intention of contesting West Salford at the next general election. The ILP, which had stood aloof from the Labour Party for some years, finally affiliated in 1914. The most important reason for the surprising weakness of Labour, however, was the failure of the Manchester and Salford Labour Representation Committee to create a presence. The LRC in Manchester did not affiliate to the Labour Party until as late as 1913 (though the Trades Council had done so much earlier). It was only during and after the First World War that the LRC, by that time reconstituted as a Divisional Labour Party, became a centre of political and social activity along the pattern of the ILP or the BSP.[149]

On the union front, in the years immediately preceding the Great War, the forces of Labour were undoubtedly massing. The ability of the labourers to surprise the older established unionists manifested itself in 1911–13. Union membership grew by 1 million in these years – an increase of 60 *per cent*. In particular, unions for the types of workers so numerous in Salford, transport workers, dockers and general labourers, almost all of which had been founded in the late Eighties, went up by over 300 *per cent*. The immediate pre-War years saw the fulfilment of the promise of New Unionism.[150] The role of Socialist organisers was as important now as it had been then, though the ability of these labourers to surprise Socialists as well as union officials was also a feature of this period; there were occasions when both had to run hard in order to take the lead in unofficial strikes, the start of which took them by surprise. The scale and the growing sense of Labour power engendered an optimism which was not lessened by failure to win more elections at the local level. Historians differ on the question of when 'the making' of the working class took place. There is a strong case that it was made, not in the early nineteenth, but in the early twentieth century.

If the Left was not enamoured of the Parliamentary route, some Socialists and the trades union movement increasingly were, especially after the Osborne judgement. In the first general election of 1910 the 29 seats won by Labour Party men in 1906 increased to 40, and a further two were added in the second election of that year. Already Liberals were alarmed by the growth of the Labour Party in industrial districts, though not so much perhaps in Manchester and Salford as in other places. However what really brought the demise of Liberalism nationally and locally was the Great War. The collapse was particularly dramatic in Salford. Ben

Tillett captured North Salford in a by-election in 1917 and was elected again in 1918 and 1922, Conservatives winning the other seats. In 1923 Labour won all three. The following year it lost them all, but recaptured them again in 1929. Things took rather longer in Salford Town Hall. It was not until 1935 that Labour became the majority on the Council.[151]

If George Evans was looking down from some Socialist heaven, he would have rejoiced at Labour's rise in Salford. He might not have felt the same over the subsequent life-histories of many of his contemporaries. After Socialism, Henry Reade found Christ and became an Anti-Socialist. John Trevor, who always saw the struggle as essentially a religious one, left the ILP (which he helped to found) and spent the rest of his life trying to revive the idea of a Labour Church, which had faded after 1900. Frederick Brocklehurst broke with Trevor over Trevor's withdrawal from the ILP, becoming president of the Manchester and Salford district. One of the delegates to the conference which founded the Labour Representative Committee in London in 1900, he seemed destined to be a future Labour MP. However, Brocklehurst turned patriot in the Boer War and severed his connections with Socialism. In December 1910 he unsuccessfully contested Prestwich as a Conservative, and stayed in that Party for the rest of his life. Friends of Evans such as William Horrocks stayed loyal to the SDF, whilst others found a congenial political home in the ILP. Had he lived, Evans would probably have shared their ambivalence towards a Labour Party which emerged as the political arm of the organised Trades Union movement. Almost certainly, he would have gone with his SDF comrades into the British Socialist Party, and from thence perhaps into the local branch of the Communist Party at its formation in 1922.[152]

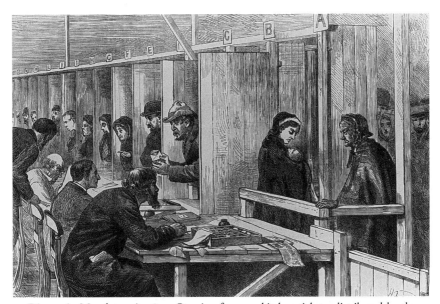

Distress in Manchester in 1879. Queuing for soup kitchen tickets, distributed by the District Provident Society, in temporary relief premisis in a warehouse in Windmill Street.
(*Illustrated London News*)

# CHAPTER 12

# Women: the Pankhursts, Feminism and the Struggle for the Vote

Early in 1910, taking the opportunity afforded by a visit of the leader of the Suffragettes to Pendleton, the *Salford Reporter* reminded its readers that Emmeline Pankhurst was a local woman. Before marrying she had been Miss Goulden, and lived in Seedley for some years after her marriage. Her father, a Pendleton calico printer, was a respected figure in his time and had been on the Borough Council in the 1870s. 'As Miss Goulden', the *Reporter* recollected, 'she was a handsome woman, and exceedingly popular'.[1] Now one of the best known figures in the country, this 'slight, delicate looking, exquisitely dressed and very fastidious woman, who seemed to embody (in her outward appearance) all that the Victorian middle and upper classes demanded of a woman',[2] had in fact become the acknowledged leader of the phenomenon of the age – militant feminism.

Although in drawing attention to Mrs Pankhurst's local origins the newspaper was doing the obvious journalistic thing, it was by no means unjustified: the women's movement owed much to Manchester. Her ideas were rooted in two strong local traditions, a middle-class feminism which went back to the 1860s, and a more modern development which drew strength from 'ethical Socialism' and found a home in the Independent Labour Party. To these she and her children were to add something distinctly Pankhurstian – an impatient anger which began when politicians rebuffed the demand for votes for women. Anger let to militance, which turned fanatical under repression. Whether or not her militant Suffragettes were one of the causes of the 'strange death of Liberal England', as has been alleged, by 1914 they had certainly demonstrated an ability to push Liberal England to the limits of its liberality.

Although patriarchy was as powerful in nineteenth century Manchester as the next place, there were reasons why a reaction to it came early there, and why Manchester was always nationally prominent in the movement for women's suffrage. That women outnumbered men in the local population at each successive census (as they did) was nothing unusual, nor was the fact that vast numbers of girls and women were employed in other people's homes as domestic servants. However, the fact that the labour force in the Lancashire textile industry was predominantly female was enough to challenge the idea that a woman's place was in the home. Although some working-class women were active in feminine issues through

Owenism and the wider popular Radical movement in the mid-century, working-class women were not drawn into feminist activity in any numbers until the later Nineties, *via* the Independent Labour Party and women's trades unionism. By that time, organised middle-class feminism had been in existence for 30 years or so. One of the places it put down early roots and where it was able to maintain a continuous existence was Manchester. Here the women's Suffrage movement was a child of the Liberalism found amongst Anti-Corn Law League families.

One of its first manifestations was a letter from 'One of the Women in England' in the *Manchester Guardian* in 1858.[3] The writer attacked John Bright as a 'half reformer' who offered nothing to women. When Bright referred to the vast numbers of male factory workers denied the vote (as he was always doing), he ignored the even larger number of women workers. In his political arithmetic the value of women's labour and capital never came into the calculations. To the end of his life, Bright argued that the main task was to widen the franchise to male householders, and that to bring women into the argument would weaken the thrust of Reform. Moreover, to grant the vote to women on the same terms as men would be to hand a huge political gift to Conservatism. If John Bright ignored the *principle* behind giving women equal political rights, his brother Jacob did not. A successful businessman and a Member of Parliament, Jacob Bright, his wife and their circle were the focus of bourgeois Manchester's support for women's suffrage.[4]

In 1865 a small group of London women with an interest in higher education formed a discussion group called the Kensington Society. That year, John Stuart Mill was elected MP for Westminster, and included women's enfranchisement in his election address. Soon after, the Kensington Society drafted the first petition to Parliament for the enfranchisement of 'all householders, without distinction of sex, who possess such property or rental qualification as your Honourable House may determine.' This excluded married women, who could not be householders since all property rights belonged to husbands, and was therefore a petition for the enfranchisement of unmarried women and widows. Signed by 1,499 women it was taken to Parliament by Mill and Henry Fawcett. The movement for votes for women had begun.[5]

The group who circulated the first petition then formed a provisional committee. In November 1866 a new petition was drawn up and the London Committee began persuading women nationally to sign. On 3rd January 1867, they wrote to Miss Lydia Ernestine Becker of Manchester, president of the Manchester Ladies' Literary Society, known to be in favour of women's suffrage, noting that a committee was in the process of being formed in Manchester. This was duly done at a meeting at the home of Dr Louis Borchardt, with Jacob Bright in the chair. At its next meeting, Lydia Becker was appointed secretary.[6] Within months, the London Committee became the London National Society for Women's Suffrage, and the Manchester Committee the Manchester National Committee for Women's Suffrage. Later that year, the two groups, together with the newly formed Edinburgh Society, formed a loose federation called the National Society for Women's Suffrage, though the individual societies remained autonomous.

Until her death in 1890, Lydia Becker was the pivotal figure in the women's movement in Manchester, and became known widely as the editor of the *Women's*

*Suffrage Journal.* This intelligent and remarkable woman, the daughter of a German *emigré*, was a friend and valued correspondent of Darwin on the subject of botanical research. She was also the first woman to be elected to the Manchester School Board. However, it is as the persistent organiser of the campaign for the widows' and spinsters' franchise that she is remembered. It was a largely thankless task, for by the time of her death, that part of the women's cause had made little real progress. Nonetheless, Miss Becker persisted, and kept the movement alive: Christabel Pankhurst was later to pay tribute to her perserverance.[7]

The Manchester National Society used similar methods to the Anti-Corn Law League. It retained itinerant lecturers, went in for holding meetings, distributed handbills and tracts and its members sought to bring the women's cause to the notice of Members of Parliament. Like the League, it sponsored a flow of petitions to the Legislature. Women, being outside the 'political nation', faced problems common to such other 'outsiders'. To prise open the doors of Parliament it was necessary to use the methods and language of the prevailing political system. In this, a Manchester barrister proved very useful. This was Dr Richard Marsden Pankhurst, the man Emmeline Goulden married in 1879.

Emmeline Pankhurst was born in 1858, the eldest daughter and third of the eleven children of Robert Goulden and his wife, Sophia Jane Craine.[8] Followers of Cobden and Bright, her parents were actively interested in a number of Radical reform movements. Both her parents were advocates of equal suffrage, and Emmeline was taken to her first suffrage meeting when she was fourteen, where she heard Lydia Becker.

Proprietor of the old established Seedley Print Works, Robert Goulden was a successful businessman, well able to afford to send his daughter as a weekly boarder to a 'ladylike' school in Manchester and then to the École Normale in Paris when she was fifteen. Emmeline arrived just after the end of the Franco-Prussian war and stayed for three years. There she acquired an admiration for French culture and a marked distaste for things German. Paris did nothing to diminish her awareness of public affairs: it was said that a daughter of Henri Rochfort turned her into a republican.[9] A member of Salford's Cotton Famine Relief committee and a borough councillor, Robert Goulden perhaps influenced Emmeline in other ways as well. An amateur actor, for a time he was owner of the Prince of Wales' Theatre, Salford. It is perhaps not too fanciful to suggest that when, after more than thirty years of 'constitutional' women's suffrage agitation, Emmeline turned to militance she did so out of an instinct that what was needed to make the public take notice of the women's issue was *theatricality.*

'Finished' in Paris, Emmeline Goulden returned home to Pendleton. Three years later, at twenty one, she married the best-known Radical in Manchester, Richard Marsden Pankhurst Ll.D., a barrister more than twice her age.[10] The marriage seems to have been fulfilling for both of them. If clothes, food and art were important to Emmeline, she was not frivolous, especially about politics. And if her husband was intensely involved in Radical causes and the Law, he was also a loving family man. They had five children, Christabel (born 1880), Estelle Sylvia (b. 1882), Henry Francis (b. 1884) who died as a child, Adela (b. 1885) and a second Henry

'The slight, delicate looking, exquisitely dressed and very fastidious woman': Emmeline Pankhurst about 1910. (Author's collection)

Francis (b. 1889). In their different ways the children, especially the daughters, were to prove as remarkable as their parents.

The son of an auctioneer and valuer, who left the Church and Conservatism to become a Baptist and a Liberal, Richard Pankhurst was born in 1834 in Stoke-on-Trent. As a youth he taught in a Sunday School, but later became agnostic. However, he never lost his Dissenter seriousness and taste for politics. Growing up in Manchester, he was educated at Manchester Grammar School and Owens' College, receiving the University of London External Degrees of BA, LL.B, and LL.D (with a gold medal of the University). Called to the Bar at Lincoln's Inn, he practiced on the Northern Circuit and in the Chancery Court of the County Palatine of Lancaster. Known as Dr Pankhurst, or simply 'the Doctor', and recognised by his red beard, rather high-pitched voice and the vehemence of his platform speeches, he soon established himself in Manchester as a leading apologist for advanced Radicalism, entering politics at the time of the Second Reform Act. He is first noticed as a member of a 'middle-class deputation', dispatched to give Gladstone the assurance of Salford's unabated confidence in him. A Radical of the Radicals, Pankhurst next became a republican. Perhaps this was what first attracted Emmeline Goulden, fresh from Paris.

Richard Pankhurst was a law reformer, a feminist and a democrat. He was also an advocate of free secular education for all. As early as 1858 he helped to start evening classes for working people at Owens' College, where he served as an unpaid member of the teaching staff and later as a governor. For thirteen years he was honorary secretary of the Lancashire and Cheshire Union of Institutes, which provided qualifications and an examination system for clerks and working men studying in the network of Mechanics' Institutes and Working Men's Colleges which had grown up since the 1840s.[11] An academic lawyer as well as a barrister, Pankhurst researched and wrote articles on bankruptcy, international law, patent law and labour law. As a member of the Manchester Chamber of Commerce, he made a close study of commercial questions and his words on these questions were always listened to with attention. He also served on the Council of the National Association for the Promotion of Social Science, and was a regular contributor to its papers and discussions.

Above all, Richard Pankhurst was devoted to the cause of women's emancipation. As a member of the Executive Committee of the Manchester National Society, he was involved from the effective start of the movement. He was one of the speakers at the first public meeting in favour of women's suffrage ever held in Britain, in the Manchester Free Trade Hall in April 1868. For some years he acted as legal adviser to Miss Becker and the MNSWS, and was able to render the movement great service. In 1869 he drafted the amendment which included women in the

Dr Pankhurst, shortly before his death in 1897. (*Manchester Faces and Places*)

Municipal Corporations Bill and, somewhat unexpectedly, secured the municipal vote for qualified (unmarried) women. That year he also acted as counsel in a test case in which women's enfranchisement was sought on the basis of 'ancient statutes and usages', though this was unsuccessful. In 1870 he drafted the Women' Disabilities Removal Bill, the first for the enfranchisement of women ever presented in Parliament. He also drafted the Married Women's Property Acts of 1870 and 1882.

In order to be free to work for public and political causes, Dr Pankhurst had decided to remain unmarried, and lived with his parents until he was forty. However, he subsequently met and married Emmeline Goulden and she was immediately drawn into the Doctor's busy political life. Thereafter, the births of her children followed in fairly close succession, preventing any further involvement for the time being, though she did take part in the campaign to give women the vote in the 1884 Reform Bill. This was prevented by Gladstone, who was always against the enfranchisement of women. In the aftermath of the Corrupt Practices Act of 1883, in which canvassing and other election work ceased to be salaried, Gladstone's alternative was that Liberal women should devote their political energies towards helping the Party in a voluntary capacity, as Conservative women were already doing through the Primrose League. At the request of Mrs Jacob Bright, a family friend, Emmeline joined the Manchester Women's Liberal Association, though she was soon to follow her husband in other political directions.

The events of 1884 plunged middle-class women's suffrage into the doldrums from which it did not recover for a decade. Lydia Becker died in 1890, and must have felt her life's work on that front had been a failure. Yet, looking at the position of women (or rather middle-class women) more closely, that seems over-pessimistic. Such measures as the Matrimonial Causes Act of 1857 and the two Married Women's' Property Acts were important. Josephine Butler's long battle for the repeal of the Contagious Diseases Act, which was to reach its conclusion within two years, had made the dual standard of sexual morality a public issue. The work of female educational reformers had led to the establishment of a few high quality schools for middle-class girls, and the battle to enter the universities was going forward. In Manchester the battle was almost won, women being awarded degrees from 1891. By 1884 women had made some headway in medicine, the first profession to open up to them. Even on the political front, women householders (mostly widows and spinsters) had gained the municipal franchise in 1869, the School Board Franchise in 1870, and by 1894 were to be qualified for all local franchises. However, the big one, the Parliamentary vote, was as far off as ever. None of these advances had been achieved without opposition. More importantly, women were divided by class into virtually two separate sets of beings. Very little of what had been achieved affected the majority of women at all. However, within a short time, working women in the trade union and Socialist movements were to make their presence felt in the revival of the movement for votes for women.

From its inception in 1868 Dr Pankhurst had been one of the leading spirits in the Manchester Liberal Association, but his temperament was too independent for him to be much of a party man. After a dispute with Liberal Imperialists in 1883, he left the Association. Thereafter he embarked upon the next phase of his career, that of free-range Radical. In October he stood as an independent Liberal in the Manchester bye-election. Going to the poll on a platform of universal adult suffrage 'for every sane human being of both sexes', the payment of MPs, free compulsory elementary education, reduced spending on the armed forces, Home Rule for Ireland, land nationalization, and the abolition of the House of Lords, he lost to a Conservative by 12,000.[12] He did not worry. His object was to publicise the Radical programme.

In 1885, to further his legal and political careers, Dr Pankhurst took his wife and young family to London, where they were soon drawn into the Socialist revival. That year, sponsored by the local Liberal and Radical Association, Richard Pankhurst stood for Parliament at Rotherhithe, losing by only 527 votes. Richard and Emmeline joined the Fabian Society, embraced the cause of Irish Home Rule, and became involved in the Women's Franchise League, a short-lived organisation which advocated full political rights for *married* as well as *unmarried* women, and equal divorce and inheritance laws, a distinct advance in their feminism.

Early in the 1890s the fortunes of the Pankhursts took a change for the worse. The Doctor began to suffer from gastric ulcers, and the necessary periods of rest and recovery impaired his earning. For the first time, they began to have financial difficulties, and the bankruptcy of Robert Goulden perhaps did not help these. In 1885 her father and his partner had turned the Seedley Print Co. into a private limited company and Emmeline had been made a director. Two years later it collapsed.[13] Five years later, her father died and the expected legacy did not materialise. Nor was Emmeline's attempts to run a fancy goods shop 'on aesthetic rather than commercial considerations' a success. 'Emersons', as they named it, lost rather than made money. To cap it all, when the lease on their Russell Square residence expired, they were faced with a large bill for delapidations. In 1893 the Pankhursts returned to Manchester.

Soon after, Dr Pankhurst and his wife joined the newly formed Independent Labour Party. For a decade, it was to be Emmeline's political home. In May 1895 Dr Pankhurst again stood for Parliament, this time as ILP candidate for Gorton. It was not a good time for the Left, and he was easily defeated. However, he was becoming prominent in the ILP, having a seat on the National Administrative Council. The following year, he attracted more public notice as a legal counsel for the Manchester branch in the dispute over holding political meetings in Boggart Hole Clough. During the course of this famous dispute several ILP leader were arrested and imprisoned for refusing to pay the nominal fines imposed. The subsequent publicity over their 'martyrdom' helped the ILP to win its battle for free speech in the parks. Emmeline was very actively involved and had been arrested. Somewhat to her disgust, instead of being fined or imprisoned, she was discharged by the magistrate.[14] However, the publicity value of demonstration, arrest and imprisonment was not lost on her.

In these years, Emmeline and her husband were active in other areas of public service. It was now possible for women to vote for, and be elected to School Boards and Boards of Guardians. After trying without success to win a seat on the School Board, Emmeline was elected a Guardian for the Chorlton Union. She found the workhouse system bureaucratic and harsh, but made her mark with several sensible suggestions to humanise it *and* save money. As a Guardian she became aware of the economic and medical problems of working-class women.[15] At this time, too, much of the Doctor's legal work was to do with municipal matters. He took on cases connected with the abatement of smoke and gas nuisances and other sanitary matters, which also affected the life of the poor. One of the Doctor's last public acts (in September 1897), was to open a new ILP club on Broad Street, Pendleton.[16] Soon after, his medical condition worsened, and on the 5 July 1898 Richard Marsden Pankhurst died. Emmeline was left a widow in reduced circumstances, with four children to educate. She was then forty. Needing an income, she gave up her seat on the Board of Guardians and obtained a post as Registrar of Births and Deaths. As with the workhouse, this proved another educative experience. She was shocked by the lives of poor women, and how little respect there was for them.

There can be little doubt of the scale of loss occasioned by Dr Pankhurst's death, both as family man and local politician. His death was felt as a particularly grievous loss by the ILP. Within months the movement commemorated him by naming a new ILP club in Higher Broughton 'Pankhurst Hall'.[17] Yet, once the grieving was over, as for many women, widowhood was to prove a liberating experience for Emmeline. She was forced to seek paid work, go out more into the world, and take responsibility for decisions once left to her husband. Perhaps not surprisingly, immediately after the Doctor' death, political involvement lessened for a time. Though her 'poverty' was never worse than genteel, Emmeline faced some financial difficulties and had to see her children through their education. The house in Victoria Park was given up, and the family moved to a more modest dwelling, 62 Nelson Street, Manchester, Emmeline's brother, Herbert Goulden, moving in 'to share expenses' with her. Mrs Pankhurst opened another 'Emersons' shop, which proved no more profitable than its predecessor. For a time, her chief public involvement was with the School Board, on which she won a seat in 1900, though the family was also actively 'unpatriotic' in the Boer War, and suffered for it. The revival of Pankhurst interest in the women's suffrage question was brought about by Christabel, who came into contact with certain leading figures in the North of England Society for Women's Suffrage at Manchester University.

At the time of the Doctor's death, Adela and Harry were still at school whilst Sylvia had just started at the Manchester School of Art, where she was extremely happy and did well. The problem was the higher education of the eighteen year-old Christabel, of whose abilities her parents had the highest opinions. When Dr Pankhurst died, Emmeline and Christabel were in Switzerland, where Christabel had been taken to spend a year 'perfecting her French'. However, she now returned to Manchester where she was rather unwillingly employed at Emersons. Christabel was uncertain of what she wanted to do. An earlier idea of being a dancer had been given up and she led a pampered self-centred existence disdaining to do more than the minimum in the shop. Eventually, Mrs Pankhurst decided it would be good for her daughter to take a course at the Victoria University (as Owens' College had now become). It was to change both their lives, because it was here that Christabel met Esther Roper and Eva Gore-Booth.[18]

A daughter of the Irish Ascendancy, Eva was brought up in the great country house of Lissadell in County Sligo. Descendants of Humphrey Booth, the 17th century Manchester merchant and benefactor, the Gore-Booths were Salford as well as Irish landowners, Lissadell and Sligo Streets in Pendleton recording the connection. Eva's father was patron of the living of Sacred Trinity, a Booth foundation, where his uncle, the Rev. H. F. Gore-Booth, was rector. Determined to end the neglect of his slum parish, this Ritualist incumbent involved himself in local matters, serving on the Salford School Board, and presided over the celebrations of the 260th anniversary of his church in 1895.[19] Brought up in the atmosphere of the Gaelic Revival, Eva was a minor poet of some distinction. She and her sister Constance (who, as Countess Markiewicz, later played an part in the Irish Rebellion of 1916) were free and unconventional spirits. Subsequently the Countess (who had married a Pole) was elected the first woman Member of the British parliament, though, as a Sinn Feiner, never took her seat. However, all that was in the future. What brought Eva Gore-Booth to industrial Manchester was not some desire to return to ancestral roots, but friendship with Esther Roper, a prominent figure in the women's suffrage movement there. The two met on holiday in Italy and began a partnership which survived until Eva's death thirty years later.

At first sight, the Irish aristocrat's daughter and the serious-minded daughter of a Manchester church missionary of humble origins, were perhaps an unlikely pair. Yet, Esther Roper was a remarkable example of the New Woman. One of the first batch of women to present themselves at Manchester University, she took her law degree in 1891, and soon began an involvement in the women's suffrage movement. Eva soon found a role in the Manchester University Settlement in Ancoats. Tall, slender, short-sighted and intensely bookish she was a teacher who inspired intense devotion in the students who attended her evening classes. She certainly inspired Christabel Pankhurst, to whom she was introduced by Esther Roper. It was Esther who suggested that Christabel should matriculate and begin studies for a law degree at the University, which was to be the making of her. This was the connection which also brought her mother back to the cause of women's suffrage, and was to be the making of *her* as well.

The revival of the movement began in 1893 when leading suffragists in London, sensing a new spirit amongst women, decided to challenge the idea that women did not care about the suffrage issue. Arguing that the old tactics of public meetings addressed to a largely middle-class audience and petitions to Parliament needed changing, what was proposed was a national petition to be signed by women *across party political and class lines*. To implement this, new organisers were appointed, and in August 1893 Esther Roper became secretary of the North of England Society for Women's Suffrage. Together with her assistant organisers, Esther revived the movement, and successfully took it across the class barrier.[20] For the first time, they gave women's suffrage the possibility of the weight of numbers.

In all this Manchester and the cotton towns was central. The local campaign started in 1894 with a great meeting at the Free Trade Hall. Welcomed by old suffrage stalwarts such as Mr and Mrs Jacob Bright and Mrs Wolstenholme Elmy, it attracted supporters from the next generation of middle-class Liberal women. One of Esther Roper's mentors was Mrs Priscilla Bright Maclaren, Jacob Bright's

Christabel Pankhurst. (Author's
collection)

daughter, who had founded the Edinburgh Suffrage Society. Other second generation supporters were Richard Cobden's daughters, Mrs Jane Cobden-Sanderson
and Mrs Annie Cobden Unwin, and Miss Margaret Ashton, sister of Lord Ashton
of Hyde, who was to be a great supporter of the cause in the next two decades.
Its president was Bertha Mason of Ashton, and prominent male supporters included
Rev. S. A. Steinthal, the Unitarian, Professors Alexander and Weiss from the Victoria
University and the Archdeacon of Manchester.[21] Esther Roper and her organisation
not only broadened the movement by taking the 'Appeal' to the factory gates, the
Manchester Society was also revitalized. In two years she doubled the membership,
and, to pay for the vast amount of publicity distributed, she doubled the subscription
of middle-class members.[22] It was at the end of a particularly busy three years'
work that she took the holiday which led to her meeting with Eva Gore-Booth,
who had gone to Italy with suspected consumption. Without hesitation, Eva gave
up Lissadell for Manchester.

   In that unhealthy place she found a rich and full life. In addition to her work
at the Ancoats Settlement, she became, in 1900, co-secretary of the Manchester
and Salford Women's Trade Union Council. Since the 1880s more and more
information had been revealed about the condition of women workers, but efforts
to organise women met with little success. In 1895 it was decided to make a new
start and to set up a separate Women's Trade Union Council for the district.
Determined to avoid party politics, it aimed to promote new organisations for

working women and to collect and publish information about conditions under which they worked with a view to influencing public opinion and legislation. The WTUC took an interest in the welfare of schoolchildren, and in 1903 Eva became its representative on the Technical Instruction Committee of the City Council. She also began to form ideas which challenged the 'separate spheres' notions of masculinity and femininity, which were to come to the fore in the next decade in campaigns to prevent the ending of work for barmaids, pit-brow workers and other women employed in occupations thought unsuited to the 'feminine ideal'. There were those who felt that Eva and Esther were 'unfeminine' for speaking in public, encouraging women to be independent, 'disrupting the family' and campaigning for the vote. But in Manchester they found a milieu where middle-class men and women were prepared to support these ideas and, just as important, working-class women prepared to accept them as mentors.[23] It was via this connection that many working-class women destined to be activists were brought into the suffrage movement for the first time.

In 1900 Esther Roper decided to renew their efforts by targeting the industrial districts of Lancashire and Cheshire with a petition to be signed only by mill women. In a year they had collected over 29,000 signatures, and Esther Roper, accompanied by a deputation of 15 Lancashire women took their petition to Parliament to present to sympathetic MPs. That evening Mrs Fawcett entertained them to dinner at an expensive restaurant. Whilst this gesture was not unappreciated, some of the working women were embarrassed by having to try to order a meal from a menu written entirely in French.[24] A vignette of contemporary class differences, it highlights the paradox of the North of England Women's Suffrage Society. Its membership was composed of well-to-do Liberals, whilst its work was mainly directed towards women workers.

The key problem for the suffragists of all classes was how to persuade Parliament to take them seriously. They tried all the ways they could to achieve this. In 1902 Miss Roper took a leading part in a deputation of women graduates to meet MPs. Another tactic was to help candidates sympathetic to women's suffrage in constituencies where women's unions were strong, which in practice meant Labour men in cotton towns. Thus, in the summer of that year, Esther, Eva, Christabel and Emmeline Pankhurst were involved in a successful campaign in Clitheroe to elect David Shackleton as Labour's third MP. Aside from the shining examples of Keir Hardie and George Lansbury, they were to find Labour politicians as unreliable as any others. Whatever was promised at elections, once in Parliament they invariably let women down. Shackleton was a case in point. Miss Roper never let them get away with it.

By 1903 there was a growing sense of frustration with conventional methods of persuasion amongst Manchester's suffragists. Yet the achievements of Esther Roper and her associates over the past decade were impressive. They had revived the women's suffrage movement, giving heart to old middle-class supporters, recruiting new men and women to the cause. They had taken the suffrage campaign to the textile workers, and thereby widened its appeal enormously. When Esther Roper's people collected those 29,000 signatures to the 'Appeal' she demonstrated a power of organisation the National Union of Women's Suffrage Societies could never match, and Mrs Fawcett was said to stand almost in awe of her.[25] For a moment it even seemed possible that the demand for women's suffrage could build up into a big movement across class. There was also the example of the way Esther, Eva and others chose to live, leading active lives independent of men, deriving strength from close female relationships. This was, of course, easier for women with money, such as Eva Gore-Booth, and was not something which, for other reasons, commended itself to most women. Nevertheless Esther Roper and Eva Gore-Booth demonstrated that, if they so chose, determined women could be free from male domination.

Certainly the two women had a great effect on Christabel Pankhurst: they transformed her life. Through them she found that serious purpose she had hitherto lacked, becoming active on both the executive of the North of England Women's Suffrage Society and on the Women's Trade Union Council. She joined Eva's Poetry Circle at the University Settlement as an adoring student, and the two became close. Her sister Sylvia noted with some surprise that, when she became ill, Christabel showed more care and solicitude for Eva Gore-Booth than for anyone else Sylvia could recall.[26] The three women became inseparable and Christabel went on holiday with Eva and Esther to Italy. Like her mother in temperament and appearance – bright, good-looking and stylish – her time at the University developed Sylvia intellectually. The study of Law brought her out as a speaker of fluency, quick understanding and the power of sharp retort.

The transformation of Christabel had interesting effects on her mother. As well as re-awakening Emmeline's interest in the suffrage question, Christabel's friendship with Eva caused her acute jealousy, as Sylvia Pankhurst makes clear in *The Suffragette Movement*, and she was not the only one who noticed.[27] It seems, in part at least, that it was to win Christabel back that, in October 1903, Emmeline Pankhurst founded the Women's Social and Political Union, a new suffrage organisation, at 62 Nelson Street. Ostensibly, the reason was to set up a Labour Women's organisation along the lines of the Women's Liberal Federation. The first thought was to call it the Woman's Labour Representation Committee, but dissatisfaction with Labour attitudes made her hesitate. Calling the new body the Women's Social and Political Union was apparently Christabel's idea.[28] Out of this embryonic organisation was to grow a movement capable of upsetting the male Establishment and becoming so identified with 'Votes for Women' in the popular mind, that the work of such people as Esther Roper and the broadly-based organisations they formed were largely forgotten for more than half a century.

Although the WSPU had to rely on the goodwill of the ILP and the North of England Society for meeting places, support and publicity, it made its own impact from the start. Emmeline Pankhurst proved a superb speaker. One early activist recalled she 'could play upon her audience with untaught art that comes from passionate sincerity'[29] and she urged women to rebel against their inferior position and voice their demands. At first, Christabel was more committed to the work of Eva and Esther, but was soon drawn into WSPU activity, developing as a speaker with as much charisma as her mother. Within a year, Emmeline had won Christabel back. The two inspired a kind of passionate loyalty amongst women not seen before and began to recruit devoted followers. Three of the earliest were Teresa Billington, a strong-willed teacher, the first woman ever to be appointed by the

ILP as a national organiser, Annie Kenney, a mill girl passionately devoted to Christabel, and Hannah Mitchell, a seamstress and ILP activist, born in rural poverty.[30] Sylvia, Adela and Harry Pankhurst also became involved. At this stage, most of those involved in the WSPU were working-class women. In 1904 and 1905, as Teresa Billington makes clear, the WSPU was built on ILP lines and intended to work through Labour organisations. Nor, at this stage, was it militant. Its energies went into intensive propaganda campaigns in Midland and Northern industrial towns, to which the Pankhursts brought formidable energy.[31]

It was Christabel who took the first step towards militancy. It happened at a Liberal meeting in the Free Trade Hall on 19 February 1904. After Winston Churchill had delivered a long speech on Free Trade, Christabel, who had obtained a seat on the platform, sought to propose an amendment asking that the Representation of the People Acts be amended so that words expressed in the masculine gender would be construed to include women. The chairman refused to allow this as having nothing to with the subject under consideration. For a few minutes Christabel refused to withdraw, but eventually did so. She later remembered moving from her place to the speakers' table and making her intervention before a huge audience as the most difficult thing she ever did.[32] It was a personal gesture, nothing to do with WSPU policy or tactics, and attracted no attention. Next time, though, she would give them something more theatrical.

Meanwhile, Christabel severed her ties with Eva Gore-Booth and Esther Roper. In 1904 she tried to persuade the committee of the Women's Trade Union Council to declare women's suffrage as one of its aims. Despite pushing very hard, she failed, and withdrew from the organisation. She then cut the two women with a finality which contrasts to her former closeness to them.[33] Increasingly, whatever Christabel Pankhurst stood for in the women's movement, it was not sisterliness.

The next stage in the development of the Pankhurstian WSPU was disillusionment with Parliament, party politics and the NUWSS. A significant step in this was the way Parliament treated a private member's Bill to extent the existing franchise to women on 12th May 1905. About 300 women, mostly from Co-operative Guilds in the London area, attended the House of Commons for its second reading and were treated to the spectacle of a deliberate filibuster. Afterwards, despite harassment from the police, a protest meeting was held, from which the women departed deeply angry.[34] This rebuff coincided with the start of the summer season in which ILP branches held open-air meetings throughout the north. In co-operation with them, the WSPU now began to campaign for votes for women on a systematic basis. For the first time, women's suffrage became a topic heatedly discussed in the world of Northern Radical politics. It was, however, not the only issue addressed by WSPU speakers. On 2nd July Christabel addressed the West Salford ILP on 'What the Labour Party would do for Children', and later she spoke on behalf of a Bill for the Relief of the Unemployed. That particular question was the big issue in Labour politics at that time, and it did not escape the notice of the WSPU that when the unemployed workers movement organised a demonstration in Manchester which was roughly broken up by the police, the government rapidly brought in the Unemployed Relief Bill, at the same time denying that it was in any way influenced by the Manchester 'riot'.[35]

The direct result of this was the demonstration at the Free Trade Hall in Manchester on 13th October 1905 which launched WSPU militancy. The plan was Christabel's, and it was to attend the meeting at which Sir Edward Grey and Churchill would speak as part of the campaign leading up to the coming General Election. She and Annie Kenney planned to attempt to question the speaker on a future Liberal government's willingness to give women the vote. Anticipating a rebuff, she and Annie would create a disturbance and get themselves arrested. Later, in court they would refuse to pay any fines, and go to prison. Martyrdom, Christabel sensed, would take women's suffrage into the headlines.

Christabel and Annie Kenney duly made their protest at the Free Trade Hall meeting, shouting 'Will the Liberal Government give women the vote?' and were removed from the meeting by the police. In order to make sure that they would be arrested and taken to court, when told by the police they were free to leave, Christabel spat in the faces of two officers and quite deliberately struck them. She and Annie were duly tried and sentenced to a fine or imprisonment. Choosing the latter, they were taken to Strangeways where they served seven and three days respectively. Christabel had not told the WSPU what was going to happen, but made plans with her family and with Teresa Billington, whose role it was to arrange protest meetings and handle publicity when the two women went to prison.[36]

The Free Trade Hall demonstration had a number of repercussions. Whilst it gave the WSPU a great boost, it precipitated a split in the North of England Society. Most argued that breaking the law was against national policy. The Liberals considered this disruption of a great public meeting would set the cause back at a time when the party seemed likely to form the next government (as it did within months). There is also evidence that some working-class activists were also offended by the Free Trade Hall demonstration. On the other hand, the dispute let to the resignation from the NEWSS of a group which included Esther Roper, Eva Gore-Booth, Sarah Dickinson, Sarah Reddish and the Rev. Steinthal, ostensibly in support of Christabel and militance. However, Eva and Esther did not join the WSPU. Eva in particular was disturbed by the way Christabel altered her version of what she had done to suit different audiences: 'She can't tell one tale in Manchester and another in Oldham.'[37] The personal and political rift was now complete. Eva and Esther from then on devoted themselves to three new organisations – the National Industrial and Professional Women's Suffrage Society; the Lancashire and Cheshire Women's Textile and Other Workers Representation Committee, which kept up their connection with organised textile women; and the Manchester and Salford Women's Trade and Labour Council, a break-away body from the politically neutral Women's Trade Union Council. Because the organisers of these bodies were more or less the same people, forming a tightly-knit group headed by Eva Gore-Booth, Esther Roper, Sarah Dickinson and Sarah Reddish, they tended to act as one.[38] In the coming years they were very active in constitutional agitation. Interestingly, they were largely ignored in the press. In the judgement of one historian 'whilst the three societies run by Esther Roper and Eva Gore-Booth were by no means insignificant, they did not generally attract either the notoriety of the militants, or the great approval accorded to the constitutionalists by the respectable middle-class Liberals.[39]

Paradoxically, the split led to a reinvigoration of the North of England Society. With the departure of Esther Roper and Eva Gore-Booth and their associates, the Society dropped its activities in the Labour movement and concentrated on a campaign directed at the middle-classes. Its membership, which had been falling since 1900, recovered, and under the leadership of Margaret Ashton it became very active. Although the action of Christabel Pankhurst and Annie Kenney was unacceptable to their members, there was a recognition that the militants had done more to bring women's suffrage within the realm of practical politics in the last twelve months than old-style campaigners had managed in nearly fifty.

The immediate effect of the 'martyrdom' of Christabel Pankhurst and Annie Kenney after the Free Trade Hall demonstration was a sharp rise in the membership of the WSPU. However, for a time there were to be no more imprisonments. Christabel received a severe warning from the University that she would be expelled if she went to prison again. Provocation was suspended.[40] As the build-up to the election began in December 1905, WSPU members started a campaign of heckling at Liberal meetings. On 21st December, Sylvia Pankhurst, who was now a London art student, and was organising working women in the East End, introduced the tactic to the capital, and, aided by Annie Kenney, heckled Campbell-Bannerman at a big Albert Hall meeting. In the election, the WSPU tried to help defeat Winston Churchill in North West Manchester, not because he was against women's suffrage (he was vaguely in favour, as were many Liberal politicians) but apparently because the constituency was easy to reach from Nelson Street. Others whose meetings were heckled included Asquith, Lloyd George and Grey. It did them no harm. The Liberals got back with the biggest majority since the first Reform Act. Nonetheless, the WSPU made its mark. Early in 1908 the *Daily Mail* began to call them *Suffragettes*,[41] a name which entered the language, usefully separating militants from the constitutional suffragists of the National Union, and the Radical suffragists who followed Eva Gore-Booth and Esther Roper's lead.

The move of the WSPU from Manchester to London followed Christabel's graduation with a first-class degree in Law in June 1906. September found the WSPU installed the ground floor of Clements Inn, close to the apartments of Frederick and Emmeline Pethick-Lawrence, two rich supporters now financing the cause. Mrs Pethick-Lawrence, who had progressed to feminism *via* charity work and Socialism, became treasurer, whilst her Old Etonian husband, who had followed his wife into Socialism and the women's movement, brought his professional skills to the WSPU as legal adviser. When his wife cracked under the strain soon after, he took over as treasurer. For the next six years this couple were the loyal and devoted lieutenants of Mrs Pankhurst and Christabel, Frederick Pethick-Lawrence being the only male ever allowed inside the all-female sanctum of the WSPU leadership.[42]

The departure from Manchester was abrupt and unheralded. The summer of 1906 saw the WSPU starting to make an impact locally, with the Pankhursts actively involved, not least in their native Salford. At meetings, invariably held under ILP auspices, they put their case with their customary flair. Late July saw a demonstration on Goulden home ground, Langworthy Road, Seedley, at which a crowd of 3,000 were addressed by Christabel, Adela Pankhurst and Annie Kenney.

Annie Kenney. (Museum of
London)

Four days later Mrs Pankhurst braved egg-throwers to denounce opponents of
votes for women, and followed this with a scene in the Salford Electoral Revision
Court.[43] Then, quite suddenly, their home base was abandoned. To be closer to
the centre of power and influence made sense and certainly the WSPU never
looked back. But more was abandoned by the move to London than merely place
of origin.

   Not quite as abrupt, but just a decisive, was the split with the ILP, which took
place over the next twelve months. One of the paradoxes surrounding the formation
of the WSPU is that, if it started as a result of the failure of ILP leaders (Snowden
in particular) to commit themselves to the enfranchisement of women, the WSPU
would never have survived its early days without ILP support. In Manchester this
could not have been closer: the WSPU shared rooms with the Manchester Central
Branch, and ILP stalwarts gave support and physical protection from local roughs
at out-door meetings. This co-operation went on after the Pankhursts departed,
when the leadership of the Manchester WSPU was left in the hands of Alice Milne
and Hannah Mitchell.[44]

   That it did not last long after the move to London was due to Christabel
Pankhurst. In the general election of 1906 she peremptorily banned the WSPU
from working with *any* political party. Now that support was beginning to come
in from rich feminists, Christabel thought it was time to distance the Union from

the ILP, and, in particular, to end the reliance on East End women at demonstrations in London. Old associations with the women's trade-union movement were severed with that unsentimental finality which was one of Christabel's least endearing characteristics. Links with the ILP were badly strained by the activities of Christabel and Teresa Billington at the Cockermouth bye-election on 1st August. Their new policy of not co-operating with any political party divided and confused Labour's supporters and the Socialist candidate coming a poor third caused bitter resentment. This caused trouble within the ILP and Emmeline and Christabel severed their connections with branch and party soon after. Even so, branch members continued to support women's suffrage, and this support survived even the formal break caused by the WSPU making the severance of all political alliances an absolute condition of membership in October 1907. After a decade and a half as an ILP stalwart, Emmeline Pankhurst was turning into something else, and the pretence that the WSPU was an organisation of working women was about to be abandoned.[45] A question suggests itself. Was Emmeline's socialism ever anything more than skin-deep?

Just a year after the Pankhursts moved in with the Pethick-Lawrences a rebellion was mounted against them within the WSPU in which Teresa Billington (now Mrs Billington-Greig) and Mrs Charlotte Despard were the leading figures. There were a number of reasons. One was the personal nature of the leadership of the Pankhurst-Pethick-Lawrence faction, and the blatant disregard for the Union's constitution. Another was the severance of ties with the ILP. A third was the intention of the Pankhursts to keep the WSPU London-dominated, despite the fact that many branches had sprung into existence in Lancashire, Yorkshire and Scotland. Fearing a successful challenge to their domination of the Council if the WSPU's first annual conference, planned for October 1907, was held, a 'London coup' was staged. It was decided to cancel the conference. Informing London, but not provincial members, a meeting was held in the Essex Hall, and the Pankhursts and Pethick-Lawrences used it to reorganise the WSPU. The constitution was revised, all power was concentrated in a committee dominated by the present leaders and their immediate associates. The WSPU became the National Women's Social and Political Union, and all members were required to sign a pledge accepting the objects and methods of the new Union, and undertake not to support candidates of any political party until women had obtained the vote. Mrs Despard and Mrs Billington-Greig left, and formed the Women's Freedom League. The Pankhurst faction completely outmanoeuvred their opponents, and captured about eighty per cent of WSPU supporters.[46] From now on, there were two militant feminist organisations. This split was reflected in Manchester, which from now on had branches of both.

Manchester was always one of the largest NWSPU centres. By 1910 it could draw 20,000 to its rallies, and sold a thousand copies a week of *Votes for Women*. The Manchester Women's Freedom League was never as large as the NWSPU. It had a central branch, and a district which united members in places such as Eccles, Swinton, Urmston and Burnage. The WFL, however, did not approve of tactics which caused injuries or damaged private property, and retained its links with the Labour movement. It sent speakers to ILP and Women's Co-operative Guild meetings, addressed workers outside factory gates, held 'at homes', and did a great deal of campaigning in local elections. Furious with Hilaire Belloc's anti-feminism, the League attacked him vigorously in the South Salford election of January 1910. Believing in militance without violence, it advocated the non-payment of taxes and boycotting the census of 1911.

In the new NWSPU, Emmeline Pankhurst was founder, spiritual leader and star orator. Having little taste for administration, which she left to the Pethick-Lawrences, she preferred to lead from the front, which she did brilliantly. Christabel concerned herself with tactics and strategy. After the split there was deliberate polarization of the Union into leaders and followers. Criticism of Christabel's or Emmeline's actions became impossible. Far from having adverse effects on support, membership grew and money poured in from sympathisers. The NWSPU received support from across the social spectrum, from titled aristocrats to factory workers. Superbly organised, it proved adept at keeping the woman question in the news almost to the moment the Great War began in August 1914.[47] Two things are, however, worth noting: an impatience, verging on the capricious, with which the leadership viewed political reality, and the fact that votes for women became an end in itself. In respect of the first, the hesitance of Liberals to hand Conservatism the votes of an army of middle-class spinsters and widows on a plate, and Radical and Labour arguments that votes for women should be part of a new Reform Bill to widen the franchise generally (an idea the Pankhursts had once held) were dismissed as masculine foot-dragging. Votes for women became a quest for the Holy Grail: the NWSPU never seems to have given thought to any legislative programme after the vote was won.

From the time of the move to London, NWSPU tactics passed through four phases. The first involved agitation and demonstrations intended to achieve publicity and the support of the public, and culminated in the great Hyde Park Rally of June 1908. On 23 October 1906 the NWSPU organised a demonstration in the Lobby of Parliament during which ten women, including Adela Pankhurst, Annie Kenney and Mrs Annie Cobden Sanderson were arrested. When they refused to be bound-over by the magistrate, they were given a harsh punishment – two months in the 2nd Division in Holloway prison (that is, imprisoned as common felons). When reported in the newspapers this caused a sensation. Money and applications for membership of the NWSPU poured in, and even Mrs Fawcett, that pillar of constitutional respectability, came out in support. The scale of this reaction quickly let to the prisoners being transferred to the less severe 1st Division, and the Home Secretary was minded to release them after they had served only a month. Upon liberation the ten were given a banquet at the Savoy. It was a turning point in the history of the NWSPU. The publicity aroused confirmed the success of deliberately seeking out the martyrdom of imprisonment, using that 'curious mental and moral duplicity' (as Teresa Billington later described it) 'which allowed us to engineer an outbreak and then lay the burden of its results upon the authorities'.[48] Moreover, the incident marked the end of the plebeian origins of the Union. Only one (or two, if Annie Kenney could still be so described) of the 'Holloway Ten' were working-class. Funded by the well-to-to and hero-worshipped by their followers the Pankhursts were now in their element.

Mrs Pankhurst arrested in Victoria Street, London, February 1908. (Museum of London)

Down to 1909, the Union developed its tactics of demonstration, provocation and civil disobedience. The basic activity was the outdoor demonstration, but the principal headline-catcher became 'the March on Parliament', which took on a ritualised form. The march on parliament of 13 February 1907 was typical. Carefully planned with volunteers of young women prepared to go to prison, it resulted in 49 arrests, including Sylvia and Christabel Pankhurst, most of whom were sentenced to 14 days in prison. The occasion of W. H. Dickens's Suffrage Bill month later, led to another. For this, Annie Kenney and Adela Pankhurst recruited 40 mill workers who, dressed in clogs and shawls, were sent to London with funds raised by Lancashire NWSPU branches. This 'raid' was blocked by 500 policemen, and 65 women went to prison for their part in it.[49] The rest of 1907 saw no further major demonstrations, but hundreds of indoor meetings were held, many on a large scale. Despite this, Liberal and Conservative party leaders made it clear that they did not favour the extension of the franchise to women. The Union therefore decided to step up the level of demonstrations in 1908. In their turn magistrates became tougher, usually sentencing those convicted to the indignities of the 2nd Division. In February, leading from the front, Mrs Pankhurst went to prison for the first time. On her release she appeared at a rally in the Albert Hall attended, by 7,000 supporters. That Easter saw Christabel in Manchester to lead the Suffragette attack on Churchill, forced into a bye-election by the appointment of Asquith as Prime Minister. At one stage, she was addressing twelve meetings a day and great was Suffragette satisfaction when Churchill lost by 419 votes, though how important the feminist contribution to this was is a matter of some dispute.[50]

In conscious emulation of the great Reform demonstration of four decades previously, the NWSPU organised a rally in Hyde Park on 21 June 1908. Arrangements were placed in the capable hands of Mrs Drummond – known thereafter as 'General' Drummond – whose plan it was to have seven great processions converging on Hyde Park. The marchers were to be 'an army', their uniform white dresses with sashes and favours in the purple, white and green of the NWSPU. Thirty trains brought the women into London on that day, and the massive columns marched behind 700 banners to the music of 40 bands. Estimates of the numbers attending vary, but all are in excess of 250,000.[51] Despite this mighty demonstration, Asquith let it be known he had not changed his mind, and refused to respond to the resolutions forwarded to him from Hyde Park. Foreseeing this, Christabel planned to escalate the campaign of militance. Indifference had to be shaken.

On 13 October, a plan to 'rush Parliament', openly advertised, led to the arrest of Mrs Pankhurst, Christabel and Mrs Drummond for 'conduct likely to lead to a breach of the peace'. Sixty thousand people had assembled in Parliament Square, and the 'rush' was stemmed only by the efforts of 5,000 policemen. Mrs Pankhurst and Mrs Drummond received sentences of three months, and Christabel ten weeks, but the publicity value to the NWSPU was far greater than anything achieved before. At a meeting at the Albert Hall a couple of weeks later, a campaign to disrupt political meetings was started. 'We do not intend to allow a single Cabinet minister to speak in public' it was announced, and big efforts in the next two months were made to carry it out. On one occasion, it took Lloyd George two hours to deliver a twenty minute speech.[52] Despite such minor successes and the fact that support was rapidly growing, victory seemed as far away as ever. Frustration mounted. Current tactics seemed to be getting nowhere. In June 1909 militance was escalated. The tactice of the NWSPU entered a second phase.

On the 29th of that month the NWSPU staged its thirteenth march on Parliament. The largest so far, in all, 108 women and 14 men were arrested. At 9 o'clock, in a move apparently not authorised by the leadership, a number of windows in Whitehall were smashed by Suffragettes. Shortly after, Marian Wallace Dunlop, sentenced to a month for defacing St Stephen's Hall, went on hunger strike. After refusing food for 96 hours she was released. Encouraged by this, the stone-throwers demanded to be treated as political prisoners in the 1st Division, refused to wear prison-clothing and went on hunger strike. Six days later they were released. 'Starving their way out of prison' seemed to be a new way to beat governmental power, and certainly embarrassed Liberals of all kinds. An orgy of window-smashing, damaging slate roofs and physical assault followed in the second half of 1909. The government retaliated by restricting entry into Liberal meetings to ticket only, and with force-feeding of hunger strikers. This was met with NWSPU outrage and a certain amount of opposition from journalists and doctors. Police action against women protesters also became more physical, working-class women being treated noticeably more roughly than middle or upper-class ladies, a matter exposed by Lady Constance Lytton when she disguised herself as 'Jane Warton'.[53]

Appalled by this escalation of events, early in 1910 the journalist, H. N. Brailsford, floated the idea of conciliation, starting a movement to promote an agreed Suffrage Bill. Fifty four pro-Suffragist MPs agreed to give one their support, and, somewhat reluctantly, Mrs Pankhurst and the NWSPU suspended 'mild militancy'. Except for one week in November 1910, the truce lasted from January 1910 to November 1911. To attract Conservative support, the Bill put forward by Brailsford's conciliation committee was drawn narrow and would have given the vote to one million women, predominantly middle-class spinsters and widows, on a household qualification. However, Asquith was determined not to let the Conciliation Bill get beyond a second reading. In July 1910 it was effectively killed.[54]

The NWSPU, by now a large organisation with a very considerable income, called for legitimate political pressure to be mounted on the Liberal government. Joined by the other suffrage societies, a great march in London was organised on 18 June, which consisted of 10,000 women with 40 bands. Another joint demonstration was held on 23 July, and the summer of 1910 saw large meetings in most provincial cities, not least in Manchester, where the NWSPU and the Women's Freedom League co-operated in demonstrations at the Urmston Fair Ground in July and the great Alexandra Park Rally in October. The North of England Society was also very active in its less militant fashion. In Salford a branch had been formed in 1909 to spread the message locally. At the election of January 1910, the North of England Society collected no less than 47,853 signatures in favour of women's suffrage in the forty constituencies covered by its branches.[55]

By this time, the main women's organisations were receiving support from a number of fringe societies. If their (often male) membership was small, it was frequently influential and helped to broaden the appeal of the movement. A minority of Church of England clergy and laity in Manchester and Salford supported it through the Church League for Women's Suffrage. Nonconformity had its branch of the Free Church League for Women's Suffrage, and the Catholic Women's Suffrage Society was also active. Manchester also had branches of the London Graduates Union for Women's Suffrage, the Actresses' League, the Celtic group and the Men's Political Union for Women's Suffrage. However, the latter was never as influential as the Men's League for Women's Suffrage, which was founded as a non party-political body in 1908. Many of its members belonged to the North of England Society and included such figures as Canon Hicks of St Phillip's, Salford, an outspoken Liberal and Temperance reformer, who became Bishop of Lincoln in 1910, and no less than seven professors from Manchester University.[56]

In these years the support for women's suffrage within Manchester injected force and vigour into the struggle nationally. Needless to say, the Anti-Suffrage Movement was also active, a Broughton audience being told by Mrs Arthur Somervell, hon. secretary of the Women's Anti-Suffrage League, that the majority of women did not want the vote, that the social system had 'for centuries' been based on the 'rule of men', and that confusion would ensue if women came into possession of the multifarious franchise qualifications currently available to members of the opposite sex.[57] It was less significant that the League was probably speaking for what most women and men thought than the fact that Manchester's opinion-formers were generally in favour of the enfranchisement of women. Strong support came from C. P. Scott's *Manchester Guardian*, though Scott was to be horrified by the future escalation of militant disturbances, and most constitutional suffragists were Liberals of the *Manchester Guardian* type. Though more lukewarm, the *Manchester Evening News* was generally in favour, and by 1910 the Conservative *Manchester Courier* had also become sympathetic, though remaining antagonistic to the Pankhursts and the NWSPU. There was also significant support from trade unionists, the ILP and the City Council, which, by a large majority, in October 1910 passed a formal motion for a petition to Parliament in support of the third reading of the 'Conciliation Bill', the second reading of which had been supported by all of Manchester's and Salford's Members of Parliament.[58]

In the summer of 1910 the various women's organisations held meetings in towns and cities across the country, but the main tactic was to await the resumption of Parliament in November. On 12th November Grey let it be known that the government would not find time for a Bill, so a militant demonstration was decided on for 18 November, the day Parliament re-assembled. Parliament duly met, only to hear of the dissolution prior to a new election to be held in December. There was no mention of a Conciliation Bill. When the NWSPU women tried to 'rush' the precincts, they received a reception at the hands of the police of a rougher nature than ever before. The immediate result was an outburst of a different militancy than the ritualised pushing and shoving of 'rushes' on Parliament. One such was 'the Battle of Downing Street' of 22nd November, in which Augustine Birrell, a Cabinet Minister, was injured. All this spelt the ruin of Brailsford's conciliation diplomacy, and the start of a new and more violent phase of militancy.[59]

But not immediately. Militancy was laid aside for the General Election of December 1910. The Liberals were returned to power and the truce was renewed in January and February 1911 pending clarification of the government's intentions. Once more, the Liberals declined to give a Women's Bill parliamentary time, but a private member's Bill was drafted, receiving a second reading in May. Inside the House of Commons there was widespread support for a Conciliation Bill, and 86 city and borough councils up and down the country passed resolutions in favour. The government also made friendly noises. By the time of the Coronation of George V, there was a feeling that this time the obstacles were going to be overturned. The movement marked the celebrations with a monster procession seven miles in length. Forty thousand women marched through the streets of London in confident anticipation of the triumph.

On 7 November the Prime Minister indicated that, in the next session, the government would introduce a measure extending manhood suffrage 'to all *bona fide* residents', and if the House desired it this could be amended to include the enfranchisement of women. Enraged by the insult of the women's franchise being passed as an extension of a manhood suffrage Bill, and suspecting a government ploy to cheat women (for which they blamed Lloyd George) the NWSPU resumed militancy. After almost two years of truce, the NWSPU no longer believed the promises of politicians. Amongst the leadership there was growing paranoia. As C. P. Scott noted in his diary, Christabel had come round to envisaging 'the whole suffrage movement in its present phase as a gigantic duel between herself and Lloyd George whom she designed to destroy'.[60] For the NWSPU, only a government-sponsored Suffrage Bill would now be acceptable, and to concentrate the minds of the politicians, a campaign of attacks on property began on 21st November 1911. A 'march on Parliament' was arranged, but at the same time a carefully organised squad of women met at another rendezvous and were issued with stones and hammers. They proceeded to smash a great number of windows in government and business properties in Whitehall. On 15th December Emily Wilding Davison, acting on her own initiative, set three post boxes ablaze with pieces of linen soaked with paraffin, for which she was sent to prison for six months. These attacks were precursors of a sustained campaign against property over the next two and a half years. The campaign entered its third phase.

The first days of March 1912 saw a carefully planned outbreak of window smashing in London. A number of arrests were made, including those of Mrs Pankhurst and the Pethick-Lawrences, and on the 28th the first hunger strikes began. Force-feeding led to NWSPU protest meetings: in Hyde Park, Sylvia appealed for support for the women 'who are dying of tortures and are at this moment facing death'.[61] In May, Emmeline and the Pethick-Lawrences were tried for conspiracy. Mrs Pankhurst argued movingly that all the militant deeds had been done for political reasons, and that they should be treated accordingly. They were all given four months in the 2nd Division, and had to pay the costs of the prosecution. They replied that if, within a week, they were not transferred to the 1st Division they would hunger-strike. A big appeal to Asquith to treat the NWSPU as political prisoners succeeded. Mrs Pankhurst and the Pethick-Lawrences were transferred to the 1st Division. They then demanded that *all* NWSPU prisoners should be treated likewise. If they were not, all would go on hunger-strike. The refusal by the authorities led to just this. Their refusal of food began on 19 June. When faced with force-feeding, Mrs Pankhurst reacted so violently that the prison authorities desisted. Eventually, weak from fasting, she was released on 24th June. By 6th July all NWSPU protesters had been released before the end of their sentences.[62]

Escalation into attacks on property had a series of consequences. It alienated some NWSPU members, amongst the first to resign being Dr Elizabeth Garrett Anderson, the pioneer physician. It also dismayed Brailsford, Nevinson and those MPs who had been involved in the Conciliation Bill initiative. Early in 1912 a second Bill failed to pass its second reading: a year before, the Bill had secured a majority at this stage. Police action against the Union led to Christabel fleeing to Paris, whence she sent directives to the movement and continued to write each week for *Votes for Women*. Disguised as 'Amy Richards' she lived in some comfort in Paris, initially as the house-guest of the Princesse de Polignac. After Mrs Pankhurst was released she joined Christabel in Paris, a city both women, being militants of the Bollinger tendency, found congenial. At that time a meeting in Boulogne was arranged with the Pethick-Lawrences, *en route* to Switzerland. There followed a disagreement over the policy of window smashing, the Pethick-Lawrences arguing against, because of its arousal of popular opposition. Christabel appeared to take their point, but Frederick recollected later that Mrs Pankhurst appeared to resent the fact that he had even ventured to question the wisdom of her daughter's policy. After the Pethick-Lawrences' Swiss holiday they went to Canada. When they returned they were to find the Pankhursts had moved the NWSPU to a new

Sylvia Pankhurst. (Museum
of London)

home, and the Pethick-Lawrences were informed that they were out. The Pethick-
Lawrences departed quietly without trying to cause a split.[63] The committee was
dissolved. Henceforth, the NWSPU was effectively Emmeline and Christabel
Pankhurst. Christabel was sole policy-maker, the London office entirely staffed by
women loyal to her. There were other changes as well. After the defeat of the
Conciliation Bill, other women's organisations, hitherto prepared to work alongside
the NWSPU, became more alienated. Mrs Fawcett and the National Union now
regarded the Pankhursts and the NWSPU as the biggest obstacle to the success of
the suffrage movement. Mrs Pankhurst diverted attention from all this by inciting
NWSPU members to all-out militancy in a speech at the Albert Hall. Attacks on
property increased. A new development was arson, first used against a cabinet
minister's country house that July. The burning of letters in mail boxes in November
was the effective end of the NWSPU's efforts to win public support. The public
were now apparently to be *coerced* into pressurising the government to give women
the vote. Needless to say, arson achieved the opposite effect.

In an atmosphere of growing NWSPU fanaticism (and ever-heavier repression),
all developments over the next year and a half seemed to make things worse. Hopes

of an amendment to a Franchise Reform Bill in early 1913 (on which non-militant Suffragists pinned their faith), were dashed by a ruling of the Speaker of the House of Commons. To the increasingly paranoid followers of Christabel and Emmeline this was merely another indication that *all* politicians were their enemies. Increasingly, desperate measures were needed: a concerted campaign of arson against public and private property was launched. The campaign was to continue until the end of July 1914 and destroyed an estimated half a million pounds' worth of property. Condemned by press and public, Mrs Pankhurst accepted responsibility for it. On 24th February 1913 she was arrested, tried and sentenced to three years' imprisonment. Her response was to go on hunger-strike. By now, political England was caught up in an appalling spiral of fanaticism and repression. The government countered hunger-strikes and politically embarrassing force-feeding with the Prisoners Temporary Discharge for Ill-Health Act of April 1913, which allowed for the release of hunger-strikers and their subsequent re-arrest.[64] The NWPSU called it 'the Cat and Mouse Act', and were able to give it a gloss of state sadism. When the police were empowered to ban NWSPU meetings, all this achieved was to make legal activity more difficult, and turned the NWSPU even more towards arson, an activity less easily prevented. The more arson increased, the uglier the public mood against Suffragettes became.

In her Cat and Mouse 'martyrdom', Mrs Pankhurst did not flinch. On 12th April she was released on a 15 day licence, recovering in Nurse Pine's Nursing Home, only to be re-arrested on 26th May. Refusing to eat or drink she was released on 30 May on a seven day licence, only to be re-arrested on 14th June attempting to go to Emily Davison's funeral. The latter had been killed by a racehorse in the Derby on 3rd June 1913 when, apparently intending to wave the NWSPU colours in front of the horses at Tattenham Corner, she got on to the course and was trampled. Whether or not her death was accident or suicide is unclear. To the NWSPU she was a martyr, and was given an a martyr's funeral. The feelings aroused generated another outburst of arson, as did the trial and imprisonment of the women arrested in a big police round-up on 30th April.[65]

By now the NWSPU was becoming Manichean. The enemy became not merely politicians, but men in general, who, in the mind of Christabel Pankhurst, came to be seen as the quintessence of moral evil. More and more, she focused on their sexual iniquities: force-feeders became identified with white-slavers. Taking up the point made by Contagious Diseases Act campaigners of forty years before about the double-standard of sexual morality, Christabel came to argue that sexual diseases and prostitution were the evils most responsible for society's ills. Her articles on the subject appeared as a book in December 1913, *The Great Scourge and How to End It*, in which she claimed that venereal disease was a 'direct consequence of men's failure to live up to the moral standards of women' and that 'the militancy of women is doing a work of purification'. Although there was a kernel of truth in all this about the social consequences of the dual sexual standard, Christabel's claim that '75 to 80 per cent of men' had been infected with VD before marriage was absurd. Her theories were the last straw for many female, a well as male supporters. NWSPU membership had been falling since its peak in 1909, arson being the most important reason.[66] By 1913, the NWSPU had reduced itself down to a fanatical organisation, and the more repressive authority became, the more anti-male the Suffragettes turned. Such was activist psychology in 1913 and 1914, it scarcely mattered how strange the ideas of their leader across the water became. By now, all the people capable of independent thought had left. The militants accepted the ideas and directives of their leader in Paris with an enthusiasm unburdened by doubt.

The most significant of those capable of independent thought to go was Sylvia Pankhurst. Since 1912 she had been carrying on a suffrage campaign of her own in the East End of London, receiving financial assistance from local NWSPU branches. Her mother and sister, who had long since lost interest in the plight of working-class women, largely ignored it until drawn into the Bromley and Bow by-election of November 1912. Sylvia Pankhurst had found a great ally in George Lansbury, Labour MP for that constituency, who, with his wife, had been ardent NWSPU supporters for some years. In October 1912 he came round to the view that Labour MPs in the House of Commons should vote against the Government until women were given the vote. The Party's refusal led to Lansbury resigning his seat to fight an election as an Independent Labour candidate on the women's suffrage issue. In the event, the campaign was a disaster. Lansbury lost, leaving Labour even more unenthusiastic over votes for women on Pankhurst/NWSPU terms, and the NWSPU further disillusioned with electoral politics.[67]

The set-back did not deter Sylvia, at home in the East End ever since coming to London as an art student. She continued to build up NWSPU branches there, creating a semi-autonomous East End Federation. Her approach and programme differed significantly to that of the official NWSPU. Deeply involved in Labour politics – Keir Hardie became her lover at this time – as Emmeline and Christabel moved right, Sylvia moved left. With its working-class membership, the East London Federation advocated universal adult suffrage and welcomed both men and women into membership. Although strongly against arson, the Federation did not eschew militance. However, it was its espousal of industrial causes, and the formation of a 'People's Army' in the East End which led to a rift with her mother and sister. In January 1914, Sylvia travelled to Paris to be peremptorily informed by Christabel that the East London Federation must separate from the NWSPU completely.[68] Expulsion did not worry Sylvia. Already moving in a significantly different direction to Emmeline and Christabel, she was now to embark on a remarkable political journey which was to take her into pacifism, communism and Ethiopia.

The life of Adela Pankhurst followed a not dissimilar pattern. An elementary school teacher, she had followed her mother, brother and sister into the ILP and the WSPU. An early activist (one of the four arrested at Belle Vue on 23rd June 1906, for which she served a week in prison for refusing the pay the fine), Adela's Socialism (like Sylvia's) was not jettisoned when the NWSPU became militant. In the end, Emmeline and Christabel forced her out as well. Shortly before the Great War, Adela emigrated to Australia.[69] If all the world's a stage, Pankhursts never doubted that there were parts for them upon it.

The year which ended on August 4th 1914, saw an intensification of the battle of wills between the NWSPU and the government. Both sides became locked into a spiral of extremism from which neither would withdraw. Who knows where it would have led, had it not been terminated upon the outbreak of war: probably in the death of a Suffragette after one hunger strike too many. When on strike, Mrs Pankhurst's will-power was quite remarkable, as were her physical powers of recovery upon release. By July 1913, her strength had been sapped by repeated hunger strikes and she retreated to the continent for a holiday with Annie Kenney, a hunger-striker of comparable strength and endurance. Whilst abroad, Mrs Pankhurst decided on a lecture tour of America. Two sea voyages would restore her health, she would be able to address meetings without fear of arrest, and could raise money for the cause. Annie Kenney, on the other hand, decided to return and risk re-arrest by speaking when public meetings resumed in the autumn.[70]

The willingness of the NWSPU activists to do this again and again led to the re-introduction of force-feeding. The Cat and Mouse Act had been introduced to avoid this, but the illegal acts of NWSPU hunger-strikers out on licence made a mockery of it. In October 1913 force-feeding was resumed.[71] The result was more arson, which the authorities were largely powerless to prevent. In February 1914, there was another split in the NWSPU. An influential middle-class group broke away to form the United Suffragists. Their view was that, in Paris, Christabel was increasingly out of touch with the movement she commanded.[72]

Mrs Pankhurst returned to England on 5th December 1913, only to be re-arrested immediately she set forth on land. Enraged militants retaliated by intensifying the campaign of arson, and Mrs Drummond's 'bodyguard' on two occasions the following February succeeded in preventing the police re-arresting Emmeline. They caught up with her in Glasgow on 9 March 1914 and, after a fight, made an arrest. For the first time, Mrs Pankhurst herself was roughed-up: policemen do not like being made to look foolish. For this, Velazquez's 'Rokeby Venus' was slashed by a Suffragette in the National Gallery. Emmeline hunger-struck, and was released in a state of exhaustion after five days. Her next arrest was in the attempt to 'rush' Buckingham Palace on 21st May, after the Home Secretary had denied her request for an audience with the King. This ensured a spectacular demonstration. Photographs filled the newspapers.[73]

In the summer of 1914 (and later) the Pankhursts tried to create the illusion that such unrest was creating a crisis so grave that the government would have to make concessions similar to those to the Ulster Unionists. The government never showed signs of doing anything of the kind.[74] It was the Suffragettes who were brought to breaking point. The public turned against them, meetings were disrupted and there was an increase in physical attacks on constitutional suffragists as well as the NWSPU. Released after her Buckingham Palace arrest, Mrs Pankhurst was re-arrested on 9th July. She refused food and drink, became ill, and had to be released two days later. On a stretcher, she attempted to attend an NWSPU meeting at Holland Park Skating Rink and was re-arrested. They released her on 18 July in a state of utter exhaustion. She was forced to retreat to St Malo to recuperate, where she was joined by Christabel: that is where they were when war broke out. The arson campaign ceased immediately and the government released all NWSPU prisoners. Mrs Pankhurst suspended all militant action until 13 August. It was never resumed. Votes for women was put on ice for the duration.

Although one cannot know what might have happened if the Great War had not come down like some cosmic guillotine, there is no doubt that, despite later claims that they were on the verge of success, the Suffragettes were failing to move the government in its opposition to 'votes for women now'. What militance had done was to make the issue headline news, and Mrs Pankhurst the best known women of her time. Even to many who saw her as personifying everything they hated about the assertiveness of the New Woman, her tenacity and sheer bravery exacted admiration. For her followers, shrinking in number, but still resolute in their militance, she retained to the end her aura of unquestioned leader in the resistance to male dominance.

It may be doubted whether such women activists as Salford's Sarah Dickinson or Nellie Keenan saw her in the same light. Both weavers, the former started work as a half-timer for Richard Haworth & Sons about 1879, beginning a lifetime's work for women's trade unionism and women's suffrage when she became a leading organiser of the tiny Manchester and & Salford Association of Machine, Electrical & Other Women Workers. Nellie Keenan, from a later generation of Salford working women, became active from 1902 as Treasurer, and later Secretary, of the Salford Power-Loom Weavers Association, and in the Lancashire & Cheshire Women Textile & Other Workers' Representative Committee, and on the Manchester and Salford Women's Trades and Labour Council.[75] To such women the blinkered 'single-cause' attitude of the middle-class Suffragettes seemed to miss the point.

The NWSPU had never lacked critics within the wider feminist movement, least of all in Lancashire. Most severe, perhaps, towards the Pankhursts was Teresa Billington-Greig, once so close. 'I don't believe in votes for women as a panacea of all evils' she wrote in 1911, complaining that the NWSPU had 'cut down its demand from one of sex equality to one of votes on a limited basis. It has suppressed free speech on fundamental issues. It has gradually edged the working-class element out of its ranks. It has become socially exclusive, punctiliously correct, gracefully fashionable, and narrowly religious.'[76] Three years later she would no doubt have added 'and stolen the limelight and tarred women's suffrage with the brush of illegality and arson.' NWSPU stridency drowned out the considered call for womanhood suffrage being made by a network of organisations, far larger in membership and more numerous on the ground than the Suffragettes. The heartlands of this movement were industrial Lancashire, Yorkshire and Cheshire. Here organisation was shared between the revived National Union of Women's Suffrage Societies and the Radical suffrage bodies built up by Esther Roper, Eva Gore-Booth and their associates. In these districts, there was a degree of co-operation between the essentially middle-class National Union and the other bodies found nowhere else. Under the leadership of Margaret Ashton, the National Union funded much of the work and employed such leading Lancashire women as Selina Cooper, Margaret Alderley, Sarah Reddish and, later, Ada Nield Chew as paid organisers. Connection with such well-supported bodies as the Women's Co-operative Guild helped advance the Suffrage cause.

Working-class activists faced difficulties of a different order to those of their better-off sisters, most movingly expressed by Hannah Mitchell 'No cause can be won between dinner and tea, and most of us who were married had to work with one hand tied behind us so to speak. Public disapproval could be faced and borne, but domestic unhappiness, the price many of us paid for our opinions and activities, was a very bitter thing.'[77] Public disapproval involving threats, verbal abuse, physical violence and pressure from employers nonetheless could be very severe. The physical demands of marches, demonstrations and open-air meetings were also a strain, and few NWSPU or National Union activists came home to the accumulation of family and household chores these women faced. On the other hand, radical suffragists nearly always worked with and found support from sympathetic members of the opposite sex in the Labour movement, and from some clergy and journalists.

By 1914 this network of organisations had achieved some remarkable results. If the vote had not been won, advanced political opinion had been converted, and the long-standing antipathy of the trade union leadership and Labour politicians overcome. The latter was finally achieved at the Labour Party conference of 1912 when a resolution in favour of adult suffrage, which said that the parliamentary Labour Party would oppose any Franchise Bill which did not include women was carried. After a decade of rejection at the TUC and Labour Party conferences, this was a triumph for Radical suffragists, who in these years had suffered conflicting loyalties to both feminism and Labour politics. But it had other effects, not the least of which as the decision of the National Union of Women's Suffrage Societies, which, up to then, had tried to keep their campaign on non-party political lines, to throw in its lot with the Labour Party. Already beset by doubts on this, when they heard of the Labour decision, they abandoned neutrality. For many constitutional suffragists this involved a considerable change in political gear, for none more so than for Margaret Ashton, a Liberal of long-standing. The renewed friendship with Labour was a vindication of the policy of the radical suffragists, and gave all activists a real stimulus. A month or so before war started in 1914, a joint women's suffrage and Labour demonstration was held in Manchester.

In August 1914 Emmeline Pankhurst embarked upon the final phase of her political life. Now a Conservative, she and Christabel became ardent supporters of the War, for which they were to be welcomed into the bosom of the Establishment. Always Francophile, they were outraged by the invasion of France and Belgium. They, Annie Kenney and many of the NWSPU threw themselves into the recruiting drive. Their newspaper, the *Suffragette*, was renamed *Britannia*. As a description of what Mrs Pankhurst had become, it was perfect. In 1915 they were prominent in the effort to recruit women workers into munitions factories. Two years later, the NWSPU became The Women's Party. Mrs Pankhurst and Christabel made a name for themselves haranguing workers against the evils of striking, pacifism and Bolshevism.[78]

The Great War changed most things. Whilst Christabel and her mother turned patriotic, Sylvia became militantly pacifist. She threw herself into defending conscientious objectors and founded a League of Rights for soldiers' and sailors' wives and relatives. Fined for speeches against the war, Derbyshire miners paid her fine. Inspired by the Russian Revolution in 1917, she began campaigning for a workers' state on the Soviet model. Her East London Federation became the Workers' Socialist Federation, her paper the *Women's Dreadnought*, the *Workers' Dreadnought*.[79] In reaction to the interventionist war against the Bolsheviks waged by Britain and her allies she organised a 'Hands off Russia' movement, and in 1920 her organisation was renamed the Communist Party (British Section of the Third International). However, her efforts to secure a united front with Lenin against 'compromising elements' within British Socialism were frustrated. Comrade Pankhurst was charged with 'amateurism' and refusal to accept that the Labour party's brand of Socialism was a necessary step on the road to Communism. A six months' visit to Socialist parties in Europe, and a subsequent visit to Moscow to attend the second congress of the Third International somewhat assuaged her feelings, but such an idealistic and tempestuous personality as Sylvia's could not be so easily diverted.

On returning to Britain she renewed her attacks on the capitalist government on the one hand, and the main body of British Socialists on the other through the *Dreadnought*. In due course, the newspaper's offices were raided by the police and Sylvia was charged under the Defence of the Realm Act with incitement to sedition, and sentenced to serve five months in prison. It was just like old times. Her sentence did not affect her activities in the slightest. More damaging was the results of her criticisms of the Communist leadership in her journal, having become disillusioned with Lenin's dictatorship and the New Economic Policy in Russia. Refusing an ultimatum to cease subversion of party unity and relinquish control of the *Dreadnought*, she was compelled to sever her ties with the official party.

During the following decade she went into the political wilderness. She moved through a succession of radical causes, from an independent Workers' Communist Party and an Unemployed Workers' Organisation to the promotion of new international languages, Esperanto and Interlingua, as a counter to rising nationalist movements in Italy and Germany. In 1924, with the Women's Socialist Federation dying and her friends deserting her, Sylvia ceased publication of the *Dreadnought*, moved to Woodford Green and bought a small café, 'The Red Cottage', serving teas and light meals. However, she did not cease from mental strife.

The divergence of the Pankhursts into the twin extremes of patriotism and pacificism had its counterpart in the wider women's movement. Once war began, the NUWSS, following Mrs Fawcett's patriotic lead, suspended political work and involved itself with relief work where the interests of women needed protecting. In 1915 a split began to appear within the NUWSS Council between those who wanted active support for the war effort and those who wanted to concentrate on relief work, but an even more serious rift came over the support of some of the leading figures for the pacifist Women's International League. This in turn led some into support for the National Council Against Conscription. In 1917 these pacifists came out in support for the Russian Revolution, which they thought would usher in a new era in European affairs.[80]

This was a path followed by Eva Gore-Booth and Esther Roper (who had moved to London in 1913) and a number of their old friends amongst the radical suffragist organisations in Lancashire, Cheshire and Yorkshire.[81] However, most women supported the war. Tens of thousands of women of all classes threw themselves in war-work and stayed resolutely behind the war effort, even when the heady patriotism of 1914 was replaced by a resolute determination to see it through in the grim days of 1917 and 1918.[82]

Before the end of 1916 the question of votes for women was being discussed again, if only because of the difficulties caused by the need to prepare a new register to include men serving with the forces. From this it was a short step to recognition of the need to introduce franchise reform. Whilst a special Speaker's Conference prepared a report, organisation began again amongst women. In this process, which resulted in the enfranchisement of women over the age of thirty in January 1918, Mrs Pankhurst had only a marginal involvement. Indeed, at first she opposed the move, on the grounds that soldiers and sailors (disenfranchised through loss of residence) should be granted the vote without the issue of women's suffrage being allowed to complicate the matter.[83]

During the summer of 1917, Mrs Pankhurst, now a British celebrity, travelled to Petrograd and Moscow, where she interviewed Alexander Kerensky. She travelled to the USA and Canada, where she spoke on women's service to the Allied cause, the menace of Bolshevism, and the need to prohibit non-Anglo-Saxon immigration. In December 1918, however, she suffered a grievous disappointment when Christabel, standing for Parliament in the 'Coupon Election' as candidate of the Women's Party was defeated at Smethwick, even though she faced no Unionist opposition. Within a year, the Women's Party had ceased to exist.[84]

In September 1919, Mrs Pankhurst returned to the North American lecture circuit. Now ardently right-wing, she proclaimed that only upper-class rule could preserve 'the values of civilisation'. For a time she settled in Canada, becoming a citizen in 1924. She began to lecture on 'Social Hygiene', a return to Christabel's old theories, and for three years travelled Canada addressing audiences on the subject of venereal disease, which she saw as one of the three major problems facing the British Empire (her other two being materialism and intemperance). Eventually, exhausted by proclaiming her message to North American audiences, she went to live in Bermuda, then a genteel British colony. Subsequently, in the late summer of 1925, she and Christabel set up 'the English Teashop of Good Hope', in another genteel British colony, Juan-les-Pins, on the Cote d'Azur. One supposes it had a different ambience to Sylvia's 'Red Cottage'. Mundane commerce however, never was their forte. A few months later they returned to London. Soon after Emmeline joined the Conservative Party, and in 1927 was adopted as a candidate for the strongly Labour seat of Whitechapel and St George's in the East End. However, before a General Election occurred, her health failed and she died on 14 June 1928, at the age of sixty-nine. Less than two year later, in March 1930, a statue of her in the Victoria Tower Gardens beside the Houses of Parliament was unveiled by Stanley Baldwin. With women now exercising the vote on the same terms as men, Baldwin was perhaps saying 'thank you' on behalf of the Conservative Party, the last love of Emmeline's remarkable political life.[85] In every sense, she had come a long way from Victorian Seedley.

So had her three daughters. Although she failed in 1918, Christabel polled a remarkable 8,614 votes, the largest for any woman in the first election in which women took part. A year later she became candidate for the Abbey division of Westminster, but her political ambitions evaporated, and she withdrew. When Mrs Pankhurst went to Canada, Christabel joined her, and subsequently lived most of the rest of her life in California, where she became a Seventh Day Adventist. In

1936 once again it was Stanley Baldwin who saw to it that she was made a Dame of the British Empire. Early in the Second World War, Dame Christabel left for the United States, and died at Los Angeles in 1958. The following year, a bronze medallion with her likeness was affixed to her mother's memorial statue in London.[86]

If the political movements of the post-war world offered so little scope to the temperaments of Emmeline and her eldest daughter, they proved more congenial to those of her other two. Adela found the Australian situation well-suited to her activities. There she organised the Women's Party and later the Australian Socialist Party, and was active in opposition to the Great War, publishing *Put up the Sword* to argue her case. In the Second World War she was interned. She married Tom Walsh, president and secretary of the Australian Seamen's Union, and had a son and three daughters, dying in May 1961.[87]

At the close of her Communist stage, Sylvia Pankhurst turned to serious writing. In her search for answers to the human dilemma, she was first attracted by the ideas of Gandhi. After months of research she wrote *India and the Earthly Paradise*, published in Bombay in 1926. British politics under what she called 'MacBaldwinism' she found depressing, and lamented the workers' failure in the General Strike of that year. What gave focus to her life at that time was the cause of Ethiopia, to which she was first drawn by another man in her life. For some years her lover had been Silvio Corio, a Socialist who had fled Mussolini's Italy. He was the father of her child, Richard Pankhurst, to whom she gave birth when she was forty-four. Later Sylvia moved from Wood Green and opened a Montessori School at West Dean in Sussex. It was Corio's influence which led to her preoccupation with the rise of Fascism. To expose fascist atrocities she initiated the Society of Friends of Italian Freedom, and in 1932 became the founder and hon. secretary of the Women's International Matteotti Committee to agitate for the release from house arrest of the murdered Italian Socialist deputy's widow. When Mussolini launched his brutal invasion of Ethiopia in 1934 she discovered the cause which dominated the rest of her life. She and Corio set out to mobilize British public opinion against the British and other western governments' attempts to appease *Il Duce* in order to gain Italian support against Germany. Her mouthpiece was the *New Times and Ethiopian News*, which she founded. Through it she condemned Italian atrocities and invoked support for Ethiopia's exiled ruler, Haile Selassie. Her journal was successful in the formation of anti-fascist sentiment not only on the left, but amongst the moderate majority. In the words of one biographer, Sylvia emerged 'from the tangled thicket – almost forest – of her luxuriantly rebel past, as a *grande dame* of the Popular Front'.[88]

It is hardly surprising that Sylvia Pankhurst supported the Second World War against the Axis powers. Characteristically, she started by forming a Women's War Emergency Council in October 1939 to prevent the exploitation of women. However, her greatest efforts were directed to rallying support for Ethiopia, and when British troops conquered that country in 1941 she urged the restoration of full national self-determination and of the Emperor. In 1944, when she visited the country, Sylvia found her promised land. Twelve years later, after pouring forth letters, pamphlets and books on Ethiopian and other issues, including a massive *Ethiopia: a Cultural History* (1955), she ceased publication of the *New Times*, and with her son (also a writer and intellectual of the left) emigrated to Ethiopia, where they founded the *Ethiopian Observer*. In that poor and harshly beautiful country Sylvia's restless soul found tranquillity, and it was there she died in September 1958. She, too, had come a long way from Victorian Pendleton.

What a remarkable family group the wife and daughters of Dr Pankhurst were. Though destined to take separate routes and end at different destinations, all imbibed or inherited his deep-felt political individuality. Of the four, closest to the Doctor's character and temperament was perhaps Sylvia. She also had her mother's resolution. Imprisoned on several occasions in the Suffragette cause, she hunger-struck thirteen times. But, as her mother and Christabel became more and more autocratic, Sylvia went the opposite way. Her passion, almost a religion, was that social pity for the poor to which other men and women of her class and generation subscribed. Utterly careless about her personal comforts, her devotion to the cause of poor women and their families, the victims of militarism, colonialism and fascism was total. Of all the children of Richard and Emmeline Pankhurst she was the most intellectual. From her pen came a stream of newspapers, pamphlets and books. On the suffrage cause she wrote two valuable books, *The Suffrage Movement* (1931 ) and *The Life of Emmeline Pankhurst* (1935). Everything she was involved in she wrote about, from *Soviet Russia as I saw it* (1921), through *British Policy in Eritrea* (1945) to *Ethiopia Today*, which appeared posthumously in 1961. She was also a talented artist and painter.

Mrs Pankhurst and Sylvia have their monument. To the best-hearted of the Pankhursts there is nothing tangible. It almost seems that there has been an official effort to ignore her. In the *Dictionary of National Biography*, that quasi-official book of the great and the good, there are no entries for Pankhurst, Estelle Sylvia, or Pankhurst, Richard Marsden, though Emmeline and Christabel (and even Adela, in passing) are there.[89] The British Establishment takes anything up to half a century to remember trouble-makers, however talented, who neglect to come to heel.

# Lancashire Fusilier: Sir Lees Knowles and 'The Territorial Family'

In 1886 Benjamin Armitage lost his seat in Parliament to a rich young barrister with local roots at least as deep as those of the Armitages. Lees Knowles was to hold West Salford through three more general elections, until ousted in his turn in the great Liberal revival of 1906. In his brand of Conservatism, old Beer and Bible politics were to some extent displaced by new sentiments powerful enough to win support across class – the determination to preserve the Union of Great Britain and Ireland, a shared enthusiasm for organised sport, and the harnessing of local patriotism to the cause of Imperial defence. In retrospect, Knowles' part in the movement which created the link between Salford and 'its' regiment in the British Army appears as nothing less than the central concern of his political life. Those who seek tangible evidence of this can do no better than to study the Boer War monument which faces Salford Royal Hospital. Atop his plinth a Lancashire Fusilier stands frozen in a silent but triumphant salute, busby raised in one hand, rifle with bayonet fixed in the other. Dedicated to the Regiment in general, and to local men who went as Active Service Volunteers to fight the Boers, it carries a proud claim: 'Daring in all Things'. This is the work of Lees Knowles and it stands testimony to once-powerful emotions. When it was unveiled by the King in 1905 it marked the high point of Knowles' career, and of his relationship with the people of Salford.

Born in 1857, the son of John Knowles of Westwood, Pendlebury, and Elizabeth, daughter of James Lees of Green Bank, Oldham, James Lees Knowles was the eldest son of an only son in one of the great Lancashire coal-owning families. In the 1880s the firm of Messrs. Andrew Knowles & Sons Ltd employed 3,400 men and boys at collieries at Pendlebury, Pendleton, Agecroft, Clifton Hall, Little Lever and Radcliffe. These workers produced about a million tons a year, a twentieth of the total annual output of the Lancashire coalfield.[1] With its main office at the Wheatsheaf Colliery, the centre of the firm's activities was the township of Pendlebury. Although there were other large employers close by, in that particular coal mining and cotton spinning township the influence of Messrs. Knowles was so pervasive that people referred to it simply as 't'firm'.[2]

Lees Knowles's father, John, a grandson of the first Andrew Knowles, was a great capitalist. On the retirement of *his* father, Thomas Knowles, and his uncles Robert and James, John Knowles became a principal in the third generation of the family firm's history. When it became a private limited company in 1873 he was made a director and eventually chairman. John Knowles was a considerable property owner, and amongst his other business interests he ran a cotton spinning factory at Pendlebury. In 1867 Knowles became the first Chairman of the Swinton and Pendlebury Local Board and in 1888 was appointed one of the first aldermen on the Lancashire County Council. A county JP, he served as a Deputy Lieutenant

'The epitome of public school manliness': Lees Knowles, about the time of his election to Parliament for West Salford. (*Manchester Faces and Places*)

# The Knowles Family Tree (SIMPLIFIED)

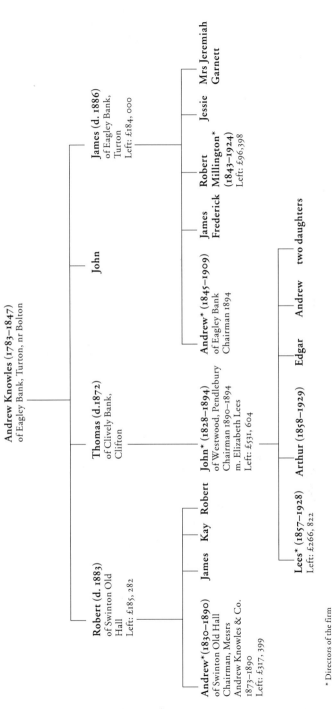

**Andrew Knowles (1783–1847)**
of Eagley Bank, Turton, nr Bolton

**Robert (d. 1883)**
of Swinton Old
Hall
Left: £185, 282

**Thomas (d.1872)**
of Clively Bank,
Clifton

John

**James (d. 1886)**
of Eagley Bank,
Turton
Left: £184, 000

**Andrew\*(1830–1890)**
of Swinton Old Hall
Chairman, Messrs
Andrew Knowles & Co.
1873–1890
Left: £317, 399

James    Kay    Robert

**John\* (1828–1894)**
of Westwood, Pendlebury
Chairman 1890–1894
m. Elizabeth Lees
Left: £531, 604

**Andrew\* (1845–1909)**
of Eagley Bank
Chairman 1894

James
Frederick

**Robert
Millington\***
(1843–1924)
Left: £96,398

Jessie

Mrs Jeremiah
Garnett

**Lees\* (1857–1928)**
Left: £266, 822

**Arthur (1858–1929)**

Edgar    Andrew    two daughters

\* Directors of the firm
In the second generation, the firm was run by Andrew Knowles' sons, Robert, Thomas and James. In 1873 the firm became a family Limited company.
In 1899 the directors were Robert M. Knowles, Andrew Knowles, Lees Knowles, Thomas Marshall (Wigan) and H. Bramhall (manager since 1886, managing director after the death of
John Knowles). (*Rep* 11 Nov 1890)

and was High Sheriff in 1892–3. If there was money in cotton, there was even more in coal: deeply involved in both, John Knowles became a very rich man. After his death his personal estate was valued at over half a million pounds.[3]

John Knowles' father had him educated to take an early and active part in the family business. On leaving a private school in Liverpool, he served an apprenticeship with a firm in Oldham, which equipped him for his future role of surveyor and mining engineer. For *his* sons John Knowles had different plans. They were sent off to public school to be made into gentlemen first and businessmen afterwards, if they were so inclined. Lees Knowles went to Rugby (where he was followed by his brothers, Arthur and Edgar) and thence to Trinity College, Cambridge. Sound enough academically, it was as a record-breaking athlete and rugby footballer that he made his mark. At school he won a string of trophies for athletics, and competed for Cambridge against Oxford four years in succession, being President of the University Athletics Club in 1878. He also played for Lancashire at rugby. His love of sport never left him. A steward at University athletics meetings on a number of occasions, he took a combined Oxford and Cambridge team to North America in 1901 to compete against McGill, Toronto, Harvard and Yale.[4] In Knowles' time the middle-class passion for athletics and team games spread to the masses, nowhere more so than in industrial Lancashire. When the young Knowles first appeared as a Unionist candidate he did so as the epitome of public school manliness.

After Cambridge Knowles studied law, and was called to the Bar at Lincoln's Inn, joining the Northern circuit in 1883. The young Knowles led an agreeable existence. He enjoyed the social connections London afforded an Old Rugbeian, a Cambridge Blue, a member of the Bar and the Junior Carlton Club. Foreign travel beckoned, and Knowles visited Germany regularly and developed a particular fondness for the the Isle of Capri. But, (though he could have been if he had wanted) Knowles was no idler. After university he returned to base. Knowles' love for Lancashire, and especially his own corner of the County Palatine, went deep, and was a mix of the down-to-earth and the romantic. Knowles' Lancashire was the pit-head and factory townships of Swinton and Pendlebury, and the teeming industrial city he represented in Parliament. It was also the country estate he bought in 1903 together with all its historic associations. A Tory Imperialist as well as a professional Lancastrian, the big question for Knowles was not what England could do for Lancashire, but what Lancashire could do for England?

Knowles entertained political ambitions from an early age, and was lucky enough to realise them before he was thirty. The timing of his entry into politics could scarcely have been more fortuitous. His first election contest was in December 1885 for the Leigh Division. It was a solid Liberal seat, and for the first time many miners had the vote. Knowles lost handsomely. But events then swung his way. Just over six months later he found himself in the House of Commons.

The new era which began with the Reform Act and the Liberal victory of 1885 led to a major Conservative reorganisation in Salford. The old Borough Party was disbanded and divided into three constituency associations. The chairmanship of the West Salford constituency party passed to Councillor T. F. Reddaway, a prominent local manufacturer, who, when Sir William Worsley declined to stand again, invited Lees Knowles. Knowles said he would accept only if Benjamin Armitage voted for the Home Rule Bill. When Armitage did so, Knowles issued his election address.[5] The conditions of the Home Rule crisis presented him with an exceptional opportunity and he took it, defeating Armitage by 274 votes. For Knowles, West Salford was an almost perfect constituency. Situated next door to Pendlebury, the family base, Messrs. Knowles owned the Pendleton and Agecroft pits at which the 500 or so local miners worked, but these miners (who were not going to vote Conservative) were not numerous enough to make life politically difficult for him. Elated by victory, but aware of how close the parties were in Pendleton, the young Knowles threw himself into constituency matters more energetically than any previous Member for Salford. When the Tory *Salford Chronicle* needed to be shored up, Knowles put money into it,[6] and over the next twenty years judiciously used his considerable wealth to underpin his political efforts. Indeed, long after he ceased to be an MP he continued to make considerable bequests in the district. A keen churchman, a trustee of three livings, Knowles, like his father before him, was churchwarden and school manager at St. John's, the Height, and was to serve on the Ecclesiastical Commission in London.

As a law-and-order man, Knowles attracted a certain amount of publicity when, in December 1890, he presented a petition from local JPs for a modification in the law to allow them to sanction the use of 'the cat' as a punishment for 'scuttling', a form of gang-warfare current amongst 'roughs' in Salford and other places. First appearing in the 1870s, outbreaks of scuttling, in which street gangs, including a few girls, fought with missiles, belts and knives, broke out from time to time, generating considerable public concern. The petition followed a particularly brutal fight between the Hope Street and Oldfield Lane gangs. In the event, scuttling was not suppressed by the 'cat-o'-nine-tails', but greater police activity, stiffer sentences and to some extent, changes in the culture of working-class males.[7]

One direction into which their energies and interests were channelled was sport. When Lees Knowles began to immerse himself in Salford life the involvement of the industrial towns in modern sport was fast becoming passionate. In particular, he was delighted to find the sports he had excelled in were now being played and watched by the masses. In athletics the old working-class tradition of 'pedestrianism' (road racing for money) was being superceded by cross-country running and organised athletics meetings, the first, or one of the first, in the district, being the Manchester Grand Athletic Festival of 1864. Held in emulation of the 'Olympic Festivals' started in Liverpool, for some years these attracted good crowds and plenty of competitors and, as was noted at the time, did much to 'popularise the athletic sports of our universities and public schools'.[8] In their modern form, athletics in Salford started in 1884 with the founding of Salford Harriers and Broughton Harriers. By 1890 Salford Harriers were national cross-country champions. Knowles had a long association with the club and boasted of being its 'oldest honorary member'.[9] Cycling made its appearence at this time and was taken up with enthusiasm: within a short time there were at least nine clubs active in the borough.[10] The sport, however, which attracted the crowds in the 1880s was Knowles' other great love, rugby football.

Salford is a sporting curiosity in that, almost alone of the big Victorian towns, it never produced an Association Football League club. Salford's name has long

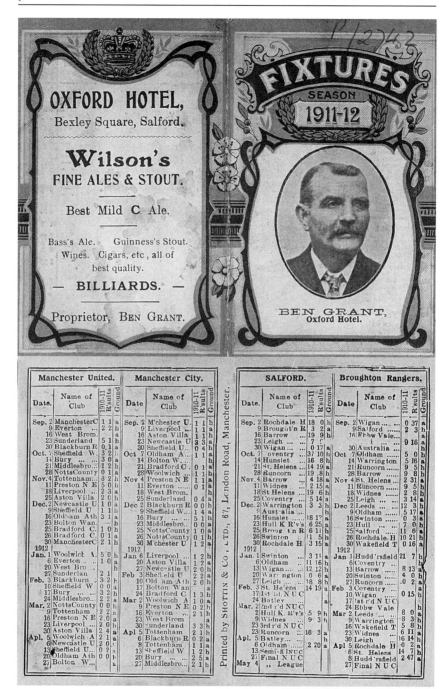

'Football-mad Manchester': Football and Northern Union rugby fixtures for the season 1911–12. (Northamptonshire Record Office)

been associated with rugby. This is not because Salford people did not (or do not) share in the love of 'the people's game'. Quite the contrary. It is partly because rugby emerged rather earlier than Association Football as a spectator sport in the district, and partly because of the geography of the great double-barrelled city. From 1909, when the club moved to its present ground at Old Trafford, just across the Ship canal from Ordsall, the Football League team Salford fans have generally supported is Manchester United.[11]

The first rugby clubs were middle-class, Knowles himself playing for Manchester (founded in 1860). In the Seventies the game began to be played more widely, reports of local matches appearing in the newspapers as early as 1872. By the end of that decade there were at least a dozen teams in the Manchester, Salford and Swinton district, out of which three – Swinton, Broughton Rangers and Salford – emerged as 'crowd pullers.' Of these Swinton (founded in 1868) was the oldest and the first to build a reputation. By the early Eighties it had emerged as one of the top teams in the North, famous enough to be invited to Oxford to do battle with the University XV in 1883. Two years later, when Swinton played Bradford, the game attracted 10,000 spectators.[12] Broughton Rangers, (founded 1877), became famous rather later, as one of the leading clubs of the Northern Union, after the split in rugby in the mid-Nineties. The club's great days were between then and the start of the first World War.[13] The club which eventually became 'Salford' started in 1873 as the football team of the Cavendish Sunday School in Hulme. For a time they played at Moss Side, migrating to Salford in search of a better ground. Eventually they amalgamated with the Crescent Club and changed their name to Salford. By 1879, at their ground in Howard Street, Eccles New Road, they had a 'gate' and were drawing good crowds. The famous red jerseys were adopted in 1883, and by the following season the team were playing many of the leading clubs in Lancashire and Yorkshire. However, it was some years before Salford was as successful as Swinton. Between 1880 and 1896 the clubs played one another thirty times and Salford won on only four occasions.[14] As with Broughton Rangers, Salford's best days came after they joined the Northern Union.

From the time Lees Knowles became MP for West Salford he associated himself with the club. He became its president and contributed a Foreword to its first history, which appeared in 1892. To encourage the game, Knowles presented a cup to be played for each season by local junior teams. In rugby, and sport in general, Knowles saw a means for the promotion of values he endorsed and believed the nation needed: 'manliness', local pride, and 'club' (as opposed to 'class') spirit.

Knowles' parliamentary apprenticeship was served as a supporter of Lord Salisbury's Government, which came to power in 1886. In those years Ireland was at the centre of events. To render Ireland governable, Balfour brought in a tough Crimes Act, in support of which Knowles made his maiden speech.[15] In these years dramatic events succeeded one another rapidly but by 1892 the Unionist Government felt itself to be on top of the problem: coercion and land purchase seemed to be doing the trick. For Unionists like Knowles, it seemed a victory. Another influence on the young MP was the upsurge of Imperialism at the time of the Queen's Jubilee in 1887. The late Eighties saw the partition of Africa by the great powers. It was the golden age of annexation by chartered companies and individual adventurers, pre-eminent amongst whom was Cecil Rhodes. Imperialism and the results of Rhodes' machinations in Southern Africa were to play no small part in Lees Knowles' political life. However, in his first Parliament, his most immediate concern was with the more mundane, but not unimportant, matter of local government. One of the most able figures in Lord Salisbury's Cabinet was C. T. Ritchie, President of the Local Government Board, whom Knowles served as private secretary for six years.[16] Amongst the most important of Ritchie's achievements was the 1888 Local Government Act. County Councils were set up to modernise rural local government, and County Boroughs (of which Salford became one) were introduced as their urban counterparts. These years also saw the passing of local legislation of real importance. The education system was improved by the Technical Institute Act of 1899 making county and county borough councils the authorities, a foreshadowing of their future roles as local education authorities. For Salford, the outcome was the building of the Royal Technical Institute in Peel Park, to which Knowles donated an organ for its great hall. The Conservatives also abolished elementary school fees in 1891, marking a change in party policy. It was now argued that if the abolition of fees was left to a future Liberal Government, free education might be confined to the board schools, placing the voluntary schools at a serious disadvantage, and possibly leading to their demise. At first, this argument proved too machiavellian for local voluntaryists. To the fury of Liberals and Non-conformists, in 1892 and 1893 the Church-dominated Salford School Board refused to implement free education.

These years saw important changes on the industrial front and in the class basis of politics, Socialism bringing a sharp new edge into both. Trades unionism, in the form of the Pendlebury, Pendleton, Clifton and Kearsley Miners Association, began to impinge on Messrs. Andrew Knowles. For more than half a century the policy of the firm had been to refuse to employ union men.[17] Although by 1870 half the colliers in the Farnworth and Kearsley District were in a union, none were employed by Andrew Knowles & Sons.[18] Things changed in the Eighties. A series of fierce disputes in the end led to the establishment of a union in the district. Almost as important as 'New Unionism' was the the enfranchisement of the miners. Now part of the political nation, miners were to find (as Chartists had predicted forty years before) that they were not so readily oppressed as hitherto. Locally, the Clifton Hall Colliery disaster which resulted in the deaths of 178 men and boys and the injuring of a further 44 others in an explosion of firedamp in June 1885, was a turning point. A public subscription to help the families of the killed and injured raised over £27,000.[19] The Pendlebury, Pendleton, Clifton and Kearsley Miners' Association was founded in June 1888, at a time when conditions took a marked turn for the better. Miners nationwide agitated for a pay rise. It was the first of several, which were to see wages increase by up to 35 per cent over the next three years. That December, Messrs. Knowles and all the other companies finally acceeded to the demand for weekly instead of fortnightly pay.[20] However, it was one thing for Knowles to agree to these advances: it was quite another to recognise the union.

The following summer the union pressed for a 10 per cent rise, already achieved in Yorkshire, threatened to strike, and won. A new mood of elation set in. In July

1889 the Pendlebury and District men joined the Lancashire Federation. The owners federated in their turn, Lees Knowles's father becoming a prominent figure on the executive committee of the Lancashire and Cheshire Coal-owners. In the boom year of 1890 the miners pressed for the eight hour day and another 10 per cent rise. The latter was won after a five day national strike. This victory took the union through the credibility barrier in the Pendlebury district.[21] In October a strike at the Wheatsheaf Colliery began over 'packing' (to prevent subsidence), though the big issue was union recognition. In the end, after eleven weeks, a compromise was arrived at on 'packing', and the firm had been forced to negotiate with union officials. With a membership of 3,202 in the Pendlebury and District Lodge at Christmas 1891, the fortunes of the union reached a peak.[22]

In January 1894, just after another big industrial dispute with the miners' union, John Knowles died. Lees Knowles inherited 'Westwood', Pendlebury, property in Manchester and estates in Pendleton (including 'Light Oaks', 'the Duchy' and

'The price of coal': monument to the victims of the Clifton Hall colliery disaster, 1885, in the churchyard of St Augustine's, Pendlebury (Photo: the author)

'Somerville'). He also inherited a seat on the board of the company.[23] He was to find his directorship of 't'firm' no easy ride: it involved playing a leading part in its running, and in the activities of the federated coal proprietors and the Institute of Mining Engineers. It also meant that, for the first time, he was going to have to relate directly to the miners. In the timing of all this, Knowles was, as always, lucky. If the bitter lock-out of 1893 had taken place a year earlier he might have lost to Benjamin Armitage in their second electoral contest. He was also fortunate that industrial relations were quiet in the mid-years of the decade.

At midsummer 1892 Lord Salisbury's government resigned and a general election was called. Despite the fact that Lancashire in general was against Home Rule, knowing how little separated the parties locally, Salford Liberals expected to do well. In fact, they carried North Salford and would have won in South Salford if the Socialists had not split the anti-Conservative vote. In Pendleton, Knowles did well to hold off Benjamin Armitage, scraping home by just 40 votes.

Though Conservatism prevailed in Salford, Gladstone won the election. With the support of Irish Nationalists he was returned with a majority in the House of Commons. In the face of widespread opposition, he introduced his second Home Rule Bill. At a Unionist rally in Broughton in April 1893, Hardcastle, the former MP, and Frederick Platt-Higgins, the prospective candidate, attacked Gladstone for the 'Great Betrayal'. From that fountainhead of Salford Protestantism, the pulpit of St. Bartholomew's, the Rev. G. W. Baile, Secretary of the Irish Sunday School Society thundered, as others before him had thundered, that Home Rule meant Rome Rule, and that most Irishmen were really against it.[24] Other parts of Gladstone's programme also had the tendency to unite Conservatives, Unionists, Protestants and businessmen more closely than ever. The threat of Welsh Disestablishment gave Churchmen the chance to invoke '69. 'Local Option' locked brewers, publicans and Salford's drinkers in an even boozier embrace. Employers' Liability (for accidents) propelled many businessmen towards Conservatism. Gladstone's programme was defeated almost in its entirety and the Grand Old Man bowed out in 1894. Rosebery's government was defeated in late June 1895 and a general election followed. In Salford it was as close as ever. The initiative lay with the Conservatives. If Home Rule, Church Defence and the position of demominational schools were the main issues, there were a range of others: duties on cotton goods imported into India, the future of the Poor Law, Jewish immigration, cheap labour and 'sweating', Employers' Liability, the eight hour day, Socialism and anti-Socialism, Trades Unionism and 'Free Labour'. All over South-East Lancashire Conservatism did well. In Manchester five Unionists and one Liberal were returned against three of each in 1892. In Salford, the closest contest was in Broughton, where Frederick Platt-Higgins ousted Sir W. H. Holland by a mere six votes. A local man, the son, and grandson, of Salford machine makers, Platt-Higgins was a modern Conservative in the Lees Knowles mould. Fighting under the slogans 'the Unity of the Empire' and 'Justice to the Voluntary Schools', he proved the ideal man to win North Salford back for the Unionists.[25] South Salford in 1895 saw a re-run of three years before. Sir Henry Howorth, the Conservative, polled 74 more votes than Alexander Forrest, who might well have won if a Socialist had not 'intervened' once more. Lees Knowles' victory in West Salford was the most comfortable of the three. On the dissolution of Parliament, Benjamin Armitage had withdrawn his candidature, and, William Agnew declining to stand, Armitage's half-brother Vernon was drafted. In the circumstances he did remarkably well, losing by only 100 out of 8,608 votes cast.

Knowles' third term in Parliament saw the most effective phase of his public life. He resumed his post as private secretary to C. T. Ritchie, now President of the Board of Trade, and over the next few years busied himself with such matters as sanitation and housing. In addition, he served on the Select Committee for Town Holdings, and had the distinction of being Chairman of a Select Committee on Plumbers' Registration Bill. His selection as hon. secretary of the Lancashire

Conservative MP's group gave him special pleasure, as did any appointment to do with his native county. In London he busied himself as a trustee of the City of London Parochial Charities, and as hon. secretary to the housing charity, the Guinness Trust. Mindfull as ever of the needs of his own class, he served on the council of Rossall, the Lancashire public school, and also spent five years as a Church Cominissioner.[26]

In the second half of the 1890s the dominating factor in national politics was Imperialism. Scarcely a year passed without its little wars, tensions with one or other of the Great Powers, and a futher racking-up of the spirit of 'Jingoism'. 1896 brought the Ashanti War and an Anglo-American rift over the British Guiana-Venezuela border. 1898 brought Kitchener's re-conquest of the Sudan and the Battle of Omdurman: the atmosphere reminded people of 40 years earlier, when Tennyson electrified England with 'The Charge of the Light Brigade'. What made the fires of Imperialism really crackle, however, was the coming of the Boer War. Events in the Transvaal were to introduce Knowles to the love of his life.

Trouble in that Boer republic began with the discovery of gold in Witwatersrand. Johannesburg sprang up as 'Uitlanders' – prospectors, financial speculators and white ruffians from all over the world swarmed in. Kruger, the Transvaal's President, made it clear that Uitlanders were expected to behave themselves, and not expect political equality with his people. Between Kruger, the Uitlanders (whose cause was championed by Cecil Rhodes) and the colonial administration in the Cape there developed serious tensions, into which the British Government, was inexorably drawn. The Jameson Raid into the Transvaal, a failed *coup d'état* by accomplices of Cecil Rhodes, exacerbated an already tense situation. For three years the situation deteriorated, and the war which was to play such a part in Knowles's Lancashire life started on 28th October 1899. By then, Knowles was hon. colonel, the 3rd Volunteer Battalion, the Lancashire Fusiliers, in which position he was to discover the intoxicating pleasure of being an armchair soldier.

Salford and the British Army had long enjoyed a relationship. Whether from wanderlust, or desire to escape poverty or the mill, many Salford men had taken the Queen's shilling, to return full of tales of soldiering. There had been an infantry barracks on Regent Road since 1795: military display and soldiers on and off duty were part of the Salford scene. As well as working-class recruits who signed up with the regulars or the Militia, ever since 1859 young men of the middle classes had joined the Volunteer Rifle Corps.[27] Encouraged by government as a way of training 'marksmen', the Volunteers had stayed quite distinct and separate from both regulars and Militia, who rather looked down on them.

By the time of Gladstone's first government, national military arrangements were in need of reform, and one of the new ideas of the time was that of 'territorial connection'. It led, in 1881, to the allocation of certain regiments of the British Army to counties. In the process, the XXth Regiment of Foot, raised in 1688, and possessed of a long and distinguished military history, was renamed 'the Lancashire Fusiliers'.[28] Since its beginnings there had scarcely been a war or 'soldiers' battle' the XXth had not been in the thick of – Dettingen, Fontenoy, Culloden, Quebec, Corunna, the Alma, Inkerman. Its finest hour had been at the Battle of Minden in 1759, when it carried out the extraordinary feat, for infantry, of putting cavalry to flight. In the late eighteenth century it had been known as the East Devonshire Regiment when it had strong connections with the city of Exeter. However, in the wars against the French Republic and Napoleon, the XXth had recruited well in Lancashire. But its Lancashire connections were not really close until 1873. In that year, the XXth's regimental barracks were moved from Exeter to Bury. In 1881 it was re-named, and, as the Lancashire Fusiliers, saw action in the Sudan in 1898 and fought at Omdurman. When the Boer War started, the 2nd Battalion (raised at the time of the Mutiny) was ordered to leave India for the Cape.

Cardwell's army reforms in the 1870s began the first moves to give the Militia and Rifle Volunteers a more modern role as 'territorial reserve forces'. In 1875 the Salford Rifle Volunteers (the '56th Lancashire') consisted of seven companies (702 men). They had a regimental band, and their headquarters and drillyard were at Duncan's Lodge, Cross Lane.[29] Further reforms converted them into the 3rd Volunteer Battalion, the Lancashire Fusiliers, though their status and role were still quite separate from the regular battalions of the regiment, who scarcely noticed their existence. Nonetheless, they gave every indication of being serious reserve soldiers. On the eve of the Boer War, now under the command of Col. Frederick Haworth, of the firm of Richard Haworth & Sons, the 3rd Volunteer Battalion's ten companies were up to strength.[30] It was at this point that Lees Knowles offered his services to the government in any capacity. He was given an honorary colonelcy in the Battalion.

For the Battalion and the Regiment Knowles was a valuable acquision: he placed his influence, enthusiasm and money at their service, and all were useful in the days to come. As the Regimental *Annual* for 1900 noted 'No one could have entered more enthusiastically into its history, traditions and customs than he has done'.[31] For Knowles, the regiment became the link between imperialism and local patriotism. He discovered a great grand-uncle, Robert Knowles, who had served as a volunteer in the Royal Lancashire Militia in the Napoleonic Wars and been killed in Spain at the age of 24. Knowles was very proud of this, and was later to edit and publish a selection of Robert's letters. Knowles was also delighted to find that the Regiment's greatest hour contained an incident, the symbolism of which modern Lancashire could not fail to appreciate. On the day of the Battle of Minden, the XXth had picked roses on the march to the fray, and maybe worn them in the fight. As the regimental *History* of 1903 records, 'The anniversary of Minden has always been celebrated by the corps … In recent years the celebrations have been worthily carried out. Trooping of the colours at noon (every officer and man wears a rose), athletic sports, Minden dinners etc.'[32] At the latter events it was the custom for newly commissioned officers to receive a red rose which was then dipped in wine and *eaten*. Whether the custom pre-dated Knowles' association with the regiment is not known. It seems to carry the Knowles stamp: county, Church and country. What *is* certain, is that over the years Knowles was responsible for adding to the Lancashire Fusiliers' customs and regalia, things upon which British regiments build cohesion.

Knowles' first duty as Hon. Colonel was to perform the opening ceremony of the new drill hall in Cross Lane on 8th December 1899, towards which he contributed a thousand pounds.[33] Shortly after, news of the setbacks and early defeats in South Africa began to fill the newspapers. The 2nd Battalion were soon in action and Salfordians were amongst the first casualties. Spion Kop was later described by Knowles as a 'Lancashire Battle'. If it was, it was no Lancashire triumph. Seventeen hundred men were killed on that hill. Well-able to separate out the bravery of the common soldier from incompetent leadership, the public cherish certain hard-fought military defeats. Spion Kop entered the vernacular: on some football grounds the name was given to the steep terrace where the home fans gathered. Shock at these setbacks soon gave way to a tremendous wave of patriotism. Efforts were re-doubled to win the South African War.

One result of this was the sending of Volunteer Active Service Companies to the Cape, the first suggestion for which came from Knowles as early as the 14th September 1899 in a letter to the commander-in-chief, Field Marshall Viscount Wolseley. Knowles said he had discussed with Col. Haworth the idea of raising and equipping a hundred men from Salford and offering them to the army:

> What I feel is this, that there ought to be some personal local contact between the Regulars, the Militia and the Volunteers. I thought that if we could arrange to have a company named the 'Salford Company', into which our Salford recruits might pass we might create such an interest ... But what I want chiefly to say is that if the Volunteers can be of service in connection with the present Transvaal difficulty, we shall be most grateful if you will give the 3rd V. B. the Lancashire Fusiliers the opportunity of showing our usefulness and our grit.

Wolseley grasped the possible future importance of the offer, replying 'I entirely endorse your opinions as to the necessity of strengthening the ties between the Army and its Auxiliary forces ... and the more we combine them together the better for the Army and for the State. I can see no insuperable difficulty in calling one company of the Battalion abroad the Salford Company to be composed of men from Salford'. In the event, the first Volunteer Active Service Company of 112 men which embarked for South Africa in March 1900 was composed of sections from each of the three Volunteer Battalions of the Lancashire Fusiliers, that is to say Rochdale and Bury men as well as Salfordians. They took part in operations with the 2nd Battalion, and the regulars praised them as competent and soldierly during the year they served in South Africa. A second Active Service Company of 111 officers and men was later despatched to the Cape.[34]

A third of Lees Knowles' initiatives was the practical idea of setting up a Compassionate Fund. At a meeting on 20th November 1899 Knowles proposed that such a fund be raised, and that its disposition of should be at the discretion of the officers of the 3rd Volunteer Battalion 'for the benefit of Lancashire Fusiliers, whether of the line, the Militia or the Volunteers.' The fund was duly inaugurated with a sum of one thousand pounds in July 1900, to which Knowles contributed handsomely. As well as being a pioneering exercise in paternalism, Knowles' scheme recognised that future regimental plans would not necessarily be the same as at present.[35]

Although public opinion was generally swept up in the mood of euphoria and

Imperialism which Knowles gloried in, not all Salford was enthused by the war. Liberal opinion was divided, with an important minority supporting the anti-war line of C. P. Scott's *Manchester Guardian*, Socialists as well as Radicals were against the war, as were Irish Nationalists, who identified with the Boers from the outset. People generally were pro-war, and the party of John Bull and Rule Britannia in Salford was headed by Knowles, Platt-Higgins and Col. Haworth. The turning point was the Relief of Mafeking. 'Bands of the rudest kind were improvised and paraded in the streets playing patriotic music, many in the procession singing loudly.' Bonfires were lit, and effigies of the Kaiser, whose support for the the Boers had enraged British public opinion, were burned.[36]

The war dragged on for two more years, but by October 1900 it was clear that there was only going to be one outcome. The government called a general election. It was one it could not lose: in the 'Khaki Election' Conservatives triumphed in all three Salford seats by massive majorities. On the eve of the election, after 14 years as the Member for South Salford, Sir Henry Howorth stood down, to be succeeded by James Grimble Groves, managing director of Groves & Whitnall the Salford brewery. Groves defeated Alfred Mond (of the chemical firm Brunner & Mond) by 1227 votes. This time there was no Socialist. In North Salford, Platt-Higgins improved his majority. In Pendleton, Knowles defeated C. E. Mallet, the Liberal, by 1,162, his biggest ever majority.[37] In an atmosphere of popular Jingoism, led by a government seen by Liberals as 'Khaki clad, khaki mad and khaki bad', public events were dominated by the war for another year. In May 1901 the Active Service Units returned to a great welcome. Arriving at Victoria Station, they marched to HQ in Cross Lane, welcomed at Bexley Square by the mayor and assembled dignitaries. Two months later there was a special dinner for the 43 Salford men who returned from active service. They were each presented with an illuminated scroll and a silver match box, the honours being done by Knowles, Groves and Col. Haworth.[38]

Knowles now busied himself with seeking official recognition for the Regiment's services in South Africa, especially for the bravery of the 2nd Battalion at Spion Kop. In June 1901 the War Office responded by conferring three honours on the Regiment. Henceforth it was to bear 'Omnia Audax' ('Daring in all things') and the Red Rose of Lancaster upon its colours, and at the same time the King was also graciously pleased to grant Knowles's request that a hackle of Toriest primrose yellow be worn on the regimental busby. The following year, Knowles decided to resign his ornamental post of honorary Colonel and take up the active position of Lieutenant-Colonel, the 3rd Volunteer Battalion, second in command to Col. Haworth. To qualify, Knowles obtained his certificate at the School of Instruction, Chelsea. His commission was celebrated by a portrait which depicts him in uniform, busby in hand, proud and stern. Now truly a Lancashire Fusilier, Knowles took every opportunity to foster the regiment's traditions and give it whatever aid and comfort he could. He bought it pictures, he encouraged and supported Major Smyth's history of the regiment, and he provided the 3rd Battalion with a firing range on land he owned in Pendleton.[39]

Above all, what Knowles and his friends sought was some 'lasting memorial' in Salford. A statue was decided on, a subscription raised, and the commission placed in the hands of George Frampton, RA. Its design, 'A Lancashire Fusilier in review order cheering for the King', was decided on at a meeting in Knowles's house. In the event, two were erected, the other being at Bury. On the 13th July 1905 the King came to Salford to unveil the monument at the Chapel Street end of Oldfield Road. He was greeted by the civic dignitaries and Lees Knowles, now a Baronet, in full uniform, bursting with pride.[40]

By the standards of what was to come, the sacrifices commemorated by this monument were tiny. Two hundred and twenty two Lancashire Fusiliers were killed in this little Imperial war and, of the Salford Company who went to South Africa as Knowles's volunteers, only one did not return. But it was not about sacrifices, but feelings and ideas: local patriotism, volunteering, comradeship and bravery in the face of the enemy. Col. Haworth saw it as 'another and lasting link in the chain that binds the teritorial family together'.[41]

'Daring in all things': the Lancashire Fusiliers monument, Chapel Street, Salford. In the background is the spire of St John's Cathedral.
(Photo: the author)

For his his contribution to the Boer war and political services to Conservatism Knowles received a baronetcy in 1903, and marked this social translation with the purchase of the Turton Estate, the manor house of which, Turton Tower, had once been the possession of Humphrey Chetham, the great 17th century Manchester merchant and benefactor. It was all the more satisfactory in that Turton had ancestral connections: many of Knowles' forebears were buried there. So, to his considerable repertoire, Knowles added yet another role: country squire. All that was lacking was a lady of the manor.

A later historian of the regiment reflected, 'South Africa was the grave of the old army of Victorian days.'[42] So it was, in more ways than one. The Boers took an unconscionable time being defeated: peace was not signed until 31 May 1902. Well before the end of the war the euphoria of Mafeking gave way to a mood of critical introspection. An army which could not be mobilised quickly, had no general staff and lacked an efficient intelligence service was dangerously out of date in the modern world. There was an urgent need to match French and German efficiency. It fell to the Liberal, Haldane, to carry out the reforms which ensured that when the Great War started the British Army was ready. However, the process of assessment and debate began under the Conservatives. The problems were how to force traditionalists to accept reform; how to do it within public spending controls; and how to avoid compulsory national service, regarded in every quarter as anathema. When the Conservative Secretary of War's proposed cuts in the regular army and changes in the role of the Volunteers were debated, Knowles spoke feelingly in the House of the past services of the XXth, the Lancashire Fusiliers, and of the county system.[43] He 'looked upon the territorial system as a sort of family connection. The territorial system was carried out, not merely into the Army, but into the Navy; our battleships now being named after counties. Everybody was now accustomed to territorial names and a county name gave a wider attachment to a regiment and a homely and sentimental attachment'.

It was left to the Haldane to work out the new arrangements in 1907–9. Though the Regiment was reduced by two battalions and the Volunteers reorganised into something different, the territorial attachment was kept, and Knowles was to find a role within the new system. Meanwhile, he continued to play a full part in the life of the regiment, and contributed articles to the Lancashire Fusiliers' *Annual*. In 1905 there had appeared 'A Day with Korps-Students in Germany', which described a visit to Heidelberg to take part in the 25th anniversary of a duelling society with which a German friend of his was associated.[44] Reflecting, without odious comparisons, on the differences between student pastimes in the two countries, Knowles simply noted what 'splendid exercise' fighting with the student duelling swords was. Making specified passes with the sword held aloft, the object was to inflict and take blows around certain unprotected parts of the head and face: 'The pluck of the German student is enormous. One gash, received without a grimance, opened a man's head about the width of an ordinary thumb, and required 14 stitches, and this without a sign of pain'. Knowles concluded 'This may not be sport from an English point of view. What at once strikes the Englishman when he visits Germany are the Schmisse, or gashes on the faces of the students, the result of duelling. This form of exercise is essential for the German Korps Students. It teaches them self-confidence and it makes Spartans of a military nation ... as we at Oxford and Cambridge have our ways of keeping ourselves in good training, so have my friends the Korps Students of Germany in general, and at Heidelberg in particular'.

Knowles was a regular summer visitor to Germany. The next year he contributed a piece on watching the German Army in training, a description of infantry and cavalry crossing the Rhine at Speyer. What impressed most was that every officer and man knew exactly what he was supposed to be doing. Although written before Anglo-German rivaly began to sharpen, even so it is surprising that in these essays Knowles gave no inkling that one day these people may be the enemy. At that time, however, his piece on the student societies attracted some interest in both Germany and this country. A German version was published in in 1908, a second English one in 1911, followed by a new and enlarged edition two years later. The

'The high point of Knowles' career': welcoming King Edward VII to the unveiling of the Boer War monument in 1905. (Local History Collection, Peel Park)

discovery of the pleasures of writing was something new. Knowles was to indulge it more fully in his retirement.

Knowles' finest years – the second half of the Nineties and the early Edwardian era – were not entirely filled by the excitement of politics, the thrills of being a Boer-warrior or the pleasures of foreign vacations. His seat on the board of the firm carried responsibilities and duties as well as financial reward. From his presidential addresses to the Institute of Mining Engineers in 1906 and the Manchester Geological and Mining Society in two years later, it is clear that Knowles had aquired an intimate knowledge of both the economic and the scientific aspects of the coal business.[45] By then he had also won his spurs as a class warrior on the industrial relations front.

In the boom of he late nineties, trade union activity revived strongly. In 1898 the miners began to press for the restoration of the pay cut of four years before and renewed the agitation for the Eight Hour Day. However, the main bone of contention with the firm was the operation of the Workmen's Compensation Act of 1897. This important piece of legislation, which replaced the Employers Liability Act of 1880, introduced a new principle. Hitherto, the injured workman had to prove employers' liability. Now liability was assumed. As with the 1880 Act, the law allowed 'contracting out', and Messrs Andrew Knowles announced its intention of so doing. A new scheme was drafted for the approval of the Registar General of Friendly Societies. The miners put up strong opposition to it but the firm had its way.[46] Its scheme was approved by the Registrar General and very soon most of their workers were in it. In the event, the firm's victory was short-lived. When the new Liberal Government came to power in 1906, one of the first pieces of legislation it promoted was a new Workmen's Compensation Act. What no-one now disputed was the need for accident schemes. In Knowles' collieries alone between November 1898 and the end of December 1905 there were 5,735 accidents (25 fatal), an average of 16 per working week.[47]

One thing the firm was powerless to stop was the Union's growth. By 1902 virtually all Knowles' workers were in the union and the Pendlebury and District Good Intent Lodge was large and prosperous. However, trade union fortunes were notoriously liable to ebb and flow with the conditions of the times, and the gains made in the boom of the Boer War were soon threatened in the post-war depression. In August 1902 – for the first time in four years – miners in the district were on short time. A sixteen week strike at Knowles' Agecroft Pit over that old bone of contention, 'packing', resulted in the men going back to work without a definite victory.[48]

The miners had long spells of short time in 1904 and 1905, and suffered two wage reductions. In February 1905 the firm reported it 'had never been so short of work since the formation of the company' (in 1873), and that prices were falling: shareholders that year had to rub along on a dividend of only 6 per cent.[49] The following month Pendleton Colliery was closed by an accident for some weeks. It was at such times the workers felt the real benefit of being in a healthy union.

By 1906, the the economy improved, which not only benefited the miners, but also the party they supported. The Liberals won the general election of 1906, and one of the local signs of victory was the elevation of Thomas Greenall, President of the Lancashire and Cheshire Miners, to the Salford Borough Magistrates Bench.[50] Under the Liberal Government the chief gains for the miners were the passing of the Employers' Liability Act and the Eight Hours Act, which came into operation on 1st. July 1909.[51] From 1908 the political awareness of the miners sharpened when, following a ballot of its members, the Lancashire and Cheshire Association affiliated to the Labour Party.[52]

However, as we have seen, 1910 and the years following saw the rise of an unprecedented wave of labour militance. In December 1910 the Pendleton miners enforced the closed shop. Three thousand men came out on 23 December because three men at the Wheatsheaf No 2 pit – the last of all the men at the Knowles pits in Pendlebury, Pendleton, Agecroft and Clifton Hall – refused to join the union when the local association called for one hundred per cent membership. The union approached the employers to put pressure on their men and, if necessary, dismiss them. Messrs Knowles replied they could not take sides. After a two-week strike the union had its way.[53] Labour troubles in the mining industry came to a climax early in 1912 with the national miners' strike over a national minimum wage. The Lancashire Miners Federation only had funds to sustain industrial action for two weeks, and the resultant scenes over the six and half weeks which followed were both harrowing and occasionally violent. The aftermath was a serious decline in the membership of the union locally. Dissatisfied with the financial support given during the strike, in November 1912 it was reported that those who left were resisting all efforts to get them to rejoin, especially at the pits of Messrs Knowles and the Clifton & Kearsley Coal Company.[54] Thus, on the eve of the Great War tensions between Capital and Labour were anything but solved. If the miners made further advances during the war, old tensions were to come back after the peace. Lees Knowles was to live though it all.

The 1906 election was the beginning of the end of Knowles' political career. The disintegration of Tory political dominance began in the depression after the Boer War, when a series of issues arose which gave the Liberals a chance to re-unite. The first was the Education Bill of 1902, which proposed to abolish school boards and replace them with local education authorities, provide secondary schools and draw the denominational schools into the new system by funding them out of the rates. The latter proposal enraged Nonconformists, who had fought it for over sixty years. A second factor in the revival of Liberalism was the question of Chinese labour in South Africa. After the war a shortage of native labour in the Transvaal led to the decision to import Chinese to work the mines. To prevent them becoming settlers the Cape government agreed to the idea of their being indentured labour. Liberals argued that this would, in effect, re-introduce slavery into the British Empire. 'Yellow Slavery' fired-up Nonconformity, giving Liberalism that sense of moral purpose on which it always thrived. In the summer of 1904 this was the main issue in Salford party politics. The capitalist/colonialist case was promoted by Platt-Higgins, and opposed by his new Liberal opponent in North Salford, W. H. Byles.[55] For trades unionists as well as Liberals, 'Yellow Slavery' was a major issue, and the TUC orchestrated rallies and meetings against the government's support for Milner's scheme. One of the first things the Liberal Party did when it came to power was to force the abandonment of the use of Chinese labour in South Africa.

An even more emotive issue for Liberalism, particularly in Manchester and Salford, was Chamberlain's proposals for protectionism. In the post-war depression some Conservatives accepted his arguments in favour of tariff reform to protect British industry and agriculture from the effects of foreign competition. Others, led by Balfour, clung to Free Trade. In Salford, Platt-Higgins argued the case for protectionism, calling into question the claims conventionally made about the benefits of Free Trade. Knowles, by contrast, was a convinced Free Trader. Groves at first had difficulty making up his mind, but eventually came out in support of Balfour, declaring that he would oppose duties on imported food and raw materials. If the issue split Conservatives, the attack on their central article of faith was the strongest elixir imaginable for Liberals. A propaganda campaign was launched by such bodies as the Cobden Society, and protectionists were given a drubbing. In the titles of such books as *The Hungry Forties* (a phrase not used before, but which entered the national vocabulary), the campaign recalled memories of the great days of the Anti-Corn Law League. As Platt-Higgins ruefully acknowledged, Conservatives had difficulty countering the 'Big and Little Loaf' simplifications of their opponents.[56] Leaders and makers of public opinion clung to the creed which said that Britain owed its economic strength to the liberalisation of trade: challenging this, protectionists were on a sure-fire loser for some time to come.

The size of the Liberal victory in 1906 took everyone by surprise. With 377 seats in the House of Commons, they had a majority of 84 over all other parties combined – the biggest since the Reform Act of 1832. In Salford the Conservatives and Unionists lost all three seats. Artifical though their victory in the Khaki election had been, such a total reversal was dramatic. Since the Boer War, issues had come to the fore which created a quite extraordinary interest in party politics: in 1906 no less than 90 per cent of Salford electors cast their votes.[57] In addition to the education, Chinese labour and protectionist controversies, the Taff Vale case in 1901 and the Aliens' Act of 1905 roused Liberals. As already noted, the decision which declared trades unions legal entities capable of being sued over a trade dispute (a reversal of the previously understood basis of labour law) was a major factor in the formation of a Labour party: for the first time the big battalions of the trades union movement began to back the Labour Representation Committee. The Aliens' Bill politicised Manchester and Salford Jewry. In the election, Jewish voters gave their support to the Liberals. From 1900 Irish Nationalism also underwent a revival locally. Branches of the United Irish League sprang up, the 'Martyrs' in South Salford, 'Archbishop Croke' in North Salford, 'St. Patrick' in Great George Street, 'Father Mathew' in Pendleton. By 1905, in addition to the United Irish, there were also the Irish National Foresters, the Gaelic League and the Gaelic Athletic Association.[58] Their ardent support for the Liberal party over Home Rule led to further friction with the Manchester Catholic Federation, who accused the United Irish League of selling out Catholicism on the schools issue, and, in the aftermath of the Saffenreuter affair, of disloyalty to the clergy. Refuting this, J. P. Byrne, the leading Irishman in Salford, replied 'the League did not wish to undermine the work of clergy, but in politics they would insist on their just rights.'[59]

In fact, Home Rule was not the main issue in the election. Nonetheless, the realisation that it was no longer the bogey of yesteryear came as a shock to Unionists. In North Salford, Platt-Higgins was defeated by W. P. Byles, by the remarkable majority of 1,187. The son of the founder of the *Yorkshire Observer*, Byles was a Home Ruler, and a politician of decidedly independent views.[60] Broughton Liberals evidently liked this: Byles was to hold the seat until his death in 1917. The big issues was Protectionism and Byles was an ardent free trader. Platt-Higgins was blown away in a gale of economic liberalism. On this and on the immigrant issue the Jewish voters of Broughton came out solidly for Byles.

James Grimble Groves was defeated in South Salford by the poet, novelist and controveralist Hilaire Belloc. Born in France, brought up English, a Catholic with an Irish American wife, Belloc was a figure of some fascination. In many ways he seemed an ideal candidate for the most proletarian and Catholic of the three Salford constituencies. Anti-puritan, anti-rationalist, (though a traditionalist at heart), Belloc was passing through his Radical phase. A Home Ruler, a Free Trader, in favour of trades unions, and (though not a teetotaller) against 'corporate brewers' and tied houses, he seemed an attractive candidate to Liberal and Radical voters. Here, as elsewhere, though, the big issues were Free Trade, Chinese Labour, and trades union questions. Despite the absence of a Labour candidate, Belloc's majority (a 'mere 852'), was the narrowest of the three, almost certainly because of his religion. In the Parliament of 1906, Belloc found himself the only Catholic MP for South Lancashire, an area with probably the highest concentration of Catholics in England.

The greatest Liberal triumph, however, was the ousting of Sir Lees Knowles in Pendleton. His vanquisher, George W. Agnew, was not a big gun, though his father, Sir William Agnew, certainly was. A millionaire art dealer, Sir William was a great provincial Liberal chieftain, with impeccably Salfordian credentials. George Agnew, now 54, was born in Pendleton and had spent his boyhood at Summer Hill, the family house on Eccles Old Road, where his father once entertained Gladstone and Lord Randolph Churchill. Like his opponent, Agnew was an old Rugbeian and Cambridge graduate. Though he now lived in London and Bury St Edmunds, he had been a subscriber to constituency party funds for many years. Backed by a powerful committee, Agnew returned to Pendleton to claim his political inheritance.[61] Remarkably, although he lost by 2,210 votes, Knowles in fact polled only 384 less than in the Khaki election. In those years, Pendleton was the fastest growing part of the borough, and the electorate had increased by 1,601 since 1900.[62] Free trader against free trader, Knowles put up a good fight but the tide was now against him. After two exciting and successful decades in Parliament, Sir Lees Knowles, Bart found himself out in the political cold.

The loss of the election by such a great margin did not shatter Unionist morale. The aristocrats who led the party had been perfectly happy to accept democratisation as long as the system led to the election of their party, which it had, almost uninterruptedly, since 1886. When it did not, they had ways to circumvent it. Balfour and Lord Lansdowne, Conservative leader in the House of Lords, made a compact that the Lords would revert to the tactics employed against Gladstone in 1893–5, and use its in-built Conservative majority to frustrate leglislation they did not like. They began by throwing out the major measure of 1906, an Education Bill, as well as a Bill to end plural voting, but, (to please the unions), 'allowed' the Trades Disputes Act to pass. There followed three more attempts to amend the 1902 Education Act, all of which were thwarted by House of Lords, Church of England, Catholic and some teacher opposition. The abandoning of the fourth and last Bill in 1908 was deplored in the strongest terms by Asquith, now Prime Minister. To Unionists its defeat was a cause for celebration. Together with Sir Arthur Percival Heywood, the Bishop of Manchester and the vicar of St Thomas's, Knowles was prominent at the victory meeting of the Pendleton Church Defence League early in 1909. Later that year he derived much satisfaction from the decision of the Salford local education authority that, henceforth, Empire Day should be celebrated anually in all its schools.[63]

Knowles enjoyed the thwarting of the Liberal programme as much as the next Unionist, and was out of politics by the time the Liberals exacted retribution on the House of Lords. However, it was to Liberal reform of the army that Knowles owed the continuation of his close relationship with the Lancashire Fusiliers. Haldane's Territorial and Reserve Forces Act of 1907 was the leglislative part of a great scheme of army reform which extended over the next few years. A General Staff was created for the first time, and, proceeding within the limitation of reducing defence expenditure and keeping the Cardwellian principle of 'linked battalions',

Haldane carried out a reorganisation of the home military forces along two lines. The first was the creation of an Expeditionary Force, ready for rapid mobilisation. The second was the merging of the non-regular non-Militia categories – the Yeomanry and the Volueers – into a single new category, the Territorial Force. In this way, Haldane arranged for 14 divisions and 14 mounted brigades which, as with regular army divisions, were to have their own transport and medical services as part of the organisation. To improve the supply of officers Haldane arranged for the conversion of the old Volunteer Corps at public and secondary schools into Officer Training Corps.[64]

Under the new arrangements, the Lancashire Fusiliers were to consist of two regular battalions, one of which was always abroad and one at home. Despite Knowles' pleadings, the old 3rd and 4th Battalions were disbanded in 1906. The old Militia gave way to the Special Reserve (which became new 3rd and 4th Battalions) designed to supply drafts to the regular battalions in the field. The Volunteers (as stated) became part of the Territorial Force. Lancashire was given the task of raising 39,200 Territorial Army reservists (two divisions) and the organising of this was discussed at a great meeting at Manchester on 29th November 1907 addressed by Lord Derby. A county Territorial Association was formed which was divided into two sub-associations, one for West Lancashire and the other for East Lancashire. Funds were appealed for, Knowles contributing his usual £1,000. The Regiment's old Volunteer Battalions became the 5th, 6th, 7th, and 8th Battalions (Territorial), the first two at Bury and Rochdale, the 7th and 8th at Salford. In all this Knowles found three roles for himself: Vice-Chairman of the County Association, Chairman of the East Lancashire Association, and Officer Commanding the 7th and 8th Battalions. Over the next year and a half the main task was to get the Eastern Division up to strength. It did not prove easy. Recourse had to be made to persuading local authorities and employers to offer full pay to men who went on T. A. training each year, if they volunteered. In Salford, 'patriotic' firms such as Groves & Whitnalls (who for many years had entertained Crimean veterans to an annual dinner) led the way. By April 1909 the two Salford Battalions had recruited 1,664 towards a full complement of 1,960 men. Finding officers was more difficult; at this date the Battalions were 33 short of the full complement of 58.[65] The recruiting and administration of the whole force was a major undertaking. In addition to one Yeomanry Regiment and 12 Infantry Battalions, there were three Brigades of Field Artillery, Royal Engineers, the East Lancashire Territorial and Transport Column and a Medical Corps unit to be raised. However, it was accomplished by July, and when the King came to review the Territorial Force at Worsley and present them with colours, the Lancashire Association had done its work.

That November, on the eve of another election, Knowles resigned as candidate for West Salford, citing ill-health. He was fifty-two. As with many sportsmen, he seems not to have enjoyed a robust middle-age. Perhaps unable to face another defeat, he had had enough of party politics. From now on he contented himself with being squire of Turton, some soldiering with the Territorials, good works and the pleasures of his library. His successor in Pendleton was Lieutenant Carlyon Bellairs, RN. The son of a General, Bellairs had won the Kings Lynn election in 1906 for the Liberals, but had abandoned that party 'on account of the Socialistic tendency of its legislation'.[66] With so little time, it was not going to be easy to put up a good show in the next Pendleton election, which came two months later.

It is, perhaps, unsurprising that Knowles found the era ushered in by the Liberal victory of 1906 not to his liking. The political climate was very different from when he set out in politics twenty years before. Imperialism on the cheap was over, 'splendid isolation' had ended with the Anglo-French Entente of 1904, the focus of British foreign policy was now back on Europe. Peace had been threatened by the Moroccan Crisis of 1905, and, from that time, Anglo-German naval rivalry became embittered. At home, the programme of social legislation which so upset Lieutenant Bellairs – which later came to be seen as 'laying the foundation of the Welfare State' – opened up a new era. Irish Home Rule was back on the agenda, a Labour Party now existed, women were demanding to be part of the political nation. Faced with all this, it is perhaps understandable why Knowles found the roles of officer, squire and scholar more congenial than that of politician.

In the first election of 1910 the main issue was Lloyd George's 'People's Budget'. Since coming to power the Liberals had passed the Trades Disputes Act, a new Workmen's Compensation Act, created Children's Courts and brought in old age pensions. The latter, by providing pensions for the over–70s with annual incomes of less than £31.10s was a blessed reform, removing the shadow of the workhouse from many old people. But it was expensive. Facing a large deficit (caused by increased naval expenditure as well as social legislation) the Chancellor devised a budget aiming to shift the tax burden away from producers to possessors of wealth. His Budget was, of course, designed as a noose for lordly bears. After a struggle, it passed the Commons, but the Lords rejected it at the end of November 'until the judgment of the country had been expressed'. Unionists were incensed at Lloyd George's tax proposals: the Conservative candidate in Broughton began making speeches on the 'danger of communism'.[67]

In addition to the People's Budget and the House of Lords' power of veto, Home Rule came to the fore again in 1907. Numerous Liberal and Irish meetings in Salford were addressed by Belloc and Byles. The North Salford Women's Liberal Association heard Mrs Byles explain that all Ireland wanted was what Canada, New Zealand and even the Isle of Man already had. That November, at the close of an address on the 'Manchester Martyrs' by W. F. Reardon at the 'Father Anderson' branch of the United Irish League in Pendleton 'the memory of the dead was sung with great spirit by those present, the proceedings closing with the singing of "God Save Ireland" by the lecturer, the audience standing.'[68] In the government's battle with the House of Lords at Westminster the Irish MPs offered their support on condition that the power of the House of Lords should be so far reduced that it could no longer defeat a Home Rule Bill.

Other significant, though less important, issues were tariff reform, whether or not it was legal for trades unions to impose political levies, and the Disestablishment of the Church in Wales, demanded by the Welsh and English Nonconformists, who wanted retribution for their defeat over the Education Bills. These were issues Beer and Bible Conservatives could react to, and the 'collectivist' trend of the times re-activated the Young England Patriotic Association, which now added 'and Anti-Socialist League' to its name. However, by the time of the election, the

Conservatives were on the defensive. In Salford the Liberals did well. In January 1910 they won all three seats, though with reduced majorities. Manchester Liberalism was solid: the cotton trade was strongly opposed to tariffs, and the people feared 'dear food'. Local support for Home Rule did not waver, and Liberal voters were also resolute on the House of Lords. Byles won by 853 votes in Salford North, in an election in which 92 per cent of the electors voted. In Pendleton, Agnew defeated Bellairs comfortably enough, despite a Socialist getting 2,396 votes.[69] By far the keenest contest was between Belloc and Montague Barlow in South Salford. Belloc was politically volatile, with a penchant for enraging his supporters by abruptly changing his views on key issues. Before the end of 1908 he had alienated Nonconformists and Temperance men by voting against the education and licensing bills and, as already noted, on the eve of the election aroused the fury of the Women's Freedom League when he described the campaign for votes for women as 'grossly immoral'. However, in January 1910 Belloc was re-elected. In a constituency where (in his estimation) one in five workers were Catholics he was sure of the Catholic vote. He was also sure of the Irish, the Free Traders and the 'sensible drinkers'. The Budget was the key issue, and Belloc attacked landowners and the House of Lords. To the strains of 'Has anyone here seen Belloc', he held off Barlow's challenge with a majority of 316.[70]

However, Barlow was a man to watch. His father, the dean of Peterborough, came of a Lancashire family. A barrister, educated at Repton and Cambridge, Barlow was, like his father, an ardent Evangelical. The captain of a company in the Church Lads' Brigade and legal adviser to the Church Schools' Association, Barlow was prominent in church politics. One of the founders of the 'True Temperance'Association, he was an opponent of 'teetotal fanaticism', advocating reform of the licensing laws on the German rather than the New England model. More churchy and less sporty than Knowles, Barlow nonetheless in some ways resembled him and was destined to do for the Lancashire Fusiliers in the Great War what Knowles had done in the South African conflict and after.[71]

The Liberal Party won the election in January 1910, but their Parliamentary majority over the Unionists was reduced to two. From now on they depended on the support of Labour and the Irish Nationalists. The People's Budget was passed, and plans were made to remove the power of the Lords. Shortly before these resolutions were passed by the House of Commons, King Edward died. To be clear that there was a mandate for the Reform of the Lords, and that King George V was prepared to carry out the threat (first used in the Reform Crisis of 1831–2) of creating enough Liberal peers to overcome the Conservative majority if need be, a second general election was called for December 1910.

Though the main issue was the House of Lords, the *Reporter* noted 'The proposal to abolish the power of the Lords failed to rouse any remarkable enthusiasm amongst Liberal audiences.' Conservatives made much of 'the attack on the Constitution',[72] but the electorate were tiring of elections. As usual, what galvanised Manchester Liberals was fiscal policy, and they voted resolutely against 'dear food'. The Conservatives tried, but failed, to make Home Rule the big issue. This election was nothing like as exciting as the previous two. Agnew, who, having inherited his father's baronetcy, was now Sir George, got in again for West Salford, and

William Byles (knighted the following year) defeated his Conservative opponent. Once again the most interesting events took place in Ordsall. At the eleventh hour, Belloc pulled out, now declaring himself an enemy to party politics and his unfortunate successor, the Hon. Charles Russell, lost a close contest with Barlow. Barlow remained South Salford's MP until 1923. He had a good war and a distinguished run in Parliament, rising to be Minister of Labour in 1922, and was made a baronet two years later.[73]

Now out of politics, Knowles busied himself with other things. He began a series of publications which, in one way or another, touched on the history of the regiment or other long term interests of his. A visit to Germany in 1909 for the celebration of the 150th anniversary of the Battle of Minden was marked by the publication of his translation of Vormbaum's *The Battle of Minden and the action at Gohfeld.* In the same year appeared *An Abstract of the Manor Court of Turton, 1737–1850,* 'Compiled by the direction of Sir Lees Knowles', and *The War in the Peninsula – Some Letters by Lieut. Robert Knowles ... Arranged by his great-great-nephew Sir Lees Knowles.* In 1911 a new edition of his essay on the German Korps Students appeared and in 1914 Knowles produced his magnum opus, *Minden and the Seven Years War.* It was nothing if not a labour of love, and, if it did not reveal anything previously unknown, it was a clear restatement of the events, complete with the range of maps and diagrams beloved of military historians and armchair soldiers.

By now the Great War had started. Almost as if in reaction to its immensity, Knowles' writings seem to bury themselves more and more in trivia. In 1915 there appeared his edition of *Letters of Captain Englebert Lutyens.* An English officer of Schleswig-Holsteiner ancestry, a captain in the XXth Regiment, Lutyens had been orderly officer at Longwood, St. Helena, in the period preceding the death of Napoleon there in 1820. Knowles was attracted to the subject no doubt by the fact that he was a student of all things appertaining to the regiment, that he was a Napoleon buff and by the existence of the letters. The Lutyens 'case' was a very minor incident. The officer apparently got on well with Napoleon in his last illness, and suffered the envy and malice of the other military guardians of the Emperor, so much so that Lutyens was relieved of his post for 'an error of judgement'. Napoleon had presented a copy of Cox's *Life of Marlborough* to the XXth and when the books were seen to carry the Imperial monogram, Lutyens was ordered to return them. When he protested he was removed. Shortly after, Napoleon died and Lutyens missed promotion, a trip to England and the reward of £500 for carrying the despatches announcing the death of the Emperor. Lutyens protested as far as the Duke of York, his commander in chief. Though badly used, he protested too much. Knowles identified strongly with Lutyens: 'To be called upon to play the spy ... was an insult and offensive to the feelings of one who had the instincts of an officer and a gentleman.'[74] In time, Cox's *Life* did find its way into the possession of the regiment, with certain other memorabilia, and in 1921 Knowles published *A Gift of Napoleon ... being a sequel to the Letters of Capt. E. Lutyens.*

In 1918 Knowles published *The British in Capri, 1806–1808,* an outcome of his love for the Isle of Capri as well as military history. It also reflected a more recent affair of the heart, being dedicated to his wife in memory of their marriage in 1915.

Knowles' bride was Lady Nina Ogilvie-Grant, daughter of the 10th Earl of Seafield. He was then 57, and there were to be no children. Virtually nothing is known of Knowles's private life, of earlier loves, or lack of them. At any rate, in 1915, the middle-aged squire brought home a lady of impeccable descent. Under them, the final phase in the history of a Lancashire landed estate was acted out. Knowles was Turton's last squire. After his death Lady Knowles gave the house to the Turton Urban District Council, who used it as a council chamber. More recently, it has become one of the Borough of Blackburn's museums.

In 1923, his mind evidently still on Capri and the Napoleonic Wars, Knowles' last work appeared, a translation from the Italian of Farrace's *The Taking of Capri*. With the exception of one or two journalist pieces, that exhaused his literary output. By no means an ungifted writer, Knowles kept resolutely to minor subjects, almost if to emphasise his amateur status. Perhaps his study was his means of escape from the immensity and pain of the Great War. Although he was not inactive in public matters between 1914 and 1918, it cannot be said he played a very prominent part in Salford's efforts in that great test of the national will.

The man who did was his Unionist 'heir', C. A. Montague Barlow. If the industrial towns like Salford had been capitalism's reserve army of labour in the nineteenth century, in the Great War they became, in a very literal way, the reserve of the nation at arms. What is more, this reserve was not forced into battle reluctantly: it volunteered. From two Regular, two Special and four Territorial Battalions at the start of the war, the Lancashire Fusiliers grew to a total of 30 Battalions (not all of which were in existence at the same time). In the Great War the XXth found itself (as usual) in some of the hardest fighting – on the Somme, 3rd Ypres (Passchendaele), Cambrai and the March Retreat of 1918. Its bloodiest battlefield was 'Lancashire Landing', Gallipoli, 25th April 1915, when six Victoria Crosses were won 'before breakfast'. In the war as a whole Lancashire Fusiliers won a total of 18 VCs – more, apparently, than any other single regiment.[75]

In the first month of the war the Territorial Battalions were expanded, large numbers of Salford Corporation employees from the tramways and other departments, rushing to join the 2nd/7th Battalion, and men from Bury, Heywood and Radcliffe joining the 2nd/5th. The first of the 'Kitchener' Battalions was the 9th (Service) Battalion, formed 31st August 1914; into it were recruited men from the mills, mines and factories around Manchester, Bury and Bolton. Appointed Secretary of State for War on 5th August, Kitchener proposed the raising of half a million men to form the 'New Armies' which would equip Britain for a war which he correctly estimated would last at least three years.

The response was truly amazing. In the first two months almost three quarters of a million men enlisted. Before the introduction of conscription in 1916, nearly two and a half million men had volunteered.[76] At the start of the war the immense political and social tensions in British society were suspended for the duration. Imminent civil war in Ulster after the passing of the Home Rule Act of 1914 was avoided, volunteers on both sides enlisting in the British Army. As we have seen, confrontations between Capital and Labour (with some of the biggest strikes ever experienced in 1911 and 1912) were suspended. To the dismay of some Socialists, who saw the conflagration as a 'capitalist war', the rank and file Labour movement proved as patriotic as any other section of society. The Women's Movement suspended its campaign and turned patriotic. The War brought some of the most powerful subterranean currents in Edwardian society to the surface – in particular a naive unquestioning patriotism and an idealism which extended across the social spectrum. Nowhere was the response more enthusiastic than in the great industrial towns, where the idea of inviting men to enlist with their 'pals' triggered an intense surge of recruiting from the last days of August, 1914. Lord Derby is credited with inaugurating the scheme at a packed meeting in Liverpool on 29th August, when he urged the city to form its own battalion, with the guarantee that 'those who joined together should serve together.' Within three days, enough volunteers had come forward for not one, but three battalions. The 'pals' idea spread like wildfire, *ad hoc* committees vying with each other to raise 'New Army' battalions.[77]

Following a packed and enthusiastic meeting at the *Hippodrome* early in September a Salford Committee was floated. It was convened by Montague Barlow, 'the raiser of the Salford Brigade'. Between September 1914 and July 1915 he and his committee, raised four active service and one Reserve 'Pals' Battalions. The committee undertook to make all arrangements for raising, clothing, housing and feeding the troops. It even saw to their pay. Over £70,000 was spent on training alone, and when equipment such as field kitchens was needed, industrial firms and rich individuals provided them in response to an appeal.[78]

In all, Salford and district contributed 11 Battalions to the Lancashire Fusiliers, as well as an uncounted number of recruits to other regiments, first under 'Lord Derby's Scheme' in 1915, then under conscription. But it was the example of the men who (in Barlow's words) 'at first call voluntarily placed their services at the disposal of the King and country for the Defence of Liberty and Civilisation'[79] who were remembered with most pride. Engaged to serve with men they worked and played with from the same town or district, they represent the closest thing to a volunteer civilian army Britain has ever produced, raised in the main by civilian recruiting committees. They were the product of that camaraderie and local pride, created in the dense network of factories, pubs, clubs and organisations of the Victorian and Edwardian industrial town. Their camaraderie and idealism seems particularly strong in Salford, which raised more 'Pals' battalions than Birmingham and as many as Glasgow.[80] If Salford's five are added to Manchester's eight, the King and Country patriotism of the great double-barrelled city in 1914–15 was outstanding. Although it cannot be said that Knowles (or Barlow, or any other individual) was responsible for this cohesion and spirit, in his encouragement of the sporting ethos, active service volunteering and tireless promotion of the Lancashire Fusiliers as 'a territorial family', Knowles surely played some part in fostering them. Although his role in the Great War was low-key, Knowles remained in the Territorials until 1918, and, in recognition, was made an Officer of the British Empire in 1920, by which time he was also a Knight of Grace of the Order of St. John of Jerusalem (for his work with the Ambulance Brigade), and a Commander of the Royal Victorian Order.

Salford, like every other place in the land, has its Great War memorials. Plaques in Sacred Trinity Church record the death toll of the 15th, 16th and 19th Battalions and there is the cenotaph in Albion Place. The contrast between its ominous plainness and the triumphalism of Knowles' Boer War memorial is marked: one great casualty of the Great War was Jingoism. In all 13,642 Lancashire Fusiliers died in the First World War.[81] How many Salford men gave their lives has never been satisfactorily computed, and the sort of monument which many towns erected, listing individual names, would perhaps be too terrible a sight to bear. The naive, boyish idealism of the 'Pals' Battalions led them straight into the mechanized slaughter of the Western Front, and there came a point when volunteering dried up and compulsion came in. When it was all over, it was to the spirit of the 'Pals' that patriotism clung to make it all seem worth while.

Another casualty was the self-confidence of coal-and-cotton capitalism. The Great War destroyed the international trade network of which Manchester was the centre. After a brief post-war boom, there came the slow realisation that old markets were now lost, or had shrunk, or found new suppliers. Salford' population growth, unchecked since censuses were first taken, reached a peak (of 234,000) in 1921: it has declined ever since. The Great war ended the awesome demographic and industrial dynamism of Victorian Salford. For at least another half century it remained a largely unreconstructed soot-black Victorian city, whose image is preserved forever in L. S. Lowry's drawings and paintings.

This fact, and the aversion of the post-war generation for the Victorians and Edwardians, should not blind us to the fact that nineteenth-century Salford was one of the centres where modern manufacturing industry was forged. It was here that some the biggest themes of Britain's nineteenth-century history emerged and worked themselves out. If the greatest was the triumph of possessive individualism, Capital was faced up to by Labour. Yet economic history alone is inadequate to do justice to the complexity of this industrial society. On this base of Capital and Labour, the themes of religion and ethnicity, localism and imperialism, gender as well as class relationships, and the politics of those both inside and outside the political nation interacted to create a rich and complex social superstructure.

Sir Lees Knowles, a Victorian who witnessed the start of the decline of the business which had made his family rich for four generations, died on 7th October 1928. He left a fortune of £227,000, all of which went to his wife, the daughter of a tenth Earl: wealth from the ground recycled to the landed.[82] Knowles, a Tory paternalist, was a benefactor as well as an expropriator. When Benjamin Armitage died and the Pendleton Club was put up for sale, Knowles bought it so that Pendleton lads would not lose their meeting place. Following the lead of his sister, Mrs Pilkington, who lived in Pendleton, he endowed a cot in Salford Royal Hospital, at a cost of £1,200. To commemorate Queen Victoria's Diamond Jubilee he gave £500 towards the Home for District Nurses on the Crescent. And always one for ritual and regalia, he gave the Salford Corporation a ceremonial mace to mark the coronation of King Edward VII. In the Twenties he gave land for an improvement scheme under the council's public works programme for the unemployed and for the last 17 years of his life was chairman of the Pendleton Old Folks Tea, presiding for one last time shortly before his death. He did not forgot his old school, endowing three exhibitions for Rugbeians, and one yearly for a graduate in his fourth year, at Trinity College, Cambridge. Cambridge, in its turn, remembers him in the Lees Knowles lectures in Military Science.[83]

Knowles was the last, or one of the last, wealthy bourgeois figures not merely to use Salford as a political or economic springboard, but to live close to, and involve himself in the life of the place. There are many reasons for the social detachment of the twentieth-century upper middle class, but one is that in the last few years of Knowles' life, both Capital and Labour were both being transformed. The pre-war years saw the nationally organised miners (and other workers as well) take on the federated employers in some of the biggest industrial conflicts ever witnessed in this country. The Great War saw the mine and transport companies nationalised: the Peace saw them return to private hands. Pre-war industrial conflicts then resumed, culminating in the General Strike of 1926, which began and ended as a coal dispute. The very month Lees Knowles died Messrs. Andrew Knowles & Sons Ltd ceased to exist. In what the newspapers called 'the fourth big Coal Fusion' since the General Strike, it amalgamated with a number of other firms to form Manchester Collieries.[83] In the old heavy industries family capitalism was being replaced by corporate capitalism, larger in scale, more remote and faceless. The likes of Lees Knowles and the Armitages had become figures of the past.

Imperialism and the Volunteer spirit: Lees Knowles' inscription on the Lancashire Fusilier Monument, Chapel Street. (Photo: the author)

# Notes

## Abbreviations used in the Notes

| | |
|---|---|
| B Lib | British Library |
| LRO | Lancashire Record Office |
| M | Manchester |
| *M Chron* | *Manchester Chronicle* |
| MCL | Manchester Central Library |
| *MG* | *Manchester Guardian* |
| *M Merc* | *Manchester Mercury* |
| MRL | Manchester Reference Library |
| *N Star* | *Northern Star* |
| Peel Park | Local History Collection, Salford Central Library, Peel Park |
| PP | Parliamentary Papers |
| *Rep* | *Pendleton Reporter* (1879), later (1884) the *Salford Reporter,* then the *Reporter* |
| S | Salford |
| *S Chron* | *Salford (Weekly) Chronicle* |
| *SWN* | *Salford Weekly News* |
| *W Man Chron* | *Wheeler's Manchester Chronicle* |

## Notes to Introduction

1. T. R. Marr, *Housing Conditions in Manchester and Salford* (Manchester, 1904), p. 1.
2. For the decennial census statistics for Salford from 1801 to 1911, and eighteenth-century population calculations, see Appendix One.
3. Analysis based on firms listed in Slater's *Manchester, Salford and Suburban Directory* (1901).
4. For Frankenburgs, see *Reporter*, 31 December 1892 (25th year of the business), 19 August 1893 (Our Local Industries series, No. VIII), 2 March 1901, 2 March 1901 (Isidor Frankenburg on the early years of the firm).
5. For Mandelburgs, see *Reporter*, 21 February 1885, 21 January 1886, 6 April 1889 (Private Limited Co. formed), 22 March 1913, 28 March 1914 (profits and dividends).
6. J. Aikin, *A Description of the Country from Thirty to Forty Miles Round Manchester* (1795), p. 176.
7. For Odd Fellows origins, see *Reporter*, 23 November 1889. 'Victory' Lodge commenced in the *Ropemakers Arms*, Chapel Street in 1809. *Jubilee Record of the Independent Order of Rechabites (Salford Unity) Friendly Society* (1885), p. 12.

## Notes to Chapter 1

1. Minutes of evidence taken before the Committee on the Factory Bill ('Sadler's Committee'). pp. XV, 1831–32, pp. 439–48, answers to questions 9512 and 9500.

2. City of Westminster Archives, Baptismal Register of St James, Piccadilly. Parish of St James Workhouse Admissions Registers, 1791–94, pp. 55, 147, 193, 220, and 1794–96, p. 168.

3. Minute Book of the Governors and Directors of the Poor of the Parish of St James, 10 Feb., 29 Feb., and 10 March, 1797.

4. As described by John Douglas in a letter to the St James Parish authorities dated 21 January 1797, copied into the minutes of 10 February, *Ibid.*

5. Sadler's Committee, *op. cit.* Answers to questions 9532, 9551 and 9552. Aberdeen married Sarah at Eccles Parish Church, 25 March 1805 (St Mary Parish Register, 1802–12).

6. Frances Collier, *The Family Economy of the Working Classes in the Cotton Industry 1784–1833* (Manchester, 1964), p. 14.

7. *M Mercury*, 7 January 1777. Birmingham Reference Library, Boulton and Watt papers, letter from W. Douglas & Co., dated 1 January 1792.

8. Elizabeth Raffald, *The Manchester Directory for the year 1772* (1889), p. 14. E. J. Foulkes, 'The Cotton Spinning Factories of Flintshire 1777–1866', *Publications of the Flintshire Historical Society*, vol. 21 (1964), pp. 91–7. A. H. Dodd, *The Industrial Revolution in North Wales* (1951), pp. 283–7. S. D. Chapman, 'The Cost of Power in the Industrial Revolution in Britain: the Case of the Textile Industry', *Midland History*, I, 2, (1971), pp. 8–7, and 'The Peels in the Early English Cotton Industry', *Business History*, XI, 1 (1969), p. 85f.

9. Cooke's map is in Peel Park Library. For Taylor, Weston & Co., see Parliamentary Papers, Factory Commission, 1834. Inquiries D1, pp. 264–5.

10. *M Mercury*, 24 June 1777.

11. For Walness see *M Mercury*, 7 March 1797. For Gee see *M Mercury*, 16 August 1763. For Seedley Printworks see Manchester Archives, J. Graham 'MS History of Printworks in the Manchester District from 1760 to 1846' (MS 1847), p. 423.

12. LRO, Will of William Douglas, 25 January 1810. A. G. Veysey (ed.), *Guide to Flintshire Record Office* (1974), p. 84, for Gyrn Hall. P. S. Richards 'The Holywell Textile Mills, Flintshire', *Industrial Archaeology*, vol. 6, no. 1 (1969), pp. 28–51. E. J. Foulkes, 'The Cotton Spinning Factories of Flintshire', *op. cit.*, p. 94. For the fire see *MG*, 4 December 1850.

13. Ipswich and East Suffolk Record Office, Fitzgerald Papers, HB 56, Box 21, New lease of Pendelton Hall estate to John Douglas Esq. of Grantham, and others.

14. *SWN*, 27 June 1863. *M City News*, 19 March 1892. Walter Greenwood, *Lancashire* (1951), pp. 143, 145–6. See also F. A. Bruton, *A Short History of Manchester and Salford* (1924), p. 213.

15. *Poor Man's Advocate*, 3 March 1832. J. Aiken, *A Description of the Country from Thrity to Forty Miles Round Manchester* (1795) pp. 219–20.

16. Sadler's Committee, answer the question 9581.

17. A. W. Skempton and H. R. Johnson, 'The First Iron Frames', *Architectural Review* (March 1962). LRO, Will of George Augustus Lee dated 12 June 1824.

18. Sadler's Committee, 9603.

19. *Ibid.*, 9602–4.

20. *Ibid.*, p. 364. *Poor Man's Advocate, op. cit.*

21. *A Letter to the Rt Honourable Lord Viscount Althorp MP, Chancellor of the Exchequer in Defence of the Cotton Factories of Lancashire*, Manchester, 1832.

22. Sadler's Committee, 9581. See also his answers to 9573 to 9580.

23. *Ibid.*, 9506.

24. *Ibid.*, 9549

25. *Ibid.*, 9632.

26. *Ibid.*, 9636.

27. *Royal Commission into the Employment of Children in Factories*, 1833. Examinations taken by Mr Tufnell. Part I. Witnesses in favour of the Ten Hours Bill. p. 1.

28. For Carlile, see John Smith and Joel H. Wiener's account in *Dictionary of Labour Biography*, vol. vi (1982), pp. 46–53.

29. Edward Royle's account in J. O. Baylen and N. J. Gossman (eds), *Biographical Dictionary of Modern British Radicals 1780–1830* (1979), pp. 467–70.

30. *Ibid.*, p. 469.

31. *Factory Commission*, p. 117.

32. *Character, Object and Effects of Trades' Unions with Some Remarks on the Law concerning them* (London, 1834), published anonymously. For Tufnell (1806–86), see F. Boase, *Modern English Biography*, vol. vi, Supplement to vol. iii (1921).

33. *Factory Commission*, 2nd Report, 1833, Part I. Examinations taken by Mr Tufnell, p. 1.

34. *Ibid.*

35. *Ibid.*, Evidence of Roberts, p. 123.

36. *Ibid.*, p. 125.

37. Factory Commission, Supplementary Report, 1834, Part 1, Mr Tufnell's Report for Lancashire, p. 210.

38. J. T. Ward, *The Factory Movement 1830–1855* (1962), pp. 99–103.

39. *Ibid.*, pp. 106–11.

40. W. H. Hutt, 'The Factory System of the Early Nineteenth Century', *Economica* (March 1926), reprinted in F. A. Hayek (ed.), *Capitalism and the Historians* (1954).

41. *Ibid.*, p. 163.

42. The failure of both manufacturers and trades union officials to recognise Byssinosis as an industrial disease and take action to protect workers in textile factories lasted until the 1980s. See the *Guardian*, 17 August 1982, referring to a BBC TV documentary 'Dust to Dust', screened that evening.

# Notes to Chapter 2

1. For Brotherton's life see *DNB*, 11, p. 1354 (by W. E. A. Axon), Delbert F. Shafer's piece in *Biographical Dictionary of Modern British Radicals* (1979), 2, pp. 87–92 and obituaries in *MG* and *The Times*, 8 January 1857. There is an account of Brotherton's early years in the *Reporter*, 17 June 1893, and J. S. Cowan sketched his career in the *Reporter*, 4 January 1957. The principal primary source is the 22 volumes of Brotherton's newspaper cuttings and leaflets held in Peel Park Library.

2. LRO, Will of John Brotherton, dated 16 August 1809.

3. *Reporter*, 17 June 1893. LRO, Will of William Brotherton, 1 November 1818.

4. Angus Bethune Reach, *Manchester and the Textile Districts in 1848*, ed. C. Aspin (Helmshore, 1972), pp. 10, 12–13, 14.

5. *SWN*, 7 October 1871. *S Chron*, 11 September 1875.

6. *Hansard*, 3rd Series, LX, 1842, 710.

7. LRO. Will of Joseph Brotherton, 6 January 1836.

8. M. Central Lib., Joseph Brotherton's MS Commonplace Book 1809–1816, 'A catalogue of Books belonging to Joseph Brotherton Oldfield Road Salford 1811'.

9. *Report of a Conference held June 28, 29, 30, July 1 1809 in Christ Church Salford*, Manchester, 1809. W. E. A. Axon, *A History of the Bible Christian Church Salford from 1809 to 1909* (Manchester, 1909), p. 22. For Clowes, see Theodore Crompton, *The Life and Correspondence of the Rev. John Clowes MA* (London, 1874).

10. Axon, *op. cit.*, p. 37.

11. Peel Park, Brotherton Cuttings, vol. 14, p. 64, Declaration of Faith of Bible Christians. Drawn up to keep 'unity peace and harmony in the Society', 2 January 1837.

12. 'On Abstinence from Intoxicating Liquors' is printed in *Letters on Religious Subjects*, No. 8 (Salford, 1821), and was reprinted by Axon in 1890. Mrs Brotherton's *Vegetable Cooking* was first published in 1812.

13. Brotherton's arguments summarised in J. Grant, *Random Recollections of the Lords and Commons*, vol. 2 (1838), pp. 159–69.

14. 'As elementary schools they have not today, and never had, any superiors', *Reporter*, 27 April 1889. Boys from the school won three of the first five scholarships to Manchester Grammar School offered by the Salford School Board, *Reporter*, 6 February 1897.

15. Letter from Owen dated 14 September 1836 in *New Moral World*, 1 October 1836, reprinted in *M Chron*, 21 March 1840.

16. In a letter to Edward Watkin. Sir E. W. Watkin, *Alderman Cobden of Manchester* (1891), p. 80.

17. This section on local government is based on R. L. Greenall 'Local Government in Salford 1830–1853', unpublished MA Dissertation, University of Leicester (1970). pp. 9–17.

18. Brotherton's evidence to *House of Commons Committee on Select and Other Vestries*, 1830, minutes of evidence p. 48.

19. Greenall 'Local Government', *op. cit.,* p. 13.

20. *MG*, 7 November 1829, 3 April 1830.

21. Axon, *Bible Christian Church, op. cit.*, pp. 37–44.

22. Alexander Prentice, *Historical Sketches and Personal Recollections of Manchester* (1851), pp. 73–4.

23. *Ibid.*, pp. 31, 48–51.

24. *Ibid.*, pp. 132–48. W. Haslam Mills, *The Manchester Guardian: A Century of History* (1921), pp. 30–3.

25. *The Times*, obituary, 8 January 1857.

26. Particularly Prentice. See *Wh Man Chron,* 4 December 1830 (formation of the Manchester Political Union).

27. *MG*, 29 January 1831. Prentice, *Historical Sketches*, pp. 371–2.

28. *Ibid.*, 2 July 1831.

29. *Wh Man Chron*, 3, 17 and 31 December 1831.

30. *Wh Man Chron*, 4 and 11 February, 17 March 1832.

31. *MG*, 19 May 1832. *Wh Man Chron*, 9 June 1832.

32. *MG*, 9 June 1832.

33. *MG*, 28 November 1838. For his platform, see *Wh Man Chron*, 2 July 1831.

34. *MG*, 8 December 1832. See also *Wh Man Chron*, 14 July 1832.

35. For Garnett's manifesto and campaign see *Wh Man Chron*, 30 June 1832, *MG*, 21 November 1832, *Wh Man Chron*, 24 November 1832, *MG*, 22 November 1832, *Wh Man Chron*, 24 November 1832.

36. LRO, Garnett Papers. Salford Election Papers, DDQ (*A Card*).

37. *Ibid.*, Handbill dated 7 December 1832.

38. *M Herald*, 19 December 1832.

39. *Hogg's Weekly Instructor*, Edinburgh, 15 May 1847 (Brotherton Cuttings, vol. 22, pp. 28–9). See also J. Grant, *op. cit.,* pp. 156–7, 176.

40. *MG*, 7 February 1856. *Grant*, op. cit., p. 172.

41. *Wh Man Chron*, 10, 24 January 1835, *M and Salford Advertiser*, 10 January 1851.

42. On the insults, see letters about Brotherton cheating one Charles Lamb out of money, *Wh Man. Chron*, 14 February 1835. On Tory organisation, see Manchester Archives, J. B. Smith's Election Papers, vol iii, item 86, Smith to Brotherton, 11 March 1835.

43. *Wh Man Chron*, 21 Mar, 1 August 1835, 12 March 1836, 1 April 1837, 21 April 1838, 26 December 1840. W. Paul, *History of the Organisation and Progress of Operative Conservative Societies* (Durham, 1838), p. 13.

44. For Stowell, see Chapter Four.

45. *MG*, 7 January 1837.

46. *Wh Man Chron*, 5 July 1834.

47. *Reporter*, 13 October 1894 for Garnett's election address.

48. Recalled in *SWN*, 26 May 1877, and in articles in the *Reporter*, 23 September, 13, 20, 27 October 1894, based on the material in the Brotherton Cuttings collection.

49. *MG*, 29 July 1837.

50. *MG*, 16 August, 12 October and 25 November 1837. LRO, Garnett's Election Papers, Evidence presented before House of Commons Committee, 7 February 1838.

51. *MG*, 4 April 1838.

52. *MG*, 30 May 1838.

53. *MG*, 7, 10 July 1838.

54. Archibald Prentice, *History of the Anti-Corn Law League*, 1853. Second Edition with a new introduction by W. H. Chaloner, 1968, vol. 1, pp. 73, 74.

55. Norman McCord, *The Anti-Corn Law League*, (1958) p. 36.

56. Prentice, *op. cit.*, vol. 1, pp. 257, 318.

57. *Ibid.*, vol. 2, p. 131.

58. *Ibid.*, pp. 415, 429.

59. *MG*, 12 May 1852.

60. Peel Park. Brotherton Cuttings, vol. 12, Speech in a debate upon the 1833 Bill.

61. See Brotherton's speech to a meeting in Manchester: *Wh Man Chron*, 13 April 1833 on his role from 1816 to 1825.

62. *M Gazette*, 12 July 1825.

63. *Wh Man Chron*, 5 March and 20 August 1836, *MG*, 28 September 1836.

64. *MG*, 14 December 1836.

65. *M and S Advertiser*, 7 August 1841.

66. *M and S Advertiser*, 18 October 1845. One notable manufacturer who reduced hours in his Preston Mill was Robert Gardner, the Evangelical churchman.

67. C. Driver, *Tory Radical* (1946), p. 476. *The Scotsman*, 3 March 1847. *S Reporter*, 11 May 1895, quoting from the Brotherton Cuttings collection.

68. This account is based on J. S. Cowan, 'Joseph Brotherton and the Public Library Movement', *The Library Association Record*, vol. 59, no. 5 (May 1957). R. L. Greenall, 'Local Government in Salford 1830–1853', *op. cit.*

69. *Ibid.*, pp. 88–91.

70. *Wh Man Chron*, 23 January 1830.

71. *MG*, 12 November 1851.

72. *MG*, 1 November 1854.

73. Axon, *Bible Christian Church, op. cit.*, p. 78.

74. *MG*, 24 July 1852.

75. *MG*, 3 November 1849.

76. S. E. Maltby, *Manchester and the Movement for National Elementary Education* (Manchester, 1918).

77. *MG*, 6 April 1833.

78. Greenall, 'Local Government', *op. cit.*, pp. 22–3.

79. *Ibid.*, ch. 2.

80. *Ibid.*, pp. 60–5.

81. *Ibid.*, pp. 65–70.

82. *Ibid.*, pp. 76–80.

83. *Ibid.*, pp. 98–108.

84. Quoted by Playfair, p. 385.

85. J. Roberton, *Health of Towns Commission. Report on the amount and causes of death in Manchester* (London, 1845), p. 2.

86. Greenall, 'Local Government' *op. cit.* pp. 108–12.

87. *Ibid.*, pp. 112–15.

88. Library of the London School of Economics and Political Science. Webb Local Government Collection, vol. 160, quoted in Greenall, 'Local Government', p. 80.

89. Greenall, *op. cit.* pp. 92–7.

90. *Borough of Salford. Despotic Tyranny. Statement of the circumstances connected with the abitrary dismissal of Mr Stephen Neal, Chief Constable, by the Watch Committee*, Manchester, 1852.

91. *MG*, 3 November 1847. Gendall was the Ratepayers Association president, 1847–48.

92. This section is based on Greenall 'Local Government' *op. cit.*, pp. 123–34.

93. J. G. de T. Mandley, *Broughton: History of its Union with Salford* (Manchester, 1884), p. 3.

94. *MG*, 7 July 1852.

95. *MG*, 13 March 1852.

96. *MG*, 7 November 1856.

97. *MG*, 3 August 1858.

98. *SWN*, 9 February 1861.

## Notes to Chapter 3

1. The principal sources are the *Northern Star*, the *Manchester Guardian* and the *Salford Weekly News*, Richardson's pamphlets and booklets, a volume of his press cuttings in Manchester Archives entitled 'Richardson's Works', and some correspondence about him in 1905, chiefly a letter from his son, in the Local History Collection in Manchester Central Library. See also Jack Ridley in the entry on Richardson in J. O. Baylen and N. J. Gossman (eds), *Biographical Dictionary of Modern British Radicals* (1984), vol. 2, pp. 433–5.

2. *Poor Man's Advocate*, 13 October 1832.

3. *M and S Advertiser*, *MG*, 9 March 1833, *Wh Man Chron*, 12 April 1834.

4. *Wh Man Chron*, 10 May 1834; *MG*, 26 January and 6 February 1838, *N Star*, 24 February 1838; Broadside in Home Office Papers, PRO, H040/38, item 692 dated 28 June 1838.

5. *Wh Man Chron*, 31 May 1834.

6. *MG*, 31 December 1836, 7 January 1837.

7. *M and S Advertiser*, 30 December 1837 for Richardson's 'Proclamation! Poor Law Amendment Act', *MG*, 6 February 1838. *MG*, 29 March 1837, *Wh Man Chron*, 1 April 1837, *MG*, 19 April 1837. *Ibid.*, 27 May 1837.

8. *Ibid.*, 6 February, 14 March, 21 March, 4 April 1838.

9. Successive issues of *MG*, 11 May to 21 July 1838.

10. *M Chron*, 28 March 1840.

11. *MG*, 14 March 1838, *M Courier*, 10 February 1839.

12. PRO MH 32/64, letter from Power to the Poor Law Board, Jan.–Feb. 1839.

13. Dorothy Thompson, *The Chartists, Popular Politics in the Industrial Revolution* (1986 edn), pp. 51–2.

14. *N Star*, 12 March 1838.

15. *MG*, 18 April 1838, R. G. Gammage, *History of the Chartist Movement 1839–1854*, 1894 edn (1969), pp. 41.

16. *MG*, 19 September 1838, Gammage, *op. cit.*, pp. 52–3.

17. PRO, HO 40/38, item 201, large poster announcing the demonstration.

18. See *MG*, 26 September 1838, *N Star*, 29 September 1838.

19. PRO, HO 40/38, December 1838, ban on torchlight processions; HO 40/37 Broadsheet issued by Richardson, 15 December 1838; *MG*, 29 December 1838.

20. PRO, HO 40/37, Lord Derby to Lord John Russell 25 April 1839; HO/43, D. Maude to Russell 25 April 1839.

21. *MG*, 6 December 1837, *N Star*, 8 December 1838, *N Star*, 13 April, 4 May, 18 May and 1 June 1839; PRO HO 40/37/390.

22. PRO HO 40/53 file of intercepted letters, f. G28. The Home Secretary had authorised the opening of Richardson's letters in February 1839, J. T. Ward, *Chartism* (1973), p. 120.

23. *N Star*, 5 January, 9 March 1839. Gammage, *op. cit.*, p. 119.

24. 9 February 1839.

25. Gammage, *op. cit.*, p. 111–12.

26. *MG*, 29 May, 4 June 1839. *N Star*, 1 June 1839. Ward, *op. cit.*, pp. 121, 124.

27. Gammage, *op. cit.*, p. 119.

28. Ward, *op. cit.*, pp. 130, 131; Gammage, op. cit., p. 148. PRO HO/43/465–6, handbill addressed to the Manchester trade unionists, signed by Richardson.

29. *N Star*, 27 July 1839. *MG*, 31 July 1839.

30. *M Chron*, 3, 10 August 1839. *MG*, 14 August 1839.

31. *N Star*, 21 September 1839.

32. *Ibid.*, 26 October, 21 December 1839.

33. *Ibid.*, 8, 22 February 1840. Gammage, *op. cit.*, p. 182. *N Star*, 22 February to 25 April 1840.

34. *Ibid.*, 11 April 1840.

35. *N Star*, 23 May, 6 and 20 June 1840, 1, 8 August 1840.

36. *Ibid.*, 25 April 1840, 24 October 1840, 21 November 1840, 12 December 1840.

37. *Ibid.*, 5, 12, 19, 26 September, 3, 17 October 1840.

38. *M Chron*, 26 December 1840, *M and S Advertiser*, 2 January 1841.

39. *N Star*, 13, 27 February 1841.

40. R. G. Kirby and A. E. Musson, *The Voice of the People* (Manchester, 1975), pp. 447–8, *M and S Advertiser*, 13 March 1841. PRO MH/12/6220.

41. M Archives, 'Richardson's Works', cuttings on pages 9 and 10.

42. *Ibid.*, p. 3.

43. *Ibid.*, cutting from *Dundee Chronicle*, 4 November 1841.

44. *Ibid.*, 23 December 1841.

45. *Ibid.*, p. 10.

46. Ward, *op. cit.*, p. 159.

47. *N Star*, January 1841 to December 1842, *passim*, contains many reports of the activities of the Salford Chartists.
48. *Ibid.*, 19 June 1841, 16 July 1842.
49. *Ibid.*, 29 May 1841.
50. *M Times*, 16 July 1842.
51. This 'account' is based on reports in *MG*, 9, 11, 13, 17, 18, 24 August 1842. *M Chron and S Standard*, 20 August 1842; *Illustrated London News*, 13, 20 August 1842.
52. Cutting in 'Richardson's Works'.
53. Preserved in 'Richardson's Works'.
54. In a letter to the chief librarian of the Manchester Central Library in 1905, Richardson's son Thomas, writing from Cardiff, lists six unpublished manuscripts by his father – four plays, including 'Hulme Hall, or, The Recusant's Vengeance. Based on a Tale of the Plague' (1830), a story, and a volume of 'Poetic Fragments'. There were also two other items relating to the South Lancashire Beersellers Association, of which Richardson was secretary in 1860. Apart from the latter, there was nothing of a political nature. (MCL, Newspaper Cuttings.)
55. *MG*, 13 April 1844.
56. James Spry, *The History of Odd Fellowship, Manchester Unity* (1867), pp. 56–68, Report of the Select Committee on the Friendly Societies Bill, PP, Sessional Papers, 1849, vol. xiv, pp. 138–93, *List of the Lodges comprising the Manchester Unity of Odd Fellows, with a table of Lodge Nights Compiled by William Ratcliffe CS of the Order*, Oldham, 1845.
57. *N Star*, 19, 26 July, 2, 16, 23 August, 13, 27 September 1845.
58. See below, chapter 5.
59. *The Annual Black Book and Political Almanac for 1848*, pp. 19, 41.
60. *MG*, 27 February 1850.
61. *MG*, 13 February 1850, 8 September 1852. MCL, Ms Volume of Writings by R. J. Richardson on the dialect and etymology of Lancashire, dated 1852. It seems he was planning a book on the subject. See also a letter from Richardson in *MG*, 23 April 1857 on the etymology of the word 'ley': 'England is a country of dialects'.
62. *N Star*, 20 October 1849.
63. Obituary of Alfred Richardson, *Reporter*, 14 September 1901. M Archives, 'Richardson's Works', printed 'Threnody on the Death of Henry Richardson son of Reginald and Elizabeth Richardson of Salford who closed his transitory life July 20th 1844, aged seven months and ten days'.
64. *Wh Man Chron*, 11 September, 30 October 1830, *MG*, 13 June 1849, 25 September 1852.
65. *MG*, 20 October, 8 December 1852.
66. *MG*, 8 February, 8 March, 5 April 1854.
67. *Ibid.*, 4 April 1855.
68. *Ibid.*, 8 April 1856, 15, 29 June 1858.
69. *SWN*, 30 July 1859.
70. *MG*, 21 April 1855.
71. *Ibid.*, 5 November 1857.
72. *Ibid.*, 7 April 1858.
73. M. Archives, Wilson Papers. Richardson to George Wilson, 2 February 1858.
74. *MG*, 15 January, 18 September, 5 October 1858.
75. *Ibid.*, 2 May 1859.
76. *SWN* and *M Weekly Times*, 26 January 1861.

## Notes to Chapter 4

1. (The Revd) J. B. Marsden, *Memoirs of the Life and Labours of the Rev. Hugh Stowell* (1868), pp. 445, 449. Marsden had been Stowell's curate.
2. For the life of Stowell see Marsden, *op. cit.*; (The Revd) C. D. Bullock, *Hugh Stowell: A Life and its Lessons* (1881); obituaries in *MG*, 6 October 1865, *Times*, 10 October 1865, *SWN*, 14 October 1865., *DNB*, vol. lv (1898), p. 7.; Boase, *Modern English Biography*, vol. iii (1901, repr. 1965), col. 781.

3. The founder was the Rev. N. M. Cheek. For the early history of St Stephen's see *S. Chron*, 6 November 1875. Other early chapels of ease in Manchester and Salford were St Thomas's Pendleton (1776), St James's (1788), St Clement's (1793), St George's (1799), and St Luke's, Chorlton (1804).

4. Marsden, *op. cit.*, p. 38–40.

5. *S Chron*, 24 April 1875 gives a good account of these two Acts, and the circumstances behind them.

6. LRO, DR Ch 37/114, Salford Christ Church Papers, 1831–48. *MG*, 9 January 1830, 1 May 1836, 1 November 1845.

7. John Evans, *Lancashire Authors and Orators* (1850), p. 268.

8. Bullock, *op. cit.*, p. 26.

9. Marsden, *op. cit.*, pp. 36–7.

10. Evans, *op. cit.*, p. 269.

11. Marsden, *op. cit.*, pp. 176–7.

12. *Ibid.*, pp. 47–8.

13. *Ibid.*, pp. 271, 273.

14. And received an accolade in *N Star* (26 April 1845), on the first anniversary of his reducing hours from 12 to 11 per day in his mills.

15. For obituaries of Heelis, see *S Chron* and *SWN*, 2 September 1871.

16. For obituary of Goulden, see *S Chron*, 12 October 1878.

17. *Wh Man Chron*, 20 February 1836, public meeting of the 'United Dissenters' on the bringing of religious liberty to Ireland and the grievances of Dissenters in England.

18. *MG*, 23 February 1850 gives a local history of church rate since 1831.

19. Marsden, *op. cit.*, p. 171.

20. Chetham's Library, pamphlets bound in a volume titled *Manchester Rectory Division Bill*. See also 'A Manchester Rector', *The Manchester Parish Divison Act 1850. The Charter of the Privileges of the Manchester Parishes*, Manchester, 1887, *The Manchester Rectory Divison Bill. Report of the Evidence Given Before the Committee of the House of Commons, together with a Full Report of the Speeches of Council*, Manchester, 1850. The attack on the Collegiate Church began in 1846, when Canon Parkinson accepted the principalship of St Bees, and went on until 1851. See *MG*, 29 November 1851, presentation of plate to the churchwardens of Manchester who saw through the Rectory Division Bill. Present were Gardner and Heelis.

21. *Wh Man Chron*, 27 June 1835, 27 February 1836.

22. *Appeal from the Association for Building and Endowing Ten Churches in the Boroughs of Manchester and Salford*, Manchester, 1841, pp. 1–2, 3, *M Chron*, 13 February 1841. See also *The First Report of the Committee of the Association for Building and Endowing Ten Churches*, Manchester, 1842.

23. For the early history of St Bartholomew, see *SWN*, 10 April 1875; *Reporter*, 10 February 1883 and 12 July 1902. For St Matthias, see *SWN*, 8 May 1875, *S Chron*, 4 December 1875. For St Simon, see *MG*, 20 March 1845, 28 February 1849, *SWN*, 7 August 1875, *Reporter*, 11 January 1908.

24. Out of the 478 clergy in the Diocese in 1866, 21 per cent were graduates of Trinity College, Dublin, *SWN*, 24 March 1866.

25. *MG*, 8 November 1851, 9 April 1858, *S Chron*, 7 April 1877.

26. See Appendix 2. The Church of England in Salford in Canon Stowell's time.

27. Birley was chairman of the Salford School Board 1870–90, and Manchester School Board 1870–85 and 1888–90, *Manchester Faces and Places*, vol. 2, No. 3 (1891); *Reporter*, 22 November 1890 (obituary).

28. *Reporter*, 7 July 1906.

29. A. V. Parsons, 'Education in the Salford District 1780–1870', unpublished M.Ed. thesis, Manchester, 1963.

30. Marsden, *op. cit.*, p. 186. *MG*, 1 November 1837. S. E. Maltby, *Manchester and the Movement for National Elementary Education* (Manchester, 1918), p. 53.

31. Parsons, *op. cit.*, p. 306.

32. Marsden, *op. cit.*, p. 186.

33. *MG*, 17 May 1854.

34. Parsons, *op. cit.*, p. 133 for 1861. The figures for 1903 were: Church of England places 18,163; Nonconformist and undenominational 3,088; Roman Catholic 6,758; total voluntary places 27,929;

Board School places 19,072. I. R. Cowan, 'The work of the Salford School Board', unpublished M. Ed. thesis, Durham, 1965, p. 179.

35. The Revd T. G. Lee at the AGM of the Borough of Salford Ragged and Industrial School, *SWN* 2 February 1867.

36. *SWN*, 17 March 1866.

37. Stowell advocated giving Palestine to the Jews after the Crimean War was over, *MG*, 1 November 1854, *SWN* 2 May 1860.

38. Marsden, *op. cit.,* p. 43.

39. *Ibid.,* pp. 451, 163.

40. For details see D. Newsome, *Godliness and Good Learning* (1961), Chapter 2. *S Chron*, 1 January 1870.

41. *MG*, 1, 8 February 1851, *The Ecclesiologist,* vol. 12 (1851), pp. 45–9.

42. Bullock, *op. cit.,* pp. 47–8.

43. *MG*, 12 August 1848.

44. See, for instance, *The Importance of the Controversy between the Church of England and the Church of Rome. A lecture delivered at St Matthew's Church Manchester, 1839, by the Rev. Hugh Stowell MA,* 1839.

45. *Ibid.,* p. 52.

46. See E. R. Norman, *Anti-Catholicism in Victorian England* (1968), *passim;* and G. F. A. Best, 'Popular Protestantism', in R. Robson (ed.), *Ideas and Institutions of Victorian Britain* (1967), pp. 115–42.

47. A. de Tocqueville, *Journeys to England and Ireland* (1835), ed. J. P. Meyer (Yale, 1958), p. 108.

48. *Wh Man Chron*, 24 March 1832.

49. *Ibid.,* 25 October, 22 November 1834, 21 November 1835.

50. *Ibid.,* 10 March 1832.

51. *MG*, 6 Mar 1844, 1 May 1850.

52. For Gavazzi see *MG*, 21 January 1852 and 8 August 1855; for Wlodarski see *SWN*, 15 February 1862; for the Camins see *MG*, 28 June 1859. There were Orange riots in Liverpool in 1851 and 1857, anti-Catholic riots in Stockport 1852, an Irish riot in Hulme 1852 and in Wigan 1859.

53. *M Chron*, 23 March 1839, *Great Protestant Meeting of Lancashire and Cheshire at Manchester on Thursday, September 26 1839,* London, 1839, *M and S Advertiser,* 19 April 1845, *The Proposed Endowment of Maynooth. A Speech Delivered at a Great Meeting of the Churchmen of Manchester Opposed to the Endowment of Maynooth College, on Thursday April 22 1845 by the Rev. Hugh Stowell AM,* London and Manchester, 1845, price 2*d.,* *MG*, 14 April 1855, 22 April 1856.

54. Marsden, *op. cit.,* p. 249. *A Complete Memoir of the Late Rev. Canon Stowell,* 1865, a 2*d.* pamphlet.

55. *MG*, 27 February 1850, 6 October 1852, 13 December 1854.

56. *MG*, 12 August 1848, 'Reminiscences of Catholicity in the early part of the century', *The Harvest,* Vol. II, p. 229.

57. *MG*, 19, 28 September 1855. *'One Body and One Spirit'. A Sermon preached at Christ Church Salford on Sunday evening October 7th 1855 by the Rev. Canon Stowell MA in reply to the controversial sermon of Dr. Wiseman Preached at the Opening of the Church of St John's Catholic Chapel Salford,* Manchester, 1855.

58. In 1859 Catholics began a long campaign to have priests appointed as chaplains in workhouses, see *MG*, 2 July 1859. It was to take over 20 years to win it. In 1864 Daniel Lee, a leading layman, one of the few Catholic merchants in Manchester, noted that, despite their numbers, 'no candidate for office ... ever thinks of consulting their wishes', *SWN*, 31 December 1864.

59. A. de Tocqueville, *op. cit.,* p. 108 (f.n.).

60. *Wh Man Chron*, 22 February 1834.

61. *MG*, August 1849, *passim,* 24 November 1852, 8 October 1858.

62. L. E. Mather (ed.), *The Rt. Hon. Sir William Mather* (1929), pp. 208–9.

63. *SWN*, 3, 10 November 1860.

64. *Ibid.,* 10, 24 August 1861.

65. *Ibid.,* 16, 30 November 1861.

66. *Ibid.,* 7, 21 December 1861, 8, 22 February 1862.

67. *The Duty of England in Regard to the Traffic in Intoxicating Drinks by the Rev. Canon Stowell. Reprinted from the 'Alliance' a weekly newspaper price one penny,* Leeds, 1840.

68. *MG*, 26 July 1854.
69. *SWN*, 5 October 1861.
70. As 'Doctors U Sto-ill and Holland Ool'. Manchester Archives, J. B. Smith's Election Papers.
71. *Wowell versus Stowell or the Reverend Hugh Stowell's letter to the Electors of Salford, (Being never intended for the Electors of Great Britain) on their Duty to their representative at the present crisis, made to answer itself, by Hugh Wowell*, Manchester, 17 June 1841.
72. *No Revolution. A Word to the People of England by the Rev. Hugh Stowell*, 1848. pp. 3.
73. Marsden, *op. cit.,* p. 235.
74. *MG*, 10 July 1852.
75. *MG*, 22 November 1854.
76. Marsden, *op. cit.,* p. 171.
77. *MG*, 30 January 1861.
78. *SWN*, 21 October 1865.
79. *SWN*, 13 January 1866, 26 October 1867, 15 May 1869. *Manchester Faces and Places*, vol. 4, 1893–94, pp. 107–8.
80. *Reporter*, 4 December 1886.
81. For T. A. Stowell see *Manchester Faces and Places*, vol. 1, 1889–90, p. 158–9.

## Notes to Chapter 5

1. On Armitage the most informative sources are the detailed obituary notices in the local press, particularly in the *M Examiner and Times, M Courier* and *MG*, 27 November 1876, the *SWN* and the *Eccles Advertiser*, 2 December 1876. See also Cyrus Armitage, *Some Account of the Armitages from 1662 to the Present Time* (1850), (dedicated to his uncle, Sir Elkanah) and B. l'Anson, *The History of the Armytage or Armitage Family* (1915). In M Archives there is a volume of (mainly) letters of condolence on the death of Sir Elkanah. In LRO there is a collection of newspaper cuttings, including the obituaries cited above (Armitage Family Papers), and in Chetham's library there are a few papers.
2. Cyrus Armitage, *op. cit.,* pp. 87–94.
3. *Northampton Mercury*, 5 September 1829, quoting the *M Advertiser.*
4. Obituary in *SWN, op. cit., The English Independent*, 30 November 1876; W. G. Robinson, *William Roby and the Revival of Independency in the North* (1954). The Missionary Society hoped Elijah would introduce the Tahitians to the benefits of textile manufacture.
5. Obituary, *Eccles Advertiser, op. cit.*
6. Obituary, *SWN, op. cit.*
7. *Ibid.*
8. *Trades Union Magazine and Precursor of a People's Newspaper*, 8 March 1851 (Peel Park). (Hereinafter *TU Mag*).
9. *MG*, 1 July 1854, 2 July 1857; *SWN*, 1 December 1860; *Reporter*, 19 March 1881.
10. Ipswich and East Suffolk Record Office, Fitzgerald papers. Lease from Duchy of Lancaster in 1824 recited in a lease from J. P. Fitzgerald to J. Kerrich in 1840 (HB 56 Box 22). For Stephenson's drilling see *MG*, 15 September 1832. C. E. Lee, 'Robert Stephenson the Elder (1788–1857) Railway and Mining Engineer: His Lancashire Connections', *Trans. of the Lancs. & Cheshire Antiquarian Society for 1967* (1974), pp. 128–36; B. Library, Add. MS 54181, correspondence of Robert Stephenson mainly with J. P. Fitzgerald. For flooding see *Wh Man Chron*, 30 May 1835; *MG*, 5 August 1843. For Fitzgerald's bankruptcy see *Northampton Herald*, 14 July 1849. For transfer of the lease to Knowles, see Fitzgerald papers (Ipswich), indenture of 3 September 1858. For the 1897 sale see indenture dated 30 August 1897.
11. J. B. Smethurst, 'Ermen & Engels in Eccles', Eccles and District History Society Lectures, typescript (1969–70), pp. 19–26. *S. Chron*, 22 August 1896 (Ermen & Roby became a public company); *Reporter*, 11 August 1900 (death of Godfrey Ermen).
12. James Richardson, 'Charlestown Reminiscences No. 23', *Reporter*, 24 March 1900.
13. For Sir Elkanah's will, see *Illustrated London News*, 13 January 1877, p. 47.
14. Obituary, *Reporter*, 18 June 1887.

15. Obituary of Sir Elkanah, *Eccles Advertiser, op. cit.*

16. For Vernon Armitage, see *Reporter*, 25 July 1885, 13 May 1911 (obituary), 17 June 1911 (will).

17. *MG*, 26 November 1838.

18. A. Redford and I. S. Russell, *The History of Local Government in Manchester*, vol. 2 (1950 edn), chapters XV and XVI.

19. *Ibid.*, chapter XVII.

20. A. Prentice, *History of the Anti-Corn Law League* (1968 edn) vol. 1., p. 398; vol. 2., p. 416.

21. *M. Examiner and Times*, 27 November 1876, Redford and Russell, *op. cit.*, chapter XX for the story of Longdendale Valley water works, though the authors have little to say about Armitage.

22. *N Star*, 18 April, 19 February 1848.

23. *MG*, 6 March 1847. For 'Famine Fever' in Manchester see *MG*, June 1847 *passim*.

24. *MG*, 27 February 1847.

25. This account is largely based on J. H. Treble, 'O'Connor, O'Connell and and the Attitudes of Irish Immigrants towards Chartism in the North of England', in J. Butt and I. F. Clarke (eds), *The Victorians and Social Protest* (Newton Abbott, 1973), pp. 33–70.

26. *Ibid.*, p. 49.

27. *Ibid.*, p. 68.

28. *MG*, 11, 15, 29 March, 1, 5, 8, 12, 19 April 1848.

29. *MG*, 8, 12 April 1848. See also Armitage's obituary, *MG*, 27 November 1876.

30. *MG*, 3 June 1848.

31. *MG*, 19, 26, 29 July, 19, 30 August 1848.

32. Redford and Russell, *op. cit.*, pp. 206–7.

33. *MG*, 13 October 1852.

34. Obituary, *M Courier*, 27 November 1876.

35. T. G. Lee, *TU Mag*, 25 January 1851.

36. *MG*, 5 October 1850.

37. *M Spectator*, 2 November 1850.

38. *TU Mag*, 23 November 1850, 19 April 1851.

39. D. A. Farnie, 'The English Cotton Industry 1850–1896', unpublished MA dissertation, Manchester (1953), p. 227.

40. *MG, M Spectator*, 4 January 1851.

41. *MG*, 15, 18 January, 2, 6 April 1851.

42. *MG*, 1 February 1857, *M Spectator*, 1 and 8 February 1851.

43. *Reporter*, 27 February 1909.

44. J. Clayton in his *The Story of the Salford Central Mission* (Blackburn, 1928), notes Lee was said 'to have three times emptied the church and three times, by his eloquence and zeal, filled it again' (p. 25). See *S Chron*, 19 May 1877, for Lee's retirement from New Windsor.

45. For Heywood see J. O. Baylen & N. J. Gossman, (eds), *Biographical Dictionary of Modern British Radicals*, vol ii, 1830–1870 (1984), pp. 238–40.

46. *Reporter*, 5 December 1876.

47. *MG*, 3, 13, 17 May 1848.

48. *MG*, 7 June 1848.

49. *MG*, 25, 29 January 1851.

50. *MG*, 19, 23 April 1851.

51. *MG*, 28 February, 3 March 1852.

52. *MG*, 28 April, 22, 26, 29 May, 2, 5, 12 June, 3, 10 June 1852.

53. *MG*, 3 November 1852.

54. *MG*, 20 December 1854. The press was almost wholly anti-Bright, the only paper supporting him being the *Examiner and Times*.

55. *MG*, 20, 24 January, 28 February, 7, 14, 31 March 1855.

56. *MG*, 1, 6, 10 December 1855, 5 February 1856, *MG*, 6 November 1856.

57. *MG*, 5, 6 March 1857. Cobden to Wilson, 6 March 1857, Wilson Papers, M. Archives.

58. *MG*, 6, 7, 11, 14, 18, 19, 21 March 1857.

59. *MG*, 17, 20 March 1857. See also Cobden's letters to Wilson, 6, 10, 13 March, Wilson Papers, *op. cit.*

60. *MG*, 24 March 1857.

61. *MG*, 30 March 1857.
62. *MG*, 18 March 1857.
63. Wilson Papers, *op. cit.*, letter from W. Warburton to Wilson 8 May 1857; *MG*, 21 January, 2 February 1858. See also *MG*, 1 April 1858.
64. *MG* 18 September 1858.
65. *MG*, 15 January 1858.
66. *MG*, 27 October 1858.
67. *MG*, 18 November 1858.
68. *MG*, 25 November, 8, 11 December 1858.
69. *MG*, 9, 14, 15 April 1859.
70. *MG*, 18, 21 April 1859. *MG*, 2 May 1859.
71. The first number is dated 28 May 1859.
72. *SWN*, 4 and 11 February, 15 July 1865.
73. *The Times*, 27 November 1862.

## Notes to Chapter 6

1. At a rally at Pomona Gardens, Manchester, *S Chron*, 6 April 1872.
2. *S Chron*, 11 December 1869.
3. For Cawley's life, see his entry in *Debrett's House of Commons and the Judicial Bench* (1874), and his obituaries in *SWN* and *S Chron*, 7 April 1877.
4. *MG*, 3, 24 January 1852.
5. *MG*, 24 March 1852.
6. *MG*, 29 January 1858.
7. *MG*, 18 February 1858.
8. *MG*, 7 October and 10 November 1858.
9. *SWN*, 8 September and 6 October 1866.
10. *MG*, 14 September 1855.
11. *MG*, 20 March 1852.
12. *MG*, 21 May 1859.
13. *SWN*, 4 and 11 February 1865.
14. *SWN*, 15 August 1868. The electorate in Salford was increased from 5,960 to 14,859.
15. *S Chron*, 19 January 1867.
16. For Daniel Hall's obituary see *Reporter*, 3 December 1898. For John's see *Reporter*, 4 September 1886.
17. *S Chron*, 4 January 1869. The first issue was on 24 October 1868. It declared 'We confidently expect the support and encouragement of all those inhabitants of the Borough whose motto is "Loyalty to the throne; Protestant reforms in the Church; and all needful reforms in the State: but Popish revolution in neither Church nor State."' Its proprietor was named as William Henry Wood.
18. *SWN*, 20 July 1967.
19. *SWN*, 10, 17 August 1867, 15 February 1868.
20. *S Chron*, 14 November 1868.
21. For Haworth's views, see *S Chron*, 14 November 1868.
22. Wood was secretary of the Manchester and Salford Trades Council from 1866 to 1877. He was a Freemason, a Salford Councillor 1884–87 and the author of a short history of Salford. For Wood's trades union work see Chapter 11 below. Short obituaries appeared in the *Reporter*, and *S. Chron*, 20 April 1901.
23. *SWN*, 18 April 1868.
24. *Marx Engels on Britain* (Moscow, 1962), pp. 545–6.
25. *SWN*, 29 August 1868.
26. *S Chron*, 7 November 1868. Mead stumped Salford as the missioner of the Manchester-based Protestant Reformation Society. Ratteners were trades union saboteurs, locally in the brickyards.
27. 'One Who Knows Lancashire' in *The Times*, 23 November 1868, quoted in *SWN*, 28 November 1868.

28. The pivot of the district was Christ Church School, Hope Street. See the article by 'An old Hope Street boy' in the *Reporter*, 8 February 1890, who remembered an 'Irish Penny man' who used to visit once a year, and 'instil into the boys more bigotry, uncharitableness, and hatred of their fellow creatures of the Roman Catholic persuasion than a lifetime could properly uproot.'

29. For the Fenian incident see *SWN*, 21 September, 9, 16, 30 November 1867. See also Paul Rose, *The Manchester Martyrs* (1970), *passim*.

30. *SWN*, 6 March 1869.

31. *S Chron*, 16 June 1869.

32. These included Loyal Orange Lodge No. 141 'Charley's True Blues'; No. 250 'Hugh Stowell'; No. 169 'Rt Hon. Benjamin Disraeli's True Blues of Salford'; and No. 256 'Earl of Derby's "No Surrender"'. Their appearance is recorded in the pages of the *S Chron* in 1869 and 1870. Only two new lodges have been noticed after the end of 1870. It is clear immigrant Scots and Irish Protestants were an important part of the membership of the Salford Orange Lodges.

33. *SWN*, 10 April 1869.

34. *SWN*, 8 October 1870.

35. *SWN*, 3 December 1870.

36. In the twenty years of the Salford School Board the population grew from 124,805 (in 1871) to 198,100 (in 1891) and the number of children attending school from 16,631 to 35,132, *Manchester Faces and Places*, IV (1893), p. 11.

37. The figures (for school places) were 28,655 in voluntary schools and 18,108 in Board Schools, I. R. Cowan 'The Work of the Salford School Board', unpublished MA dissertation, Durham, 1965, p. 179.

38. *S Chron*, 7, 14 February 1874.

39. *SWN*, 7 September 1878.

40. *SWN*, 28 December 1872. Catholics were particularly annoyed at the termination of Fr. Saffenreuter's position as priest and teacher of Catholics in the workhouse in that year.

41. *Ibid.*

42. Professor Beasley, *Beehive*, 16 May 1874, quoted by a Socialist in a letter to the *Reporter*, 25 February 1899.

43. In a letter to Pendleton Conservative Club, *S Chron*, 30 January 1875.

44. Walker was head of Walker & Lomax, one of the largest spinning and manufacturing firms in Bury. He was strongly endorsed by Richard Haworth, and other leading supporters in Salford and Manchester were J. L. Barrett, E. Hardcastle MP, Hugh Birley, Thomas Dickens and James Worrall, *SWN*, 12 April 1877.

45. *SWN*, 21 April 1877.

46. *SWN*, 5 May 1877.

47. *SWN*, 1 February 1879.

## Notes to Chapter 7

1. *SWN*, 6 January 1872.

2. Davies's life has been reconstructed from the newspapers and other sources indicated below. Obituaries appeared in the *MG*, 19 October 1885 and the *Reporter* and *S Chron*, 24 October 1885.

3. A. de Tocqueville, *Journey to England and Ireland* (1883) ed. J. P. Meyer (Yale, 1958), p. 105.

4. There is a good account of the early history of Methodism locally in *SWN*, 24 July 1875.

5. *Slater's Royal National Commercial Directory of Manchester and Salford and their Vicinities* (1876), pp. 197–8.

6. For Brunswick see *History of the Brunswick Chapel, Pendleton. With Notices of Early Methodism in Manchester and Salford*, compiled by William Daynes (1880). For Pendleton Congregational see *SWN*, 18 September 1875 and *Reporter*, 27 January 1906. The reference to Whitby Abbey and Armitage and Hewitt largesse is in *M Courier*, 5 September 1846. For Broad Street Primitive Methodists, see *Reporter*, 17 August 1907. For the history of the Welsh Calvinists in Manchester and Salford, see *Reporter*, 16 February 1901. The congregation began to form in 1788 and moved to Salford in 1833 and to Pendleton in 1879. For the building and opening of the Chapel on Broad

Street see *SWN*, 30 November 1878 and 19 July 1879. For Bathesda's early history, see *SWN*, 21 August 1875 and *Reporter*, 24 March 1883. For the opening of the new chapel, see *SNW*, 1 March 1862 and 7 March 1863.

7. For early Sunday Schools, see *SWN*, 15 January 1870. The statistics for 1831 are from *Wh Man Chron*, 19 February 1831. For Gravel Lane Sunday school see *SWN*, 28 April 1860.

8. See *SWN*, 12 January 1870 for Davies's part in its fifth annual general meeting.

9. For the Ragged School Union see *SWN*, 31 March 1866. For Spaw Street see *SWN*, 8 February 1862, 26 November 1864, 18 March 1865. For Davies's support, see *SWN*, 23 February 1867.

10. *SWN*, 26 November 1864.

11. *MG*, 13 October 1856.

12. Figure quoted in *SWN*, 26 January 1861 in an article voicing anxiety about the political situation in the USA.

13. A. Silver, *Manchester Men and Indian Cotton 1847–72* (Manchester, 1966). See also *SWN*, 15 June 1861 for anxieties and hopes that other sources of supply could be developed by the investment of Manchester capital in other countries such as India.

14. *SWN*, 19 April 1862. See also that newspaper 21 September, 30 November and 21 December 1861.

15. *SWN*, 25 January, 8 February, 17 May and 19 July 1862.

16. *SWN*, 26 July 1862.

17. *SWN*, 15 November 1862.

18. *SWN*, 19 April, 3 and 17 May, 28 June, 11 October 1862.

19. *SWN*, 8 November 1862.

20. *SWN*, 31 May 1862.

21. *SWN*, 27 September, 25 October 1862, 15 July 1865.

22. *SWN*, 18 July 1863. See also *SWN*, 8 November 1862 and 7 and 14 February 1863.

23. For the hatred of labour tests see *SWN*, 28 June and 11 October 1862. The latter reported that there was an 'incipient revolt among the able bodied men' in Manchester. In March 1863 there were riots against attendance centres in Staleybridge (*SWN*, 28 March 1863).

24. *SWN*, 14 February 1863.

25. Parsons 'Education in the Salford District 1780 to 1870', *op. cit.*, p. 299. In late December 1862 there was a peak of 5,238 'cases' involving 17,793 persons receiving relief from the Committee *SWN*, 27 December 1862.

26. *SWN*, 13 September 1865 (editorial).

27. *SWN*, 27 December 1862.

28. *SWN*, 13 September 1862.

29. *SWN*, 28 March, 18 and 25 April 1863.

30. *SWN*, 18 July 1863. For the Associations see *SWN*, 4 and 25 April 1863.

31. *SWN*, 28 March, 9 and 23 May, 26 September 1863, 6 February, 26 March 1864.

32. *SWN*, 8 August 1863.

33. *SWN*, 22 August 1863.

34. *SWN*, 3 July 1869 (editorial).

35. *SWN*, 3 October 1864.

36. *SWN*, 10 December 1864 and 15 July 1865.

37. *SWN*, 15 October 1864.

38. *SWN*, 18 March 1865, on the occasion of the re-opening of Mr James Aspinall Turner's mill in Booth Street, Salford after a standstill of two years.

39. *MG*, 25 August 1857. For the background see that newspaper 20 May and 6 September 1854; 1, 6, 9, 10, and 12 May and 17 December 1856; 6 August, and 24 August 1857.

40. Quoted in L. M. Mather, *The Rt. Honourable Sir William Mather* (1925), p. 279.

41. David Chadwick, *Proposed Establishment of Public Baths and Wash-Houses in Salford* (Salford, 1854). *MG*, 25 July and 27 August 1856.

42. *SWN*, 3 November 1860.

43. For Pickering's mortality rates in Salford (by Districts) see Appendix 4, Table 2.

44. For the vital statistics of Salford 1844–60 see Appendix 4, Table 1.

45. Anti-cholera placard *SWN*, 19 August 1865. See also *SWN*, 6 July 1867 for the cases of cholera in Salford in 1866.

46. See Appendix 4, Table 4.
47. See Appendix 4, Table 5.
48. *Vital Statistics* (1864), *op. cit.*
49. See Appendix 4, Table 3.
50. *SWN*, 16 November 1861. LSE, Webb Collection, *Proceedings of the Salford Borough Council*, Report of the Borough Surveyor of Bolton, who was called to report.
51. *SWN*, 24 October 1863; 6 and 27 February, 10 September 1864.
52. *SWN*, 4 September 1869 gave the official figures.
53. *SWN*, 15 April 1865, letter signed 'S. E. R.'
54. *SWN*, 5 August 1865.
55. *SWN*, 19 August 1865.
56. Vital statistics for Salford, 1866, in *SWN*, 6 July 1867. See also Table 3 above.
57. *Ibid.*
58. For details of the 1867 Act see *SWN*, 15 December 1866, 19 January 1867.
59. *SWN*, 16 May 1868.
60. LSE Library. Jevons Collection. *Vital Statistics and the Medical Officer of Health's Report on the Sanitary Condition of the Borough of Salford for the year 1868.*
61. *SWN*, 13 November, 24 December 1869, 1 January and 23 July 1870.
62. *SWN*, 5 August 1871.
63. *SWN*, 31 August 1871, 8 February 1873, 5 April 1873.
64. *S Chron*, 19 November 1870.
65. *Ibid.*, see also *SWN*, 12 December 1868.
66. *SWN*, 20 June 1868. *Reports of the Rivers Pollution Commission (1868)*, British Parliamentary Papers, XL, 1870.
67. *S Chron*, 8 August 1874.
68. Tatham's Annual Report for 1873 is summarised in *SWN*, 22 August 1874.
69. *S Chron*, 5 April 1879.
70. See Appendix 4, Table 4.
71. *SWN*, 24 September, 8 October 1870.
72. *SWN*, 10 April and 1 May 1875.
73. *SWN*, 17 February 1877.
74. *SWN*, 3 March 1877.
75. *SWN*, 4 August 1877.
76. *Reporter*, 4 September 1880. For the three new parks, see *SWN*, 8 August 1874, 24 July 1875 and 12 May 1877. For the playground in Greengate, see *S Chron*, 2 October 1875 and *SWN*, 1 June 1878.
77. For Salford Improved Industrial Dwellings see *SWN*, 25 Apr, 20 June, 11 July 1868, 9 April 1870, and 4 March 1871.
78. *Reporter*, 23 October 1886.
79. See Appendix 4, Table 4. According to an editorial in *SWN*, 11 November 1871. The Medical Officer's statistics placed it fourth (after Sunderland, Liverpool and Manchester) in his annual report for 1871, published in *SWN*, 30 March 1872.
80. *Annual Report of the Medical officer for 1900*, Table 12.

## Notes to Chapter 8

1. *Reporter*, 24 December 1898. Levy was a leading figure in the David Lewis Trust, which had recently donated 25 acres to the Council to extend Peel Park.
2. For Benjamin Armitage's life see *Manchester Faces and Places*, vol. iii (1892), pp. 129–31, B. I'Anson, *The History of the Armytage or Armitage family* (1915), p. 110; and W. B. Tracey and W. T. Pike, *Manchester and Salford at the Close of the 19th Century: Contemporary Biographies* (1899), p. 101. The *Reporter* of 13 August 1898 reprinted an account of him from the *Manchester Evening Mail* series 'Portraits on 'Change', and an obituary on 9 December 1899. The same newspaper printed details of his personal estate (gross value sworn under £277,472) in its number dated 27 January 1900.

3. For G. A. Southam's obituary and Southam family history, see *Reporter*, 24 September 1898.

4. *Reporter*, 17 February 1900. The writer was J. Richardson. Armitage was president of the Manchester Chamber of Commerce 1878–81, and thereafter a director.

5. For the Ford Lane Club, see *SWN*, 26 April 1862, 28 January 1865 (children's Sunday Evenings), 27 May 1865 ('botanising'), 10 February 1872 (sale of drinks). For Pendleton Lads' club, see *Reporter*, 19 October 1889.

6. For works' treats, see *SWN*, 9 February 1867, for Armitage's houses, see *Reporter*, 24 November 1883, and 31 March 1900 (sale of Benjamin Armitage properties). For the playground, see *SWN*, 7 September 1878. For the chapels, see *SWN*, 20 March and 18 September 1875.

7. *SWN*, 19 November 1859 (first annual meeting of the Ballot and Reform Association), 22 June 1861. See also Wilson Papers (M Archives), Printed Prospectus, the Garibaldi Reception Committee, 1864.

8. *SWN*, 6 January 1866.

9. *SWN*, 21 August 1866.

10. *SWN*, 20 July 1867.

11. *SWN*, 1 May 1869.

12. *SWN*, 30 October 1869, 29 January 1870 (first annual meeting of the Liberal Association).

13. *SWN*, 9 February 1867 (Nassau mills), *Reporter*, 19 March 1881 (account of the firm), *Reporter*, 12 February 1881 (Family Ltd. Company).

14. For Benjamin Armitage of Sorrel Bank see J. Richardson's 'Charlestown Reminiscences', Letter VIII, *Reporter*, 9 September 1899. There are also references to his business in that newspaper in 3 March 1888, 16 January 1892, 24 June 1893 and 18 June 1898. For the sale of his pictures, see *Reporter*, 5 November 1887 ('Work') and 29 May 1897.

15. *SWN*, 31 March 1877, *SC*, 13 November 1875, *SWN*, 5 January 1878 (on Rylett's work).

16. *SWN*, 24 February 1877.

17. Arnold's obituary appeared in the *Reporter*, 24 May 1902. After the Cotton Famine Arnold travelled in Greece, the Near East, Russia and Persia publishing his accounts in book form. He was editor of the *Echo* for seven years and published a couple of novels. An ardent land nationalizer, he was the author of *Free Land* and *Social Politics* and was president of the Free Land League (1885). He became an alderman on the London County Council in 1889 and was chairman 1895–96. He was knighted in 1895.

18. *SWN*, 23 November 1878.

19. *Reporter*, 17 April 1880.

20. *SWN*, 25 October 1879.

21. *Reporter*, 22 January 1881.

22. *Reporter*, 1 October 1881 ('John Dillon' branch); 8 December 1883 ('Thomas Brennan'); 29 August 1885 (Pendleton).

23. *Reporter*, 20 May 1882.

24. *Reporter*, 14 August 1880 noted the formation of the Parliamentary Debating Society. For its progress, see that newspaper, *passim*, down to 20 January 1883, when it notes the winding up of the Society and the passing of the balance of its funds to the Salford Royal Hospital.

25. See *Reporter*, 28 August 1880 for the Radical Reform Union, and the same paper from 7 May 1881 to 11 February 1882, *passim*, for the Democratic League. For the Secular Society, see *Reporter*, 17 June, 14 October 1882 (Bradlaugh) and 30 June 1883 (Mrs Besant).

26. *Reporter*, 25 February and 28 October 1882, 21 April 1883, 26 April 1884.

27. *Reporter*, 21 January and 25 March 1882.

28. For Goulden, see *S Chron*, 21 October 1878. For Haworth, who died aged 63, see W. B. Pope, *Memorials of Richard Howarth, Manchester* (privately printed, 1885), and full obituaries in *MG*, 3 December 1883, *Reporter*, 8 December 1883. *Reporter*, 28 October 1882 (Working Men's Constitutional Union).

29. For Hardcastle, see M. Stenton and S. Lees (eds), *Who's Who of British Members of Parliament, Vol. 2, 1886–1916* (1978), and *Reporter*, 7 November 1885 for his platform. For Bowles, see R. T. Matthews and P. Mellini, *In 'Vanity Fair'* (1982), *passim*, and *MG*, 24 November 1885. For Sir William Worsley, see *Reporter*, 23 May 1885. First choice for the Conservatives in West Salford had been a local man, James Worrall, Jun., who turned the offer down 'for business reasons'.

30. *Reporter*, 7 November 1885.

31. *Reporter*, 28 November 1885.

32. *Reporter*, 10 April 1886.

33. *Reporter*, 15 May 1886 (Broughton meeting), M Archives, Misc/473/1–4, Bright to Armitage, 6 May 1886.

34. *Reporter*, 15 May 1886.

35. *Reporter*, 10 July 1886.

36. *Ibid.*

37. M Archives, Letters of John Bright to Armitage, *op. cit.*, Bright to Armitage, 29 December 1886.

38. *Reporter*, 31 July 1886, 28 May 1887.

39. *Reporter*, 16 October and 20 November 1886.

40. *Reporter*, 16 July 1887, 3 March 1888.

41. *Reporter*, 21 June 1890.

42. *Proposal to open the Free Reference Libraries and Reading Rooms of Salford on Sunday Afternoons by Mr Benjamin Armitage (Chomlea). Price One Penny*, Manchester, 1888.

43. *Reporter*, 11 February, 10 March, 14 April 1888.

44. From 10 January 1891, the *Salford Reporter* (which had started life as the *Pendleton Reporter and Salford and Weaste Times* in 1879) became simply the *Reporter*. The last issue of *SWN* was 23 March 1889, after which it was incorporated with the *Manchester Weekly Times*.

45. *Reporter*, 25 February 1892.

## Notes to Chapter 9

1. *SWN*, 10 August 1878.

2. For a differing account of this episode see John Garrard's 'The Great Gas Scandal of 1887', duplicated typescript, British Gas North Western, Manchester, 1987. Mr Garrard focuses on Hunter as a new type of manager existing on a then hazy borderland between professional and entrepreneurial activity, importing into municipal service habits and attitudes that were, he argues, commonplace in large areas of the commercial world. He points out that whilst what Hunter was doing was quite clearly wrong, it was not then legally defined as corrupt. In general Mr Garrard chiefly differs from this writer in his estimate of Hunter's abilities as a gas engineer, his underplaying of the correctness of Mandley's accusations and the value of his anti-Hunter campaign.

3. *S Chron*, 7 August 1869, *SWN*, 20 August 1870.

4. Information given by the new gas engineer, Hunter, to a Parliamentary Select Committee, reported in *SWN*, 7 June 1879.

5. For Mandley's obituary, see *Reporter*, 22 August 1903.

6. *Manchester Faces and Places*, IV (1893), p. 57.

7. *SWN*, 7 September 1878.

8. *Ibid.*

9. *Salford Gas Management* (Manchester, 1878), p. 6. The text is prefaced 'Why is our Gas so Bad and yet so Dear?'

10. *Ibid.*, p. 15.

11. *S Chron*, 11 January 1879.

12. *Reporter*, 4, 18 September 1880.

13. *Reporter*, 13 November 1880.

14. *Reporter*, 12 March 1881.

15. *Reporter*, 21 January 1882.

16. *Reporter*, 25 March, 8, 22 April 1882.

17. See Mandley's accusations in *Reporter*, 22 April 1882 and 6 November 1886. When it all came out in 1888 the *Reporter* (24 March) informed its readers: 'He has travelled through the East in the garb of an Arab, he has taken the waters at Carlsbad, and has seen many continental cities. He has kept men and maid servants, driven his carriage and pair, has a shooting box and hunters in Cheshire; he has lectured and preached and addressed public meetings; and he has hob-nobbed with the great and distinguished. Members and ex-members of Parliament, mayors and ex-mayors,

magistrates, aldermen and common councillors have played billiards at Beech House, drunk his wine and smoked his cigars and partaken of his cold turkey.'

18. *Reporter*, 22 January 1881.

19. As the *Wigan Examiner* put it, 'Samuel Hunter, the manager, was apparently held in mysterious awe by the members. He had cast a glamour over their mental visions which nothing could remove'. The paper reported the story of Hunter attending meetings dressed for the hunt. Quoted in the *Reporter*, 19 February 1887.

20. Hunter's life-story came out at his eventual trial, *Reporter*, 5 February 1887.

21. *SWN*, 3 November 1877. Big improvements to the Liverpool Street Gas works were reported in *S Chron*, 25 January 1879.

22. *Reporter*, 9 October 1886.

23. *Reporter*, 8 August 1885, 16 October and 6 November 1886.

24. *Reporter*, 22 January 1887.

25. *Reporter*, 5 February 1887.

26. *Reporter*, 12 February, 5 March 1887.

27. *Reporter*, 3 September 1887.

28. *Ibid.*

29. *Reporter*, 8 October 1887.

30. *Reporter*, 26 November 1887, 3, 24 March, 7 July 1888.

31. *Reporter*, 24 March 1888.

32. *Reporter*, 10 March, 2, 9, 16 June 1883. For the 1888 discussions see *Reporter*, 24 March 1888 to 27 April 1889, *passim*.

33. *Reporter*, 25 August, 29 September 1888.

34. *Reporter*, 24 November 1888, 18 August 1889.

35. *Reporter*, 24 August 1889.

36. *Reporter*, 31 August 1889.

37. *Reporter*, 29 March 1890.

38. *Reporter*, 5, 19 April, 3 May 1890.

39. *Reporter*, 10, 17, 24 May, 7 June 1890.

40. *Manchester City News*, 5 July, 1 November 1890.

41. *Ibid.*, 8 August 1891.

42. Hunter was released in March 1892, having served three years and four months.

43. *Reporter*, 8 January 1887.

44. *Reporter*, 21 February, 7 March 1891. The amalgamation of the townships became operative, April 1892.

45. *Reporter*, 12, 20 October, 10 November 1894.

46. *Reporter*, 26 January 1895.

47. *Reporter*, 9 February 1895. For the Socialist analysis, see J Hempsall, *The Muddle in Salford*, Salford Social Democratic Federation Pamphlet No. 1 (Manchester, 1895).

48. *Reporter*, 27 April 1895.

49. *Reporter*, 28 September, 5 October, 9, 16 November 1895.

50. Library of the London School of Economics and Political Science, Webb Local Government Collection, vol. 160 (Lancs, 20).

51. *Reporter*, 9 May 1908, 17 April, 12 June 1909.

52. *Reporter*, 10 August 1912.

53. *Reporter*, 24 August 1912.

54. For half a century Phillips was a powerful figure in Salford's local government. For his obituary, see *MG*, 3 March 1931.

55. *Reporter*, 22 August 1903.

## Notes to Chapter 10

1. *Reporter*, 11 January 1890.

2. Cardinal Manning, when he opened the Catholic Church at Market Harborough, Leicestershire, in 1877, *Northampton Mercury*, 18 August 1877

3. For the history of the St James Mission, see *SWN*, 19 June 1875 and *Reporter*, 14 October 1905.

4. *SWN*, 15 July 1871 and 19 June 1875.

5. *SWN*, 19 June 1875.

6. *SWN*, 1 May 1875. Two years later it was dedicated to the Mother of God as well as St James, *SWN*, 14 July 1877.

7. *Reporter*, 21 June 1890.

8. *MG*, 12 August 1848. For the consecration of Dr Turner as Bishop of Salford, see *MG*, 26 June 1851.

9. For St Peter's school, see *SWN*, 14 June 1862; St Peter's Church, *SWN*, 7 October and 12 December 1872; Mount Carmel School, *SWN*, 7 October 1865, 6 March and 11 September 1875; Mount Carmel Church, *Reporter*, 31 August 1907; St Joseph's, *Reporter*, 31 August 1907; St Anne's, *SWN*, 10 September 1870; St Thomas of Canterbury, *Reporter*, 3 May 1880 and 7 December 1901; St Boniface, *Reporter*, 19 December 1891.

10. Bishop Bilsborrow's first Pastoral Letter, *Reporter*, 3 September 1892.

11. *Reporter*, 30 May 1908.

12. For a full obituary of Bishop Turner, see *SWN*, 20 July 1872.

13. For Herbert Vaughan, J. G. Snead-Cox, *Life of Cardinal Vaughan* (1910), and *DNB*, 2nd Supplement, Vol. III (1912); A. McCormack, *Cardinal Vaughan: The Life of the third Archbishop of Westminster* (1966); see also G. A. Beck (ed.), *The English Catholics 1850–1950* (1950); D. Gwynn, *The Second Spring 1818–1852* (1942), and E. R. Norman, *The English Catholic Church in the 19th Century* (1984); see also S. Leslie (ed.), *Letters of Herbert Cardinal Vaughan to Lady Herbert of Lea 1867–1903* (London, 1942).

14. *DNB*, *op. cit.*, p. 550.

15. McCormack, *op. cit.*, *passim*. On his father's death in 1880 Vaughan became the recipient of an income of £1000 a year.

16. *Ibid.*, p. 136.

17. G. B. Pagani, *Life of the Rev. Aloysius Gentili* (London, 1851), p. 245; *SWN*, 25 March 1862; *SWN*, 23 July 1866.

18. *SWN*, 23 July 1866.

19. I. R. Cowan, 'The Work of the Salford School Board', unpublished MEd dissertation, Durham, 1965, p. 179.

20. *Reporter*, 7 November 1885.

21. *MG*, 2 July 1859; *SC*, 26 March 1870.

22. *Reporter*, 26 January 1889.

23. *SWN*, 18 May 1878.

24. *SWN*, 26 July 1865, 10 September 1870 (Catholic Grammar School); *SC*, 27 September 1873, 24 April 1875 (Seminary); *DNB* (St Bede's); *Reporter*, 1 November 1902 (Adelphi House).

25. *SWN*, 28 April 1877.

26. *Reporter*, 25 February 1893. Dr O'Gorman was a Broad Street surgeon who had served eleven years on the Board of Guardians. He was also Surgeon-major to the 4th Manchester Regiment of Volunteers.

27. *DNB*, p. 554.

28. The *Reporter* in 1887 referred to a dispute in the Anglo Irish Catholic press over whether or not Vaughan had a preference for Belgian and German priests over Irishmen. The Irish believed he had.

29. *Reporter*, 7 May, 10 September 1892.

30. *Reporter*, 16, 30 September 1893.

31. *Reporter*, 2 December 1893.

32. *Reporter*, 6, 20 January, 10 February 1894.

33. *Reporter*, 5 May 1894, 28 December 1895, 25 July 1896, 18 June and 24 September 1898.

34. *Reporter*, 7 Jan, 11 February 1899

35. *Reporter*, 18 February 1899.

36. *Reporter*, 25 March, 17 June 1899.

37. *Reporter*, 22, 29 July 1899.

38. *Reporter*, 12 August 1899.

39. *Reporter*, 19 August, 28 October 1899.

40. *Reporter*, 14 October 1899, 6 January 1900, 30 April 1904.

41. *Reporter*, 14 June 1902.

## Notes to Chapter 11

1. *Reporter*, 15 April 1893. See also Naomi Reid's account of Evans' life in Joyce M. Bellamy and John Savile (eds), *Dictionary of Labour Biography*, vi (1982), pp. 109–10. In addition to references to Evans in the local press much of the information in this chapter derives from G. C. Goldberg's unpublished Manchester University MA dissertation, 'The Socialist and Political Labour Movement in Manchester and Salford 1884–1914', 1975.

2. *Reporter*, 24 January 1885.

3. *Reporter*, 7 March 1885. Apart from Horrocks, a Socialist, other speakers included Messrs Ball (Liberal), Edeson and Marsden (Conservatives) and Murray (Irish Nationalist). Horrocks attacked Benjamin Armitage for a recent speech on Free Trade.

4. Edmund and Ruth Frow, *Radical Salford: Episodes in Labour History* (Swinton, 1984), p. 18.

5. *S. Chron*, 8 March 1873.

6. *Reporter*, 7, 14, 21, 28 May, 2 July, 20 August and 8 October 1881 (for the Democratic League) and for pro and anti-Bradlaugh groups see *Reporter*, 24 September 1881, 11 and 25 February and 17 June 1882. The Pendleton Secular Club's inaugural lecture (by Bradlaugh) led to 'uproarious proceedings', *Reporter*, 14 October 1882. In the years 1880–83 there were also 'Parliamentary Debating Societies' in Salford and Pendleton.

7. E. and R. Frow, *op. cit.*, p. 18, and Goldberg, chapter 1.

8. *Ibid.*

9. *Reporter*, 31 December 1894.

10. *The Draper's Record*, 18 April 1903 (quoted in the *Reporter*).

11. *SWN*, 15 February 1879.

12. Attention to the plight of the unemployed was drawn in a series of harrowing articles in the *SWN* in December 1878.

13. *Reporter*, 1 March 1884.

14. *See Principles, Objects and Laws of the First Salford Co-operative Society. Established October 1829* (Manchester: Hignett and Jackson, 1831). There are informative articles on this Owenite experiment and the men involved in *SWN*, 30 January 1864, *SWN*, 1 February 1879 (on Craig); *Reporter*, 23 June 1883, *Reporter*, 14 July 1888 (on G. F. Mandley); *Reporter*, 27 April 1895 (on Joseph Smith); *Manchester Faces & Places*, IV, p. 55 (on Mandley). See also R. and E. Frow, *op. cit.*, pp. 10–11.

15. *N Star*, 8 and 15 February, 13 June 1840, *M Chron*, 13 June 1840.

16. *N Star*, 20 June 1840, 20 March 1841.

17. Recalled in a piece in the *Reporter*, 19 July 1884.

18. *N Star*, 28 October 1848.

19. *MG*, 14 September 1850.

20. For the 'Industrial' and the 'Equitable' see *SWN*, 31 December 1859, 20 January 1866; *S Chron*, 23 January 1875; *Reporter*, 1 December 1883. For PICS see W. F. Cottrell, *The Jubilee Record of the Pendleton Industrial Co-operative Society Ltd 1860–1910* (Manchester, 1910), *passim*. By 1904 the PICS employed over 700 people and had nearly 24,000 members. Its share capital was £240,000: *Reporter*, 30 January 1904.

21. Cottrell, *op. cit.*, pp. 113–14. The Society also sen £500 to the Amalgamated Society of Engineers in the big lock-out in 1897, *Reporter*, 18 September 1897.

22. *SWN*, 9 February 1878. *S Chron*, 9 July 1870. An editorial in the *SWN*, 19 October 1878 declared 'Building Societies are the savings banks of the mass of the people'.

23. *SNW*, 20 January 1872.

24. *Reporter*, 23 November 1889. This was 'Victory' Lodge. A second, 'Clarence', opened in 1812.

25. See above, Chapter Three.

26. *SWN*, 2, 9 August 1879.

27. Based on an analysis of Friendly Societies mentioned in the *Reporter* in 1891. A great deal of space in local newspapers was given to meetings, together with a plethora of the local and national statistics of the several orders.

28. See *Jubilee Record of the Independent Order of Rechabites (Salford Unity) Friendly Society* (1885).

29. Jubilee of the Sons of Temperance, Grand Division 1864–1914, *Reporter*, 28 November 1914. It then claimed to be the most numerous Friendly Society in Salford.

30. *Reporter*, 22 November 1890.

31. *SWN*, 14 October 1871; *Reporter*, 28 February 1891.

32. *Reporter*, 1 October 1887; *SWN*, 7 June 1879.

33. *Reporter*, 4 December 1897.

34. See Chapter 1 of his *The Classic Slum* (Manchester, 1971). The quotations here are from a talk he gave on 'Class Development in an Industrial Society', Eccles and District History Society Lectures (typescript, 1972–73).

35. These figures were given by W. H. Wood, Secretary of the Manchester and Salford Trades Council: *SWN*, 21 January 1872.

36. See Alan Fox, *History and Heritage: The Social Origins of the British Industrial Relations System* (1985), Chapter 4, especially pp. 131–7.

37. *SWN*, 18, 26 August 1866.

38. *SWN*, 2 July 1864, 19 August 1865, 13 July, 7, 21 September 1867.

39. *SWN*, 28 July, 15 September 1866.

40. *Reporter*, 24 September 1887.

41. S. and B. Webb, *The History of Trade Unionism* (1913 edn), p. 236.

42. *Ibid.*, pp. 264–5.

43. *S Chron*, 14 August 1875.

44. *S. Chron*, 27 June 1874; *SWN*, 14 September 1872; *S Chron*, 18 January and 1 March 1873; 24 September 1870; 19 April 1877; *SWN*, 23 February 1878; *S Chron*, 1 March 1873 (the 'garrett master' case); *SWN*, 17 May 1873 (carters); *S Chron*, 21 August 1873 (dyers).

45. *S Chron*, 20 February 1875 (Atlas); *SWN*, 27 February 1875, *S Chron*, 20 February 1875 (miners); *S Chron*, 29 June 1875 (Cottrill's).

46. *SWN*, 25 May 1878.

47. *SWN*, 2 February, 25 May, 1 June, *Reporter*, 13 September 1878.

48. The following account is based on reports in *SWN*, and *S Chron* from 5 May 1877 to 20 July 1878.

49. *S Chron*, 7, 14 November 1868.

50. *S Chron*, 4 December 1869, 9 July 1870.

51. *SWN*, 27 October 1877.

52. *SWN*, 15 September 1866, 19 January 1867.

53. *SWN*, 13 July 1867.

54. See *SWN*, 18, 24 December 1869 (Jones); *SWN*, 8 April 1871 (Jones Memorial in Ardwick cemetery).

55. *SWN*, 11 November 1871.

56. *Reporter*, 15 September 1888.

57. *Reporter*, 7 September 1889.

58. *Reporter*, 22 March, 30 August 1890.

59. *Reporter*, 25 July 1885.

60. *Reporter*, 7 November 1885.

61. G. C. Goldberg's dissertation *op. cit.* (hereinafter Goldberg), pp. 14, 18.

62. Goldberg, *op. cit.*, p. 40; Blatchford, *My Eighty Years*, pp. 192–8; H. Pelling, *The Origins of the Labour Party, 1880–1900* (1954), pp. 101–2.

63. Goldberg, *op. cit.*, p. 43.

64. For Trevor see *Dictionary of Labour Biography*, vol. vi, pp. 249–53.

65. For Brocklehurst see *ibid.*, vi, pp. 39–46.

66. *S Chron*, 12 December 1892; *Reporter*, 27 January 1894 (Hardie); *Reporter*, 12 October 1895 (Hempsall).

67. *Reporter*, 10 March 1894.

68. *Reporter*, 7 July 1906 (Wilson); 14 December 1907, 28 November 1908, 6 February 1909.

69. For Batty see *Reporter*, 11 January, 22 February, 4 April, 29 May 1909.

70. *Reporter*, 29 May 1909 (Fr. Carroll); Millie Toole, *Our Old Man* (1948), pp. 14–15.

71. *Reporter*, 9 February, 31 August 1895.

72. *Reporter*, 22 August, 5 September, 17 October, 21 November 1891.

73. *Reporter*, 19 September 1891.

74. Goldberg, *op. cit.*, p. 52; *Reporter*, 21 May 1892.

75. *Reporter*, 16 November 1901.

76. Goldberg, *op. cit.*, p. 57.

77. *Reporter*, 14 May 1898.

78. Goldberg, *op. cit.*, pp. 53–5.

79. Quoted by Naomi Reid in *Dictionary of Labour Biography*, vi, p. 110.

80. *Reporter*, 25 February, 13 May 1893.

81. Alexander Thompson (quoting the *MG*) in the Preface to Blatchford's *My Eighty Years*, op. cit.

82. Goldberg, *op. cit.*, pp. 60–1.

83. *Reporter*, 25 February, 4 November 1893; *Reporter*, 23 May 1896 (Watters). For Sunley see *Reporter*, 18 June 1898.

84. *Reporter*, 2 March (for Hobart), 20 July 1895.

85. Goldberg, *op. cit.*, p. 69. For Brocklehurst, who was sent to Strangeways for a month for disobeying the prohibition on public speaking in the Park, see *Dictionary of Labour Biography*, vi, pp. 39–46, which also has an appendix on the Boggart Hole Clough contest.

86. *Reporter*, 11 August 1894, 16 February 1895. For Macartney's obituary (he died at 52) see *Reporter*, 21 November 1914. See also *Reporter*, 27 June 1896, 18 May 1897, 30 April and 11 June 1904.

87. *Reporter*, 3 November, 10, 31 December 1892.

88. *County Telephone*, 20 February 1892, 19 March 1893; *Reporter*, 15 September 1894. Railway companies were known as tyrannical employers and pay was low as a corollary to railway work being regarded as a 'safe' employment (though in fact work on the railways was frequently dangerous: see *Reporter*, 19 January 1878 for national accident figures).

89. For the United Carters see *Reporter*, 1 August 1891. For Kelly's union see *Reporter*, 12 September, 10 October, 26 December 1891. For the Tramway and Hackney Carriage men see *Reporter*, 12 September 1891, *County Telephone*, 7 May 1892; *Reporter*, 25 February 1893.

90. *Reporter*, 11 August 1906. For Jackson himself see *Manchester and Salford at the Close of the 19th Century: Contemporary Biographies* (Brighton, 1900), p. 117.

91. *Reporter*, 6 January, 26 May 1894.

92. *Reporter*, 11 October 1890, 7 March, 9 May, 29 August 1891.

93. *Reporter*, 13 January 1894.

94. *Reporter*, 1, 15, 29 June; *S Chron*, 6 July 1895; *Reporter*, 12 December 1896.

95. For the bleachers and finishers see *Reporter*, 28 June 1890, 10 October 1891, 5 March, 8 October 1892, 11 February, 22 April 1893. For shirtmakers and macintosh workers see *Reporter*, 8 March, 19 April, 30 August 1890, 7 May 1892; *S Chron*, 16 July 1892. For block and roller cutters and smallwares workers, see *Reporter*, 24 January 1891, 6 February 1892.

96. *Reporter*, 12 September 1891, 14 March 1895. For ETU origins see 6 February 1892, 18 July 1896.

97. *Reporter*, 18 July 1891, 19 March 1892, 24 August and 2 November 1895 (paper mill workers); *County Telephone* 27 February 1892 (shopworkers); *Reporter*, 11 March 1893 (insurance workers); *Reporter*, 13 September 1890, 30 July 1892 (carpenters); *County Telephone*, 30 April 1892 (house painters).

98. *Reporter*, 18 January 1890.

99. *Reporter*, 7 May 1892, 16 September 1893 11 May 1895.

100. *Reporter*, 9 September, 2 December 1893, 13 January 1894.

101. *Reporter*, 29 January 1898. The paper printed articles regularly on the dispute between 4 September 1897 and May 1898.

102. *Reporter*, 22 January 1898 for a full report on the local aspects of the battle – which firms applied the lock-out and which did not. For the local aftermath, see *Reporter*, 5 February 1898. For Mather & Platt adopting the 48-hour week see *Reporter*, 7 May 1898.

103. It was this campaign that first made Abraham Wilkinson's name as a working-class Conservative politician. See the profile of him in *Reporter*, 16 December 1905.

104. *Reporter*, 11 and 18 May, 1 June 1889.

105. *Reporter*, 22 June 1889 (Marshall); 13 July, 7, 14, 21 September (Settle's articles); 8 June, 28 September, 2 November 1889 (Council Housing Committee).

106. *Reporter*, 18 January 1890 (Municipal League).

107. *Reporter*, 14 June 1890. Fraser's pamphlet was published in Manchester in 1890 and his articles

were in the *Reporter*, 12, 19, 26 July and 2 August of that year. These were reprinted as a pamphlet entitled *Sanitary Salford*.

108. *Reporter*, 14 June, 29 November 1890.

109. *Reporter*, 27 November 1891 (slum clearance); 15 April 1893 (Queen Street Dwellings). In the latter year the Lancashire and Yorkshire Railway Co. erected two blocks of model industrial dwellings in Oldfield Road for the benefit of its workers. *Reporter*, 20 October 1894 (Model Lodging House, Bloom St, opened).

110. *Reporter*, 14 February 1914; *Reporter*, 23 October 1897 (back-to-backs); *Reporter*, 26 January 1895 (end of the Sanitary Association).

111. For the 'Muddle' see *Reporter*, 13, 20 October, 10 November 1894, and January to November 1895, *passim*.

112. '... there was no serious trouble until the outbreak of the Boer War when nearly all the Socialists and Labour people declared themselves pro-Boer and I remained pro-British': Blatchford, *My Eighty years, op. cit.*, p. 200.

113. *Reporter*, 17 October 1904 (John Street children).

114. *Reporter*, 1 April 1905.

115. *Reporter*, 4 February (Manchester Scheme); 20 May ('Hunger March') 1905.

116. *Reporter*, 2 September (Trades Council Committee – which included Mrs Pankhurst), 9 and 30 September 1905.

117. *Reporter*, 16, 23 September, 5 December 1905. *Reporter*, 21, 28 April (Gregory's sermon). 21 July 1906 ('Camp of the unemployed').

118. *Reporter*, 18 February 1899 (*Darkest Salford*). See also *Reporter*, 4 October 1902, the first of a series of articles by Hunt on 'municipal trading'.

119. *Reporter*, 11 July 1896, 8 July 1899 ('finest piece of corporation property'); 27 September 1902 (Ratepayers Association); 8 February 1902 (rents); 14 February 1914 (council loss).

120. *Reporter*, 8 October 1904 (Marr); *Reporter*, 22 March 1902 and 2 May 1903 (physique of children) quoted in Cowan's dissertation 'The Work of the Salford School Board', *op. cit.* p. 369.

121. *Reporter*, 8 July 1899 (Barracks); 21 November 1903 (slum clearance and Seaford Road development), 9 January, 28 May, 2 July 1904 (further details); 4 July 1914 (Salford's 'council housing' since 1894).

122. *Reporter*, 8 October 1904 (Storey).

123. Goldberg, *op. cit.*, pp. 103–4.

124. For Nuttall see *Reporter*, 2 June 1906; *Reporter*, 7 November 1903 (Hayes); 23 April 1904 (Thompson); 4 November 1905 (Mottershead); 3 November 1906 (Purcell). For Purcell see also *Dictionary of Labour Biography*, i, pp. 275–9. Goldberg, *op. cit.*, p. 139.

125. *Reporter*, 23 April, 17 September 1904 (Hempsall); 7 May, 20 June 1904 (Jewish Unionists); 22 May 1909 (union growth).

126. *Reporter*, 26 August and 2 September 1905; Goldberg, *op. cit.*, p. 93.

127. Goldberg, *op. cit.*, pp. 125–7; *Reporter*, 20 January 1906.

128. Goldberg *op. cit.*, Chapter 8, especially pp. 150–4. The *Reporter* reference is 27 February 1909.

129. *Reporter*, 16 July 1904. For Fearneley see the obituary in *Reporter*, 23 March 1907.

130. *Reporter*, 9 September 1905 (Hampson Lodge and Conservative Labour Party Van); 16 December 1905 (for Wilkinson). Alongside the Conservative Labour Party the Young England patriotic Association was active in the summer of 1907. In 1908 it added 'and Anti-Socialist League' to its title.

131. Goldberg, *op. cit.*, pp. 93–4 (for the LRC locally), and 139–40 for electoral statistics.

132. Goldberg, *op. cit.*, pp. 137–8; *Reporter*, 22 January 1910.

133. Goldberg, *op. cit.*, p. 140; *Reporter*, 10 December 1910.

134. *Reporter*, 3 January 1914.

135. *Reporter*, 22 April 1911.

136. *Reporter*, 17, 24 June, 1 July 1911.

137. *Reporter*, 8 July 1911.

138. *Reporter*, 19 August 1911.

139. *Reporter*, 26 August 1911.

140. *Reporter*, 26 August 1911 and 2 September 1911. See also 9 September for a very full account of the 'Irish' conditions at Renshaw's.

141. Goldberg, *op. cit.*, pp. 152–4.

142. *Reporter*, 2, 23 March, 13 April, 18 May, 22 June 1912.

143. *Reporter*, 11 May 1912, See also *Reporter*, 23 March, 25 May and 26 June.

144. *Reporter*, 15 June 1912.

145. *Reporter*, 11, 18 May, 7 September 1912 (Furnishing Trades); 29 June 1912 and 1 February 1913 (Railwayman); 11 January 1913 (Engineers).

146. *Reporter*, 27 September 1913. See also 13 and 20 September for the Docks strike, and 7 June 1913 for the strike at Connolly & Steele.

147. *Reporter*, 2 May 1914.

148. *Reporter*, 22 March 1913.

149. Goldberg, *op. cit.*, pp. 93–4.

150. H. Pelling, *Popular Politics and Society in late Victorian Britain* (1968), p. 150, 'The Labour Unrest, 1911–14'.

151. For national election figures, *ibid.*, p. 102, 'Labour and the Downfall of Liberalism'. For Salford see John A. Garrard and Michael Goldsmith 'Salford Elections 1919–1969' (duplicated typescript, Dept of Sociology, Government and Administration, University of Salford, 1970), and E. and R. Frow, *Radical Salford, op. cit.*, p. 25.

152. For Reade see his *Christ or Socialism. A Human Autobiography*, 1909, Chapter VI; for Trevor see *Dictionary of Labour Biography*, vi, pp. 249–53. For Brocklehurst, see *ibid.*, pp. 39–42. For Horrocks see *Reporter*, 1 June 1901. For the formation of the CP branch in 1922, see Goldberg, *op. cit.*, p. 17, and R. and E. Frow, *op. cit.*, p. 26.

## Notes to Chapter 12

1. *Reporter*, 26 February 1910. For Mrs Pankhurst see also *Reporter*, 19 April 1913; Ray Strachey's account in *DNB* (1922–1930); Roger Fulford. *Votes for Women* (1957); A. Rosen, *Biographical Dictionary of Modern British Radicals*, vol. 3, ed. J. O. Baylen and N. J. Grossman (Brighton, 1988), pp. 631–5, and the same author's *'Rise up, Women'. The Militant Campaign of the Women's Social and Political Union, 1903–1914* (1974); *The Times*, 15 June 1928; E. Sylvia Pankhurst, *The Life of Emmeline Pankhurst* (1935). The unpublished Masters' dissertation by Catherine E. Leech, 'The Feminist Movement in Manchester, 1903–14', Manchester, 1971, is particularly valuable for the local history of the women's movement in Manchester and Salford.

2. Leech, *op. cit.*, p. 72.

3. *MG*, 13 December 1858.

4. For Jacob Bright see Boase, *Modern British Biography*, iv (1908; repr. 1965), col. 496.

5. Rosen, *'Rise up, Women', op. cit.*, pp. 5–7.

6. *Ibid.*

7. Christabel Pankhurst, *Unshackled* (1959), p. 26. For Lydia Ernestine Becker, see Leech's dissertation, Appendix I, p. 49, and Jill Liddington and Jill Norris, *One Hand Tied Behind Us* (Virago, 1978), pp. 69–74.

8. For Robert Goulden's obituary see *Reporter*, 30 April 1892.

9. *Reporter*, 19 April 1913.

10. For Richard Pankhurst, see Andrew Rosen's account of him in *Biographical Dictionary of Modern British Radicals.*, pp. 640–3; and *Manchester Faces and Places*, iv (1893), pp. 33–4.

11. *Manchester Faces and Places.*

12. *Biograhical Dictionary of British Radicals*, p. 641.

13. For details see *Reporter*, 17 January 1885, 7 April, 11 June and 5 November 1887.

14. Rosen, *Biographical Dictionary of British Radicals*, p. 632.

15. *Reporter*, 19 April 1913.

16. *Reporter*, 18 September 1897.

17. *Reporter*, 3 December 1878. Bruce Glasier opened it two years later in the presence of Mrs Pankhurst and her family: *Reporter*, 17 November 1900.

18. For Esther and Eva see Gifford Lewis, *Eva Gore-Booth and Esther Roper. A Biography* (1988), which is particularly valuable on the women's movement in Manchester before the rise of the WSPU.

19. For the Rev. Gore-Booth see *Reporter*, 10 October 1903, and Gifford Lewis, *op. cit.*, p. 65.

20. *Ibid.*, p. 84.

21. Leach, *op. cit.*, p. 19; Gifford Lewis, *op. cit.*, p. 85.

22. Gifford Lewis, *op. cit.*, p. 85.

23. *Ibid.*, pp. 70–2.

24. *Ibid.*, p. 87. For Selina Cooper see Jill Liddington, *The Life and Times of a Respectable Radical: Selina Cooper (1864–1946)* (1984). The quotation about Miss Roper is on p. 103.

25. *Ibid.*, p. 92.

26. *Ibid.*, p. 97.

27. *Ibid.*, p. 95.

28. Rosen says that it was because a body called the Women's Labour Representation Committee was then being formed by Esther Roper and Eva Gore-Booth, *'Rise Up Women'*, *op. cit.*, p. 30.

29. See *Reporter*, 19 April 1913 for an appreciation of her oratorical gifts.

30. For those three see Rosen, *'Rise Up Women'*, *op. cit.*, pp. 39–46. Hannah Mitchell's autobiography *The Hard Way Up*, ed. Geoffrey Mitchell (1968), was reprinted in 1977.

31. Leach, *op. cit.*, p. 4.

32. In her book *Unshackled*, *op. cit.*, p. 46; See also Rosen, *op. cit.*, p. 33.

33. Gifford Lewis, *op. cit.*, pp. 97–8.

34. Rosen *op. cit.*, pp. 37–9.

35. *Ibid.*, pp. 47–8.

36. Rosen, *op. cit.*, pp. 49–52.

37. *Ibid.*, p. 54. Gifford Lewis, *op. cit.*, pp. 111–15.

38. Leach, *op. cit.*, pp. 35–6.

39. *Ibid.*, p. 38.

40. Rosen, *op. cit.*, p. 54.

41. *Ibid.*, p. 65.

42. *Ibid.*, pp. 61–4.

43. *Reporter*, 27 May 1905, 1, 22, 29 September 1906.

44. Leach, *op. cit.*, pp. 8–9.

45. Rosen, *op. cit.*, pp. 69–71.

46. *Ibid.*, pp. 88–93.

47. Rosen, *op. cit.*, pp. 93–4.

48. *Ibid.*, pp. 73–8.

49. *Ibid.*, pp. 80–2.

50. *Ibid.*, pp. 99–101.

51. *Ibid.*, pp. 102–4.

52. *Ibid.*, pp. 110–13.

53. *Ibid.*, pp. 118–30.

54. *Ibid.*, pp. 131–7.

55. *Ibid.*, p. 137; Leach *op. cit.*, p. 18; *Reporter*, 20, 27 March 1909; Leach, p. 29.

56. Leach, *op. cit.*, pp. 32–4. For Canon Hicks see *Who Was Who, 1916–28*, pp. 493–4.

57. *Reporter*, 3 April 1909.

58. Leach, *op. cit.*, pp. 40–3.

59. Rosen, *op. cit.*, pp. 138–45.

60. *Ibid.*, pp. 146–52.

61. *Ibid.*, pp. 152–65.

62. *Ibid.*, pp. 166–7.

63. *Ibid.*, pp. 159, 163–5, 167–9, 171, 173–5.

64. *Ibid.*, pp. 176, 189–93.

65. *Ibid.*, pp. 198–201.

66. *Ibid.*, pp. 203–12.

67. *Ibid.*, pp. 180–4. For Sylvia see John D. Fair's article in *Biographical Dictionary of Modern British Radicals*, pp. 635–9, and *Who Was Who, 1951–1960*, pp. 846–7.

68. Rosen, *op. cit.*, pp. 217–18, 223.

69. For Adela see Roger Fulford's account of Sylvia Pankhurst in *DNB*, 1951–60. The post 1914

history of all the family is covered in D. Mitchell, *The Fighting Pankhursts: A Study in Tenacity* (1967).

70. Rosen, *op. cit.*, pp. 202, 213.

71. *Ibid.*, p. 215.

72. *Ibid.*, pp. 220, 223–6.

73. *Ibid.*, pp. 226–33.

74. *Ibid.*, p. 237.

75. For these two local women see Liddington and Norris, *One Hand Tied Behind Us*, pp. 290–1.

76. In her *The Militant Suffrage Movement: Emancipation in a Hurry* (1911), pp. 2 and 13, quoted in Leach's dissertation, *op. cit.*, p. 50.

77. Geoffrey Mitchell (ed.), *The Hard Way Up: The Autobiography of Hannah Mitchell* (1968), p. 130.

78. Rosen, *op. cit.*, pp. 250–2, 266–9; Mitchell, *The Fighting Pankhursts*, pp. 50–3.

79. The best short account of Sylvia Pankhurst's career from 1914 is Fair's in *Biographical Dictionary of British Radicals*. See also Mitchell, *ibid.*, and Patricia W. Romero, *E. Sylvia Pankhurst: Portrait of a Radical* (1987).

80. Jo Vellacott Newberry, 'Anti-War Suffragists', *History*, vol. 62 (1977), pp. 414–23.

81. Gifford Lewis, *op. cit.*, pp. 163–72.

82. The number of women employed rose from 3,224,600 in July 1914 to 4,814,600 by January 1918: Rosen, *op. cit.*, pp. 255–6.

83. *Ibid.*, 258–60.

84. Rosen, *Biographical Dictionary of Modern British Radicals*, pp. 634; and *'Rise Up Women'*, p. 269

85. Rosen, *Biographical Dictionary of Modern British Radicals*, pp. 634–5.

86. For Christabel Pankhurst see Rosen, *'Rise Up Women'*, pp. 269–71.

87. For Adela see Roger Fulford, *DNB*.

88. The words are David Mitchell's, quoted in Fair, *ibid.*, p. 638.

89. This will be redressed in the forthcoming *New DNB*.

## Notes to Chapter 13

1. *Reporter*, 15 December 1888. See also *Reporter*, 12, 19 February 1881 and 24 February 1883. For accounts of the firm, *MG*, 3 October 1855; *Reporter*, 20 February 1892 and 11 November 1899.

2. *Reporter*, 3 February 1883.

3. For John Knowles' obituary see *Reporter*, 27 January 1894, which is also very informative on the history of the family and the firm. See also F. Boase, *Modern English Biography*, vol. v (Supplement to Vol 11, D–K) (1912; repr. 1965), col. 834.

4. For obituaries of Lees Knowles see *The Times*, 8 October (p. 18) and *Reporter*, 12 October 1928. See also *Who's Who* (1921), col. 1506; M. Stenton and C. Lees (eds), *Who's Who of British Members of Parliament, Vol II, 1886–1918* (1978), pp 204–5. For his (and his brothers') school days see F. J. Salt (ed.), *Rugby School Register, 1885–1891* (Revised edn, 1952), pp. 195, 209, 353. Knowles wrote an account of sport at Rugby for the *English Illustrated Magazine*, November 1891, pp. 87–97.

5. *Reporter*, obituary, *op. cit.*

6. *S Chron*, 18 November 1893.

7. For 'scutting' see *S Chron*, 4 April 1874, 6 February 1875; *Reporter*, 17 February 1881, 11, 18 April 1885, 8 June 1889, 1 February 1890 (for 'Buffalo Bill's' gang in Pendleton) and 26 April and 20 December 1890 for the Hope Street/Oldfield Lane gang fight. For John Joseph Elliott, 'the king of the scuttlers', see *Reporter*, 29 July 1899.

8. *Wh Man Chron*, 6 September 1834, 21 November 1835 (Foot races on Kersal Moor). 'Pedestrianism' was much reported in the papers in the Sixties and early Seventies, e.g. *SWN*, 8 August 1863, 29 July 1871. For the first Manchester Grand Athletic Festival, *SWN*, 30 July, 6 August, 7 September 1864.

9. For their early history see *Reporter*, 22 March and 6 September 1884, 25 January and 30 August 1890.

10. The first report of cycling notice is *Reporter*, 12 June 1886. In 1894 nine clubs sent cards with their 'runs' to the paper at Easter.

11. The first reports in the local papers were in the 1885–86 season. An association football league was formed for Salford and district in 1891. Foremost among the clubs then was Seedley AFC, *Reporter*,

24 August 1895. The first mention of Manchester City in the *Reporter* is 29 August 1903. In April 1904 City won the FA cup and also came second in the 1st Division: Manchester United, however, narrowly missed promotion to that division that year, (*Reporter*, 30 April 1904). For the latter club's removal to Old Trafford see *Reporter*, 25 September 1909.

12. For the Oxford match see *Reporter*, 17 February 1883. Oxford won by one try and one goal to nil: 'They were much taller and heavier than the Swinton men; in fact, the least of the Oxford men appeared to be bigger than R. Seddon, the biggest of our local players'. For the Bradford game *Reporter*, 24 October 1885. For Swinton's record over the past decade *Reporter*, 30 September 1890.

13. By 1897 there were two other clubs in Broughton, both of which remained members of the Rugby Union – Broughton (founded 1868) and Broughton Park. The Broughton club collapsed in 1898 (*Reporter*, 14 May).

14. For Salford RFC, *S Chron*, 20 December 1879; *Reporter*, 12 March 1892 (reviewing J. Higson's *History of the Salford Football Club*) lists each season's results from 1880 to 1891. For Salford *versus* Swinton 1880–1896, *Reporter*, 31 October 1896.

15. Knowles's obituary, *Reporter*, *op. cit.*

16. *Ibid.*

17. As Lees Knowles' father made clear when giving evidence to the *Trade Union Commission Manchester Outrages Inquiry, 1867* (Parliamentary Papers 1868). 'In fact we will not employ union men', p. 269. This was because of industrial disputes between 1844 and 1846, and the 'turn-out' in 1863. For the 1863 dispute there is much detail on p. 270. See also *SWN*, 9 September 1865, 17 November 1866, 16, 23 February 1867.

18. The struggles of this union is recorded in the columns of *SWN* from 31 July 1869 to 29 April 1871, *passim.*

19. For Clifton Hall, see *Reporter*, 20, 27 June, 4, 11 July 1885. John Knowles' evidence at the inquest is reported in the last of these issues.

20. *Reporter*, 8, 15, 22 December 1888.

21. *Reporter*, 8, 22 March, 3 May 1890.

22. *Reporter*, 29 August, 17 October, 21, 28 November, 26 December 1891, 30 January 1892.

23. *Reporter*, 10 March 1894. Details of John Knowles' personalty and will.

24. *Reporter*, 25 March (Baile); 15 April 1873 (Broughton meeting).

25. *S Chron*, 27 April 1895. For the election, see *Reporter*, 20 July.

26. *The Times*, obituary 8 October 1928.

27. For the formation of the Salford Company of Volunteer Rifles (56th Lancashire) see *SWN*, 31 December 1859 and 10 March 1860.

28. For the history of the Regiment, see B. Smyth, *A History of the Lancashire Fusiliers Formerly XX Regiment*, 2 vols (Dublin, 1903); C. J. Latter, *The History of the Lancashire Fusiliers 1914–18*, 2 vols (Aldershot, 1949); Cyril Ray, *Famous Regiments: The Lancashire Fusiliers (The 20th Regiment of Foot)* (1971).

29. 'An Occasional Paper', *S Chron*, 10 July 1875, outlines the history of the Salford Volunteers from 1859 to 1875.

30. *Reporter*, 16 December 1899.

31. *The Lancashire Fusiliers' Annual* (1900), p. 101–2.

32. Smyth, *Lancashire Fusiliers*, vol. 1, footnote pp. 123–4.

33. *Reporter*, 16 December 1899.

34. Smyth, *Lancashire Fusiliers*, vol 2, Appendix VIII, pp. 447–50.

35. *Ibid.*, Appendix IX, pp. 451–2.

36. *Reporter*, 26 May 1900. For the popular mood nationally see P. Price, *An Imperial War and the British Working Class* (1972).

37. *Reporter*, 6 October 1900.

38. *Reporter*, 25 May, 27 July 1901. In the latter report is the reference to Knowles describing Spion Kop as a 'Lancashire battle'.

39. Smyth, *Lancashire Fusiliers*, vol. 2, p. 358. *L. F. Annual* (1902), pp. 134–5; *L. F. Annual* (1903), p. 104.

40. *Reporter*, 25 March, 16 July 1905.

41. *L. F. Annual*, 1902, p. 136.

42. C. J. Latter, *op. cit.*, p. 1.

43. *L. F. Annual*, 1904, p. 5.

44. Pages 57–70. The piece was reproduced from *C. B. Fry's Magazine*.

45. *Transactions of the Institute of Mining Engineers*, 1906. Knowles spoke on Workmen's compensation with special reference to contracting out, p. 38. *Manchester Geological and Mining Society General Meeting 8 December 1908*, Manchester, Presidential Address.

46. *Reporter*, 21 July 1906.

47. *Reporter*, 2, 23 August 1902, 14 February 1903. In December 1902 the Clifton, Kearsley, Pendlebury and Pendleton Miners Association had 3,400 members. Messrs Knowles employed 3,408 men at that time.

48. *Reporter*, 25 February 1905.

49. *Reporter*, 2 June 1906.

50. *Reporter*, 19 June, 17, 24, 31 July 1909.

51. *Reporter*, 23 May 1908.

52. *Reporter*, 31 December 1910, 7 January 1911.

53. *Reporter*, 2 November 1912.

54. *Reporter*, 19 March, 4 June, 9 July 1904.

55. *Reporter*, 23 January 1904. See also 3 June, 16 December 1905, 20 January 1906.

56. *Reporter*, 20 January 1906.

57. *Reporter*, 11 February 1905. See also 3 August and 30 November 1901 (for branches of the United Irish League).

58. *Reporter*, 30 May, 4 July 1908. In 1914 Byrne, as president of the Salford branch of the United Irish League, was presented with a portrait in oils for his services to the cause.

59. For a good obituary of Byles, see *Reporter*, 20 October 1917.

60. For Agnew see *Reporter*, 11 October 1902 and 14 February 1914 (when he resigned).

61. *Reporter*, 6, 20 January 1906.

62. *Reporter*, 9 January, 29 May 1909.

63. R. C. K. Ensor, *England 1870–1914* (Oxford, 1936; repr. 1960), pp. 395–6.

64. *Reporter*, 7 December 1907, 19 September 1908, 3 April 1909. See also Knowles' account, 'Lancashire and the New Act', in *L. F. Annual* (1907), pp 38–41.

65. *Reporter*, 13 November 1909.

66. Ian Malcolm, quoted in *Reporter*, 23 October 1909.

67. *Reporter*, 16, 30 November 1907.

68. *Reporter*, 22 January 1910.

69. *Reporter*, 30 December 1908, 22 January 1910.

70. For Barlow, see *Reporter*, 26 June 1909.

71. *Reporter*, 10 December 1910.

72. For Barlow (who died in 1951) see *Who's Who of British Members of Parliament, op. cit.*, Vol VIII, p. 19.

73. *Letters of Captain Englebert Lutyens*, p. vii.

74. This account of Salford's efforts in the Great War is based on C. J. Latter, *The History of the Lancashire Fusiliers 1914–18*; C. Ray, *Famous Regiments: the Lancashire Fusiliers*; and Sir C. A. Montague Barlow (ed.), *The Lancashire Fusiliers. The Roll of Honour of the Salford Brigade, 15th, 16th, 19th, 20th and 21st Lancashire Fusiliers* (1919). For new light on Gallipoli and the 'six VCs before breakfast' episode, see G. Moorhouse, *Hell's Foundations. A Town, its Myths and Gallipoli* (1992), pp. 124–40.

75. For this phenomenon, see P. Simkins, *Kitchener's Armies: the Raising of the New Armies, 1914–16* (Manchester), 1988. p. xiv.

76. *Ibid.*, pp. 84–5.

77. Latter, *op. cit.*, pp. 96–7.

78. Barlow, *Lancashire Fusiliers*.

79. *Ibid.*

80. Ray *op. cit.*, p. 116.

81. *The Times*, 25 February 1929.

82. Obituary, *Reporter*, 12 October 1928; *Who's Who of British MPs*, pp. 204–5.

83. *The Times*, 1 October 1928.

# Population of Salford, 1773–1911

## 1. The three townships before 1853

| Year | Salford | Pendleton | Broughton | Total | Manchester |
|------|---------|-----------|-----------|-------|------------|
| 1773 | 4,765 | c. 2,000* | 563 | c. 7,328 | 22,481 |
| 1788 | 9,120 | – | – | – | – |
| 1801 | 13,611 | 3,611 | 866 | 18,088 | 75,000 |
| 1811 | 19114 | 4,805 | 825 | 24,744 | 89,000 |
| 1821 | 22,772 | 5,948 | 880 | 32,600 | 126,000 |
| 1831 | 40,786 | 8,435 | 1,589 | 50,810 | 182,000 |
| 1841 | 53,200 | 11,032 | 3,794 | 68,026 | 235,000 |
| 1851 | 63,423 | 14,224 | 7,126 | 84,773 | 303,000 |

## 2. The Municipal (later County) Borough of Salford

| 1861 | 70,967 | 20,900 | 9,885 | 101,752 | 339,000 |
|------|--------|--------|-------|---------|---------|
| 1871 | 82,280 | 26,560 | 14,961 | 124,801 | 351,000 |
| 1881 | 101,583 | 43,117 | 31,533 | 176,233 | 462,000 |
| 1891 | 109,732 | 50,543 | 37,864 | 198,139 | 505,000 |
| 1901 | 105,335 | 66,574 | 49,048 | 220,957 | 544,000 |
| 1911 | 99,466 | 78,783 | 53,108 | 231,357 | 714,000 |

*Note*: * An estimate of 1776

*Sources*: For each date except 1773 and 1788 printed Census Abstracts have been used. For 1773 see *MS. Euumeration of the Houses and inhabitants of Manchester containing the Town and Township of Salford* (and Broughton), 1773, Chetham's Library. The figure for Pendleton in 1776 is given in J. Aikin *A Description of the County from Thirty to Forty Miles round Manchester*, 1795, and the Salford figure for 1788 was given by Joseph Brotherton to the Select Committee of the House of Commons on Select and Other Vestries, 1830. *Minutes of Evidence* p. 51.

# *The Church of England in Salford in Canon Stowell's time*

## 1. Churches consecrated before 1831

| | Name | Date of consecration | Patronage | Population in 1871 |
|---|---|---|---|---|
| 1. | Sacred Trinity | 1635 | Gore-Booth family | 10,622 |
| 2. | St Thomas, Pendleton | 1776 (demolished 1848) | The Proprietors | 9,477 |
| 3. | St Stephen | 1794 | The Proprietor | 11,636 |
| 4. | St Philip | 1825 | Warden & Fellows Manchester Collegiate Church | 10,907 |

## 2. Churches consecrated in Stowell's time

| | | | | |
|---|---|---|---|---|
| 5. | Christ Church | 1831 | Trustees | 9,316 |
| 6. | St Thomas, Pendleton | 1831 (rebuilt anew) | Vicar of Eccles | 9,477 |
| 7. | St John, Higher Broughton | 1839 | S.W. Clowes and 4 trustees | 8,515 |
| 8. | St Matthias | 1842 | Trustees | 6,962 |
| 9. | St Bartholomew | 1842 | Trustees | 19,003 |
| 10. | St Simon | 1848 | Trustees | 6,524 |
| 11. | St Paul, Kersal | 1852 | Trustees | 1,424 |
| 12. | St Paul, Pendleton | 1856 | Crown and Bishop alternately | 8,339 |
| 13. | St George, Pendleton | 1858 | Bishop | 6,917 |
| 14. | St James, Hope | 1861 | Trustees | 766 |
| 15. | St Anne, Pendleton | 1863 | Vicar of Eccles | (Part of St Thomas's district) |
| 16. | St Luke, Weaste | 1865 | Bishop, Vicar of Eccles and Trustees | 1,665 |
| 17. | Holy Ascension, Lower Broughton | 1866 | S.W. Clowes and 4 trustees | 6,439 |

*Source*: An 1871 Religious Census, quoted in *Salford Weekly News*, 13 May 1871.

## 3. Churches and chapels in Salford in 1861

| | | |
|---|---|---|
| Church of England | 13 | |
| Old Dissent | 6 | (Independent 4; Baptist 2) |
| Bible Christian | 1 | |
| New Jerusalem | 1 | |
| Methodists | 10 | (Wesleyan 3; Primitives 2; Methodist Association 2; Methodist Free Church 1; New Connexion 1; Welsh Calvinistic 1) |
| Roman Catholic | 1 | (Plus 2 School/Chapels) |

*Source*: Slater's *Directory*, 1861.

# *Public Health in Salford –*
# *A Chronology*

| | |
|---|---|
| 1765, 1776, 1792 | Police (Improvement) Acts for Manchester and Salford. |
| 1797 | Henceforth each has a separate body of Commissioners. |
| 1830 | Salford's first Improvement Act. |
| 1832 | Salford becomes a Parliamentary borough. |
| 1844 | Salford becomes a Municipal borough. Salford's second Improvement Act. |
| 1845 | Playfair's Report on the *State of large Towns in Lancashire.* |
| 1848 | Cholera. Peel Park opened. |
| 1850 | Salford Water and Improvement Act. Rawlinson's Report on the *Sanitary State of Broughton.* |
| 1851 | Rawlinson's *Report on Pendleton.* |
| 1853 | Salford Extension and Improvement Act:- the borough takes in Broughton and Pendleton, establishing a 'Trinity without Unity'. |
| 1859 | Salford Gas Works Act. |
| 1861 | Sanitary Inspector's Reports on the State of the Borough begin. |
| 1862 | Salford Consolidating and Amending Act. |
| 1866 | Cholera. Important national Sanitary Act passed. |
| 1867 | Salford gets a second MP under the new Reform Act. |
| 1868 | Appointment of Salford's first Medical Officer of Health. |
| 1870 | Salford Improvement Act, mainly for the New Blackfriars Street scheme. |
| 1871 | Salford Drainage and Improvement Act, to build the Intercepting Sewer and Sewage Works. |
| 1874 | The first of three new parks made. |
| 1875 | Artisans and Labourers Dwellings Act. |
| 1880 | First public baths opened in Salford. |
| 1891 | Local Act to Unite the Salford Districts ends the 'Trinity without Unity'. |
| 1892 | After Liverpool, Salford the second most unhealthy of the 33 large towns in England and Wales. |
| 1894 | All new houses to have water closets. |
| 1900 | Salford still has the second highest death rate and third highest infant mortality rate in England and Wales. |

# *Vital statistics of the Borough of Salford 1844-1912*

## 1. Population totals and death rates in Salford, 1844-60

| Year | Population | Death-rate |
|------|------------|------------|
| 1844 | 75,414 | 24.6 |
| 1845 | 77,144 | 23.8 |
| 1846 | 78,874 | 32.7 |
| 1847 | 80,604 | 28.0 |
| 1848 | 82,334 | 29.9 |
| 1849 | 84,064 | 30.6 |
| 1850 | 85,794 | 25.8 |
| 1851 | 87,523 | 25.1 |
| 1852 | 88,953 | 28.0 |
| 1853 | 90,406 | 27.2 |
| 1854 | 91,883 | 28.9 |
| 1855 | 93,384 | 27.1 |
| 1856 | 94,910 | 24.1 |
| 1857 | 96,460 | 26.1 |
| 1858 | 98,036 | 30.4 |
| 1859 | 99,640 | 24.9 |
| 1860 | 101,277 | 24.4 |

Source: *Annual Report of the Medical Officer of Health*, 1911, Table M.7, p. 27.

## 2. Mortality rates in the borough of Salford in 1860 (by districts)

| District | | Dwelling Houses | Estimated Population | Death Rate per 1,000 |
|----------|--|-----------------|----------------------|----------------------|
| Salford | | | | |
| 1. | Blackfriars | 719 | 4,071 | 22.35 |
| 2. | Islington | 1,096 | 6,608 | 23.46 |
| 3. | Oldfield Road | 2,141 | 11,240 | 23.58 |
| 4. | Crescent | 2,525 | 13,256 | 32.36 |
| 5. | St Philip's | 2,883 | 15,136 | 21.21 |
| 6. | St Stephen's | 1,000 | 5,250 | 24.19 |
| 7. | Trinity | 2,254 | 11,833 | 24.76 |
| 8. | Greengate | 1,731 | 9,088 | 21.57 |
| | | 14,349 | 76,482 | 24.55 (average) |

| District | Dwelling Houses | Estimated Population | Death Rate per 1,000 |
|---|---|---|---|
| Pendleton | | | |
| 9. St Thomas's ⎱<br>10. Seedley ⎰ | 4,026 | 20,130 | 20.86 |
| Broughton | | | |
| 11. Kersal ⎱<br>12. St John's ⎰ | 1,781 | 9,340 | 12.74 |
| Totals | 20,156 | 105,952 | 22.81<br>(borough average) |

Source: Pickering's first report, *The Vital Statistics of the Borough of Salford for the year ending 1860*, Table E.


### 3. Population totals and district densities, five year intervals, 1861 to 1901

| | Population | | | | | Density (persons per acre) | | | | |
|---|---|---|---|---|---|---|---|---|---|---|
| Year | Borough | Regent Road | Green-gate | Pendle-ton | Brough-ton | Borough | Regent Road | Green-gate | Pendle-ton | Brough-ton |
| 1861 | 102,920 | 33,756 | 37,519 | 21,649 | 9,996 | 19.9 | 31.7 | 142.8 | 9.0 | 7.0 |
| 1866 | 113,614 | 39,949 | 37,144 | 24,136 | 12,385 | 22.0 | 37.4 | 141.2 | 10.0 | 8.7 |
| 1871 | 125,890 | 47,195 | 36,517 | 26,920 | 15,258 | 24.3 | 44.2 | 138.8 | 11.1 | 10.7 |
| 1876 | 149,591 | 58,219 | 34,393 | 34,617 | 22,362 | 28.9 | 54.7 | 130.6 | 14.3 | 15.7 |
| 1881 | 177,760 | 70,346 | 31,725 | 43,598 | 32,091 | 34.4 | 66.0 | 120.6 | 18.0 | 22.5 |
| 1886 | 188,238 | 74,802 | 31,261 | 47,143 | 35,032 | 36.4 | 70.4 | 118.8 | 19.5 | 24.6 |
| 1891 | 198,775 | 79,341 | 30,579 | 50,891 | 37,964 | 38.3 | 74.5 | 116.2 | 21.1 | 26.6 |
| 1896 | 209,703 | 71,879 | 36,055 | 58,394 | 43,375 | 40.4 | 75.3 | 92.5 | 24.1 | 30.4 |
| 1901 | 221,587 | 71,435 | 33,743 | 67,023 | 49,386 | 42.6 | 74.8 | 86.5 | 27.6 | 34.6 |

Source: *Annual Report of the Medical Officer for the Year 1902*, p. 62.

Notes:1. The population of the borough grew by 22–23,000 per decade from 1860, except in the Seventies, when the growth was more than double that figure.
2. Within the township of Salford the Greengate District lost population over these four decades. The population for the Regent Road Registration District overtook it in 1864, and by 1901 more than twice as many people lived in the new Salford districts such as Ordsall and Eccles New Road than in Greengate District.
3. Pendleton's population grew by a factor of 3 in these four decades, the chief expansion coming in the Seventies and the Nineties. In the same period Broughton grew by a factor of almost 5, the chief expansion being in the Seventies and Eighties.
4. The density of persons per acre in Greengate declined from 1861 to 1901, whilst that of all other districts intensified.
5. The growing density of persons per acre in the new districts never approached that of Greengate at its most crowded in 1861.

## 4. Marriage, birth and death rates in Salford by districts, 1861-1900 (five year averages, annual rates per 1,000 of the population)

| Year | Marriages | | Births | | | | Deaths | | | |
| | Boro' | Regent Road | Green-gate | Pendle-ton | Brough-ton | Boro' | Regent Road | Green-gate | Pendle-ton | Brough-ton |
|---|---|---|---|---|---|---|---|---|---|---|
| 1861-65 | 11.9 | 38.6 | 38.2 | 43.1 | 37.8 | 26.2 | 26.3 | 29.3 | 29.4 | 22.2 | 14.6 |
| 1866-70 | 13.8 | 38.9 | 39.7 | 43.0 | 37.5 | 28.0 | 27.9 | 31.6 | 31.1 | 23.8 | 15.1 |
| 1871-75 | 15.5 | 42.0 | 45.5 | 42.6 | 38.8 | 35.9 | 28.3 | 32.7 | 30.5 | 24.6 | 17.7 |
| 1876-80 | 18.0 | 43.8 | 45.6 | 41.8 | 43.1 | 43.0 | 27.5 | 31.0 | 30.0 | 23.7 | 21.7 |
| 1881-85 | 16.3 | 38.4 | 40.5 | 39.2 | 37.1 | 34.8 | 23.4 | 25.5 | 27.8 | 21.4 | 17.5 |
| 1886-90 | 16.0 | 36.8 | 38.2 | 38.4 | 36.3 | 33.2 | 25.7 | 27.5 | 31.5 | 23.8 | 19.5 |
| 1891-95 | 17.1 | 35.4 | 37.0 | 40.1 | 34.7 | 29.9 | 24.3 | 26.0 | 31.9 | 22.5 | 17.5 |
| 1896-1900 | 18.3 | 34.6 | 36.3 | 38.2 | 35.1 | 28.4 | 23.8 | 25.8 | 32.5 | 21.3 | 17.5 |

*Source*: *Annual Report of the Medical Officer of Health, 1902*, p. 62.

*Notes*: 1. Marriage rates reflect the economic fortunes of the district – low in the Sixties, at their height in the Seventies, slightly higher in the Nineties than the Eighties.
2. To some extent birth-rates follow this pattern: peaking in the Seventies, from the Eighties the rate is falling faster in the middle-class Broughton (with the adoption of birth control) than in the other more industrialised districts. (See Table 5 for the period after 1900)
3. From its peak in the early Seventies, the death rate is falling in the borough, though it had a tendency to rise again in hard times, as in the second half of the Eighties. The most marked fall shows in 'New Salford', the Regent Road District, where public health provision and housing bye-laws had their effect. In Greengate, by contrast, despite all the efforts on the public health front, the rate shows little improvement and is rising again after 1885. In Pendleton and Broughton rising death rates from the mid-Eighties reflect the tension between industrial and population growth and sanitary improvements.

## 5. Birth, death and infant mortality rates, and rates of mortality from 'the seven principal zymotic diseases', and from phthisis, cancer, nervous diseases, heart diseases, bronchitis and pneumonia in Salford 1878-1912

| Years (five year averages) | Rates per 1,000 population from | | | | | | | | Deaths under 1 year old to 1,000 births |
| | Births | Deaths, all causes | Seven Principal Zymotic Diseases | Phthisis | Cancer | Nervous Diseases | Heart Diseases | Bron-chitis | Pneu-monia | |
|---|---|---|---|---|---|---|---|---|---|---|
| 1878-82 | 41.5 | 25.6 | 4.8 | 2.6 | 0.4 | 3.4 | 1.1 | 3.5 | 1.8 | 178 |
| 1883-87 | 37.8 | 24.3 | 4.1 | 2.6 | 0.5 | 3.0 | 1.2 | 3.0 | 1.9 | 184 |
| 1888-92 | 36.2 | 25.6 | 4.3 | 2.1 | 0.5 | 2.3 | 1.2 | 3.1 | 2.7 | 189 |
| 1893-97 | 35.1 | 23.6 | 4.5 | 1.8 | 0.6 | 2.1 | 1.3 | 2.3 | 2.4 | 207 |
| 1898-1902 | 33.1 | 22.6 | 3.9 | 1.8 | 0.7 | 2.2 | 1.5 | 2.5 | 2.3 | 199 |
| 1903-07 | 31.7 | 19.2 | 3.1 | 1.7 | 0.7 | 1.8 | 1.6 | 2.0 | 1.9 | 162 |
| 1908-12 | 28.7 | 17.7 | 2.4 | 1.5 | 0.9 | 1.5 | 1.4 | 2.0 | 1.9 | 142 |

*Source*: *Annual Report of the Medical Officer of Health, 1912*, Table M.14, p. 39.

*Notes*: 1. The improving public health of the borough, especially after 1900, is reflected in this table.

2. Overall the birth rate fell steadily from the early Eighties, though the pattern (not shown here) varied by district and social class. This fall was as much to do with the declining incidence of marriage (which in turn reflected economic circumstances) as with the adoption of birth control.

3. The fall in the death rate, which becomes more marked in the Edwardian years, was partly due to reductions in the 'Seven Principal Zymotic (infectious) Diseases' which resulted from the more effective public health provision of the time, and partly from improved personal health care, the product of recent government legislation. 'Zymotic Diseases' included smallpox, measles, scarlet fever, whooping cough and diarrhoea. Despite all this, death from Pthisis ('Consumption'), Heart Disease, Bronchitis and Pneumonia all remained high in the borough.

4. Improved personal health care had much to do with the fall in the Infant Mortality rate, apparent from the late Nineties and becoming marked from 1906.

# Index

Aberdeen, Charles, 13–27 *passim*
Agnew, George W., 181, 323, 326
Agnew, Thomas, 53 *et seq*
Agnew, Sir William, 53, 177, 179–192 *passim*, 312, 323
Albert Mill, 179
Althorp, Lord, 25
Anti-Catholicism, 42 *et seq*, 94–107 *passim*, 135–6
Anti-Corn law League, 10, 44–46, 117, 125, 130
Anti-Irish feelings, 142–3
Anti-Poor Law movements, 62–4, 159, 231, 241, 257
Anti-Popery, *see* Anti-Catholicism
Armitage, Benjamin, of Chomlea, 111, 128, 140, 173–192 *passim*
Armitage, Benjamin, of Sorrel Bank, 179, 181, 189, 190, 230, 312
Armitage, Elijah, 110
Armitage,'Old Elkanah', 108–9
Armitage, Sir Elkanah, 44, 79, 80, 108–133 *passim*, 137, 140, 153, 173, 177, 240
Armitage, firm of Sir Elkanah & Sons, 6, 108–133, 178, 190, 192
Armitage, Godfrey, of Lydgate, 109
Armitage, Vernon Kirk, 111, 115, 189, 192, 312
Arnold, Sir Robert Arthur, 179–189 *passim*
art galleries, 179, 181
Art Treasures Exhibition, *see* Manchester Art Treasures Exhibition
Ashley, Lord, *see* Shaftesbury, Lord
ashpits, *see* Public Health
Ashton, Margaret, 279, 284
Ashworth, Henry, 131
Atherton, Miss, 81,92
Athletics, 307
Axon, W. E. A., 190

Bailey, Sir William Henry, 189
Bardsley, Rev. James, 135
Barlow, Montague, 326 *et seq*
Barrowclough, Jabez, 67, 70
Bateman & Sherratt, firm of, 7
Batty, Joshua, 245

Bazley, Thomas, 130,
Becker, Lydia E., 271 *et seq*
Bellairs, Carlyon, 324 *et seq*
Belloc, Hilaire, 260 *et seq*, 287, 322, 326, 327
Beswick, Father, 221
Bible Christians, 31 *et seq*
Billington, later Billlington-Grieg, Teresa, 281 *et seq*
Bilsborrow, Rt. Rev. Dr. John, 222 *et seq*
Birley, Herbert, 92 *et seq*, 135
birth rates, *see* Public Health and Appendix Four
Blatchford, Robert, 243 *et seq*
Boer War, 249
Borchardt, Louis, 271
Bowles, Thomas Gibson, 186 *et seq*
Brailsford, H. N., 289 *et seq*
Bradlaugh, Charles, 182, 229, 243
Bright, Jacob, 138, 271, 278
Bright, Mrs Jacob, 275, 278
Bright, John, 10, 44 *et seq*, 58, 79, 104, 117, 124–7, 141, 173, 179–80, 188–9, 271–2
Broad Street, Pendleton, 151, 152
Brocklehurst, Frederick, 227 *et seq*
Broughton, 2, 3, 57–8, 136
Broughton Harriers, 307
Broughton, population of, 2, Appendix One
Broughton Rangers, 309
Brotherton, James, 29
Brotherton, John, 28,
Brotherton, Joseph, 28–60 *passim*, 63, 103, 108, 115, 116, 124, 126, 137
Brotherton, Martha, 28 *et seq*
Brotherton, William, 28–9
Brothertons, Harvey & Co., firm of, 28, *see also* Harvey, Tysoe & Co.
Brown, John, 242
Buffaloes Friendly Society, 234–5
Building Societies, 233
Burns, John, 242
Burns, W., 224 *et seq*
Byles, W. H., 321 *et seq*
Byrne, J. P., 224 *et seq*

Campbell, James, 69, 71,75
Carlile, Richard, 22–3

canals *see* Manchester, Bolton & Bury,
   Manchester Ship
Cardwell's Army Reforms, 314
Carroll, Father, 245
Carruccio, Father S., 221
Casartelli, Rt. Rev. Dr. Louis, 220
'Cat and Mouse Act', 294 *et seq*
Catholic Bishops of Salford *see* Bilsborrow,
   Casartelli, Turner and Vaughan
Catholic Schools, 100, 213
Catholics, Roman, 11, 96, 100–1, 146–7,
   212–26, 245
Cawley, C. E., 134–49 *passim*
Chadwick, David, 54 *et seq*, 153
Chadwick, W. H., 120
Charlestown, Pendleton, 15, 213, 222 *et seq*
Chalmer, Rev. E. B., 103
Charley, W. T., 140–49
Chartism, 9, 64–80 *passim*, 117–20, 124, 129,
   130–31, 231
Cheetham, John, 125, 132, 140
Chester, Bishop of, 89
Christ Church, King Street, *see* Bible Christians
Christ Church, Acton Square, 86–107 passim
Christian Socialism, 122, 245, *see also* Labour
   Church
Church Building in Salford, 84–107 *passim. See
   also* Salford, churches
Church Schools *see* Salford, Schools in
Church Defence, 90–4, 323
Churchill, Winston, 282, 288
*Clarion* newspaper, 243 *et seq*
Clifton Hall Colliery Disaster, 310–11
Clifton Viaduct, 135
Clothing industry, 7,
Clowes, Rev. John, 31
Clowes, Samuel William, 81, 141
Clynes, J. R., 260 *et seq*
Cobbett, William, 63, 65, 243
Cobden, Richard, 10, 44 *et seq*, 58, 126–7, 272
Cobden-Saunderson, Mrs. Annie, 279 *et seq*
Collegiate Church, Manchester, 86, 89, *see also*
   Manchester Cathedral
Conservative Labour Party, 261
Coombes, Rev. J. A., 49
Cooper, J. R., 80
Co-operative movement, 8, 69, 122, 231–3
Corio, Sylvio, 301
Cotton *see* Textiles,
Cotton Famine, 6, 132, 154–61, 179, 180
'Council Housing', pre-Great War, 254–59
Court Leet of the Hundred of Salford *see*
   Salford, Local Government of
Cowherd, Rev. William, 31 *et seq*
Crilly, Father, 225

Crimean War, 104–5, 125–6
Cross Lane, 81

Davies, Thomas, 150–72 *passim*
Davison, Emily, 194
de Clerc, Monsignor, 221
de Tocqueville, A., 98, 101, 150
Dean, Christopher, 68, 74
death rates *see* Public Health and Appendix Four
Denman, Capt., 125, 31
Derby, Lord, 67, 125, 138, 141, 157, 329
Despard, Charlotte, 286 *et seq*
Dickens, Alfred L., 188
Dickenson, Sarah, 297
Diggles, John, 56
Disraeli, Benjamin, 134, 138, 177
Dissenters Committee, Manchester United, 90
Dixon, Elijah, 240
Dob Lane Chapel, Failsworth, 108
Doherty, John, 16–27 *passim*, 47
Donovan, Daniel, 119
Douglas, William, and family, 14 *et seq*
Douglas & Co., firm of, 14
'Douglas Greeners', 16
Doyle, Rev. William, 107
Dreydel, Thomas, 191
Druids, Ancient Order of, 234
Drummond, Mrs., 289 *et seq*
Duchy of Lancaster, 35, 112
Drink Trade, 145
Dugdale, John, 41
Dundee, 72–7 *passim*
Dunlop, Marian W., 289
Duxbury, Anyon, 67, 69

Eccles New Road, 84
Eccles, parish of, 2
Economic fluctuations, 8, 18, 20, 65, 79,
   112, 118, 121, 154–62, 180–1, 230–1,
   249–50
Edeson, E., 183
Education, 32, 50, 93, 121, 144–5, 152–3,
   157, 176, 213–4, 219
Egerton of Tatton, Lord, 92, 141
Ellis, Hughes & Co., firm of, 18
Ellor Street. 15
Elmy, Mrs. Wolstenholme, 278 *et seq*
Emigration, 159, 220
Engineering, 4, 6, 7, 252–4
Engels, Friedrich, 142
Ermen & Engels, firm of, 16, 113
Eugenie, Empress, 112
Evans, George, 227–69 *passim*
Every Street Chapel, Ancoats, 33
Ewart, William, 48

Fabian Society *see* Socialism
Factory Movement *see* Ten Hours Bill
Famine Relief Committee, 156–61
Fawcett, Henry, 271
Fawcett, Mrs., 280
Fearneley, Frank, 261
Fenians, 143–4, 182, 223–4
Fielden, John, 48–8
First Salford Co-operative Society *see*
   Co-operative Movement
Fitzgerald, John Purcell, 81, 92, 112,141
Foresters, Orders of, Friendly Societies, 234

Forrest, Alexander, 191, 312,
Footpaths Preservation, 80–1
Frankenburg, Isidore, 7, 257
Fraser, Dr. William, 255
Freethinkers, Freethought *see* Secularists
Free Labour League, National, 241 *et seq*
Free Trade, 44–5, 117, 125, 181 321, *see also*
   Anti- Corn Law League
Friendly Societies, 8, 78–9, 233–35
Frost, James Garrett, 69

Gadd, Father C. J., 218 *et seq*
Gaelic League, 322
Garibaldi Reception Committee, Manchester,
   177
Gardner, Robert, 39, 89–107 *passim*, 135
Garnett, Jeremiah, 125, 129
Garnett, William, 39 *et seq*
Gendall, Peter, 56, 69
George, Henry, 228 *et seq*
Gibson, Charles, 54 *et seq*
Gibson, Thomas Milner, 104, 124, 130, 186
Gladstone, Robert, 92
Gladstone, William Ewart, 127–7, 132, 145,
   147, 181, 191, 228, 275, 312, 323
Gooch, Thomas L., 134
Gore-Booth, Eva, 277–302 *passim*
Gore-Booth, Rev. H. F., 278
Gore-Booth, Sir Robert, 92, 141
Gould, Nathan, mill of, 69
Goulden, Herbert, 27
Goulden, Robert, 270, 272, 276
Goulden, William Whitelegge, 90–107 *passim*, 184
Gravel Lane Wesleyan Chapel, 15
Grayson, Victor, 261 *et seq*
Greengate Rubber & Cable Works *see*
   Frankenburg, Isidore
Greenall, Thomas, 320
Greenwood, Walter, 16
Groves, James Grimble, 316 *et seq*, 322
Groves & Whitnall, firm of, 316, 324
Good Templars, Independent Order of, 234

Haldane's Army Reforms, 318, 323–4
Hall, Daniel, 139–40
Hall, John, 140
Hall, J. K., 244 *et seq*
Hall, Leonard, 247 *et seq*
Hall i' th'Wood, Bolton, 81
Hall of Science, Campfield, 72, 80
Hampson, Frederick, 261
Handloom Weavers, 65, 110, 118
Hankinson, Richard, 188
Hardcastle, Edward, 186 *et seq*
Hardie, Keir, 243, 244, 248, 253, 256, 280,
   295
Harford, Edward, 80
Harris, T. W., 243 *et seq*
Harry, Henry, 239, 242
Harrison, H. B., 191
Harry, Henry, 239, 242
Harvey, Joseph, 28
Harvey, William, 28 *et seq*
Harvey, Tysoe & Co., firm of, 29
Haworth, Frederick, 314 *et seq*
Haworth, George C., 203, 231
Haworth, firm of Richard & Sons, 6, 154,
   297
Hayes, J., 259
Hearne, Father, 100, 118
Heelis, Stephen, 90
Hempsall, John, 255 *et seq*
Heywood, Abel, 79, 80, 83, 122, 124, 130,
   240
Heywood, Sir Arthur, 323
Heywood family, 92
Heywood, Oliver, 127, 138, 181
Hicks, Canon, 245 et seq, 290
Higgins, William, 49
Higgins *see also* Platt-Higgins
Higgins & Sons, firm of, 140
Hodgetts, Joseph, 62
Home Rule *see* Irish Home Rule
Hooson, Edward, 130
Hope Hall, 114
Holland, W. H., 191, 312
Horrocks, William, 183, 227 *et seq*
Holywell, North Wales, 14 *et seq*
Hoole, Holland, 20 *et seq*
Hopwood, Robert Gregg, 134
Howorth, H. H., 188, 312, 316
Hughes, Thomas, 122
Hunt, Henry, 65, 240
Hunt, W., 210
Hunter, Samuel, 93–211 *passim*
Huntington, Rev. George, 143
Husband, Richard, 243
Hyndman, H. M., 228 *et seq*

Imperialism, 180, 182, 309–10, 313
Improvement Commissioners *see* Salford, Local
    Government
Independent Labour Party *see* Socialism
Infidels *see* Secularists
Ireland, Established Church of, 98 *et seq*,
    142–44
Irish Confederate Clubs, 118–20
Irish Famine, 100
Irish Home Rule, 181–3, 187–90 , 309
Irish Land League, 182, 245
Irish League, United, 322
Irish National League, 189
Irish Repealers, 118–20
Irish Republicanism, 143–4 *see* also Fenianism
Irish Society of London, 98
Irlams o' th'Height, 110
Irwell Bleach Works, 16
Irwell, River, 2, 9, 162, 165–6, 168
Irwell Street Wesleyan Chapel, 151–3
Isherwood, R., 191

Jackson, George G., 191, 245 *et seq*
Jenkinson, William, 119
Jews in Salford, 2, 7, 94, 173, 253, 260, 322
Jingoism, 180
Jones, Ernest, 83, 129, 239–40

Kay, firm of James & Sons, 112
Kay, Joseph, 145–7
Keenan, Nellie, 297
Keevney, 199 *et seq*
Kelley, G. D., 260
Kelly, John, 245, 250 *et seq*
Kenney, Annie, 282 *et seq*
Kersal Moor, 66, 68, 81
Kirk family, 115
Knowles, Andrew & Co,. firm of, 303 *et seq*
Knowles, Sir James Lees, 189, 191, 308–31
    *passim*
Knowles, family, 304, 305, 314
Knowles, John, 303, 304, 311
Knowles, Lady, 328, 330
Knowles, Thomas, 183

Labour Church, 227, 244 *et seq*
Lalor, James F., 119
Lambert, Hoole & Jackson, firm of, 18 *et seq*
Lancashire Fusiliers, 313 *et seq*
Lancashire Reform Union, 130–1
Langton, William, 92
Langworthy, Edward Ryley, 48 *et seq*, 60, 105,
    126, 153, 181
Lansbury, George, 280, 295
Leake, Robert, 177, 179–92 *passim*

Lee, Henry, 145,
Lee, Herbert, 191
Lee, Rt. Rev. James Prince, 95, 135
Lee, Rev. Thomas Gardner, 122–4
Leigh, 66
Le Mare, E. R., 90–107 *passim*
Lever, Ellis, 197–211 *passim*
Levy, B. W., 173
Leyburne, George, 141
Liberal Party, 132 *see also* Salford, parliamentary
    elections
Liberal Unionists, 189 *et seq*
Licensing Act, 145
Liberation Society, The, 90, 112
Lightbown, Henry, 189
Loch, James, 125
Lodging houses, 166
Lockett, Willliam, 44 *et seq*
Lowry, L. S., 86, 87, 330
Lytton, Lady Constance, 289

McCarthy, Father N. C., 223 *et seq*
McCartney, R. J., 183, 249 *et seq*
McGrath, Rev. W. H., 135
McLaren, Mrs. P. B., 278 *et seq*
McNeile, Rev. Hugh, 84, 98 *et seq*
Makinson, Charles,198 *et seq*
Marr, T. R., 1, 258
Markiewicz, Constance, 278
Manchester and Salford Sanitary Association,
    137, 163
Manchester Art Treasures Exhibition, 58, 112, 200
Manchester, Bolton & Bury Canal, 28, 112
Manchester Church Reform Association, 91,
    95, 135
Manchester Docks, 6, 252 *et seq*
Manchester Financial & Reform Association,
    124–5
Manchester Grammar School, 121, 192
Manchester Municipal Council, 116, 207
Manchester,Parliamentary Elections in, 104,
    124 *et seq*, 130–1, 137, 187, 240, 260–2,
    276, 284, 312
Manchester, relations with Salford, 1, 2, 34,
    37, 203
Manchester Ship Canal, 251 *et seq*
Manchester United, 308–9
Manchester University, 273–95 *passim*
Manchester University Settlement, Ancoats, 278
    *et seq*
*Manchester Courier*, 291
*Manchester Evening News*, 205, 291
*Manchester Gazette*, 37
*Manchester Guardian*, 37, 58, 66, 69, 122–3,
    125, 127, 128, 136, 290, 291, 316

*Manchester Spectator*, 122–4
Mandleburg, J. & Co., firm of, 7, 112
Mandley, G. F., 62, 194
Mandley, J. G. de T., 16, 179, 191, 193–211
   *passim*
Mann, Tom, 242
Manning, Cardinal, 214
Marx and Engels, 228
Mason, Bertha, 279
Mason, George, 183
Massey, W. N., 105, 127–8, 131–2, 137, 177
Mather & Platt, firm of, 7, 176, 253, 254
Mather, John, 188
Mather, Sir William, 102, 163, 179–92 *passim*
Maule, Fox, 72
Maurice, F. D., 122
Mead, Henry, 103, 142–3
Methodism, 151, Appendix Two, 3
midden problem *see* Public Health
Middlehurst, J. E., 184
Mill, John Stuart, 271
Milner, George, 188
Miller, Rev. 84, 98
Mitchell, Hannah, 282 *et seq*, 297
Mode Wheel, 81, 167, 168
Morris, William, 228 *et seq*
Mosley, Sir Oswald, 117
Murphyism, 144
Murray, George, 182

Nadin, George & Nephew, firm of, 110
Napier, General, 68
Nassau Mills, Patricroft, 132
National Reform League, 140
National Reform Union, 140, 177
National Womens' Social and Political Union,
   302 *passim*
Neal, Chief Constable, 56
Near Eastern Crisis, 180 *see also* Crimean War
New Church *see* Swedenborgians
New Unionism *see* Trades Unions
New Windsor Independent Chapel, 122–4
New Windsor and Pendleton Burial Society, 235
New Jerusalem Temple, Bolton Street, *see*
   Swedenborgians
Newton Heath Local Board, 81
Nicholson, S. C., 142, 237 *et seq*
Noar, William, 166
Nuttall, Joseph, 248 *et seq*
*Northern Star*, 65–79 *passim*, 117
Northern Union rugby football, 309

O'Brien, James Bronterre, 65, 78, 80, 83
O'Brien, Smith, 120
O'Connellites, Manchester, 75–6 , 118–20

O'Connor, Feargus, 65, 70, 71, 75, 118, 119, 240
O'Gorman, Dr. R., 191, 221
Oastler, Richard, 20 *et seq*
Oddfellows, Orders of, various, 8, 78–9, 140,
   233–34
Oldfield road, 18
Openshaw, James, 261
Orangemen, 99 *et seq*
Ordsall, 141, 185, 186, 232, 246, 247, 251,
   260, 262
Ordsall Lane, 81
Owen, Robert, 32
Owenites, 32
Owens' College *see* Manchester University

Paine, Thomas, 30
Palmerston, Lord, 58–9, 83, 108, 112, 125–9,
   132, 137, 138, 177
Pankhurst, Adela, 272, 295 *et seq*
Pankhurst, Christabel, 272, 277–302 *passim*
Pankhurst, Emmeline, 248–302 *passim*
Pankhurst, Harry, 272
Pankhurst, Richard, 179, 224, 246, 248, 253,
   272–77
Pankhurst, Richard, son of Sylvia, 301
Pankhurst, Sylvia, 272, 281, 295 *et seq*
Pankhurst Hall, 246–7, 277
Parkinson, Canon R., 135
Parnell, Charles Stuart, 181
Parliamentary Reform, 37–40, 184–5
Pauper apprentices, 14 *et seq*
Pauperism *see* Poor Law
Peace Society, the, 31, 50, 59
Peel, Sir Robert, 45–6, 73
Pendlebury, 303 *et seq*
Pendleton, 1, 2, 15–16, 57–8, 112–3, 323
Pendleton Club, the, 174–5
Pendleton Lads' Club, 176, 330
Pendleton, maps of, 3, 17
Pendleton Mechanics' Institute, 122, 124
Pendleton New Mills, 112 *et seq* 175–6
Pendleton Old Hall, 14, 16
Pendleton Pit, 112–3
Pendleton Pole, 15
Pendleton, population of, 2, 113, Appendix One
Pendleton Weavers' lock-out, 121–4
Permissive Bill *see* Teetotalism
Perth, 72
Pethick-Lawrence, Mr. and Mrs. Frederick,
   284–93
Philips & Lee, firm of, 18 *et seq*
Philips, Mark, 50, 58, 117
Phillips, F. S., 209–11
Phoenix Park murders, 183
Pickering, James, 163–7

Pickles, W., 267 *et seq*
Platt-Higgins, Frederick, 312, 321
Plug Plot riots, 75
Plunkett, James, 250 *et seq*
Pochin, Henry Davies, 188
Police *see* Salford, local government
Police Commissioners *see* Salford, local
   government
Political Unions, 62, 65
Pollution *see* Public Health
Pomona Gardens, 180
Poor Law, 42–3, 62–4, 155–61
Pope, Samuel, 80
Potter family, 38, 44, 80, 108
Potter, Sir John, 127, 129
Potter, Thomas, 116
Potter, Thomas Baines, 127
Power, Alfred, 63–4
Prentice, Archibald, 38, 80
Priory, The, 114
Protectionism, 142, 181
Protestant & Reformation Society, 99 *et seq*
Public Baths, 163
Public Health, 9, 54–8, 137, 146, 162–72,
   254–59, Appendix Four
Public Works, 159
Purcell, A. A., 259 *et seq*
Purves, T. M., 244 *et seq*

Queen Victoria, 112, 120

Ragged Schools, 88, 84, 153
Railway workers *see* Trade Unions
Railways, 135
Ratcliffe, William, 78–9
Rawson, Henry, 140
Reade, Henry M., 229 *et seq*
Rechabites, Independent Order of, 8, 234
Reciprocal Free Trade, Reciprocity *see*
   Protectionism,
Reddaway, T. F., 306
Reddaway & Co., firm of, 253
Reddish, Sarah, 283
Rice, Joseph, 90–107 *passim*
Richardson, Alfred, 80
Richardson, Reginald John, 43 *et seq*, 61–83
   *passim*, 233
Richardson, Elizabeth, 62, 67
Ritchie, C. T., 310, 312
River Pollution *see* Irwell, River
Roberts, Robert, 235–6
Roberts, W. P., 130
Roby, Rev. William, 110
Roper, Esther, 277–302 *passim*
Royle, John, 249

Rugby Football, 308–9
Rusden, R. D., 179, 183
Russel, Bellringer & Co., firm of, 16
Rylett, Harold, 179

Sabbath Observance, 101–4, 190
Sadler, Michael, 20 *et seq*
Sadler's Committee on Textile Factories, 13–27
   *passim*
Saffenreuter, Father G., 212–226 *passim*
St. Bede's College, Manchester, 220
**Salford**
  Barracks, Regent Road, 313
  Board of Guardians *see* Poor Law
  Borough Council *see* Local government
  Booth Charities, 35 *et seq*, 82
  Broughton, relations with, 37, 42, 57–8, 64, 208
  Cemeteries, 60
  Churches
    Sacred Trinity, 329
    St. Anne, Brindleheath, 92
    St. Anne, Adelphi, (R. C.) 215
    St. Bartholomew, 92, 312
    St. Boniface, 215
    St. Charles, 213 *et seq*
    St. George, 92
    St. James (Hope), 115
    St. James, Ellor Street (R. C.), 213 *et seq*
    St. John, Broughton, 2
    St. John's Cathedral, 96, 97, 215
    St John (Height), 307
    St Joseph, 215
    St. Luke, 92
    St. Matthias, 92
    Mount Carmel, 215
    St. Paul, Paddington, 92
    St. Paul, Kersal, 92
    St. Peter, 215, 217
    St. Philip, 19, 86, 91
    St. Sebastian, 223
    St. Simon, 92
    St. Stephen, 85–6, 143
    Stowell Memorial, 84, 107
    St. Thomas, 15, 323
    see also Appendix Two.
  Education *see* Schools
  Elections, local government, 53, 145, 248,
    261–2
  Elections, parliamentary, 37 *et seq*, 125–32,
    144–49, 176–92, 248–49, 260, 311–12,
    316, 321–23, 326
  Famine Relief Committee, 157–62
  'Financial Muddle', the, 255–56
  Funeral Friendly Society, 235
  Firms in *see* individual business entries

**Salford** *continued*

Gas works, 51, 193–211, 242

Improved Industrial Dwellings Co., 171

Great War, 328 *et seq*

Harriers, 307

Labour force in, 5–6, 152, 227–70 *passim*

Irish, *see under* Irish

Lyceum, 77

Library and Museum, 48–9, 190

Local goverment, 2, 9, 33 *et seq*, 50 *et seq*, 57, 63–4, 78, 193–211

Improvement Acts *see* Local Government

Manchester, relations with, *see* Manchester, relations with Salford

Market charter, 35

Modern City of, 1

Parks, 48–9, 171

Parliamentary constituencies, 9, 134, 138, 185–56

Pendleton, relations with, 37, 42,57–8, 64, 208

Police, 56

Poor law, 9, 42–4, 63–4, 219

Population, 1, 2, 113, 161–62, Appendix One

Police, 56

Ratepayers Associations, 56–7

Royal Hospital, 19, 330

Royal Technical Institute, 310

Royal visits, 120, 317, 319

Rugby club, 307

School Board, 144–45

Schools, 32, 50, 144–45, 176, 214, 218–20

Statues, 46, 59, 303, 316–7, 319

Town hall, 35, 36

Working Men's College, 60, 153

Working Men's Sanitary Association, 254–55.

*Salford Chronicle*, 140, 142, 184,307

*Salford Weekly News*, 131, 138, 142

*Salford Reporter*,190, 203 *et seq*

Sanitation *see* Public Health

Schepercel, Father A. M., 221

Schneiders, Father F., 221,

Scholefield, Rev. James, 31, 33

Scott, C,P., 290, 291, 316

Second Spring *see* Catholics

Secularists, 22,183, 229, 230,

Seedley, 3, 270

Seedley Print Works, 16, 77, 232, 276

Sefton, Earl of, 33, 50

Settle, Alfred, 244 *et seq*

sewers see public Health,

Shackleton, David, 280

Shaftesbury, Earl of, 25 *et seq*, 47–8

Sharp,William, 193–211

Shaw, Sir Charles, 116

Sheppard, Chief Constable, 56

Ship Canal *see* Manchester Ship Canal

Sick and Burial Societies, 235

Sinclair, Alderman, 195

Slink trade, 82

Slums, 54–5, 167, 171

Smart, George, 243

Smart, Rev. Henry, 254

Smart, T. R., 73

Smith, John Benjamin, 37 *et seq*, 72

Smith, Father., 222 *et seq*

Smith, F. H., 19

Social Democratic Federation *see* Socialism

Socialism, 32–3 (Owenite), 227–69 *passim*, 276, 285

Socialist League *see* Socialism

Somervell, Mrs A., 290

Soup kitchens, 155, 231

Southam, George Armitage, 173, 189, 190, 192

Southam family, 173–74

Spaw Street Ragged School, 153

Spion Kop, 315

Steinthal, Rev. S. A., 279, 283

Stephens, Rev. J. R., 64, 66

Stephenson, Robert, 112

Stowell, Rev. Hugh, 42, 49, 84–107 *passim*, 125, 134–5, 143, 159

Stowell, Rev. Thomas Alfred, 106–7, 190

Strettles, Rev. J. B., 36

Strikes and lock-outs *see* Trades Unions

Sturge, Joseph, 73, 75

Sunday Observance see Sabbath Observance

Suffragettes, 284–302 *passim*

Sunley, George, 191

Surat cotton, 154, 160

Swedenborgians, 31 *et seq*

Swinton Park, 115

Swinton Rugy Club, 309

Syndicalism *see* Socialism

Syson, Dr J. E., 167

Tatham, Dr. R., 168–71

Taylor, James, chief constable, 57

Taylor, John Edward, 36 *et seq*, 116

Taylor, Rev. Robert, 22–3

Taylor, Weston & Co., 15

Teetotalism, 32, 49–50, 103

Temperance *see* Teetotalism

Temperance, Sons of, 227, 234

Ten Churches Association *see* Church Building in Salford

Ten Hours Bill, 20 *et seq*, 46–8, 141

Textiles, 3 *et seq*, 14 *et seq*, 28 *et seq*, 110 *et seq*, 154 *et seq*, 179 *et seq*, 252

Thompson, A. M., 243 *et seq*

Thompson, James, 224 *et seq*

Thompson, Rev. Joseph, 36
Tillett, Ben, 267 *et seq*
Tolpuddle Martyrs, protest over, 62
Tootal, Edward, 92
Tractarians, 95, 143
Trades Council, Manchester and Salford, 236 *et seq*
Trades unionism, 8, 62, 80, 121–3, 147, 178, 236–9, 279–80, 310–11, 319–21
*Trades Union Magazine & Precursor of a People's Newspaper*, 122–3
Trafford Road, 84
Trevor, John, 244 *et seq*
Trustees Church Building Act, 86
Tufnell, E. C., 23 *et seq*
Turner, James Aspinall, 127
Turner, Wright, 161, 177
Turner, Rt. Rev. Dr. William, 216, 220
Turton Tower, 317
Tysoe, Charles, 29 *et seq*
Tysoe, John, 29

United Kingdom Alliance for the Suppression of the Liquor Trade, 50, 103
Unwin, Mrs. Annie Cobden, 279 *et seq*

Vaughan, Rt. Rev. Dr. Herbert, 183, 214, 216 *et seq*
Vegetarian Society, the, 50
Vegetarianism, 32
Vestry, Manchester Parish *see* Salford, Local government
Vestry, Salford Select, 35 *et seq*
Victoria Mill, Weaste, 77
Vincent, Henry, 130

Walker, Thomas, trial of, 36
Walks, Whit, 152

Walness, 81,
Watkin, Absalom, 50
Walker, J. W., 195 *et seq*
Walker, Olver Ormerod, 148
Walmsley, Dr. Francis, 180
Watters, R. W., 248
Weaste, 3, 16
Webb, Sidney, 56, 209
Wesleyan Home Missions, 153,
Wesleyans, 151
Westminster, parish of, 13, 14
Whit Lane, 16,
Whit Lane Weaving Co., 122, 179
Wigley, J., 179
Wilkinson, Abraham, 249 *et seq*
Willis, William, 62, 67
Winks, A. F., 183
Winterbottom, Archibald & Co., 113
Wilson, Rev. C. P., 245
Wilson, George, 44 *et seq*, 82, 130
Wilson & Co., Adelphi Print Works, 76
Wolseley, Field-Marshall Viscount, 315
Workmens' Compensation Act, 319–20
Wood, William Henry, 142, 237 *et seq*
Woodhead reservoir, 117
Worrall's Dye Works, 80
Worsley, 66
Worsley, Sir William, 186 *et seq*
Wright, Thomas, architect, 86
Wright Turner & Son, 6
Womens' Suffrage Societies, 217–302 *passim*
Womens' Social & Political Union, 281 *et seq*, *see also* National WSPU

Young England Patriotic Association, 249 *et seq*, 325
Young Ireland, 168